Architectural Issues of Web-Enabled Electronic Business

Nan Si Shi, Ph.D.
University of South Australia, Australia

V.K. Murthy, Ph.D.
University of New South Wales at Australian
Defence Force Academy, Australia

IDEA GROUP PUBLISHING
Hershey • London • Melbourne • Singapore • Beijing

Acquisition Editor:	Mehdi Khosrowpour
Senior Managing Editor:	Jan Travers
Managing Editor:	Amanda Appicello
Development Editor:	Michele Rossi
Copy Editor:	Jane Conley
Typesetter:	Tamara Gillis
Cover Design:	Integrated Book Technology
Printed at:	Integrated Book Technology

Published in the United States of America by

Idea Group Publishing (an imprint of Idea Group Inc.)
701 E. Chocolate Avenue, Suite 200
Hershey PA 17033
Tel: 717-533-8845
Fax: 717-533-8661
E-mail: cust@idea-group.com
Web site: http://www.idea-group.com

and in the United Kingdom by

Idea Group Publishing (an imprint of Idea Group Inc.)
3 Henrietta Street
Covent Garden
London WC2E 8LU
Tel: 44 20 7240 0856
Fax: 44 20 7379 3313
Web site: http://www.eurospan.co.uk

Library of Congress Cataloging-in-Publication Data

JK

Shi, Nan Si, 1953-
  Architectural issues of Web-enabled electronic business / Nan Si Shi,
V.K. Murthy
      p. cm.
Includes bibliographical references and index.
  ISBN 1-59140-049-X (hardcover) -- ISBN 1-59140-081-3 (ebook)
  1. Computer network architectures. 2. Business--Data processing. 3.
Electronic information resources. I. Murthy, V. K., 1963- II. Title.
  TK5105.52 .N35 2002
  658.8'4--dc21
                              2002014185

British Cataloguing-in-Publication Data
A Cataloguing-in Publication record for this book is available from the British Library.

NEW from Idea Group Publishing

- **Digital Bridges: Developing Countries in the Knowledge Economy**, John Senyo Afele/ ISBN:1-59140-039-2; eISBN 1-59140-067-8, © 2003
- **Integrative Document & Content Management: Strategies for Exploiting Enterprise Knowledge**, Len Asprey and Michael Middleton/ ISBN: 1-59140-055-4; eISBN 1-59140-068-6, © 2003
- **Critical Reflections on Information Systems: A Systemic Approach**, Jeimy Cano/ ISBN: 1-59140-040-6; eISBN 1-59140-069-4, © 2003
- **Web-Enabled Systems Integration: Practices and Challenges**, Ajantha Dahanayake and Waltraud Gerhardt ISBN: 1-59140-041-4; eISBN 1-59140-070-8, © 2003
- **Public Information Technology: Policy and Management Issues**, G. David Garson/ ISBN: 1-59140-060-0; eISBN 1-59140-071-6, © 2003
- **Knowledge and Information Technology Management: Human and Social Perspectives**, Angappa Gunasekaran, Omar Khalil and Syed Mahbubur Rahman/ ISBN: 1-59140-032-5; eISBN 1-59140-072-4, © 2003
- **Building Knowledge Economies: Opportunities and Challenges**, Liaquat Hossain and Virginia Gibson/ ISBN: 1-59140-059-7; eISBN 1-59140-073-2, © 2003
- **Knowledge and Business Process Management**, Vlatka Hlupic/ISBN: 1-59140-036-8; eISBN 1-59140-074-0, © 2003
- **IT-Based Management: Challenges and Solutions**, Luiz Antonio Joia/ISBN: 1-59140-033-3; eISBN 1-59140-075-9, © 2003
- **Geographic Information Systems and Health Applications**, Omar Khan/ ISBN: 1-59140-042-2; eISBN 1-59140-076-7, © 2003
- **The Economic and Social Impacts of E-Commerce**, Sam Lubbe/ ISBN: 1-59140-043-0; eISBN 1-59140-077-5, © 2003
- **Computational Intelligence in Control,** Masoud Mohammadian, Ruhul Amin Sarker and Xin Yao/ISBN: 1-59140-037-6; eISBN 1-59140-079-1, © 2003
- **Decision-Making Support Systems: Achievements and Challenges for the New Decade**, M.C. Manuel Mora, Guisseppi Forgionne and Jatinder N. D. Gupta/ISBN: 1-59140-045-7; eISBN 1-59140-080-5, © 2003
- **Architectural Issues of Web-Enabled Electronic Business**, Nansi Shi and V.K. Murthy/ ISBN: 1-59140-049-X; eISBN 1-59140-081-3, © 2003
- **Adaptive Evolutionary Information Systems**, Nandish V. Patel/ISBN: 1-59140-034-1; eISBN 1-59140-082-1, © 2003
- **Managing Data Mining Technologies in Organizations: Techniques and Applications**,   Parag Pendharkar/ ISBN: 1-59140-057-0; eISBN 1-59140-083-X, © 2003
- **Intelligent Agent Software Engineering**, Valentina Plekhanova/ ISBN: 1-59140-046-5; eISBN 1-59140-084-8, © 2003
- **Advances in Software Maintenance Management: Technologies and Solutions**, Macario Polo, Mario Piattini and Francisco Ruiz/ ISBN: 1-59140-047-3; eISBN 1-59140-085-6, © 2003
- **Multidimensional Databases: Problems and Solutions**, Maurizio Rafanelli/ISBN: 1-59140-053-8; eISBN 1-59140-086-4, © 2003
- **Information Technology Enabled Global Customer Service**, Tapio Reponen/ISBN: 1-59140-048-1; eISBN 1-59140-087-2, © 2003
- **Creating Business Value with Information Technology: Challenges and Solutions**, Namchul Shin/ISBN: 1-59140-038-4; eISBN 1-59140-088-0, © 2003
- **Advances in Mobile Commerce Technologies**, Ee-Peng Lim and Keng Siau/ ISBN: 1-59140-052-X; eISBN 1-59140-089-9, © 2003
- **Mobile Commerce: Technology, Theory and Applications**, Brian Mennecke and Troy Strader/ ISBN: 1-59140-044-9; eISBN 1-59140-090-2, © 2003
- **Managing Multimedia-Enabled Technologies in Organizations**, S.R. Subramanya/ISBN: 1-59140-054-6; eISBN 1-59140-091-0, © 2003
- **Web-Powered Databases**, David Taniar and Johanna Wenny Rahayu/ISBN: 1-59140-035-X; eISBN 1-59140-092-9, © 2003
- **E-Commerce and Cultural Values**, Theerasak Thanasankit/ISBN: 1-59140-056-2; eISBN 1-59140-093-7, © 2003
- **Information Modeling for Internet Applications**, Patrick van Bommel/ISBN: 1-59140-050-3; eISBN 1-59140-094-5, © 2003
- **Data Mining: Opportunities and Challenges**, John Wang/ISBN: 1-59140-051-1; eISBN 1-59140-095-3, © 2003
- **Annals of Cases on Information Technology** – vol 5, Mehdi Khosrowpour/ ISBN: 1-59140-061-9; eISBN 1-59140-096-1, © 2003
- **Advanced Topics in Database Research** – vol 2, Keng Siau/ISBN: 1-59140-063-5; eISBN 1-59140-098-8, © 2003
- **Advanced Topics in End User Computing** – vol 2, Mo Adam Mahmood/ISBN: 1-59140-065-1; eISBN 1-59140-100-3, © 2003
- **Advanced Topics in Global Information Management** – vol 2, Felix Tan/ ISBN: 1-59140-064-3; eISBN 1-59140-101-1, © 2003
- **Advanced Topics in Information Resources Management** – vol 2, Mehdi Khosrowpour/ ISBN: 1-59140-062-7; eISBN 1-59140-099-6, © 2003

Architectural Issues of Web-Enabled Electronic Business

Table of Contents

Preface

In the not too distant future, the Web will be everywhere in the world. By the year 2003, the explosion of Web-enabled electronic business (e-Business) will be worth more than US $1 trillion and the Web users will be more than 600 million. This is offering organizations previously unheard of opportunities. To be successful or survive, industry leaders have made strategies towards e-Business, and others, sooner or later, more or less, will have to become certain kinds of e-Business.

Web technologies play a critical role in today's Web-enabled e-Business. A key to success in applying the Web-based technologies to real world problems lies in understanding the architectural issues and developing the appropriate methodologies and tools for building e-Business systems. The main purpose of this book, therefore, is to provide the e-Business professionals with a holistic perspective of this field that covers a wide range of topics.

At the very outset of this project, we realized that it is impossible for any one author to write a book of this type and cover all the important aspects of this rapidly emerging field, maintaining the same depth, width and consistency. With this in mind, the main philosophy that was followed in organizing this handbook was to invite experts around the world to contribute their knowledge. Therefore, we identified some of the key topics in this area and invited a wide range of professionals across the globe to contribute a chapter in the area of their expertise to this handbook. This had an overwhelming and enthusiastic response from authors in different parts of the world: Australia, Canada, Germany, Singapore, the United Kingdom, and the United States. We also tried to avoid a hasty approach in the compilation of this book and gave adequate time for it to grow over months of preparation and consultation with the publishers, authors, and reviewers.

The success of this book is to a large extent, due to the collective effort of a great team consisting of the authors and other reviewers. The blind review process included the authors besides other reviewers. The inclusion of the authors in the blind review process improved the quality of the book and also served as an incentive to each author to strengthen his/her write-up. Although the editors initially received many proposals and manuscripts, the stringent quality control measures taken permitted us ultimately to include only 26 chapters, contributed by 51 professionals from 27 universities and five industry organizations in different parts of the world.

READERSHIP

The primary readers of this handbook are professionals, executives and undergraduate/postgraduate students in IT and Computer Science-related areas. Professionals will be able to use this book as an informative technical introduction to areas of their interest in Web-based technologies and architectures. The references provided in each chapter provide additional background to the reader to pursue a more detailed study of any particular aspect.

ORGANIZATION

This handbook is organized in nine sections, with the following major themes:

1. Globalization of E-Business
2. Intelligent Portal Architecture
3. Scalability and Performance
4. Web-based Distributed Data Mining
5. Web Search and Data Retrieval
6. Web Information Systems (WIS) Development: Design, Environment and Standards
7. E-Marketing and Virtual Marketplace
8. Security Architecture
9. E-Business Applications

Each section is organized into chapters. Therefore, the chapters are numbered by Section number followed by the Chapter number in that section.

OVERVIEW

As the book is devoted to a very diverse range of topics written by a large number of professionals and academics, it is felt necessary to provide a bird's eye view of the contents of the chapters at the expense of a longer than a usual preface.

Section I deals with **"Globalization of E-Business"** and consists of two chapters.

Chapter 1 by Daniel Brandon on **"Issues in the Globalization of Electronic Commerce,"** presents globalization aspects of e-Business. While "Globalization" is the marketing and selling of a product outside a company's home country, "Localization" is the process of customizing Web content so that it is most understandable and usable to a person residing in a particular locale. That process involves several aspects, including Language, Culture, Laws/Regulations, Payment/Currency, Dates/Units, and Logistics. This chapter describes the key issues in each these areas and then analyzes approaches that could be used to address these issues.

Chapter 2, **"Electronic Architectures for Bridging the Global Digital Divide: A Comparative Assessment of E-Business Systems Designed to Reach the Global Poor,"** by Nikhilesh Dholakia and Nir Kshetri, presents a comparative view of e-business systems designed to extend the benefits of e-business to the poor demographic segments of the developing world and to reach populations that are on the "wrong side of the digital divide." It aims to fill the research gap by providing a comparative assessment of the architecture of four e-Business networks, across various network architecture dimensions. The architectures discussed in this chapter are designed to provide such services as telemedicine, international trade, e-government, environmental protection, and entertainment to the people in developing countries.

Section II is concerned with **"Intelligent Portal Architecture"** and consists of two chapters.

In Chapter 3 **"Intelligent Business Portals,"** Xue Li describes how portals can be regarded as an information gateway for exchanging business information over the Internet and for delivering the right information to the right user, at the right time, to the right place, to make the right decisions. In order to implement Intelligent Portals, this chapter introduces a three-layer architecture that reflects the usage of the modern information technology infrastructure. At the development layer, Portals are packaged according to the needs. At the deployment layer, Portals are allocated to their applications. At the top control layer, Portals become knowledgeable and knows how, where, and when to deliver their services. An Information Broker is the key component responsible for implementing the three-layer Intelligent Portal architecture.

In Chapter 4, **" Expert Database Web Portal Architecture,"** Anthony Scime outlines the components of an expert database Web portal, its design, and population. The creation of such a database requires an architecture that captures the expert's domain knowledge and finds and evaluates applicable Web pages from which data is extracted. With expert database Web portals, searchers will be able to locate valuable knowledge on the Web and to access information that has been organized by a domain expert to increase accuracy and completeness. This chapter also discusses a Web page miner architecture.

Section III deals with **"Scalability and Performance"** and consists of two chapters.

Chapter 5, **"Scheduling and Latency—Addressing the Bottleneck"** by Michael J. Oudshoorn, addresses the growing need to distribute the server side of the application in order to meet business objectives and to provide maximum service levels to customers. It focuses on two performance bottlenecks: scheduling and communication latency. Then it discusses an adaptive scheduling system to automatically distribute the application across the available resources such that the distribution evolves to a near optimal allocation tailored to each user, and introduces the concept of ambassadors to minimize communication latency in wide-area distributed applications.

Chapter 6, **"Integration of Database and Internet Technologies for Scalable End-to-end E-commerce Systems"** by K. Selçuk Candan and Wen-Syan Li, describes the state of art of e-commerce acceleration services and points out their disadvantages, including failure to handle dynamically generated Web content. More specifically, it addresses the two questions faced by e-commerce acceleration systems: (1) what changes do the characteristics of the e-commerce systems require in the popular content delivery architectures and (2) what is the impact of end-to-end (Internet + server) scalability requirements of e-commerce systems on e-commerce server software design. It also introduces an architecture for integrating Internet services, business logic, and database technologies for improving end-to-end scalability of e-commerce systems.

Section IV is concerned with **"Web-Based Distributed Data Mining"** and consists of two chapters.

Chapter 7, **"Internet Delivery of Distributed Data Mining Services: Architectures, Issues and Prospects"** by Shonali Krishnaswamy, Arkady Zaslavsky and Seng Wai Loke, presents on-going research and the operations of commercial data mining service providers. It evaluates different distributed data mining architectural models in the context of their suitability to support Web-based delivery of data mining services and describes emerging technologies and standards in the e-services domain and discusses their impact on a "virtual marketplace of data mining e-services." This chapter is a useful resource for the construction of systems that support Web-based delivery of data mining services and facilitates enhanced understanding of the architectural models, the operational semantics and the underlying technologies.

Chapter 8, **"Data Mining For Web-Enabled Electronic Business Applications"** by Richi Nayak presents data mining concepts and issues that are associated with Web-enabled e-business applications such as: (1) analysis of the pattern of user behaviour that reflects the acceptability and satisfaction with a Web site, (2) correlation analysis between Web contents, be it products or documents, and (3) analysis of Web usage data to assist e-business in real-time personalization and cross-marketing strategies. The data mining techniques can provide companies with previously unknown buying patterns and the behaviour of their online customers and other meaningful information.

Section V deals with **"Web Search and Data Retrieval"** and consists of four chapters.

Chapter 9, " **Intelligent Web Search Through Adaptive Learning From Relevance Feedback"** by Zhixiang Chen, Binhai Zhu, and Xiannong Meng, deals with the machine learning approaches to real-time intelligent Web search. The goal is to build an intelligent Web search system that can find the user's desired information with as little relevance feedback from the user as possible. The system can achieve a significant search precision increase with a small number of iterations of user relevance feedback. A new machine learning algorithm is designed as the core of the intelligent search component. With the new algorithm, three intelligent Web search engines, *Websail, Yarrow* and *Features,* are built that are able to achieve a significant search precision increase with just four to five iterations of real-time learning from user relevance feedback. It also describes the performances and characteristics of the three search engines and discusses the future research issues regarding real-time intelligent Web search.

Chapter 10, **"World Wide Web Search Engines"** by Wen-Chen Hu and Jyh-Haw Yeh, provides an overview of the current technologies for Web search engines with an emphasis on non-traditional approaches. Numerous search technologies have been applied to Web search engines; however, the dominant search method has yet to be identified. The major reason for this is that the amount of information posted on the WWW is huge and the page formats vary widely. This chapter classifies existing technologies for Web search engines into six categories: 1) hyperlink exploration, 2) information retrieval, 3) metasearches, 4) SQL approaches, 5) content-based multimedia searches, and 6) others. Also it provides a comparative study of major commercial and experimental search engines and some future research directions for Web search engines.

Chapter 11, **"Retrieval of Multimedia Data on the Web: An Architectural Framework"** by Mohammed Moharrum, Stephen Olariu and Hussein Abdel-Wahab, proposes a general architectural framework for a broad array of retrievals of multimedia data required by various applications. This framework has three objectives: (1) proposing a layered architecture to facilitate design and separate different issues, (2) covering a large number of multimedia applications, and finally, (3) making use of existing and well-established technology, such as Mobile Agents, SQL databases, and cache managements schemes. The framework separates issues involved in multimedia retrieval into five layers, namely: keyword searching and data servers, proxy servers, domain and department archives, mobile user agents, and the users. Through these five layers, various customized solutions to a large array of problems will be proposed and applied. The chapter also offers solutions for different problems that arise in retrieval of multimedia data and identifies critical issues involved in multimedia retrieval over the Internet.

In Chapter 12, **"Navigation in e-Business Web Sites,"** Roland Hübscher, Tony Pittarese, and Patricia Lanford focus on certain aspects related to content and usability, two of the most important keys to successful Web sites. They discuss existing problems and point out a series of important user and task characteristics that need to be considered when designing an online store. They concentrate on usability issues of content organization and navigation that are inherently intertwined. Also they discuss the checkout process, an important element of many e-Business, whose design requires not only the usual usability guidelines but also trust issues.

Section VI is concerned with **" Web Information Systems (WIS) Development: Design, Environment and Standards"** and consists of six chapters.

Chapter 13 by V.K. Murthy on **"E-Business Transaction Management in Web Integrated Network Environment"** describes the Operational Models, Programming Paradigms, and Software Tools needed for building a Web-integrated network computing environment. Various interactive distributed computing models (client server- CS, code on demand, remote evaluation, mobile agents, three and N-tier systems) and different logical modes of programming (imperative, declarative, subjunctive, and abductive) are described. Also, transaction and workflow models (that relax atomicity, consistency, isolation, durability, and serializability properties), and new protocols and software tools (PJava/JDBC) are described. Some important application areas of these models are for telediagnosis and cooperative problem solving.

Chapter 14 on **"System Development Methodologies for Web-Enabled E-Business: A Customization Framework"** by Linda V. Knight, Theresa A. Steinbach and Vince Kellen, explores the fit between typical Web-based information system characteristics and existing development methodologies, from the traditional System Development Life Cycle (SDLC) to some of the newer rapid response models. It concludes that, contrary to common practice in most organizations, one standardized development methodology is not best suited for all, or even most, e-business projects. Fifteen variables that are key to identifying the best methodology for a given e-business project are distilled, and a framework is constructed to aid development teams in the process of formulating a customized development methodology to serve as a basis for project management and control. This framework provides a storehouse of options from which project managers can select and tailor methodologies to suit their organizational needs including the unique nature of Web-enabled e-business.

An important key in achieving more effective Web system development within the rapidly changing environment will be a design approach that facilitates the creation of architectures that actively encompass both functional and informational elements, and links it to the business model creating a strong cohesion. This requires an appropriate architectural modeling language and a process for carrying out the architectural design. Chapter 15 by David Lowe and Brian Henderson-Sellers on **"Characterizing Web Systems: Merging Information and Functional Architectures,"** discusses the above aspects, looking at a model of Web systems that emphasizes the links between the various architectural elements and process level support for design activities.

In Chapter 16 , **"Customisation of Internet Multimedia Information Systems Design Through User Modelling,"** Sherry Y. Chen and Marios C. Angelides attempt to incorporate cognitive and interpersonal styles into the design of Internet multimedia information systems. Based on the findings of previous studies, this chapter presents a user model to customize the design of Internet multimedia information systems for different cognitive and interpersonal styles. This model can help designers to decide which levels of navigation support and presentational structures work best for different types of users; it can be applied for providing personalization for users with different preferences. Also, this chapter discusses the implications for the design of Internet multimedia information systems.

Chapter 17, **"A Software Model, Architecture and Environment to Support Web-Based Applications"** by David Kearney and Weiquan Zhao, describes a model, an architecture and an associated Web Application Support Environment (WASE) that hide the low-level complexity of the existing Web infrastructure and at the same time empower enterprise Web application programmers in their objective of writing modular and easily maintainable software applications for electronic commerce. WASE is not a compiler and does not completely abstract away the unique features of Web infrastructure. It is being constructed using XML documents in its API to allow the function and configurability of applications to be defined in a Web-like fashion.

Chapter 18, **"XML - Digital Glue for the Modern World—Electronic Business Standards Fuelling Intra- and Inter-Enterprise Interoperability for Global Collaboration,"** by Frank Jung, provides information about current XML-related standards for the electronic interchange of business documents. It introduces the principles of the major standards in this area, such as XML, DTDs, XML Schema, XSL, XSLT, XPath, XPointer, DOM and SAX. Also it explains why XML is not only an ideal data interchange format, but is very likely to earn its merits as a very effective format for persistently storing XML-based documents required in the modern e-business world. Finally, the chapter provides a brief introduction to industry initiatives aimed at optimizing the standardized exchange of business documents, such as BizTalk, and others.

Section VII deals with **"E-Marketing and Virtual Marketplace"** and consists of four chapters.

In Chapter 19, **"Designing Agent-Based Negotiation For E-Marketing"**, by V.K. Murthy describes how to design agent-based negotiation systems in E-marketing. Such a negotiation scheme requires the construction of a suitable set of rules, called a protocol, among the participating agents. The use of AI planning and the logic and algebra of specifications to devise multi-agent-based negotiation protocols are explained. The construction of the protocol is carried out in two stages: first expressing a program into an object-based rule system and then converting the rule applications into a set of agent-based transactions on a database of active objects represented using high-level data structures. Also it describes an algorithm to detect the termination of the negotiation process.

Chapter 20, **"Virtual Marketplace for Agent-Based Electronic Commerce"** by Chuen Hwee Ng, Sheng-Uei Guan, and Fangming Zhu, proposes an architecture for a mobile agent-based virtual marketplace. As the Internet grows, the potential for conducting electronic commerce grows as well. However, given the explosion of online shopping, searching for particular products amongst the sea of commercial content could become a fundamental obstacle for electronic commerce. Hence, an agent-based virtual marketplace is designed to facilitate agent negotiations by providing a trusted and secure environment. A novel dynamic pricing mechanism has also been implemented in the context of the airline ticketing industry and found to be rather successful.

In Chapter 21, **"Integrated E-Marketing—A Strategy-Driven Technical Analysis Framework."** Simpson Poon, Irfan Altas, and Geoff Fellows propose a framework that addresses the issue of real-time objective-driven E-marketing. They also present approaches that combine real-time data packet analysis integrated with data mining techniques to create a responsive E-marketing campaign. Finally, they discuss some of the potential problems facing E-marketers in the future. This chapter has only explored some preliminary concepts of objective-driven E-marketing, and the challenge is how to integrate the business and technology strategies to maximize the understanding of E-marketing in a dynamic way.

Chapter 22, **"An Agent-Based Architecture for Product Selection and Evaluation under E-Commerce"** by Leng Woon Sim and Sheng-Uei Guan, proposes the establishment of a trusted Trade Services entity within the electronic commerce agent framework. A Trade Services entity may be set up for each agent community. All products to be sold in the framework are to be registered with the Trade Services. The main objective of the Trade Services is to extend the current use of agents from product selection to include product evaluation in the purchase decision. To take advantage of the agent framework, the Trade Services can be a logical entity that is implemented by a community of expert agents. Each expert agent must be capable of learning about the product category it is designed to handle, as well as the ability to evaluate a specific product in the category. An approach that combines statistical analysis and fuzzy logic reasoning is proposed as one of the learning methodologies for determining the rules for product evaluation.

Section VIII is concerned with **"Security Architecture"** and has two chapters.

Chapter 23, **"An Architecture for Authentication and Authorization of Mobile Agents in E-Commerce"** by Wee Chye Yeo, Sheng-Uei Guan, and Fangming Zhu, describes the design and implementation of agent authentication and authorization schemes. By combining the features of the Java security environment and the Java Cryptographic Extensions, a secure and robust infrastructure is built. Public Key Infrastructure (PKI) is the main technology used in the authentication module. In developing this module, care was taken to protect the public and private keys generated. To verify the integrity of the agent, digital signature is used. The receiving party would use the public keys of the relevant parties to verify that all the information on the agent is intact. In the authorization module, the agent is checked regarding its trustworthiness and a suitable user-defined security policy will be recommended based on the level of authentication the agent has passed.

In Chapter 24, **"Security and Trust of Online Auction Systems in E-Commerce"**, P.W. Lei, L.K. Lo, C.R. Chatwin, R.C.D. Young, M. I. Heywood and N. Zincir-Heywood offer some architectural solutions for reducing online auction fraud in online auction trading.. The discussion herein is restricted to those factors that are deemed critical for ensuring that consumers gain the confidence required to participate in online auctions and hence a broader spectrum of businesses are able to invest in integrating online auction systems into their commercial operations.

Section IX deals with **"E-Business Applications,"** and consists of two chapters.

In Chapter 25 **"E-Commerce and Digital Libraries,"** Suliman Al-Hawamdeh and Schubert Foo discuss a number of outstanding issues, such as those of access control, content management, information organization, and challenges confronting digital libraries in their adoption of e-commerce, including e-commerce charging models.

Chapter 26, **"Electronic Business Over Wireless Device: A Case Study"** by Richi Nayak and Anurag Nayak, presents the basic concepts necessary to understand e-Business over wireless devices (mobile-business or m-business). This paper also presents a case study of the voice-driven airline-ticketing system that can be accessed at any time and anywhere by mobile phones. This application offers maximum functionality while still maintaininga high level of user convenience in terms of input and navigation. Many optimists see m-business as a technology that is just one step before it becomes an everyday occurence.

Acknowledgments

Credit for the successful accomplishment of this book is due to many people's contributions and help. It is our pleasant duty to acknowledge with thanks the insights and excellent contributions provided by all the authors. We also want to thank all of the blind reviewers who assisted us in the reviewing process. Special thanks also go to all the staff at Idea Group Publishing, particularly to Mehdi Khosrow-Pour, Jan Travers and Michele Rossi. Shi would like to acknowledge all of the people who encouraged and supported me in this project, especially Professors Kevin O'Brien and Rod Oxenberry, and Associate Professor Graham Arnold from University of South Australia; Mr. Han Tsi Fung and Ms. Marilyn Ling from Singapore Pools (Private) Limited; and Mr. Andrew Chen. Murthy wishes to thank Professor C. Newton for support in the editorial process of this book. Also, thanks are due to Dr. H. Abbass, University of New South Wales at ADFA, and Professor E.V. Krishnamurthy, Australian National University, for their help in the review process. Finally, we want to thank our family members for their love and support throughout this project.

Nan Si Shi and V.K. Murthy
19 April 2002

Section I:

Globalization of E-Business

Chapter I

Issues in the Globalization of Electronic Commerce

Daniel Brandon, Jr., Ph.D.
Christian Brothers University

ABSTRACT

This chapter presents globalization aspects of electronic commerce, describes the key issues in each area, and then analyzes approaches that could be Used to address these issues. "Globalization" is the marketing and selling of a product outside a company's home country, and the most effective way to do that on the Internet is via localization of Web content. 'Localization' is the process and product of customizing Web content so that it is most understandable and usable to a person residing in a particular locale. That process involves several aspects including: Language, Culture, Laws/Regulations, Payment/Currency, Dates/ Units, and Logistics. In each of these areas there are a number of both business and technical issues that are illustrated and analyzed in this chapter.

INTRODUCTION

This chapter presents globalization aspects of electronic commerce. According to Computerworld: "Globalization is the marketing and selling of a product outside a company's home country. To successfully do that on the Internet, a company needs to *localize* – make its Web site linguistically, culturally, and in all other ways accessible to customers outside its home territory" (Brandon, 2001). The objectives of this chapter are to identify and describe the key issues in the globalization of electronic commerce and to present architectural and other solutions available.

BACKGROUND

"Ever since the end of the Cold War, the world has been rushing toward ever-higher levels of national convergence, with capital markets, business regulation, trade policies, and the like becoming similar" (Moschella, 1999). The value of cross-border mergers grew sixfold from 1991 to 1998 from U.S. $85 billion to $558 billion. The world has not witnessed such a dramatic change in business since the Industrial Revolution (Korper, 2000). More than 95%

of world population lives outside of the U.S., and for most countries the majority of their potential market for goods and services is outside of their borders. Currently (11/2000) over 60% of the world's online population resides outside of the United States (IW, 2000):

United States 36.2%	Japan 7.2%	Germany 5.1%
United Kingdom 4.8%	China 4.2%	Canada 4.0%
South Korea 3.9%	Italy 3.1%	Brazil 2.8%
France 2.4%	Australia 2.2%	Russia 1.8%
Taiwan 1.7%	Netherlands 1.4%	Spain 1.3%

Today the majority of the Fortunes 100's Web sites are available only in English (Betts, 2000). In our rush to get on the WWW, we sometimes forget that WW is for "World Wide" (Giebel, 1999). Wal-Mart (a $165 billion U.S. company) has a global work force of more than 1 million and runs more than 1000 of its 3406 retail outlets outside of the U.S.; yet its Web site (Wal-mart.com) is only for Americans (Sawhney, 2000). Today's average Web site gets 30% of its traffic from foreign visitors, and only 1% of small and midsize American businesses export overseas (Grossman, 2000).

KEY ISSUES

"Localization" (shortened to L12N in Internet terms) considers five global dimensions: geographic, functional, regulatory, cultural, and economic (Bean, 2000). We shall examine each of these somewhat overlapping and interrelated issues in these groupings: Language, Cultural, Legal, Payment/Currency, Dates/Units, Logistics; and then discuss other general business issues. Technical issues will also be identified, before we present architectural solutions and recommendations.

Language

Currently (1/2001) the breakdown of Internet User languages is roughly 50% English, 8% Japanese, 6% German, 6% Spanish, 6% Chinese, 4% French, and 20% other. That means if one does not localize their Web site soon, he/she will be ignoring more than half of the world. According to IDC, by 2005 more than 70% of the one billion Web Users around the world will be non-English speakers (Wonnacott, 2001). For the immediate future most of the Internet community will still understand English, but overall English is the native language of only 8% of the world. Most Users in foreign countries prefer content in their own language; for example, 75% of Users in China and Korea have such a preference (Ferranti, 1999). It was found that visitors spend twice as long, and are three times more likely to buy from a site presented in their native language (Schwartz, 2000).

Multiple languages are Used in many areas. Belgium has both French and Dutch. In Switzerland, German, French, and Italian are Used. Also, we have to take into account differing dialects that are Used across various countries speaking a specific language. One cannot use "Classic German" in Germany, Austria, or Belgium, since they all speak a different German. The combination of language and dialect is called a "locale."

When one installs an operating system on his/her computer, they may specify a locale. Then to view content that has been localized for another language, one has to have the Internet browser properly equipped with the correct scripts (characters and glyphs/symbols). In some locals there may be one spoken language but several writing systems for it, such as in Japanese. The current versions of Netscape and Microsoft Internet Explorer support most languages directly or via a "download" of needed scripts. You still may have to adjust option settings in these products accordingly in order to associate the proper character set with the proper language (Brandon, 2001) .

One can convert Web pages by hiring a translator or using a computer-based translation product or service. Hiring a translator will provide the best localization but is more costly than the automatic methods. Translators can easily be found in the Aquarius directory (http:// aquarius.net) or Glenn's Guide (www.glennsguide.com). It is best to Use a translator that "lives" in the local region; if a translator has not lived in a region for a decade, he has missed ten years of the local culture. There are also many companies that provide translation services such as: Aradco, VSI, eTranslate, Idiom, iLanguage, WorldPoint, and others. The cost of these services is about 25 cents per word per language (Brandon, 2001).

Automatic translation software is another option, but it is still in its infancy (Reed, 1999). Some popular software products for translation are: www.e-ling.com, www.lhs.com, and www.systransoft.com. The automatically translated text typically does not convey the meaning of the original text. For example, some English elevator signs translated to then from another language may read:

–   Bucharest: "The lift is being fixed for the next day. During that time we regret that you will be unbearable."
–   Leipzig: "Do not enter the lift backwards, and only when lit up."
–   Paris: "Please leave your values at the front desk."

There are several Web sites that provide free translation services such as: http:// babelfish.altavista.com, http://translator.go.com, and www.freetranslation.com. For example, Figure 1 shows the "BabelFish" Web site where we are requesting a translation of an English sentence into Spanish. Figure 2 shows the translation results. Another alternative, although certainly not optimal, is to provide a link on your English Web page to these free services so that visitors can translate your content themselves. Figure 3 shows a portion of the CBU School of Business English version Web site. The automatic Spanish translated version (using BableFish) is shown in Figure 4. Note that the automatic version, while syntactically and grammatically correct, does not convey the exact intended meaning to most of the titles

Figure 1

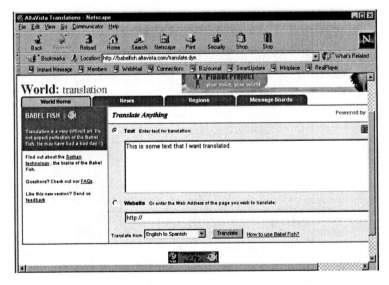

Figure 2

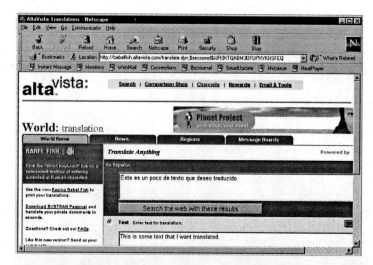

Figure 3

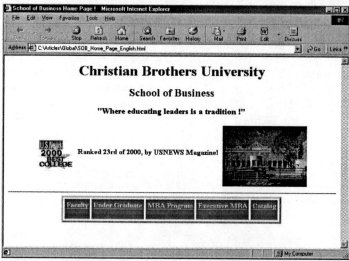

Figure 4

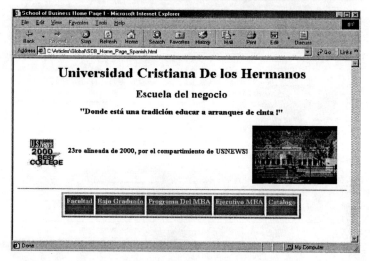

Figure 5

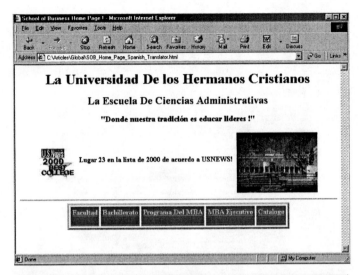

Figure 6

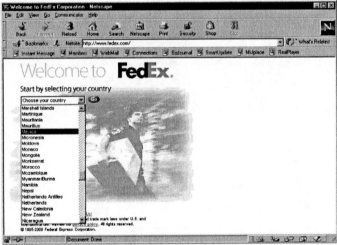

Figure 7

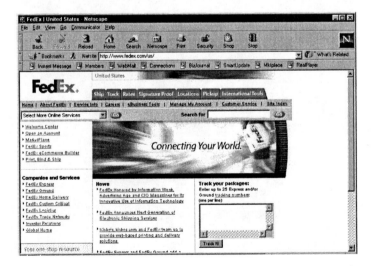

Figure 8

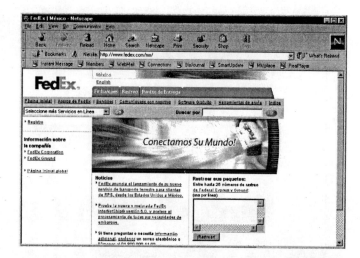

Figure 9

Figure 10

and phrases. Figure 5 is the version converted by a translator manually, and even though you may not speak Spanish, you can see the extent of the differences (Brandon, 2000).

Shown in Figure 6 is the home page for FedEx (www.fedex.com). One can select from over 200 countries for specific language and content. Figure 7 show the U.S. FedEx page, and Figure 8 shows the FedEx site for Mexico.

Another example is Nike's home page shown in Figure 9, and its Japan version shown in Figure 10.

Culture

Creating an effective foreign Web site involves much more than just a good language translation. Not only do languages differ in other countries, but semantics (the meaning of words and phrases) and cultural persuasions in a number of key areas are different. "Sensitivity to culture and national distinction will separate success from failure" (Sawhney, 2000). To be effective, a Web site has not only to be understandable and efficient, but has to be culturally pleasing and inoffensive. To accomplish that, it may be necessary that not only language be localized, but that content, layout, navigation, color, graphics, text/symbol size, and style may be different. Many companies have put forth global Web sites simply by translating the English into the targeted language, but then had to pull back and re-plan and redesign the localized site due to cultural offenses.

A country's humor, symbols, idioms, and marketing concepts may not send the same messages to other countries in the world. Oriental "manners" can be much different and more subtle than in other parts of the world (www.gwjapan.com); for example, avoid groups of four on Japanese sites. Sometimes even your product names may be offensive or inappropriate. General Motors tried to market the Chevy Nova in Mexico (in Spanish "No Va" means "doesn't go")! Some areas of global disagreement to avoid are: equality of the sexes or races, body parts and sexuality, abortion, child labor and majority age, animal rights, nudity, guns, work hours and ethic, capital punishment, scientific theories, and religious particulars (Brandon, 2001).

Cultural persuasions work both ways. For example, many American Web sites offend other countries, but Americans are sometimes offended by foreign material. A European branch of a major U.S. software company ran an advertisement with a woman straddling a chair with her legs which said "Sometimes size is not important if you have the right tool." The advertisement did well in Europe but offended Americans.

Colors have symbolic and special meaning in most locales. In the U.S., red/white/blue signify patriotism, and red and green signify Christmas. In India, pink is considered too feminine. Purple is a problem in many places; it symbolizes death in Catholic Europe and prostitution in the Middle East. Euro Disney had to rework its European sites after the first version used too much purple. Overall blue is the most culturally accepted color (Brandon, 2001). Much of the world is still using eight colors not 256 colors, thus it is best, for the immediate future, to use primary colors. An individual's perception of color depends not only on the ability to see it, but also on the ability to interpret it within the context of his/her emotional and cultural realities. "Ninety percent of Web sites are colored poorly, they are simply overdone, and there is no sense of harmony" (Holzschlag, 2000).

It is also very important to respect other cultures "symbols" (heroes, icons, etc.), both positive and negative (swastika). One guide site is Merriam Webster's Guide to International business (www.bspage.com/address.html). The classic books on these cultural subjects are excellent guides for Web pages also: "Kiss, Bow, or Shake Hands: How to do Business in

60 Countries (Morrison, 1995), Do's and Taboos Around the World (Axtell, 1993), and Dun & Bradstreet's Guide to Doing Business Around the World (Morrison, 1997).

Laws and Regulations

This year a French court's ruling that Yahoo! must make auctions of Nazi memorabilia unavailable in France indicates how uncertain and risky international e-business can be. "The troubling aspect of this case is that different countries can say that content not even targeted at their population breaks the law" (Perrotta, 2000). With the Internet, it is not possible to know for sure from where a user is logged in due to "IP tunneling" possibilities.

"Freedom" laws (such as the U.S. First Amendment) are not universal, and saying/ printing some things can be illegal in some parts of the world. In the U.S., you can say what you like about "public figures," but not so in most of the rest of the world. There have even been several lawsuits in the U.S. concerning pornographic sites and the like due to different interpretations of laws in different states (different geographic/political parts of U.S.).

Another legal issue concerns the privacy of personal data collected online. Many parts of the world have stricter laws than does the U.S., and U.S. companies have had judgments rendered against them in foreign courts. Recently an agreement has been reached between the U.S. and the European Union that would, among other things, mandate that all companies doing business in Europe notify users when personal data is being collected. Under that agreement, companies have four options in compliance to the new policy: register with the data-protection authority for the European Union, subscribe to a self-regulatory organization like Trust-e, prove they are subject to laws similar to the European Union, or agree to refer disputes to European regulators (Whiting, 2000).

There are other areas that could cause legal problems, too. One is foreign advertising restrictions; for example, in Germany, you cannot directly compare your product with that of a competitor. In some other countries this comparison may not be illegal but may leave a in bad taste. Other areas consider safety, consumer protection laws, health, and other standards; for example in the U.K., currently one cannot sell the drug Viagra, even though its sale is legal in the rest of the world; in Germany, companies are not allowed to provide an unlimited return guarantee.

Payment and Currency

Nearly half of the U.S. Web sites refuse international orders because they are unable to process them (Grossman, 2000). You could always ask for advance payment in native currency (cash, cashier's check, International Money Order), but you had better have a very unique product for that approach to be successful. Foreign exchange rates vary daily so indicating that your prices are in your country's funds (exclusive of local taxes and custom duties) and using credit cards (so the credit card company does the conversion) are two ways to deal with that issue. You can also link to a converter site (www.xe.net/ucc, www.oanda.com) or place a calculator on your page (www.xe.net/currency or www.bloomberg.com/markets/ currency/currcalc.cgi); see Figure 13 as a utility for your customers or do your own conversions. Also, in many countries traditional pricing may be much lower or higher, so product pricing is important. For example, computer products are typically 50% more expensive in Europe than in the U.S.

However, credit cards are rare in Japan, as is the use of checks. There postal workers collect COD's, and some companies send goods to "brick & mortar" places for consumers to pick up. In Germany, only 5% of Web users (second to U.S. in overall net usage) use credit cards. 88% of European merchants use invoice billing (with a long net payment due time). So while credit cards are a convenient and popular mechanism in the U.S., it is not so in the rest of the world.

To complicate matters even further, there are many (and always changing) international sales taxes, Value Added Taxes (VAT) in Europe, with different exempt items in each country. Selling in Europe may involve VAT registration in countries; one needs to get rulings and advise in writing from each country. Typically a company pays VAT based on the country it's based in, but that can depend on the country and item being sold.

One approach to avoid all these problems is to use an escrow service such as Paymentech (www.paymentech.com) which now handles about 3 billion transactions/year; others are: www.tradesafe.com, www.internetclearing.com, www.iescrow.com, www.worldpay.com.

Time-Date and Units of Measure

Dates are very important in E-Commerce being used for events such as: delivery dates, credit card expiration dates, product expiration dates, etc. There is an international standard on dates (ISO 8601 Date Format), and even though you may not use it internally in your programs (for database operations and calculations), your Web display should be in the localized format. For example, the common U.S. format of 10/6/2000 is not uniformly understood; instead use Oct-6-2000. Major databases (i.e., Oracle) allow you to switch date formats per session or connection so the way a date is input (inserted into table) or output (selected from table) is automatically converted to the internal table representation of the date. Some popular Web databases (ie., MySQL) do not provide this capability, so you will have to do the conversion in your own code (via client side JavaScript or Java Applets, or server side CGI programs or Java Servlets). Some popular Web programming languages have features to facilitate these conversions (i.e., Java's GregorianCalendar class or Perl's Date::Manip). Related to dates but not to the display problem, is the fact that each locale has it's own set of holidays; this will affect daily volumes and delivery schedules. Some locales may use a special calendar: Arabic Lunar Calendar, Jewish calendar, Iranian calendar, or the Japanese Imperial Calendar.

In the U.S., a 12-hour clock is common, except in U.S. military establishments. The rest of the world uses mostly a 24-hour clock, so it is best to display time in the 24-hour format. Of course time zones will be different, so include your time zone along with the phone numbers for personal customer support. It is best to spell out the time zone in the native language. You could instead give your support time in Greenwich 2000 Standard (GMT) and use or link to www.timeanddate.com for a customizable world clock and calendar.

In addition to dates and times, other units of measure will be different also. Only the U.S. and Canada still use the "English System," the rest of the world is on the metric system now, even Britain. This may or may not affect the goods you are selling, but overall the lack of adoption of the metric system will now begin to put the U.S. and Canada at a disadvantage in world E-Commerce. Even for an English-only Web site, to do business internationally, it will prove advantageous to display product information in both English and metric measurements or allow the user to dynamically change units (Hickman, 1998).

Figure 11 shows an example of a fictitious Web site selling "combat outfits." Here JavaScript is used to switch the HTML content from English units to Metric units; Figure 12 shows the Web site after hitting the button to switch to Metric units. The JavaScript code is shown in Appendix Listing 1. Dynamic HTML generation could have been done in a similar manner on the server using CGI in Perl or C/C++, or with Java Servlets.

Figure 11

Figure 12

Figure 13

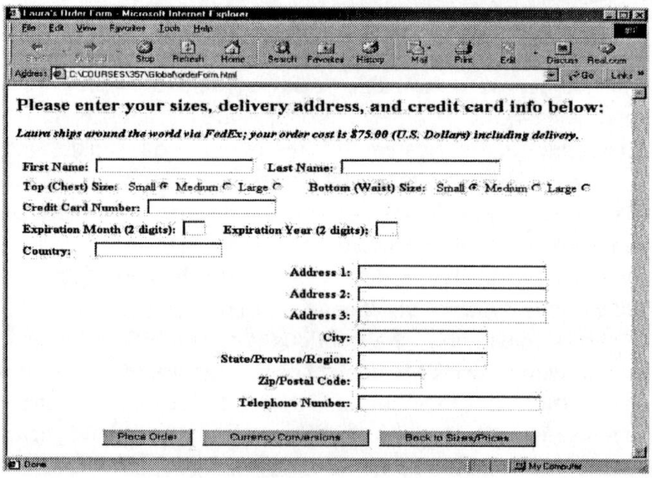

"Addressing" a customer may be more involved; some foreign addresses may have longer and more address fields. "For Europeans, trying to buy from American e-commerce companies is a lot like shopping in the Third World. While delivery address forms let you specify any country, the forms demand an American state, a five-digit zip code, a 3-3-4 formatted phone number, and they assume your street address only takes up one line" (Grossman, 2000). There is a universal standard, of sorts, here called the Universal Address Formats ("UPU"). Generally, it is of good advice including a country code (and base validation of remaining fields upon this country code), at least three address lines (40 characters each), city field (30 characters), a "state/province/region" field (20 characters), a postal code/zip field (10 characters), and a contact phone number (20 characters). Figure 13 shows an order form using these specifications for the "combat outfit" example in Figure 12.

Logistics

Logistics involve both getting your products to the customer, as well as allowing the customer to return unwanted goods. Some parts of the world have relatively primitive transportation networks. In China, villages don't have postal service. Also, each locale typically has a set of customs and tariffs that you may need to add to the price of your goods. This "landed cost" of an order is the sum of the price of goods, shipping charges, insurance, duties/customs, value added tax (VAT), and any import or export fees. You may need a "Shippers Export Declaration" depending on value and mode of transportation (www.census.gov/foreign-trade/www/correct.way.html) or other documents depending on countries and goods. As well as normal shipping insurances, you may need to consider export insurance (www.exim.gov). Of course, the language as well as logistic terminology varies; however there is a standard set of international logistic acronyms ("incoterms" - www.schenkerusa.com/incoterms.html).

Many countries have foreign import restrictions and/or quotas on such things as: animals, plants, items made from certain animals or endangered species, arms, explosives, bulletproof clothing, weapons or things that look like weapons, pornographic material, controlled substances, poisons, and treasonable items. In addition, many countries have certain export restrictions. One should "classify" his/her product according to the "Harmonized Schedule," but that schedule will vary somewhat by country plus it changes in time. To further complicate matters, many countries have sanctions or embargos against other countries, and some companies or individuals may be "denied" or "debarred." Japan has more than 200 trade laws and 17,000 regulations on imports (Pfenning, 2001). Today, 85% of U.S. companies do not ship to customers seeking delivery abroad, and the 15% that do ignore these compliance issues and push the responsibility of customs, restrictions, and payment onto their customers. (Shen, 2000)

There are several ways to handle all these logistics issues. One is to use shipping companies that handle all these problems for you (at a nominal charge) such as FedEx (www.fedex.com) or UPS (www.ups.com). These organizations can provide export documentation requirements, lists of prohibited articles, cost calculators, package tracking, etc. The different organizations have different degrees of global coverage. FedEx offers an interactive "Global Trade Manager" that walks you through a dialog about your shipment and indicates the forms you will need; you can even print out the forms from this Web site.

Another alternative is to use software or services that handle all these payment, custom, and restrictions issues by preparing the paperwork and calculating "landed costs; One example can be found at www.mycustoms.com, and this system can be integrated into your Web site by sending an XML-formatted document describing your product to its server.

Still another alternative is to use a centralized distribution center in foreign regions to reduce shipping costs and eliminate some import taxes and tariffs (Tapper, 2000), either directly or with a partner. There are also total fulfillment providers such as: National Fulfillment Services, DupliSoft, Fill It, SubmitOrder, Equire, FedexLogistics, etc. These organizations not only handle delivery but also inventory, returns, customer service, and in some cases Web ordering and payment.

For tracking and customer service, toll-free numbers are not always accessible in all countries, so provide direct-dial numbers and fax numbers. Also, on your foreign Web page version, supply the local country code for these numbers (Georgia, 1999). Try to encourage the use of e-mail for customer service and logistic issues. For further help in these areas contact your country's commerce office (in the U.S., the United States Department of Commerce Regional Export Assistance Office), and look at www.vastera.com, www.clearcross.com, www.intership.com, www.worldtrade.com, www.bxa.doc.gov or www.arentfox.com/features/tradeleg/home.html.

Other Business Issues

There are many other issues that may affect your global E-Commerce. "Building a global e-business calls for hosts of strategies that include partnering with or acquiring foreign companies, assembling sales and support operations, understanding new laws, languages, cultures, and implementing technology that can sustain a global endeavor" (Bacheldor, 2000). Many organizations have been successful by using foreign partners such as: E-Steel, GlobalFoodExchange, and Office Depot. There are many possible levels of "partnering," the simplest is perhaps just swapping e-mail lists and cross-listing each other's links. Hiring foreign personnel may be a lengthy process, in some countries a 2-3 month notice to current employers is customary. Trusted partners may be easy to find in some areas like Europe, but harder to find in other areas.

Demand and demographics are certainly different in other countries. For example, in the U.S. the average age is 41 with 41% having college degrees and 50% female; however, in France the average age is 35 with 64% having college degrees and 24% female. Thus, research and experience in international marketing is a must. If your company does not have such expertise, consider hiring a consultant (GlobalReach – www.euromktg.com, IDC – www.idc.com, or BlueSky – www.bluesky-inc.com), using government assistance where available (such as the U.S. Export Offices), or available guides (i.e. www.unzco.com/basicguide/index.html). There are numerous advertising channels around the world including international classified ads (www.profnet.org/classifieds.htm) and foreign press release services.

Being listed in all the major Web site directories may be very important. The major directories also have localized sites. Yahoo has directories for 24 countries. Another important consideration are domain names and URLs. If your URL is myCompany.com, you would likely also want to use myCompany.fr, etc. One can register for many international domain names (about 50 currently) through Network Solutions (www.idnames.com) or directly at the register for each country (registries exist in 192 countries) (Cohen, 2000). A list of country codes and links to their registers is found at Internet Assigned Numbers Authority (www.iana.org or www.icann.org). Of course, using and defending your brand name may also become an issue.

A problem some companies face with an international Web presence involves corporate internal political issues. Is the Web site content and/or operation to be managed centrally (i.e., in the home country) or locally. "Achieving complete centralization is too time-consuming said Compaq. It's better to agree on standards and allow customization around that." (Robb, 2000) Localization won't work well without some degree of regional autonomy.

TECHNICAL ISSUES

"Language is often the least challenging aspect of customizing, or localizing, a Web site for a foreign audience. The hard part is all the technical challenges." (Yunker, 2000) These include date/currency formats, bandwidth capabilities, tagging HTML properly, correct character sets to use, managing multilingual pages on the server, directing users to the language specific content, etc. Bandwidth and response time are vastly different around the world. In China, the 28.8 Kbp is standard, so one must minimize graphics and/or have a text-only version for China and similar bandwidth limited areas. In Europe and Japan, "wireless" or Mobile-commerce is more popular than currently in the U.S., and this affects bandwidth and display sizing (Brandon, 2001).

Whether your HTML pages are manually created, statically created by an HTML editor (e.g. FrontPage, DreamWeaver, etc.) or dynamically created on the server, the HTML code will have to identify both the character set and encoding. Character sets are the common ASCII, an ISO standard (eg.. ISO 2022-JP for Japanese) or a special set. The encoding to use is identified via the HTML META tag, such as: <META http-equiv="content-type" content="text/html; charset=Shift_JIS"><HTML Lang="ja"> for Japanese. You may also need to add ISO country codes to specify further dialect particulars (Brandon, 2001). The new standard is Unicode (ISO 10646, www.unicode.org) which Uses 16 bits (double byte) to store up to 65,536 characters/symbols versus ASCII 8 bit codes (256 symbols). With Unicode you do not have both a character set and an encoding; it is one and the same ("charset=utf-8"). It probably is less of a problem with the Web browser's handling of international characters than with the database where order information and customer information are stored. Latest versions of database products also support Unicode, and those are the versions needed for full global support.

Navigation varies with some scripts from the more common left to right then top to bottom; Arabic and Hebrew are (usually) right to left, and Kana is vertical. The latest version of HTML contains tags to handle navigational direction. As well as navigational issues, other issues are: hyphenation, stressing (underline, italics, bold in Roman, but different in other languages), bullet items, fonts, symbols above and below others, text justification, text sort orders, and GUI controls (text boxes and their labels, check boxes, radio buttons, drop downs, etc.) Field size is often a problem, and the layout of graphical User interfaces may need to be redesigned; for example, German words are longer than words in other languages (Brandon, 2001).

When translating your content, you need to separate out the scripts (JavaScript, ASP, JSP, etc.) or just let the translators work from the displayed page, not the underlying HTML. Not all HTML editors support both displaying and saving "double-byte" characters/symbols, so be sure to choose one that does such as Frontpage 2000. Also with the symbolic Asian languages, you may need to add language support kits to the operating system (unless you have the latest version of Windows 2000, for example) for most graphics applications to work correctly. Also, icons that have embedded text will be a problem, so it is best to separate the text from the icons. In a of review of Howard Johnson's new Web site, Squier stated: "Hojo has made a big deal about this site being bilingual (English and Spanish), but I found little substance to back up the hype. The graphics, most of which contain text, are not translated into Spanish. This is sort of important, since we're talking about words like

'Reservations' and 'Free Vacation Giveaway'" (Squier, 2000). One can use both language specific text and visual international symbols to convey meaning and focus users. Common symbols in the world include light bulbs, telephones, books, envelopes, computers, flashlights, nature, tools, umbrellas, the globe, binoculars, eyeglasses, scissors, audio speakers, VCR/tape controls, microphones, arrows, magnifying glasses, cars/trains/boats/planes, a smile, and a frown (Fernandes, 1995).

ARCHITECTURAL SOLUTIONS

For all of the above issues, it is evident that different Web content must be used in different locales. How to deploy and maintain these differences is a large and complex software architectural problem.

The first consideration is directing users to the locale-specific pages, and there are several methods that are typically used. One method is to put buttons, drop downs, or links on your native home page that the user can click to go to a locale-specific page (see the FedEx example in Figure 6). It is best to have the text on those buttons display the language name in the foreign language, although there are many sites that do not do it that way. For example on the button for Spanish say "Españoles" not "Spanish." The URLs of the locale version of your home page should be the same as your home page except end with the name of the country or locale, or end with the ISO standard country code abbreviation. That way it is easy for Users to link directly to their native version also. For example, with a home page URL of www.mycompany.com, have the Spanish version called www.mycompany.com/es or www.mycompany.com/espanole. Cookies can also be Used to maintain a User's language choice, so that when they return to the main URL they are switched to the locale-specific version automatically, assuming most Users of a specific PC will not be switching languages. The FedEx site (Figure 6) works in this manner.

With the capabilities of modern operating systems and using the Java language, there is an automatic way of placing a user on the correct native page (Davis & Smith, 1999). When users install an operating system on their computer (such as Microsoft Windows 95/98/2000),

Figure 14

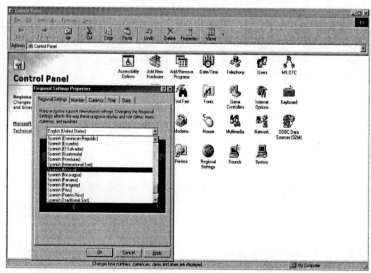

they will specify a locale (via Control Panel/Regional Settings); for most computers, the manufacturer sets this up upon assembly based upon the "ship to" address. This is shown in Figure 14.

Your home page can simply be a container for a Java Applet that interrogates the operating system to find the regional setting. Then the Applet can load the correct locale/language version. A simple example of such an Applet is shown in Appendix Listing 2. The Applet has a label to display the URL being linked to, but in practice the linking may be so fast that the label is never seen. Appendix Listing 3 is an example of the home page HTML. Be sure to put your "meta" information in this file also, so the search engines will find it. For international sites, foreign language search words should also be included (and the Web pages manually register with foreign search engines). It is still best to put buttons or a drop down on each locale version, in case the User wants to select a language other than the one for which he has set up his workstation.

The capability within the Java language for this is called "Resource Bundles" (Patten & Grandlienard, 1999). These bundles may be simple text files or Java classes. In the previous example, a text file was used for each locale. The text file "IntlRes.resource" contains the URL for the English version (or whatever your default version will be). In our example here it contained the one line: "page=SOB_Home_Page_English.html." The text file "IntlRes_fr.resource" would contain the base French version, here: "page=SOB_Home_Page_French_Translator.html," "IntlRes_es.resource" would contain the base Spanish version, here: "page=SOB_Home_Page_Spanish_Translator.html".and so on using the ISO 3166 codes. These text files (containing the URLs) can be specialized to a second level for dialects.

Instead of maintaining the URLs in the bundles (text files here), the actual phrases, codes, image filenames, video file names, etc. can be stored in the bundles. Then using Java server programming, dynamic HTML can be produced (under program control) "on the fly" to generate the native pages. "The biggest and most costly problem … is having to re-create Web sites from scratch because the original was programmed with English text embedded in the code" (DiSabatino, 2000). Appendix Listing 4 shows how this is done conceptually with a simple Java Applet that displays three messages in the foreign language of the workstation's regional setting. For dynamic HTML, this is typically done with a Java Servlet running on the server. Although technically more challenging, there are several advantages. First, the HTML is generated dynamically and can be a function of time, date, or anything else as well as locale. Second, when some information has to be changed, you do not have to open up and modify every language page; only the object that is being changed (phrase, image, etc.). Another key advantage is that the bundles can be classes, and as such an inheritance hierarchy can be set up. Dialects would be subclasses of the language and would inherit the properties of the language. In the subclasses, only those dialect properties that were different would have to be maintained.

There are products that facilitate this task of producing resource bundles or the like. Products such as Sun's Internationalization and Localization Toolkit (JILT), Multilizer Java Edition, or Catalyst Enterprise (Apicella, 2000) will capture all the textual references in a computer program (such as Java, C++, or PERL) and let you build a dictionary of translations in different languages. JILT Uses resource bundles, and the other products take different approaches. This is a great aid in modern dynamic HTML, Java Applet, or Java Servlet-based Web sites.

Then there is the enormous problem of version and configuration control with Web pages, just as there is in any software-based system. Maintaining many language and or country/locale versions of a company's Web site will be a major task in the future. Over time, the English text changes as products, their features, and policies are changed. There must be a method to keep everything in synchronization. There are some "content management" products such as Idiom's WorldServer or BroadVision's Web-Publishing System that have some of those needed localization capabilities. For example, each text item, logo, graphic, and other items are tagged with a rule to indicate how it is to be handled in different languages and/or regions (Robb, 2000).

Some Web sites that provide aid in all these technical areas include: Unicode (www.unicode.org), International Technical Issues (www.w3.org/International), Basis Technology (www.basistech.com), and the Microsoft Internationalization Whitepaper (http://msdn.microsoft.com/workshop/management/intl/locprocess.asp).

GENERAL RECOMMENDATIONS

Is globalization right for an organization ? It can be very costly to build and maintain a foreign presence. A full business plan must be set up: market analysis (product demand, pricing, and competition), total entry costs, then ROI must be considered (Tapper, 2000). Without doubt it is more expensive and time consuming to design and build an effective global Web presence than just a domestic site. Forbes has a list of ten key general questions for companies considering going global (Klee, 2001):

– Do you have a good reason? Is exporting central to your company's strategy ?
– Do you have the right "stuff" to pull it off (talent, technology, leadership, …) ?
– Can you identify a market(s) ?
– Are you flexible ?
– Can you find a good distributor (partner) ?
– Can you cope with all the complexity ?
– Can you brave the "nonlegal" barriers (ways of "doing business") ?
– Are you willing to extend credit and deal with currency turmoil ?
– Are you ready to run a much different kind of company ?
– Do the rewards outweigh the costs ?

"A company must have commitment from the top to make the endeavor of designing for international markets a success (Fernandes, 1995). Know your audience, See who your visitors are. Many companies are surprised when they analyze their log files and see who visits their site. There is software to facilitate this type of analysis and there is a new breed of application servers such as HitBox Enterprise from WebSideStory (www.Websidestory.com) addressing visitor analysis. These application servers do not Use log files (since they gather the information online from your static or dynamic Web pages) and thus do not require programming resources on your side.

Finally, to be most effective in the long run, an organization must get totally immersed in foreign and Web-related matters. One can join global organizations like The Global Trading Web Organization (www.commerceone,com), subscribe to international trade newsletters (www.newsletteraccess.com/subject/intetrade.htm), and Use other international services: www.worldbusiness.net/marketplace, www.digilead.com, ciber.bus.msu.edu/busres/tradlead.ht, Global Information Network (www.ginfo.net), Global Business Centre (www.glreach.com/gbc), GoingGlobal (www.going-global.com), WorldPoint (www.worldpoint.com), Internationalization of the Internet: (www.isoc.org:8080), InvestinEurope (www.investineurope.com).

FUTURE TRENDS

As statistically shown earlier, U.S. Web Users will play a smaller role each year in the "World Wide Web." China and Asian markets will grow dramatically. The "Euro" will become standard, and Europe may require U.S. based companies to charge VAT.

Communication infrastructures are building up in second and even third world countries (both government and private). Major communication build ups are currently occurring in the Pacific rim, Latin America, and South America (Ferranti, 1999). Companies such as FedEx will offer more sophisticated international shipping and logistic services to more parts of the world.

More sophisticated software for translation, localization, and version control is being developed each month. In addition, more companies will discover how to Use the technology available within Java (JSP, Servlets, Applets, Beans). The Internet will become pervasive and become an integral part of our everyday lives via WevTV, Net "Applicances," Wireless devices, handheld devices, smart cards, etc.

CONCLUSION

In the not too distant future, the Web will be everywhere, and by "everywhere" we mean not only in all our electronic devices, but everywhere in the world. It has been said that the "Net brutally punishes latecomers." (Sawhney & Mandai, 2000), so it is essential to start planning the internationalization and localization of E-Commerce now. Also remember the Web is a two-way street; foreign corporations will be coming after your customers soon!

REFERENCES

Apicello, Mario, (2000). Multilizer for java powers your apps to travel the globe, *Infoworld*, January.

Axtell, Rodger, (1993). *Do's and Taboos Around the World*, New York: John Wiley & Sons

Bacheldor, Beth , (2000). Worldwide E-Commerce: It's more than a web site, *Information Week*, May.

Bean, James, (2000). A framework for globalization, *Enterprise Development*, March.

Betts, Mitch, (2000). Global Web Sites Prove Challenging, *Computerworld*, August.

Brandon, Daniel, (2001). Localization of Web Content, 15th Southeastern Small College Computing Conference, 17(1), Nashville TN, November.

Cohen, Alan, (2000). Going global, *PC Magazine*, October.

Currid, Cheryl, (2000). Global strategy, *WebTechniques*, September.

Davis, Mark and Helena Smith, (1999). The Java international API: Beyond JDK 1.1, *Java Report*, February.

Disabatino, Jennifer, (2000). Web site globalization, *ComputerWorld*, July.

Fernandes, Tony, (1995). *Global Interface Design*, New York: Academic Press.

Ferranti, Marc, (1999). From global to local, *Infoworld*, October.

Ferranti, Marc, (2000). Globalization tidal wave, *Infoworld*, November.

Georgia, Bonny, (1999). The world is your marketplace, *Home Office Computing*, November.

Giebel, Tom, (1999). Globalize your web site, *PC Magazine*, November.

Grossman, Wendy, (2000). The outsiders, *Smart Business*, July.

Grossman, Wendy, (2000). Go global, *Smart Business*, October.

Harvey, David, (2000). Going global, *Home Office Computing*, October.

Hickman, Nancy, (1998). Internationalizing Your Web Site, *WebTechniques*, March.

Hoffman, Thomas, (2000). Euro projects bumped by e-commerce, ERP, *Computerworld* February.

Holzschlag, Molly, (2000). Color my world, *WebTechniques*, September.

IW (staff), (2000). Weekly stats, *InternetWeek*, November 20.

Kiplinger, Knight, (2000). Globalization – Alive & well, *Fidelity Outlook*, November.

Klee, Kenneth, (2001). "Going global: Out ten tests can help you get started. *Forbes Small Business,* March.

Korper, Steffano, and Juanita Ellis, (2000). *The E-Commerce Book, Building the E-Empire*, New York: Academic Press.

Lagon, Olin, (2000). Culturally correct site design, *WebTechniques*, September.

Morrison, Terri, (2000). *Kiss, Bow, or Shake Hands: How to do Business in 60 Countries,* Adams Media.

Morrison, Teresa, (1997). *Dun & Bradstreet's Guide to Doing Business Around the World*, Prentice Hall

Moschella, David, (2000). Ten key IT challenges for the next 20 years, *Computerworld,* December.

Neuman, Chuck, (2000). Considering the color-blind, *Webtechniques*, August.

Patten, Bob and Garry Grandlienard, (1999). Using resource bundles to international text, *Java Report*, February.

Perrotta, Tom, (2000). Yahoo! Ruling exposes risks of being global, *InternetWorld*, July.

Peterson, Constance, (2000). Accessible web sites matter, *Enterprise Development*, June.

Pfenning, Art, (2001). E-Biz must chart international path, *InternetWeek*, March 19.

Reed, Sandy, (2000). Want to limit the audience for you web site ? Keep it English only, *Infoworld*, August.

Robb, Drew, (2000). Act Globally, Serve Locally, *Information Week*, July.

Sawhney, Mohanbir and Sumant Mandai, (2000). Go Global, *Business*, May.

Schwartz, Howard, (2000). Going global, *WebTechniques*, September.

Shen, Jay, (2000). The commerce diplomats, *WebTechniques*, November.

Squier, Joseph and Nielsen, Jakob, (2000). Deconstructing—Hojo.com, *Internet World*, June.

Tapper, Sandy, (2000). Is globalization right for you, *WebTechniques*, September.

Uniscape Corporation, (2000). Global Content Manager.

Whiting, Rick, (2000). U.S. companies to comply with European privacy rules, *Information Week*, February.

Wilson, Tim, (2001). Spotty infrastructure impairs world view, *InternetWeek*, March.

Wonnacott, Laura ,(2001). Going global may bring new opportunities for existing customers, *InfoWorld*, April.

Yunker, John, (2000). Speaking in Charsets, *WebTechniques*, September.

APPENDIX

Listing 1

```
<HTML><HEAD><TITLE>Laura's Combat Outfits</TITLE>
<SCRIPT LANGUAGE="javascript">
var firstTime = true;
var heading = " "; var caption =" "; var sizeTable = " ";
var chestSize = new Array(3); var waistSize = new Array(3);

function size(type, fromSize, toSize){
```

```
        this.type= type; this.fromSize = fromSize; this.toSize = toSize;
    }


    function setHeading() {
        heading = "<HTML><BODY BGCOLOR='gray'><H1 ALIGN='Center'>Laura's
Combat Outfits for Women</H1>";
    }


    function English() {
        setHeading();
        heading += "<H3 ALIGN='Center'>(U.S./Canada Sizes)</H3>";
        heading += "</BODY></HTML>";
        caption = "<B>Sizes in Inches, $75 U.S. Dollars</B>";
        chestSize(0) = new size("small", "34","35");
        chestSize(1) = new size("medium","36","37");
        chestSize(2) = new size("large", "38","40");
        waistSize(0) = new size("small","22","23");
        waistSize(1) = new size("medium","24","25");
        waistSize(2) = new size("large", "26","28");
        buildTable(0);
        if(firstTime == false)
                {setContent();}
        firstTime = false;
    }


    function Metric(){
        setHeading();
        heading += "<H3 ALIGN='Center'>(Metric Sizes)</H3>";
        heading += "</BODY></HTML>";
        caption = "<B>Sizes in Centimeters, $75 U.S. Dollars</B>";
        chestSize(0) = new size("small", "85", "89");
        chestSize(1) = new size("medium","90","94");
        chestSize(2) = new size("large", "95","105");
        waistSize(0) = new size("small", "55", "59");
        waistSize(1) = new size("medium", "60", "64");
        waistSize(2) = new size("large", "65", "70");
        buildTable(1);
        setContent();
    }


    function buildTable(units) {
        sizeTable = "<HTML><BODY BGCOLOR='gray'> <P>"+
                    "<IMG                         SRC='laura_croft.jpg'
ALIGN=left> <P> <P> <P> <P>"+
                    "<P        ALIGN=Center><TABLE        BORDER=1
CELLPADDING=8><CAPTION><FONT COLOR='white'>"+caption+"</CAPTION>"+
                    "<TR><TD><FONT COLOR='white'><B>Sizes</B></TD>"+
                    "<TD ALIGN=CENTER><FONT COLOR='white'><B>Small</
```

```
B></TD>"+
                    "<TD ALIGN=CENTER><FONT COLOR='white'><B>Medium</
B></TD>"+
                    "<TD ALIGN=CENTER><FONT COLOR='white'><B>Large</
B></TD>"+
                    "</TR>"+
                    "<TR><TD ALIGN=LEFT><FONT COLOR='white'><B>Chest</
B>"+
                    "</TD><TD ALIGN=CENTER><FONT COLOR='black'>"+
chestSize(0).fromSize+"-"+chestSize(0).toSize+
                    "</TD><TD ALIGN=CENTER><FONT COLOR='black'>"+
chestSize(1).fromSize+"-"+chestSize(1).toSize+
                    "</TD><TD ALIGN=CENTER><FONT COLOR='black'>"+
chestSize(2).fromSize+"-"+chestSize(2).toSize+
                    "</TD></TR>"+
                    "<TR><TD ALIGN=LEFT><FONT COLOR='white'><B>Waist</
B>"+
                    "</TD><TD ALIGN=CENTER><FONT COLOR='black'>"+
waistSize(0).fromSize+"-"+waistSize(0).toSize+
                    "</TD><TD ALIGN=CENTER><FONT COLOR='black'>"+
waistSize(1).fromSize+"-"+waistSize(1).toSize+
                    "</TD><TD ALIGN=CENTER><FONT COLOR='black'>"+
waistSize(2).fromSize+"-"+waistSize(2).toSize+
                    "</TD></TR>"+
                    "</TABLE></P>";
        if(units == 1)
                    sizeTable += "<P ALIGN='center'><FORM><INPUT
type='button'  name='measurement'  value='U.S./Canada  Measurements'
onClick='parent.English()'>";
        else
                    sizeTable += "<P ALIGN='center'><FORM><INPUT
type='button'   name='measurement'   value='Metric   Measurements'
onClick='parent.Metric()'>";
        sizeTable+="   <INPUT TYPE=button VALUE='Place Order'
onClick=parent.location='orderForm.html'>"+
                    "   <INPUT TYPE='button' VALUE='Exit'
onClick=parent.close()></FORM></P></BODY></HTML>";
    }

    function setContent(){
        parent.bodyPart.location="javascript:parent.sizeTable";
        parent.headPart.location="javascript:parent.heading";
    }

    English();

    </SCRIPT></HEAD>
    <frameset rows='80,*' frameborder='no'>
```

```
<frame src="javascript:parent.heading" name="headPart" Border=none
        scrolling=no marginwidth=0 marginheight=0>
<frame src="javascript:parent.sizeTable" name="bodyPart" Border=none
        scrolling="auto" marginwidth=0 marginheight=0>
</frameset>
</HTML>
```

Listing 2
```
import java.applet.*;
import java.net.*;
import java.util.*;
import java.awt.*;

public class LanguageSelector extends Applet {
    public void init() {
     // get resource bundle corresponding to global setting
     ResourceBundle rb = ResourceBundle.getBundle("IntlRes");
     // construct string representation of URL
     String s = getCodeBase() + rb.getString("page");
     Label l = new Label ("Linking to: " + s);
     add(l);
     URL url = null;
     try {url = new URL(s); }
       catch ( MalformedURLException e) {
       System.out.println("Bad URL: " + url);
       }
     // link to specific language page
     getAppletContext().showDocument(url);
   }
}
```

Listing 3
```
<HTML>
<HEAD>
<TITLE>Language Selector</TITLE>
</HEAD>
<BODY>
<H2 ALIGN=center>Checking regional settings on workstation...</H2>
<APPLET CODE="LanguageSelector.class" WIDTH=500 HEIGHT=200></APPLET>
</BODY>
</HTML>
```

Listing 4
```
// simple Java applet to display three labels in default client locale
import java.applet.*;
import java.awt.*;
import java.util.*;
public class Intl extends Applet {
```

```
    Label l1;
    Label l2;
    Label l3;
    public void init() {
     // get resource bundle 'rb' using file (or class) 'IntlResource'
     ResourceBundle rb = ResourceBundle.getBundle("IntlResource");
     l1 = new Label(rb.getString("msg1")); // get text called 'msg1' in rb
     add(l1); // add label to applet
     l2 = new Label(rb.getString("msg2")); // get text called 'msg2' in rb
     add(l2); // add label to applet
     l3 = new Label(rb.getString("msg3")); // get text called 'msg3' in rb
     add(l3); // add label to applet
     }
    }
```

Chapter II

Electronic Architectures for Bridging the Global Digital Divide: A Comparative Assessment of E-Business Systems Designed to Reach the Global Poor

Nikhilesh Dholakia
University of Rhode Island

Nir Kshetri
University of Rhode Island

ABSTRACT

This chapter presents a comparative view of e-business systems designed to extend the benefits of e-business to the poor demographic segments of the developing world and to reach populations that are on the "wrong side of the digital divide." Four such systems are selected: the Global Trade Point Network (GTPN) of the United Nations, Alcatel Telemedicine Network, Little Intelligent Communities (LINCOS), and Johns Hopkins International's (JHI) Telemedicine Network. The four networks are compared across various network architecture dimensions. Our analysis indicates that LINCOS offers reduced capital cost, flexible architectures, and at the same time access to worldwide information systems, and hence has the highest potential to reach effectively the most excluded population in developing countries. Collaborations among technology marketers, national governments and international agencies are needed to identify the needs of the digitally excluded population and select appropriate architectures to serve the needs.

INTRODUCTION

Used appropriately, the Internet may deliver higher value to the people in developing countries than those in developed countries (World Bank, 2000). Arnold and Quelch (1998), for instance, argue that firms and individuals from developing countries can benefit more by using the Internet as a distribution channel than those from developed countries:

> [T]he power of new electronic media, notably the Internet, is not restricted to developed economies. Indeed, given the limits of conventional distribution channels in EMs [emerging markets], their value may be higher, albeit in only a small market. Worldwide electronic marketplaces allow local businesses access to a range of product choices and price quotes that can diminish the local distributors' often exclusive power. Industrial customers in particular are likely to find it economically attractive to establish electronic links with suppliers and customers outside their country. (p. 18)

There is, however, a wide gap between rich and poor nations in terms of their capabilities of accessing, delivering, and exchanging information in digital forms (Carter & Grieco, 2000). Developing countries, comprising more than 80% of the world population, account for a tiny fraction of global e-commerce. An estimate suggests that 99.9% of business-to-consumer e-commerce in 2003 will take place in the developed regions of North America, Europe, and Asia Pacific (Computer Economics, 2000). This "global digital divide" is the outcome of the complex interactions between information and communication technologies (ICT) and various factors in the environment.

If larger numbers of firms and individuals from developing countries are connected to the Internet, the utility value of the network will increase because of the well-known network externality effects (Katz and Shapiro, 1985, 1986). Apart from economic benefits such as more choices and the convenience of shopping at home, the Internet can facilitate progress on educational and scientific development, mutual aid, and world peace (Fink, 1997; Mansell & When, 1998). It can also foster democracy and offer exposure to and knowledge of other cultures (Fink, 1997). The benefits of widening and deepening of Internet access in the poorer countries thus not only accrue to the developing countries but also to the developed countries and the world as a whole.

The global digital disparity is attracting the attention of academicians and policymakers (Petrazzini & Kibati, 1999; UNDP, 2001). In recent years, several initiatives are being taken at different levels to exploit fully the potential of the Internet and e-commerce and to bridge the existing digital divide. Some of the initiatives are purely philanthropic; some are commercial, while others are a combination of the two. The extent to which individuals and organizations from developing countries will be able to enjoy the benefits of the Internet is a function of the characteristics of the network architectures designed to reach them. Several networks are emerging in an attempt to reach the global poor. The emerging networks that entail "*at least* one of the activities – production, distribution, marketing, sale *or* delivery – of goods and services by electronic means" fall in the domain of e-commerce (WTO, 1998). Little research exists on such emerging networks. This chapter aims to fill the research gap by providing a comparative assessment of the architecture of four of such networks – Global Trade Point Network (GTPN) of the United Nations, Little Intelligent Communities (LINCOS), Alcatel Telemedicine Network in Senegal (and proposed E-government Network in Mali), and the Johns Hopkins Global Access System. In a broad sense, these four networks try to accomplish *at least one* of the four e-commerce activities – production, distribution, marketing, sale *or* delivery of goods or services – and thus qualify as e-commerce networks.

BACKGROUND: RAPID EMERGENCE OF THE DIGITAL DIVIDE

All individuals and organizations are not equally likely to adopt a new technology. The adoption rate is influenced by economic variables such as profitability or relative advantage and social variables such as compatibility (Rogers, 1983). A technology is not likely to offer the same level of profitability to all potential adopters and/or is not equally compatible with all social systems, and hence adoption rates vary across individuals and organizations. Consequently, different types of "divide" emerge. In the case of the Internet and e-commerce, for instance, there are more male users than females (GVU Center, 1998). Also, more educated and high-income people are more likely to adopt the Internet than less educated and low-income people. Large enterprises have higher e-commerce adoption rates than small and medium-sized enterprises (SMEs) (Coppel, 2000). In addition, there is a "digital divide" across different races, age groups, etc. The global digital divide between the rich and poor nations is thus embedded in and enmeshed with these other types of "digital divides."

GLOBAL DIGITAL DIVIDE: PATTERNS AND CAUSES

Whereas high-income countries have income 63 times that of low-income countries, the respective ratios are 97 for PCs, 133 for mobile phones, and over 2100 for Internet hosts (Table 1). While reliable data on e-commerce transactions are not available, the ratio is likely to be even higher for e-commerce transactions since e-commerce is virtually non-existent in many developing countries. The pattern indicates that the gap between developed and developing countries is wider for more recent technologies such as PC, mobile phone, and the Internet than for technologies that were introduced earlier. Edejer (2000) states that the "current digital divide is more dramatic than any other inequity in health or income." Simply put, if the inequity of Internet access (a ratio of 2100) was as low as that for TV (a ratio of 9), the world would

Table 1: A comparison of countries in different income groups according to the penetration of several ICT products

Income group of Country	GNP per capita (1999)	TV per 1,000 (1998)	Telephone per 1,000 (1998)	PC per 1,000 (1998)	Mobile phones per 1,000 (1998)	Internet hosts per 10,000 (2000)
Low	410	76	23	3.2	2	0.37
Lower middle	1200	250	90	13.6	18	2.83
Upper middle	4900	285	176	53.1	76	35.88
High	25730	661	567	311.2	265	777.22
Ratio of High to Low income	*63*	*9*	*25*	*97*	*133*	*2101*

Source: Authors' calculations based on data from World Bank (2001)

be transformed dramatically. Policy measures at different levels would largely influence the extent to which the gap in Internet access will widen or become narrower in the future.

There are several causes of the digital divide. First, a large majority of potential users in developing countries cannot afford a telephone line, a personal computer, and the telephone and Internet services provider (ISP) access charges. Whereas the cost of a PC is 5% of per capita GDP in high-income countries, it is as high as 289% in low-income countries (ITU, 2001). For example, in January 2001, the cheapest Pentium III computer cost US$ 700 (UNDP, 2001), which is much higher than the average per capita GDP of most developing countries (Table 1). Furthermore, monthly Internet access charge as a proportion of per capita GDP in the world varies from 1.2% in the U.S. to 118% in Sierra Leone (ITU, 2001).

Second, even if consumers are willing to pay for the connection of a telephone line, there is a big gap between demand and supply in many developing countries. High import taxes on ICT products, monopoly in the telecommunications sector, and unfavorable geographical structures such as rugged mountains, wet and swampy ground, and deserts are partly responsible for the low availability and higher prices of ICT in these countries.

A third problem is related to the lack of skills. A majority of potential users in developing countries lack English language and computer skills – prerequisites to the use of Internet. For instance, in 1998 about 85% of the text in 2.5 million Web pages that were surveyed was in English (Nunberg, 2000). This proportion decreased to about 80% in 1999 and is estimated to reduce to 50% by 2003 (Nua, 1999b). Although a shift of Internet content to non-English languages is underway (Nua, 1999a), some knowledge of English is still necessary to use the Internet as the bulk of software used in the Internet is in English (Hedley, 1999) and most of the human-computer interfaces favor English language users (Goodman, 1994).

A fourth problem is related to the lack of relevant content. Although there are an estimated four billion Web pages in existence with a daily addition of about seven million new pages (Nua, 1999b) – an annual growth rate of about 100% (Nielsen, 2001) –the content remains largely geared to the needs of advanced nations. Edejer (2000) observes the difficulty of finding reliable health related information relevant to developing countries online:

> Few reports of health research from developing countries are published in journals indexed by Western services such as *Medline*. Western indexing services cover some 3000 journals, of which 98% are from the developed world. The whole of Latin America accounted for 0.39% of the total number of articles referenced by Medline in 1996... Because only a small number of journals from developing countries are indexed by Medline, research from these countries is almost invisible.

In the case of e-commerce, Avinash Persaud of State Street Bank points out at least three forces that are likely to widen the global divide (Economist.com, 2000). First, the "network" is likely to help first movers to establish a dominant position, giving firms from developed countries an edge. Second, e-commerce has shifted power from sellers to buyers. Since most of the firms from developing countries are commodity producers that are low down in the supply chain, buyer firms from developed countries will squeeze the profit margins of supplier firms from developing countries. Third, developing countries may get low investment inflows in the high-tech sector because the combination of risks and returns in these countries is less attractive than in developed countries.

Thus in the absence of appropriate policy measures, it is likely that the global digital divide will become wider rather than narrower. Policy measures directed at making appropriate network architectures available to the digitally excluded populations at reasonable costs could bridge the gap or at least decrease the rate at which it widens. Such policy measures include national-level actions like providing tax and other incentives to establish appropriate networks and entice foreign investors; international-level actions like providing loans and ICT-related assistance; and company-level actions such as designing and implementing networks that satisfy the needs of people in developing countries.

APPROACHES TO BRIDGING THE DIGITAL DIVIDE

The Internet is a versatile technology that can be used for a variety of purposes including education (such as distance learning to provide access to rural areas), civic participation (online government information to increase efficiency, disseminating information, community networking, etc.), urban and rural development, transportation (such as advanced transport telematics to improve road conditions and traffic flows), health (for example, improved, efficient communications and health education on the Web), access to information (library, language translation for multilingual nations, etc.), and e-commerce (to change/enhance buyer-seller relationships, business information online, etc.). The relative importance of such functions – for firms as well as individuals – is likely to be different in the developing countries than in the developed ones. The effectiveness of a network in bridging the digital divide is, thus, dependent on: (1) the network's ability to identify priorities of digitally excluded populations, and (2) the network's ability to attack the major barriers to Internet and e-commerce adoption.

In the following section, we discuss the network architectures of four e-business system designed to reach the global poor: the Global Trade Point Network (GTPN) of the United Nations Conference on Trade and Development (UNCTAD) (Figure 1), Alcatel Telemedicine Network (Figure 2), Little Intelligent Communities (LINCOS) (Figure 3) and Johns Hopkins International's (JHI) Telemedicine Network (Figure 4). A comparison of the functioning of the four networks is provided in Table 2.

Figure 1: UNCTAD GTPN

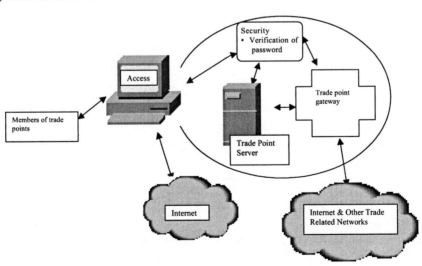

Figure 2: Alcatel Telemedicine Network in St Luis, Senegal

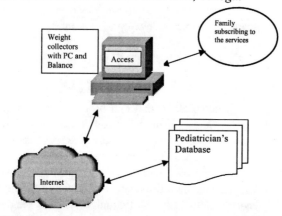

Figure 3: LINCOS Network

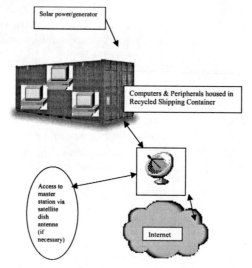

Figure 4: JHI Telemedicine Network

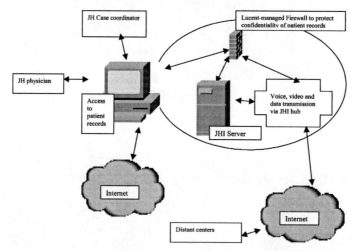

Table 2: A comparison of the four networks designed to reach the global poor

Attributes	UNCTAD GTPN	LINCOS	Alcatel Telemedicine	JHI Telemedicine
Services operating at	• Global level	• Latin America (Costa Rica and Dominican Republic)	• Senegal • Mali • Other African nations	• Middle East, Far East, South America and Europe
Primary services	• International-trade related, mainly for SMEs	• Health, education, banking, and government service • Electronic trading • Technical support for SMEs • Telecom and Information center • Video conference and entertainment • Forest, soil and water analysis	• Telemedicine	• Telemedicine, clinical services, discovery research, and medical education
Alliances with	• Over 35 universities, government organizations, and private companies (like Sun, Informix, Netscape, Oracle and Cisco).	• Over 10 academic institutions and at least 10 technical companies	• National governments	• Lucent, DoxSys
Salient features/ functions of the network	• A database-driven, interactive Internet system with password-protected areas that uses state-of-the-art tools for uploading, downloading, automatically updating and searching for information • Clients access the network through "trade points" that compile, standardize, centralize and update information on a national or local basis • Information on each trade point is formatted into standardized categories and codes. Data on member enterprises are verified periodically.	• Use recycled shipping containers to house computers, peripherals and generators • Solar power enabled • Multipurpose, multimedia mobile units • Can provide high Internet access • Can operate independently of traditional infrastructures • Satellite dish antennae link them to telecom networks or "master stations" if necessary.	• Weight collectors (equipped with PCs and a balance) take the weight of children of families subscribed to the system. • The data is loaded via Internet into the database of a Pediatrician, who detects the 10% of those children who require further attention. • The pediatrician sends emails to the concerned weight collector who informs the families and invites them for a medical visit.	• A referring physician can request a second opinion from Johns Hopkins physicians. • The patient's records are sent to the Hopkins campus and placed into an electronic medical folder. • The electronic folder is then sent to a hub at Johns Hopkins. • The case coordinator reviews the medical record and assigns it to a physician for review. • The physician's review is automatically forwarded to the case coordinator who then forwards it to the referring physician.

NETWORKS FOR BRIDGING
THE DIGITAL DIVIDE

United Nations Trade Point Program

UNCTAD launched the Global Trade Point Program in 1992 to facilitate the access to international markets for small and medium-sized enterprises (SMEs). There are more than 140 trade points in different parts of the world. In a trade point, participants in foreign trade transactions (e.g., customs authorities, foreign trade institutes, banks, chambers of commerce, freight forwarders, transport and insurance companies) are grouped together under a single physical or virtual roof to provide all required services at a reasonable cost.[1] It is a source of trade-related information providing actual and potential traders with data about business and market opportunities, potential clients and suppliers, trade regulations and requirements, etc.

The Secure Electronic Authentication Link (SEAL) project and concept were developed by the United Nations Trade Point Development Center. Its "smart card" project facilitates payment flows in international trade. The first level smart card allows users to automatically authenticate their user profile to the SEAL and secure an electronic trading opportunity (ETO) on the GTPN. The second level smart card allows confidentiality of information, payment information integrity, cardholder account authentication, merchant authentication, and interoperability with the ETO system on the Internet and the GTPN.

LINCOS: Little Intelligent Communities

The LINCOS initiative was developed jointly by the Fundación Costa Rica para el Desarrollo Sostenible, the Media Lab at the MIT, and the Instituto Tecnológico de Costa Rica in 1998 (Saxe et al., 2000). It has alliances with over ten academic institutions, and at least ten technology companies (United Nations, 2000). LINCOS uses recycled shipping containers[2] to house computers, peripherals and generators; thus allowing intelligent uses of ICTs in the regions with few development opportunities.

LINCOS integrate multiple ICTs into a single technology platform. The units are installed in a container equipped with five computers and other facilities to provide a broad range of services including Internet access, health, education, banking, government services, electronic trading, technical support for SMEs, telecom and Information center, video conference and entertainment, forest, soil and water analysis, etc. Each unit is satellite operated and solar power enabled and can operate independently of traditional infrastructures. The satellite dish antennae link them to any telecom network or "master station" as needed. Although the cost was about US$70,000 in the pilot stage, it is expected to decrease significantly with the increase in production (United Nations, 2000).

The prototype LINCOS sites, which have already been deployed in Costa Rica, are providing several benefits. For instance, coffee growers use LINCOS sites to find the best prices in the world as well as next week's weather.[3] Thirty such communities are being planned in the Dominican Republic and another 30 in Central America (Proenza, 2001).

Alcatel Telemedicine and E-Government Networks

Alcatel, the Europe-based telecommunications giant, has designed an Internet platform to offer services to end users aimed at solving a part of daily population concerns (OECD, 2001). In St. Louis, Senegal, weight collectors – women living in the area equipped with a laptop and a balance – take the weight of the children of families subscribed to Alcatel's telemedicine system.[4] The weight of children is surveyed regularly – twice a week – as a significant indicator of children's health. The data is loaded via Internet into the database of a pediatrician, who then detects the 10% of those children requiring further attention.[5] Then, the cyber-pediatrician sends emails to the concerned weight collector who informs the families and invites them for a medical visit. During February 2001, three children were saved from malnutrition, but one child died since his mother did not follow the pediatrician's prescription. The families are paying their subscription, and the waiting list for the service is long. This pilot project, led by Afrique Initiatives, serves as an example of how the Internet can leverage very weak health care resources.

In addition, Alcatel is taking initiatives to build Africa-based application domains for the Internet. It will provide local-content services to the general public related to health care as well as product transport chain, training dissemination, etc.

Along similar lines, in Mali, a nationwide project is being prepared that has the potential to impact the entire organization of civil society. To increase the decentralization process, the proposed system will connect 700 new local authorities to the central government authority via the Internet. It will also be possible to access both public and private services over the same infrastructure. All these services will be accessed via the community cyber-center. The network architecture is based on broadband IP access, used as a leapfrog technology solution. The cost is about US$2000, which is considered to be reasonable since the Telecenter's mean revenue in already-served areas varies between US$500 and US$1000 a month for the telephone service only (OECD, 2001).

The program will be conducted in cooperation with local partners strongly involved in Internet services, such as ISPs, project incubators, software developers, IS designers and local International Non-Government Organizations (INGOs). Although the program is more business-oriented than philanthropic, it is expected to generate benefits for the population.

Johns Hopkins Global Access System

Johns Hopkins Global Access System is based on the premise that anyone who wishes to have a second opinion on a diagnosis from anywhere in the world can receive it from a physician at the Johns Hopkins University. The system combines advancements in technologies such as imaging internetworking and workflow systems to create state-of-the-art telemedicine-based patient referral systems (Billie, 2001). When a referring physician requests a second opinion from a Johns Hopkins physician, the patient's records are sent to the Hopkins campus and placed into an electronic medical folder. The electronic folder is then sent to a hub at Johns Hopkins. The case coordinator reviews the medical record within two hours and then assigns it to a physician for review.

Once assigned, the physician gets five hours to accept or decline the case. Once accepted, the physician is required to complete the review process within 40 hours using a standard Web browser. After reviewing, the physician produces a report using a dictation service that is incorporated into the patient's medical record. This report is automatically forwarded to the case coordinator who then retrieves the report and forwards it to the referring physician. The entire process is completed within 48 hours (24 hours for emergencies). Through the global access system, Johns Hopkins provides telemedicine services in Europe, the Far East, Middle East and South America.[6]

A COMPARISON OF THE FOUR NETWORKS IN TERMS OF SEVERAL NETWORK ARCHITECTURE DIMENSIONS

The architecture of a network is likely to serve its purpose if it is simple, functionally adequate, affordable, immediately implementable, meets actual end client requirements, employs and nurtures local expertise, and employs locally available components if it is feasible to do so (Huston, 1994). Additional characteristics of a good network design include obvious and beneficial capabilities: user friendly, use of "state of the practice" rather than "state of the art" technology, upgradeable, secure, predictable, robust, and reliable (Hancock, 1990, pp. 68-69). It should be noted that the above characteristics are not mutually exclusive. Moreover, it is very unlikely for a given network architecture to satisfy all of the above criteria at once and the relative importance of a criterion is a function of several contextual factors.

The following is a comparison of the architectures of the four networks along some important dimensions. Table 3 presents a summary of the effectiveness of the four networks in terms of various network architecture dimensions.

Scalability

A scalable computer application or product continues to function well as it is changed in size or volume and also takes full advantage of the rescaled situation.[7] Three of the four networks – UNCTAD GTPN, Alcatel Telemedicine, and Johns Hopkins global access system—are mainly based on the Internet. The most important component of growth on the Internet is the demand for greater speed in the communications lines that make up the end-to-end Internet. Since the basic design of the Internet is remarkably scalable,[8] these three networks are likely to perform well on the scalability dimension. The performance, however, is likely to vary significantly from one country to another. Since 2-Channel ISDN is already available in many developing countries and some Asian cities are connected with the major

Table 3: A comparison of the four networks in terms of various network architecture dimensions

Dimension	UNCTAD GTPN	LINCOS	Alcatel Telemedicine	JHI Telemedicine
Scalability	• Very effective	• Not very effective	• Effective	• Effective
Robustness/ reliability/ predictability	• Very effective	• Depends upon the quality of the elements used in the network	• Very effective	• Very effective
Security	• Very effective	• Not much effective	• Not much effective	• Very effective
Quality	• High	• Moderate	• Moderate	• High
Use of local resources and expertise	• Not effective	• Very effective	• Not effective	• Not effective
Use of state of the practice technology	• Not effective	• Very effective	• Effective	• Not effective
Obvious and beneficial capabilities	• Effective	• Very effective	• Very effective	• Effective

U.S. cities with OC-48 Network (Dholakia & Kshetri, 2001), scalability is not a major problem in these countries. Although available bandwidth at present is very low in African countries, several initiatives are being taken that have the potential to bring a bandwidth boom in the near future. For instance, Africa ONE Limited is undertaking a project to build, own and operate a 32,000-kilometer undersea fiberoptic telecommunication cable system,[9] that will link African nations to each other and the rest of the world.

Although Alcatel[10] and Johns Hopkins Global Access System are relatively newer and are yet to be tested, GTPN is performing relatively well on scalability dimension. The United Nations Trade Point Development Center (UNTPDC) incubates a significant proportion of GTPN and a huge amount of data content.[11] GTPN architecture has been viewed as an appropriate model to assist least developed countries and those without the capability to establish Intranet or to use the Internet efficiently (Moreira, 1997).

For LINCOS, Internet access is only one of the several services it provides. The units are installed in a container equipped with five computers. Additional LINCOS units are to be provided if more computers need to be added. The investment for each unit was as high as US$ 85,000 in Dominican Republic and US$ 50,000 in San Marcos de Terazu, Costa Rica (Proenza, 2001). Thus, in terms of scalability dimension, LINCOS is not as good as the other three networks.

Robustness, Reliability and Predictability

A robust system continues to provide service even if some of its components or capabilities are lost to failure or it is subject to malicious attack. Reliability is a measure of whether a system provides the expected level of service. Reliability is typically achieved by combining component reliability, component redundancy, and a robust system design. While a robust system typically provides a reliable service, a reliable system need not be robust. The Internet has been quite resilient against failures so far, and since most of the networks mainly rely on the Internet, they are reasonably robust and reliable. Although about 3% of the routers may be down at any moment, major disruptions are rarely observed since the protocols governing the switching of data packets have built-in mechanisms to tolerate significant amount of error (Barabási, 2001).

Predictability, on the other hand, has to do with the user's expectations about the availability and quality of the services. A service can be predictably poor, but predictable services are often meant to be reliable whose occasional failures can be anticipated. Since the reliability of supporting infrastructure such as telephone lines varies widely across the world, so do user expectation and hence the predictability of a network.

In case of LINCOS, each unit is satellite operated and solar power-enabled and can operate independently of traditional infrastructures. Thus, robustness, reliability and predictability of LINCOS are more dependent on the quality of the elements that constitute each unit, such as the solar power generator and computer. The satellite dish antennae link them to any telecom network or "master station" as necessary, which enhances the robustness, reliability and predictability of LINCOS.

Affordability and Adoptability

The affordability and hence adoptability of a network is partly determined by its size. Since GTPN is one of the highest volume services on the Internet today, per unit cost is likely to be very low; hence the services are affordable and adoptable even for SMEs.[12] A survey found that 85.7% of trade point customers are SMEs and micro-enterprises (UNCTAD, 1997).

Affordability and adoptability of a network are also functions of supporting infrastructures and services. Since telephone and Internet access in many developing countries in general and African nations in particular are more expensive than in the U.S.,[13] the services provided by the networks are also likely to be more expensive in these countries.

For LINCOS, although the initial cost to establish each unit seems high, it should be noted that – unlike other networks – it is designed to work independently of traditional infrastructure. Since a large proportion of people in developing countries lack electricity and a still higher proportion do not have a telephone connection, a network that needs electricity and telephone for its operation is of no use to them. If the costs to provide electricity and telephone to the rural community are taken into account, LINCOS networks become relatively more affordable and adoptable.

Security

While robustness refers to a network's capability to provide service even if some of its components or capabilities are lost to failure or it is subject to malicious attack, security refers to the proneness to such attack. It should be noted that security is not equally important for the end users of all the networks discussed in this chapter. For instance, security tends to be less important than affordability for networks like Alcatel and LINCOS. On the other hand, security might be crucial in the case of GTPN and Johns Hopkins Global Access System – networks that handle sensitive trade or medical records.

Password-restricted areas have been added to the Global Trade Point Web site that uses state-of-the-art tools for uploading, downloading, automatic updating, and searching for information. Only Trade Points and members of Trade Points can send electronic trading opportunities (ETOs) and see "hot" ETOs.[14] Java is used to control access, certify trading partners, and handle payments. The Java-based secure infrastructure ensures integrity and confidentiality of all trade information.

Certification is the first step in secure trading. Prospective traders download the UNTPDC's 100% Pure Java-based applet and use it to provide the UN with reference data about their banking, trading, and services. After the UN certifies it, the company uses the Java applet residing in its standard Internet browser to access the network. Similarly, the smart card project of the UNCTAD is facilitating the payment flow in international trade. As discussed in the previous section, the first and second level smart cards allow secure ETO, confidentiality, payment information integrity, authentication, etc.

The Johns Hopkins Global Access System has similarly taken sufficient measures to ensure the confidentiality of patient records by using the Lucent Managed Firewall.

Quality of Services

Quality of service provided by a network should be evaluated in terms of customer expectation and the quality of alternative services. Since the networks discussed in this chapter are mainly designed to reach the global poor (or disadvantaged enterprises) who were previously unconnected by any other networks, it is difficult to judge the quality expected by the customers. The networks, however, are designed to provide as much benefits as possible to the poor people or disadvantaged enterprises, though not necessarily in philanthropic ways.

For the GTPN, interactivity and decentralization have been the keywords of the new network architecture. Users have access to the state-of-the-art tools for uploading, downloading, automatically updating and searching for information.

The "quality" of a telemedicine network is partly determined by its ability to diagnose and provide the required treatment at the earliest. Alcatel Telemedicine performs well on this dimension, given the fact that there is only one pediatrician for every 10,000 children in St. Luis, Senegal, and a child is very unlikely to get alternative diagnosis and treatment. In the Alcatel network, within less than five minutes, the pediatrician detects the 10% of those children showing odd curves that require further attention. Then she sends an email alert to the concerned weight collector who informs the family and invites them to come for a medical visit.

In the Johns Hopkins Global Access System, the medical consulting process is completed in less than 48 hours. As the treatment progresses, follow-up consultation can be provided which also includes video-conferencing. To facilitate communication and information transmission efficiently and effectively, the entire patient process will be available to all involved staff at Johns Hopkins as well as referring physicians in real time. A Customer Relationship Management (CRM) system based on Lucent's CRM products and services is also used, including a comprehensive suite of software to assist in customer contact and information management and integration of quality assurance and billing software.

Other Dimensions

Use of local resources and expertise: Alcatel and LINCOS are using local expertise and locally available components whereas JHI and GTPN have not given much attention to this dimension. For instance, Alcatel's proposed e-government network in Mali will be conducted with local partners strongly involved in Internet services, such as ISPs, project incubators, software developers, IS designers and local INGOs. Similarly, LINCOS is using recycled shipping containers mainly because of their local availability.

State-of-the-art vs. state- of- the- practice: GTPN and Johns Hopkins Global Access System are emphasizing state-of-the-art rather than state-of-the-practice technologies and hence are likely to be of little use for the people really excluded digitally. ALCATEL and LINCOS fare better on this dimension.

Obvious and beneficial capabilities: In terms of this dimension, again Alcatel and LINCOS perform better than the other two networks. Alcatel Telemedicine Network has already saved the lives of many children in Senegal. Likewise, LINCOS is providing a variety of services that are most essential for the rural community. Johns Hopkins Global Access System, on the other hand, can serve only those people who already have access to physicians. Likewise, GTPN's main role lies in bundling the services previously provided by several parties.

In sum, LINCOS performs the best on the dimensions of the use of local resources and expertise, use of state of the practice technology, and obvious and beneficial capabilities. Alcatel Telemedicine is the next best on these dimensions. UNCTAD GTPN and JHI Telemedicine, on the other hand, are not focusing on the population that is really excluded digitally.

FUTURE PROSPECTS FOR THE DIGITALLY EXCLUDED POPULATIONS

Rapidly dropping costs of ICTs, developments of user-friendly software and interfaces, and versatility of the Internet offer the potential for leapfrogging many of the development obstacles. Civil society, governments, and entrepreneurs of developing countries can take actions to bridge the digital divide by targeting highly excluded communities, by designing appropriate combination of new and old technologies, and by setting projects in the context of a longer-term plan to extend the benefits more widely.

The extent to which e-business companies can exploit the opportunity provided by a market size of over 4 billion digitally excluded people depends upon the architecture of their networks. Some of the important dimensions of network architecture that need special attention to serve developing market include affordability, state-of-the-practice rather than state-of-the-art technology, and utilization of locally available resources and expertise.

DISCUSSION, CONCLUSIONS AND IMPLICATIONS

The electronic architectures discussed in this chapter are designed to provide such services as telemedicine, international trade, e-government, environmental protection, and entertainment to the people in developing countries. Although, such networks are helping to bridge the digital divide between the developing and developed countries to some extent, most of them are not yet able to reach really excluded population in developing countries. The existing digital divide can be bridged to a large extent if appropriate policies are put in place at various levels.

Technology Developers and Marketers

The long waiting list and people's willingness to pay for the services provided by Alcatel Telemedicine Network in Senegal indicates that there is a huge untapped market for modern ICTs in developing countries if the services are *affordable* and *appropriate* to the target population and e-business companies need not provide their services in philanthropic ways. Lyle Hurst, director of HP e-inclusion, a partner of LINCOS, says that the mobile digital community centers "will be a significant market opportunity for all involved."[15] To exploit the potential, comprehensive research on the needs of the digitally excluded population and on the most appropriate networks to satisfy such needs by using locally available expertise and resources is needed.

National Governments and International Agencies

National governments and international agencies should collaborate with technology developers and marketers to identify and implement the most appropriate architecture to exploit the leapfrogging potential of the modern ICTs and to benefit the digitally excluded populations. Use of locally available resources and expertise can ensure the availability of networks with appropriate architecture at reasonable prices, thus accelerating the diffusion of modern ICTs, and at the same time producing multiplier effects with the creation of other economic activities. National governments can encourage technology marketers to create and implement networks that use local resources and expertise by providing appropriate policies as well as tax and other incentives. International agencies can influence the diffusion path of modern ICTs in developing countries by finding foreign investors, influencing national government policies, providing loan assistance, etc.

Of the four networks considered in this chapter, LINCOS makes use of locally available resources and has low capital costs (when infrastructure expenditures are added), flexible architectures, and at the same time access to worldwide information system and hence have the highest potential to reach effectively the most excluded populations in developing countries. National governments, international agencies, and technology marketers can work together to develop and implement this and other similar networks in developing countries.

ENDNOTES

[1] See http://www.unctad.org .

[2] The container is selected for its availability, ease of transport, durability and convenience (Saxe et al., 2000).

[3] See http://www.smartbusinessmag.com/article.

[4] Personal communications with Susanne Wahler, Marketing Manager, Voice Networks Division, Alcatel.

[5] See http://digitalbridges.gdbe.org/compendium.html.

[6] See http://www.hopkinsmedicine.org/international/global/.

[7] See http://search390.techtarget.com/sDefinition/0,,sid10_gci212940,00.html.

[8] See http://www.nap.edu/html/coming_of_age/ch2.html.

[9] See http://www.africaone.com/english/about/technical_description.cfm.

[10] In fact, the long waiting list indicates that Alcatel is not performing well in scalability dimension.

[11] In 1997, UNTPDC incubated 97% of the GTPN and over 12 GB of data content (Moreira, 1997).

[12] More than 1.6 billion electronic trading opportunities (ETOs) were exchanged in the GTPN between 1993 and 2000, with 4-5 million hits per day (see http://www2.asianconnect.com/untpdc/info/sunpress.html).

[13] For instance, a study conducted by the Organization for Economic Cooperation and Development found that an Internet account in Africa is over eight times more expensive than in the U.S.

[14] ETOs that are less than eight days old.

[15] See http://www.smartbusinessmag.com/article.

REFERENCES

Arnold, D. J & Quelch, J.A. (1998). New strategies in emerging markets. *Sloan Management Review*, (40:1), 7-21.

Barabási, A. (2001). The physics of the Web. *Physics World*, 14 (7) http://physicsweb.org/article/world/14/7/09.

Billie, K. (2001). Can I get a second opinion? *eDoc Magazine HTTP://WWW.EDOCMAGAZINE.COM/EDOCDIS.CFM?ID=83.*

Carter, C. & Grieco M. (2000) New deals, no wheels: Social exclusion, tele-options and electronic ontology. *Urban Studies, 37* (10), 1735-1748.

Computer Economics. (2000) The global economy is not so global. *Internet & E - Business Strategies*, 4 (4), 1-3.

Coppel, J. (2000). E-Commerce: Impacts and policy challenges. Economics Department Working Paper No. 252, *Organization of Economic Cooperation and Development* (OECD).

Dholakia, N. & Kshetri, N. (2001). The webs and the web-nots in the global economy: Electronic commerce, the digital divide, and policy options. In Wolfgang Fritz (Ed.) *Internet Marketing* (2nd ed.), 401-22, Stuttgart, Germany: Schaeffer-Poeschel.

Economist.com. (2000). Falling through the net. September 23.

Edejer, Tessa Tan-Torres. (2000). Disseminating health information in developing countries: The role of the Internet. *British medical Journal*, 321: 797-800.

Fink, K. (1999). Information networking as an instrument of sustainable development: Connectivity, content, and (co—)capacity building. *Social Science Computer Review*, 17(1):107-114.

Goodman, S.E., Press, L.I., Ruth, S.R. & Ruthowski, A.M. (1994). The global diffusion of the Internet: patterns and problems. *Communications of the ACM*, 37, 8: 27-31.

Gore, A. (1996). Bringing information to the world: The global information infrastructure. *Harvard Journal of Law and Technology*, 9 (1).

GVU Center. *GVU's 10th WWW User Survey,"Graphic, Visualization, & Usability Center*. (1998).

Hancock, B. (1998). *Issues and Problems in Computer Networking*. New York: American Management Association.

Hedley, R. A. (1999). The information age: Apartheid, cultural imperialism, or global village?. *Social Science Computer Review*, 17 (1), 78-87.

Huston, G. (1994). *The Architecture and Design of the Network, http://www.telstra.net/gih/prestns/inet94/wkshp/wkshp1.html*.

ITU. (2001). *The Internet: Challenges, Opportunities and Prospects*, 17 May- World Telecommunication Day, http://www.itu.int/newsroom/wtd/2001/ExecutiveSummary.html accessed 1 July, 2001.

Katz, M. L. & Shapiro, C. (1985). Network externalities, competition, and compatibility. *American Economic Review*, June, 424-440.

Katz, M. L. & Shapiro, C. (1986). Technology adoption in the presence of network externalities. *Journal of Political Economy*, 94, 822-41.

Mansell, R. & When, U. (1998). *Knowledge Societies: Information Technology for Sustainable Development*. New York: Oxford University Press.

Moreira, C. (1997). United Nations Trade Point Development Center (UNTPDC) Economic and Social Commission for Asia and the Pacific (ESCAP)," June 4, The UNCTAD/ESCAP Conference on Information Technologies and Electronic Trading in the Asia-Pacific Region. http://www.arraydev.com/commerce/jibc/9703-08.htm.

Nielsen, J. Kill the 53-day Meme, http://www.useit.com/alertbox/9509.html.

Nua Internet Surveys. (1999a). The Global Internet Market, April 5. http://www.nua.ie/surveys/trendmuncher/archives/1999/issue1.html.

Nua Internet Surveys. (1999b). May 29, Internationalization of the Web.

Nunberg, G. (2000). Will the Internet always speak English?. The American Prospect, March 27- April 10, 40-43.

OECD. (2001). Donor Information and Communications Technology (ICT) Initiatives and Programs. Joint OECD/UN/UNDP/World Bank Global Forum Exploiting the Digital Opportunities for Poverty Reduction, OECD, Paris, 5-6 March 2001. http://www.oecd.org/dac/digitalforum/docs/DO_Session1_MatrixAnnex.pdf.

Petrazzini, B & Kibati, M. (1999). The Internet in developing countries. *Communications of the ACM*, 42(6), 31-36.

Proenza, F. J. (2001). Telecenters for socioeconomic and rural development in Latin America and the Caribbean, *FAO, ITU, IADB*, Washington DC. May, http://www.iadb.org/ict4dev/telecenters/fullrep.pdf.

Rogers, E.M. (1983). *The Diffusion of Innovations*, 3rd ed. New York: Free Press.

Saxe, E. B. (2000). Taskforce on Bridging the Digital Divide through Education, October 23, 2000 http://www.worldbank.org/edinvest/lincos.htm.

UNCTAD. (1997). Trade point survey results, United Nations Conference on Trade and Development, Geneva, 1997 http://www.untpdc.org/untpdc/library/te/survey/.

UNDP. (2001). *Human Development Report 2000*, United Nations Development Program, New York. http://www.undp.org/hdr2001/completenew.pdf.

United Nations. (2000). Report of the high-level panel of experts on information and communication technology. General Assembly, economic and Social Council, 22 May, http://www.un.org/documents/ga/docs/55/a5575.pdf.

World Bank. Economic Toolkit for African policy makers. (2000). http://www.worldbank.org/infodev/projects/finafcon.htm.

World Bank. (2001). *World Development Report 2000/2001: Attacking Poverty*. Washington D.C.: The World Bank.

WTO. (1998). Declaration on Global Electronic Commerce, Ministerial Conference, Second Session, Geneva, 18 and 20 May, WT/MIN(98)/DEC/2, Geneva: World Trade Organization.

Section II:

Intelligent Portal Architecture

Chapter III

Intelligent Business Portals

Xue Li
University of Queensland

ABSTRACT

Portals can be regarded as an information gateway for exchanging business information over the Internet. They are for delivering the right information to the right user, at the right time, to the right place, to make the right decisions. A portal is a packaged piece of information with the properties of self-servicing, personalization, and real-time delivery. From a business point of view, a portal is a mobile, self-explanatory, and just-in-time delivered piece of information. In e-Commerce, business information is the set of timed transactions that can be triggered by events in business activities. This chapter will illustrate and explain the architecture of intelligent business portals for Web-enabled business applications.

INTRODUCTION

The portal concept was introduced by Merrill Lynch (Shilakes & Tylman, 1998). It was estimated that by the year 2002, the portal market value in Business Intelligence (Bergert, 2000) will reach US$7 billion, in Content Management will reach US$ 4.5 billion , and in Data Warehousing & Mart will reach US$ 2.5 billion. The main reason for this fast growth is because of the World Wide Web on the Internet and the high-speed network infrastructure.

Portals can be regarded as an information gateway (Li, 2000a & 2000b; Finkelstein, 2000; Firestone, 1999; Nielsen, 1999; Sullivan, 2001; Walker et al., 1999). Portals originated from the question of how we could deliver the right information to users. In traditional *pull technology* (Arnold, 1999; Buchwitz,1999; Käpylä, 1999), individual Web users have to initiate the search operation to find information from the Web, while when we consider *push technology* (Arnold, 1999; Buchwitz, 1999; Käpylä, 1999), information is sent to the individual users with or without solicitation. On the other hand, a user may need to interact with a system to provide information (such as filling a survey form). Thus, there is a need to provide an application independent mechanism for switching information between information providers and requestors. This requirement has generalized the traditional many-to-one client-server relation into a many-to-many client-server relation. Inevitably, an information explosion is introduced on the Web. Many Web users are frustrated in dealing with the overwhelming information bombardment. To solve the problem, the Portal as a packaged piece of information is used for delivering the right information to the right person, at the right time, to the right place, to make the right decisions (Li, 2000a & 2000b). A portal has the properties of self-servicing, personalization, and real-time delivery. For **self-servicing**, a user would be able to use pre-defined templates to re-design personalized Web pages. An example is given in Figure 1 (Wei, 2000). In this case every university student is given a Web site. The individual student can modify the Web site according to personal interests.

For **personalization**, a user would be able to deliver and receive information that is dedicated to the person. Figure 2 and Figure 3 show two implemented portals that are used for the students to select subjects and view personalized enrolment information. For **real-time delivery**, a portal is used as a messaging tool to deliver instant messages to an individual. For example, Oracle9iAS (http://www.oracle.com) Wireless Edition can provide information to any wireless device, such as mobile phones, hand-held computers, and pagers.

From a business point of view, a portal provides mobile, self-explanatory, and just-in-time delivered information. The information could be supplied as a set of timed transactions

Figure 1: A sample self-servicing personalised website

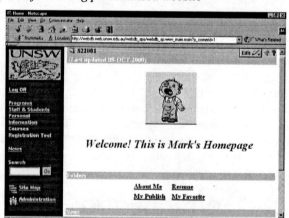

Figure 2: A sample personalised website with user input

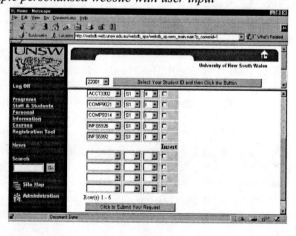

Figure 3: A sample personalised website with personal information

triggered by events in business activities. In business intelligence, knowledge is used to make business decisions, to search for useful information, or to control the routine business processes.

When portals are used as an approach to the fundamental information infrastructure of e-businesses, we need to know how to maximize their usefulness in order to improve our business performance, competitiveness, and viability. Intelligent Portals would be portals with knowledge in order to be driven around on an intranet or the World Wide Web. In other words, by capturing the domain-specific business knowledge, we can deploy Portals on the Web and let their behaviour be controlled by a knowledge base. In this case, a knowledge management system (Choo, 1998; Liebowitz & Wilcox, 1997) would play an important role in an e-business environment.

This chapter will discuss the theoretical issues on the integration of knowledge management systems with portal deployment mechanisms. Then, we will illustrate and explain the technological issues in designing and implementing intelligent business portals for Web-enabled business applications.

The next section introduces the concept of Intelligent portals. This concept is differentiated from the concept of Intelligent Agents. We then address the architecture issues. Finally, we discuss the tools and technology used in building Intelligent Portals. Some applicable cases will be given before the conclusions of the chapter.

INTELLIGENT PORTALS

Intelligence is the execution of knowledge. When a reasoning mechanism is invoked by a question or a problem, the relevant knowledge is retrieved and a possible answer or solution is then concluded. Intelligence also implies the capability to find the best solution for a problem. In a business environment, knowledge can be in different forms. It could be a set of "if-then" production rules for decision-making problems, a set of facts for corporate infrastructure descriptions, or a set of procedural descriptions for the business transactions. Business activities are event driven, so the timely execution of certain business processes is crucial to the success of business. This research area is mainly covered by workflow management (WFMC, 1996; Marin, 2001). A portal in this context is an information feeder that

Figure 4: Three-dimensional space for the workflow control

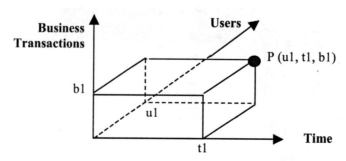

will satisfy the information needs of different users at different times for different business processes. In Figure 4, it can be seen that a point *P* in the 3-D space is the information about who is doing what at what time. Since the business activities can be the predefined workflows (like an application for an insurance policy will go through a step-by-step process to get an approval), a workflow control system should be able to check the information requirements for a particular business process and a particular person. For example, in Figure 4, point *P* may be interpreted as a person "John" at "Monday, 2 Nov, 2001, 9am" is "placing an order to buy a product."

In an e-business, if a Web site is designed for online ordering, the system should be able to deliver context sensitive information to the order form while a user is online (e.g., user Account Number, Best Sales, etc.). Furthermore, a reasoning mechanism may be triggered for context-sensitive reasoning and decision making.

In this case, an intelligent portal is a context sensitive information/service supplier that will accompany the user through the lifetime of the transaction. The 3-D space of the workflow control illustrated in Figure 4 shows the demands of the Intelligent Portals.

Intelligent Portals vs. Intelligent Agents

Here we need to differentiate Intelligent Portals from Intelligent Agents. Intelligent Agents are mobile software programs and are task oriented, while Intelligent Portals are information carriers and are content based. By using agents, we get things done; by using portals, we know what happened and what information should be supplied. One of the advantages of Intelligent Portals over Intelligent Agents concerns the acceptance from general users: agents are the programs to be executed on the clients' machines, while Intelligent Portals are the pieces of information driven by knowledge to deliver Web services. Consequently, there is no fear from users about potential virus attacks.

Integrating Knowledge Management with Portals

In a business environment, knowledge management has many aspects, from low-level day-to-day business process control to high-level executive decision making. A knowledge management system should be able to: collect relevant knowledge, store knowledge in a sharable enterprise memory, communicate the knowledge with parties, and maintain consistencies. In all these activities, a portal can play an important role within an enterprise; that is, as an information carrier to shift information around the organization.

One important task relating to portals in knowledge management is Workflow Management (WFMC, 1996; Allen, 2001). Workflow management involves:

- Specification of process control for business transactions, which concerns data coordination, exception handling, recovery, etc. The workflow specifications provide execution plans.
- Verification of the feasibility and correctness of a design, while allowing for redesign and implementations for coping with changes.
- Execution control for carrying out business transactions. A Workflow Engine is responsible for execution of the processes. During any given execution, a workflow plan may be applied to many individual users. As a result, many concurrent workflow instances will be generated. The Workflow Engine is responsible for concurrency control (process dependencies), exception handling, and recovery.

In Workflow Management, portals can be used as basic constructs to build workflow tasks (Marin, 2001). For example, in processing a procurement request (e.g., purchasing a laptop computer), one may need some information about competing offers from different suppliers. In this context, a portal should play a role not unlike a real-life broker that can assess the buyer's requests and evaluate the seller's offers in order to make a deal.

Intelligent Portal Deployment and Development

Knowledge about portals is presented from three aspects: **ontological services**, **location services**, and **directory services**. These three services answer the questions of what portals are, where they are found, and what they are used for. Ontological services are facilities that categorize business information into a searchable, indexed structure with the **meaning of the data** (i.e., Classification dimension). Location services provide maps of portals over the Internet for their **availability** (i.e., Location dimension), while **directory services** are a view of the information tailored for **personalized service** (i.e., Customization dimension). These three aspects are orthogonal in the sense that they make up the key information required for providing business data over the Internet. Figure 5 shows the idea of the deployment of the Intelligent Portals.

Figure 5: Deployment of the intelligent business portals

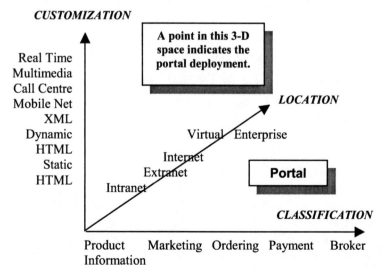

Figure 6: The paradigm of intelligent business portals

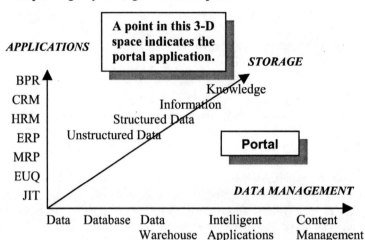

In the following discussion (see Figure 6), we show the Intelligent Portal in a three-dimensional paradigm for representation purposes. In the *Storage* dimension, the business data is packaged as structured data, unstructured data, or knowledge in a ready-to-use format. In the *Data Management* dimension, the business data are the objects managed within databases, data warehouses, intelligent applications, and content management systems. In the *Applications* dimension, the business data are the objects in Business Process Restructuring (BPR), Customer Resource Management (CRM), Enterprise Resource Planning (ERP), Material Resource Planning (MRP), or Just In time Delivery (JID), applications.

By identifying these three dimensions of business portals, we will be able to design and manage portals in a way that they are "intelligent" – i.e., that the portals as packaged business data will be "living" in a business transaction management environment and will be "clever" enough to deliver the business data on the Internet at the right time, to the right places.

In contrast with Figure 5, which illustrates the application deployment of portals, Figure 6 represents the development of portals.

In order to use intelligent portals, we need to design the business workflow so that an event-driven workflow engine can be integrated with a portal delivery system.

SYSTEM ARCHITECTURE OF INTELLIGENT PORTALS

In this section, we continue the discussions in the previous section with the architecture issues. We first introduce the layers of Intelligent Portals. Then we introduce the overall system architecture that uses Intelligent Portals.

Layers of Intelligent Portals

We identify that Intelligent Portals are organized in three layers (see Figure 7). From the top, the Portal Control Layer is used to describe the Portal's application logic, which concerns how and when Portals are used in e-business applications. Figure 4 shows this aspect in a 3-D space. The Portal Control Layer provides information to applications. The middle layer is the Portal Deployment Layer. The Portal Development Layer concerns how and where

Figure 7: Three layers of intelligent portals

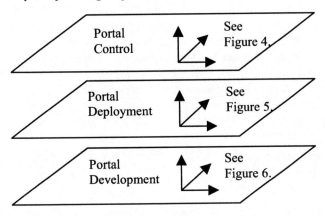

portals are deployed. Figure 5 details a 3-D space for portal deployment. At the bottom layer, we discuss portal development. The portal is conceptualized in a 3-D space in order to package data into highly structured and managed pieces of information.

Key Component: The Information Broker

The intelligence of portals relies on the performance of a kernel system component called the Information Broker (see Figure 8). It is responsible for pushing portals to users at the right time. The Information Broker is also capable of searching information for user needs. It is an executor of business workflows that is context sensitive to user requests for information. Its input consists of the User Profile (UP) and the stored information of the Business Workflow (BW). By using UP, the system knows the requirements of individual users. By using the BW, the system knows how and when to deliver what information. For example, an instance in UP indicates a user John Smith is a lecturer in Computer Science. A schedule for Teaching Preparation in the BW will then be executed by the system (i.e., the Information Broker) to deliver the information relevant to John Smith. The information is

Figure 8: Architecture of a Web site that uses intelligent portals

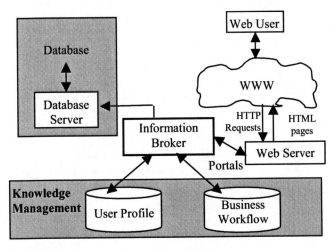

personalized by checking which subject John Smith is teaching. Information about student enrollment, the student tutorial group preferences, classroom details, deadlines, etc., will then be automatically delivered to John Smith. Moreover, the state of John Smith's profile will be updated to a new state that assumes John Smith is going to upload the teaching materials (e.g., lecture notes in PDF format, etc.) to the database in order to deliver them to students who have enrolled for the subject. Figure 8 shows the architecture of a Web site that uses the Information Broker as a key component of portals.

We will discuss some cases to use portals in business environment in a later section. The following section introduces the tools to build Intelligent Portals.

TOOLS FOR BUILDING INTELLIGENT PORTALS

In order to build Intelligent Portals, we need to select the right tools to put them together. However, there is currently no consensus on a standard for portals or Intelligent Portals. In the following discussion, we provide some suggestions of currently available tools.

Figure 9 shows the architecture of the Information Broker – the key component that needs to be built. It is an integrated system that carries out information brokering. The Workflow Engine is a subsystem with knowledge on how portals are used. The Search Engine is a sub-system that knows where to find and collect information, while Portal Management is a sub-system that knows what information is available.

Lotus provides tools such as *Portals Builder* and *K-station* (http://mirror.iian.ibeam.com/lotus/shst/kstation/index.html) for portal development. K-station is a knowledge Portal with out-of-the-box collaborative capabilities. It uses a Web browser user interface to access virtually any information source from Web applications to Microsoft Office documents to back-end data. With integrated instant collaboration features and a highly customizable environment, K-station offers a complete Knowledge Management solution.

Portals can be implemented in XML. Many tools provided by major companies (e.g., Microsoft, Oracle, IBM, etc.) are now supporting XML (Finkelstein, 2000). When using XML to represent knowledge, the domain structural knowledge must be specified in a standard Document Type Definition (DTD) as a set of rules to validate the Portals. Microsoft's version

Figure 9: Architecture of Information Broker

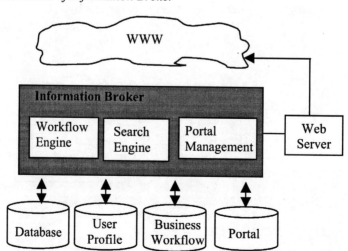

of Portals is called Sharepoint Portal Server, http://www.microsoft.com/sharepoint/evalua-tion/overview/techhighlights.asp.

Oracle (http://www.oracle.com) provides a tool called Portal Development Kit (PDK). Using this tool, *Portles* (the raw material building blocks for portals) can be created and managed from a variety of resources including databases and URL addressed components. *Oracle9iAS Portal* is its latest product to support the deployment of portals.

Other companies also provide tools for building Intelligent Portals, such as *Viador* (http://www.viador.com) and CORVID (http://www.exsys.com/products.htm). By using *CORVID*, a Web-deliverable built-in Inference Engine can be used to execute the inference rules for an enterprise knowledge management system.

There are also many Workflow Management tools that can be integrated with Intelligent Portals, such as IBM FlowMark (now called MQ Series, http://www.ibm.com), Oracle Workflow (http://www.oracle.com), Woflan and WF-net (van der Aalst et al., 1997, 1998), among others.

INTELLIGENT PORTALS IN BUSINESS

In this section we introduce some e-business cases where Intelligent Portals are applicable.

e-Marketing

e-Marketing is one of the hottest, fastest growing e-businesses on the World Wide Web. By using Intelligent Portals, one-to-one marketing is possible to keep abreast of a user's demands for specific products. In such a case, the intelligence is embodied as the application of the knowledge about the online user profile and the knowledge about available products. Consequently, users should not feel "spammed" when receiving advertisements, as the incoming information is within the user's interests.

e-Broker

Many Web sites are now providing an e-marketplace for Web users to visit, for buying and selling products. (e.g., http://www.vfm.net). In a free market where prices move toward equilibrium, effective communication between buyers and sellers is critical.

In the marketplace, a broker's role is to understand the needs of an individual customer and provide the customer with the best service available. Furthermore, a broker also serves businesses, facilitating fair and productively conducted business competition. It is very important that a broker is trusted by both customer and vendor so that in any business transactions between the parties fair market values are achieved, no more and no less. Thus, the commission of the broker can be justified.

An e-broker (also called Web Broker) can be implemented as Intelligent Portals that make profit by selling nothing but intelligence (Li, 2001). To this end, Intelligent Portals may be allowed to view the information of both requestors and suppliers. By using their individual experiences and their knowledge of the marketplace, they smooth the relationship between buyers and sellers and satisfy both by providing the best matches in the marketplace. The modern matchmakers are getting more and more popular by guaranteeing a win-win situation for sellers and buyers. Ultimately the e-brokers win as well. The e-broker's business is guaranteed because of the complex Web-enabled transactions that handle the buy-sell-payment-shipping in one integrated system. The only problem is in establishing trust between the involved parties. In many cases the third party offering e-broker services can be a mutually trusted entity, such as a financial institution (e.g., a bank), a security control system, or a well-known consultant company. There is no doubt that the e-broker is becoming increasingly common in Internet commerce Web sites for a wide range of businesses.

e-Business Management

In the area of e-business management, Intelligent Portals should be applicable to both business-to-business (B2B) and business-to-customer (B2C) types of electronic commerce. Portals are categorized as *horizontal* and *vertical* portals for inter/intra-organizational information exchanges (Li, 2000a & 2000b; Zirpins, 2001).

CONCLUSIONS

Currently the contents on the World Wide Web are evolving from passive hypertext documents to active distributed services (Zirpins, 2001). By providing self-servicing, personalization, and real-time delivery, portals can actively deliver information to Web users. In this chapter, we have discussed the following problems:

- What are Intelligent Business Portals?
- What potential do they provide?
- What is the architecture of Intelligent Portals?
- What are the technical issues in implementing them?
- How can we use them in Internet Commerce?

In order to implement Intelligent Portals, we have introduced a three-layer architecture that reflects the usage of the modern information technology infrastructure. At the development layer, portals are packaged according to needs. At the deployment layer, portals are allocated to their applications. At the top control layer, portals become knowledgeable and know how, where, and when to deliver their services.

The key component in our architecture is the Information Broker that is responsible for implementing the three-layer Intelligent Portal architecture.

REFERENCES

Allen, R. (2001). Workflow: An Introduction, in Fischer L. (Ed), *Workflow Handbook 2001*, WFMC (Workflow Management Coalition), 15-38.

Arnold, S.E. (1997). Push technology, driving traditional online into a corner. Retrieved January 9, 2002 from http://www.onlineinc.com/database/AugDB97/arnold8.html.

Bergert, S. (2000). Power to the people, *Intelligent Enterprise,* 3(18): 47-51, December.

Buchwitz, L. (1999). Monitoring competitive intelligence using Internet push technology. Retrieved October 19, 2000, from http://tor-pw1.netcom.ca/~lillyb/CI_paper.html.

Choo, C.W. (1998). *The knowing organization: How organizations use information to construct meaning, create knowledge and make decisions*, Oxford, UK: Oxford University Press.

Finkelstein, C. & Aiken, P. (2000). *Building Corporate Portals with XML.* New York: McGraw-Hill.

Firestone, J. (1999). *Defining the Enterprise Information Portal.* White Paper, Executive Information Systems, retrieved January 10, 2002, from http://www.dkms.com/EIPDEF.html

Käpylä, T., Niemi, I., & Lehtola, A. (1999). *Towards an accessible Web by applying PUSH technology,* Retrieved January 10, 2002, from http://www.vtt.fi/tte/samba/projects/ida-push/Ercim_WS_UI_paper.htm.

Li, X. (2000a). Engineering issues in Internet commerce. Chapter 1. In *Internet Commerce and Software Agents: Cases, Technologies and Opportunities,* S. M. Rahman and R.J. Bignall (Ed.), Hershey, PA: Idea Group Publishing.

Li, X. (2000b). Information gateway—Portals. Keynote Speech, IEEE TOOL's 36, June, Xi'an.

Li, X. (2001). Web brokers in e-Marketplace. Project in INFS2200 Relational Database Systems, University of Queensland, Australia, http://www.itee.uq.edu.au/~infs2200.

Liebowitz, J. & Wilcox, L. (1997). *Knowledge Management and its Integrative Elements,* Boco Raton, FL: CRC Press.

Marin, M. (2001). The role of workflow in portal environments. In Fischer L. (Ed,) *Workflow Handbook* 2001, WFMC (Workflow Management Coalition), 79-90.

Nielsen, J. (1999). Intranet portals: The corporate information infrastructure. Retrieved January 9, 2002, from http://www.useit.com/alertbox/990404.html.

Shilakes, C.C. & Tylman, J. (1998). Enterprise information portals, in-depth report. Merrill Lynch & Co. Global Securities Research & Economics Group. Retrieved April 17, 2001, from http://www.sagemaker.com/company/WhitePapers/eip_indepth.pdf.

Sullivan, D. (2001). The end for search engines? Search Engine Report, internet.com Cooperation, Retrieved January 9, 2002, from http://www.searchenginewatch.com/sereport/01/02-theend.html.

van der Aalst, W.M.P. (1998). The application of petri nets to workflow management. *The Journal of Circuits, Systems and Computers,* 8(1), 21-66.

van der Aalst, W.M.P. et al., (1997). A Petri net-based tool to analyze workflows, *Proceedings of Petri Nets in System Engineering,* University of Hamburg, Hamburg, 78-90.

Walker, J., Schadler, T., Ciadelli, A., & Overby, C. (1999). Building an Intranet portal, *Forrester Report,* Cambridge, Forrester Research Inc, January.

Wei, Q. (2000). Student Portals, Master Thesis. Supervised by Xue Li. University of New South Wales, Sydney, Australia.

WFMC (1996). Workflow Management Coalition Terminology and Glossary (WFMC-TC-1011), Technical Report, Workflow Management Coalition, Brussels, 1996.

Zirpins, C., etc. (2001). Advanced concepts for next generation portals. *Proceedings of the 1st Workshop on Web Based Collaboration (WBC'01),* September.

Chapter IV

Expert Database Web Portal Architecture

Anthony Scimé
State University of New York College at Brockport

ABSTRACT

The volume of data available on the World Wide Web makes it difficult for a domain novice to find reliable, accurate information. Such a novice may call upon a domain expert for information and advice. On the Web, this expert advice can be organized as an expert database behind a Web portal for the domain. The creation of such a database requires an architecture that captures the expert's domain knowledge and finds and evaluates applicable Web pages from which data is extracted. This chapter outlines the components of an expert database Web portal, its design, and population.

INTRODUCTION

One of the advantages of the World Wide Web is that information is available in virtually every domain. This information, however, must be found to be of value. Two general methods of finding information on the Web are to conduct a search and to access a Web portal. A Web search is typically conducted by the use of a search engine. A Web portal provides access to information in a specific domain. The Web portal maybe a domain-specialized search engine or a Web-accessible domain specific database. The specialized search engine portals are search engines with search indices for Web pages in the specific domain. These portals are sometimes referred to as consumer portals (Bordner, 1999). The database Web portals, also known as commerce or industry portals (Bordner) or knowledge portals (Staab & Maedche, 2001), provide information on the domain collected from specific sources in advance of the searcher's request. This database Web portal approach to accessing information is especially useful for the novice searcher unfamiliar with the domain being accessed (Bordner; Maedche & Staab, 2001).

To access information on the Web, a user must either know the URL of desired pages, or find pages with the needed information by some search process. Searching for Web pages requires the user to be able to express his/her information need in terms understandable to the search engine. That is, the searcher must choose keywords. The search engine must recognize the keywords as keywords representing Web pages that will satisfy the searcher's information need (Hoelscher & Strube, 1999; Lawrence & Giles, 1999; Turtle & Croft, 1996). After conducting a search, the searcher must have sufficient knowledge to determine the validity of the found pages and be able to sift through the excessive volume typically returned by search engines (Hoelscher & Strube). The sheer volume of pages makes it difficult to find comprehensive and valid pages on the Web for any given information need (Lawrence & Giles).

On the Web, the process of searching for information that is new to the searcher is difficult. The novice domain searcher does not know the keywords necessary to achieve the desired result. Most searchers limit the keyword search to one or two keywords and search within a single search engine (Hoelscher & Strube, 1999). The search typically ranks the resulting hits. Ranking brings to the top of the results list the Web pages that most closely match the searcher's keyword query. The results of most searches may be flawed, because the searcher is not expert in developing quality query expressions. Nor, do most searchers select a search engine based on the domain to be searched (Hoelscher & Strube). Searcher frustration, or more specifically a searcher's inability to find the information he/she needs, is common.

The lack of domain context leads the novice to find a domain expert, who can then provide information in the domain and may satisfy the novice's information need. The domain expert should have the ability to express domain facts and information at various levels of abstraction and provide context for the components of the domain. This is one of the attributes that makes him or her the expert (Turban & Aronson, 2001). Because the novice has no personal context, he/she uses the expert's context. A domain expert database Web portal can provide domain expertise on the Web. In this portal, relevant information has been brought together—not as a search engine, but as a storehouse of previously found and validated information.

The use of an expert database Web portal to access information about a domain relieves the novice searcher of the responsibility to know about, access, and retrieve domain documents. A Web mining process has already sifted through the Web pages to find domain facts. This Web-generated data is added to domain expert knowledge in an organized knowledge repository/database. The value of this portal information is then more than the sum of the various sources. The portal, as a repository of domain knowledge, brings together data from Web pages and human expertise in the domain.

EXPERT DATABASE WEB PORTAL OVERVIEW

An expert database-driven domain Web portal can relieve the novice searcher of having to decide on validity and comprehensiveness. Both are provided by the expert during portal creation and maintenance (Maedche & Staab, 2001). To create the portal, the database must be designed and populated. In the typical database design process, experts within a domain of knowledge are familiar with the facts and the organization of the domain. In the database design process, an analyst first extracts from the expert the domain organization. This organization is the foundation for the database structure and specifically the attributes that represent the characteristics of the domain. In large domains, it may be necessary to first identify topics of the domain, which may have different attributes from each other and occasionally from the general domain. The topics become the entity sets in the domain data model. Using database design methods, the data model is converted into relational database tables. The expert's domain facts are used to initially populate the database (Hoffer, George, & Valacich, 2002; Rob & Coronel, 2000; Turban & Aronson, 2001).

However, it is possible that the experts are not completely knowledgeable or can not express their knowledge about the domain. Other sources for expert level knowledge can be consulted. Expert level knowledge can be contained in data, text, and image sources. These sources can lead to an expansion of domain knowledge in both domain organization and domain facts.

In the past, the expert was necessary to point the analyst to these other sources. The expert's knowledge included knowledge such as where to find information about the domain, what books to consult, and the best data sources. Today, the World Wide Web provides the analyst with the capability of finding additional information about any domain from a little bit of knowledge about the domain. Of course, the expert must confirm that the information found is valid.

In the Web portal development process, the analyst and the expert determine the topics in the domain that define the specializations, topics, of the domain. These topics are based on the expert's current knowledge of the domain organization. This decomposition process creates a better understanding of the domain for both the analyst and the expert. These topics become keyword queries for a Web search, which will now add data to the expert's defined database architecture.

The pages retrieved as a result of the multiple topic-based Web searches are analyzed to determine both additional domain organizational structure and specific facts to populate the original and additional structures. This domain database is then made available on the Web as a source of valid knowledge about the domain. It becomes a Web portal database for the domain. This portal allows future novice searchers access to the expert's and the Web's knowledge in the domain.

RELATED WORK

Web search engine queries can be related to each other by the results returned (Glance, 2000). This knowledge of common results to different queries can assist a new searcher in finding desired information. However, it assumes the common user has domain knowledge sufficient to develop a query with keywords or is knowledgeable about using search engine advanced features for iterative query refinement. Most users are not advanced and use a single keyword query on a single search engine (Hoelscher & Strube, 1999).

Some Web search engines find information by categorizing the pages in their indexes. One of the first to create a structure as part of its Web index is Yahoo! (http://www.yahoo.com). Yahoo! has developed a hierarchy of documents that is designed to help users find information faster. This hierarchy acts as a taxonomy of the domain, which helps by directing the searcher through the domain. Still, the documents must be accessed and assimilated by the searcher; there is no extraction of specific facts.

An approach to Web quality is to define Web pages as authorities or hubs. An authority is a Web page with in-links from many hubs. A hub is a page that links to many authorities. A hub is not the result of a search engine query. The number of other Web pages linking to it may then measure the quality of a Web page as an authority (Chakrabarti et al., 1999). This is not so different from the how experts are chosen.

Domain knowledge can be used to restrict data mining in large databases (Anand, Bell, & Hughes, 1995). Domain experts are queried as to the topics and subtopics of a domain. This domain knowledge is used to assist in restricting the search space. DynaCat provides knowledge-based, dynamic categorization of search results in the medical domain (Pratt,

Hearst, & Fagan, 1999). The domain of medical topics is established and matched to predefined query types. Retrieved documents from a medical database are then categorized according to the topics. Such systems use the domain as a starting point but do not extract information and create an organized body of domain knowledge.

Document clustering systems, such as GeoWorks, improve user efficiency by semantically analyzing collections of documents. Analysis identifies important parts of documents and organizes the resultant information in document collection templates, providing users with logical collections of documents (Ko, Neches, & Yao, 2000). However, expert domain knowledge is not used to establish the initial collection of documents.

MGraphs formally reasons about the abstraction of information within and between Web pages in a collection. This graphical information provides relationships between content showing the context of information at various levels of abstraction (Lowe & Bucknell, 1997). The use of an expert to validate the abstract constructs as useful in the domain improves upon the value of the relationships.

An ontology may be established within a domain to represent the knowledge of the domain. Web sites in the domain are then found. Using a number of rules the Web pages are matched to the ontology. These matches then comprise the knowledge base of the Web as instances of the ontology classes (Craven et al., 1998). In ontology-based approaches, users express their search intent in a semantic fashion. Domain-specific ontologies are being developed for commercial and public purposes (Clark, 1999); OntoSeek (Guarino, Masolo, & Vetere, 1999), On2Broker (Fensel, et al., 1999), GETESS (Staab et al., 1999), and WebKB (Martin & Eklund, 2000) are example systems.

The ontological approach to creating knowledge-based Web portals follows much the same architecture as the expert database Web portal. The establishment of a domain schema by an expert and the collection and evaluation of Web pages are very similar (Maedche & Staab, 2001). Such portals can be organized in a Resource Description Framework (RDF) and associated RDF schemas (Toivonen, 2001).

Web pages can be marked up with XML (Decker, et al., 2001), RDF (Decker, et al.; Maedche & Staab, 2001; Toivonen, 2001), DAML (Denker, Hobbs, Martin, Narayanan, & Waldinger, 2001), and other languages. These Web pages are then accessible through queries, and information extraction can be accomplished (Han, Buttle, & Pu, 2001). However, mark-up of existing Web pages is a problem and requires expertise and wrapping systems, such as XWRAP (Han et al.,). New Web pages may not follow any of the emerging standards, exasperating the problem of information extraction (Glover, Lawrence, Gordon, Birmingham, & Giles, 2001).

Linguistic analysis can parse a text into a domain semantic network using statistical methods and information extraction by syntactic analysis (Deinzer, Fischer, Ahlrichs, & Noth, 1999; Iatsko, 2001; Missikoff & Velardi, 2000). These methods allow the summarization of the text content concepts but do not place the knowledge back on the Web as a portal for others.

Automated methods have been used to assist in database design. By applying common sense within a domain to assist with the selection of entities, relationships, and attributes, database design time and database effectiveness is improved (Storey, Goldstein, & Ding, 2002). Similarly, the discovery of new knowledge structures in a domain can improve the effectiveness of the database.

Database structures have been overlaid on documents in knowledge management systems to provide a knowledge base within an organization (Liongosari, Dempski, & Swaminathan, 1999). This database knowledge base provides a source for obtaining organizational knowledge. However, it does not explore the public documents available on the Web.

Semi-structured documents can be converted to other forms, such as a database, based on the structure of the document and word markers it contains. NoDoSE is a tool that can be trained to parse semi-structured documents into a structured document semi-automatically. In the training process, the user identifies markers within the documents which delimit the interesting text. The system then scans other documents for the markers and extracts the interesting text to an established hierarchical tree data structure. NoDoSE is good for homogeneous collections of documents, but the Web is not such a collection (Adelberg, Bell, & Hughes, 1998).

Web pages that contain multiple semi-structured records can be parsed and used to populate a relational database. Multiple semi-structured records are data about a subject that is typically composed of separate information instances organized individually (Embley et al., 1999). The Web Ontology Extraction (WebOntEx) project semi-automatically determines ontologies that exist on the Web. These ontologies are domain specific and placed in a relational database schema (Han & Elmasri, 2001). These systems require multiple records in the domain. However, the Web pages must be given to the system; it can not find Web pages or determine if they belong to the domain.

EXPERT DATABASE CONSTRUCTOR ARCHITECTURE

The expert database Web portal development begins with defining the domain of interest. Initial domain boundaries are based on the domain knowledge framework of an expert. An examination of the overall domain provides knowledge that helps guide later decisions concerning the specific data sought and the representation of that data.

Additional business journals, publications, and the Web are consulted to expand the domain knowledge. From the expert's domain knowledge and consultation of domain knowledge sources, a data set is defined. That data is then cleansed, reduced and decisions about the proper representation of the data are made (Wright, 1998).

The Expert Database Constructor Architecture (see Figure 1) shows the components and the roles of the expert, the Web, and page mining in the creation of an expert database portal for the World Wide Web. The domain expert accomplishes the domain analysis with the assistance of an analyst from the initial elicitation of the domain organization through extension and population of the portal database.

Topic Elicitor. The Topic Elicitor tool assists the analyst and the domain expert in determining a representation for the organization of domain knowledge. The expert breaks the domain down into major topics and multiple subtopics. The expert identifies the defining characteristics for each of these topics. The expert also defines the connections between subtopics. The subtopics, in turn, define a specific subset of the domain topic.

Domain Database. The analyst creates a database structure. The entity sets of the database are derived from the expert's domain topic and subtopics. The attributes of these entity sets are the characteristics identified by the expert. The attributes are known as the domain knowledge attributes and are referred to as DK-attributes. The connections between the topics become the relationships in the database.

Taxonomy Query Translator. Simultaneously with creating the database structure, the Taxonomy Query Translator develops a taxonomy of the domain from the topic/subtopics. The taxonomy is used to query the Web.

Figure 1: Expert database constructor architecture

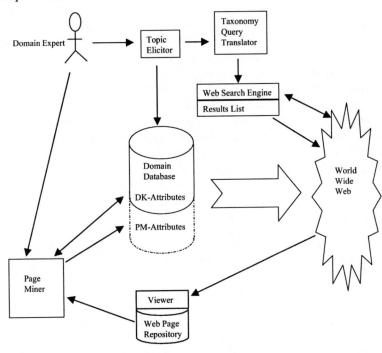

The use of a taxonomy creates a better understanding of the domain, thus resulting in more appropriate Web pages found during a search. However, the creation of a problem's taxonomy can be a time-consuming process. Selection of branch subtopics and sub-subtopics requires a certain level of knowledge in the problem domain. The deeper the taxonomy, the greater specificity possible searching the Web (Scime, 2000; Scime & Kerschberg, 2000).

The domain topic and subtopics on the taxonomy are used as keywords for queries of the World Wide Web search engine indices. Keyword queries are developed for the topic and each subtopic using keywords, which represent the topic/subtopic concept. The queries may be a single keyword, a collection of keywords, a string, or a combination of keywords and strings. Although a subtopic may have a specific meaning in the context of the domain, the use of a keyword or string could lead to the retrieval of many irrelevant sites. Therefore, keywords and strings are constructed to convey the meaning of the subtopic in the domain. This increases the specificity of the retrievals (Scime, 2000).

Web Search Engine and Results List. The queries search the indices of Web search engines, and the resulting lists contain meta data about the Web pages. This meta data typically includes each found page's complete URL, title, and some summary information. Multiple search engines are used, because no search engine completely indexes the Web (Selberg & Etzioni, 1995).

Web Page Repository and Viewer. The expert reviews the meta data about the documents, and selected documents are retrieved from the Web. Documents selected are those that are likely to provide either values to populate the existing attributes (DK-attributes) of the database or will provide new, expert-unknown information about the domain. The selected documents are retrieved from the Web, stored by domain topic/subtopic and prepared for processing by the page miner. The storage by topic/subtopic classifies the retrieved documents into categories, which match the entity sets of the database.

Web Page Miner. The Web pages undergo a number of mining processes that are designed to find attribute values and new attributes for the database. Data extraction is applied to the Web pages to identify attribute values to populate the database. Clustering the pages provides new characteristics for the subtopic entities. These new characteristics become attributes found in the Web pages and are known as page-mined attributes or PM-attributes. Likewise, the PM-attributes can be populated with the values from these same pages. The PM-attributes are added as extensions to the domain database. The found characteristic values of the topic and subtopics populate the database DK- and PM-attributes (see section below).

Placing the database on a Web server and making it available to the Web through a user interface creates a Web portal for the domain. This Web portal provides significant domain knowledge. Web users in search of information about this domain can access the portal and find an organized and valid collection of data about the domain.

WEB PAGE MINER ARCHITECTURE

Thus far the architecture for designing the initial database and retrieving Web pages has been discussed. An integral part of this process is the discovery of new knowledge from the Web pages retrieved. This page mining of the Web pages leads to new attributes, the PM-attributes, and the population of the database attributes (see Figure 2).

Page Parser. Parsing the Web pages involves the extraction of meaningful data to populate the database. This requires analysis of the Web page's semi- or unstructured text.

Figure 2: Web page mining

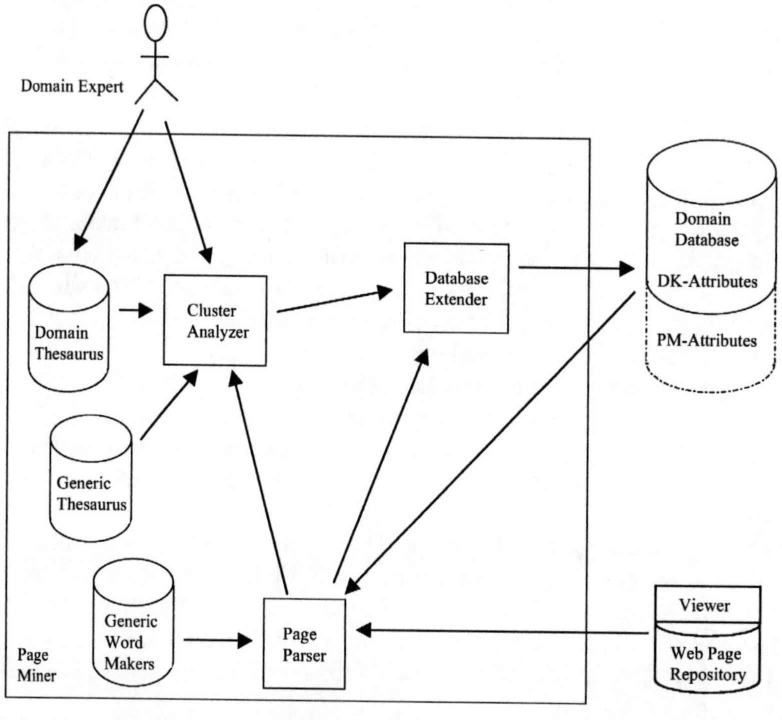

The attributes of the database are used as markers for the initial parsing of the Web page. With the help of these markers textual units are selected from the original text. These textual units may be items on a list (semi-structured page content) or sentences (unstructured page content) from the content. Where the attribute markers have an associated value, a URL-entity-attribute-value quadruplet is created. This quadruplet is then sent to the database extender.

To find PM-attributes, generic markers are assigned. Such generic markers are independent of the content of the Web page. The markers include names of generic subject headings, key words referring to generic subject headings, and key word qualifiers divided into three groups – nouns, verbs, and qualifiers (see Table 1) (Iatsko, 2001).

A pass is made through the text of the page. Sentences are selected that contain generic markers. When a selected sentence has lexical units such as next or following, it indicates a

Table 1: Generic markers

Subject Headings	Key Words	Nouns	Verbs	Qualifiers
Aim of Page	article, study, research	aim, purpose, goal, stress, claim, phenomenon	aim at, be devoted to, treat, deal with, investigate, discuss, report, offer, present, scrutinize, include, be intended as, be organized, be considered, be based on	present, this
Existing method of problem solving	device, approach, methodology, technique, analysis, theory, thesis, conception, hypothesis	literature, sources, author, writer, researcher	be assumed, adopt	known, existing, traditional, proposed, previous, former, recent
Evaluation of existing method of problem solving	device, approach, methodology, technique, analysis, theory, thesis, conception, hypothesis	misunderstanding, necessity, inability, properties	be needed, specify, require, be misunderstood, confront, contradict, miss, misrepresent, fail	problematic, unexpected, ill-formed, untouched, reminiscent of, unanswered
New method of problem solving	device, approach, methodology, technique, analysis, theory, thesis, conception, hypothesis	principles, issue, assumption, evidence	present, be developed, be supplemented by, be extended, be observed, involve, maintain, provide, receive support	for something, doing something, followed, suggested, new, alternative, significant, actual
Evaluation of new method of problem solving	device, approach, methodology, technique, analysis, theory, thesis, conception, hypothesis	limit, advantage, disadvantage, drawback, objection, insight into, contribution, solution, support	recognize, state, combine, gain, refine, provide, confirm, account for, allow for, make possible, open a possibility	for something, doing something, followed, suggested, new, alternative, significant, actual, valuable, novel, meaningful, superior, fruitful, precise, advantageous, adequate, extensive
Results	Conclusion		obtain, establish, be shown, come to	

connection with the next sentence or sentences. In these cases the next sentence is also selected. If a selected sentence has lexical units such as demonstrative and personal pronouns, the previous sentence is selected.

From selected sentences, adverbs and parenthetical phrases are eliminated. These indicate distant connections between selected sentences and sentences that were not selected. Also eliminated are first person personal pronoun subjects. These indicate the author of the page is the speaker. This abstracting does not require domain knowledge and therefore expands the domain knowledge beyond that of the expert.

The remaining text becomes a URL-subtopic-marker-value quadruplet. These quadruplets are passed to the cluster analyzer.

Cluster Analyzer. URL-subtopic-marker-value quadruplets are passed for cluster analysis. At this stage the values of quadruplets with the same markers are compared, using a general thesaurus to compare for semantic differences. When the same word occurs in a number of values, this word becomes a candidate PM-attribute. The remaining values with the same subtopic-marker become the values, and new URL-subtopic-(candidate DM-attribute) value quadruplets are created.

It is possible the parsed attribute names are semantically the same as DK-attributes. To overcome these semantic differences, a domain thesaurus is consulted. The expert previously created this thesaurus with analyst assistance. To assure reasonableness, the expert reviews the candidate PM-attributes and corresponding values. Those candidate PM-attributes selected by the expert become PM-attributes. Adding these to the domain database increases the domain knowledge beyond the original knowledge of the expert. The URL-subtopic-(candidate DM-attribute) value quadruplets then become URL-entity-attribute-value quadruplets and are passed to the populating process.

Database Extender. The attributes-values in the URL-entity-attribute-value quadruplets are sent to the database. If an attribute does not exist in an entity, it is created, thus extending the database knowledge.

Final decisions concerning missing values must also be made. Attributes with missing values may be deleted from the database or efforts must be made to search for values elsewhere.

AN EXAMPLE: THE ENTERTAINMENT AND TOURISM DOMAIN

On the Web, the Entertainment and Tourism domain is diverse and sophisticated offering a variety of specialized services (Missikoff & Velardi, 2000). It is representative of the type of service industries emerging on the Web.

In its present state, the industry's Web presence is primarily limited to vendors. Specific vendors such as hotels and airlines have created Web sites for offering services. Within specific domain subcategories, some effort has been made to organize information to provide a higher activity level of exposure. For example, there are sites that provide a list of golf courses and limited supporting information such as address and number of holes.

A real benefit is realized when a domain comes together in an inclusive environment. The concept of an Entertainment and Tourism portal provides advantages for novices in Entertainment and Tourism in the selection of destinations and services. Users have quick access to valid information that is easily discernible.

Imagine this scenario: a business traveler is going to spend a weekend in an unfamiliar city – Cincinnati, Ohio. He checks our travel portal. The portal has a wealth of information about travel necessities and leisure activities from sports to the arts available at business and vacation locations. The portal relies on a database created from expert knowledge and the application of page mining of the World Wide Web (Cragg, Scime, Gedminas, & Havens, 2002).

Travel Topics and Taxonomy. Applying the above process to the Entertainment and Tourism domain to create a fully integrated Web portal, the domain comprises those services and destinations that provide recreational and leisure opportunities. An expert travel agent limits the scope to destinations and services in one of fourteen topics typically of interest to business and leisure travelers. The subtopics are organized as a taxonomy (see Figure 3, adapted from Cragg et al., 2002) by the expert travel agent based upon their expert knowledge of the domain.

The expert also identifies the characteristics of the domain topic and each subtopic. These characteristics become the DK-attributes and are organized into a database schema by the analyst (Figure 4 shows three of the 12 subtopics in the database, adapted from Cragg et al., 2002). Figure 4a is a partial schema of the expert's knowledge of the travel and entertainment domain.

Search the Web. The taxonomy is used to create keywords for a search of the Web. The keywords used to search the Web are the branches of the taxonomy, for example "casinos," "golf courses," "ski resorts."

Mining the Results and Expansion of the Database. The implementation of the Web portal shows the growth of the database structure by Web mining within the entertainment and tourism domain. Figure 4b shows the expansion after the Web portal creation process. Specifically,

Figure 3: Travel taxonomy

destination
- casinos
- golf courses
- ski resorts
- restaurants
- live theater
- national parks
- museums
- movie theaters
- biking trails
- hiking
- cruises
- nightclubs
- bars
- amusement parks

the casino entity gained four new attributes. The expert database Web portal goes beyond just the number of golf course holes by adding five attributes to the category. Likewise, ski_resorts added eight attributes.

Returning to the business traveler who is going to Cincinnati, Ohio, for a business trip, but will be there over the weekend. He has interests in golf and gambling. By accessing the travel domain database portal simply using the city and state names, he quickly finds that there are three riverboat casinos in Indiana less than an hour away. Each has a hotel attached. He finds there are 32 golf courses, one of which is at one of the casino/hotels. He also finds the names and phone numbers of a contact person to call to arrange for reservations at the casino/hotel and for a tee time at the golf courses.

Figure 4: Partial AGO Schema

a. Defined by the Tourism and Entertainment Expert

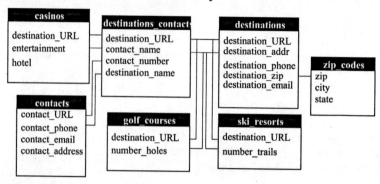

b. After the Web Portal Creation Process

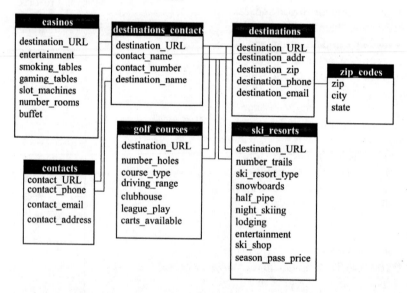

Doing three searches using the Google search engine (www.google.com) returns hits more difficult to interpret in terms of the availability of casinos and golf courses in Cincinnati. The first search used the keyword "Cincinnati" and returned about 2,670,000 hits; the second, "Cincinnati and Casinos," returned about 17,600 hits; and the third, "Cincinnati and Casinos and Golf," returned about 3,800 hits. As the specificity of the Google searches increases, the number of hits decreases, and the useable hits come closer to the top of the list. Nevertheless, in none of the Google searches is a specific casino or golf course Web page within the top 30 hits. In the last search, the first Web page for a golf course appears as the 31st result, but, the golf course (Kings Island Resort) is not at a casino. However, the first hit in the second and third searches and the third hit in the first search do return Web portal sites. The same searches were done on the Yahoo! (www.yahoo.com) and Lycos (www.lycos.com) search engines with similar results. The Web portals found by the search engines are similar to the portals discussed in this chapter.

ADDITIONAL WORK

The Web portal's knowledge discovery process is not over. Significant gains are possible by repetition of the process. Current knowledge becomes initial domain knowledge, and the process steps are repeated.

Besides the expert database, the important feature of the Web portal is the user interface. The design of a suitable knowledge query interface that will adequately represent the user's location and activity requirements is critical to the Web portal's success. An interface that provides a simple but useful design is encouraging to those novice searchers unfamiliar with the Web portal itself.

CONCLUSION

It is fairly common to construct databases of domain knowledge from an expert's knowledge. With the vast source of information on the World Wide Web, the expert's knowledge can be expanded upon and the combined result provided back to the Web as a portal. Novices in the domain can then access information through the portal.

To accomplish this Web-enhanced extension of expert knowledge, it is necessary to find appropriate Web pages in the domain. The pages must be mined for relevant data to compliment and supplement the expert's view of the domain. Finally, the integration of an intrinsically searchable database and a suitable user interface provide the foundation for an effective Web portal.

As the size of the Web continues to expand, it is necessary that available information be logically organized to facilitate searching. With expert database Web portals, searchers will be able to locate valuable knowledge on the Web. The searchers will be accessing information that has been organized by a domain expert to increase accuracy and completeness.

REFERENCES

Adelberg, B. (1998). NoDoSE - A tool for Semi-Automatically Extracting Structured and Semistructured Data from Text Documents. *Proceedings of ACM SIGMOD International Conference on Management of Data*, 283-294.

Anand, S., Bell, A., and Hughes, J. (1995). The Role of Domain Knowledge in Data Mining. *Proceedings of the 1995 International Conference on Information and Knowledge Management*, Baltimore, Maryland, 37-43.

Bordner, D. (1999). Web Portals: The Real Deal. *InformationWeek, 7*(20), from http://its.inmar-inc.com/wp/InmarWebportals.htm.

Chakrabarti, S., Dom, B. E., Kumar, S. R., Raghaven, P., Rajagopalan., S., Tomkins, A., Gibson, D. & Kleinberg, J. (1999). Mining the Web's link structure. *IEEE Computer, 32*(8), 60-67.

Clark, D., (1999). Mad cows, metathesauri, and meaning. *IEEE Intelligent Systems, 14*(1), 75-77.

Cragg, M., Scime, A., Gedminas T. D., & Havens, S. (2002). Developing a domain specific Web portal: Web mining to create e-business. *Proceedings of the World Manufacturing Conference*, Rochester, NY. (forthcoming).

Craven, M., DiPasquo, D., Freitag, Da., McCallum, A., Mitchell, T., Nigam, K., & Slattery, S. (1998). Learning to extract symbolic knowledge from the World Wide Web. *Proceed-

ings of the 15th National Conference on Artificial Intelligence (AAAI-98), Madison, WI., AAAI Press, 509-516.

Decker, S., van Harmelen, F., Broekstra, J., Erdmann, M., Fensel, D., Horrocks, I., Klein, M., & Melnik, S. (2001). The semantic web—on the respective roles of XML and RDF. Retrieved December 5, 2001 from http://www.ontoknowledge.org/oil/downl/IEEE00.pdf.

Deinzer, F., Fischer, J., Ahlrichs, U., & Noth, E. (1999). Learning of domain dependent knowledge in semantic networks. *Proceedings of the European Conference on Speech Communication and Technology*, Budapest, Hungary, 1987-1990.

Denker, G., Hobbs, J. R., Martin, D., Narayanan, S., & Waldinger, R. (2001). Accessing information and services on the DAML-enabled web. *Proceedings of the Second International Workshop on the Semantic Web—SemWeb'2001*, Hong Kong, China, 67–78.

Embley, D.W., Campbell, D.M., Jiang, Y.S., Liddle, S.W., Lonsdale, D.W., Ng, Y.K., & Smith, R.D. (1999). Conceptual-model-based data extraction from multiple-record web pages. *Data & Knowledge Engineering, 31*(3), 227-251.

Fensel, D., Angele, J., Decker, S., Erdmann, M., Schnurr, H., Staab, S., Studer, R., & Witt, A. (1999). On2broker: Semantic-based access to information sources at the WWW. *Proceedings of the World Conference on the WWW and Internet (WebNet 99)*, Honolulu, 25-30.

Glance, N. S. (2000). Community search assistant. *AAAI Workshop Technical Report of the Artificial Intelligence for Web Search Workshop*, Austin, Texas, 29-34.

Glover, E.J., Lawrence, S., Gordon, M. D., Birmingham, W. P., Giles, C. L. (2001). Web Search— Your Way. *Communications of the ACM, 44*(12), 97 - 102. Guarino, N., Masolo, C., & Vetere, G. (1999). OntoSeek: Content-based access to the Web. *IEEE Intelligent Systems, 14*(3), 70-80.

Han, H. & Elmasri, R. (2001). Analyzing unstructured Web pages for ontological information extraction. *Proceedings of the International Conference on Internet Computing (IC'2001)*, Las Vegas, NV, 21-28.

Han, W., Buttler, D., & Pu, C. (2001). Wrapping web data into XML. *SIGMOD Record, 30*(3), 33-45.

Hoelscher, C. & Strube, G. (1999). Searching on the Web: Two types of expertise. *Proceedings of SIGIR '99*, Berkeley, CA, 305-306.

Hoffer, J. A., George, J. F., Valacich, J.S. (2002). *Modern Systems Analysis and Design* (3rd ed.). Upper Saddle River, NJ: Prentice Hall.

Iatsko, V. A. (2001). Text summarization in teaching English. *Academic Exchange Quarterly* (forthcoming).

Ko, I. Y., Neches, R., Yao, Ke-Thia (2000). Semantically-based active document collection templates for web information management systems. *Proceedings of the ECDL 2000 Workshop on the Semantic Web*, Lisbon, Portugal.

Lawrence, S. & Giles, C.L. (1999). Accessibility of information on the Web. *Nature* 400 107–109.

Liongosari, E. S., Dempski, K. L., & Swaminathan, K. S. (1999). In search of a new generation of knowledge management applications. *SIGGROUP Bulletin, 20*(2), 60 - 63.

Lowe, D. B. & Bucknell A. J. (1997). Model-based support for information contextualisation in Hypermedia. In P. H. Keng and C. T. Seng (Eds.), *Multimedia Modeling: Modeling Multimedia Information and Systems*. Singapore: World Scientific Publishing.

Maedche, A. & Staab, S. (2001). Learning ontologies for the semantic web. *Proceedings of the Second International Workshop on the Semantic Web - SemWeb'2001*, Hong Kong, China, 51-61.

Martin, P., & Eklund, P. W. (2000). Knowledge retrieval and the World Wide Web. *IEEE Intelligent Systems, 15*(3), 18-25.

Missikoff, M., & Velardi, P. (2000). Mining text to acquire a tourism knowledge base for semantic interoperability. *Proceedings of the International Conference on Artificial Intelligence (IC-AI'2000)*, Las Vegas, NV, 1351-1357.

Pratt, W., Hearst, M., & Fagan, L. (1999). A knowledge-based approach to organizing retrieved documents. *AAAI-99: Proceedings of the Sixteenth National Conference on Artificial Intelligence*, Orlando, FL, 80-85.

Rob, P. & Coronel, C. (2000). *Database Systems: Design, Implementation, and Management*, Cambridge, MA: Course Technology.

Scime, A. (2000). Learning from the World Wide Web: Using organizational profiles in information searches, *Informing Science, 3*(3), 135-143.

Scime, A. & Kerschberg, L. (2000). WebSifter: An ontology-based personalizable search agent for the Web. *Proceedings of the 2000 Kyoto International Conference on Digital Libraries: Research and Practice*, Kyoto, Japan, IEEE Computer Society, 203-210.

Selberg, E. & Etzioni, O. (1995). Multi-service search and comparison using the MetaCrawler. Proceedings of the 4th International World Wide Web Conference, Boston, MA, 195–208.

Staab, S., Braun, C., Bruder, I., Düsterhöft, A., Heuer, A., Klettke, M., Neumann, G., Prager, B., Pretzel, J., Schnurr, H., Studer, R., Uszkoreit, H., & Wrenger, B. (1999). A system for facilitating and enhancing Web search. *Proceedings of IWANN '99 - International Working Conference on Artificial and Natural Neural Networks*, Berlin.

Staab, S. & Maedche, A. (2001). Knowledge portals ontologies at work. *AI Magazine, 21*(2).

Storey, V. C., Goldstein, R. C., Ding, J. (2002). Common sense reasoning in automated database design: An empirical test. *Journal of Database Management, 13*(1), 3-14.

Toivonen, S. (2001). Using RDF(S) to Provide Multiple Views into a Single Ontilogy. *Proceedings of the Second International Workshop on the Semantic Web - SemWeb'2001*, Hong Kong, China, 61-66.

Turban, E. & Aronson, J. E. (2001). *Decision Support Systems and Intelligent Systems* (6th ed). Upper Saddle River, NJ: Prentice Hall.

Turtle, H. R., & Croft, W. B. (1996). Uncertainty in information retrieval systems. In A. Motro and P. Smets (Eds.), *Uncertainty Management in Information Systems From Needs to Solutions*. Boston: Kluwer Academic Publishers.

Wright, P. (1998). Knowledge discovery preprocessing: Determining record useability. *Proceeding of the 36th Annual Conference ACM SouthEast Regional Conference*, Marietta, GA, 283-288.

Section III:

Scalability and Performance

Chapter V

Scheduling and Latency – Addressing the Bottleneck

Michael J. Oudshoorn
University of Adelaide, Australia

ABSTRACT

As e-business applications become more commonplace and more sophisticated, there is a growing need to distribute the server side of the application in order to meet business objectives and to provide maximum service levels to customers. However, it is well known that the effective distribution of an application across available resources is difficult, especially for novices. Careful attention must be paid to the fact that performance is critical – business is likely to be lost to a competitor if potential customers do not receive the level of service they expect in terms of both time and functionality. Modern globalised businesses may have their operational units scattered across several countries, yet they must still present a single consolidated front to a potential customer. Similarly, customers are becoming more sophisticated in their demands on e-business systems and this necessitates greater computational support on the server side of the transaction. This chapter focuses on two performance bottlenecks: scheduling and communication latency. The chapter discusses an adaptive scheduling system to automatically distribute the application across the available resources such that the distribution evolves to a near-optimal allocation tailored to each user, and the concept of Ambassadors to minimize communication latency in wide-area distributed applications.

INTRODUCTION

The effective distribution of an e-business application across available resources has the potential to provide significant performance benefits. However, it is well known that effective distribution is difficult, and there are many traps for novices. Despite these difficulties, the average programmer is interested in the benefits of distribution, provided that his/her program continues to execute correctly and with well-defined failure semantics. Hence we say that the programmer is "all care." Nevertheless, the reality is that the average programmer does not want to be hampered with managing the distribution process. He/she is not interested in dealing with issues such as the allocation of tasks to processors, optimisation, latency, or process migration. Hence we say that the programmer is "no responsibility." This gives rise to the "all care and no responsibility" principle of distribution whereby the benefits of distributed systems are made available to the average programmer without burdening him or her with the mechanics behind the distributed system.

The customer, or end user, of an e-business application has similar demands to the E-business applications developer, namely, the need for performance. As end users become more sophisticated and place more complex and computationally intensive demands on the e-business application, the need for distribution across multiple processors become necessary in order to obtain increased throughput so as to meet these demands.

As businesses themselves become more globalised and distributed, no one business unit provides all of the information/resources required to satisfy a complex request. Consider a business that has interests in steel, glass and rubber products. It is likely that all of its products are manufactured in the same place, but all of its products may be related to motor vehicles (sheet steel, windscreens, rubber hoses and floor mats). A vehicle producer may want to place an order for components for 1,000 vehicles. The vehicle producer will act as the client and attempt to order the necessary components from the manufacturer in a single E-business transaction. The e-business application may, however, need to contact several business units within the organisation to ensure that the order is met. The problem of latency across a wide area network now becomes apparent.

The ongoing Alchemy Project aims to provide automated support for the "all care and no responsibility" principle. The Alchemy Project aims to take user applications and perform appropriate analysis on the source code prior to automatically distributing the application across the available resources. The aim is to provide a near-optimal distribution of the application that is tailored to each individual user of the application, without burdening the applications developer with the details of, and issues related to, the physical distribution of the application. This permits the developer to focus on the issues underlying the application in hand without clouding the matter with extraneous complications. The project also examines issues surrounding fault tolerance, load balancing (Fuad & Oudshoorn, 2002), and distributed simulation (Cramp & Oudshoorn, 2002)

The major aim of the Alchemy Project is to perform the distribution automatically. This chapter focuses on two aspects of the project – namely, the scheduling of tasks across the available distributed processors in a near-optimal manner, and the minimisation of communication latency within distributed systems. These two features alone provide substantial benefits to distributed application developers. Existing applications can be easily modified readily to utilise the existing benefits provided, and new applications can be developed with minimal pain. This provides significant benefits to developers of e-business systems who are looking to develop distributed applications to better harness the available resources within their organisations or on the internet without having to come to terms with the intricacies of scheduling and communication within hand-built distributed systems. This frees developers from the need to be concerned with approaches such as Java RMI (Sun Microsystems, 1997) typically used to support distribution in e-business applications, and allows developers to concentrate more on the application itself.

The chapter focuses on scheduling through the discussion of an adaptive system to allocate tasks to available processors. Given that different users of the same application may have vastly different usage patterns, it is difficult to determine a universally efficient distribution of the software tasks across the processors. An adaptive system called ATME is introduced that automatically allocates tasks to processors based on the past usage statistics of each individual user. The system evolves to a stable and efficient allocation scheme. The rate of evolution of the distribution scheme is determined by a collection of parameters that permits the user to fine-tune the system to suit his or her individual needs.

The chapter then broadens its focus to examine distributed systems deployed on the worldwide scale where latency is the primary determinant of performance. The chapter introduces Ambassadors, a communication technique using mobile Java objects in RPC/RMI-like communication structures. Ambassadors minimise the aggregate latency of sequences of interdependent remote operations by migration to the vicinity of the server to execute those operations. At the same time, Ambassadors may migrate between machines while ensuring well-defined failure semantics are upheld, an important characteristic in distributed systems. Finally, the chapter discusses the future directions of the Alchemy Project.

These two focal points of the Alchemy Project deliver substantial benefits to the applications programmer and assist in reducing development time. For typical e-business applications the performance delivered by ATME and Ambassadors is adequate. Although manual fine-tuning or development of the distributed aspects of the application is possible, the cost and effort does not warrant the performance gains.

SCHEDULING

A programming environment can assist in significantly reducing a programmer's workload and increase system and application performance by automating the allocation of tasks to the available processing nodes. Such automation also minimises errors through the elimination of tedious chores and permits the programmer to concentrate on the problem at hand rather than burdening him or her with details that are somewhat peripheral to the real job. Such performance gains have a direct benefit to the client of a large, complex e-business system.

Most scheduling heuristics assume the existence of a task model that represents the application to be executed. The general assumption that is made is that the task model does not vary between program executions. This assumption is valid in domains whereby the problem presents itself in a regular way (e.g., solving partial differential equations). It is, however, generally invalid for general-purpose applications where activities such as the spawning of new tasks and the communication between them may take place conditionally, and where the interaction between the application and a user may differ between executions, as is typical in e-business applications. Consequently, such an approach does not lead to an optimal distribution of tasks across the available processors. This means that it is not possible to statically examine the code and determine which tasks will execute at runtime and perform task allocation on that basis. The best that is achievable prior to execution is an educated guess. The scheduling problem is known to be NP-complete (Ullman, 1975). Various heuristics (Casavant & Kuhl, 1988; El-Rewini & Lewis, 1990; Lee, Hwang, Chow & Anger, 1999) and software tools (Wu & Gajski, 1990; Yang, 1993) have been developed to pursue a suboptimal solution within acceptable computation complexity bounds

A probabilistic approach to scheduling is explored here. El-Rewini and Ali (1995) propose an algorithm based on simulation. Prior to execution, a number of simulations are conducted of possible task models (according to the execution probability of the tasks involved) that may occur in the next execution. Based on the results of these simulations, a scheduling algorithm is employed to obtain a scheduling policy for each task model. These policies are then combined to form a policy to distribute tasks and arrange the execution order of tasks allocated to the same processor. The algorithm employed simplifies the task model in order to minimise the computational overhead involved. However, it is clear that the computational overhead involved in simulation remains excessive and involves the applications developer having *a priori* knowledge of how the application will be used. In essence, this technique derives an average scheduling policy based on probability that each task may run in the next execution of the application. This is inappropriate for e-business applications.

The simulation-based static allocation method of El-Rewini and Ali (1995) clearly suffers from computational overhead and furthermore assumes that each user will interact with the software in a similar manner. The practical approach advocated in this chapter is coined ATME – an Adaptive Task Mapping Environment. ATME is predictive and adaptive. It is sufficiently flexible that an organisation can allow it to adapt on an individual basis, regional basis, or global basis. This leads to a tailored distribution policy, which delivers good performance, to suit the organisation.

Conditional Task Scheduling

The task-scheduling problem can be decomposed into three major components:
1. the task model which portrays constituent tasks and the interconnection relationships among tasks of a parallel program,
2. the processor model which abstracts over the architecture of the underlying parallel system on which the parallel program is to be executed, and
3. the scheduling algorithm, which produces a scheduling policy by which tasks of a parallel program are distributed onto available processors and possibly ordering for execution on the same processor.

The aim of the scheduling policy is to optimise the performance of the application relative to some performance measurement. Typically, the aim is to minimise total execution time of the application (El-Rewini and Lewis, 1990; Lee et al, 1999) or the total cost of the communication delay and load balance (Chu, Holloway, Lan & Efe, 1980; Harary, 1969; Stone, 1977). The scheduling algorithm and the scheduling objective determine the critical attributes associated with the tasks and processors in the task and processor model respectively. Assuming a scheduling objective of minimising the total parallel execution time of the application, the task model is typically described as a weighted directed acyclic graph (DAG) (El-Rewini & Lewis, 1990; Sarkar, 1989) with the edges representing relationships between tasks (Geist, Beguelin, Dongarra, Jiang, Manchek & Sunderam, 1995). The DAG contains a unique start and exit node. The processor model typically illustrates the processors available and their interconnections. Edges show the cost associated with the path between nodes. Figure 1 illustrates a typical processor model. It shows three nodes, P1, P2 and P3, with relative processing speeds of 1, 2, and 5, respectively. Edges represent network bandwidth between nodes.

Figure 1: Processor model

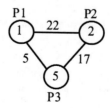

Applications supported by ATME are those based on multiple processors that are loosely coupled, execute in parallel, and communicate via message-passing through networks. With the development of high-speed, low-latency communication networks and technology (Detmold & Oudshoorn, 1996a, 1996b; Detmold, Hollfelder & Oudshoorn, 1999) and the low cost of computer hardware, such multiprocessor architectures have become commercially viable to solve application problems cooperatively and efficiently. Such architectures are becoming increasingly popular for e-business applications in order to realise the potential performance improvement.

An e-business application featuring a number of interrelated tasks owing to data or control dependencies between the tasks is known as a conditional task system. Each node in the corresponding task model identifies a task in the system and an estimate for the execution time for that task should it execute. Edges between the nodes are labelled with a triplet which represents the communication costs (volume and time) between the tasks, the probability that the second task will actually execute (i.e., be spawned) as a consequence of the execution of the first task, and the preemption start point (percentage of parent task that must be executed before the dependent task could possibly commence execution).

Figure 2 shows an example of a conditional task model: Task A and C depend on the successful execution of Task S, but Task C has a 40% probability of executing if S executes, whereas A is certainly spawned by S. A task, such as C, which may not be executed, will have a "ripple effect" in that it cannot spawn any dependent tasks unless it itself executes. If S spawns A, then at least 20% of S will have been executed.

The task model and the processor model are provided to ATME in order to determine a scheduling policy for the application. The scheduling policy determines the allocation of tasks to processors and specifies the execution order on each processor. The scheduling policy performs this allocation with the express intention of minimizing total parallel execution time based on the previous execution history. The attributes of the processors and the network are taken into consideration when performing this allocation. Figure 3 provides an illustration of the task scheduling process. To avoid cluttering the diagram, all probabilities are set to 1.

Figure 2: Conditional task model

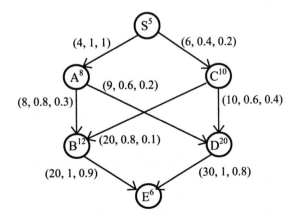

Figure 3: The process of solving the scheduling problem

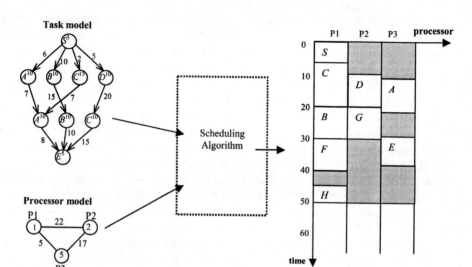

The ATME System

Input into ATME consists of the user defined parallel tasks (i.e., the e-business application), the task interconnection structure, and the processor topology specification. ATME then annotates and augments the user source code and distributes the tasks over the available processors for physical execution. ATME is developed over the PVM platform (Geist et al, 1994). The user tasks are physically mapped onto the virtual machines provided by PVM, but the use of PVM is entirely transparent to the user. This permits the underlying platform to be changed with ease and ensures that ATME is portable. In addition, the programmer is relieved of the need to be concerned with the subtle characteristics of a parallel and distributed system.

Figure 4 illustrates the functional components and their relationships. The *target machine description* component presents the user with a general interface to specify the available processors, processor interconnections and their physical attributes such as processing speed and data transfer rate. The user supplied application code is preprocessed, instrumented and analyzed by the *program preprocessing and analysis component,* which enables it to execute under PVM and produces information to be captured at run-time. The task interconnection structure is also generated in this component. ATME provides explicit support through PVM-like run-time primitives to realize task spawn and message-passing operations.

With the task model obtained from the *task model construction* and the processor model from the *target machine description*, the *task scheduling* component generates a policy by which the user tasks are distributed onto the underlying processors. At run-time, the *runtime data collection* component collects traces produced by the instrumented tasks, which is stored, after the execution completes, into program databases to be taken as input by the *task model construction* to predict the task model for the next execution. The *post-execution analysis* and *report generation* provide various reports and tuning suggestions to the E-business applications developer and to ATME for program improvement.

The underlying target architecture is generally stable; that is to say, the system generally does not change along with the application program. In this case, the processor model of the target machines, once established, does not have to be reconstructed every time an application program is executed. There is also no need to undertake further program preprocessing and analysis until the application code is modified.

A feedback loop exists in the ATME environment starting with the *task model construction*, through *task scheduling, runtime data collection* and back to *task model construction*. This entire procedure makes ATME an adaptive environment in that the task model offered to the scheduling algorithm is incrementally established based on the past usage patterns of the application. Accurate estimates of task attributes are obtained for relatively stable usage patterns and thus admit improvement in execution efficiency. The data collected in the program databases is aged so that the older data has less influence on the determination of the task attributes. This ensures that ATME responds to evolving usage patterns but not at such a rapid rate that a single execution, which does not fit the usual profile, forces a radical change in the mapping strategy.

Experimental results (Huang & Oudshoorn, 1999b) support theoretical analysis (Huang & Oudshoorn, 1998; Huang & Oudshoorn, 1999a) and demonstrate that the use of ATME

Figure 4: Structure of the ATME environment

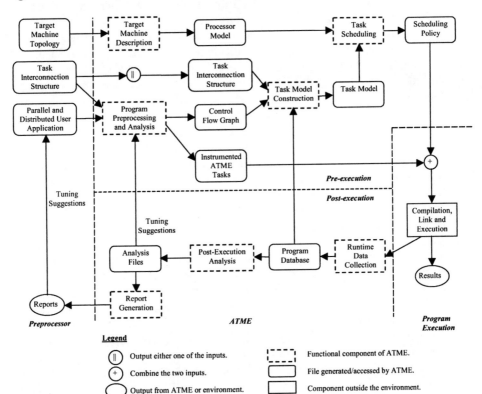

leads to considerable reduction in total parallel execution time for a large variety of applications when compared to a random and round-robin distribution of tasks. This includes applications that have constant usage patterns as well as those that evolve over an extended period of time and those whose usage pattern varies significantly. The key to this improvement is the scheduling algorithm employed and the adaptive nature of the ATME environment. From the perspective of the e-business application, this means that ATME evolves to a near-optimal distribution strategy based on the available resources and the manner in which the application is used. This means that there is no work required on behalf of the application developer if the manner in which the public interacts with the e-business application varies over time, as ATME will deal with this. However, on a global scale these performance gains are lost due to the effect of communication latency. The next section addresses the issue of communication latency and proposes a technique to minimise this cost.

LATENCY MINIMIZATION

A major difference between worldwide distributed computing and LAN-based distributed computing is that the latencies of message sends are several orders of magnitude higher in the former case than in the latter. This factor has an immense impact on the time taken to complete operations in a worldwide distributed e-business application, as is demonstrated by the detailed example below. Some element of latency is inherent in worldwide distribution of resources and, as such, is unavoidable. However, much of the impact stems from characteristics of the technologies used to build distributed systems. As such, this additional latency is unnecessary.

Optimised Remote Procedure Call (RPC) (Birrell & Nelson, 1984; Bogle & Liskov, 1994) mechanisms provided by commercial operating systems over ATM LANs can provide message send latencies of the order of one millisecond. Such latencies are three orders of magnitude above the theoretical minimum time for information transfer implicit in fundamental physics (information can propagate across a LAN with a 300 metre diameter in one microsecond at the speed of light). Recent research has led to communication technologies providing latencies of the order of ten microseconds. Nevertheless, even with millisecond latencies, RPC has proven to be a viable technology for the construction of LAN-based distributed systems, although improvements are of course desirable.

Now consider a worldwide network with a 15,000 kilometre average diameter. In this case, the theoretical minimum latency for a message send is 50 milliseconds. In the time taken for a message to propagate across this network, a modern microprocessor can execute several million instructions, possibly enough processing capacity to satisfy the requests of several additional e-business users. Worldwide distributed systems exhibit a completely different ratio between the time taken in the computational part of a distributed systems task and the time taken in communication to support that computation. This ratio is heavily skewed towards communication. Consequently, the best performing worldwide distributed systems technologies will be those, which minimise the time spent in communication. To be more precise, the best performance is obtained from those mechanisms that minimise the time during which computational elements of an interaction must wait for the completion of communication elements.

The latency of message sends over worldwide networks is currently within an order of magnitude of the fundamental limitation on the speed of information transfer (the speed of light). This is a fundamental obstacle to significant improvement in the latency of message transmission across the world. Consequently, significant improvement must be sought through new communication techniques that minimise the number and impact of the worldwide message transmissions necessary to support a given distributed systems interaction.

Suppose that a client has a batch of n remote operations to execute against a server on the other side of the world. Using RPC or RMI, $2n$ messages across the world will be required to effect these operations and with a single threaded client, these messages will be sent serially (alternately by client and server). Consequently, the aggregate delay for the batch will be at least $2nl$, where l is the latency of a single message transmission.

A multi-threaded client ameliorate the situation somewhat, in that batches of mutually independent operations may be in progress concurrently, but multi-thread gains nothing in the common situation where there are dependencies between operations in the batch. These dependencies may be classified as follows:

1. *Order Dependency* – an operation O_2 is order dependent on an operation O_1 if the computation associated with O_2 must be executed after the computation associated with O_1.

2. *Result Dependency* – an operation O_2 is result dependent on an operation O_1 if a parameter (for this purpose, the target object of a remote method call is a parameter) of O_2 is a result of O_1. This is implicitly an order dependency.

3. *Functional Dependency* – an operation O_2 is functionally dependent on an operation O_1 if a parameter (or the target object) of O_2 is a non-identity result of O_1. This is implicitly both a result dependency and an order dependency. This kind of dependency also includes the case where the execution of O_2 is conditional on the result of O_1.

Mechanisms such as Futures (Walker, Floydd & Neves, 1990), Promises (Liskov & Shrira, 1988) and Wait-by-necessity (Caromel, 1991, 1993) allow order interdependent operations to be in progress concurrently. Mechanisms such as Batched Futures (Bogle & Liskov, 1994) and Responsibilities (Detmold and Oudshoorn, 1996a, 1996b) go further in allowing result interdependent operations to be in progress concurrently. In order to allow functionally dependent operations to progress concurrently it is necessary that the function that determines a parameter of a later operation from the result(s) of earlier operations be executed on the server. This in turn entails migration of the code of this function from client to server.

The Impact of Latency: An Example

To illustrate the impact of latency, a detailed example is presented. This example operates in the context of three LANs operating within a business environment: a client LAN, a remote store LAN, and a head-office LAN. These LANs are distributed worldwide, and messages between processes on different LANs are assumed to take 100 milliseconds to propagate.

The remote store LAN contains a resource directory object and several objects representing various product lines currently handled by the store. The head office LAN contains an object maintaining a record of product sales for various stores. These records are used to assess product and store success. Any store can initiate the process in order to ensure up-to-date information is available in order to evaluate its performance relative to all other stores. Consequently, the data may be gathered by an ad hoc process initiated in a third LAN (the client LAN) rather than from the head office. An outline of the algorithm used by the client to perform the interaction is shown in Figure 5.

Figure 5: An example remote interaction containing interdependent operations

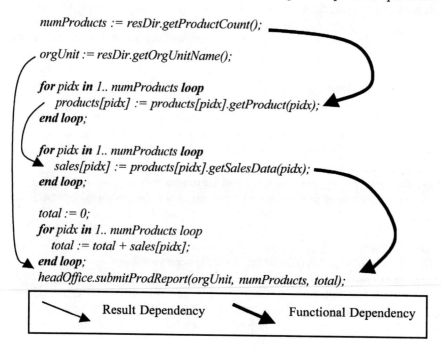

Now, supposing that the remote store LAN currently has twenty product lines, one can model the performance of various communication mechanisms in terms of the number of worldwide message transmission required.

RPC/RMI

For RPC/RMI with a single-threaded client, each remote operation requires two worldwide message transmissions, and all messages must occur serially. There is one call to each of *getProductCount*, *getOrgUnitName* and *submitPUReport*, and (with twenty product lines) twenty calls to each of *getProduct* and *getSalesData*, giving a total of 43 remote calls and 86 serial worldwide message transmissions. At 100 milliseconds per transmission, communication will contribute 8.6 seconds to the latency of the interaction.

Multi-Threaded RPC/RMI and Futures

If the client is multi-threaded (and also if it uses a Futures or Promises mechanism), then the calls to *getProductCount* and *getOrgUnitName* can proceed concurrently. More importantly, all the calls to *getProduct* can proceed concurrently, as can all the calls to *getSalesData*. Each group of concurrent calls contributes only two worldwide transmissions to the overall latency. There are four such collections of calls (the call to *submitProductReport* is in a group by itself), so the aggregate contribution to latency is 800 milliseconds, a speed-up of ten times.

Batched Futures and Responsibilities

Batched Futures and Rresponsibilities give further improvement in that the calls to *getSalesData* may be in progress concurrently with the calls to *getProduct*. This reduces the number of collections of concurrent calls to three and consequently the contribution to latency to 600 milliseconds.

The Ideal Latency

To achieve the ideal aggregate latency, the interaction should be structured as follows:
1.   Migrate code for the interaction from the client LAN to the remote store LAN. This costs one worldwide message transmission.
2.   Execute the loops and all the calls, except for the final call, to *submitProductReport*. This does not require any worldwide message transmissions.
3.   Migrate to the head office LAN. This costs one worldwide message transmission.
4.   Execute the call to *submitProductReport*. Again, this does not require any worldwide message transmissions.
5.   Return to the client. This costs one worldwide message transmission. This step is necessary in order that the client is able to determine that the interaction has completed successfully.

Therefore, only three worldwide message transmissions are required. These contribute only 300ms to aggregate latency, a speed-up of nearly thirty times over the single-threaded RPC/RMI case and nearly three times over the multi-threaded case. The critical difference with this approach is that it involves the migration of code.

Ambassadors Concept

Human ambassadors served an essential function in international diplomacy in the age prior to electronic communication. They were posted to a foreign state and empowered to act on behalf of their home state, thereby enabling diplomatic relations between the two states to proceed without a multi-week delay (or latency) between each round of negotiations.

Ambassadors as a distributed communication mechanism perform a role analogous to that of their human counterparts. A client needing to execute a batch of interdependent operations against a remote server packages those operations into an Ambassador, which is then dispatched to the location of the server. Upon arrival at the server, the Ambassador executes the remote operations, subject only to small local latency, and then returns to the client, delivering the results. The only high latency message transmissions are those used to transport the Ambassador between client and server, that is, two messages for the entire functionally interdependent batch of operations.

The communication structure and failure semantics of Ambassadors follows that of at-most-once RPC. In at-most-once RPC (Birrell & Nelson, 1984), timeouts are used to detect failure of a remote call. If the success of an RPC is not confirmed (by reception of a reply message) prior to expiration of the timeout, the call is declared failed (even though a reply may subsequently arrive). A similar approach is used for Ambassadors. If an Ambassador does not return from the server it is visiting prior to expiration of a timeout, then that Ambassador is reported to have failed and an exception is raised at the client.

The elements of a distributed e-business system can fail independently. Therefore, it is usually not sufficient to simply initiate remote operations and then assume that they will be carried out. Instead, clients usually desire feedback as to the success or failure of the remote interaction. Therefore, if mobile objects are to be used as a communication mechanism, it is very important that they be subject to constraints on communication (migration) structure, such as support-defined failure semantics and feedback regarding failures. In particular, it is not sufficient to have mobile objects without a constrained communication structure and defined-failure semantics.

Semantics of Ambassadors

Ambassadors are to provide a means whereby a method is invoked against a local object, but the object is migrated so that the invocation actually takes place on some remote node (in this case, nodes are Java virtual machines). Typically, the remote node would be close to the node containing server object with which the method called against the Ambassador was to interact.

The operation causing a method invocation to occur against a given object, but on a remote node, is called a *migrate-and-invoke* operation. It entails sending a message to the node where the invocation of the object is to take place. This message contains (the transitive closure of) the state of the object, an indication of the method to be invoked, and the parameters to pass to that invocation. The node receiving the message executes the method as appropriate; this execution can of course contain further migrate-and-invoke operations.

Two kinds of migrate-and-invoke operations are provided in the current Ambassador system. These are:

> **void**   visit   *(ImmigrationServerProxy, Ambassador,MethodID, Object[]);*
> **void**   migrate   *(ImmigrationServerProxy, Ambassador, MethodID, Object[]).*

In each case, the first parameter is a reference to a proxy for an object on a remote virtual machine where the invocation is to take place. The second parameter is the object to migrate (which must be of a class inheriting from the *Ambassador* class). The third parameter is the method to invoke against this object when it reaches the remote node. Finally, the fourth parameter provides the parameters to pass to the remote invocation.

The *visit* operation passes a copy of the object and parameters (including the respective closures) to the remote virtual machine, validates that the invocation is type-safe and, all being well, starts the invocation executing. This invocation then has low-latency access to objects residing in the remote virtual machine, via standard (local) Java method invocations. The thread that initiates the *visit* operation waits for an acknowledgment indicating either that the invocation was started successfully or that it could not be started due to a type error. Importantly, this acknowledgment is sent by the remote node concurrently with the execution of the remote invocation. If the invocation started executing successfully, then the initiating thread is suspended; otherwise, the *AmbassadorInvocationError* exception is raised to the caller of the *visit* operation.

Initiating a *visit* operation entails an eventual reply. This reply contains an updated copy of the object that was migrated. When the reply is received, the thread that issued the *visit* operation is resumed. This thread then copies the state of the updated copy over the state of the local copy of the Ambassador object. The thread then returns normally from the call to *visit*. Ambassador objects are implicitly monitors; hence the copy of an Ambassador object left behind during a visit is inaccessible until the visit returns.

Normally, the acknowledgment that the invocation associated with a visit has started successfully would arrive at the visit's origin node before the reply from that visit. If the reply arrives first, processing is delayed until the acknowledgment has also arrived. It is possible to optimise the system so that the reply is treated as an implicit acknowledgment in this case and the explicit acknowledgment was then discarded when it arrived.

The *migrate* operation differs from *visit* in that the thread initiating a migrate operation terminates (after establishing that the remote invocation has been started successfully) instead of being suspended. Consequently, no reply is expected for a *migrate* operation and no copy back of the object occurs.

Reply messages are sent when remote invocations return. The reply message is sent to the point of the most recent *visit* operation. If the execution of a remote invocation initiated by a *visit* performs a *migrate* operation, then that invocation does not return (and does not send a reply). Instead, the invocation resulting from the *migrate* is responsible for the reply— either it is sent when the invocation returns, or the invocation performs a further *migrate*.

The first *migrate-and-invoke* operation on an Ambassador is required to be a *visit* operation. This ensures that the client (who initiates the *visit*) is informed when the interaction implemented by the "tour" undertaken by the Ambassador is complete. The tour of an Ambassador is hence a cycle, completed by a reply message, potentially with sub-cycles hanging off the main cycle, and recursively so.

The copies of the object that are left behind whilst a *visit* is in progress are called *anchors*. These anchors will eventually be updated when the reply to the *visit* is received. Attempts to perform migrate or visit operations on anchors are not permitted and raise an exception. These semantics ensure there is only one "live" copy of an Ambassador at any given time. Hence, the flow-of-control of an Ambassador tour is sequential and consequently is easily understood.

The result(s) of a *visit* can be obtained by the execution of local methods defined by the Ambassador subclass. Since, as described previously, Ambassadors are monitors, a blocked thread holds the monitor lock for the duration of a visit and accesses are blocked until the visit has returned.

Implementation Status

The Ambassadors system has been implemented in Java (JDK 1.1). This implementation has produced experimental results in line with predictions from the model presented in this chapter. The implementation and results are reported below and in Hollfelder et al, 1999). A prototype running on top of RMI (Nelson, 1981) has been produced prototypes running directly on the Java socket facilities and using the standard Java serialisation facilities for marshalling and unmarshalling. The Java reflection interface (Object Management Group, 1991) is used to perform method invocations on Ambassadors.

The system was tested using the interaction described in Figure 5 with the head office at The University of Adelaide, the client at the Australian National University (Canberra), and the remote store at the University of Southern California. Ping round-trip times are 420ms between Adelaide and Southern California, 430ms between Canberra and Southern California, and 33ms between Canberra and Adelaide.

The performance of the code is benchmarked against the performance of pure RMI. Consequently, the code in Figure 5 is initially run using only RMI. The initial implementation of Ambassadors is also over RMI. This is achieved by placing standard RMI code (with minor modifications) into an Ambassador object. The Ambassador was then sent to the server that executed the RMI operations. A second implementation of Ambassadors over TCP/IP was also developed and compared to RMI and to the initial Ambassadors implementation.

When using the Ambassadors implementation, the client sends an Ambassador to the remote store to gather data on the product lines. The Ambassador then migrates to the Head Office to submit the report. Finally, the Ambassador returns to the client.

It is important to note that there was no fundamental change to the code in each case. When using pure RMI, each interaction requires an RMI call across the entire distance; in the case of Ambassadors, there were two high latency RMI calls (to send and receive the Ambassador) and a number of low latency RMI calls between the server and the Ambassador code. The difference between the two Ambassador implementations lies solely in the transport mechanism employed.

Figure 6 shows the mean interaction times obtained for the example interaction with various mechanisms. The experiment was conducted 30 times for each mechanism for various numbers of product lines. Tests of different mechanism were interleaved in order to distribute the effects of variation in the underlying network performance across all mechanisms. In addition to the results, theoretical minima for the interaction using sequential RMI, multi-threaded RMI, and the ideal case are presented for comparison. It is clear that more complex interactions do not necessarily require additional time to execute because of the nature of Ambassadors. This represents a significant performance improvement for e-business applications that mimic this style of interaction.

Several things are noteworthy in the results. These include:
1.   The implementation of Ambassadors over RMI is significantly slower than any of the implementations over TCP. In contrast, in an experiment conducted on a LAN, the

Figure 6: Performance of RMI, Ambassadors over RMI and TCP/IP

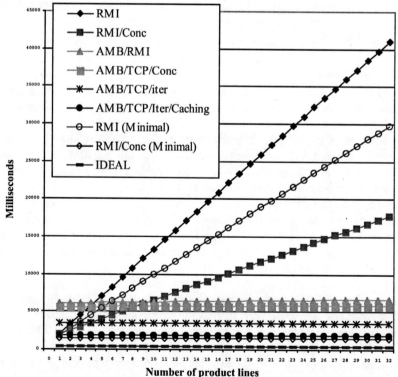

AMB/RMI implementation outperforms all but the fastest AMB/TCP implementation. The most likely explanation is that the use of TCP by RMI is optimised for local networks.

2. The fastest implementation of Ambassadors caches TCP connections for re-use. This avoids an extra round trip (for connection establishment) for every message send, and results in this implementation exhibiting performance at least twice as good as any of the others.

3. The fastest implementation with 32 product lines, is about 24 times faster than RMI and about 10 times faster than multi-threaded RMI. It is, at 1600 milliseconds, still nearly four times slower than the ideal $(441 = (420 + 430 + 33)/2$ milliseconds) but is within 30% of the theoretical minimum for concurrent RMI.

4. Concurrent RMI does not scale properly. The aggregate interaction time should be (almost) independent of the number of product lines, which it clearly is not. The experiment was conducted under JDK 1.1 without native thread support, and these results indicate flaws in that JDK implementation.

5. Further to this, the only difference between AMB/TCP/ITER and AMB/TCP/CONC is that the latter executes each invocation as a separate thread. The difference in performance between the two implementations is quite marked and cannot be accounted for as thread creation overhead. Instead, most of the difference in performance must be due to inefficiencies in the interaction between threading and network I/O, pointing to another flaw in the JDK 1.1 implementation.

In summary, the results for the best implementation of Ambassadors are quite promising, whilst still leaving room for improvement. Note that Figure 6 provides results in the case of a cached Ambassadors system, meaning the server virtual machine caches the Ambassador object class, obviating the need to load the class over the network for subsequent calls. Usually, the RMI calls from the Ambassador to the server are RMI calls between two virtual machines. These virtual machines would typically be on the same physical computer, at worst on the same LAN. Although the comparison only involved RMI as the *defacto* standard technology, the results prove the advantage of the Ambassadors system over RPC-RMI for complex interactions consisting of interrelated operations.

CONCLUSIONS

The Alchemy Project is successful in its aims of allowing the average programmer to engineer his or her software without excessive concern for issues involved in producing a distributed application. The issues of scheduling are handled by the adaptive subsystem ATME and lead to an application whose allocation of tasks to processors evolves over time to a near optimal distribution tailored for each individual user's interaction with the application. Minimizing the effects of latency in globally distributed systems is handled by the use of Ambassadors which frees the user from the need to physically be concerned with the details involved in code migration. Performance gains have been made in both local-area and wide-area networks.

The "all care and no responsibility" principle which has guided the Alchemy Project has led to a collection of tools (ATME and Ambassadors) that provide the average e-business applications developer with the potential performance benefits of a distributed system without the burden of having to address the complexities associated with physically undertaking the distribution manually. Although the Alchemy Project does not aim to deliver optimal performance, it provides a significant improvement over naïve distribution strategies, while liberating the programmer from many issues associated with distribution, allowing his/ her to focus on issues related to the problem domain and the development of a solution. This should result in more correct and maintainable code. The benefits are not reserved for the developer of distributed e-business systems. The end-user/customer also benefits directly through the improved throughput delivered. In a world where customers have limited patience, it is necessary to exploit all means by which improved performance can be delivered so as to ensure the customer does not get bored waiting for a response and start thinking of the competitors.

Future work in this project will focus on to application of the "all care and no responsibility" principle to provide automated support for fault tolerance, load balancing and code/object migration through the use of autonomous software agents.

ACKNOWLEDGMENTS

The author acknowledges the work of former research students within the Alchemy Project, Drs. Henry Detmold and Lin Huang, as the basis for this chapter.

REFERENCES

Birrell, A. D. & Nelson, B.J. (1984). Implementing remote procedure calls, *ACM Transactions on Computer Systems*, 2:1, 39–59.

Bogle, P. & Liskov, B. (1994). Reducing cross domain call overhead using batched futures, *Proceedings of OOPSLA '94, ACM SIGPLAN Notices*, 29:10, 341–354.

Caromel, D. (1991). *Programmation Parallele Asynchrone et Imperative: Etudes et Propositions*, Doctorat de l'Universitè de Nancy I, Spècialitè Informatique.

Caromel, D. (1993). Toward a method of object–oriented concurrent programming, *Communications of the ACM*, 36:9, 90–102.

Casavant, T.L. & Kuhl, J.G. (1988). A Taxonomy of Scheduling in General-Purpose Distributed Computing Systems, *IEEE Transactions on Software Engineering*, 14:2, 141–154.

Chu, W.W., Holloway, L.J., Lan, M.-T., & Efe, K. (1980) Task allocation in distributed data processing, *Computer*, 13:11, 57–69.

Cramp, A. & Oudshoorn, M.J. (2002), Employing hierarchical federation communities in the virtual ship architecture. Submitted for publication.

Detmold, H. & Oudshoorn, M.J. (1996a). Communication constructs for high performance distributed computing, *Australian Computer Science Communications*, 18:1, 252–261.

Detmold, & Oudshoorn, M.J. (1996b). Responsibilities: Support for contract–based distributed computing, *Australian Computer Science Communications*, 18:1, 224–233.

Detmold, H., Hollfelder, M., & Oudshoorn, M.J. (1999). Ambassadors: Structured object mobility in world-wide distributed systems, *Proceedings of the 19th IEEE International Conference on Distributed Computing Systems*, Austin, TX, 442–449.

El-Rewini, H., & Ali, H.H. (1995). Static scheduling of conditional branches in parallel programs, *Journal of Parallel and Distributed Computing*, 24:1, 41-54.

El-Rewini, H., Ali, H.H., & Lewis, T. (1995). Task Scheduling in Multiprocessing Systems, *Computer*, 28:12, 27–37.

El-Rewini, H., & Lewis, T. (1990). Scheduling Parallel Program Tasks onto Arbitrary Target Machines, *Journal of Parallel and Distributed Computing*, 19:2, 138–153.

Fuad, M. & Oudshoorn, M.J. (2002). adJava – Automatic distribution of Java applications. Submitted for publication.

Geist, A., Beguelin, A., Dongarra, J., Jiang, W., Manchek, R. & Sunderam, V. (1994). PVM: Parallel Virtual Machine. *A User's Guide and Tutorial for Networked Parallel Computing,* Cambridge, MA: The MIT Press.

Harary, F. (1969). *Graph Theory,* New York: Addison-Wesley.

Hollfelder, M., Detmold, H., & Oudshoorn, M.J. (1999). A Structured Communication Mechanism using Mobile Objects as Ambassadors, *Australian Computer Science Communications,* 21:1, 265–276.

Huang, L., & Oudshoorn, M.J. (1998). Preemptive task execution and scheduling of parallel programs in message passing systems, Technical Report TR98-04, Department of Computer Science, University of Adelaide.

Huang, L. & Oudshoorn, M.J. (1999a) Static scheduling of conditional parallel tasks. *Chinese Journal of Advanced Software Research,* 6:2, 121–129.

Huang, L. & Oudshoorn, M.J. (1999b). Scheduling Preemptive Tasks in Parallel and Distributed Systems. *Australian Computer Science Communications,* 21:1, 289–301.

Lee, C.Y., Hwang, J.J., Chow, Y.C., & Anger, F.D. (1999). Multiprocessor scheduling with interprocessor communication delays. *Operations Research Letters,* 7:3, 141–147.

Liskov, B. & Shrira, L. (1988). Promises: Linguistic support for efficient asynchronous procedure calls in distributed systems. *Proceedings of the Sigplan '88 Conference on Programming Language Design and Implementation,* 260–267.

Nelson, B.J. (1991). *Remote Procedure Call.* PhD, thesis, Department of Computer Science, Carnegie–Mellon University.

Object Management Group (1991). *Common object request broker architecture.* Object Management Group Document Number 91.12.1, Revision 1.1.

Sarkar, V. (1989). *Partitioning and Scheduling Parallel Programs for Execution on Multiprocessors,* Cambridge, MA: The MIT Press.

Stone, H.S. (1977). Multiprocessor scheduling with the aid of network flow algorithms, *IEEE Transactions on Software Engineering,* 3:1, 85–93.

Sun Microsystems (1997). *Java Remote Method Invocation Specification.*

Ullman, J. (1975). NP-complete scheduling problems, *Journal of Computing System Science,* 10, 384–393.

Walker, E.F., Floyd, R., & Neves, P. (1990) Asynchronous remote operation execution in distributed systems. *Proceedings of the Tenth International Conference on Distributed Computing Systems,* 253–259.

Wu, M.Y. & Gajski, D. (1990). Hypertool: A programming aid for message-passing systems. *IEEE Transactions on Parallel and Distributed Systems,* 1:3, 330–343.

Yang, T. (1993). *Scheduling and Code Generation for Parallel Architectures,* PhD Thesis, Rutgers, The State University of New Jersey.

Chapter VI

Integration of Database and Internet Technologies for Scalable End-to-End E-commerce Systems

K. Selçuk Candan
Arizona State University

Wen-Syan Li
C&C Research Laboratories, NEC USA, Inc.

ABSTRACT

The content of many Web sites changes frequently. Especially in most e-commerce sites, Web content is created on request, based on the current state of business processes represented in application servers and databases. In fact, currently 25% of all Web content consists of such dynamically generated pages, and this ratio is likely to be higher in e-commerce sites. Web site performance, including system up-time and user response time, is a key differentiation point among companies that are eager to reach, attract, and keep customers. Slowdowns can be devastating for these sites, as shown by recent studies. Therefore, most commercial content-providers pay premium prices for services, such as content delivery networks (CDNs), that promise high scalability, reduced network delays, and lower risk of failure. Unfortunately, for e-commerce sites, whose main source of content is dynamically generated on demand, most existing static content-based services are not applicable. In fact, dynamically generated content poses many new challenges for the design of end-to-end (client-to-server-to-client) e-commerce systems. In this chapter, we discuss these challenges and provide solutions for integrating Internet services, business logic, and database technologies, and for improving end-to-end scalability of e-commerce systems.

INTRODUCTION

The content of many Web sites change frequently: (1) entire sites can be updated during a company restructuring or during new product releases; (2) new pages can be created or existing pages can be removed as incremental changes in the business data or logic, such as inventory changes, occur; (3) media contents of the pages can be changed while HTML contents are left intact, for instance when advertisements are updated; and (4) (sub)content of pages can be dynamically updated, for instance when product prices change. Some of these changes are administered manually by Webmasters, but most are initiated automatically by the changes in the underlying data or application logic. Especially in most e-commerce sites, Web content is created on-request, based on the current state of business processes represented in application servers and databases. This requires close collaboration between various software modules, such as Web servers, application servers, and database servers (Figure 1), as well as Internet entities, such as proxy servers.

Web site performance is a key differentiation point among companies and e-commerce sites eager to reach, attract, and keep customers. This performance is measured using various metrics, including system up-time, average response time, and the maximum number of simultaneous users. Low performance, such as slowdowns, can be devastating for content providers, as shown by recent studies (Zona Research, 2001), which indicate that even with response times of 12 seconds, Web sites find 70% abandonment rates (Table 1).

Figure 1: Database-driven dynamic content delivery versus static content delivery

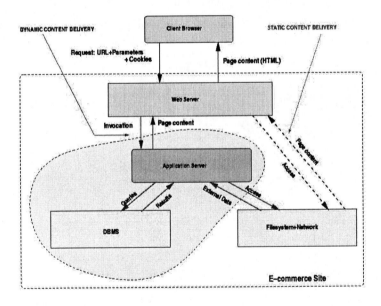

Table 1: Relationship between the time required to download a page and the user abandonment rate

Download time	Abandonment rate
< 7 seconds	7%
8 seconds	30%
12 seconds	70%

As a result, most commercial Web sites pay premium prices for solutions that help them reduce their response times as well as risks of failure when faced with high access rates. Most high-volume sites typically deploy a large number of servers and employ hardware- or software-based load-balancing components to reduce the response time of their servers. Although they guarantee better protection against surges in demand, such localized solutions can not help reduce the delay introduced in the network during the transmission of the content to end-users. In order to alleviate this problem, content providers also replicate or mirror their content at *edge caches,* i.e., caches that are close to end-users. If a page can be placed in a cache closer to end-users, when a user requests the page, it can be delivered promptly from the cache without additional communication with the Web server, reducing the response time. This approach also reduces the load on the original source as some of the requests can be processed without accessing the source.

This gives rise to a multi-level content delivery structure, which consists of (1) one or more local servers and reverse proxies, which use load distribution techniques to achieve scalability, (2) Content Delivery Networks (CDNs) paid by the e-commerce site that deploy network-wide caches that are closer to end-users, (3) caches and proxy servers that are employed by Internet Service Providers (ISPs), to reduce the bandwidth utilization of the ISPs, and (4) browser caches that store content frequently used by the user of the browsers. This structure is shown in Figure 2. Note that, although different caches in this structure are deployed by different commercial entities, such as CDNs and ISPs, with different goals, the

Figure 2: Components of a database-driven Web content delivery system

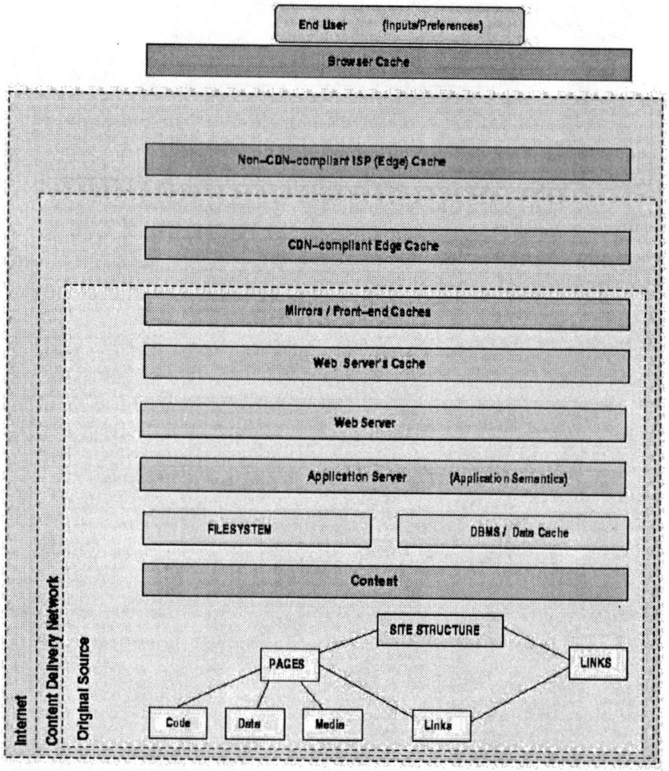

Table 2: Dynamic content versus static content

Common ...	Static Content	Dynamic Content
Format	Text, Images, Video, Audio	Mostly text
Storage	File system	Databases (data) and application servers (business logic)
Source of Delay	Network delay	Data access and application processing delay
Scalability Bottleneck	Web server	Database and application server

performance of an e-commerce site depends on the successful coordination between various components involved in this loosely coupled structure.

A static page, i.e., a page that has not been generated specifically to address a user request and which is not likely to change unpredictably in the future, can easily be replicated and/or placed in caches for future use. Consequently, for such content, the hierarchy shown in Figure 2 works reasonably well. For instance, caching works because content is assumed to be constant for a predictable period of time and it can be stored in the caches and proxies distributed in the network without risking staleness of accesses. In addition, CDNs provide considerable savings on network delays, because static content is media rich.

For dynamically generated pages, however, such assumptions do not always hold (Table 2). One major characteristic of this type of content is that it is usually text oriented and therefore small (4k). Consequently, the delay observed by the end-users is less sensitive to the network bottlenecks compared with large media objects.

In contrast, the performance of dynamic content-based systems is extremely sensitive to the load variations in the back-end servers. The number of concurrent connections a Web server can simultaneously maintain is limited and new requests have to wait at a queue until old ones are served. Consequently, system response time is a function of the maximum number of concurrent connections and the data access/processing time at the back-end systems. Unfortunately, the underlying database and application servers are generally not as scalable as the Web servers; they can support fewer concurrent requests, and they require longer processing times. Consequently, they become bottlenecks before the Web servers and the network; hence, reducing the load of application and database servers is essential.

Furthermore, since the application servers, databases, Web servers, and caches are independent components, it is not trivial to reflect the changes in data (stored in the databases) to the cached Web pages that depend on this data. Since, most e-commerce applications are sensitive to the freshness of the information provided to the clients, most application servers have to specify dynamically generated content as non-cacheable or make them expire immediately. Hence, caches can not be useful for dynamically generated content. Consequently, repeated requests to dynamically generated Web pages with the same content result in repeated computation in the back-end systems (application and database servers).

In fact, dynamically generated content poses many new challenges to the efficient delivery of content. In this chapter, we discuss these challenges and provide an overview of the content delivery solutions developed for accelerating e-commerce systems.

OVERVIEW OF CONTENT DELIVERY ARCHITECTURES

Slowdowns observed by major Web sites, especially during their peak access times, demonstrate the difficulty companies face trying to handle large demand volumes. For e-commerce sites, such slowdowns mean that potential customers are turned away from the electronic stores even before they have a chance to enter and see the merchandise. Therefore, improving the scalability of Web sites is essential to companies and e-commerce sites eager to reach, attract, and keep customers.

Many e-commerce sites observe non-uniform request distributions; i.e., although most of the time the request load they have is manageable, in certain occasions (for example, during Christmas for e-shops and during breaking news for news services), the load they receive surges to very high volumes. Consequently, for most companies, investing in local infrastructure that can handle peak demand volumes, while sitting idle most other times, is not economically meaningful. These companies usually opt for *server farm-* or *edge-based* commercial services to improve scalability.

Server Farms vs. Edge Services

Server *farms,* provided by various companies including Digital Island (www.digitalisland.com), Exodus, and MirrorImage (www.mirrorimage.com) are one possible external scalability solution. A server *farm,* in essence, is a powerhouse that consists of hundreds of colocated servers. Content providers *publish,* or upload, the content into the server farm. It is then the responsibility of the server farm to allocate enough resources to ensure a quality of service to its customers. Note that, by their nature, server farms are expensive to create. Therefore, companies that provide such services tend to establish a few server farm sites, usually at sites closer to where most of their content providers are. These sites are then linked with high-bandwidth leased land or satellite connections to enable distribution of data within the server farm network. Some of the server farm companies also provide *hosting* services, where they host the entire site of their customers, relieving them from the need of maintaining a copy of the Web site locally.

Although the server farm approach provides protection against demand surges by leveraging the differences between the demand characteristics of different content providers, because the farms can not permeate deep into the network, they can not reduce the network distance between the end-users and the data sources (farms). This, however, may contribute to the overall delay observed by the end-users. For example, Figure 3 shows a user in Japan

Figure 3: Network delays observed by the end-users.

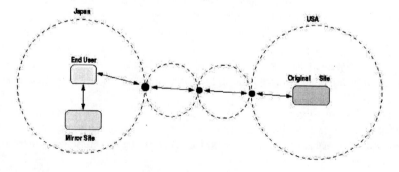

who wants to access a page in a Web site in US. The request will pass through several ISP gateways before reaching the original Web site in the US. Since gateways are likely to be the main bottlenecks and since there are many others factors along the Internet paths between the user and the origin that may contribute to delays, even if the response time of the source is close to zero, the end-user in Japan may observe large delays.

One obvious way to eliminate network delays is by using a high-speed dedicated line to deliver the contents without or reducing passing through Internet gateways. This solution sometimes is used by large companies to link their geographically dispersed offices and by server farms to ship content quickly between their content centers. However, it is clear that implementing such an approach as a general solution would be prohibitively expensive.

An alternative approach for reducing the network delay is to use intelligent caching techniques; i.e., deploying many cheap mirror servers, proxies, and other intermediary short-term storage spaces in the network and serving users from sources closer to them. This approach is commonly referred to as edge-based content delivery service and the architectures that provide content delivery services are referred to as edge-based content delivery networks (CDNs). Akamai (www.akamai.com), and Adero (www.adero.com) are some of the companies that provide edge-based services.

Content Delivery Services

Several high-technology companies (Digital Island; Akamai Technologies; Adero Inc.; CacheFlow Inc., www.cacheflow.com; InfoLibria Inc., www.infolibria.com) are competing feverishly with each other to establish network infrastructures referred to as *content delivery networks (CDNs)*. The key technology underlying all CDNs is the deployment of network-wide caches which replicate the content held by the origin server in different parts of the network: front-end caches, proxy caches, edge caches, and so on. The basic premise of this architecture is that by replicating the HTML content, user requests for a specific content may be served from a cache that is in the network proximity of the user instead of routing it all the way to the origin server.

In CDNs, since the traffic is redirected intelligently to an appropriate replica, the system can be protected from traffic surges and the users can observe fast response times. Furthermore, this approach can not only eliminate network delays, but it can also be used to distribute the load on the servers more effectively. There are several advantages of this approach:

- User requests are satisfied in more responsive manner due to lower network latency.
- Since requests are not routed completely from the user site to the origin server, significant bandwidth savings can be potentially realized.
- Origin servers can be made more scalable due to load distribution. Not all requests need to be served by the origin server; network caches participate in serving user requests and thereby distributing the load.

Of course these advantages are realized at the cost of additional complexity at the network architecture level. For example, new techniques and algorithms are needed to route/forward user requests to appropriate caches. Akamai enables caching of embedded objects in an HTML page and maintains multiple versions of the base HTML page (index, html), such that the HTML links to the embedded objects point to the cached copies. When a user request arrives at the origin server that has been *akamized,* an appropriate version of index, html is returned to the user to ensure that the embedded objects in the base HTML page are served from the Akamai caches that are close to the user site. In general, current architectures restrict themselves to the caching of static content (e.g., image data, video data, audio data, etc.) or content that is updated relatively infrequently. The origin server and the caches have to rely on manual or hard-wired approaches for propagating the updates to the caches in the latter case. We see that there are two major approaches for developing architectures for content delivery networks:

- Network-level solutions: In this case, context delivery services are built around existing network services, such as domain name servers (DNSs), IP multicasting, etc. The advantage of this approach is that it does not require a change in the existing Internet infrastructure and can be deployed relatively easily. Also, since in most cases the network protocols are already optimized to provide these services efficiently, these solutions are likely to work fast. However, since most existing network services are not built with integrated content delivery services in mind, it is not always possible to achieve all desirable savings using this approach.

- Application-level solutions: In order to leverage all possible savings in content delivery, another approach is to bypass the services provided by the network protocols and develop an application-level solutions, such as application level multicasting (e.g., FastForward networks by Inktomi (www.inktomi.com). These solutions rely on constant observations of network-level properties and responding to the corresponding changes using application-level protocols. Since providers of these solutions can finetune their application logic to the specific needs of a given content delivery service, this approach can be optimized to provide different savings (such as, bandwidth utilization, response time, prioritized delivery of content) as needed and can provide significant benefits. The main challenges with this approach, however, are to be able to observe the network state accurately and constantly and to deploy a costly Internet-wide application infrastructure.

In this chapter, we mostly focus on the application-level architectures for content delivery services. Figure 4(a) shows the three entities involved in a content delivery architecture: the original source, a potential main server (or redirection server), and mirror servers. The original site is the e-commerce site maintained by the customer; i.e., the e-commerce business owner. The main redirection server is where the redirection decisions are

Figure 4: (a) Content delivery architecture and (b) a mirror server in this architecture

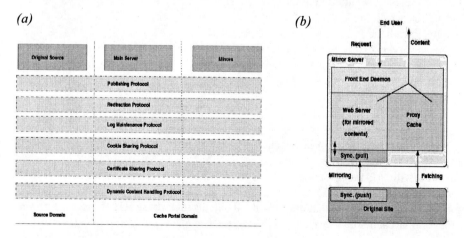

given (note that in some architectures the redirection decision may be given in a truly distributed fashion). In effect, this server is similar in function to a domain name server, except that it functions at the application level instead of functioning at the IP-level. The mirror servers, on the other hand, are the servers in which content is replicated/cached. In Figure 4(a), we show the architecture of a generic mirror server, which integrates a Web server and a proxy server:

- The Web server component serves the data that has been published by the original Web server in advance (before the request is received by the mirror server).
- When a user request arrives at the mirror server, it is first processed by the Web server and the proxy cache. If the content is found in either compo nent, the content is delivered. If the content is not found, it has to be fetched from the original Web site and copied into the proxy cache if the attribute of the content is not specified as "non-cacheable."
- If the server is too overloaded to perform these tasks, it can redirect traffic to other mirror sites.

Various protocols are required for these three entities to cooperate. Figure 4(a) lists these protocols. Note that different service providers implement these protocols differently. Consequently, achieving interoperability between providers requires agreements on protocols and development of common infrastructures (Content Bridge, www.content-bridge.com).

Publishing Protocol

Publishing protocol enables the content available at the original site to be replicated and distributed to the mirror sites. Depending on the architecture, the protocol can be push- or pull-based, can be object- or site-dependent, and can be synchronous or asynchronous– In a push-based protocol, the source decides when and which objects to push to the mirrors. In a pull-based protocol, on the other hand, the mirrors identify when their utilization drops below a threshold and then request new objects from the original source. Note that it is also possible that mirrors will act as simple, *transparent* caches, which store only those objects that pass through them. In such a case, there is no publishing protocol required. In an object-based protocol, the granularity of the publishing decision is at the object-level; i.e., the access rate to each object is evaluated separately and only those objects that are likely to be requested at a particular mirror will be published to that mirror server. In a site-based protocol, however, the entire site is mirrored. In a synchronous protocol, publication is performed at potentially regular intervals at all mirrors; whereas, in an asynchronous protocol, publication decisions between the original server and each mirror are given separately.

The publishing protocol is the only protocol that is not directly involved in servicing user requests. The other protocols, shown in Figure 4a, are all utilized in request-processing time for:

1. capturing the initial user request,
2. choosing the most suitable server for the current user/server/network configuration, and
3. delivering the content to the user.

Next, we discuss these protocols and their roles in the processing of user requests.

Cookie and Certificate Sharing Protocols

Most user requests arrive at the original source and, if necessary, they are directed to the appropriate mirror servers. Some user requests, though, may directly arrive at mirror servers. Therefore, both the original source and the mirror servers must be capable of capturing and processing user requests. There are two aspects of this task:

- masquerading as the original source while capturing the user (transaction) requests at the mirrors/caches, and
- running the application logic and accessing/modifying the underlying data in the databases on the behalf of the original source.

Masquerading as the original source may require the mirror site to authenticate itself as the original source (i.e., have the same certificates). Furthermore, for state-dependent inputs (e.g., user history or preferences), mirrors should have access to state information (i.e., cookies that are placed into the memory space of client browsers by servers for enabling stateful browsing) maintained by other mirror servers or the original source.

However, cookies can not be read by any domain except the ones that set them in the first place.

In DNS-based solutions where all the replicas are seen as if they are under the same domain, this task does not cause any problems. However, if mirror servers have their own domain names, they require special attention (Figure 5). One way to share cookies across servers is shown in Figure 6:

1. Assign a unique ID to the user *the first time* user accesses the source and exchange this ID along with *the first redirection message.*
2. Use this ID to synchronize the cookie information between the original source and the mirror.
3. Performs these tasks without modifying existing applications:
   - intercept inputs and outputs through a synchronization module that sits between the Web server and the application server, and
   - hide this process from the clients through the *server rewrite* option provided by Web servers.

The cookie synchronization module manages this task by keeping a cookie information-base that contains the cookie information generated by the original site. Although, keeping the cookie data may be costly, it enables dynamic content caching with no modification of the application semantics. Furthermore, once the initial IDs are synchronized, irrespective of how many redirections are performed between mirrors and the original source, the cookie information will always be fresh. At any point in time, if the original site chooses to discontinue the use of the service, it can do so without loosing any client state information.

Running the applications of the original source can be done either by replicating the application semantics at the mirror site or by delegating the application execution to a separate application server (or the original source).

Replicating the application semantics not only requires replicating the application and the execution environment, but also replicating/distributing the input data and synchronizing the output data. In other words, this task is equivalent to a distributed transaction processing task. Although it is possible to provide a solution at the Web-content level, the more general case (implementing a distributed database + application environment) is generally beyond the scope of current CDNs. However, due to the increasing acceptance of the Java 2 Enterprise

Figure 5: Problem with cookies in multi-domain CDNs: (a) The original site writes a cookie into the clients browser, (b) when the client is directed to a mirror, the cookie available at the client can no longer be accessed, therefore (c) while the client is being redirected to a mirror, the system must create a copy of the existing cookie at the client

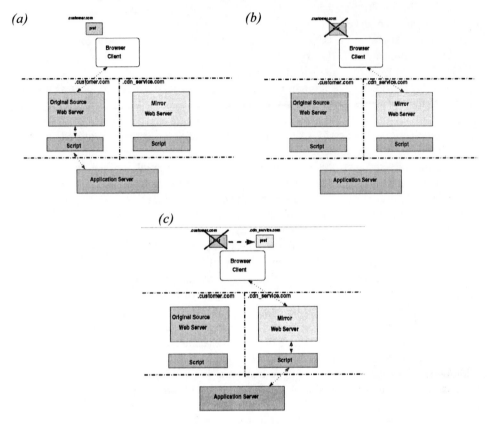

Figure 6: Handling cookies in multi-domain CDNs without modifying the application programs

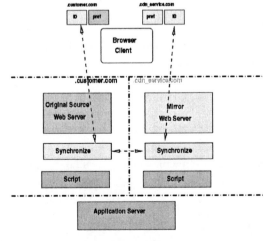

Edition (J2EE) (Javatm 2 Platform, www.java.sun.com/jzee.), a platform-independent distributed application environment, by the application server vendors, this is becoming a relevant task.

An application server is a bundle of software on a server or group of servers that provides the business logic for an application program. An application server sits along with or between the Web server and the backend, which represents the database and other legacy applications that reside on large servers and mainframes. The business logic, which is basically the application itself and which acts as the middleware glue between the Web server and the back-end systems, sits within the application server.

J2EE platform enables application builders to integrate pre-built application components into their products. Since many applications, such as those involved in e-commerce, contain common modules, independent software developers can save a great deal of time by building their applications on top of existing modules that already provide required functionality. This calls for a distributed architecture, where different modules can locate each other through directory services and can exchange information through messaging systems. In addition, for such a system to be practical, it has to support a container framework that will host independently created modules and the transaction services that enable these modules to perform business transactions. J2EE-compliant application servers act as containers for business logic/modules (Enterprise Java beans) that provide their services to other modules and/or end-users. Note that J2EE-compliant application servers provide the necessary framework for a replication environment, where applications and the data on which they run can be replicated at the edges. The resulting replicated application architecture enables dynamic load balancing and removes the single points of failure.

JXTA (Project JXTA, www.jxta.org) is another recent technology that can be used for developing distributed, interoperable, peer-to-peer applications. It includes the protocols for finding peers on dynamically changing networks, sharing content with any peer within the network, monitoring peer activities remotely, and securely communicating with peers. Although JXTA lacks many essential protocols required for facilitating the development of replicated/distributed applications, it provides some of the basic building blocks that would be useful in creating a CDN with many independent peer mirror servers.

J2EE is widely accepted by most major technology vendors (including IBM, SUN, BEA, and Oracle). A related technology, Microsoft's .NET strategy (Microsoft, www.microsoft.com/servers/evaluation/overview/net.asp.), uses an application server built using proprietary technology. But, in its essence, it also aims at hosting distributed services that can be integrated within other products.

Note that whichever underlying technology is utilized, delivering Web content through a replicated/distributed application architecture will need to deal with dynamically changing data and application semantics. We will concentrate on the issues arising due to dynamicity of data in the next section.

Redirection Protocol

A redirection protocol implements a policy that assigns user requests to the most appropriate servers. As we mentioned earlier, it is possible to implement redirection at the network or application levels, each with its own advantages and disadvantages. Note that there may be more than one redirection policy used for different e-commerce systems therefore, a redirection protocol should be flexible enough to accommodate all existing redirection policies and be extendible to capture future redirection policies.

There are two ways that a request redirection service can be implemented: domain name server (DNS) redirection and application-level redirection.

In DNS Redirection, the DNS at the original Web site determines the mirror site closest to the end-user based on his/her IP address and redirects the user to that mirror site. In Figure 7(a), end-users 1 and 2, who are far from the content providers original server are redirected to local mirror servers, whereas end-user 3 gets the content from the original server. Since DNS redirection applies to all requests the same way, object-based solutions, where different objects or object types are redirected differently, can not be implemented.

In application-level solutions can be implemented in various ways. In this approach, shown in Figure 7(b), all page requests are directed to the original site. Given a request, the original site checks the user's location based on the IP address associated with the request and then, finds the closest mirror sites *(Site 1* and *Site2* in this example) containing the objects embedded in the requested page. The system then rewrites the HTML content of the Web page by specifying these most suitable object sources. When the browser parses this customized page, it learns that it has to go to these servers to fetch the objects; i.e., in this example, the browser contacts *Site* 1 to fetch the object *Obj1* and *Site2* to fetch objects *Obj2* and *Obj3*.

Although DNS redirection has a very low overhead, it's the main disadvantage is that it can not differentiate between semantics of different requests (e.g., media versus HTML page) as well as capabilities of the servers that are using the same domain name. Consequently, irrespective of what type of content (media, text, or stream) is requested, all servers must be ready to serve them. Furthermore, all content must be present at all servers. Therefore, this approach does not lend itself to intelligent load balancing. Since dynamic content delivery is very sensitive to the load on the servers, however, this approach can not be preferred in e-commerce systems.

Note that it is also possible to use various hybrid approaches. Akamai Technologies (www.akimi.com), for instance, is using an hybrid of the two approaches depicted in Figures 7(a) and (b). But whichever implementation approach is chosen, the main task of the redirection is, given a user request, to identify the most suitable server for the current server and network status.

The most appropriate mirror server for a given user request can be identified by either using a centralized coordinator (a dedicated redirection server) or allowing distributed decision making (each server performs redirection independently).

Figure 7: Content delivery: (a) DNS redirection and (b) embedded object redirection

(a)   *(b)*

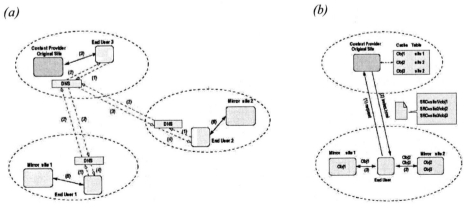

In Figure 8(a), there are several mirror servers coordinated by a main server. When a particular server experiences a request rate higher than its capability threshold, it requests the central redirection server to allocate one or more mirror servers to handle its traffic.

In Figure 8(b), each mirror server software is installed to each server. When a particular server experiences a request rate higher than its capability threshold, it checks the availability at the participating servers and determines one or more servers to serve its contents.

Note, however, that even when we use the centralized approach, there can be *more than one* central server distributing the redirection load. In fact, the central server(s) can broadcast the redirection information to all mirrors, in a sense converging to a distributed architecture, shown in Figure 8(b). In addition, a central redirection server can act either as a passive directory server (Figure *9*) or an active redirection agent (Figure 10):

- As shown in Figure *9,* the server which captures the user request can communicate with the redirection server to choose the most suitable server for a particular request. Note that in this figure, arrow *(4)* and *(5)* denote a subprotocol between the first server and the redirection server, which act as a directory server in this case.

- Alternatively, as shown in Figure 10, the first server can redirect the request to the redirection server and let this central server choose the best content server and redirect the request to it.

Figure 8: (a) Content delivery through central coordination and (b) through distributed decision making

(a)

(b)

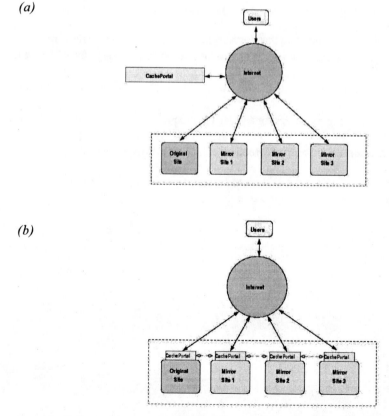

Figure 9: Redirection process, Alternative I

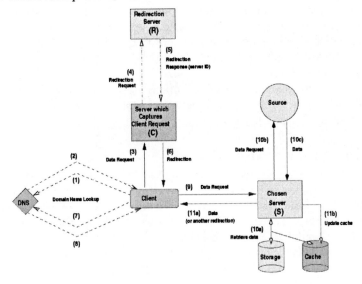

Figure 10: Redirection process, Alternative 2 (simplified graph)

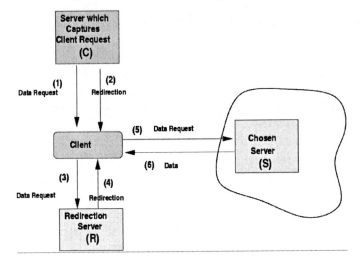

The disadvantage of the second approach is that the client is involved in the redirection process twice. This reduces the transparency of the redirection. Furthermore, this approach is likely to cause two additional DNS lookups by the client: one to locate the redirection server and the other to locate the new content server. In contrast, in the first option, the user browser is involved only in the final redirection (i.e., only once). Furthermore, since the first option lends itself better to caching of redirection information at the servers, it can further reduce the overall response time as well as the load on the redirection server.

The redirection information can be declared *permanent* (i.e., cacheable) or *temporary* (non-cacheable). Depending on whether we want ISP proxies and browser caches to contribute to the redirection process, we may choose either permanent or temporary redirection. The advantage of the permanent redirection is that future requests of the same nature will be redirected automatically. The disadvantage is that since the ISP proxies are also involved in the future redirection processes, the CDN loses complete control of the redirection (hence load distribution) process. Therefore, it is better to use either temporary redirection or permanent redirection with a relatively short expiration date. Since most browsers may not recognize temporary redirection, the second option is preferred. The expiration duration is based on how fast the network and server conditions change and how much load balancing we would like to perform.

Log Maintenance Protocol

For a redirection protocol to identify the best suitable content server for a given request, it is important that the server and network status are known as accurately as possible. Similarly, for the publication mechanism to correctly identify which objects to replicate to which servers (and when), statistics and projections about the object access rates, delivery costs, and resource availabilities must be available.

Such information is collected throughout the content delivery architecture (servers, proxies, network, and clients) and shared to enable the accuracy of the content delivery decisions. A log maintenance protocol is responsible with the sharing of such information across the many components of the architecture.

Dynamic Content Handling Protocol

When indexing the dynamically created Web pages, a cache has to consider not only the URL string, but also the cookies and request parameters (i.e., HTTP GET and POST parameters), as these are used in the creation of the page content. Hence, a caching key consists of three types of information contained within an HTTP request (we use the Apache (http://httpd.apache.org) environment variable convention to describe these):

- the HTTP_HOST string,
- a list of (cookie,value) pairs (from the HTTRCOOKIE environment variable),
- a list of (GET parameter name,value) pairs (from the QUERYSTRING), and
- a list of (POST parameter name,value) pairs (from the HTTP message body).

Figure 11: Four different URL streams mapped to three different pages; the parameter (cookie, GET, or POST parameter) ID is not a caching key

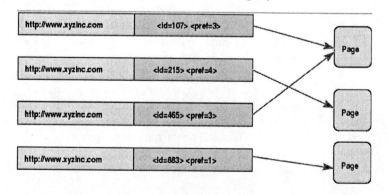

Note that given an HTTP request, different GET, POST, or cookie parameters may have different effects on caching. Some parameters may need to be used as keys/indexes in the cache, whereas some others may not (Figure 11). Therefore, the parameters that have to be used in indexing pages have to be declared in advance and, unlike caches for static content, dynamic content caches must be implemented in a way that uses these keys for indexing.

The architecture described so far works very well for static content; that is, content that does not change often or whose change rate is predictable. When the content published into the mirror server or cached into the proxy cache can change unpredictably, however, the risk of serving stale content arises. In order to prevent this, it is necessary to utilize a protocol which can handle dynamic content. In the next section, we will focus on this and other challenges introduced by dynamically generated content.

IMPACT OF DYNAMIC CONTENT ON CONTENT DELIVERY ARCHITECTURES

As can be seen from the emergence of J2EE and .NET technologies, in the space of Web and Internet technologies, there is currently a shift toward service-centric architectures. In particular, many "brick-and-mortar" companies are reinventing themselves to provide services over the Web. Web servers in this context are referred to as *e-commerce* servers. A typical e-commerce server architecture consists of three major components: a database management system (DBMS), which maintains information pertaining to the service; an application server (AS), which encodes business logic pertaining to the organization; and a Web server (WS), which provides the Web-based interface between the users and the e-commerce provider. The application server can use a combination of the server side technologies, such as to implement application logic:

- the Java Servlet technology (http://java.sun.conitproducts/servlet.), which enables Java application components to be downloaded into the application server;
- JavaServer Pages (JSP) (http://java.sun.conilproducts/jsp) or Active Server Pages (ASP) (Microsoft ASP.www.asp.net), which use tags and scripts to encapsulate the application logic within the page itself; and
- JavaBeans (JavaBeans(TM), http://java.sun.comlproducts/javabeans.), Enterprise JavaBeans, or ActiveX software component architectures that provide automatic support for services such as transactions, security, and database connectivity.

In contrast to traditional Web architectures, user requests in this case invoke appropriate program scripts in the application server which in turn issues queries to the underlying DBMS to dynamically generate and construct HTML responses and pages. Since executing application programs and accessing DBMSs may require significant time and other resources, it may be more advantageous to cache application results in a *result cache* (Labrinidis & Roussopoulos, 2000; Oracle9i Web cache, www.oracle.com//ip/deploy/ias/caching/index.html?web_caching.htm), instead of caching the data used by the applications in a data cache (Oracle9i data cache, www.oracle.com//ip/deploy/ias/caching/index.html?database_caching.html).

The key difference in this case is that database-driven HTML content is inherently *dynamic,* and the main problem that arises in caching, such content is to ensure its *freshness.* In particular, if we blindly enable dynamic content caching we run the risk of users viewing stale data specially when the corresponding data-elements in the underlying DBMS are updated. This is a significant problem, since the DBMS typically stores inventory, catalog, and pricing information which gets updated relatively frequently. As the number of e-commerce sites increases, there is a critical need to develop the next generation of CDN architecture which would enable dynamic content caching. Currently, most dynamically generated HTML pages are tagged as non-cacheable or expire-immediately. This means that every user request to dynamically generated HTML pages must be served from the origin server.

Several solutions are beginning to emerge in both research laboratories (Challenger, Dantzig, & Iyengar, 1998; Challenger, Iyengar, & Dantzig, 1999; Douglis, Haro, & Rabinovich, 1999; Levy, Iyengar, Song, & Dias, 1999; Smith, Acharya, Yang, & Zhu, 1999) and commercial arena (Persistence Software Systems Inc., www.dynamai.com; Zembu Inc., www.zembu.com; Oracle Corporation, www.oracle.com). In this section, we identify the technical challenges that must be overcome to enable dynamic content caching. We also describe architectural issues that arise with regard to the serving dynamically created pages.

Overview of Dynamic Content Delivery Architectures

Figure 12 shows an overview of a typical Web page delivery mechanism for Web sites with back-end systems, such as database management systems. In a standard configuration, there are a set of Web/application servers that are load balanced using a traffic balancer, such as Cisco LocalDirector (Cisco, www.cisco.com/warp/public/cc/pd/cxsn/yoo/). In addition to the Web servers, e-commerce sites utilize database management systems (DBMSs) to maintain business-related data, such as prices, descriptions, and quantities of products. When a user accesses the Web site, the request and its associated parameters, such as the product name and model number, are passed to an application server. The application server performs the necessary computation to identify what kind of data it needs from the database and then sends appropriate queries to the database. After the database returns the query results to the application server, the application uses these to prepare a Web page and passes the result page to the Web server, which then sends it to the user.

In contrast to a dynamically generated page, a static page i.e., a page which has not been generated on demand can be served to a user in a variety of ways. In particular, it can be placed in:

- a proxy cache (Figure 12(A)),
- a Web server front-end cache (as in reverse proxy caching, Figure 12(B)),
- an edge cache (i.e., a cache close to users and operated by content delivery services, Figure 12(C)), or
- a user side cache (i.e., user site proxy cache or browser cache, Figure 12(D))

for future use. Note, however, that the application servers, databases, Web servers, and caches are independent components. Furthermore, there is no efficient mechanism to make database content changes to be reflected to the cached pages. Since most e-commerce applications are sensitive to the freshness of the information provided to the clients, most application servers have to mark dynamically generated Web pages as *non-cacheable* **or make** them expire immediately. Consequently, subsequent requests to dynamically generated Web pages with the same content result in repeated computation in the back-end systems (application and database servers) as well as the network roundtrip latency between the user and the e-commerce site.

In general, a dynamically created page can be described as a function of the underlying application logic, user parameters, information contained within cookies, data contain within

Figure 12: A typical e-commerce site (WS: Web server; AS: Application server; DS:Database server)

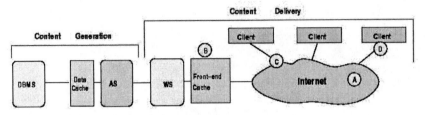

databases, and other external data. Although it is true that any of these can change during the lifetime of a cached Web page, rendering the page *stale,* it is also true that

- application logic does not change very often and when it changes it is easy to detect;
- user parameters can change from one request to another; however, in general many user requests may share the same *(popular)* parameter values;
- cookie information can also change from a request to another; however, in general, many requests may share the same *(popular)* cookie parameter values;
- external data (filesystem + network) may change unpredictably and undetectably; however, most e-commerce Web applications do not use such external data; and
- database contents can change, but such changes can be detected.

Therefore, in most cases, it is unnecessary and very inefficient to mark all dynamically created pages as *noncacheable,* as it is mostly done in current systems. There are various ways in which current systems are trying to tackle this problem. In some e-business applications, frequently accessed pages, such as catalog pages, are pre-generated and placed in the Web server. However, when the data on the database changes, the changes are not immediately propagated to the Web server. One way to increase the probability that the Web pages are fresh is to periodically refresh the pages through the Web server (for example, Oracle9i Web cache provides a mechanism for time-based refreshing of the Web pages in the cache) However, this results in a significant amount of unnecessary computation overhead at the Web server, the application server, and the databases. Furthermore, even with such a periodic refresh rate, Web pages in the cache can not be guaranteed to be up-to-date.

Since caches designed to handle static content are not useful for database-driven Web content, e-commerce sites have to use other mechanisms to achieve scalability. Below, we describe three approaches to e-commerce site scalability.

Configuration I

Figure 13 shows the standard configuration, where there are a set of Web/application servers that are load balanced using a traffic balancer, such as Cisco LocalDirector. Such a configuration enables a Web site to partition its load among multiple Web servers, therefore achieving higher scalability. Note, however, that since pages delivered by e-commerce sites are database dependent (i.e., put computation burden on a database management system), replicating only the Web servers is not enough for scaling up the entire architecture. We also need to make sure that the underlying database does not become a bottleneck. Therefore, in this configuration, database servers are also replicated along with the Web servers. Note

Figure 13: Configuration I (replication); RGs are the clients (requests generators) and UG is the database where the updates are registered

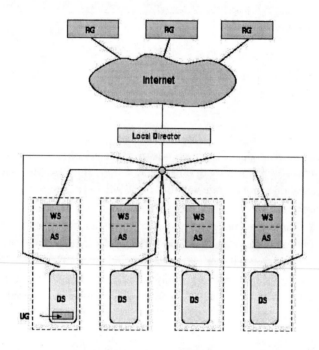

that this architecture has the advantage of being very simple; however, it has two major shortcomings. First of all, since it does not allow caching of dynamically generated content, it still requires redundant computation when clients have similar requests. Secondly, it is generally very costly to keep multiple databases synchronized in an update-intensive environment.

Configuration II

Figure 14 shows an alternative configuration that tries to address the two shortcomings of the first configuration. As before, a set of Web/application servers are placed behind a load balancing unit. In this configuration, however, there is only one DBMS serving all Web servers. Each Web server, on the other hand, has a middle-tier database cache to prevent the load on the actual DBMS from growing too fast. Oracle 8i provides a middle-tier data cache (Oracle9i data cache, 2001), which serves this purpose. A similar product, Dynamai (Persistence Software Systems Inc., 2001), is provided by Persistence software. Since it uses middle-tier database caches *(DCaches),* this option reduces the redundant accesses to the DBMS; however, it can not reduce the redundancy arising from the Web server and application server computations. Furthermore, although it does not incur database replication overheads, ensuring the currency of the caches requires a heavy database-cache synchronization overhead.

Figure 14: Configuration II (middle-tier data caching)

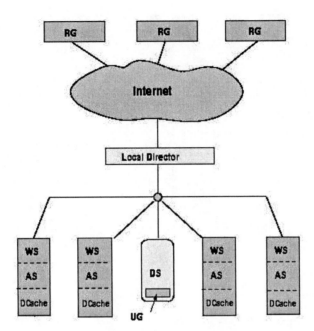

Configuration III

Finally, Figure 15 shows the configuration where a dynamic Web-content cache sits in front of the load balancer to reduce the total number of Web requests reaching the Web server farm. In this configuration, there is only one database management server. Hence, there is no data replication overhead. Also, since there is no middle-tier data cache, there is also no database-cache synchronization overhead. The redundancy is reduced at all three levels (WS, AS, and DS).

Note that, in this configuration, in order to deal with dynamicity (i.e., changes in the database) an additional mechanism is required that will reflect the changes in the database into the Web caches. One way to achieve invalidation is to embed into the database update sensitive triggers which generate invalidation messages when certain changes to the underlying data occurs. The effectiveness of this approach, however, depends on the trigger management capabilities (such as tuple versus table-level trigger activation and join-based trigger conditions) of the underlying database. More importantly, it puts heavy trigger management burden on the database. In addition, since the invalidation process depends on the requests that are cached, the database management system must also store a table of these pages. Finally, since the trigger management would be handled by the database management system, the invalidator would not have control over the invalidation process to guarantee timely invalidation.

Another way to overcome the shortcomings of the trigger-based approach is to use materialized views whenever they are available. In this approach, one would define a materialized view for each query type and then use triggers on these materialized views. Although this approach could increase the expressive power of the triggers, it would not

Figure 15: Configuration III (Web caching)

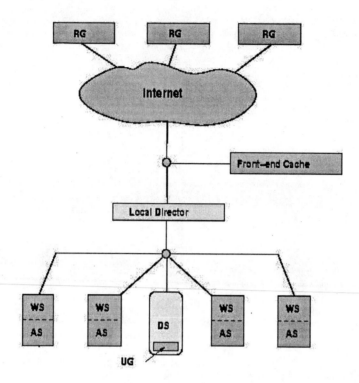

solve the efficiency problems. Instead, it would increase the load on the DBMS by imposing unnecessary view management costs.

Network Appliance NetCache4.O (Network Appliance Inc., www.networkappliance.com) supports an extended HTTP protocol, which enables demand-based *ejection* of cached Web pages. Similarly, recently, as part of its new application server, Oracle9i (Oracle9i Web cache, 2001), Oracle announced a Web cache that is capable of storing dynamically generated pages. In order to deal with dynamicity, Oracle9i allows for time-based, application-based, or trigger-based invalidation of the pages in the cache. However, to our knowledge, Oracle9i does not provide a mechanism through which updates in the underlying data can be used to identify which pages in the cache to be invalidated. Also, the use of triggers for this purpose is likely to be very inefficient and may introduce a very large overhead on the underlying DBMSs, defeating the original purpose. In addition, this approach would require changes in the original application program and/or database to accommodate triggers. Persistence software (Persistence Software Systems Inc., 2001) and IBM *(Challenger, Dantzig, & Iyengar, 1998;* Challenger, Iyengar, & Dantzig, 1999; Levy, Iyengar, Song, & Dias, 1999) adopted solutions where applications are finetuned for propagation of updates from applications to the caches. They also suffer from the fact that caching requires changes in existing applications

In (Candan, Li, Luo, Hsiung, & Agrawal, 2001), CachePortal, a system for intelligently managing dynamically generated Web content stored in the caches and the Web servers, is described. An invalidator, which observes the updates that are occurring in the database identifies and invalidates cached Web pages that are affected by these updates. Note that this configuration has an associated overhead: the amount of database polling queries generated to achieve a better-quality finer-granularity invalidation. The polling queries can either be directed to the original database or, in order to reduce the load on the DBMS, to a middle-tier data cache maintained by the invalidator. This solution works with the most popular components in the industry (Oracle DBMS and BEA WebLogic Web and application server).

Enabling Caching and Mirroring in Dynamic Content Delivery Architectures

Caching of dynamically created pages requires a protocol, which combines the HTML *expires* tag and an *invalidation* mechanism. Although the expiration information can be used by all caches/mirrors, the invalidation works only with compliant caches/mirrors. Therefore, it is essential to push invalidation as close to the end-users as possible. For time-sensitive material (material that users should not access after expiration) that reside at the non-compliant caches/mirrors, the *expires* value should be set to 0. Compliant caches/mirrors also must be able to validate requests for non-compliant caches/mirrors.

In this section we concentrate on the architectural issues for enabling caching of dynamic content. This involves reusing of the unchanged material whenever possible (i.e., incremental updates), sharing of dynamic material among applicable users, prefetching/precomputation (i.e., anticipation of changes), and invalidation.

Reusing unchanged material requires considering the Web content that can be updated at various levels; the structure of an entire site or a portion of a single HTML page can change. On the other hand, due to the design of the Web browsers, updates are visible to end-users only at the page level. That is whether the entire structure of a site or a small portion of a single Web page changes, users observe changes only one page at a time. Therefore, existing cache/mirror managers work at the page level; i.e., they cache/mirror pages. This is consistent with the access granularity of the Web browsers. Furthermore, this approach works well with changes at the page or higher levels; if the structure of a site changes, we can reflect this by removing irrelevant pages, inserting new ones, and keeping the unchanged pages.

The page level management of caches/mirrors, on the other hand, does not work well with subpage level changes. If a single line in a page gets updated, it is wasteful to remove the old page and replace it with a new one. Instead of sending an entire page to a receiver, it is more effective (in terms of network resources) to send just a delta (URL, change location, change length, new material) and let the receiver perform a page rewrite (Banga, Douglis, & Rabinovich, 1997). Recently, Oracle and Akamai proposed a new standard called Edge Site Includes (ESI) which can be used to describe which parts of a page are dynamically generated and which parts are static (ESI, www.esi.org). Each part can be cached as independent entities in the caches, and the page can be assembled into a single page at the edge. This allows the static content to be cached and delivered by Akamai's static content delivery network. The dynamic portion of the page, on the other hand, is to be recomputed as required.

The concept of independently caching the fragments of a Web page and assembling them dynamically has significant advantages. First of all, the load on the application server is reduced. The origin server now needs to generate only the non-cacheable parts in each page. Another advantage of ESI is the reduction of the load on the network. ESI markup language also provides for environment variables and conditional inclusion, thereby allowing personalization of content at the edges. ESI also allows for an explicit invalidation protocol. As we will discuss soon, explicit invalidation is necessary for caching dynamically generated Web content.

Prefetching and Precomputing can be used for improving performance. This requires anticipating the updates and prefetching the relevant data, precomputing the relevant results, and disseminating them to compliant end-points in advance and/or *validating* them:

- either on demand (validation initiated by a request from the end-points or
- by a special validation message from the source to the compliant end-points.

This, however, requires understanding of application semantics, user preferences, and the nature of the data to discover what updates may be done in the near future.

Chutney Technologies (Chutney Technologies, www.chutneytech.com/) provides a PreLoader software that benefits from precomputing and caching. PreLoader assumes that the original content is augmented with special Chutney tags, as with ESI tags. PreLoader employs a predictive *least-likely to be used* cache management strategy to maximize the utilization of the cache.

Invalidation mechanisms mark appropriate dynamically created pages cacheable, detect changes in the database that may render previously created pages invalid, and invalidate cache content that may be obsolete due to changes.

The first major challenge an invalidation mechanism faces is to create a mapping among the cached Web pages and the underlying data elements (Figure 16(a)). Figure 16(b) shows the dependencies between the four entities (pages, applications, queries, and data) involved in the creation of dynamic content. As shown in this figure, knowledge about these four entities is distributed on three different servers (Web server, application server, and the database management server). Consequently, it is not straightforward to create an efficient mapping between the data and the corresponding pages.

The second major challenge is that timely Web content delivery is a critical task for e-commerce sites and that any dynamic content cache manager must be very efficient (i.e.,

Figure 16: (a) Data flow in a database driven web site, and (b) how different entities are related to each other and which Web site components are aware of them

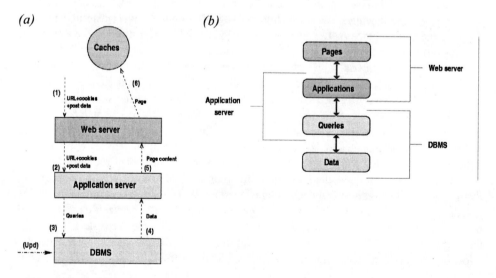

should not impose additional burden on the content delivery process), robust (i.e., should not increase the failure probability of the site), independent (i.e., should be outside of the Web server, application server, and the DBMS to enable the use of products from different vendors), and non-invasive (i.e., should not require alteration of existing applications or special tailoring of new applications).

CachePortal (Candan, Li, Luo, Hsiung, & Agrawal, 2001) addresses these two challenges efficiently and effectively. Figure 17(a) shows the main idea behind the CachePortal solution:

- Instead of trying to find the mapping between all four entities in Figure 17(a), CachePortal divides the mapping problem into two: it finds (1) the mapping between Web pages and queries that are used for generating

This bi-layered approach enables the division of the problem into two components: *sniffing* or mapping the relationship between the Web pages and the underlying queries and, once the database is updated, *invalidating* the Web content dependent on queries that are affected by this update. Therefore, CachePortal uses an architecture (Figure 17(b)), which consists of two independent components, a *sniffer*, which collects information about user requests and an *invalidator*, which removes cached pages that are affected by updates to the underlying data.

The sniffer/invalidator sits on a separate machine, which fetches the logs from the appropriate servers at regular intervals. Consequently, as shown in Figure 17(b), the sniffer/invalidator architecture does not interrupt or alter the Web request/database update processes. It also does not require changes in the servers or applications. Instead it relies on three logs (the HTTP request/delivery log, the query instance/delivery log, and the

Figure 17: Invalidation-based dynamic content cache management: (a) the bi-level management of page to data mapping, and (b) the server independent architecture for managing the bi-level mappings

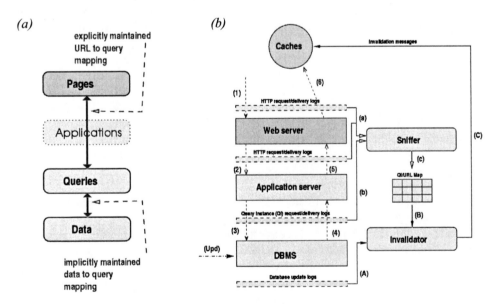

database update logs) to extract all the relevant information. Arrows **(a)-(c)** show the sniffer query instance/URL map generation process and arrows **(A)-(C)** show the cache content invalidation process. These two processes are complementary to each other; yet they are asynchronous.

At the time of the writing, various commercial caching and invalidation solutions exist. Xcache (Xcache, www.xcache.com) and SpiderCache (SpiderSoftware, www.spidercache.com) both provide solutions based on triggers and manual specification of Web content and the underlying data. No automated invalidation function is supported. Javlin (Object Design, www.objectdesign.com/htm/javlin_prod.asp) and Chutney (www.chutneytech.com/1) provide middleware level cache/pre-fetch solutions, which lie between application servers and underlying DBMS or file systems. Again, no real automated invalidation function is supported by these solutions. Major application server vendors, such as IBM WebSphere (WebSphere Software Platform, www.ibm.com/websphere), BEA WebLogic (BEA Systems, www.bea.com), SUN/Netscape I-planet (iPlanet, www.iplanet.com), and Oracle Application Server (www.oracle.com/ip/deploy/ias.) focus on EJB (Enterprise Java Bean) and JTA (Java Transaction API *(Java(TM)Transaction API, 2001))* level caching for high performance computing purpose. Currently, these commercial solutions do not have intelligent invalidation functions either.

Impact of Dynamic Content on the Selection of the Mirror Server

Assuming that we can cache dynamic content at network-wide caches, in order to provide content delivery services, we need to develop a mechanism through which end-user requests are directed to the most appropriate cache/mirror server. As we mentioned earlier, one major characteristic of e-commerce content is that it is usually small (~4k); hence, the network delay observed by the end-users is less sensitive to the network delays compared with large media objects, unless the delivery path crosses (mostly logical) geographic location barriers. In contrast, however, dynamic content is extremely sensitive to the loads in the servers. The reason for this sensitivity is that, it usually takes three servers—a database server, an application server, and a Web server—to generate and deliver those pages; and the underlying database and application servers are generally not very scalable and they become bottleneck before the Web servers and the network.

Therefore, since the characteristics of the requirements for dynamic content delivery is different from delivering static media objects, we see that the content delivery networks need to employ suitable approaches depending on their data load. In particular, we see that it may be desirable to distribute end-user requests across geographic boundaries if the penalty paid by the additional delay is less the gain observed by the reduced load on the system. We also note that, since the mirroring of dynamically generated content is not as straightforward as mirroring of the static content, in quickly changing environments, we may need to use servers located in remote geographic regions if no server in a given region contains the required content.

However, when the load is distributed across network boundaries, we can no longer use pure load balancing solutions, as the network delay across the boundaries also becomes important (Figure 18). Therefore, it is essential to improve the observed performance of a dynamic content delivery network by assigning the end-user requests to servers intelligently, using the following characteristics of CDNs:

Figure 18: Load distribution process for dynamic content delivery networks—The load of customers of a CDN comes from different geographic locations; however, a static solution where each geographic location has its own set of servers may not be acceptable

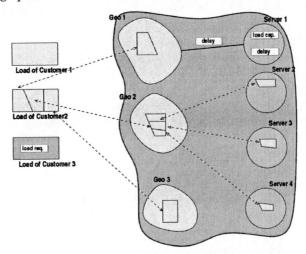

- the type, size, and resource requirements of the published Web content (in terms of both storage requirements at the mirror site and transmission characteristics from mirror to the clients),
- the load requirement (in terms of the requests generated by their clients per second),
- the geographic distribution of their load requirement (where are their clients at a given time of the day), and
- the performance guarantees that they require (such as the response time observed by their end-users).

Most importantly, these characteristics, along with the network characteristics, can change during the day as the usage patterns of the end-users shift with time of the day and the geographic location. Therefore, a static solution (such as a predetermined optimal content placement strategy) is not sufficient. Instead, it is necessary to dynamically adjust the client-to-server assignment.

RELATED WORK

Various content delivery networks (CDNs) are currently in operation. These include Adero (Adero Inc., http://www.adero.com/), Akamai (Akamai Technologies, http://www.akamai.com), Digital Island (Digital Island, http://www.digitalisland.com/), MirrorImage (Mirror Image Internet, Inc., http://www.mirrorimage.com/) and others. Although each one of these services are using more or less different technologies, they all aim to utilize a set of Web-based network elements (or servers) to achieve efficient delivery of Web content. Currently, all of these CDNs are mainly focused on the delivery of static Web content. (Johnson, Carr, Day, Kaashoek, 2001) provides a comparison of two popular CDNs (Akamai and Digital Island) and concludes that the performance of CDNs is more or less the same. It also suggests that the goal of a CDN should be to choose a *reasonably* good server, while avoiding *unreasonably* bad ones, which in fact justifies the use of a heuristic algorithm. (Paul & Fei, 2000), on the other hand, provides concrete evidence that shows that a distributed architecture of coordinated caches perform consistently better (in terms of hit ratio, *response time,* freshness, and *load balancing).* These results justify the choice of using a centralized load assignment heuristic.

Other related works include (Heddaya & Mirdad, 1997; Heddaya, Mirdad, & Yates, 1997), where authors propose a diffusion-based caching protocol that achieves load-balancing, (Korupolu & Dahlin, 1999) which uses meta-information in the cache-hierarchy to improve the hit ratio of the caches, (Tewari, Dahlin, Vin, & Kay, 1999) which evaluates the performance of traditional cache hierarchies and provides design principles for scalable cache systems, and (Carter & Crovella, 1999) which highlights the fact that static client-to-server assignment may not perform well compared to dynamic server assignment or selection.

CONCLUSIONS

In this chapter, we described the state of art of e-commerce acceleration services. We point out their disadvantages, including failure to handle dynamically generated Web content. More specifically, we addressed two questions faced by e-commerce acceleration systems: (1) what changes the characteristics of the e-commerce systems require in the popular content delivery architectures and (2) what is the impact of end-to-end (Internet+server) scalability requirements of e-commerce systems on e-commerce server software design. Finally, we introduced an architecture for integrating Internet services, business logic, and database technologies, for improving end-to-end scalability of e-commerce systems.

REFERENCES

Banga, G., Douglis, F., & Rabinovich, M. (1997). Optimistic deltas for WWW latency reduction. In *Proceedings of the USENIX Technical Conference.*

Candan, K. Selçuk, Li, W., Luo, W., Hsiung, W., & Agrawal, D., (2001). Enabling dynamic content caching for database-driven Web sites. In *Proceedings of the 2001 ACM SIGMOD ,* Santa Barbara, CA, USA, May.

Carter, R.L., & Crovella, M.E., (1999). On the network impact of dynamic server selection. In *Computer Networks,* 31, 2529–2558.

Challenger, J., Dantzig, P., & Iyengar, A., (1998). A scalable and highly available system for serving dynamic data at frequently accessed Web sites. In *Proceedings of ACM/IEEE Supercomputing '98,* Orlando, Florida, November.

Challenger, J., Iyengar, A., & Dantzig, P., (1999). Scalables system for consistently caching dynamic Web data. In *Proceedings of the IEEE INFOCOM'99,* 294-303. New York: March IEEE.

Douglis, F., Haro, A., & Rabinovich, M. (1997). HPP: HTML Macro-preprocessing to support dynamic document caching. In *Proceedings of USENIX Symposium on Internet Technologies and Systems.*

Heddaya, H., & Mirdad, S., (1997). WebWave: Globally load balanced fully distributed caching of hot published documents. In *ICDCS.*

Heddaya, A., Mirdad, S., & Yates, D. (1997). Diffusion-based caching: WebWave. In *NLANR Web Caching Workshop,* June 9–10.

Johnson, K.L., Carr, J.F., Day, M.S., & Kaashoek, M.F. (2000). The measured performance of content distribution networks. *Computer Communications* 24(2), 202-206.

Korupolu, M.R. & Dahlin, M., (1999). Coordinated placement and replacement for large-scale distributed caches. In *IEEE Workshop on Internet Applications,* 62—71.

Labrinidis, A., & Roussopoulos, N., (2000). Webview materialization. In *Proceedings of the ACM SIGMOD,* 367-378.

Levy, E., Iyengar, A., Song, J., & Dias, D., (1999). Design and performance of a Web server accelerator. In *Proceedings of the IEEE INFOCOM* '99, 135-143. New York: March 1999. IEEE.

Paul, S. & Fei, Z. (2000). Distributed caching with centralized control. In *5th International Web Caching and Content Delivery Workshop*, Lisbon, Portugal, May.

Smith, B., Acharya, A., Yang, T., & Zhu, H., (1999). Exploiting result equivalence in caching dynamic Web content. In *Proceedings of USENIX Symposium on Internet Technologies and Systems*.

Tewari, R., Dahlin, M., Vin, H.M. & Kay, J.S. (1999). Beyond hierarchies: Design considerations for distributed caching on the Internet. In *ICDCS,* 273-285.

Section IV:

Web-Based Distributed Data Mining

Chapter VII

Internet Delivery of Distributed Data Mining Services: Architectures, Issues and Prospects

Shonali Krishnaswamy
Monash University, Australia

Arkady Zaslavsky
Monash University, Australia

Seng Wai Loke
RMIT University, Australia

ABSTRACT

The recent trend of Application Service Providers (ASP) is indicative of electronic commerce diversifying and expanding to include e-services. The ASP paradigm is leading to the emergence of several Web-based data mining service providers. This chapter focuses on the architectural and technological issues in the construction of systems that deliver data mining services through the Internet. The chapter presents ongoing research and the operations of commercial data mining service providers. We evaluate different distributed data mining (DDM) architectural models in the context of their suitability to support Web-based delivery of data mining services. We present emerging technologies and standards in the e-services domain and discuss their impact on a "virtual marketplace of data mining e-services."

INTRODUCTION

Application Services are a type of e-service/Web service characterised by the renting of software (Tiwana & Ramesh, 2001). Application Service Providers (ASPs) operate by hosting software packages/applications for clients to access through the Internet (or in certain cases through dedicated communication channels) via a Web interface. Payments are made for the usage of the software rather than the software itself. The ASP paradigm is leading to the emergence of several Internet-based service providers in the business intelligence applications domain such as data mining, data warehousing, OLAP and CRM. This can be attributed to the following reasons:

- The economic viability of paying for the usage of high-end software packages rather than having to incur the costs of buying, setting-up, training and maintenance.
- Increased demand for business intelligence as a key factor in strategic decision-making and providing a competitive edge.

Apart from the general factors such as economic viability and emphasis on business intelligence in organisations, data mining in particular has several characteristics, which allow it to fit intuitively into the ASP model. The features that lend themselves suitable for hosting data mining services are as follows:

- *Diverse Requirements.* Business intelligence needs within organisations can be diverse and vary from customer profiling and fraud detection to market-basket analysis. Such diversity requires data mining systems that can support a wide variety of algorithms and techniques. Data mining systems have evolved from stand-alone systems characterised by single algorithms with little support for the knowledge discovery process to integrated systems incorporating several mining algorithms, multiple users, various data formats and distributed data sources. This growth and evolution notwithstanding, the current state of the art in data mining systems makes it unlikely for any one system to be able to support all the business intelligence needs of an organisation. Application Service Providers can alleviate this problem by hosting a variety of data mining systems that can meet the diverse needs of users.
- *Need for immediate benefits.* The benefits gained by implementing data mining infrastructure within an organisation tend to be in the long term. One of the reasons for this is the significant learning curve associated with the usage of data mining software. Organisations requiring immediate benefits can use ASPs, which have all the infrastructure and expertise in place.
- *Specialised Tasks.* Organisations may sometimes require a specialised, once-off data mining task to be performed (e.g. mining data that is in a special format or is of a complex type). In such a scenario, an ASP that hosts a data mining system that can perform the required task can provide a simple, cost-efficient solution.

While the above factors make data mining a suitable application for the ASP model, there are certain other features that have to be taken into account and addressed in the context of Web-based data mining services, such as: very large datasets and the data intensive nature of the process, the need to perform computationally intensive processing, the need for confidentiality and security of both the data and the results. Thus, while we focus on data mining Web services in this paper, many of the issues discussed are relevant to other applications that have similar characteristics.

The potential benefits and the intuitive soundness of the concept of hosting data mining services is leading to the emergence of a host of commercial data mining application service providers. The current modus operandi for data mining ASPs is the "managed

Figure 1: Current model of client interaction for data mining ASPs

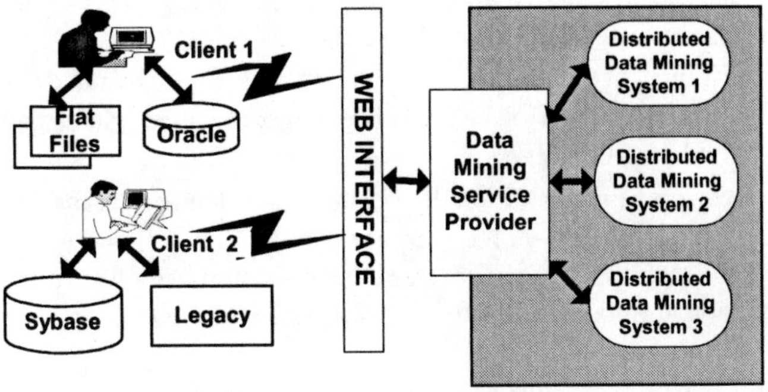

applications" model (Tiwana and Ramesh, 2001). The operational semantics and the interactions with clients are shown in figure 1.

Typically a client organisation has a single service provider who meets all the data mining needs of the client. The client is well aware of the capabilities of the service provider and there are predefined and legally binding Service Level Agreements (SLAs) regarding quality of service, cost, confidentiality and security of data, and results and protocols for requesting services. The service provider hosts one or more distributed data mining systems (DDM), which support a specified number of mining algorithms. The service provider is aware of the architectural model, specialisations, features, and required computational resources for the operation of the distributed data mining system.

The interaction protocol for this model is as follows:

1.   Client requests a service using a well-defined instruction set from the service provider.
2.   The data is shipped from the client's site to the service provider.
3.   The service provider maps the request to the functionality of the different DDM systems that are hosted to determine the most appropriate one.
4.   The "suitable" DDM system processes the task and the results are given to the client in a previously arranged format.

This model satisfies the basic motivations for providing data mining services and allows organisations to avail the benefits of business intelligence without having to incur the costs associated with buying software, maintenance and training. The cost for the service, metrics for performance and quality of service are negotiated on a long-term basis as opposed to a task-by-task basis. For example, the number of tasks requested per month by the client and their urgency may form the basis for monthly payments to the service provider.

The main limitation of the above model is that it implicitly lacks the notions of competition and that of an "open market place" that gives clients the highest benefit in terms of diversity of service at the best price. The model falls short of allowing the Internet to be a virtual market place of "services" as envisaged by the emergence of integrated e-services platforms such as E-Speak (http://www.e-speak.hp.com) and technologies to support directory facilities for registration and location such as Universal Description, Discovery and Integration (UDDI) (http://www.uddi.org). The concept of providing Internet-based data mining services is still in its early stages, and there are several open issues such as: performance metrics for the quality of service, models for costing and billing of data mining services, mechanisms to describe task requests and services, and application of distributed data mining systems in ASP environments. This chapter focuses on the architectural and technological issues of Web-based data mining services. There are two fundamental aspects that need to be addressed. The first question pertains to the architectures and functionality of data mining systems used in Web-based services.

- What is the impact of different architectural models for distributed data mining in the context of Web-based service delivery? Does any one model have features that make it more suitable than others?
- DDM systems have not traditionally been constructed for operation in Web service environments. Therefore, do they require additional functionality, such as a built-in scheduler and techniques for better resource utilisation (which are principally relevant due to the constraints imposed by the Web-services environment)?

The second question pertains to the evolution of data mining ASPs from the current model of operation to a model characterised by a marketplace environment of e-services where clients can make ad-hoc requests and service providers compete for tasks. In the context of several technologies that have the potential to bring about a transformation to the current model of operation, the issues that arise are the interaction protocol for such a model and the additional constraints and requirements it necessitates.

The chapter is organised as follows. We review related research and survey the landscape of Web-based data mining services. We present a taxonomy of distributed data mining architectures and evaluate their suitability for operating in an ASP environment. We present a virtual marketplace of data mining services as the future direction for this field. It presents an operational model for such a marketplace and its interaction protocol. It also evaluates the impact of emerging technologies on this model and discusses the challenges and issues in establishing a virtual marketplace of data mining services. Finally, we present the conclusions and contributions of the chapter.

RELATED WORK

In this section we review emerging research in the area of Internet delivery of data mining services. We also survey commercial data mining service providers. There are two aspects to the ongoing research in delivering Web-based data mining services. In Sarawagi and Nagaralu (2000), the focus is on providing data mining *models* as services on the Internet. The important questions in this context are standards for describing data mining models, security and confidentiality of the models, integrating models from distributed data sources, and personalising a model using data from a user and combining it with existing models. In (Krishnaswamy, Zaslavsky, & Loke, 2001b), the focus is on the exchange of messages and description of task requests, service provider capabilities and access to infrastructure in a marketplace of data mining services. In Krishnaswamy et al. (2002), techniques for estimating metrics such response times for data mining e-services are presented. The potential benefits and the intuitive soundness of the concept of hosting data mining services are leading to the emergence of a host of business intelligence application service providers: digiMine (http://www.digimine.com), iFusion (http://www.kineticnetworks.com), ListAnalyst.com (http://www.listanalyst.com), WebMiner (http://www.Webminer.com) and Information Discovery (http://www.datamine.aa.psiWeb.com). For a detailed comparison of these ASPs, readers are referred to Krishnaswamy et al. (2001b). The currently predominant modus operandi for data mining ASPs is the single-service provider model. Several of today's data mining ASPs operate using a client-server model, which requires the data to be transferred to the ASP servers. In fact, we are not aware of ASPs that use alternate approaches (e.g., mobile agents) to deploy the data mining process at the client's site. However, the development of research prototypes of distributed data mining (DDM) systems, such as Java Agents for Meta Learning (JAM) (Stolfo et al., 1997), Papyrus (Grossman et al., 1999), Besiezing Knowledge through Distributed Heterogeneous Induction (BODHI) (Kargupta et al., 1998) and DAME (Krishnaswamy et al., 2000) show that this technology is a viable alternative for distributed data mining. The use of a secure Web interface is the most common approach for delivering results (e.g., digiMine and iFusion), though some ASPs such as Information Discovery sends the results to a "pattern-base" (or a knowledge-base) located at the client site. Another interesting aspect is that most service providers host data mining tools that they have developed (e.g., digiMine, Information Discovery and ListAnalyst.com). This is possibly because the developers of data mining tools are seeing the ASP paradigm as a natural extension to their market. This trend might also be due to the know-how that data mining tool vendors have about the operation of their systems.

DISTRIBUTED DATA MINING

Traditional data mining systems were largely stand-alone systems, which required all the data to be collected at one centralised location (typically, the user's machine) where mining would be performed. However, as data mining technology matures and moves from a theoretical domain to the practitioner's arena, there is an emerging realisation that distribution is very much a factor that needs to be accounted for. Databases in today's information age are inherently distributed. Organisations operating in global markets need to perform data mining on distributed and heterogeneous data sources and require cohesive and integrated knowledge from this data. Such organisational environments are characterised by a physical/geographical separation of users from the data sources. This inherent distribution of data sources and the large volumes of data involved inevitably lead to exorbitant communications costs. Therefore, it is evident that the traditional data mining model involving the co-location of users, data and computational resources is inadequate when dealing with environments that have the characteristics outlined previously. The development of data mining along this dimension has lea to emergence of *distributed data mining (DDM)*.

Broadly, data mining environments consist of users, data, hardware and the mining software (this includes both the mining algorithms and any other associated programs). Distributed data mining addresses the impact of distribution of users, software and computational resources on the data mining process. There is general consensus that distributed data mining is the process of mining data that has been partitioned into one or more physically/geographically distributed subsets. In other words, it is the mining of a distributed database (Note: we use the term "distributed database" loosely to include all flavours of homogeneity and heterogeneity). The process of performing distributed data mining is presented as follows (Chattratichat et al, 1999):

- Performing traditional knowledge discovery at each distributed data site.
- Merging the results generated from the individual sites into a body of cohesive and unified knowledge.
- The characteristics and objectives of DDM makes it highly suited for application in the domain of ASP hosted data mining services due to the following reasons:
- The inherent distribution of data and other resources resulting as a consequence of client organisations being distributed.

- The transfer of large volumes of data (from client data sites to the service provider) results in exorbitant communication costs. Certain DDM architectural such as the mobile agent and hybrid models allow on-site mining to alleviate communication costs. Further, this facility can also be used in cases where the client does not wish to send sensitive data outside.

- The need for integrated results from heterogeneous and distributed data sources. Client organisations typically require heterogeneous and distributed data sets to be mined and results to be integrated and presented in a cohesive form. Knowledge integration is an important aspect of distributed data mining and this functionality is built-in to DDM systems.

- The performance and scalability bottlenecks of data mining. Distributed data mining provides a framework that allows the splitting up of larger datasets with high dimensionality into smaller subsets that require less computational resources individually. This can facilitate the ASP to process large data sets faster.

Several DDM systems and research prototypes have been developed including: Parallel Data Mining Agents (PADMA) (Kargupta, Hamzaoglu, & Stafford, 1997), Besiezing Knowledge through Distributed Heterogeneous Induction (BODHI) (Kargupta et al., 1997), Java Agents for Meta-Learning (JAM) (Stolfo et al., 1997), InfoSleuth (Martin, Unruh, & Urban, 1999), IntelliMiner (Parthasarathy & Subramonian, 2001), DecisionCentre (Chattratichat et al., 1999) and Distributed Agent-based Mining Environment (DAME) (Krishnaswamy et al., 2000; Krishnaswamy et al., 2000). We now present a taxonomy of DDM architectural models and evaluate their relative advantages and disadvantages with respect to ASP-hosted data mining services. Research in distributed data mining architectures studies the processes and technologies used to construct distributed data mining systems. There are predominantly three architectural frameworks for the development of distributed data mining systems – the

Figure 2: Taxonomy of distributed data mining architectural models

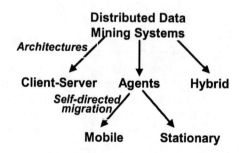

Table 1: Classification of distributed data mining systems

DDM Architectural Models	DDM Systems
Client-Server	DecisionCentre, IntelliMiner
Agents • Mobile Agent • Stationary Agent	JAM, Infosleuth, BODHI, Papyrus, PADMA
Hybrid	DAME

client-server model, the agent-based model and the hybrid approach which integrates the two former techniques. The agent-based model can be further classified into systems that use mobile agents and those that use stationary agents. This taxonomy is illustrated in Figure 2.

A summary classification of distributed data mining systems based on this taxonomical categorisation is presented in Table 1.

Client-Server Model for Distributed Data Mining

The client-server model illustrated is characterised by the presence of one or more data mining servers. In order to perform mining, the user requests' are fed into the data mining server that collects data from different locations and brings them into the data mining server. The mining server houses the mining algorithms and generally has high computational resources. In some instances, the server is a parallel server, in which case the distributed data sets are mined using parallel processors prior to knowledge integration.

However, this model for distributed data mining process involves a lot of data transfer. Since all the data required for mining has to be brought from the distributed data sources into the mining server (and this could run into gigabytes of data), the communication overhead associated with this model is very expensive. The advantage of this model is that the distributed data mining server has well-defined computational resources that have the ability to handle resource-intensive data mining tasks. The most prominent DDM system developed using this architectural model is DecisionCentre (Chattratichat et al., 1999) and IntelliMiner (Parthasarathy & Subramonian, 2001). The important technologies used to develop client-server DDM systems are the Common Object Request Broker Architecture (CORBA), Distributed Component Model (DCOM), and Java (including Enterprise Java Beans (EJB), Remote Method Invocation (RMI), and Java Database Connectivity (JDBC).

In the context of ASP-hosted data mining services, this architectural model provides the following advantages:

- Computational resources that can handle high-intensity jobs. This is very important for ASPs, who have to meet the response time needs of several clients. The DecisionCentre approach of has a fast, parallel server is a good option in this context.
- ASPs have complete control over the computational resources and the mining environment.
- The model gives ASPs the flexibility to split client data sets to facilitate faster processing.
- The disadvantages of this model are:
- It doesn't provide the facility to perform mining at the client's site; and
- The communication bottlenecks associated with transferring large volumes of data.

Agent-Based Model for Distributed Data Mining

The agent-based model is the more commonly used approach to constructing distributed data mining systems and is characterised by a variety of agents coordinating and communicating with each other to perform the various tasks of the data mining process. One of the widely recognised application areas for agent technology in general is distributed computing, since it has the scope and ability to reduce the complexity of such environments. The motivation for the use of agent technology in distributed data mining stems is twofold. Firstly, there is the underlying basis of distributed data mining being an application that has the characteristics, which are intuitively suited for an agent-based approach. These characteristics are modular and well-defined sub-tasks, the need to encapsulate the different mining algorithms to present a common interface (and thereby address the heterogeneity issue), the requirement for interaction and cooperation between the different parts of the system and the ability to deal with distribution. Secondly, agent technology (with a particular emphasis on agent mobility) is seen as being able to address the specific concern of increasing scalability and enhancing performance by reducing the communication overhead associated with the transfer of large volumes of data. Using mobility of agents as a distinguishing criterion, we classify distributed data mining systems into two groups. The principal technologies used in the construction of agents are agent development toolkits and environments. We now discuss the mobile agent model and the stationary agent model for distributed data mining.

Mobile Agent Model for Distributed Data Mining

The principle behind this model for distributed data mining is that the mining process is performed via mobile code executing remotely at the data sites and carrying results back to the user. Usually, such systems have one agent that acts as a controlling and coordinating entity for a task. It is this agent's responsibility to ensure successful completion of a task.

The advantage of this model is that it overcomes the communication overhead associated with the client-server systems by moving the code instead of large amounts of data. However, there are several issues, such as the agent communication languages and the interaction and coordination between the various agents in the system. In the context of ASP-hosted data mining services, the advantage of this model is that it provides the flexibility of perform mining remotely at the client site. This can be of particular importance in cases where the client is unwilling to ship sensitive data or in cases where mining remotely can provide better response times (in view of the overhead of data transfers). The disadvantage of this model is the fact that clients will need to have a mobile agent server (i.e., the layer through which a mobile agent interacts with a remote host) installed and running at the various data sites. The technology used to build such systems is largely agent development toolkits. The important DDM systems that fall under this category are JAM (Stolfo et al, 1997), BODHI (Kargupta et al., 1998), Papyrus (Grossman et al., 1999) and InfoSleuth (Martin et al., 1999).

Stationary Agent Model for Distributed Data Mining

This architecture differs from the mobile agent model discussed previously in that it does not have agents that have the ability to move on their own and roam from host to host. Thus, in a stationary agent system, the mining agents would have to be "fixed" at the location of the data resources. This brings with it the additional constraint that the mining algorithm to be used for a given task cannot be dynamically changed and is limited by the functionality of the mining agent at the location of the data. Alternatively, it is possible to replicate a variety of mining agents at each data site. Further, the results would have to be dispatched via traditional data transfer techniques as opposed to having an agent carry the results. In the context of ASP-hosted data mining services, this model has the following limitations:

- The inability to dispatch agents remotely limits the scope of this model. Unlike the mobile agent model, this model is less viable in cases where there is a short-term contractual agreement with the client and where the relationship is ad hoc and determined on task-by-task basis.

- The inability to dynamically configure the algorithm of the agent does not provide the requisite flexibility to deal with changes in client needs.

Thus, the mobile agent model is more suited than the stationary agent approach for operation in a Web services environment. A DDM system that uses this architectural framework is Parallel Data Mining Agents (PADMA) (Kargupta et al, 1997). It must be noted that we are presenting a generic view of the agent model and different distributed data mining systems can vary in the type of agents they incorporate, the inter-agent communication and interaction models. Further, it must be noted that DDM systems may have some of the components implemented as agents and some others as software components (without the attributes of agency).

Hybrid Model for Distributed Data Mining

The hybrid model for distributed data mining integrates the client-server and mobile agent model. We have developed the Distributed Agent-based Mining Environment (DAME), which focuses on Internet delivery of distributed data mining services by incorporating metrics such as application run time estimation and optimisation of the distributed data mining process (Krishnaswamy et al., 2000). The principal motivation for the hybrid model comes from studies by Straßer and Schwehm (1997), which have shown that a combination of the client-server and mobile agent techniques leads to improved response time for distributed applications than employing one or the other approaches. Further, a hybrid approach combines the best features of both models in terms of the reducing the communication overhead, providing the flexibility to support remote mining (mobile agent model), and having well-defined computational resources for situations where the data is located on servers which do not have the ability to perform intensive data mining tasks. The DAME system is similar to IntelliMiner in that it also focuses on improving the performance of distributed data mining by better utilisation of resources. The principal difference is that the cost of mining in IntelliMiner is computed on the basis of data resources required, and the cost of mining is computed in DAME as response time based on application run-time estimation and communication time. Further, in DAME the emphasis is on determining the most appropriate combination strategy of client-server and mobile agent techniques to meet the preferred response time constraints of users in an ASP context. The distinguishing feature of this model is the optimiser and its emphasis on utilisation of resources to best meet the response time requirements of clients. For a detailed discussion on the design of the optimiser and the application run time estimator, readers are referred to (Krishnaswamy et al., 2000). The advantages of this system with respect to ASP hosted data mining services are as follows:

- The hybrid model combines the best features of the client-server and the mobile agent approaches. It facilitates incorporation of client preferences with respect to the location of the data mining process. Clients who are concerned about shipping their sensitive data might opt for the mobile agent model, and clients who do not have the computational resources can benefit from the client-server model.
- The focus on cost-efficiency is important for ASP-hosted services. The optimiser determines the best combination of mobile agent and client-server techniques to meet the response time constraints of clients. Further, the application run time estimator helps in scheduling tasks so as to improve utilisation of resources.
- The application run time estimator can also be used as a quality-of-service metric to provide clients with a priori estimates of response times.

We have presented a taxonomy of DDM architectural models and discussed their suitability for Web-based data mining services. While the classification pertains specifically

Table 2: Comparison of implementation aspects

DDM System	Status	OS Platforms	Language	Special Software Technologies
JAM	Implemented	Independent	Java	-
InfoSleuth	Implemented	Independent	Java	KQML, LDL++, JDBC, CLIPS
BODHI	Implemented	Independent	Java	-
Papyrus	Implemented	Not Specified	Not Specified	Agent TCL, Ptool, HTML, CGI, Perl
PADMA	Implemented	Unix	C++	MPI, Parallel Portable File System
DAME	Currently on-going	Independent	Java	-
Decision Centre	Implemented	Independent	Java	CORBA, JDBC, EJB, RMI
IntelliMiner	Implemented	Windows NT	C++	CORBA, COM

to DDM systems, the architectural models are generic and the issues in terms of their use in Web services environments would be relevant to any distributed computing application. We now present a comparison of the distributed data mining systems with a focus on the implementation. This comparison, presented in Table 2, provides an insight into the implementation aspects for future developers of DDM systems. The comparison of implementation details brings to the fore the fact that most DDM systems, irrespective of the architectural model in use, are platform independent, and Java is the preferred language for development.

The development of DDM systems has thus far been motivated by the issues of data distribution and scalability bottlenecks in mining very large datasets. However, ASP-hosted environments provide a new avenue of application for DDM systems, and promises to provide a fertile research area. In the context of DDM systems adapting to operate in ASP-hosted environments, several components and functionality need to be incorporated including: costing of the DDM process to support billing of tasks; quality of service metrics such as response time; availability and reliability for incorporation into Service Level Agreements; support for meeting client preferences such as response time needs and location requirements (e.g., performing the task at the client's site using technologies such as mobile agents); optimisation for improved resource utilisation; and task allocation and task description languages to support automated capturing of specific client requirements and preferences. There is an emerging interest in the issues of optimisation and scheduling of DDM tasks that are being addressed by systems like DAME and IntelliMiner. The DAME system also focuses on the need for QoS metrics in this domain, but is nevertheless concerned specifically with response time. Efforts by Grossman et al. (1999), who have developed Predictive Model Markup Language (which facilitates description and integration of models generated from distributed data sets) and Krishnaswamy et al (2001b) who have developed schemas to specify task requirements, focus on the issue of task description languages for Web-based data mining services. These initiatives notwithstanding, DDM research in ASP hosted data mining services is in a very nascent stage. We have thus far presented and analysed current work in DDM architectures from the perspective of data mining e-services. We now present our view of a future model for Web-based data mining service providers - namely, a virtual marketplace of Web-based data mining services.

A VIRTUAL MARKETPLACE OF DATA MINING SERVICES

The current model of operation for Web-based data mining ASPs does not reflect a marketplace of data mining services. As discussed in the Introduction, this model does not give clients the highest benefit in terms of diversity of service at the best price and does not meet the needs of situations where clients might require a specialised one-off task to be performed. It does not facilitate comparison of different service providers in terms of who is best able to meet the task requirements/preferences of the client. However, there are several emerging technologies and standards that have the potential to transform the current scenario and bring into effect a "virtual marketplace of data mining services." In this section, we first present emerging technologies and standards that have an impact on the realisation of this concept. We then present a multiple service provider model of operation for data mining ASPs, including an interaction protocol to support a marketplace of e-services where clients can make ad hoc requests and service providers compete for tasks. Finally, we discuss the issues and challenges that lie ahead.

Emerging Technologies and Standards

There are several emerging trends that have the potential to bring about a transformation to the current model of operation. In this section, we present an overview of the following emerging standards and systems that support e-services on the Internet:

- E-Speak (http://www.e-speak.hp.com) is an e-services infrastructure developed by Hewlett Packard. It provides the underlying technology to support registration of services by service providers and location of services by clients. A service provider registers a service by providing a description using a "vocabulary."
- Web Services Description Language (WSDL) (http://www.w3.org/TR/wsdl) is an XML format developed by Microsoft to support the communication and network details to support exchanging messages over the Web. Elements in a WSDL document include information such as the port, the port type, the network bindings, and the actual message that is being exchanged. It facilitates Web services at the lower level of data.
- Universal Description, Discovery and Integration (UDDI) (http://www.uddi.org), is a standard developed and supported by Ariba, IBM and Microsoft. UDDI is a universal registry that allows global registration and description of Web services to facilitate the location of services by clients and the interaction to enable usage of the service.
- E-Business-XML (eb-XML) (http://www.ebxml.org) is an initiative supported by the United Nations and OASIS. The stated objective of eb-XML is to support open and interoperable e-business. The eb-XML architecture provides mechanisms to define business processes and their associated messages and the registration and discovery of business process sequences with the related message exchanges.

- Web Services Flow Language (WSFL) is an IBM initiative for the composition of Web services. There are two parts to the WSFL model: The first part describes the business process and the second part describes the interactions.

In addition to these e-services infrastructures, there are several emerging data mining standards and initiatives that facilitate more open interaction and interoperation for Web-based data mining ASPs.

- Predictive Model Markup Language (PMML) (Grossman et al., 1999) is an XML-based approach for describing the predictive models that are generated as the output of data mining processes. PMML is primarily used for knowledge integration of results obtained by mining distributed data sets.
- Microsoft's OLE DB for Data Mining is a description of a data mining task in terms of the data sets that are being mined and allows specification of the attributes to be mined, the attributes to be predicted, and the type and format of the attributes. It incorporates a version of PMML and is primarily intended to allow "plug and play" of data mining algorithms.
- In Krishnaswamy et al. (2001b), XML schemas to support the interaction between clients and service providers in a virtual marketplace environment have been presented. These schemas facilitate description of client task preferences, service provider capabilities, and information to support access to data and computational resources for mining.

In view of these trends, it is not unfeasible to envision an environment where data mining ASPs compete for tasks on the basis of how well they meet client preferences and requirements. We now present such a scenario with a multiple service provider model.

Multiple Service Provider Model of Interaction for Data Mining ASPs

This model, as illustrated in Figure 3, is characterised by clients being able to request data mining services from one or more service providers. This is an illustrative example of a "virtual marketplace" of data mining services. The multiple service provider model operates in the form of a "federation" (Krishnaswamy et al., 2001a). The "federation manager" is a coordinating component in the system that manages the interactions between the client and the data mining service providers.

The interaction protocol for this model is as follows:

1. The client requests a service by providing a task specification to the federation manager. It must be noted that the parameters for specifying the task must be well defined and must facilitate the requests to be made at the level of granularity that the client deems appropriate.
2. The federation manager broadcasts the client's requests to the data mining service providers that are registered with it. The federation manager maintains information about each data mining service provider such as the name, address, contact information, DDM systems hosted, algorithms, architectures and functionality supported by those systems, and the computational resources that the service provider has.
3. The data mining service providers evaluate the requested task against the capabilities and functionality of the DDM systems that they host.

Figure 3: Multiple service provider model

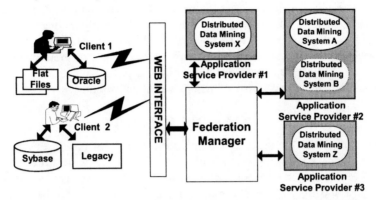

4. If they can meet the needs of the requested task, the data mining service providers respond by presenting an estimate of the cost, possible time frame for completion of the task, and liabilities for not meeting the targeted response time. This information is presented to the federation manager in a specific, structured format.

5. The federation manager can either present the responses it receives along with the information that it already maintains about the respective service providers to the client or, in more sophisticated environment, can perform matching of client preferences with the capabilities of the service providers, rank the service providers on that basis, and present this to the client. There is also scope for automated negotiation to be incorporated into this stage of the interaction protocol. It must be noted that service-provider ranking, preference matching, and automated negotiation are emerging research issues in the e-services domain.

6. The client decides which service provider it deems most appropriate and informs the federation manager and the chosen service provider.

7. The service provider gives the client a legal document/contract, which makes the commitment to maintain the confidentiality of the data that is mined and the consequent knowledge that is produced.

8. The client is then required to provide a security deposit in the form of a credit card number to the federation manager. The actual payment is made on completion of the task and provision of results to the client.

9. The client and the data mining service provider exchange information regarding the transfer of data, passwords to access systems, and the mode of transfer of results.

10. The data mining service provider processes the task, provides the results to the client (in the agreed format and method), and informs the federation manager of task completion.

11. The client acknowledges the completion of the task to the federation manager and the payment is made to the service provider.

This model overcomes the limitations and restrictions imposed by the previous approach in meeting the needs of the requirements outlined at the outset of this chapter. It is evident that the emergence of the standards and technologies presented facilitate the realisation of this model. We believe that these trends and the emerging emphasis on a more "semantic" Web have substantial potential to realise a marketplace of data mining services. However, we recognise that there are several open issues and challenges that need to be addressed for this model to materialise, such as matching and ranking of services (Tewari & Maes, 2000), negotiation, QoS metrics (Sahai, Ouyang, Machiraju, & Werster, 2001) and security. In summary, we believe that emerging trends facilitate an online market place for data mining services. We have presented an operational model for data mining ASPs, which provides a wider choice of data mining services for clients and caters to selection of the most appropriate and cost-efficient service provider by the implicit competition in the approach. We see this as a step towards a virtual marketplace of data mining services.

CONCLUSIONS

The hosting of Internet-based data mining services is an emerging area of interest. This chapter focuses on the architectures, technologies, and issues in the construction of systems that deliver data mining services through the Internet. We have discussed the underlying motivations for the provision of Web-based data mining services. We have surveyed the current research and commercial systems that deliver such services. We have presented an overview of distributed data mining and evaluated different DDM architectural models in the context of their application in Web-based delivery of data mining services. We have identified issues that need to be addressed for the application of DDM systems in the ASP domain. We believe that emerging e-services technologies and standards such as E-Speak and UDDI will lead to a virtual marketplace of data mining services. This will provide clients with a wider choice and the benefits that come with a competitive market. We have presented an illustrative model of such an environment and outlined the interaction protocol between clients and service providers to support this model. We see this as a first step in advocating such a model, and we realise that there are several technological challenges ahead. The chapter primarily targets an audience that includes data mining service providers and developers of DDM systems to support such services. The chapter provides a comprehensive understanding of the issues and questions involved in the Internet delivery of ASP-hosted data mining services. In summary, the chapter is a useful resource for the construction of systems that support Web-based delivery of data mining services and facilitates enhanced understanding of the architectural models, the operational semantics, and the underlying technologies.

REFERENCES

Chattratichat, J., Darlington, J., Guo, Y., Hedvall, S., Köhler, M., & Syed, J., (1999). An architecture for distributed enterprise data mining. In *Proceedings of the 7th International Conference on High Performance Computing and Networking* (HPCN Europe'99), New York: Springer-Verlag LNCS 1593.

Grossman, R. L., Bailey, S., Ramu, A., Malhi, B., Hallstrom, P., Pulleyn, I., & Oin, X., (1999). The management and mining of multiple predictive models using the predictive modelling markup language (PMML), *Information and Software Technology*, 4. 589-595.

Kargupta, H., Hamzaoglu, I. & Stafford, B., (1997). Scalable, distributed data mining using an agent based architecture. In *Proceedings of the 3rd International Conference on Knowledge Discovery and Data Mining*, Newport Beach, CA, (Eds), D. Heckerman, H. Mannila, D. Pregibon, and R. Uthurusamy, Madison, WI: AAAI Press. pp. 211-214.

Kargupta, H., Park, B., Johnson, E., Riva Sanseverino, E., Di Silvestre, L., & Hershberger, D., (1998). Collective Data mining from distributed vertically partitioned feature space. In *KDD-98 Workshop on Distributed Data Mining*, New York: AAAI Press.

Krishnaswamy, S., Loke, S, W., & Zaslavsky, A., (2002). Application run time estimation: A quality of service metric for Web-based data mining services, To Appear in *ACM Symposium on Applied Computing (SAC 2002)*. Madrid, March.

Krishnaswamy, S., Zaslavsky, A., & Loke, S, W., (2000). An Architecture to Support Distributed Data Mining Services in E-Commerce Environments, in *Proceedings of the 2nd International Workshop on Advanced Issues in E-Commerce and Web-Based Infor*mation Systems, pp.238-246.

Krishnaswamy, S., Zaslavsky, A., & Loke, S, W. (2001a), Federated data mining services and a supporting XML markup language, In *Proceedings of the 34th Annual Hawaii International Conference on System Sciences (HICSS-34)*. "e-Services: Models and Methods for Design, Implementation and Delivery" mini-track of the "Decision Technologies for Management" track.

Krishnaswamy, S., Zaslavsky, A., & Loke, S, W, (2001b), Towards data mining services on the Internet with a multiple service provider model: An XML based approach, *Journal of Electronic Commerce Research-Special Issue on Electronic Commerce and Service Operations*. 2(3).

Martin, G., Unruh, A., & Urban, S., (1999). An agent infrastructure for knowledge discovery and event detection, Technical Report MCC-INSL-003-99, Microelectronics and Computer Technology Corporation (MCC).

Microsoft OLE DB for Data Mining. [Online]. Available at: http://www.microsoft.com/data/ oledb/dm.htm [2000 March 26].

Parthasarathy, S., & Subramonian, R., (2001). An interactive resource-aware framework for distributed data mining, in *Newsletter of the IEEE Technical Committee on Distributed Processing, Spring*, 24-32.

Sahai, A., Ouyang, J., Machiraju, V., & Werster, K., (2001). BizQoS: Specifying and gauranteeing quality of service for Web services through real time measurement and adaptive control. [Online] Hewlett-Packard abs Technical Report HPL-2001-96, Available: http:/ /www.hpl.hp.com/techreports/2001/HPL-2001-134.html [2001 September 2].

Sarawagi, S., & Nagaralu, S, H., (2000). Data mining models as services on the Internet, *SIGKDD Explorations*. 2(1) [Online]. Available: http://www.acm.org/sigkdd/explorations/.

Stolfo, S, J., Prodromidis, A, L., Tselepis, L., Lee, W., Fan, D., & Chan, P, K., (1997), JAM: Java Agents for meta-learning over distributed databases, in *Proceedings of the Third International Conference on Data Mining and Knowledge Discovery (KDD-97)*, California, Menlo Park, CA: AAAI Press, 74-81.

Straßer, M., & Schwehm, M., (1997), A performance model for mobile agent systems, in *Proceedings of the International Conference on Parallel and Distributed Processing Techniques and Applications (PDPTA '97)*, (Eds) H. Arabnia, Vol II, CSREA, 1132-1140.

Tewari, G., & Maes, P. (2000). A generalized platform for the specification, valuation, and brokering of heterogeneous resources in electronic markets, pp. 7–24. LNAI 2033. New York: Springer-Verlag.

Tiwana, A., & Ramesh., B. (2001). E-Services: Operations, Opportunities and Digital Platforms, *Proceedings of the Thirty-fourth Annual Hawaii International Conference on System Sciences (HICSS-34)*, I "e-Services: Models and Methods for Design, Implementation and Delivery" mini-track.

Web Services Flow Language (WSFL), [Online]. Available: http://www-4.ibm.com/software/ solutions/Webservices/pdf/WSFL.pdf [2001 December 17].

Chapter VIII

Data Mining For Web-Enabled Electronic Business Applications

Richi Nayak
Queensland University of Technology, Australia

ABSTRACT

Web-enabled electronic business is generating massive amounts of data on customer purchases, browsing patterns, usage times, and preferences at an increasing rate. Data mining techniques can be applied to all the data being collected for obtaining useful information. This chapter attempts to present issues associated with data mining for Web-enabled electronic-business.

INTRODUCTION

Web-enabled electronic business (e-business) is generating massive amounts of data such as customer purchases, browsing patterns, usage times, and preferences at an increasing rate. What can be done to utilize this large volume of Web data with rich description? One possible solution is the processing of all the data being collected to obtain some useful information. For instance, mining of such Web-enabled e-business data can provide valuable information on consumer buying behaviour, which is buried deep within the data otherwise, resulting in an improved quality of business strategies.

As corporations look toward the next phase of e-business (i.e., Web-enabled), one thing is clear—it will be hard to continue to capture customers in the future without the help of data mining. Examples of data mining in Web-enabled e-business applications are generation of user profiles, enabling customer relationship management, and targeting Web advertising based on user access patterns that can be extracted from the Web data. E-business companies can improve product quality or sales by anticipating problems before they occur with the use of data mining techniques. Data mining, in general, is the task of extracting implicit, previously unknown, valid and potentially useful information from data (Fayyad, Piatetsky, Shapiro, & Smyth, 1995).

Data mining in Web-enabled e-business domain is currently a "hot" research area. The objective of this chapter is to present and discuss issues associated with data mining for Web-enabled e-business applications. This chapter starts with brief description of basic concepts and techniques of data mining. This chapter then extends these basic concepts for the Web-enabled e-business domain. This chapter also discusses challenges for data mining techniques when faced with e-business data, and strategies that should be implemented for better use of Web-enabled electronic business.

WHAT IS DATA MINING?

A typical data mining process starts with identifying a data mining problem depending on the goals and interest of a data analyst. Next, all sources of information are identified and a subset of data is generated from the accumulated data for the data mining application. To ensure quality, the data set is preprocessed by removing noise, handling missing information, and transforming to an appropriate format. A data mining technique or a combination of techniques appropriate for the type of knowledge to be discovered is then applied to the derived data set. The discovered knowledge is then evaluated and interpreted, typically involving some visualization techniques. Finally, the information is presented to the user to incorporate into the company's business strategies.

A data mining task can be decomposed into many sub-tasks when dealing with Web-enabled e-business data. Figure 1 illustrates a typical data mining process for Web documents. The process starts with locating and then retrieving intended Web documents or Web access logs. The next and most important task is analysis of data obtained from Web document(s) or logs. This includes preprocessing, actual mining process, and knowledge assimilation. In the end, the discovered knowledge is presented to user in a format that is appropriate to its goal. The analysis may indicate how a Web site is useful to a user in making decision or not. Information for a company to improve its Web site can be concluded from this analysis. The analysis may indicate business strategies to acquire new customers and retaining the existing one.

Figure 1: A mining process for Web-enabled e-business data

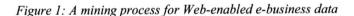

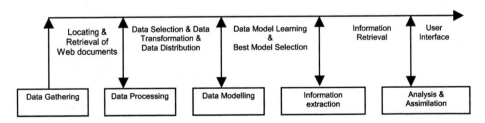

Various Data Mining Tasks and Techniques

Depending on the goals and interests of an end-user, a data mining process can have three possible tasks—predictive modelling, clustering, and link analysis.[1]

Predictive Modelling The goal of predictive modelling is to make predictions based on essential characteristics about the data (Berry & Linoff, 2000). These goals are achieved by classification and regression tasks of data mining. The classification task of data mining builds a model to map (or classify) a data item into one of several predefined classes. The regression task of data mining builds a model to map a data item to a real-valued prediction variable. Both the tasks have same basic objective—to make a prediction about variable(s) of interest. The difference lies in the nature of the variable(s) being predicted - categorical variable(s) for the classification data mining task and continuous variable(s) for the regression data mining task.

Any supervised machine-learning algorithm that learns a model on previous or existing data can be used to perform predictive modelling on the data set. The model is given some already known facts with correct answers, from which the model learns to make accurate predictions. Mainly three techniques—neural induction, tree induction and bayesian classifiers—are used for classification data mining tasks (Lim & Loh, 2000). Some other classification methods are K-nearest neighbour classifiers, case-based reasoning, genetic algorithms, rough set, and fuzzy set approaches (Berry & Linoff, 2000; Han & Kamber, 2001). Mainly three techniques—linear regression, nonlinear regression and radial basis function are used for regression data mining tasks (Cabena, Hadjinien, Stadlem, Verhees, & Zanasi, 1997).

Clustering The goal of clustering a data mining task is to identify items with similar characteristics, and thus creating a hierarchy of classes from the existing set of events. A data set is partitioned into segments of elements (homogeneous) that share a number of properties. Elements in a cluster are in close proximity to each other, and elements in different clusters are far apart from each other. Usually, the proximity is measured by some distance between elements or clusters.

Any unsupervised machine-learning algorithm, for which a predetermined set of data categories is not known for the input data set, can be used to perform clustering on the data set. The model is given some already known facts, from which the model derives categories of data with similar characteristics. When a new fact or event comes across, the learned model is capable of categorizing that fact to an appropriate cluster. Some major clustering methods are partitioning, hierarchical, density-based and model-based algorithms (Han & Kamber, 2001).

Link analysis The goal of link analysis is to establish internal relationship among items in a given data set. This goal is achieved by association discovery, sequential pattern discovery, and similar time sequence discovery tasks (Cabena et al., 1997). These data mining tasks expose samples and trends by predicting correlation of items that are otherwise not obvious. Association discovery builds a model to find items implying the presence of other items (with a certain degree of confidence and support) in the given data set. This process reveals hidden affinity among the items, i.e., which items are frequently purchased together or which Web sites are accessed together. Sequential discovery builds a model to detect an interesting trend between actions or events such that the presence of one set of item is followed by other set of items in a sequence of actions or events over a period of time. The resulting model detects association among events with certain temporal relationships. Similar time sequence discovery builds a model to find similar occurrences in a time series data set.

This process reveals hidden information (similar or dissimilar) about patterns of sales (or browsing) of two different products (or Web sites) over time.

The link analysis techniques are based on counting occurrences of all possible combination of items. The basic association discovery algorithms are considered very simple. Some of the most widely used algorithms are a priori and its variation (Agrawal & Srikant, 1994).

DATA MINING IN WEB-ENABLED E-BUSINESS DOMAIN

A small shop owner builds relationships with his customers by noticing their needs, remembering their preferences and buying behaviour. A Web-enabled e-business will like to accomplish something similar. It is a relatively easy job for the small shop owner to learn from past interactions to serve his customers better in the future. But, this may not be easy for Web-enabled e-businesses when most customers may never interact personally with its employees, and there may be a lot more customers than a small shop owner has. Data mining techniques can be applied to understand and analyse such data, and turn it into actionable information that can support a Web-enabled e-business improve its marketing, sales, and customer support operations. This seems to be more appealing, especially when (1) data is being produced and stored with advance electronic data interchange methods, (2) the computing power is affordable, (3) the competitive pressure among businesses is strong, and lastly (4) efficient and commercial data mining tools have become available for data analysis.

The general statistical approaches of data analysis fail due to the large amount of data available for analysis (Cabena et al., 1997). These traditional approaches to data analysis generally start by reducing the size of data. The reduced data facilitates data analysis on the available hardware and software systems. Data mining, on the other hand, is the process of searching for trends and valuable anomalies in the entire data. The process benefits from the availability of large amount of data with rich description. The rich descriptions of data, such as wide customer records with many potentially useful fields allow data mining algorithms to search beyond obvious correlations.

Data Mining Opportunities

One of the challenges in Web-enabled e-businesses is to develop ways of gaining deep understanding of the behaviour of customers based on the data collected from a Web site. Observing customer behaviour is important information for predicting future customer behaviour. Data mining provides a new capability to company managers by analysing data derived from the interaction of users with the Web.

In general, data obtained from Web-enabled e-business transactions is (1) primary data that includes actual Web contents, and (2) secondary data that includes Web server access logs, proxy server logs, browser logs, registration data, if any, user sessions, user queries, cookies, etc. (Cooley, Mobasher, Srivastave, 1997; Kosala & Blockeel, 2000).

Mining of primary Web data Given the primary Web data, the goal is to effectively interpret the searched Web documents. Web search engines discover resources on the Web but have many problems such as (1) the abundance problem, where hundreds of irrelevant data are returned in response to a search query, (2) limited coverage problem, where only a few sites are searched for the query instead of searching the entire Web, (3) limited query interface, where user can only interact by providing few keywords, (4) limited customization to individual users, etc. (Garofalakis., Rastogi, Seshadri, & Hyuseok, 1999). Mining of primary data i.e. actual Web contents can help e-business customers to improve the organization of retrieved result and to increase the precision of information retrieval (Jicang, Huan, Gangshan, & Fugan, 1997). The basic categorization, clustering, association analysis, and trend prediction techniques can be utilized within the retrieved information for better organization. Some of the data mining applications appropriate for such type of data are:

- applying trend prediction within the retrieved information to indicate future values. For example, an e-auction company provides information about items to auction, previous auction details, etc. Predictive modelling can be utilized to analyse the existing information and to estimate the values for auctioneer items or their number of people participating in future auctions.

- applying text clustering within the retrieved information to understand efficiently. For example, structured relations can be extracted from unstructured text collections by finding the structure of Web documents and presenting a hierarchical structure to represent the relation among text data in Web documents (Wong & Fu, 2000).

- applying association analysis to monitor a competitor's Web site. Data mining techniques can help e-businesses to find unexpected information from its competitor's Web sites, e.g., offering unexpected services and products (Liu, Ma, & Yu, 2001). Because of the large number of competitors' Web sites and the huge information in them, automatic discovery is required. For instance, association rule mining can be used to discover frequent word combination ins a page that will lead a company to learn about competitors (Liu et al., 2001).

- discovering similarity and relationships between different Web sites so to categorize Web pages. This categorization will lead to efficiently searching the Web for the requested Web documents within the categories rather than the entire Web. The categorization can be obtained by using either clustering or classification techniques. Cluster hierarchies of hypertext documents can be created by analysing semantic information embedded in link structures and document contents (Kosala & Blockeel, 2000). Documents can also be given classification codes according to keywords present in them.

- using Web query languages to providing a higher level of organization for semi-structured or unstructured data available on the Web. Users do not have to scan the entire Web site to find the required information; whereas they can use Web query languages to search within the document or to obtain structural information about Web documents. A Web query language restructures extracted information from Web information sources that are heterogenous and semi-structured (Abiteboul, Quass, McHugh, Widom, & Weiner, 1997; Fernandez & Suciu, 1999). An agent-based approach involving artificial intelligent systems can also be used to organize Web-based information (Dignum & Cortes, 2001).

Mining of secondary Web data Secondary Web data includes Web transaction data extracted from Web logs. Given the secondary Web data, the goal is to capture the buying and traversing habits of customers in an e-business environment. Any existing pattern recognition method such as a traditional classification and clustering method can be utilized for this task after applying some preprocessing steps to the data. Some of the data mining applications appropriate for such type of data are:

- promoting campaign by cross-marketing strategies across products. Data mining techniques can analyse logs of different sales indicating customers' buying patterns (Cooley, Mobasher, & Srivastaves., 1997). Classification and clustering of Web access log can help a company to target their marketing (advertising) strategies to a certain group of customers. For example, classification rule mining is able to discover that a certain age group of people from a certain locality are likely to buy a certain group of products. Web-enabled e-business can also benefit from link analysis for repeat buying recommendations. Schulz et al (1999) applied link analysis in traditional retail chains and have found that 70% cross-selling potential exists. Associative rule mining can be applied to find frequent products bought together. For example, association rule mining can discover rules such as "75% customers who place an order for product1 from the /company/product1/ page place the order for product2 from the /company/product2/ page as well."

- maintaining or restructuring Web sites in order to better serve the needs of customers. Data mining techniques can assist in Web navigation by discovering authority sites of a user's interest and overview sites for those authority sites. For instance, association rule mining can be applied to discover correlation between documents in a Web site and thus estimate the probability of documents being requested together (Lan, Bressan, & Ooi, 1999). An example of association rule resulting from analysis of a travelling e-business company Web data is: "79% of visitors who browsed pages about *Hotel* also browsed pages on *visitor information: places to visit.*" This rule can be used in redesigning the Web site by directly linking the authority and overview Web sites.

- personalization of Web sites according to each individual's taste. Data mining techniques can assist in facilitating the development and execution of marketing strategies such as dynamically changing a particular Web site for a visitor (Mobasher, Cooleg, & Srivastar, 1999). This is achieved by building a model representing correlation of Web pages and users. The goal is to build groups of users performing similar activities. The built model is capable of categorizing Web pages and users, and matching between and across Web pages and/or users (Mobasher et al., 1999). According to the clusters of user profiles, recommendations can be made to a visitor on return visit or to new visitors (Spiliopoulou, Pohle, & Faulstich, 1999). For example, people accessing educational products on a company Web site between 6-8 p.m. on Friday can be considered academicians and can be focused accordingly.

Difficulties in Applying Data Mining

The general idea of discovering knowledge in large amounts of data with rich description is both appealing and intuitive, but technically it is significantly challenging and difficult. There must be some data mining strategies that should be implemented for better use of data collected from Web-enabled e-business sources. Some of the difficulties faced by data mining techniques in the Web-enabled e-business domain and their possible solutions are suggested in this section.

Data Format Data collected from Web-enabled e-business sources is semi-structured and hierarchical, i.e., the data has no absolute schema fixed in advance, and the extracted structure may be irregular or incomplete (Abiteboul, Buneman, Suciu, 2000).

This type of data requires additional steps before applying to traditional data mining models and algorithms, whose source is mostly confined to structured data. The additional steps include transforming unstructured data to a format suitable for traditional data mining methods. Web query languages can be used to obtain structural information from semi-structured data. Based on this structural information, data appropriate to traditional data mining techniques are generated. Web query languages that combine path expressions with an SQL-style syntax such as Lorel (Abiteboul et al., 2000) or UnQL (Fernandez & Suciu, 1999) seem to be good choices for extracting structural information.

Data Volume Collected e-business data sets are large in volume. The traditional data mining techniques should be able to handle such large data sets.

Enumeration of all patterns may be expensive and not necessary. In spite, selection of representative patterns that capture the essence of the entire data set and their use for mining the data set may prove a more effective approach. But then selection of such data set becomes a problem. A more efficient approach would be to use an iterative and interactive technique that takes into account real time responses and feedback. An interactive process involves human analyst in the process, so an instant feedback can be included in the process. An iterative process first considers a selected number of attributes chosen by the user for analysis, and then keeps adding other attributes for analysis until the user is satisfied. The novelty of this iterative method will be that it reduces the search space significantly (due to the less number of attributes involved). Most of the existing techniques suffer from the (very large) dimensionality of the search space (Mitchell, 1997).

Data Quality One major source of difficulties for data mining is data quality. Web server logs may not contain all the data needed. Also, noisy and corrupt data can hide patterns and make predictions harder. (Kohavi & Provost, 2001).

Nevertheless, quality of data is increased with the use of electronic interchange, as there is less space for noise due to electronic storage rather than manual processing of them.

Data warehouses provide a capability for good quality data storage. A warehouse integrates data from operational systems, e-business applications, and demographic data providers, and handles issues such as data inconsistency, missing values, etc. A Web warehouse may be used as a data source for mining data if available.

There has been some initiative to warehouse the Web data generated from e-business applications, but still long way to go in terms of data mining (Madria, Bhowmick, Ng, & Lim, 1998).

Another solution of collecting good quality Web data is the use of (1) a dedicated server recording all activities of each user individually, or (2) cookies or scripts in the absence of such server. Activities of the users include access, inspection and selection of products, retrieval of text, duration of an active session, traversing patterns of Web pages (such as number, types, sequence, etc.), and collection of users' demographic information such as gender, sex, and location for the user anonymously accessing the Web site, etc. The combination of tags from Web pages, product correlation, and feedback from the customer to companies can also be used (Chan, 1999; Kohavi, 2001).

Also, when searching for documents, methods of evaluating the usefulness of this document are important. The agent-based approaches that involve artificial intelligence systems can be used to discover such Web-based information.

Data Adaptability Data on the Web is ever-changing. Data mining models and algorithms should be adapted to deal with real-time data in which new transaction data is incorporated for analysis and the constructed data model are updated as the new data approaches.

User-interface agents can be used to try to maximize the productivity of current users' interactions with the system by adapting behaviours. Another solution can be to dynamically modify mined information as the database changes (Cheung, Han, Ng, & Wong, 1996) or to incorporate user feedback to modify the actions performed by the system (Chundi & Dayal, 1997).

XML Data It is assumed that in few years XML will be the most highly used language of Internet in representing documents including business. XML documents may not be completely in the same format thus resulting in missing values.

Assuming the metadata stored is in XML, the integration of the two disparate data sources becomes much more transparent, field names can be matched more easily, and semantic conflicts may be described explicitly (Abiteboul et al., 2000). As a result, the types of data input to and output from the learned models and the detailed form of the models can be determined. Various techniques, such as tag recognition, can be used to fill in missing information if there is a mismatch in attributes, tags or DTDs (Abiteboul et al., 2000). Moreover, many query languages such as XML-QL, XSL (Deutsch, Florischu, Fernandez, Levy, & Suciu., 1999) and XML-GL (Ceri et al., 1999) are designed specifically for querying XML and getting structured information from these documents.

Privacy Issues There are always some privacy concerns of proper balancing between a company's desire to use personal information versus individual's desire to protect it (Piastesky-Shapiro, 2000).

The possible solution is to (1) ensure users of secure and reliable data transfer by using high speed, high-valued data encryption procedures, and/or (2) give a choice to a user to reveal the information that he/she wants to and give some benefit in exchange for revealing his or her information (such as discount on certain shopping product etc.).

CONCLUSION

This chapter attempts to present data mining concepts and issues that are associated with Web-enabled e-business applications.

It is easy to collect data from Web-enabled e-business sources as all visitors to a Web site leave a trail which automatically is stored in log files by Web server. The data mining tools can process and analyse such Web server log files or actual Web contents to discover meaningful information. The data mining techniques provide companies with previously unknown buying patterns and behaviours of their online customers. More importantly, the fast feedback the companies obtained using data mining is very helpful in increasing the company's benefit.

Earlier data mining tools such as C5 (http://www.rulequest.com) and several neural network softwares (QuickLearn, Sompack, etc.) were limited to some individual researchers. These individual algorithms are capable of solving a single data mining task. But now the second generation data mining system produced by commercial companies [such as clementine (http://www.spss.com/clementine/), AnswerTree (http://www.spss.com/ answertree/), SAS (http://www.sas.com/), IBM Intelligent Miner (http://www.ibm.com/ software/data/iminer/) and DBMiner (http://db.cs.sfu.ca/DBMiner)] incorporate multiple discoveries (classification, clustering, etc.), preprocessing (data cleaning, transformation, etc.) and postprocessing (visualization) tasks, and are becoming known to the public and successful.[2] Moreover, tools that combine ad hoc query or OLAP (Online analytical processing) with data mining are also developed (Wu, 2000). Faster CPU, bigger disks and wireless net connectivity make these tools able to analyse large volumes of data.

Utilization of data mining techniques in assisting the Web-enabled e-business content providers and consumers is overall a beneficial transaction (Eckerson, 1999). There are several important aspects of Web-enabled e-business where data mining can be beneficial. Some of them are (1) analysis of patterns of user behaviour that reflect the acceptability of and satisfaction with a Web site, (2) correlation analysis between Web contents, be it products or documents, (3) analysis of Web usage data to assist e-businesses in real-time personalization and making cross-marketing strategies.

A Web-enabled e-business company that incorporates data mining results with its strategy is sure to be successful.

ENDNOTES

[1] This chapter will not go into depth regarding data mining techniques. Interested readers can refer to data mining textbooks for the detailed description of these techniques.
[2] An interesting review of data mining softwares compiled by Peter Spirtes can be found at http://crl.research.compaq.com/vision/multimedia/dm/DataMiningSurvey.html.

REFERENCES

Abiteboul, S., Buneman, P., & Suciu, D. (2000). *Data on the Web: From Relations to substructured data and XML*, San Francisco: Morgan Kaufmann.

Abiteboul, S., Quass, D., McHugh, J., Widom, J., & Weiner, J. (1997). The Lorel query language for semi structured data. *Journal of Digital Libraries, 1*(1), 68-88.

Agrawal, R., & Srikant, R. (1994). *Fast algorithms for mining association rules*. IBM Research Report RJ9839, IBM Almaden Research Centre.

Berry, M. & Linoff, G. S. (2000). *Data mining: Concepts and techniques*. New York: John Wiley and Sons, INC.

Cabena, P., Hadjinian, P., Stadler, R., Verhees, J. & Zanasi, A. (1997). *Discovering data mining from concept to implementation*. Upper Saddle River, NJ: Prentice Hall PTR.

Ceri, S., Comai, S., Damiani, E., Fraternali, P., Paraboschi, S., & Tanca, L. (1999) XML-GL: A graphical language for querying and restructuring XML Documents. In *Proceedings of the Eighth International WWW Conference*, Toronto.

Chan, P. K. (1999). A non-invasive learning approach to building Web user profile. In B. Masand & M. Spiliopoulou, Eds.), *KDD'99 workshop on web usage and user profiling (WEBKDD'99) Aug. San Diego, CA. ACM.*

Cheung, D. W., Han, J., Ng, V. T., & Wong, C. Y. (1996). Maintenance of discovered association rules in large databases: An incremental technique. In *Proceedings of the Twelfth International Conference on Data Engineering*, New Orleans, USA, 106-114.

Chundi, P. & Dayal, U. (1997). An application of adaptive data mining: Facilitating Web information access. In *Proceedings of the ACM SIGMOD Workshop on Research Issues in Data Mining and Knowledge discovery*, 31-38.

Cooley, R., Mobasher, B., & Srivastave, J., (1997). Web mining: Information and pattern recovery on the World Wide Web. In *Proceedings of the Ninth International Conference on Tools with Artificial Intelligence*.

Deutsch, A., Florescu, D., Fernandez, M., Levy, A., & Suciu, D. (1999). A query language for XML. In *Proceedings of the Eighth International WWW Conference*, Toronto.

Dignum, F. & Cortes, U. (Eds.). (2001). *Agent-Mediated Electronic Commerce III: Current Issues in Agent-Based Electronic Commerce Systems*. Lecture Notes in Artificial Intelligence. New York: Springer Verlag.

Eckerson, W. E. (1999). Marrying e-commerce and customer intelligence. In *Patricia Seybold*

Group's Information Assets Service. June. Retrieved October 1, 2001, from http://www.psgroup.com/doc/products/1999/6/PSGP6-18-99IA/PSGP6-18-99IA.asp.

Fayyad, U. M., Piatetsky-Shapiro, G., & Smyth, P. (1995). From data mining to knowledge discovery: An overview. In U. M. Fayyad, G. Piatetsky-Shapiro, P. Smyth, & R. Uthurusamy, (Eds.), *Advances in knowledge discovery and data mining.* 1-34. Menlo Park, CA: AAAI Press.

Fernandez, M. & Suciu, D. (1999). UNQL: A query language for Web site. Retrieved September 21, 2000, from http://www.cs.huij.ac.il/~yarivi/unql-htom.html.

Garofalakis, M. N., Rastogi, R., Seshadri, S., & Hyuseok, S. (1999). Data mining and the Web: Past, present and future. In *Proceedings of the Second International Workshop on Web Information and Data Management.* 43-47.

Han, J. & Kamber, M. (2001). *Mastering data mining.* San Francisco: Morgan Kaufmann.

Jichang, W., Huan, H., Gangshan, W., & Fugan, Z. (1997). Web mining: Knowledge discovery on the Web. In *Proceedings of the Ninth International Conference on Tools with Artificial Intelligence.* Nov.

Kohavi, R. (2001). Mining e-commerce data: The Good, the Bad and the Ugly. In *Proceedings of the seventh ACM SIGKDD International Conference on Knowledge Discovery and Data Mining* (KDD 2001).

Kohavi, R. & Provost, F. (2001). Applications of data mining to electronic commerce. *Data Mining and Knowledge Discovery, 5* (1/2).

Kosala, R. & Blockeel, H. (2000). Web mining research: A survey. *SIGKDD Explorations. 2*(1), 1-15, July.

Lan, B., Bressan, S., & Ooi, B. C. (1999). Making Web servers pushier. In B. Masand & O. Spiliopoulou, (Eds).

Lim, T. S. & Loh, W. Y. (2000). A comparison of prediction accuracy, complexity and training time of thirty-three old and new classification algorithms. *Machine Learning, 40*(3), Sep. 203-228.

Liu, B., Ma, Y., & Yu, P. H. (2001). Discovering unexpected information from your competitor's Web sites. In *Proceedings of the Seventh ACM SIGKDD International Conference on Knowledge Discovery and Data Mining (KDD 2001).* Aug. San Francisco, USA.

Madria, S. K., Bhowmick, S. S., Ng, W. K., & Lim, E. P. (1998). Research issues in Web data mining. *Applied Artificial Intelligence, 12,* 303-312.

Masand, B. & Spiliopoulou, M. (1999). *KDD '99 workshop on Web usage analysis and user profiling (WEBKDD '99).* Aug. San Diego, CA. ACM.

Mitchell, T. M. (1997). *Machine learning.* New York: McGraw-Hill.

Mobasher, B., Cooley, R., & Srivastave, J. (1999). Automatic personalization based on Web usage mining. In B. Masand & M. Spiliopoulou, (Eds).

Piastesky-Shapiro, G. (2000). Knowledge discovery in databases: 10 years after. *SIGKDD Explorations, 1*(2), Jan, 59-61. ACM SIGKDD.

Schulz, A. G., Hahsler, M., & Jahn, M. (1999). A customer purchase incidence model applied to recommendation service. In B. Masand & M. Spiliopoulou, (Eds).

Spiliopoulou, M., Pohle, C., & Faulstich, L. C. (1999). Improving the effectiveness of a Web site with Web usage mining. In (Masand & Spiliopoulou, (Eds).

Wong, W. C. & Fu, A. W. (2000). Finding structure and characteristic of Web documents for classification. In *Proceedings of the ACM SIGMOD Workshop on Research Issues in Data Mining and Knowledge discovery.* July. ACM.

Wu, J. (2000). Business intelligence: What is data mining? in *Data Mining Review Online.* August.

Section V:

Web Search
and
Data Retrieval

Chapter IX

Intelligent Web Search Through Adaptive Learning From Relevance Feedback

Zhixiang Chen
University of Texas-Pan American

Binhai Zhu
Montana State University

Xiannong Meng
Bucknell University

ABSTRACT

In this chapter, machine-learning approaches to real-time intelligent Web search are discussed. The goal is to build an intelligent Web search system that can find the user's desired information with as little relevance feedback from the user as possible. The system can achieve a significant search precision increase with a small number of iterations of user relevance feedback. A new machine-learning algorithm is designed as the core of the intelligent search component. This algorithm is applied to three different search engines with different emphases. This chapter presents the algorithm, the architectures, and the performances of these search engines. Future research issues regarding real-time intelligent Web search are also discussed.

INTRODUCTION

This chapter presents the authors' approaches to intelligent Web search systems that are built on top of existing search engine design and implementation techniques. An intelligent search engine would use the search results of the general-purpose search engines as its starting search space, from which it would adaptively learn from the user's feedback to boost and to enhance the search performance and accuracy. It may use feature extraction, document clustering and filtering, and other methods to help an adaptive learning process. The goal is to design *practical* and *efficient* algorithms by exploring the nature of the Web search. With these new algorithms, three intelligent Web search engines—*WEBSAIL*, *YARROW* and *FEATURES* are built that are able to achieve significant search precision increase with just four to five iterations of real-time learning from a user's relevance feedback. The characteristics of those three intelligent search engines are reported in this chapter.

BACKGROUND

Recently, three general approaches have been taken to increase Web search accuracy and performance. One is the development of *meta-search engines* that forward user queries to multiple search engines at the same time in order to increase the coverage and hope to include what the user wants in a short list of top-ranked results. Examples of such meta-search engines include *MetaCrawler* (MC), *Inference Find* (IF), and *Dogpile* (DP). Another approach is the development of *topic-specific* search engines that are specialized in particular topics. These topics range from vacation guides (VG) to kids' health (KH). The third approach is to use some group or personal profiles to personalize the Web search. Examples of such efforts include *GroupLens* (Konstan et al., 1997), *PHOAKS* (Terveen, Hill, Amento, McDonald, & Creter, 1997), among others. The first generation meta-search engines address the problem of decreasing coverage by simultaneously querying multiple general-purpose engines. These meta-search engines suffer to certain extent the inherited problem of *information overflow* that it is difficult for users to pin down specific information for which they are searching. Specialized search engines typically contain much more accurate and narrowly focused information. However, it is not easy for a novice user to know where and which specialized engine to use. Most personalized Web search projects reported so far involve collecting user's behavior at a centralized server or a proxy server. While it is effective for the purpose of e-commerce where vendors can collectively learn consumer behaviors, this approach does present the privacy problem. Users of the search engines would have to submit their search habits to some type of servers, though most likely the information collected is anonymous.

The clustering, user profiling, and other advanced techniques used by these search engines and other projects (Bollacker, Lawrence, & Giles, 1998, 1999) are *static* in the sense that they are built before the search begins. They cannot be changed dynamically during the real-time search process. Thus, they do not reflect the changing interests of the user at different time, at different location or on different subjects. The *static nature* of the existing search engines makes it very difficult, if not impossible, to support the *dynamic changes* of the user's search interests. The augmented features of personalization (or customization) certainly help a search engine to increase its search performance, however their ability is very limited. An intelligent search engine should be built on top of existing search engine design and implementation techniques. It should use the search results of the general-purpose search engines as its starting search space, from which it would adaptively learn in real-time from the user's relevance feedback to boost and to enhance the search performance and the relevance accuracy. With the ability to perform real-time adaptive learning from relevance feedback, the search engine is able to learn the user's search interest changes or shifts, and thus provides the user with improved search results.

Relevance feedback is the most popular query reformation method in information retrieval (Baeza-Yates & Ribeiro-Neto 1999, Salton 1975). It is essentially an adaptive learning process from the document examples judged by the user as relevant or irrelevant. It requires a sequence of iterations of relevance feedback to search for the desired documents. As it is known in (Salton, 1975), a single iteration of similarity-based relevance feedback usually produces improvements from 40 to 60 percent in the search precision, evaluated at certain fixed levels of the recall ,and averaged over a number of user queries. Some people might think that Web search users are not willing to try iterations of relevance feedback to search for their desired documents. However, the authors think otherwise. It is not a question of whether the Web search users are not willing to try iterations of relevance feedback to perform their search. Rather it is a question of whether an adaptive learning system can be built that supports high search precision increase with just a few iterations of relevance feedback. The Web search users may have no patience to try more than a dozen iterations of relevance feedback. But, if a system has a 20% or so search precision increase with just about four to five iterations of relevance feedback, are the users willing to use such a system? The authors believe that the answer is "*yes*." Intelligent Web search systems that dynamically learn the user's information needs in real-time must be built to advance the state of art in Web search. Machine-learning techniques can be used to improve Web search, because machine-learning algorithms are able to adjust the search process dynamically so as to satisfy the user's information needs. Unfortunately, the existing machine-learning algorithms (e.g., Angluin, 1987; Littlestone, 1988), including the most popular similarity-based relevance feedback algorithm (Rocchio, 1971), suffer from the large number of iterations required to achieve the search goal. Average users are not willing to go through too many iterations of learning to find what they want.

WEB SEARCH AND ADAPTIVE LEARNING
Overview
There have been great research efforts on applications of machine-learning to automatic extraction, clustering and classification of information from the Web. Some earlier research includes *WebWatcher* (Armstrong, Freitage, Joachims, & Mitchell, 1995) that interactively help users locate desired information by employing learned knowledge about which hyperlinks are likely to lead to the target information; *Syskill and Webert* (Pazzani, Muramatsu, & Billus, 1996), a system that uses a Bayesian classifier to learn about interesting Web pages for the user; and *NewsWeeder* (Lang, 1995), a news-filtering system that allows the users to rate each news article being read and learns a user profile based on those ratings. Some research is aimed at providing adaptive Web service through learning. For example, *Ahoy! The Homepage Finder* in (Shakes, Langheinrich, & Etzioni, 1997) performs dynamic reference shifting; *Adaptive Web Sites* in (Etzioni & Weld 1995, Perkowitz & Etzioni 2000) automatically improve their organization and presentation based on user access data; and *Adaptive Web Page Recommendation Services* (Balabanovi, 1997) recommends potentially interesting Web pages to the users. Since so much work has been done on intelligent Web search and on learning from the Web by many researchers, a comprehensive review is beyond the scope and the limited space of this chapter. Interested readers may find good surveys of the previous research on learning the Web in Kobayashi and Takeda (2000).

Dynamic Features and Dynamic Vector Space
In spite of the World Wide Web's size and the high dimensionality of Web document index features, the traditional vector space model in information retrieval (Baeza-Yates & Ribeiro-Neto,1999; Salton, 1989; Salton et al., 1975) has been used for Web document

representation and search. However, to implement real-time adaptive learning with limited computing resource, the traditional vector space model cannot be applied directly. Recall that back in 1998, the AltaVista (AV) system was running on 20 multi-processor machines, all of them having more than 130 Giga-Bytes of RAM and over 500 Giga-Bytes of disk space (Baeza-Yates & Ribeiro-Neto, 1999). A new model is needed that is efficient enough both in time and space for Web search implementations with limited computing resources. The new model may also be used to enhance the computing performance of a Web search system even if enough computing resources are available.

Let us now examine indexing in Web search. In the discussion, keywords are used as document index features. Let X denote the set of all index keywords for the whole Web (or, practically, a portion of the whole Web). Given any Web document d, let $I(d)$ denote the set of all index keywords in X that are used to index d with non-zero values. Then, the following two properties hold:

- The size of $I(d)$ is substantially smaller than the size of X. Practically, $I(d)$ can be bounded by a constant. The rationale behind this is that in the simplest case only a few of the keywords in d are needed to index it.
- For any search process related to the search query q, let $D(q)$ denote the collection of all the documents that match q, then the set of index keywords relevant to q, denoted by $F(q)$, is

$$F(q) = \mathop{Y}_{d \in D(q)} I(d)$$

Although the size of $F(q)$ varies from different queries, it is still substantially smaller than the size of X, and might be bounded by a few hundreds or a few thousands in practice.

Definition 1. *Given any search query q, F(q), which is given in the above paragraph, is defined as the set of dynamic features relevant to the search query q:*

Definition 2. *Given any search query q, the dynamic vector space V(q) relevant to q is defined as the vector space that is constructed with all the documents in D(q) such that each of those documents is indexed by the dynamic features in F(q).*

The General Setting of Learning

Let S be a Web search system. For any query q, S first finds the set of documents $D(q)$ that match the query q. It finds $D(q)$ with the help of a general-purpose search strategy through searching its internal database, or through external search engine such as AltaVista (AV) when no matches are found within its internal database. It then finds the set of dynamic features $F(q)$, and later constructs the dynamic vector space $V(q)$. Once $D(q)$, $F(q)$ and $V(q)$ have been found, S starts its adaptive learning process with the help of the learning algorithm that is to be presented in the following subsections. More precisely, let $F(q) = \{K_1, ..., K_n\}$ such that each K_i denotes a dynamic feature (i.e., an index keyword). S maintains a common weight vector $w = (w_1, ..., w_n)$ for dynamic features in $F(q)$. The components of w have non-negative real values. The learning algorithm uses w to extract and learn the most relevant features and to classify documents in $D(q)$ as relevant or irrelevant.

Algorithm TW2

As the authors have investigated (Chen, Meng, & Fowler, 1999; Chen & Meng, Chen, Meng, Fowler, & Zhu, 2000), intelligent Web search can be modeled as an adaptive learning process such as adaptive learning, where the search engine acts as a learner and the user as a teacher. The user sends a query to the engine, and the engine uses the query to search the index database and returns a list of URLs that are ranked according to a ranking function. Then the user provides the engine relevance feedback, and the engine uses the feedback to improve its next search and returns a refined list of URLs. The learning (or search) process ends when the engine finds the desired documents for the user. Conceptually, a query entered by the user can be understood as the logical expression of the collection of the documents wanted by the user. A list of URLs returned by the engine can be interpreted as an approximation of the collection of the desired documents.

Let us now consider how to use adaptive learning from equivalence queries to approach the problem of Web search. The vector space model (Baeza-Yates & Ribeiro-Neto, 1999; Salton, 1989; Salton et al., 1975) is used to represent documents. The vector space may consist of Boolean vectors. It may also consist of discretized vectors, for example, the frequency vector of the index keywords. A target concept is a collection of documents, which is equivalent to the set of vectors of the documents in the collection. The learner is the search engine and the teacher is the user. The goal of the search engine is to find the target concept in "*real-time*" with a minimal number of mistakes (or equivalence queries).

The authors designed the algorithm *TW2*, a tailored version of *Winnow2* (Littlestone 1988), which is described in the following. As described in the general setting of learning, for each query q entered by the user, algorithm *TW2* uses a common weight vector w and a real-valued threshold q to classify documents in $D(q)$. Initially, all weights in w have a value of 0. Let $a > 1$ be the promotion and demotion factor. Algorithm *TW2* classifies documents whose vectors $x = (x_1, ..., x_n)$ satisfy $\sum_{i=1}^{n} w_i x_i > \theta$ as relevant, and all others as irrelevant. If the user provides a document that contradicts the classification of TW2, then TW2 is said to have made a mistake. When the user responds with a document that may or may not contradict to the current classification, TW2 updates the weights through promotion or demotion. It should be noticed that in contrast to algorithm *Winnow2* to set all initial weights in w to 1, algorithm *TW2* sets all initial weights in w to 0 and has a different promotion strategy accordingly. Another substantial difference between *TW2* and *Winnow2* is that *TW2* accepts document examples that may not contradict its current classification to promote or demote its weight vector, while *Winnow2* only accepts examples that contradict its current classification to perform promotion or demotion. The rationale behind setting all the initial weights to 0 by algorithm *TW2* is to focus attention on the propagation of the influence of the relevant documents, and to use irrelevant documents to adjust the focused search space. Moreover, this approach is computationally feasible because existing effective document-ranking mechanisms can be coupled with the learning process.

In contrast to the linear lower bounds proved for Rocchio's similarity-based relevance feedback algorithm (Chen & Zhu, 2002), algorithm *TW2* has surprisingly small mistake bounds for learning any collection of documents represented by a disjunction of a small number of relevant features. The mistake bounds are independent of the dimensionality of the index features. For example, one can show that to learn a collection of documents represented by a disjunction of at most k relevant features (or index keywords) over the n-dimensional

---

ALGORITHM TW2 (THE TAILORED WINNOW2):

Input q :   the user's query.

               $\alpha > 1$:   the promotion and demotion factor.

               θ :   the real-valued classification threshold

Preparation: Finding the dynamic features $F(q) = \{K_1,..., K_n\}$ and

               the dynamic vector space $V(q)$ of $D(q)$.

Step 0:   Set $w_0 = (w_{01},..., w_{0n}) = (0,...,0)$.

Step $i > 0$: Classify documents in $D(q)$ with $\sum_{j=1}^{n} w_{ij}x_j > \theta$.

               While (user judged a document $x = (x_1,..., x_n)$) do

                    If (x is relevant) do //promotion

                         For ($j = 1; j \leq n; j + +$)

                              If ($x_j = 0$) set $w_{i+1, j} = w_{ij}$

                              If ($x_j \neq 0$ & $w_{ij} = 0$) set $w_{i+1, j} = \alpha$

                              If ($x_j \neq 0$ & $w_{ij} \neq 0$) set $w_{i+1, j} = \alpha w_{ij}$

                    If (x is irrelevant) do //demotion

                         For ($j = 1; j \leq n; j + +$)

                              Set $w_{i+1, j} = \dfrac{w_{ij}}{\alpha}$

               If (user has not judged any document) stop

               Else set $i = i + 1$ and go to step $i + 1$.

Boolean vector space, *TW2* makes at most $\dfrac{\alpha^2 A}{(\alpha - 1)\theta} + (\alpha + 1)k \ln \alpha\theta - \alpha$ mistakes, where A is the number of dynamic features that occurred in the learning process. The actual implementation of algorithm *TW2* requires the help of document ranking and equivalence query simulation that are to be addressed later.

Feature Learning Algorithm FEX (Feature EXtraction)

Given any user query q, for any dynamic feature $K_i \in F(q)$ with $1 \leq i \leq n$, define the rank of K_i as $h(K_i) = h_0(K_i) + w_i$. Here, $h_0(K_i)$ is the initial rank for K_i. Recall that K_i is some index keyword. With the feature ranking function h and the common weight vector w, FEX extracts and learns the most relevant features as follows.

ALGORITHM FEX:

Input: p :   the feature promotion and demotion factor.

          w :   the common weight vector of dynamic features.

Stage 0: Sort dynamic features in $F(q)$ with ranking function h,

          and extract 10 top-ranked features for the user to judge their relevance.

Stage 1: While (user judged feature K_j) do

               If (K_j is relevant) //promotion

                    Set $w_{ij} = pw_{ij}$

          Else //demotion

                    Set $w_{ij} = \dfrac{w_{ij}}{p}$.

Document Ranking

Let g be a ranking function independent of *TW2* and *FEX*. Define the ranking function f for documents in $D(q)$ for any user query q as follows. For any Web document $d \in D(q)$ with vector $d = (x_1,...,x_n) \in V(q)$, define

$$f(d) = \gamma(d)[g(d) + \beta(d)] + \sum_{j=1}^{n} w_j x_j.$$

Here, g remains constant for each document d during the learning process of the learning algorithm. Various strategies can be used to define g, for example, PageRank (Brin & Page, 1998), classical *tf-idf* scheme, vector spread, or cited-based rankings (Yuwono & Lee, 1996). The two additional tuning parameters are used to do individual document promotions or demotions of the documents that have been judged by the user. Initially, let $\beta(d) \geq 0$ and $\gamma(d) = 1$. $\beta(d)$ and $\gamma(d)$ can be updated in a similar fashion as the weight value w_i is updated by algorithm TW2.

Equivalence Query Simulation

Our system will use the ranking function f that was defined above to rank the documents in $D(q)$ for each user query q, and for each iteration of leaning, it returns the top 10 ranked documents to the user. These top 10 ranked documents represent an approximation to the classification made by the learning algorithm that has been used by the system. The quantity 10 can be replaced by, say, 25 or 50. But it should not be too large for two reasons: (1) the user may only be interested in a very small number of top ranked documents, and (2) the display space for visualization is limited. The user can examine the short list of documents and can end the search process, or, if some documents are judged as misclassified, document relevance feedback can be provided. Sometimes, in addition to the top 10 ranked documents, the system may also provide the user with a short list of other documents below the top 10. Documents in the second short list may be selected randomly, or the bottom 10 ranked documents can be included. The motivation for the second list is to give the user some better view of the classification made by the learning algorithm.

THE WEBSAIL SYSTEM AND THE YARROW SYSTEM

The WebSail System is a real-time adaptive Web search learner designed and implemented to show that the learning algorithm TW2 not only works in theory but also works practically. The detailed report of the system can be found in Chen et al. (2000c). WebSail employs TW2 as its learning component and is able to help the user search for the desired documents with as little relevance feedback as possible. WebSail has a graphic user interface to allow the user to enter his/her query and to specify the number of the top matched document URLs to be returned. WebSail maintains an internal index database of about 800,000 documents. Each of those documents is indexed with about 300 keywords. It also has a meta-search component to query AltaVista whenever needed. When the user enters a query and

Figure 1: The display format of WEBSAIL

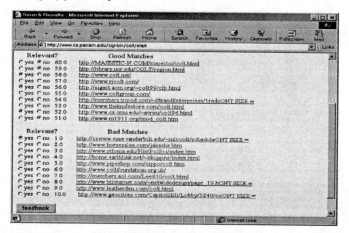

starts a search process, WEBSAIL first searches its internal index database. If no relevant documents can be found within its database then it receives a list of top matched documents externally with the help of its meta-search component. WEBSAIL displays the search result to the user in a format as shown in Figure 1.

Also as shown in Figure 1, WEBSAIL provides at each iteration the top 10 and the bottom 10 ranked document URLs. Each document URL is preceded with two radio buttons for the user to judge whether the document is relevant to the search query or not. The document URLs are clickable for viewing the actual document contents so that the user can judge more accurately whether a document is relevant or not. After the user clicks a few radio buttons, he/she can click the feedback button to submit the feedback to TW2. WEBSAIL has a function to parse out the feedback provided by the user when the feedback button is clicked. Having received the feedback from the user, TW2 updates its common weight vector w and also performs individual document promotions or demotions. At the end of the current iteration of learning, WEBSAIL re-ranks the documents and displays the top 10 and the bottom10 document URLs to the user.

At each iteration, the dispatcher of WEBSAIL parses query or relevance feedback information from the interface and decides which of the following components should be invoked to continue the search process: TW2, or Index Database Searcher, or Meta-Searcher. When meta-search is needed, Meta-Searcher is called to query AltaVista to receive a list of the top matched documents. The Meta-Searcher has a parser and an indexer that work in real-time to parse the received documents and to index each of them with at most 64 keywords. The received documents, once indexed, will also be cached in the index database.

The following relative Recall and relative Precision are used to measure the performance of WEBSAIL. For any query q, the relative Recall and the relative Precision are

$$Rrecall = \frac{|Rm|}{|R|}, \ Rprecision = \frac{|Rm|}{m},$$

where R is the total number of relevant documents among the set of the retrieved documents, and Rm is the number of relevant documents ranked among the top m positions in the final search result of the search engine. The authors have selected 100 queries to calculate the average relative Recall of WEBSAIL. Each query is represented by a collection of at most five keywords. For each query, WEBSAIL is tested with the returning document number m as 50, 100, 150, 200, respectively. For each test, the number of iterations used and the number of documents judged by the user were recorded. The relative Recall and Precision were calculated based on manual examination of the relevance of the returned documents. The experiments reveal that WEBSAIL achieves an average of 0.95 relative Recall and an average of 0.46 relative Precision with an average of 3.72 iterations and an average of 13.46 documents judged as relevance feedback.

The Yarrow system (Chen & Meng, 2000) is a multi-threaded program. Its architecture differs from that of WEBSAIL in two aspects: (1) it replaces the meta-searcher of WEBSAIL with a generic Query Constructor and a group of meta-searchers, and it does not maintain its own internal index database. For each search process, it creates a thread and destroys the thread when the search process ends. Because of its light-weight size, it can be easily converted or ported to run in different environments or platforms. The predominant feature of YARROW, compared with existing meta-search engines, is the fact that it learns from the user's feedback in real-time on client side. The learning algorithm TW2 used in YARROW has some surprisingly small mistake bound. YARROW may be well used as a plug-in component for Web browsers on client side. A detailed report of the Yarrow system is given in Chen and Meng (2000).

THE FEATURES SYSTEM

The FEATURES system (Chen, Meng, Fowler, & Zhu, 2001) is also a multi-threaded system, and its architecture is shown in Figure 2. The key difference between FEATURES and WEBSAIL is that FEATURES employs the two learning algorithms—FEX and TW2—to update the common weight vector w concurrently.

For each query, FEATURES usually shows the top 10 ranked documents, plus the top 10 ranked features, to the user for him/her to judge document relevance and feature relevance. The format of presenting the top 10 ranked documents together with the top 10 ranked features

Figure 2: The architecture of FEATURES

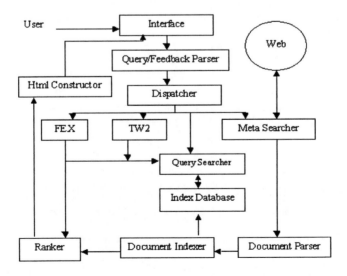

Figure 3: The display format of FEATURES

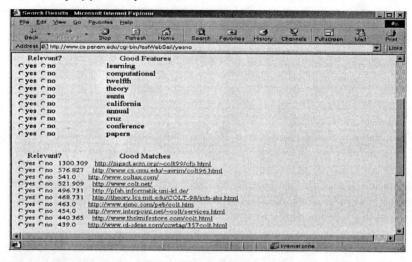

is shown in Figure 3. In this format, document URLs and features are preceded by radio buttons for the user to indicate whether they are relevant or not.

If the current task is a learning process from the user's document and feature relevance feedback, Dispatcher sends the feature relevance feedback information to the feature learner FEX and the document relevance feedback information to the document learner TW2. FEX uses the relevant and irrelevant features as judged by the user to promote and demote the related feature weights in the common weight vector w. TW2 uses the relevant and irrelevant documents judged by the user as positive and negative examples to promote and demote the weight vector. Once FEX and TW2 have finished promotions and demotions, the updated weight vector w is sent to Query Searcher and to Feature Ranker. Feature Ranker re-ranks all the dynamic features, that are then sent to Html Constructor. Query Searcher searches Index Database to find the matched documents that are then sent to Document Ranker. Document Ranker re-ranks the matched documents and then sends them to Html Constructor to select documents and features to be displayed. Empirical results (Chen et al., 2001) show that FEATURES has substantially better search performance than AltaVista.

TIMING STATISTICS

On December 13th and 14th of 2001, the authors conducted the experiments to collect the timing statistics for using WEBSAIL, YARROW and FEATURES. Thirty (30) query words were used to test each of these meta-search engines. Every time a query was sent, the wall-clock time needed for the meta-search engine to list the sorted result was recorded in the program. Also recorded was the wall-clock time to refine the search results based on the user's feedback. Since YARROW supports multiple external search engines, ALTAVISTA and NORTHERN LIGHT were selected as the external search engines when YARROW was tested. The external search engine used by WEBSAIL and FEATURES is ALTAVISTA. The following tables show the statistical results at 95% confidence interval level. The original responding time is t_{orig} and the refining time is t_{refine}, and C.I. denotes the confidence interval.

Table 1: Response time of WEBSAIL (in seconds)

t_{orig}	Deviation	95% C.I.	t_{refine}	Deviation	95% C.I.
7.29	1.42	0.789	1.166	0.461	0.255

Table 2: Response Time of YARROW (in seconds)

	t_{orig}	deviation	95% C.I.	t_{refine}	Deviation	95% C.I.
Via ALTAVISTA	5.51	1.85	1.03	0.988	0.435	0.241
VIA FEATURES	18.44	5.48	3.03	0.884	0.352	0.195

Table 3: Response time of FEATURES (in seconds)

t_{orig}	Deviation	95% C.I.	t_{refine}	Deviation	95% C.I.
6.90	2.38	1.32	0.865	0.434	0.240

The statistics from the table indicate that while the standard deviations and the confidence intervals are relatively high, they are in a reasonable range that users can accept. It takes WEBSAIL, YARROW and FEATURES in the order of a few seconds to 20 seconds to respond initially because they need to get the information from external search engines over the network. However, even for the initial response time is not long and hence is acceptable by the user.

THE COMMERCIAL APPLICATIONS

Intelligent Web search can find many commercial applications. This section will concentrate on the applications to E-commerce. E-commerce can be viewed as three major components, the service and goods suppliers, the consumers, and the information intermediaries (or infomediaries). The service and goods suppliers are the producer or the source of the e-commerce flow. The consumers are the destination of the flow. Informediaries, according to Grover and Teng (2001), are an essential part of E-commerce. An enormous amount of information has to be produced, analyzed and managed in order for e-commerce to succeed. In this context, Web search is a major player in the infomediaries. Other components of infomediaries include communities of interest (e.g., online purchase), industry magnet sites (e.g., www.amazon.com), e-retailers, or even individual corporate sites (Grover & Teng, 2001). The machine-learning approaches in Web search studied in this chapter are particularly important in the whole context of E-commerce. The key feature of the machine-learning approach for Web search is interactive learning and narrowing the search results to what the user wants. This feature can be used in many e-commerce applications. The following are a few examples.

Building a partnership: As pointed out in Tewari et al. (2001), building a partnership between the buyers and the seller is extremely important for the success of an e-Business. Tewari et al. used Multi-Attribute Resource Intermediaries (MARI) infrastructure to approximate buyer and seller preferences. They compare the degree of matching between buyers and sellers by computing a distance between the two vectors. When interactive learning features explored in this chapter are used in this process, the buyers and the sellers can *negotiate* the deal in real-time, thus greatly enhancing the capability of the system. A collection of sellers may provide an initial list of items available at certain prices for buyers to choose. The buyers may also have a list of expectations. According to the model proposed in (Tewari et.al, the possibility of a match is computed statically. If a machine-learning approach is taken, the buyers and the sellers may interactively find a best deal, similar to the situation where a face-to-face negotiation is taking place.

Brokering between buyers and sellers: Brokerage between the producers and the consumers is a critical E-commerce component. Given a large number of producers and a large number of consumers, how to efficiently find a match between what is offered on the market and what a buyer is looking for? The work described in Meyyappan (2001) and, Santos et al. (2001) provided a framework for e-commerce search brokers. A broker here is to compare price information, product features, the reputation of the producer, and other information for a potential buyer. While in the previous category the seller and the buyer may negotiate interactively. Here the buyer interacts with the broker(s) only, very similar to the real-world situation. The interactive machine-learning and related Web search technology can be applied in this category as well. The machine-learning algorithm will use the collection of potential sellers as a starting space, interactively search the optimal seller for the user based on the information collected by the brokerage software. (Meyyappan 2001) and (Santos et.al. 2001) provided a framework for this brokerage to take place. The machine-learning algorithm discussed in this chapter can be used for a buyer to interact with the broker to get the best that is available on the market. For example, a broker may act as a *meta-search engine* that collects information from a number of sellers, behaving very much like general-purpose search engines. A buyer asks her broker to get certain information; the broker, which is a meta-search engine equipped with TW2 or other learning algorithms may search, collect, collate and rank the information returned from seller sources to the buyer. The buyer can interact with the broker, just as if in the scenario of Web search. The broker will refine its list until the buyer finds a satisfactory product and the seller.

Interactive catalog: The service providers or the sellers can allow consumers to browse the catalog interactively. While browsing the learning algorithm can pick up users' interests and supply better information to the customer, much like what *adaptive Web sites* (Perkowitz & Etzioni, 2000) do for the customers. Here the learning can take place in two forms. The seller can explicitly ask how the potential buyers (browsers of the catalog) feel about the usefulness of the catalog. This can be analogous to the interactive learning using algorithms such as TW2. Researchers have reported approaches of this type (though they didn't use TW2 explicitly.) See (Herlocker and Konstan 2001) for an example and other similar projects. In the second approach, the provider of the catalog (seller) would learn the user interests and behaviors implicitly as reported in Claypool *et.al.* (2001). The learning algorithm such as TW2 can be embedded in the catalog software. The buyers' interests and intention can be captured through modified browser software. The learning algorithm can then revise the catalog listings by taking the buyers' Web page clicks as feedback. This is very similar to the Web search situation.

Web commerce infrastructure: Chaudhury, Mallick, and Rao (2000) describe using the Web in e-commerce as various *channels*. The Web can be used as *advertising channel, ordering channel*, and *customer support channel*. All these channels should be supported by an interactive system where customer feedback can be quickly captured, analyzed and used in updating the e-commerce system.

FUTURE WORK

In the future, the authors plan to improve the interface of their systems. Right now, the systems display the URLs of the documents. If the user wants to know the contents of the document, he/she needs to click the URL to view the content. The authors plan to display the URL of a document together with a good preview of its content. The authors also want to highlight those index keywords in the preview and allow them to be clickable for feature extracting and learning.

The authors also plan to apply clustering techniques to increase the performance of their system. It is easy to observe that in most cases documents that are relevant to a search query can be divided into a few different clusters or groups. The authors believe that document clustering techniques such as graph spectral partitioning can be used to reduce the number of the iterations of the learning process and to increase the performance of the system.

ACKNOWLEDGMENT

The authors thank the two anonymous referees and the editor, Dr. Nansi Shi, for their valuable comments on the draft of this chapter. The final presentation of the chapter has greatly benefited from their comments.

URL REFERENCES

(AV) AltaVista: www.altavista.com (DP) Dogpile: www.dogpile.com
(IF) Inference Find: www.infind.com (IS) Infoseek: www.infoseek.com
(KH) Kidshealth.com: www.kidshealth.com (MC) MetaCrawler: www.metacrawler.com
(VG) Vacations.Com: www.vacations.com

REFERENCES

Angluin, D. (1987). Queries and concept learning. *Machine-learning, 2*, 319-432.
Armstrong, R., Freitag, D., Joachims, T., & Mitchell, T. (1995). Webwatcher: A learning apprentice for the World Wide Web. In *Working Notes of the AAAI Spring Symposium on Information Gathering from Heterogeneous, Distributed Environments*, 6-12. AAAI Press.
Balabanovi, M. (1997). An adaptive Web page recommendation service. In *Proceedings of the First International Conference on Autonomous Agents*, 378-387. New York: ACM Press.
Baeza-Yates, R., & Ribeiro-Neto, B. (1999). *Modern Information Retrieval*. Reading, MA: Addison-Wesley.
Bollacker, K., Lawrence, S., & Giles, C.L. (1998). Citeseer: An autonomous Web agent for automatic retrieval and identification of interesting publications. In *Proceedings of the Second International Conference on Autonomous Agents*, 116-113. New York: ACM Press.
Bollacker, K., Lawrence, S., & Giles, C.L. (1999). A system for automatic personalized tracking of scientific literature on the Web. In *Proceedings of the Fourth ACM Conference on Digital Libraries*, 105-113. New York: ACM Press.
Brin, S., & Page, L. (1998). The anatomy of a large-scale hypertextual Web search engine. In *Proceedings of the Seventh World Wide Web Conference*.

Chaudhury, A., Mallick, D.N. & Rao, H.R. (2001). Web channels in E-commerce. Communications of the ACM, 44(1), 99-103.

Chen, Z., & Meng, X. (2000). Yarrow: A real-time client site meta search learner. In *Proceedings of the AAAI 2000 Workshop on Artificial Intelligence for Web Search* (the full version will appear in *Journal of Intelligent Information Systems*), pp. 12-17.

Chen, Z., Meng, X., & Fowler, R.H. (1999). Searching the Web with queries. Knowledge and Information Systems 1, 369-375.

Chen, Z., Meng, X., Fowler, R. H., & Zhu, B. (2001). FEATURES: Real time adaptive features and document learning for Web search. Journal for the American Society for Information Science, 52(8), 655–665.

Chen, Z., & Zhu, B. (2002). Some formal analysis of the Rocchio's similarity-based relevance feedback algorithm. Information Retrieval, 5(1), 61-86.

Chen, Z., Meng, X., Zhu, B., & Fowler, R. (2000). Websail: From on-line learning to Web search. In *Proceedings of the 2000 International Conference on Web Information Systems Engineering* (the full version will appear in *Journal of Knowledge and Information Systems, 4, 219-227.*

Claypool, M., Brown, D., Le, P., and Waseda, M. (2001). Inferring user interest, *IEEE Internet Computing*, 5(6), 32-39, November.

Etzioni, O. & Weld, D. (1995). Intelligent agents on the Internet: Fact, fiction and forecast. *IEEE Expert*, 10(3), 44-49.

Grover, V. & Teng, J.T.C. (2001). E-commerce and the information market. *Communications of the ACM,* 44(4), 79-86.

Herlocker, J.L. & Konstan, J.A. (2001). Content-independent task-focused recommendation, *IEEE Internet Computing*, 5(6), 40-47, November.

Ide, E. (1971). New experiments in relevance feedback. In G. Salton (Ed.), The Smart Retrieval System – Experiments in automatic document processing,, 337-354. Englewood Cliffs, NJ: Prentice Hall Inc.

Kobayashi, M. & Takeda, K. (2000). Information Retrieval on the Web. *ACM Computing Surveys,* 32(2), 144-173.

Konstan, J., Miller, B., Maltz, D., Herlocker, J., Gordon, L., & Riedl, J. (1997). GroupLens: Applying collaborative filtering to Usernet news. *Communications of ACM,* 40(3), 77-87.

Lang, K. (1995). Newsweeder: Learning to filter news. In *Proceedings of the Twelfth International Conference on Machine-learning,* 331-339.

Lewis, D. (1991). Learning in intelligent information retrieval. In *Proceedings of the Eighth International Workshop on Machine-learning,* 235-239.

Littlestone, N. (1988). Learning quickly when irrelevant attributes abound: A new linear-threshold algorithm. *Machine-learning,* 2, 285-318.

Meng, X., & Chen, Z. (1999). Personalize Web search using information on client's side. In *Advances in Computer Science and Technologies* (985-992). Denver, CO: International Academic Publishers.

Meyyappan, A. (2001). Proposing a new multi-routing agent architecture for E-marketplace. In *Proceedings of the 2001 International Internet Computing Conference,* 275-277.

Pazzani, M., Muramatsu, J. & Billus, D. (1996). Syskill & Webert: Identifying interesting Web Sites. In *Proceedings of the Thirteenth National Conference on Artificial Intelligence,* 54-61.

Perkowitz, M. & Etzioni, O. (2000). Adaptive Web sites: Concept and case study. *Artificial Intelligence,* 118, 245-275.

Rocchio, J. (1971). Relevance feedback in information retrieval. In G. Salton (Ed.), The smart retrieval system—Experiments in Automatic Document Processing,. 313-323. Englewood Cliffs, NJ: Prentice Hall, Inc.

Salton, G. (1989). Automatic text processing: The transformation, analysis, and retrieval of information by computer. Reading, MA: Addison-Wesley.

Salton, G., Wong, A., & Yang, C. (1975). A vector space model for automatic indexing. *Communications of ACM,* 18(11), 613-620.

Santos, S.C., Anglim, S., & Meira, S.R.L. (2001). A framework for Web-commerce search brokers. In *Proceedings the 2001 International of the Internet Computing Conference,* 261-267.

Shakes, J., Langheinrich, M., & Etzioni, O. (1997). Dynamic reference sifting: A case study in the homepage domain. In *Proceedings of the Sixth International World Wide Web Conference,* 189-200.

Terveen, T., Hill, W., Amento, B., McDonald, D., & Creter, J. (1997). Phoaks: A system for sharing recommendation. *Communications of ACM,* 40(3), 50-62.

Tewari, G., Berkovich, A., Gabovich, V., Liang, S., Ramakrishnan A., & Maes, P. (2001). Sustaining individual incentives while maximizing aggregate social welfare: A mediated brokering technique for trading agents in next-generation electronic markets. In Proceedings of the 2001 International Internet Computing Conference, pp. 247-253.

Yuwono, B., & Lee, D. (1996). Search and ranking algorithms for locating resources on the World Wide Web. In *Proceedings of the International Conference on Data Engineering,* 164-171.

Chapter X

World Wide Web Search Engines

Wen-Chen Hu
University of North Dakota

Jyh-Haw Yeh
Boise State University

ABSTRACT

The World Wide Web now holds more than 800 million pages covering almost all issues. The Web's fast growing size and lack of structural style present a new challenge for information retrieval. Numerous search technologies have been applied to Web search engines; however, the dominant search method has yet to be identified. This chapter provides an overview of the existing technologies for Web search engines and classifies them into six categories: 1) hyperlink exploration, 2) information retrieval, 3) metasearches, 4) SQL approaches, 5) content-based multimedia searches, and 6) others. At the end of this chapter, a comparative study of major commercial and experimental search engines is presented, and some future research directions for Web search engines are suggested.

INTRODUCTION

One of the most common tasks performed on the Web is to search Web pages, which is also one of the most frustrating and problematic. The situation is getting worse because of the Web's fast growing size and lack of structural style, as well as the inadequacy of existing Web search engine technologies (Lawrence & Giles, 1999a). Traditional search techniques are based on users typing in search keywords which the search services can then use to locate the desired Web pages. However, this approach normally retrieves too many documents, of which only a small fraction are relevant to the users' needs. Furthermore, the most relevant documents do not necessarily appear at the top of the query output list. A number of corporations and research organizations are taking a variety of approaches to try to solve these problems. These approaches are diverse, and none of them dominate the field. This chapter provides a survey and classification of the available World Wide Web search engine techniques, with an emphasis on nontraditional approaches. Related Web search technology reviews can also be found in (Gudivada, Raghavan, Grosky, & Kasanagottu, 1997; Lawrence & Giles, 1998b; Lawrence & Giles, 1999b; Lu & Feng, 1998).

Requirements of Web Search Engines

It is first necessary to examine what kind of features a Web search engine is expected to have in order to conduct effective and efficient Web searches and what kind of challenges may be faced in the process of developing new Web search techniques. The requirements for a Web search engine are listed below, in order of importance:

1. effective and efficient location and ranking of Web documents;
2. thorough Web coverage;
3. up-to-date Web information;
4. unbiased access to Web pages;
5. an easy-to-use user interface which also allows users to compose any reasonable query;
6. expressive and useful search results; and
7. A system that adapts well to user queries.

Web Search Engine Technologies

Numerous Web search engine technologies have been proposed, and each technology employs a very different approach. This survey classifies the technologies into six categories: i) hyperlink exploration, ii) information retrieval, iii) metasearches, iv) SQL approaches, v) content-based multimedia searches, and vi) others. The chapter is organized as follows: Section 2 introduces the general structure of a search engine, and Sections 3 to 8 introduce each of the six Web search engine technologies in turn. A comparative study of major commercial and experimental search engines is shown in Section 9 and the final section gives a summary and suggests future research directions.

SEARCH ENGINE STRUCTURE

Two different approaches are applied to Web search services: genuine search engines and directories. The difference lies in how listings are compiled:

- Search engines, such as Google, create their listings automatically.
- A directory, such as Yahoo!, depends on humans for its listings.

Some search engines, known as hybrid search engines, maintain an associated directory. Search engines traditionally consist of three components: the crawler, the indexing software, and the search and ranking software (Greenberg & Garber, 1999; Yuwono & Lee, 1996). Figure 1 shows the system structure of a typical search engine.

Crawler

A crawler is a program that automatically scans various Web sites and collects Web documents from them. Crawlers follow the links on a site to find other relevant pages. Two search algorithms—breadth-first searches and depth-first searches—are widely used by crawlers to traverse the Web. The crawler views the Web as a graph, with the nodes being the objects located at Uniform Resource Locators (URLs). The objects could be (Hypertext Transfer Protocols (HTTPs), File Transfer Protocols (FTPs), mailto (e-mail), news, telnet, etc. They also return to sites periodically to look for changes. To speed up the collection of Web

Figure 1: System structure of a Web search engine

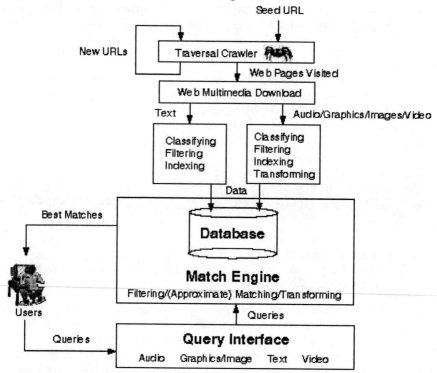

documents, several crawlers are usually sent out to traverse the Web at the same time. Three simple tools can be used to implement an experimental crawler:

- lynx: Lynx is a text browser for Unix systems. For example, the command "lynx -dump -source http://www.w3c.org/" downloads the Web page source code at http://www.w3c.org/.
- java.net: The java.net package of Java language provides plenty of networking utilities. Two classes in the package, java.net.URL and java.net.URLConnection, can be used to download Web pages.
- Comprehensive Perl Archive Network (CPAN): Perl has been used intensively for Web-related applications. Some scripts provided by CPAN at http://www.cpan.org/ are useful for crawler construction.

To construct an efficient and practical crawler, some other networking tools have to be used.

Indexing Software

Automatic indexing is the process of algorithmically examining information items to build a data structure that can be quickly searched. Filtering (Baeza-Yates, 1992) is one of the most important pre-processes for indexing. Filtering is a typical transformation in information retrieval and is often used to reduce the size of a document and/or standardize it to simplify searching. Traditional search engines utilize the following information, provided by HTML scripts, to locate the desired Web pages:

- Content: Page content provides the most accurate, full-text information. However, it is also the least-used type of information, since context extraction is still far less practical.

- Descriptions: Page descriptions can either be constructed from the metatags or submitted by Web masters or reviewers.
- Hyperlink: Hyperlinks contain high-quality semantic clues to a page's topic. A hyperlink to a page represents an implicit endorsement of the page to which it points (Chakrabarti et al., 1999).
- Hyperlink text: Hyperlink text is normally a title or brief summary of the target page.
- Keywords: Keywords can be extracted from full-text documents or metatags.
- Page title: The title tag, which is only valid in a head section, defines the title of an HTML document.
- Text with a different font: Emphasized text is usually given a different font to highlight its importance.
- The first sentence: The first sentence of a document is also likely to give crucial information related to the document.

Search and Ranking Software

Query processing is the activity of analyzing a query and comparing it to indexes to find relevant items. A user enters a keyword or keywords, along with Boolean modifiers such as "and," "or," or "not," into a search engine, which then scans indexed Web pages for the keywords. To determine in which order to display pages to the user, the engine uses an algorithm to rank pages that contain the keywords (Zhang & Dong, 2000). For example, the engine may count the number of times the keyword appears on a page. To save time and space, the engine may only look for keywords in metatags, which are HTML tags that provide information about a Web page. Unlike most HTML tags, metatags do not affect a document's appearance. Instead, they include such information as a Web page's contents and some relevant keywords. The following six sections give various methods of indexing, searching, and ranking the Web pages.

HYPERLINK EXPLORATION

Hypermedia documents contain cross references to other related documents by using hyperlinks, which allow the user to move easily from one to the other. Links can be tremendously important sources of information for indexers; the creation of a hyperlink by the author of a Web page represents an implicit endorsement of the page being to which it points. This approach is based on identifying two important types of Web pages for a given topic:

- Authorities, which provide the best source of information on the topic, and
- Hubs, which provide collections of links to authorities.

For the example of professional basketball information, the official National Basketball Association site (http://www.nba.com/) is considered to be an authority, while the ESPN site (http://www.espn.com/) is a hub. Authorities and hubs are either given top ranking in the search results or used to find related Web pages (Dean & Henzinger, 1999).

Analyzing the interconnections of a series of related pages can identify the authorities and hubs for a particular topic. A simple method to update a non-negative authority with a weight x_p and a non-negative hub with a weight y_p is given by Chakrabarti et al. (1999). If a page is pointed to by many good hubs, its authority weight is updated by using the following formula:

$$x_p = \sum_{q \text{ such that } q \to p} y_q \, ,$$

where the notation $q \circledR \eth p$ indicates that q links to p. Similarly, if a page points to many good authorities, its hub weight is updated via

$$y_p = \sum_{q \text{ such that } p \to q} x_q \, .$$

Unfortunately, applying the above formulas to the entire Web to find authorities and hubs is impracticable. Ideally, the formulas are applied to a small collection $S_{s\eth}$ of pages that contain plenty of relevant documents. The concepts of a root set and a base set have been proposed by Kleinberg (1999) to find $S_{s\eth}$. The root set is usually constructed by collecting the t highest-ranked pages for the query $s\eth$ from a search engine such as Google or Yahoo!. However, the root set may not contain most of the strongest authorities. A base set is therefore built by including any page pointed to by a page in the root set and any page that points to a page in the root set. Figure 2 shows an example of a root set and a base set. The above formulas can then be applied to a much smaller set, the base set, instead of the entire Web.

In addition to the methods used to find authorities and hubs, a number of search methods based on connectivity have been proposed. A comparative study of various hypertext link analysis algorithms is given in (Borodin et al., 2001). The most widely used method is a Page Rank model (Brin & Page, 1998), which suggests the reputation of a page on a topic is proportional to the sum of the reputation weights of pages pointing to it on the same topic. That is, links emanating from pages with high reputations are weighted more heavily. The concepts of authorities and hubs, together with the Page Rank model, can also be used to compute the reputation rank of a page; those topics for which the page has a good reputation are then identified (Rafiei & Mendelzon, 2000). Some other ad hoc methods include an Hyperlink Vector Voting (HVV) method (Li, 1998) and a system known as WebQuery (Carriere & Kazman, 1997). The former method uses the content of hyperlinks to a document to rank its relevance to the query terms, while the latter system studies the structural relationships among the nodes returned in a content-based query and gives the highest ranking to the most highly connected nodes. An improved algorithm obtained by augmenting with content analysis is introduced in Bharat and Henzinger (1998).

Figure 2: Expanding the root set into a base set

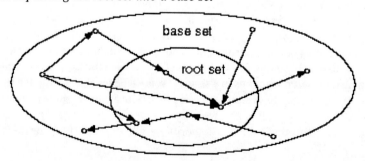

INFORMATION RETRIEVAL (IR)

IR techniques are widely used in Web document searches (Gudivada et al, 1997). Among them, relevance feedback and data clustering are two of the most popular techniques used by search engines. The former method has not so far been applied to any commercial products because it requires some interaction with users, who normally prefer to use a keyword-only interface. The latter method has achieved more success since it does not require any interaction with users to achieve acceptable results.

Relevance Feedback

An initial query is usually a wild guess. Retrieved query results are then used to help construct a more precise query or modify the database indexes (Chang & Hsu, 1999). For example, if the following query is submitted to a search engine—which TOYOTA dealer in Atlanta has the lowest price for a Corolla 2002?, the engine may produce the following list of ranked results:

1. Get the BEST price on a new Toyota, Lexus car or truck. http://www.toyotaforless.com/
2. Toyota of Glendale¾ðYour #1 Toyota dealer. http://www.toyota-of-glendale.com/
3. Leith Toyota¾ðRaleigh, North Carolina. http://www.leithtoyota.com/ f_more_about_us.html
4. Atlanta rental cars & auto rentals. http://www.bnm.com/atl2.htm

This list includes three relevant results: 1, 2, and 3, and one irrelevant result: 4. The following two relevance feedback methods can be used to improve the search results:

- Query modification: Adjusts the initial query in an attempt to avoid unrelated or less-related query results. For example, the above query could be modified by adding a condition excluding rental cars.
- Indexing modification: Through feedback from the users, system administrators can modify an unrelated document's terms to render it unrelated or less related to such a query. For example, the information concerning rental cars could be removed from the database indexes of car sales and prices.

For the above example, the search results after modification should not include Result #4.

Data Clustering

Data clustering is used to improve the search results by dividing the whole data set into data clusters. Each data cluster contains objects of high similarity, and clusters are produced that group documents relevant to the user's query separately from irrelevant ones. For example, the formula below gives a similarity measure:

$$S_{D_i, D_j} = \frac{2 \sum_{k=1}^{L} \left(weight_{ik} \cdot weight_{jk} \right)}{\sum_{k=1}^{L} weight_{ik}^2 + \sum_{k=1}^{L} weight_{jk}^2},$$

where $weight_{ik}$ is the weight assigned to $term_k$ in a document D_i (Baeza-Yates, 1992). Clustering should not be based on the whole Web resource, but on smaller separate query results. In Zamir and Etzioni (1998), a Suffix Tree Clustering (STC) algorithm based on phrases shared between documents is used to create clusters. Beside clustering the search results, a proposed similarity function has been used to cluster similar queries according to their contents as well as user logs (Wen, Nie, & Zhang, 2001). The resulting clusters can provide useful information for Frequently Asked Queries (FAQ) identification. Another Web document clustering algorithm is suggested in Chang and Hsu (1999).

METASEARCHES

None of the current search engines is able to cover the Web comprehensively. Using an individual search engine may miss some critical information that is provided by other engines. Metasearch engines (Dreilinger & Howe, 1997; Howe & Dreilinger, 1997; Selberg & Etzioni, 1997) conduct a search using several other search engines simultaneously and then present the results in some sort of integrated format. This lets users see at a glance which particular search engine returned the best results for a query without having to search each one individually. They typically do not use their own Web indexes. Figure 3 shows the system structure of a metasearch engine, which consists of three major components:

- Dispatch: Determines to which search engines a specific query is sent. The selection is usually based on network and local computational resources, as well as the long-term performance of search engines on specific query terms.
- Interface: Adapts the user's query format to match the format of a particular search engine, which varies from engine to engine.
- Display: Raw results from the selected search engines are integrated for display to the user. Each search engine also produces different raw results from other search engines and these must be combined to give a uniform format for ease-of-use.

Current search engines provide a multiplicity of interfaces and results that make the construction of metasearch engines a very difficult task. The STARTS protocol (Gravano,

Figure 3: System structure of a metasearch engine

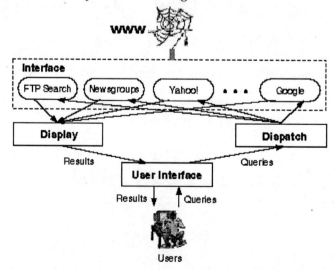

Chang, Garcia-Molina, Lagoze, & Paepcke, 1997) has been proposed to standardize Internet retrievals and searches. The goals are to choose the best sources (search engines) to evaluate a query, submit the query to the sources selected, and finally merge the query results obtained from the different sources. However, this protocol has received little recognition since none of the most-often-used search engines apply it. Another approach (Huang, Hemmje, & Neuhold, 2000) to solving this problem is to use an adaptive model which employs a "mediator-wrapper" architecture. The mediator provides users with integrated access to multiple heterogeneous data sources, while each wrapper represents access to a specific data source. It maps a query from a general mediator format into the specific wrapper format required by each search engine.

Metasearch engines rely on the summaries and ranks of URLs returned by standard search engines. However, not all standard search engines give unbiased results and this will distort the metasearch results. The NEC Research Institute (NECI) metasearch engine (Lawrence & Giles, 1998a) solved this problem by downloading and analyzing each document and then displaying results in a format that shows the query terms in context. This helps users more readily determine if the document is relevant without having to download each page. The authors of Q-pilot (Sugiura & Etzioni, 2000) noticed that thousands of specialized, topic-specific search engines are accessible on the Web, and these topic-specific engines return far better results for "on topic" queries than standard search engines. Q-pilot dynamically routes each user query to the most appropriate specialized search engines by using two methods: neighborhood-based topic identification, and query expansion.

SQL APPROACHES

Learning how to use a new language is normally an arduous task for users. However, a new system which uses a familiar language is usually adopted relatively smoothly by the users. Structured Query Language (SQL) is a well-known and widely-used database language. SQL approaches (Florescu, Levy, & Mendelzon, 1998; Mendelzon & Milo, 1998) view the World Wide Web as a huge database where each record matches a Web page, and use SQL-like languages to support effective and flexible query processing. A typical SQL-like language syntax (Konopnicki & Shmueli, 1998; Mendelzon, Mihaila, & Milo, 1997; Spertus & Stein, 2000) is

Query := **select** Attribute_List **from** Domain_Specifications
[**where** Search_Conditions];

Three query examples are given below to show the use of the language.

SQL Example 1: *Find pages in the World Wide Web Consortium (W3C) site where the pages have fewer than 2000 bytes.*
        select url **from** http://www.w3c.org/ **where** bytes < 2000;
url is a page's URL and each page has attributes such as bytes, keywords, and text.

SQL Example 2: *Find educational pages containing the keyword "database."*
        select url **from** http://%.edu/ **where** "database" **in** keywords;

Regular expressions are widely used in the query language, e.g., the symbol "%" is a wild card matching any string. The **in** predicate checks whether the string "database" is one of the keywords.

SQL Example 3: *Find documents about "XML" in the W3C Web site where the documents have paths of length two or less from the root page.*

> select   d.url, d.title
>> from   Document d **such that** 'http://www.w3c.org/' =|®ð|® ® d
>> where   d.text **like** '%XML%';

The symbol "|ð" is an alternation and the symbol "®ð" is a link. The string "=|®|®®" is a regular expression that represents the set of paths of length of one or two. The **like** predicate is used for string matching in this example.

Various SQL-like languages have been proposed for Web search engines. The methods introduced previously treat the Web as a graph of discrete objects; another object-oriented approach (Arocena & Mendelzon, 1998) considers the Web as a graph of structured objects. However, neither approach has achieved much success because of its complicated syntax, especially for the latter method.

CONTENT-BASED MULTIMEDIA SEARCHES

In order to allow for the wide range of new types of data that are now available on the World Wide Web, including audio, video, graphics, and images, the use of hypermedia was introduced to extend the capabilities of hypertext. The first Internet search engine, Archie, was created in 1990; however, it was not until the introduction of multimedia to the browser Mosaic that the number of Internet documents began to increase explosively. Only a few multimedia search engines are available currently, most of which use name or keyword matching where the keywords are entered by Web reviewers rather than using automatic indexing. The low number of content-based multimedia search engines is mainly due to the difficulty of automated multimedia indexing. Numerous multimedia indexing methods have been suggested in the literature (Chang & Hsu, 1992; Yoshitaka & Ichikawa, 1999), yet most do not meet the efficiency requirements of Web multimedia searches, where users expect both a prompt response and the search of a huge volume of Web multimedia data. A few content-based image and video search engines are available online (Benitez, Beigi, & Chang, 1998; Gevers & Smeulders, 1999; Lew, 2000; Smith & Chang, 1997; Taycher, Cascia, & Sclaroff, 1997). Various indexing methods are applied to locate the desired images or video. The major technologies include using camera/object motion, colors, examples, locations, positional color/texture, shapes, sketches, text, and texture, as well as relevance feedback (Flickner et al., 1995). However, a de facto Web image or video search engine is still out of reach because the system's key component¾ðimage or video collection and indexing¾ðis either not yet fully automated or not practicable. Similarly, effective Web audio search engines have yet to be constructed since audio information retrieval is considered to be one of the most difficult challenges for multimedia retrieval (Foote, 1999).

OTHERS

Apart from the above major search techniques, some ad hoc methods worth mentioning include:

• Work aimed at making the components needed for Web searches more efficient and effective, such as better ranking algorithms and more efficient crawlers. In Zhang and

Dong (2000), a ranking algorithm based on a Markov model is proposed. It synthesizes the relevance, authority, integrativity, and novelty of each Web resource, and can be computed efficiently through solving a group of linear equations. A variety of other improved ranking algorithms can be found in Dwork, Kumar, Naor, and Sivakumar and Singhal and Kaszkiel (2001, 2001).

- Various enhanced crawlers can be found in the literature (Aggarwal, Al-Garawi, & Yu, 2001; Edwards, McCurley, & Tomlin, 2001; Najork & Wiener, 2001). Some crawlers are extensible, personally customized, relocatable, scalable, and Web-site-specific (Heydon & Najork, 1999; Miller & Bharat, 1998). Web viewers usually consider certain Web pages more important. A crawler which collects those "important" pages first is advantageous for users (Cho, Garcia-Molina, & Page, 1998).

- Artificial Intelligence (AI) can also be used to collect and recommend Web pages. The Webnaut system (Nick & Themis, 2001) learns the user's interests and can adapt as his or her interests change over time. The learning process is driven by user feedback to an intelligent agent's filtered selections.

- To make the system easier to use, an interface has been designed to accept and understand a natural language query (Ask Jeeves, http://www.askjeeves.com).

MAJOR SEARCH ENGINES

Some of the currently available major commercial search engines are listed in Table 1, although many table entries are incomplete as some of the information is classified as

Table 1: Major commercial Web search engines. SE: Search Engine and AS: Answering Service

No.	Name	URL	Type	Backup	Method
1	AOL Search	http://search.aol.com/	Hybrid SE	Open Directory	
2	AltaVista	http://www.altavista.com/	SE	LookSmart	
3	Ask Jeeves	http://www.askjeeves.com/	AS		natural language
4	Direct Hit	http://www.directhit.com/	SE	HotBot	hyperlink
5	Excite	http://www.excite.com/	SE	LookSmart	
6	FAST Search	http://www.alltheweb.com/			scalability
7	Google	http://www.google.com/	SE		hyperlink
8	HotBot	http://www.hotbot.com/	Hybrid SE	Direct Hit	
9	IWon	http://www.iwon.com/	Hybrid SE	Inktomi	
10	Inktomi	http://www.inktomi.com/	SE		
11	LookSmart	http://www.looksmart.com/	Directory	Inktomi	reviewers
12	Lycos	http://www.lycos.com/	Directory	Open Directory	
13	MSN Search	http://search.msn.com/	Directory	LookSmart	
14	Netscape Search	http://search.netscape.com/	SE	Open Directory	
15	Northern Light	http://www.northernlight.com/	SE		filtering
16	Open Directory	http://dmoz.org/	Directory		volunteers
17	RealNames	http://www.realnames.com/			keywords
18	Yahoo!	http://www.yahoo.com/	Directory	Google	reviewers

Table 2: Major experimental Web search engines

No.	Name	URL	Method
1	Clever	http://www.almaden.ibm.com/cs/k53/clever.html	hyperlink
2	Grouper	http://longinus.cs.washington.edu/grouper2.html	clustering
3	HuskySearch	http://huskysearch.cs.washington.edu/	metasearch
4	ImageRover	http://www.cs.bu.edu/groups/ivc/ImageRover/Home.html	image
5	ImageScape	http://skynet.liacs.nl/	image
6	Inquirus	http://www.neci.nj.nec.com/homepages/lawrence /inquirus.html	metasearch
7	Mercator	http://www.ctr.columbia.edu/metaseek/	image
8	MetaSEEk	http://www.research.compaq.com/SRC/mercator/	crawler
9	PicToSeek	http://zomax.wins.uva.nl:5345/ret_user/	image
10	W3QS	http://www.cs.technion.ac.il/~konop/w3qs.html	SQL
11	WebOQL	http://www.cs.tornoto.edu/~gus/weboql/	Object SQL
12	WebSQL	http://www.cs.toronto.edu/~websql/	SQL

confidential due to business considerations (Search Engine Watch, http://www.searchenginewatch.com). Most search services are backed up by or are cooperating with several other services. This is because an independent or stand-alone service contains less information and thus tends to lose its users. In the table, the column Backup gives the major backup information provider, and most unfilled methods use keyword matching to locate the desired documents. Most search engines on the list not only provide Web search services but also act as portals, which are Web home bases from which users can access a variety of services, including searches, e-commerce, chat rooms, news, etc. Table 2 lists some major experimental search engines, which use advanced search technologies not yet implemented by the commercial search engines. The list in Table 2 is a snapshot of the current situation; the list is highly volatile, either because a successful experimental search engine is usually commercialized in a short time or because a prototype system is normally removed after its founders leave the organization. The two tables list major general-purpose search engines; special-purpose search engines, including specialty searches, regional searches, kid searches, etc., are not considered in this chapter. They use much smaller databases and therefore give more precise and limited search results.

SUMMARY

In less than a decade, the World Wide Web has become one of the three major media, with the other two being print and television. Searching for Web pages is both one of the most common tasks performed on the Web and one of the most frustrating and problematic. This chapter gave an overview of the current technologies for Web search engines with an emphasis on non-traditional approaches and classified the technologies into six categories. However, apart from the traditional keyword matching techniques, no one method dominates Web search engine technologies. The major reason for this is that the amount of information posted on the World Wide Web is huge and the page formats vary widely.

Future Directions

Users of search engines often submit ambiguous queries. Ambiguous queries can be categorized into four types: 1) disorderly, 2) incomplete, 3) incorrect, and 4) superfluous queries. Below are examples of perfect and ambiguous queries, and the ranked search results from Infoseek at http://www.infoseek.com/ for the book *Intelligent multimedia information retrieval,* edited by Mark T. Maybury (1997).

- Perfect query: *Intelligent multimedia information retrieval*
  1. Intelligent multimedia information retrieval
- Disorderly query: *Multimedia information intelligent retrieval*
  1. Artificial intelligence, fuzzy logic and neural networks
  2. Intelligent access to information: research in natural language, information retrieval, computer vision, multimedia and database
  3. Multimedia color PC notebooks
  4. Intelligent multimedia information retrieval
- Incomplete query: *Multimedia information retrieval*
  1. Abstract Stein Mulleller Thiel 95
  2. Corpora Oct 1998 to -: Corpora: TWLT 14: language technology in multimedia information
  3. 3 2.1 Introduction to the workplan
  ...
  6. Intelligent multimedia information retrieval
- Incorrect query: *Intelligent multimedia information retrieval*
  1. Artificial intelligence research laboratory at Iowa State University
  2. Vasant Honavar's home in cyberspace
  3. CIIR multimedia indexing
  ...
  31. Intelligent multimedia information retrieval
- Superfluous query: *Intelligent multimedia information retrieval systems*
  1. Research in multimedia and multimodal parsing and generation
  2. Intelligent multimedia information retrieval

This example shows that even a slight variation in the query produces significant differences among the search results. Users tend to submit ambiguous queries to search engines, most of which use the technology of keyword matching to look for the desired pages. The ambiguity creates undesired search results if keyword matching is used.

Since the introduction of eXtensible Markup Language (XML) (http://www.w3c.org/XML), more and more Web documents are published in XML. An XML document not only provides the same information, such as keywords, hyperlinks, descriptions, etc., that a function-like HTML document supplies, but also structural information. The structural information is one of the most crucial features of an XML document, and is not supplied by an HTML document. XML document searches (Hu, Zhong, Lin, Chen, 2001) are expected to be the next major research direction for Web search engines, as using this structural information is likely to give much better search results.

REFERENCES

Aggarwal, C.C., Al-Garawi, F., & Yu, P.S. (2001). Intelligent crawling on the World Wide Web with arbitrary predicates. In *Proceedings of the 10th International World Wide Web Conference*, Hong Kong.

Arocena, G.O., & Mendelzon, A.O. (1998). WebOQL: Restructuring documents, databases and Webs. In *Proceedings of the 14th International Conference on Data Engineering*, Orlando, Florida.

Baeza-Yates, R.A. (1992). Introduction to data structures and algorithms related to information retrieval. In W. B. Frakes and R. A. Baeza-Yates, (eds.), *Information Retrieval Data Structures & Algorithms*, 13-27, Upper Saddle River, NJ: Prentice Hall.

Benitez, A.B., Beigi, M., & Chang, S.F. (1998). Using relevance feedback in content-based image metasearch. *IEEE Internet Computing*, 2(4):59-69.

Bharat, K., & Henzinger, M., (1998). Improved algorithms for topic distillation in a hyperlinked environment. In *Proceedings of the 21st International ACM SIGIR Conference on Research and Development in Information Retrieval*, pages 104-111.

Borodin, A., Roberts, G.O., Rosenthal, J.S., & Tsaparas, P., (2001). Finding authorities and hubs from link structures on the World Wide Web. In *Proceedings of the 10th International World Wide Web Conference*, Hong Kong.

Brin, S., &. Page, L., (1998). The anatomy of a large-scale hypertextual Web search engine. *Computer Networks and ISDN Systems*, 30:107-117.

Carriere, J., & Kazman, R., (1997). WebQuery: Searching and visualizing the Web through connectivity. *Computer Networks and ISDN Systems*, 29(11):1257-1267.

Chakrabarti, S., Dom, B.E., Kumar, S.R., Raghavan, R., Rajagopalan, S., Tomkins, A., Gibson, D., & Kleinberg, J., (1999). Mining the Web's link structure. *IEEE Computer*, 32(8): 60-67.

Chang, S.-K., & Hsu, A., (1992). Image information systems: Where do we go from here? *IEEE Transactions on Knowledge and Data Engineering, Special Issue Celebrating the 40th Anniversary of the Computer Society*, 4(5):431-442.

Chang, C.-H., & Hsu, C.-C., (1999). Enabling concept-based relevance feedback for information retrieval on the WWW. *IEEE Transactions on Knowledge and Data Engineering*, 11(4):595-609.

Cho, J., Garcia-Molina, H., & Page, L., (1998). Efficient crawling through URL ordering. In *Proceedings of the 7th World Wide Web Conference*, Brisbane, Australia.

Dean, J., & Henzinger, M.R. (1999). Finding Related Web Pages in the World Wide Web. In *Proceedings of the 8th International World Wide Web Conference*, pages 389-401, Toronto, Canada.

Dreilinger, D., & Howe, A.E., (1997). Experiences with selecting search engines using metasearch. *ACM Transactions on Information Systems*, 15(3):195-222.

Dwork, C., Kumar, R., Naor, M., & Sivakumar, D., (2001). Rank aggregation methods for the Web. In *Proceedings of the 10th International World Wide Web Conference*, Hong Kong.

Edwards, J., McCurley, K., & Tomlin, J., (2001). An adaptive model for optimizing performance of an incremental Web crawler. In *Proceedings of the 10th International World Wide Web Conference*, Hong Kong.

Flickner, M., et al. (1995). Query by image and video content: The QBIC system. *IEEE Computer*, 28(9):23-32.

Florescu, D., Levy, A. & Mendelzon, A., (1998). Database techniques for the World Wide Web: A survey. *ACM SIGMOD Record*, 27(3):59-74.

Foote, J. (1999). An overview of audio information retrieval. *Multimedia Systems*, 7(1):2-10.

Garofalakis, J., Kappos, P., & Mourloukos, D., (1999). Web site optimization using page popularity. *IEEE Internet Computing*, 3(4):22-29.

Gevers, T., & Smeulders, A., (1999). The PicToSeek WWW image search system. In *Proceedings of the IEEE International Conference on Multimedia Computing and Systems*, 264-269, Florence, Italy.

Gravano, L., Chang, K, Garcia-Molina, H., Lagoze, C., & Paepcke, A., (1997). STARTS: Stanford protocol proposal for Internet retrieval and search. In *Proceedings of the ACM SIGMOD International Conference on Management of Data*.

Greenberg, I., & Garber, L., (1999). Searching for new search technologies. *IEEE Computer*, 32(8):4-11.

Gudivada, K. N., Raghavan, V.V., Grosky, W.I., & Kasanagottu, R., (1997). Information retrieval on the World Wide Web. *IEEE Internet Computing*, 1(5):58-68.

Heydon, A., & Najork, M., (1999). Mercator: A scalable, extensible Web crawler. *World Wide Web*, 2(4):219-229.

Howe, A. E., & Dreilinger, D., (1997). SavvySearch: A meta search engine that learns which search engines to query. *AI Magazine*, 18(2).

Hu, W.-C., Zhong, Y., Lin, W.-C.,&. Chen, J.-F., (2001). An XML World Wide Web search engine using approximate structural matching. In *Proceedings of the 5th World Multi-Conference on Systemics, Cybernetics and Informatics*, Orlando, Florida, July 22-25.

Huang, L., Hemmje, M., & Neuhold, E.J., (2000). ADMIRE: An adaptive data model for meta search engines. *Computer Networks (The International Journal of Computer and Telecommunications Networking)*, 33(1-6):431-448.

Kleinberg, J. M (1999). Authoritative sources in a hyperlinked environment. *JACM*, 46(5):604-632.

Konopnicki, D., & Shmueli, O., (1998). Information gathering in the World Wide Web: The W3QL query language and the W3QS system. *ACM Transactions on Database Systems*, 23(4):369-410.

Lawrence, S., & Giles, C.L., (1998a). Context and page analysis for improved Web search. *IEEE Internet Computing*, 2(4):38-46.

Lawrence, S., & Giles, C.L., (1998b). Searching the World Wide Web. *Science*, 280:98-100.

Lawrence, S., and C. L. Giles (1999a). Accessibility of information on the Web. *Nature*, 400:107-109.

Lawrence, S., & Giles, C.L, (1999b). Searching the Web: General and scientific information access. *IEEE Communications*, 37(1):116-122.

Lew, M. S. (2000). Next generation Web searches for visual content. *IEEE Computer*, 33(11):46-53.

Li, Y. (1998). Toward a qualitative search engine. *IEEE Internet Computing*, 2(4):24-29.

Lu, H., & Feng, L., (1998). Integrating database and World Wide Web technologies. *World Wide Web*, 1(2):73-86.

Maybury, M. T. (1997). *Intelligent multimedia information retrieval*. Cambridge, MA: MIT Press.

Mendelzon, A.O., & Milo, T., (1998). Formal models of Web queries. *Information Systems*, 23(8):615-637.

Mendelzon, A.O., Mihaila, G., & Milo, T., (1997). Querying the World Wide Web. *International Journal on Digital Libraries*, 1(1):54-67.

Miller, R. C., &. Bharat, K., (1998). SPHINX: A framework for creating personal, site-specific Web crawlers. In *Proceedings of the 7th International World Wide Web Conference*, Brisbane, Australia.

Najork, M. A., & Wiener, J., (2001). Breadth-first search crawling yields high-quality pages.

In *Proceedings of the 10th International World Wide Web Conference*, 114-118, Hong Kong.

Nick, Z. Z., Themis, P., (2001). Web search using a genetic algorithm. *IEEE Internet Computing*, 5(2):18-26.

Rafiei, D., & Mendelzon, A.O., (2000). What is this page known for? Computing Web page reputations. In *Proceedings of the 9th International World Wide Web Conference* Amsterdam, Netherlands.

Selberg, E., & Etzioni, O., (1997). The MetaCrawler architecture for resource aggregation on the Web. *IEEE Expert*, 12(1):8-14.

Singhal, A., & Kaszkiel, M., (2001). A case study in Web search using TREC algorithms. In *Proceedings of the 10th International World Wide Web Conference*, 708-716, Hong Kong.

Smith, J. R., & Chang, S.-F. (1997). An image and video search engine for the World-Wide Web. In *Proceedings of the Symposium on Electronic Imaging: Science and Technology¾δStorage and Retrieval for Image and Video Databases V, IS&T/SPIE*, San Jose, California.

Spertus, E., & Stein, L.A., (2000). Squeal: A structured query language for the Web. In *Proceedings of the 9th International World Wide Web Conference*, Amsterdam, Netherlands.

Sugiura, A., & Etzioni, O., (2000). Query routing for Web search engines: Architecture and experiments. In *Proceedings of the 9th International World Wide Web Conference*, Amsterdam, Netherlands.

Taycher, L., Cascia, M.L., & Sclaroff, S., (1997). Image digestion and relevance feedback in the ImageRover WWW search engine. In *Proceedings of the International Conference on Visual Information*, San Diego.

Wen, J.-R., Nie, J.-Y., & Zhang, H.-J., (2001). Clustering user queries of a search engine. In *Proceedings of the 10th International World Wide Web Conference*, Hong Kong.

Yoshitaka, A., & Ichikawa, T., (1999). A survey on content-based retrieval for multimedia databases. *IEEE Transactions on Knowledge and Data Engineering*, 11(1):81-93.

Yuwono, B., & Lee, D.L., (1996). WISE: A World Wide Web resource database system. *IEEE Transactions on Knowledge and Data Engineering*, 8(4):548-554.

Zamir, O., and O. Etzioni (1998). Web document clustering: A feasibility demonstration. In *Proceedings of the 19th International ACM SIGIR Conference on Research and Development in Information Retrieval*, 46-54, Melbourne, Australia.

Zhang, D., & Dong, Y., (2000). An efficient algorithm to rank Web resources. In *Proceedings of the 9th International World Wide Web Conference*, Amsterdam, Netherlands.

Chapter XI

Retrieval Of Multimedia Data On The Web: An Architectural Framework

Mohammed Moharrum, Stephan Olariu, and Hussein Abdel-Wahab
Old Dominion University

ABSTRACT

The objective of this chapter is to introduce the reader to a general architectural framework for a broad array of retrievals of multimedia data required by various applications. This framework contains more than the traditional client/server architecture and even more than the existing three-tier architectures. This chapter introduces the reader to many critical issues involved in multimedia retrieval over the Internet. A new architectural framework is proposed to cover a variety of multimedia applications over the Internet and the World Wide Web. This framework has the three main objectives of (1) proposing a layered architecture to facilitated design and separate different issues, (2) covering a large number of multimedia applications, and finally, (3) making use of existing and well-established technology, such as Mobile Agents, SQL databases, and cache managements schemes. The proposed architectural framework separates issues involved in multimedia retrieval into five layers, namely: keyword searching and data servers, proxy servers, domain and department archives, mobile user agents, and the users. Through these five layers, various customized solutions to a large array of problems will be proposed and applied. The chapter offers, but is not limited to, solutions for different problems that arise in retrieval of multimedia data. A list of important open problems is identified at the end of the chapter.

INTRODUCTION

Multimedia data plays an essential role in today's e-business applications. Indeed, a large array of e-business applications relies directly or indirectly on multimedia data, ranging from simple news lines to sophisticated multimedia libraries. We can say without hesitation that most of data being transferred nowadays through the Internet involves some multimedia component.

Overview of the Architecture

The objective of this chapter is to propose a general architectural framework for a broad array of retrievals of multimedia data required by various applications. This framework contains more than the traditional client/server architecture and even more than the existing three-tier architectures. To the best of our knowledge, our model subsumes all the currently existing models.

The most severe problem with multimedia applications is performance. This problem may incorporate many issues that are beyond the control of the application vendor, or even the network administrator. In our proposal, we suggest different architectural levels to act as performance degradation protectors. The main goal of the architectural level hierarchy is to hide the technical details of the search process from the user. The second major goal of the hierarchy is the intelligent filtering of data in order to avoid undue overload on the system.

The proposed framework supports different types of multimedia data retrieval that will serve different application areas. These types include meta-data retrieval and both feature and semantic Content-Based Retrieval (CBR) that will support Content-Based Video on Demand Applications.

As one of the goals of the e-business system is to hide all complicated details from the user, making the most complicated transactions look straightforward, we employ mobile agents to represent the user at different levels and to perform all the necessary work for him.

Our proposal for employing mobile agents includes two entities for each user, namely, a Home base and Mobile Agent Instances. The Home base resides at the server closest to the user, represents the user, and acts on his behalf. In addition, the Home base applies suitable data reduction techniques to data before sending it back to the user. Moreover, the Home base is responsible for collecting data returned by mobile agent instances and for organizing it into media presentations.

Every mobile agent instance propagates and replicates itself in the system, moving as close to the data servers as possible, in order to extract the data requested by the user. In order to reduce network traffic, different mobile units may also apply some data filtering techniques before sending data back.

The proposed architecture contains the following five layers:
1. keyword searching and data servers;
2. proxy servers;
3. domain and department archives;
4. mobile agents for the users; and
5. the users.

Review of Multimedia Content-Based Retrieval Models

In the early days of multimedia databases, multimedia data was being handled externally. As multimedia data is inserted into the database, less effort is devoted to identify, analyze and determine its contents, considering it as black boxes knowing everything about their locations, labels, creators, etc., but knowing nothing about their contents. However, most of the listed applications incorporate queries not only about the external data, but also about the contents of the black boxes. Content-based modeling, indexing, and retrieval makeup the research area that deals with such contents of multimedia data. There are two types of multimedia CBR described below.

Feature content-based querying, indexing, and retrieval (Moharrum, 2000) of multimedia data incorporate retrieving multimedia data based on visual or audible features extracted

Figure 1: The proposed architectural framework

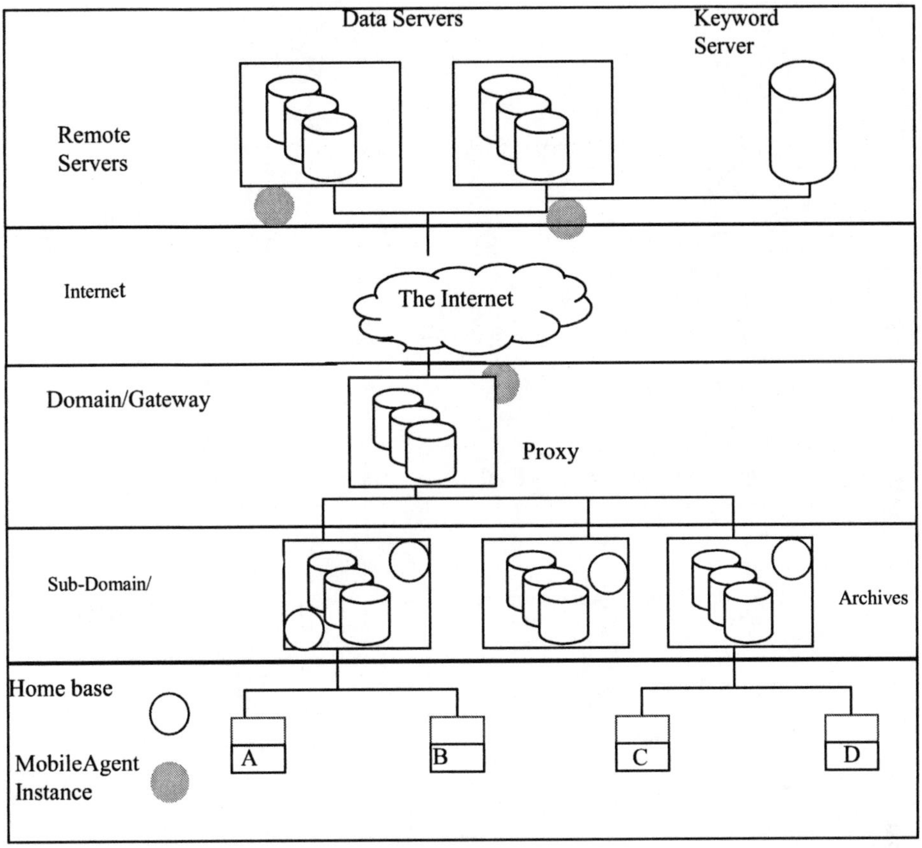

from it (e.g., video frames, audio clips, or still images). These features include color, texture, shape, or motion in video and image data, as well as frequency range, tone and any other audio-specific features that can be extracted from audio data. Most of these features are automatically extracted and indexed using techniques borrowed from image processing and analysis, computer vision and Artificial Intelligence (Hampapur, Jain & Weymouth, 1994). An example of feature content-based multimedia querying and retrieval systems is VisualSeek (Smith & Chang, 1996).

Semantic content-based querying, indexing, and retrieval (Moharrum, 2000) of multimedia data incorporate the access to multimedia data by their semantic contents as well as logical relationships among those contents. Semantic contents include every item of interest to the multimedia database user, such as people, places, buildings, etc. Logical relationships among contents include everything that may relate different items of contents, such as relationships among people (e.g., father, mother, brother, husband, wife, etc.), among places (e.g., near, far, next to, etc.), and any other types of relationship. Examples of semantic content-based multimedia querying and retrieval data models and systems include AVIS (Adali et al., 1996), VIQS (Hwang, & Subrahmanian, 1996), OVID (Oomoto & Tanaka, 1993), and SMDS (Marcus & Subrahamanian, 1996).

Although semantic content-based multimedia data modeling and querying is the core function of many modern applications, no standard unified model exists which satisfies all

Figure 2: Classification of content-based retrieval models

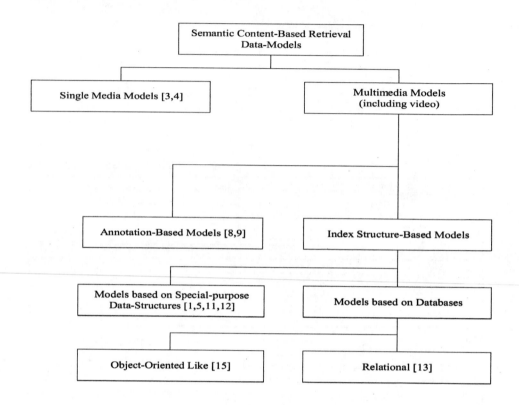

needs of such applications. A close study of existing semantic content-based querying models (Moharrum, 20000) reveals that the main problems with existing models are: lack of methodology, domain dependency, and complexity.

A classification of existing semantic content-based multimedia models is shown in Figure 2. This classification is done according to the type(s) of media involved and the type of data organization/model. However, each of these models can form the backend of an Internet-based retrieval system.

The previous subsection gave a brief introduction to Multimedia CBR. This will form the core data server part located at the top layer in our proposed framework.

This chapter contains three other sections, describing the different layers of the architecture starting from the top and going down to the user. Finally, the section suggests some extensions and future work. We will also describe in some detail the database design of the content database, a brief introduction to the agent technology, and the different caching techniques used.

LAYER I: DATA SERVERS

The main goal of this section is to describe the topmost layer of the architecture. In this layer, there are two types of services, namely, the keyword search and the multimedia data retrieval. In order to understand the need for these two types of services, consider the following example. Assume that a user submits a data query searching for some type of multimedia data (say MOV video clip) that contains some information about *Nefertiti* (queen of Egypt and wife of King *Akhenaton*) with some more detailed specifications such as a picture of a golden statue of her, belonging to a certain archeological discovery, etc. This query will finally arrive at our topmost layer through the user agent. It is convenient to find/ locate, in the first step, all the servers that contain some information about Nefertiti. Next, we dispatch mobile agents to communicate with those servers extracting all relevant data considering more specific details applying some filtering, and so on.

In the following subsection, we show how to use existing Internet search engines, such as AltaVista or Yahoo search, to perform the first task. In the next subsection, we will describe the internal structure of data servers

Keyword Search

The keyword search problem

Given a set of keywords belonging to some query, it is required to identify the locations of all servers that contain data about these keywords. A possible solution that comes to mind is to have some kind of an index server that contains a database of all possible keywords and the locations of servers that contain data about them. An example would be a search function similar to

Locate_Servers(Keyword_List L)

that returns a list of servers (represented by IP addresses and port number to communicate with the service). This database that is being looked up, can be updated upon any data insertion at any of the data servers.

In order to build such a service, we will need to decide whether it should be decentralized, or better yet, replicated in order to avoid having a single point of failure. Also, we will need to solve all kinds of problems that will arise due to replication.

Using the Internet search engines

As described in the previous subsection, implementing a separate service for the keyword search will consume much time and resources. In fact, there already exists a very similar service and widely used service, the current search engines. The function of a search engine is simply, given a set of keywords, to return the addresses (URLs) of all Internet web pages that contain documents/information about these keywords. Thus, all we need is to wrap this service to return server addresses instead of web pages URLs. Also, to return them through an API that fits the architecture rather than a generated HTML page.

A quick look at well-known search engines (Yahoo, Google search, Lycos, AltaVista) reveals that they support an almost standard search syntax for inclusion/exclusion operations as well as Boolean logic for keywords (AND, OR, and NOT). In most search engines, the exact phrases are supported as well as searching for roots and variations of a certain keyword.

What is really required is to communicate with those search engines through an API (already existing and widely used in many other web pages) and apply some data processing/ filtering to extract the relevant servers information.

This process is illustrated in Figure 3.

Figure 3: Using the Internet search engines

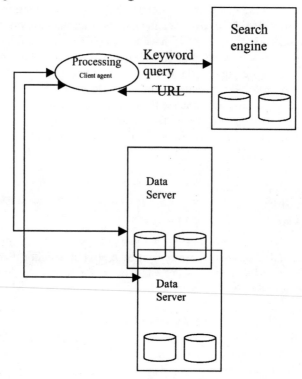

A Model for Multimedia Semantic CBR

Semantic content-based querying, indexing, and retrieval of multimedia data, as described Section 1, incorporates the access to multimedia data according to semantic and logical relationships among physical objects existing in the multimedia data streams.

The main function of the data servers in this layer is to deliver relevant data according to queries that incorporates such semantic and logical concepts. Several models have been proposed, designed and implemented to perform this task.

In this subsection, we will focus on the SQL-based model (Abugabal, Saad, Ahmed, & Moharrum, 2000). This model is easier to understand as it uses standard relational database to store meta-data as well as standard SQL as a query language. The main idea behind this model is the storage of a meta-database that contains textual data describing the actual multimedia streams. Querying this meta-database will retrieve a set of references to the actual multimedia data that will be sent back to the user. Finally, the actual multimedia data will be physically retrieved and displayed according to further user requests.

The contents database stores meta-data that reflects the contents of the multimedia objects. The data model for this content database is based on the Content-based retrieval concepts. These concepts represent an abstraction for a data model used as the semantic basis for the SQL-based model (Abugabal, Saad, Ahmed, & Moharrum, 2000), which supports different query types and allows them to be specified in SQL. Detailed query types supported as well as detailed description of the relational design can be found in the original paper by Moharrum (2000).

How a Query is Processed in this Layer

In this subsection, we describe the steps followed in processing queries from the time they are submitted by the user home base agent to the search engine server, until the reply is returned by different servers to the user agent. In order to describe these steps, we recall that a user, at the lowest layer, submits his query to a home base agent. Then the following sequence of actions will take place:

1.   The home-base agent processes the query and extracts relevant keywords.
2.   The home-base agent submits a search request to a well-known Internet search engine, such as AltaVista, and obtains results.
3.   These results will experience further processing to extract the server locations, and port numbers of the meta-database service.
4.   Different instances of the mobile agent will travel to those servers and start communicating with them to obtain relevant data.
5.   Mobile agents send the data back to the home base, which will apply some further processing before sending it to the user.

In order to illustrate the idea, we consider a simple query that tries to retrieve video clips containing information about both the pharaoh queen, Nefertity, and the Sphinx. The user agent receives the query and applies some processing to extract the two keywords "Nefertiti" and "Sphinx." Then it will also recognize that the query requests items that contain both of them, and then will submit this to the search engine as an expression like

$$+\text{"Nefertiti" AND}+\text{"Sphinx"}$$

The search engine will reply with a set of 100 URLs. Then the agent will process these URLs to identify a set of say five servers—A, B, C, D and E. An instance of the agent that carries the query will travel to each of these servers. Residing at the servers, the agents will submit the query in SQL such as:

```
SELECT      M.MediaInstance_ID
FROM        MediaInstance M, Object O1, Object O2,
            InstanceMap IM
WHERE       M.StreamName=videoStream
            and
            M.MediaInstance_ID=IM.MediaInstance_ID
            and
            O1.Object_ID=IM.Object_ID
            and
            O1.Name="Nefertiti"
            and
            O2.Object_ID=IM.Object_ID
            and
            O2.Name="Sphinx"
```

Summary

In this section, we described the topmost layer of the proposed hierarchical architecture. Two major tasks were involved, the keyword searching and the semantic CBR of data. The role of agents was touched upon and showed to be very important. The upcoming section will discuss further the details of the home base and mobile agent.

Given that all this work to be done for every query, with the mobile agent traveling across the Internet to different servers, the performance of the system will degrade significantly. Thus, a proxy server should be close enough to the user side to save multiple routes through the Internet for every query. This will be the layer to be discussed in the next section.

LAYER II AND III: CACHING

As one of the major objectives of the proposed architecture is to achieve the required performance assuming large data volumes, the key point towards this goal is to reduce network traffic. Reducing network traffic depends mainly on elimination of redundant data, and not sending anything across the network (specially the external network such as the Internet), unless it is really needed.

In this section, we will discuss the proxy servers and caches that reside in Layers II and III. The idea of all caching techniques is to achieve better user response time by accessing objects from the cache rather than from their sources, and to reduce network traffic by not resending objects across the network when not needed.

A cache is a store of recently used objects (multimedia data files/stream in our case) that is closer than the objects themselves (Coulouris, Dollimore & Kindberg, 2000). Caches can be stored locally at the user machine, or can reside in a nearby server.

Proxy servers are servers that provide a shared cache of resources (i.e., multimedia data) for the user machines at a site or across several sites.

In the following two subsections, we will discuss the proxy servers proposed in our architecture and their roles. We will also discuss the local servers caches and how they will maintain recently accessed data locally. Then, we will discuss how the nature of the applications will affect the use of these caching facilities.

Layer II: The Proxy Server

The purpose of proxy servers in our architecture is to increase availability and performance of the service by reducing the load on the wide area network and the data servers. This is achieved by letting the proxy server keep a copy of every data stream that passes through it. Thus, it will be able to supply the same data stream later, if requested. This depends mainly on the principle of temporal locality. Temporal locality states that if a user (or program) accesses some object at a certain point of time, it is likely that he/she will access the same object at a close later point of time.

The most important point here is that the proxy server will provide the objects accessed by some user at a certain instance of time not only to this user, but also to any other user in the domain that asks for the same data at a later time.

Another important point is that the proxy will not only keep the exact data items accessed by some user, but also some other data items that will be brought after the search criteria is broadened by the agent. However, we will discuss this point in more details in the next section.

In order to illustrate how will this server works, let's apply our architecture to a university environment. The university will have some gateway to the Internet, and a proxy server will reside on that gateway. Some departments within the university will have local servers that provide some sort of local cache. Each department will have a set of user machines.

Let's assume "historical library project" as a joint project between the history department and the computer science department. Let's assume that User A, from the history department, submitted the "Nefertiti and Sphinx" query described in the last section.

After User A's agent has retrieved all the tuples and multimedia data that satisfies the query, before they reach A's machine, they will be captured and copied at the proxy gateway for later use. The next day, User C, from computer science, tries to execute the same query. While his mobile agent is propagating, it will find the same query and results at the university proxy server time stamped with yesterday's date. The mobile agent will then send this data back from that level, without going again through the Internet search engines and the data servers.

Here, we raise an important question. How will the agent recognize the multimedia data stored on the proxies that satisfy the same query? One simple case is that the two users submitted exactly the same query. In such cases, all that it has to do is compare the query text submitted against the query text stored. If they exactly match, simply send back all the stored query results.

A more complicated case that needs some intelligence is when the two queries are different in query text, but share some results. In order to solve this problem, we will define some data descriptors to be attached to each multimedia data item. Then, the following scenario will occur:
1.   After the mobile agent retrieves the server locations that contain relevant data, it will propagate to the servers.
2.   The agent will retrieve the data descriptors first from the data servers (rather than the actual data items) and send them back.
3.   These data descriptors will be compared with the existing ones' and then only the non-existing data items will be ordered from the servers.

A way to enhance this solution is to store the data descriptors in the Internet search engine rather than in the data servers to save one path of going back and forth for the agent. However, this solution is very costly since it requires some changes to the Internet search engines or creating our own search engines. This contradicts the philosophy of using the existing subsystems and components instead of building new ones.

Layer III: The Departmental Local Caches/Archives
The departmental local caches are a set of smaller caches attached to each department/sub-domain. They are smaller than the proxy server as they serve only the set of users at that specific department.

All the ideas discussed with the proxy server are also applicable to the departmental caches. They depend on the temporal locality among users of the same sub-domain, and keep a copy of everything accessed for later usage. It may be advisable in some cases that the departmental caches keep their copies of multimedia objects for a longer time than the proxy servers. This may be normal for the computer science department, for example, if some people there are working on some application and spending a week or so fixing some bug.

An important point to discuss is the relationship between these two levels of cashes. The normal way of filling in these caches is top-down, as the proxy server will capture the data first, then the departmental local caches/archives.

This data will be accessed in the opposite order, as the mobile agent will search the departmental cache first and the proxy last. However, in some cases when the departmental archives keep caches for a longer period of time, the proxy will have to search for the required data at the lower level departmental archives, excluding the server from where the agent originated.

Cache Consistency Problem and Time Scale

The most important problem regarding maintaining caches is consistency. In simple words, for the cache to be consistent, it is required that the different copies of the same data are the same at any point of time. The caches generally can be inconsistent due to changes of data at the server, or due to the updates made by users. As our architecture does not assume the user ability to change data on a server, then the only source of problems is the servers. This also determines how long should the cache content be valid, and how frequently should it be refreshed or updated. The point here is that this rate depends mainly on the application and on the nature of data we are manipulating.

For example, if we are considering our historical information application, the data is unlikely to change. The most probable type of change is the addition of new data on the data servers. For this application, this can occur in terms of days or even weeks. Therefore, if we find the streams we are looking for cached and dated a week ago, they are most probably still valid.

Another example is a news episode application that looks for news videos and audio clips for a certain topic or a certain part of the world. Clearly this will not be valid that long: however, it also depends on the type of news and how frequently it is subject to change. If the news is about some hot areas that have some war going on, they will be completely different from news episodes about environmental protection efforts, for instance.

Summary

In this section, we navigated through two intermediate levels of our architecture. The importance of using different caching techniques was depicted, and two levels of such techniques were discussed. We discussed also the relationship between these two proposed levels of caching as well as the cache consistency issues.

LAYER IV: THE AGENTS

As performance is the key goal of our architecture, we propose the use of mobile agent technology mainly to reduce network traffic and to perform several tasks simultaneously. In this section we discuss how we propose to use mobile agent technology to achieve the goals described earlier.

The term "mobile agent" refers to a software entity that has two major features, namely mobility and agency (Pham, Karmouch & El-Rewini, 1998). Mobile agents are self-contained programs that move throughout the network and perform tasks on behalf of the user. On behalf of the user means that an agent will exist permanently representing a certain user, while this user might be off-line, and makes decision according to policies set by the user. The main idea of mobile agents is to replace the traditional client-server architecture by self-controlled program execution near the data source.

Mobile agents are currently a hot research topic that finds applications for various fields. This includes mainly all application in which the client-server approach was applicable. In addition, some other distributed applications such as network management and intelligent network services. (Pham, Karmouch & El-Rewini, 1998). This architecture is illustrated in Figure 4.

There are many proposed models for mobile agents; many of them still under research/ construction. Examples include, Alget from IBM, Agent TCL from Dartmouth College, ARA from University of Kaiserlautern, and many others. However, our discussion here will not

Figure 4: The mobile agent versus client/server architecture

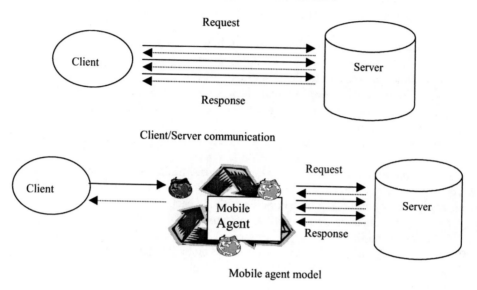

Client/Server communication

Mobile agent model

assume any of these models and simply will apply generally to any specific agent technology used.

We have our agent as two parts, one of them is immobile, namely the home base, which will reside in the nearest server to the user, and will permanently represent him even while he/she is off-line. The other part will be the mobile agent (MA) that will be roaming in the network to perform all the data search/retrieval tasks. In the next sub-section, we will discuss the home base part, then we will move to the MA part.

The Home Base

The home base is an immobile agent that represents the user permanently. In our architecture, we have one home base for every user. The home base will reside in the nearest server to the user (most probably on the same LAN to which the user is connected). This will provide high bandwidth for communication between the user and his home base.

The home base has to be configured by the user to take into consideration the capabilities of the user machine to display different types of multimedia data (this will range from powerful multimedia workstations to PDAs). Also, this configuration will include the properties of the connection between the home base and the user, such as contacting information about the available bandwidth, the quality of service parameters (Coulouris, Dollimore & Kindberg, 2000), and the availability of the network connection (this may be useful for mobile users).

The role of the home base includes two major parts:

- The transmission part gets user requests/queries and sends them over the network using the mobile agents (transmission role); and

- The receiving part receives the data delivered by mobile agents and prepares it to the user configurations in order to send it to him (receiving role).

For the transmission part, the scenario goes as follows:
1. Receive the user query.
2. Process the query to extract the relevant keywords.
3. Send different instances of MA with the keywords to Internet search engines.
4. Receive the server locations and do some processing to the user query to broaden the search space (optional).
5. Send MA instances to the data servers located in previous step to extract data.

It should be noted that the separation of the multimedia data retrieval into two stages—data descriptor and multimedia stream—is not considered at this level and can be considered as the responsibility of the MA collaborating with the caches.

For the receiving part, the scenario can be summarized as follows
1. Receive the multimedia data (descriptor and streams) from MA instances.
2. Customize data to the user configuration, and including the following:
3. Applying format transformation routines for data formats not supported by the user machine.
4. Applying resolution reduction routines to reduce data transfer to low bandwidth users. In case of failure to customize data to user's configuration, inform user, send the data descriptors, and allow user to select which data items to be retrieved.
5. Send the actual multimedia data streams to the user.

From the above description, the home base can be thought to represent the agent part of the mobile agent functionality. It should be noted also that other user-related functionality could be added to both the transmission and receiving parts of the home-base, as needed.

The Mobile Agent Instances

The mobile agent instances are the mobile part of the agent technology in the proposed architecture. This piece of software is intended to perform many tasks and represent the mobility part of the agent functionality. We do not restrict our discussion to any specific design or implementation of the mobile agents. We focus on the use of this technology to perform set of tasks making use of the mobility property.

The MA instances will interact with different architectural components of our proposal. We will use the mobility property to allow the MA instance to travel freely through all the layers of our architecture. We will assume also that the MA instance has a certain buffer (theoretically infinite) to carry on all the required information for the tasks it performs. For simplicity of the model, we will assume all communications to be vertical between the MA instance and its home base. However, a better and more complex model for horizontal communication among different MA instances can be proposed.

From the previous section, we can notice that the MA instance makes two trips per query, one of them to get locations of relevant data servers, and the second one is to get the actual multimedia data. In order to illustrate the function of the MA instance, we will follow these two trips step-by-step.

For the first trip, the MA instance will travel to contact the Internet search engines and to retrieve the data server locations. However, this task can even be done by direct contact between the home base and the Internet search engines, since the amount of data transferred before and after processing is relatively small.

The second data retrieval trip for the MA instance is summarized as follows:

1. The MA instance will travel in the network starting from the home base and holding a copy of the query.
2. When it arrives at the departmental server local caches, it will compare the query with the existing ones.
3. In the case of finding the same query, it will retrieve the data and send it back to the home base. In this case, there will be no need for the second trip.
4. The same procedure at Step 3 will occur at the proxy/gateway caches, and if data is found; sending the data back to the home base will end the task.
5. In case of not finding the required data on the proxy, the MA instance will fork itself to a number of identical instances, one for each located data server.
6. Upon arriving at the data server, the MA instance will retrieve all the data descriptors that satisfy the query, hold them in the buffer, and travel back to the proxy server.
7. At this point, the MA instance will search the proxy cache for the existence of the multimedia streams attached to the data descriptor, and will retrieve the difference set between what it has and what is cached.
8. The MA instance will record the difference set as existing, not for any instance to retrieve the same data again.
9. Then, it will travel back to the data server, and retrieve the appropriate multimedia data streams according to its set of data descriptors, and travel all the way back.
10. Upon arriving at the proxy, the retrieved multimedia streams will be cached.
11. The same caching process will happen at the departmental servers.
12. Finally, the MA instance will end its task by handing the data to its home base.

The above scheme achieves many performance goals by reducing the network traffic over the Internet to a minimum. The mobile agent will neither retrieve any unnecessary multimedia data, nor will the multiple instances of the same MA retrieve the same data stream.

The above scheme can be considered a basic functional proposal, and some enhancements can be added to achieve better performance. However, the exact performance characteristics can't be estimated unless a simulation model is developed and implemented.

DISCUSSION

In this chapter, we proposed a generic architecture for multimedia data retrieval over the Internet. We focused on two goals: first to provide the best possible performance, and second to reutilize existing components/technologies to build this architecture. The architecture proposed uses the Multimedia Content-Based Retrieval (CBR) as the theoretical model for retrieving multimedia data, based on semantic contents. We used the SQL-based model (Moharrum, 2000) as the core function of the data servers. However, no model can be suitable for all types of applications. Thus, in the case of employing this architecture to a different application domain, it will be recommended to find the suitable data retrieval model for that area, and fit it into the architecture.

We used a two-level hierarchy of caches to keep track of previously retrieved data. These two levels were proposed to interact minimally. Cache consistency problems were mostly ignored as the time scale addressed for this area of application allows very relaxed consistency. However, in other application domains, a more sophisticated caching scheme can be proposed and also fit into the general architecture.

The mobile agent technology was employed to enhance the performance by reducing network traffic. A certain scenario was proposed for the mobile agents to move throughout the network. More intelligent schemes can be proposed for application areas that requires for example, intelligent on-site data processing/filtering.

There are some other ideas to employ different technologies in an extended architecture. Among these ideas is the use of agents to perform some on-site data mining to retrieve different frequently accessed patterns of data at each data server/client domain. Then, these patterns can be used to predict user behavior and prefetch the most likely accessed data according to the frequent data access patterns.

Another idea is to use the mobile agent to perform some kind of intelligent data filtering at the data server site. This will include some learning schemes and AI to perform more sophisticated analysis of the data before sending it back. Applying such techniques may further reduce the network traffic and enhance the performance.

Peer-to-peer networks are getting wide acceptance nowadays. Such a truly distributed system will allow users to exchange data freely and easily. Napster, Gnutella, and Freenet are well known examples for such systems. The idea is to use the same scheme to exchange the multimedia data, based on its semantic contents. The architecture proposed here can't be considered a client/server one; neither can it be considered a simple N-tier architecture. In addition, moving to the peer-to-peer option will need to have nodes acting as both data sources and clients. Many issues are to be researched, such as query processing, availability, and using hyper nodes (acting mostly as servers) versus simple user nodes (acting mostly as clients).

REFERENCES

Abugabal, M., Ahmed, m., Saad, A., & Moharrum, M., (2000). Modeling and semantic content-based querying of multimedia databases. *Proceedings of the 6th International Workshop on Multimedia Information Systems,* Chicago.

Adali, S., Kasim, S., Candan, Chen, S., Erol, K., & Subrahamanian, V.S., (1996). Advanced video information systems: Data structures and query processing. *Multimedia Systems* (4)4, 172-186.

Coulouris, G., Dollimore, J., & Kindberg, T., (2000). *Distributed Systems: Concepts and Design* (3rd ed). Reading, MA: Addison-Wesley.

Day, Y.F., Dagtas, S., Lino, M., Khokhar, A., & Ghafoor, A., (1995). Object-oriented conceptual modeling of video data. *Proceedings of the Eleventh International Conference on Data Engineering,* 401-408.

Gudivada, V.N., & Ragahavan, V.V., (1996). Modeling and retrieval of images by contents. *Information processing and Management,* .33(4), 427-452.

Gudivada, V.N., Ragahavan, V.V., & Vanapipat, K., (1996). A unified approach to data modeling and retrieval for a class of image databases. In: S. Jajodio and V. S. Subrahamanian, (eds.) *Multimedia Database Systems: Issues and Research Directions,* New York: Springer Verlag, 37-78.

Hampapur, A., Jain, R., & Weymouth, T.E., (1994). Digital video indexing in multimedia systems. *Proceedings of the Workshop on Indexing and Reuse in Multimedia Systems.*

Hampapur, A., Jain, R., & Weymouth, T.E., (1995). Feature based video indexing. *Proceedings of the 3rd IFIP 2.6 Working Conference on Visual Database Systems,* 115-141.

Hwang, E., & Subrahmanian, V.S., (1996). Querying video libraries. *Journal of Visual Communication and Image Representation,* 7(1), 44-60.

Jiang, H., Montesi, D., & Elmagarmid, A.K., (1997). Videotext database systems. *Proceedings of the Fourth IEEE International Conference of Multimedia Computing and Systems,* 344-351.

Jiang, H., &. Elmagarmid, A.K., (1998). WVTDB- A semantic content-based video database system on the World Wide Web. *IEEE Transactions on Knowledge and Data Engineering,* 10(6), 947-966.

Jiang, H., Elmagarmid, A.K., Helal, A.A., Joshi, A., & Ahmed, M., (1997). *Video Database Systems Issues, Products and Application.* New York: Kluwer Academic Publishers.

Kamal, A., & El-Rewini, H., (1998). On the optimal select of proxy agents in mobile network backbones. *IEEE Communications,* 36(7), 26-37.

Khoshafian, S., & Baker, A.B., (1997). *Multimedia and Imaging Databases.* San Fransisco: Murgan Kufman publishing.

Marcus, S., (1995), Querying Multimedia in SQL. In S. Jajodio and V. S. Subrahamanian, (Eds). *Multimedia Database Systems: Issues and Research Directions,* 263-277. New York:: Springer Verlag,.

Marcus, S., & Subrahamanian, S., (1996). Foundation of multimedia database systems, *Journal of ACM,* 43(3), 474-523.

Marcus, S., &. Subrahamanian, V.S., (1995), Towards a formal theory of multimedia database systems. In S. Jajodio and V. S. Subrahamanian, (Eds). *Multimedia Database Systems: Issues and Research Directions,* 1-35. New York: Springer Verlag.

El Masry, R., Navathe, S.B., (1995). *Fundamentals of database system* (2nd ed), Redwood City, CA: Benjamin Cummings Publishing Company.

Moharrum, M.A., (2000), Towards a unified model for semantic content-based multimedia databases. Master's thesis, Alexandria University, Egypt.

Oomoto, E., & Tanaka, K., (1993), OVID: Design and implementation of a video-object database system. *IEEE Transactions on Knowledge and Data Engineering,* 5(5), 629-643.

Pham, V.A., & Karmouch, A., (1998). Mobile software agents: An overview. *IEEE Communications,* 36(7), 26-37.

Smith, J.R., Chang, S.U. (1996). VisualSEEk: A fully automated content-based image query system. *ACM Multimedia,* 87-98.

Stonebraker, M., Rowe, L.A., & Hirohama, M., (1990). The Implementation of POSTGRES. *IEEE Transaction on Knowledge and Data Engineering,* 2(1), 125-142.

Yoshitaka, A., & Ichikawa, T., (1999). A survey on content-based retrieval for multimedia Databases. *IEEE Transaction on Knowledge and Data Engineering,* 11(1), 1999, 81-93.

Windweaver updated Search Guide (n.d.). Retrieved November 21 2001, from http://www.windweaver.com/searchguide2.htm.

Chapter XII

Navigation in E-Business Web Sites

Roland Hübscher
Auburn University

Tony Pittarese
Pensacola Christian College

Patricia Lanford
Auburn University

ABSTRACT

Two of the most important keys to successful Web sites, including e-business sites, are content and usability (Nielsen, 1999). Yet, many of these sites still suffer from flawed content organization and navigation support. In this chapter, we discuss existing problems and point out a series of important user and task characteristics that need to be considered when designing an online store. We focus on usability issues of content organization and navigation which are inherently intertwined. We will also discuss the checkout process, an important element of many e-business, whose design requires not only the usual usability guidelines but also trust issues.

INTRODUCTION

Many e-business site interfaces have serious design flaws apparent to even the casual user. For a person trained in human factors and usability, navigating through a site and the checkout process is often a torture—or a scary, yet exciting fact-finding and data-collection trip through a dangerous jungle. This criticism is also supported by the fact that a massive 65% of shoppers abandon a site before actually purchasing anything (Weiss, 2000). This criticism doesn't just apply to the "mom-and-pop" Web stores, but also to many of the big players. Shopping online can be as confusing as shopping for the first time in a large department store in a foreign country. This problem is compounded by the fact that customer service availability is often extremely limited. Although a lost shopper might attract the attention and assistance of a clerk in a store, almost no parallel exists in an online environment. Many e-business sites are not nearly as usable as they should be.

We will address this usability issue by examining the role of store content organization, site visitor characteristics, and related navigational support. Obviously, navigation and content organization must be dependent on the visitors' characteristics and their goals. The main purpose of the organization and navigation support of a Web site is to allow a user to easily navigate to the needed product and efficiently complete the transaction.

Too often, the organization of the products in an online store or the manner in which the exchange is completed reflects some kind of scheme internal to the business. For instance, in some cases, products are organized according to their product stock numbers. Quite often, the technical implementation, e.g., the database design or method of processing transactions, dictates the organization of the Web site and the checkout process. Such business and implementation-imposed schemes largely ignore the users' needs and are therefore to be avoided.

While there are many similarities between general e-business sites and those selling products, visitors to the latter sites have additional concerns. Since they are being asked to spend money and give personal information, they must have confidence that the business will not purposely or accidentally misuse this information. Consumers must trust the company, otherwise they may not complete the purchase. Trust is often a by-product of the usability and professionalism of the site.

Evaluating site usability only makes sense when considered from the perspective of what kinds of customers are going to do what kinds of tasks. E-commerce sites are interested in users finding items they wish to buy and then actually buying them. It is important that users find what they want and then also be given opportunity to expand their purchase. This can be done by presenting other items that may also be to their liking and are related to the original purchase.

Ultimately, success can be measured by whether or not the user does indeed purchase the items placed in his/her shopping cart. Too often, potential buyers leave the store and abandon a full shopping cart. Our own early pilot studies have shown that, in many cases, usability and trust issues of the site are responsible for this behavior.

In the rest of this chapter, we will analyze a few different store models and what kind of organization and navigation they support. We will make recommendations on what user characteristics need to be considered to design the appropriate organization and navigation. Then we will discuss usability and trust issues considering the checkout process design of an e-business site.

CONTENT ORGANIZATION

Content in e-commerce sites needs to be organized in such a way that the customer can easily find desired products, and the products themselves are merchandised to impact the customer's purchase decision (Goldberg, 2000). Brick-and-mortar stores arrange and present products to maximize sales given space and other, often physical, constraints (Underhill, 1999). Online stores need to take advantage of the fact that they do not suffer from these same constraints. However, as discussed below, they suffer from their own kinds of problems.

We will begin by discussing some online store models based on their brick-and-mortar equivalent. We do this to both learn from brick-and-mortar stores and to understand their limitations. We will then consider implications of this analysis on navigation and checkout designs.

Online Store Models

Many online stores use a model based on what is convenient for the seller rather than the customer. This can create serious disadvantages with respect to the site organization and navigation. We will present three models and propose that the designer should seriously consider a boutique-like specialty store as a preferred model. Although brick-and-mortar stores are a good place to start, e-business stores should not have to suffer unnecessarily from the same physical, organizational, and other constraints as real stores do.

In a physical store, products are often placed in the store based upon the paths that consumers must travel in order to reach other frequently purchased items. In grocery retailing, it is quite customary to place high-volume items like milk and eggs at the back of the store, thereby forcing customers to walk past other items that the store hopes they will impulsively add to their shopping cart. It would be disastrous if the online shopper had to similarly navigate Web sites. Online, the products need to be brought to the customer in the real store, it is the other way around. While this shortened online navigation path might reduce some merchandising opportunities, it adds the potential for new techniques to be developed. In both situations, the customer "meets" the products; however, in the online version we can take advantage of the fact that there are less physical constraints. The online store can even be improved by suggesting those items that the customer is likely to purchase based on current or even past shopping behavior.

The Warehouse and Grocery Store Model

In a warehouse store (such as Sam's Club, BJ's, and others) or a typical grocery store, products are presented to the customer in a series of parallel rows (forming a grid) containing merchandise. The method is used in order to maximize the use of physical space on the shopping floor (Hart & Davies, 1996). Since both warehouse stores and grocery stores frequently merchandise products in the cases in which they arrived from the supplier, the structure enables shelves to be quickly and efficiently filled (often with machinery used in the stocking process).

While the grid structure can make for efficient merchandise handling for the retailer and efficient shopping for the frequent customer (who knows where everything is located based upon experience), it does little to distinguish a particular store from its competitors or enhance consumer interest. This is acceptable to the consumer because the products purchased at stores using this structure are generally not products that are purchased for enjoyment; i.e., this structure may work wonderfully for toothpaste and toiletries, but it is not the best method of presenting clothes to the consumer. Utilitarian efficiency for the retailer is more prized than merchandising.

Online shopping sites that are organized based on how the retailer stores product information in its corporate database are the equivalent of the physical grid structure. Products are presented to the customer in a way that is based upon what is easiest for the retailer. Product databases are simply converted to Web pages and strung along a site in a hierarchical structure that may make little sense to consumers (Jung & Lee, 2000). A static, hierarchical organization may be useful for finding information; however, it does little to utilize the inherent power of online merchandising (Galenskas, 1997).

Since online retailers are not handling physical products in stores, the constraints of product size and physical attributes become irrelevant. Physical space is not limited online— except maybe for screen space, but that's another story altogether—and products of disparate sites can be treated without respect to this difference.

The Department-Store Model

In a department store, related products are organized into "departments" and are merchandised together. Products are presented in a more pleasing arrangement than in a grocery store model, and the utilitarian view of economy of space and stocking efficiency is set aside. Shirts and pants are located in the same section. Customers who want to buy pants might need a matching shirt or even socks, too. This makes it relatively easy for the salesperson to try to sell more products. The salesperson in a particular department is a specialist on products sold in that department (but not necessarily those sold in other departments in the same store).

For the consumer, shopping in a department store feels often like a rather lonely journey through a large maze, once in a while interrupted by a possibly qualified salesperson who might work in another store as early as next week. (This characterization may be unfair to some department stores, which show a more specialty-store like face. However, they are, unfortunately, in the minority.)

Many e-business Web sites are based on this model. Although the organization is often hierarchical, it is more targeted towards the customers' needs than in the warehouse store model. However, the customer is often either looking at pants or jackets or shirts in isolation, not at pleasing combinations. The customer is also often required to do his own research to find out what goes with a gray jacket and whether is more appropriate to wear a bow tie or a regular tie to a certain occasion. The checkout at the cash register is often a quite impersonal experience and too often, just as in a physical store, one has to make an effort to find the cashier to pay for the merchandise.

The Specialty-Store Model

Buying your clothes in a specialty store, e.g., a boutique or a men's store, can be quite a different experience. A knowledgeable sales person provides you with personalized help and recommendations. After you have selected your jacket, the salesperson will bring a set of matching pants, shirts with ties, and present them all to you together with the jacket. The attention, the qualified support, and the flexible and adaptive behavior of the salesperson make you feel more convinced of the right combinations (although you may have only wanted a jacket when you entered the store). Merchandising of physical products becomes secondary to the selective, adaptive merchandising done by the salesperson. The shopper is not presented with generic mass displays of clothing, but rather two or three shirts in exactly the right size that also match the jacket that has already been selected.

The entire process builds customer confidence. The salesperson is highly professional and the store well-appointed. As in a reputable department store, you are not worried that something funny is going to happen with your credit card number.

Another example of this type of exchange would be at a good hardware store where skilled employees are able to advise the customer as to what kinds of materials they will need for a project. They don't just know which shelf the items are on, but what they are normally used for, how many are needed, whether they will withstand the weather, etc.

Not many Web sites implement the specialty-store model. Such sites provide adaptive and context sensitive support, e.g., in the form of intelligent sales agents or collaborative filtering. They have an "aura" of expertise and the visitor feels like he can rely on the recommendations made on the Web pages. There are still many online (and brick-and-mortar) stores where the site owners do not seem to care much about the items they sell, therefore why should the customers buy the product?

Note that the above argument is rather gendered. Whereas men tend to like it when one guides them through to the purchase decision, women like the "thrill of the hunt." (Of course, we vastly overgeneralize, but we do so to make a point.) Women often like digging through racks to discover that skirt *that* perfectly goes with *that* blouse, and it's great when they find a "deal." Almost every woman we know (and some men, too) loves T.J. Maxx, a store that is horrendous in terms of organization, help, checkout, etc.

The models presented above manifest themselves most significantly in the manner of navigation afforded to customers. The layout of a physical store dictates to consumers how they will interact with a store, its staff, and its products. Significant research has been done into consumer preferences and merchandising techniques in a physical environment (Underhill, 1999), but that same research is underdeveloped in an online environment. It is known, however, that consumers find well-designed Web sites to be a significant factor in their overall satisfaction (Szymanski & Hise, 2000).

As a designer, how do we come up with the best model for our site? There is not one best model. In fact, there may be situations where even the warehouse model is the most useful given the type of users, tasks, constraints, etc. In the rest of this section, we discuss a number of issues that influence content organization and navigation.

Navigation in Large E-business Sites

In examining e-business sites and the related navigation throughout those sites, it is necessary to study the intended audience of the Web site and what its motivation would be for using the site (Smith & Whitlark, 2001). This relationship of audience and motivation will be directly related to the goals of the organization and the intended role of the Web site in company operations. If we examine the various groups that are possible visitors to a company Web site, we can categorize these groups based upon their commonalities and/or differences. Although the results of this categorization would be distinct for each organization, we can examine broad categories in a fairly generic manner. The net result will be a Web site with a navigational structure based upon the needs of particular classes of site visitors. It will create a customer-centered navigation structure.

In physical places of business, content and structure must be generic in order to accommodate a wide diversity of people and interests. There is almost no ability to customize the physicality of customer contact. For example, Wal-Mart cannot customize its store to the likes and dislikes of every individual who enters their doors. At best, they can customize certain sections, e.g., make sure that the toys are visible for a five-year-old. In an online environment, different barriers exist than in a physical environment (Mack, 2000). Customization is not only possible, it is essential in meeting the needs of those who interact with an e-business site. The question is, what to customize, for whom, and in what way (Pednault, 2000)?

The purpose or goal of a particular audience of a Web site must be reflected in the attributes of a useful navigational pattern (Wolfinbarger & Gilly, 2001). Since not every business Web site has identical goals, not all sites will be identical in their content, structure, and supported navigation patterns (Rohn, 1998). Just as there are some common business goals (sell products, support online payments, allow customer feedback), there will be some common ground in content, structure, and related navigation. Differences will come in as business goals diverge. For example, in looking at retail stores, one company may offer a wide variety of products (similar to Wal-Mart); another company may choose to have a much more limited assortment of products (similar to a small jewelry store).

The complexity for business Web sites comes not only from the fact that the Web site must be integrated with the company business processes (Dickinson, 1998) and be consistent with the company's overall goals (Rohn, 1998), but also from the fact that most business Web sites cannot be customized for only one particular group. The Web site must be generic enough to be useful and helpful to all site visitors, yet at the same time account for the great diversity in the various audiences.

Instead of viewing all site visitors as identical in their background, skills, level of interest, and commitment, or going to the other extreme and viewing each individual as unique in each of these areas, it is useful to group site visitors according to their overall goals of visiting a site. By categorizing site visitors into distinct groups according to their goals, we can look at their interests and create a navigational structure that will effectively support their intentions.versity in the various audiences.

Each user brings to his/her site visitation different Web searching and navigational skill, different levels of interest in various aspects of the Web site, and different levels of commitment to satisfy the motivation that brought him/her to the site initially. This set of interests and commitment creates complexity in designing a navigational structure that would be judged usable and effective for each of these groups.

Common audiences for a typical company Web site would include company employees, customers, competitors, suppliers, investors (both current and potential for each of these previous groups), researchers, and other individuals that may be friendly, hostile, or indifferent to the business. Each of these groups has distinct motivations for using the Web site and therefore would benefit from different types of navigational structures. Designing a Web site to support *each* of these groups would likely not be necessary for most companies; instead, the focus can be placed on meeting the goals of those groups that are most important to the organization. Instead of creating a generic Web site that is moderately useful for all site visitors, we can create a Web site whose navigational structures are customized for our target groups.

An Example of Group Analysis

For example, an investor visiting a corporate Web site would likely be interested in the business plan of the organization, its personnel, products, and other facts useful in assessing the investment worthiness of the organization. Such a visitor to a corporate Web site would likely be familiar with doing research on various organizations and would be willing to invest time in searching through the site and gleaning information from a variety of Web pages. The individual might be familiar with other corporate sites and would be making assessments throughout the site visit about not only the site content, but also the professionalism, appearance, and appropriateness of the overall Web site management.

Although the ready availability of some corporate information (company history, annual reports, letters from company officers, details on present and upcoming activities) might be viewed as essential, since the overall goal of the site visitor is to assess the company as a whole, a more explorative mode of navigation would accomplish this purpose. The level of interest and commitment to finding the desired information is high, and the potential of a thorough site visitation is likely. The navigation pattern employed is explorative, loosely focused, with a diverse set of interest points. Finding a single piece of information is not the goal, but rather making an overall assessment—a holistic view, if you will—is the motivating desire.

Contrast the above with a potential customer visiting a Web site in order to research an upcoming purchase of a product sold by the organization. Most of the interests of the above investor would not be reflected in this site visitor. Professionalism and appearance will certainly be factors in his or her judgments (Lee, Kim, & Moon, 2000), but perusing the annual report or company history of the organization would likely be of no interest to this individual. This individual follows a more targeted mode of navigation. Things not directly related to his or her upcoming purchase would be viewed as distractions or interruptions. His/her tolerance of these extraneous elements would be most significantly influenced by the importance of the purchase decision. For example, a customer researching an automobile purchase might be willing to spend a lot of time on facts peripherally related to the purchase, but a customer looking for a toner refill cartridge for their printer would evidence an entirely different level of commitment.

In this situation, the potential customer might make use of a site search engine to visit a single page containing particular information. The ease in which he or she arrives at this page will determine the willingness to continue navigating through the site (Wolfinbarger & Gilly, 2001). For example, if the user is looking for a toner cartridge for an Epson 600-e printer, he or she might choose to enter "Epson 600-e" as a search target. If the result of the search leads directly to what he or she is looking for, the consumer will continue the transaction. If the result of the search is not deemed useful, then the consumer may choose to go elsewhere rather than continuing to explore (Lohse & Spiller, 1998a; Lohse & Spiller, 1998b).

For this individual, the level of interest and commitment to finding information relevant to his or her purchase decision is a factor of the importance of the decision. Since individual Web sites do not exist in a vacuum (competing Web sites likely exist), it is helpful to view the customer's commitment as minimal, except in the case where the customer has become a "regular" of this online store. The navigational pattern employed is elemental, highly focused, with a narrowly drawn set of interest points. Finding a diversity of information and background material is not the goal, but rather finding a single set of facts to make a single decision is the motivating desire (Lohse & Spiller, 1998a). Navigation through many pages of a Web site is not useful for this customer. He or she wants to find needed items, explore a small set of alternatives, and then quickly finalize the transaction without difficulty or hassle.

As one last example, a present or potential employee of an organization would have an entirely different set of interests. For the current employee, some of his or her interests might lie in what the company is planning for the future and how well it is doing overall (similar to the investor). Additionally, some of his or her interests might lie in finding out a particular piece of information about a product or program offered by the company (similar to the potential customer). For this individual, the level of interest and commitment is likely high, and the navigational pattern may be either highly focused or explorative (in fact, both types of navigational patterns are likely to be employed over time). Background information, individual facts, and large quantities of information might all be relevant to the employee's purposes.

Characteristics Influencing Navigation

In examining a navigational structure for online selling, we must consider the motivational factors influencing site customers in light of the products offered for sale. Since these factors will differ greatly from product to product and retailer to retailer, each e-commerce Web site must consider these factors in terms of its products and customers. Understanding the motivations that impact consumers and which factors can and cannot likely be influenced is a prerequisite for designing the e-commerce sites. Unlike a brick-and-mortar store, where so called "bargain hunters" may rifle through racks and racks of merchandise in hopes to find a good buy, consumers generally don't have that type of persistence shopping online (Lohse & Spiller, 1998a).

Examples of significant motivational factors in consumer decision making include the following:

- *The degree of importance accorded to the purchase*

  Customers who view a purchase decision as "trivial" or "routine" will spend little time considering alternatives or making substantive judgments about competing products. They will buy a particular product based upon experience, the recommendation of a friend, or simply because something catches their eye. The importance of the decision itself does not warrant even moderate effort on the customer's part.

  Low-importance products are not viable targets for e-commerce sale (Mack, 2000). Although cumulatively a group of low-importance products may attract attention, singularly they do not. For example, selling only toothpaste on a company Web site would attract little consumer interest. However, a particular model of automobile may be effectively merchandised by itself on a single page or even its own Web site.

  Showing products to consumers in a way that illustrates the cumulative value of a group of products will likely be more effective than displaying lone products in isolation, especially when the weight of individual products is minimal. For example, selling a collection of cosmetics or bath products online might be viable in light of the cumulative importance afforded to the product grouping.

- *The degree of commitment assigned to a particular alternative*

  Customers may come into a particular purchase decision viewing each alternative as equal or having a predetermined preference. The level of commitment he or she has to a particular alternative will determine the amount of "shopping around" the customer does and how open he or she is to other alternatives.

  Shopping products—those for which consumers actively seek alternatives—are ideal candidates for e-commerce. Both heterogeneous products (similar products viewed as very different by consumers—for example, cameras or clothes) and homogeneous products (similar products viewed as very similar or all the same by consumers—for example, toothpaste or aspirin) can both be merchandised effectively online.

  Showing products that motivate significant "shopping around" on different Web pages communicates to consumers that they are prudently evaluating different alternatives. Showing products which do not warrant much consideration or evaluation on the same page allows the user to make ready decisions without "wasting their time" with needless exploration.

- *The complexity of making an effective decision*

  A customer may find some decisions to be a straightforward match between his or her needs and particular attributes of a product. Other decisions may be more complex and subjective. The number of facts a customer must know to make an effective decision and the degree of subjectivity in the decision have a significant impact on the reasoning process of the consumer and the confidence he or she has in the decision.

  High-complexity products should be displayed with ready access to supporting information needed to make the purchase decision. Products sold based on subjective decision making should show the outcome of using the product and should feature the "testimony" of other customers.

- *The biases, preferences, and information the consumer brings into the decision*

  Each consumer brings his or her own unique preferences, experiences, biases, and knowledge into the purchase process. The degree to which he or she is willing to set aside or change these factors is largely a process of the customer's own decision-making process and value system.

Although little can be done to make a customer abandon an established decision framework, an effort can be made to eliminate things that would cause customers to react negatively. In this area, a retailer's particular knowledge about the likes, dislikes, preferences, and similar attributes of the targeted consumer are most valuable.

- *The compatibility between the product offering and the need of the customer*
  In a situation where the relationship between the role of the product and the need of the customer is obvious, consumer choice is less influenced by subjective aspects. Previously, the example was given of a consumer needing a toner refill for his/her laser printer. In this case, the singular compatibility question is "Does this toner cartridge work in my printer?" However, in a situation where a consumer is shopping for an article of clothing, there is a larger set of compatibility questions. Some of these might include, "Does this color match another clothing item?"; "Does this item fit me?"; and "What does this fabric feel like?"

  In situations where the product being sold is based upon a single compatibility question, it is most important to make the answer to that question the primary focus. In many situations, consumers will navigate using search results based on the focus of compatibility. Lengthy supporting information on the product being offered is not necessary, as the consumer can readily determine whether or not this product does meet their goal. Items should be displayed to the consumer by grouping together compatible products. This may in fact result in a single product being shown multiple times in different groups. (A laser toner cartridge compatible with 25 different machines would be a member of 25 different compatibility groups.)

  In situations where the product being sold is a product of many consumer compatibility questions, the role of support information becomes more important. The consumer cannot as easily determine for himself or herself whether or not this product does in fact meet his or her goals. Coming up with a list of likely compatibility questions and addressing them in product support material and navigational context becomes more important. For example, for clothing items, the question of two different items working together as an outfit is a key compatibility question. By showing matching and coordinating items together and assuring the consumer that they do match, the consumer can have confidence in his or her buying choices.

- *The overall cost of the transaction*
  The more expensive an item is to a consumer, the more likely they are to view the purchase decision as important. The need for supporting information goes up as the price of the item goes up. Other factors that may influence consumers are:
  - the ease and speed with which the exchange can be accomplished (Berry, 2001);
  - the number, kind, and quality of competitors being evaluated;
  - the level of enjoyment the customer has in making the purchase;
  - the degree of anxiety the customer has about making a poor decision; and
  - the interaction between other products being purchased.

Checking Out

How many times have you added a quite a few items to your shopping cart and then just left it standing in the middle of a brick-and-mortar store? How often have you done it in an online store? Of course, in an e-business it is much easier to add an article to the shopping cart. However, the design of many e-business sites almost seem to try to make sure the customer doesn't make it through the checkout.

Trust and Usability

The success of an e-business site is strongly related to its usability and content organization. Usability of e-business sites has a dimension that is not always seen in other Web sites, namely, trust. In fact, usability may be a factor in gaining trust from consumers (Jarvenpaa & Tractinsky, 1999; Lee, Kim, & Moon, 2000). According to Jarvenpaa and Tractinsky, lack of trust has been a key element in consumers hesitating in making online transactions.

What exactly is trust with respect to e-commerce? Jarvenpaa and Tractinsky define trust as "a belief or expectation that the word or promise by the merchant can be relied upon and the seller will not take advantage of the consumer's vulnerability." Consumers don't want to be put in a position where they feel the business will take advantage of them. The consumer will then be unwilling to trust the site. The lack of trust stems from an unequal balance of power between the consumer and the site (Hoffman, Novak, & Peralta, 1999). Consumers want to be in control; when they don't feel in control, they leave and go elsewhere.

Factors stated to affect trust have been level of risk, size of merchant, design of site, ease of use, aesthetics, and reputation (Jarvenpaa & Tractinsky, 1999). If a site has a good reputation, flaws in the design of the site may be overlooked. If a friend of a consumer tells how great an experience he/she has had with an online store, that consumer is likely to overlook poor design, ugly page, etc.

Trust is a short- and long-term issue for e-commerce sites. Initially, trust is needed to get new consumers to begin shopping at a site. However, it has been found that the more experience a consumer has with the Web, the greater the perceived risk and the lack of trust. The more experienced user tends to be less concerned with looks and usability, and more concerned with privacy and store policies.

What it comes down to is this: If consumers don't trust an online store, they won't buy from that store (Hoffman et al., 1999). Online stores need to improve to gain consumer trust, but what exactly formulates online trust is still somewhat unclear. Interestingly, we can now buy VISA cards that claim to specifically protect us from such online "pirates."

Design Issues for Checkouts

We will enumerate some of "design elements" that need to be avoided in order to increase the chances the customer will actually buy some of the items in the cart. Many of these suggestions may appear obvious. However, if they are so obvious why are the same mistakes made over and over again?

- *Where's the checkout?*
  At any time on any page of the site, it must be clear to the customer how to get to the checkout. Similarly, being able to check what is in the shopping cart and what all the items cost is important information. It is naïve to think the regular customer can be "tricked" into buying more by keeping information hidden.
- *Why do I have to provide all this information up front?*
  Each time the user is required to provide some kind of information whose purpose is not obviously beneficial to the customer, the customer may decide to abandon

shopping at this site immediately. So, don't ask for the credit card information before taking care of everything else.

- *Slow secure server*

  Secure Web servers are sometimes slow and thus, the checkout is slow. Consumers may have more patience in checkout lines in brick-and-mortar stores because there is more in the store environment to distract/occupy them. They can ponder all those "impulse" buys or go through the merchandise their about to purchase. Waiting for a Web site to process your order is another story. The consumer is left in limbo anxiously looking a nondescript screen wondering if his/her order is going through. If consumers are impatient—and many are—they may interrupt the transaction process and try again, possibly having being charged multiple times. Don't expect a customer to read the "don't click twice"-warning (Shubin & Meehan, 1997).

- *The Next Store is Just One Mouse-Click Away*

  We are probably all tired of this phrase, yet if for any reason a consumer is dissatisfied with an online store the competitor is indeed only a mouse-click away (Kubilus, 2000). It takes a substantial amount of effort more to leave a brick-and-mortar store. For example, if you are in a store and decide you don't want to buy anything, you stop and head for the exit. However, this "journey" can take a minute or two depending on the store size and the layout of the aisles that generally have you walk by everything in the store before you make it to the exit. An employee may stop you and ask you if any assistance is needed, and then there are those impulse buys near the exit, and so forth. Once you stand in the checkout line, you have put so much effort into finding the items and carrying the to the checkout that you probably will stick to them.

  However, this isn't so on the Web. All it takes is one click even when we are in the middle of the checkout process. The shopper is gone and is possibly (more than likely) never even tempted to come back. With a brick-and-mortar store, it is possible to be tempted to try a store again for convenience sake; it may be on the drive home, for instance. Some brick-and-mortar stores success largely rely on their location. However, online, once you leave a site, there's no geographic temptation.

- *How much is the tax, shipping cost, etc.?*

  When shopping at a brick-and-mortar store, and even in a catalog, pricing information is known up front. So many complaints are made by consumers in not knowing shipping and tax information until the purchase is already made or placed in the shopping cart. Why do some Web sites require the customer provide all the information before the site makes information of additional costs like shipping and tax available?

CONCLUSIONS

Designing an e-business Web site is difficult and it is important to realize that the one-size-fits-all model cannot possibly work. There are still books that want people to believe that they can "build their successful Web store in 21 hours" using the provided templates. Design is known to be difficult and it is no different in the case of e-business. In this chapter, we have focused on certain aspects related to content and usability, two of the most important success factors of such a site.

Navigation and content organization need to be designed with each other in mind. However, there is no one solution because there are different site visitors to be considered with different goals and different-sized wallets. We have addressed some of the characteristics listed below the influence how navigation needs to be designed, without claiming to have a complete list. Of course, it would be easy to fill many more pages with more or less relevant characteristics.

- Degree of importance accorded to the purchase
- Degree of commitment assigned to a particular alternative
- Complexity of making an effective decision
- Biases, preferences, and information the consumer brings into the decision
- Compatibility between the product offering and the need of the customer
- Overall cost of the transaction
- Ease and speed with which the exchange can be accomplished
- Number, kind, and quality of competitors being evaluated
- Level of enjoyment the customer has in making the purchase

Note that these issues need to be considered in addition to the usual usability issues of user interface and site design. However, many of discussed issues do not show up in non-e-business sites.

Another important complex of problems arises when dealing with the issue of trust, which is always important when personal information and money transactions come into play. We have briefly touched on these issues in the context of checking out the items to be purchased. However, much more research needs to go into this area, which indeed is one of the foci of our group.

REFERENCES

Berry, L. L. (2001). The old pillars of new retailing. *Harvard Business Review, 79*(4), 131-138.

Dickinson, K. (1998). Keeping an electronic commerce shop. *StandardView, 6*(3), 106-109.

Galenskas, S. M. (1997). Interactive Shopping on the Internet. *Direct Marketing, 60*(4), 50-52.

Goldberg, A. (2000). Bad Habits: If you build it, they won't come. *MC: Technology Marketing Intelligence, 20*(11), 31.

Hart, C., & Davies, M. (1996). The location and merchandising of non-food in supermarkets. *International Journal of Retail & Distribution Management, 24*(3), 17.

Hoffman, D., Novak, T., & Peralta, M. (1999). Building consumer trust online. *Communications of the ACM, 42*(4), 80-85.

Jarvenpaa, S., & Tractinsky, N. (1999). Consumer trust in an Internet store: A cross-cultural validation. *Journal of Computer-Mediated Communication, 5*(2).

Jung, Y., & Lee, A. (2000). Design of a social interaction environment for electronic marketplaces. *Conference Proceedings on Designing Interactive Systems: Processes, Practices, Methods, and Techniques*, 129-136.

Kubilus, N. (2000). Designing an e-commerce site for users. *ACM Crossroads, 7*(1).

Lee, J., Kim, J., & Moon, J. Y. (2000). What makes Internet users visit cyber stores again? Key design factors for customer loyalty. *Proceedings of the CHI 2000 Conference on Human Factors in Computing Systems*, 305-312.

Lohse, G., & Spiller, P. (1998a). Quantifying the effect of user interface design features on cyberstore traffic and sales. *Paper presented at the Human Factors in Computing Systems CHI'98.*

Lohse, G. L., & Spiller, P. (1998b). Electronic shopping: Designing online stores with effective customer interfaces. *Communications of the ACM, 41*(7), 81-87.

Mack, A. M. (2000). E-tailers transfer self space into cyberspace. *Adweek—Southeast Edition, 21*(45), 54.

Nielsen, J. (1999). *Designing Web Usability.* Indianapolis, IN: New Riders Publishing.

Pednault, E. P. D. (2000). Representation is everything. *Communications of the ACM, 43*(8), 80-83.

Rohn, J. A. (1998). Creating usable e-commerce sites. *StandardView, 6*(3), 110-115.

Shubin, H., & Meehan, M. M. (1997). Navigation in Web applications. *Interactions, 4*(6), 13-17.

Smith, S. M., & Whitlark, D. B. (2001). Men and women online: What makes them click? *Marketing Research, 13*(2), 20-26.

Szymanski, D. M., & Hise, R. T. (2000). E-satisfaction: An initial examination. *Journal of Retailing, 76*(3), 309-323.

Underhill, P. (1999). *Why We Buy: The Science of Shopping.* New York: Touchstone.

Weiss, E. (2000). Online express line hard to find. http://www.usatoday.com/life/cyber/bonus/1200/cb002.htm: USA Today.

Wolfinbarger, M., & Gilly, M. C. (2001). Shopping online for freedom, control, and fun. *California Management Review, 43*(2), 34-56.

Section VI:

Web Information Systems (WIS) Development: Design, Environment and Standards

Chapter XIII

E-Business Transaction Management in Web-Integrated Network Environment

V. K. Murthy
University of New South Wales at ADFA, Australia

ABSTRACT

This chapter describes the Operational Models, Programming Paradigms and Software Tools needed for building a Web- integrated network computing environment. We describe the various interactive distributed computing models (client server-CS, code on demand, remote evaluation, mobile agents, three and N-tier system), different logical modes of programming (imperative, declarative, subjunctive, and abductive), transaction and workflow models (that relax atomicity, consistency, isolation, durability and serializability properties), new protocols, and software tools (PJava/JDBC) that are needed. Some important application areas of these models are for telediagnosis and cooperative problem solving.

INTRODUCTION

This chapter describes the issues involved in the design of online E-business Transaction Processing systems and the solutions available for these problems using the techniques of AI, logic, conventional database transaction processing methodology and protocol engineering principles. E-business transaction processing requires that all the parties (such as traders, customers, buyers, and sellers) involved in a transaction are in agreement before allowing the transaction to be committed; if any of the parties cannot complete its part of a transaction, the entire transaction has to be rolled back. Conventional online transaction processing (OLTP) semantics are met by the following requirements called "ACID requirements":

Atomicity (A): All changes are totally done (committed) or totally undone (rolled back).

Consistency (C): The effect of a transaction preserves the invariant properties of the system.

Isolation (I): Intermediate results are not visible to other transactions. Transactions have the effect of executing serially, although they act concurrently.

Durability (D): The effects of a transaction are persistent; changes are not lost except under catastrophic failure.

However, for e-business transaction processing we need to have:
1.   long duration transactions that lack conventional ACID properties of transactions and need externalization of intermediate results, fault tolerance and recovery under failure;
2.   location and disconnection- reconnection management for hand-held mobile devices; and
3.   new logical modes and related protocols that provide rules for conducting "dialogue" among the parties so that each party can formally express what is to be communicated clearly and unambiguously.

The above requirements demand the design of a new Information architecture for e-business transaction processing systems. Further, an e-business Web-integrated network environment (INE) needs to be rich in its problem-solving capability, since it needs to serve as a virtual logical tool for the user. Such a tool is meant for effective decision making using different logical modes to cooperatively solve a business problem. In such a cooperative business environment, it is necessary to allow data exchange between some transactions during their execution, thereby necessitating the relaxation of the Isolation property used in conventional transactions. In a e-business environment, in addition to the conventional imperative programming mode of logic, we need two other logical modes - subjunctive (what if I do this? or speculative) and abductive (how did this happen? or diagnostic) programming features that add additional logical power to the user. This added power provides for various forms of reasoning to aid planning, acquiring and analysing information, arguing, and negotiation. In a negotiation, parties communicate with one another in order to reach mutually acceptable agreements on some matter of common value to them. These modes enable us to realise the following required properties for e-business transactions:
1.   Attribute-Sensitivity: The transactions are to be committed or aborted locally or globally depending upon their exact attribute values.
2.   Attribute Tolerance: The transactions can be permitted to be locally relaxed in terms of certain constraints on attributes, but globally consistent eventually.
3.   Time-criticality: These are transactions that possess Atomicity, Consistency, Isolation, and Durability (ACID) properties and are to be permanently committed, as soon as the transactions are completed to achieve local and global consistency.
4.   Time-tolerance and eventual consistency: Some transactions can wait until reconnection takes place, and are not time-critical in the sense they will not create global inconsistency, but are only necessary to provide an eventual consistency with respect to the user and the relevant database.

Hence in an e-business environment, the isolation property needs to be removed and intermediate results are made visible, and precedence order in execution and other dependencies are taken care of, thereby removing the atomicity restrictions. This model is called a workflow (which is a collection of tasks organized to accomplish some business activity) between the customer and the trader supported by suitable protocols. A workflow can be realised by mobile agents, which are autonomous objects that execute methods when they are deployed. Workflow-based mobile agents play an important role for E-business transaction processing.

In summary, for an e-business web - integrated environment, we require the following features:

1.   Protocols for disconnection and reconnection retaining the consistency of computations;
2.   Methods for subjunctive and abductive reasoning;
3.   Approaches for over-riding the requirements of the transaction model;
4.   Storage of histories; and
5.   Facility for data sharing among mobile hosts when need arises.

The above features are realized using three basic protocols for the e-business environment:

1.   Intention-Action (IA) protocol for subjunctive mode;
2.   Disconnection-Reconnection (DC) protocol for disconnection to reconnection mode; and
3.   Propose-Revise (PR) protocol for abductive mode of tele-reasoning.

BACKGROUND

Wireless communication technologies have given a new thrust to the development of an e-business web-Integrated Network Environment (INE) that uses both wireless and wired networks. Advances in communications and satellite services will enable mobile users connected through wireless networks to access information across the globe for e-business transactions. This chapter describes the issues involved in the design of a e-business transaction processing system and the new solutions proposed for these problems using the techniques of AI, conventional database transaction processing methodology and protocol engineering principles. These techniques will be useful for improved transaction throughput and scalability in e-commerce (Brancheau & Shi, 2001; Menasce & Almeida, 2000).

E-business Transaction Processing Systems

Transaction management is a well established research area with many successful results achieved so far. Transactions that have ACID (atomicity, consistency, isolation and durability) properties have traditionally been used to ensure consistent database management through atomicity (all or none) of actions, as well as isolation of user actions (Elmagarmid, 1995; Krishnamurthy & Murthy, 1991). Recent advancements in transaction management have relaxed some of these traditional properties of transactions. An e-business transaction model for INE is yet to be fully developed. The appropriate properties for transactions in INE have been studied recently by the author and other researchers (Chen & Dayal, 2000; Ghezzi & Vigna, 1997; Murthy, 2001). These papers also discuss issues and problems, that mobility brings into transaction management, and describe new methods using workflow and mobile agents and various types of new software tools currently available, such as Java, Java database connectivity, and CORBA (Dignum & Sierra, 2001). A distributed multi-database system with many autonomous and heterogeneous component databases will provide support for the management of global e-business transactions and data resources in an INE with mobile and stationary hosts. Such global transactions can be comprised of several subtransactions to be processed at one or more stationary and/or mobile computers. Database access through mobile computers in an integrated network already exists, though not in a mature state. It is also believed that integrated distributed computing will introduce dramatic changes in the way we handle transactions in a database system. This means that solutions to many problems arising in transaction management in database systems have to be revisited to suit e-business in an INE. In short, e-business in an INE raises new issues in designing database transaction handling systems, as described in the introduction.

Operational Models for INE

The INE for distributed computing consists of a collection of dissimilar (heterogeneous) computers connected through the fixed-wired networks (such as the Ethernet), as well as wireless (mobile) networks. The INE consists of fixed host computers and mobile client computers. In view of this, we will use the terms INE and mobile computing environment synonymously. Fixed hosts (FH) are connected together via a fixed high-speed network (Mbps to Gbps). The mobile clients (called mobile client host; MH) are capable of connecting to the fixed network via a wireless link. The components in the fixed network are called fixed hosts. Fixed hosts (FH) provide mobile application services and coordinate tasks to mobile hosts. MH supports query invoking and information filtering from FH to provide personal information service. Since the computers may have different computational powers and may use different representations for data, we need to take care of not only the incompatibility among their representations, but also their interoperability in using different pieces of software. Also, to achieve high performance and reliability (that provides maximal concurrency in solving a problem and recovery under failure), we need suitable computational models to help understand and analyse their behaviour. Currently, six important models are used for the design of heterogeneous distributed systems: Client-Server (CS), Remote Evaluation (REV), Code on Demand (COD), Mobile Agents (MA), Three-Tier Systems (TTS), and N-Tier Systems (NTS). To understand these models and compare them, we assume that there are two objects, A and B, where object A is client-like that interacts with another object B that is host-like to get A's task done.

1. Client-Server (CS): Here the system is partitioned in such a way that the client and server assume fixed roles. This fixed role and the synchronous client-server communication restrict the nature of protocols and increases the complexity of implementation. The client does not have the know-how, resources, or tools and requests service from the server at the location of Object B. A suitable analogy is a patient (Object A) seeking surgical treatment in a hospital (Object B). This system is resource intensive since B carries out all the required management and bears all the overhead involved. For example, to obtain a single value from a table of data for the client, the entire table has to be transferred to the server, where the table is searched. If the table is large, a good bandwidth is needed and the computational overhead is high.

2. Code on Demand (COD): Here Object B (e.g., a business firm) owns the resources and tools needed to perform a service, but lacks the know-how (code) needed to perform the task, while Object A, (e.g., a consultant) has the know-how. Thus, only know-how is transported through Object A who performs services at the location of Object B. In this model, to obtain a single value from a table of data, the searching routine is transmitted to the remote station.

3. Remote Evaluation (REV): Here Object A (like a user of a common kitchenette) owns the code (know-how, what to cook and eat) needed, while Object B owns resources and tools and provides for self-service to Object A at the location of Object B. Thus know-how and self-service facilities are transported. For obtaining a single value from a table of data, the searching routine is implemented in the remote station and the routine is activated by remote invocation or by a trigger. This scheme gets complex when a large number of routines are implemented.

   4. Mobile Agent (MA): The Object A (a gold prospector) owns the code (know-how) to perform a service, but does not own the resources (gold mine) needed. It is allowed to migrate its virtual machine (tools) to a host (Object B) where the needed resources (gold mines) are located. Object A executes its self-service at the location of Object B. Thus mobile agents transmit know-how and tools to execute self-service at a location where resources exist. Hence, they permit increased flexibility, reduced traffic, and balanced load distribution. To obtain a single value from the table, we send the search routine to the location where the table is stored, search locally, and send the result. This reduces bandwidth since only the result is shipped back and the load is distributed among different routines. Also since it is autonomous, it can—without being connected to its owner—collect information in a local station. On the other hand, the traditional approach would require many data interchanges on slow links between the owner and stations that are liable to fail.

   5. Three-Tier System (TTS): Here an intermediate object I exists between objects A and B. The resources from B migrate to I and know-how, service and tools are provided from A. This can also be achieved by agent migrating from A to I. It has been suggested that a three-tier architecture consisting of client A, a service proxy I and a server B will be efficient. A is connected to I through a narrowband network, while I is connected to B through a broadband network. I performs the function of relaying requests from clients to database servers and replying messages from servers to clients. The broadband network permits transfer of large volumes of data in a short period of time (gigabits / second). In fact due to the broadband

Table 1: Operational models for INE

Model	Object A	Object B
CS e. g.	NIL *(patient)*	know-how + service + tools+ resources *(Hospital)*
COD e . g.	know-how *(Consultant)*	service + tools+ resources *(Business firm)*
REV e . g.	know-how + service *(user)*	tools + resources *(kitchenette)*
MA e. g	know-how +self- service +tools *(Prospector)*	resources *(Gold-mine)*

TTS Here an **object I** exists between **objects A** and **B.** The resources from **B** migrates to **I** and know-how, service and tools are provided from **A.** This can also be achieved by an agent migrating from **A** to **I.**

NTS Here an **object I** in **TTS** is implemented as a collection of components that are used in client-initiated business transactions.

connection, the database can be migrated to a proxy and transactions can be processed there. This would reduce the mobile transaction processing time, provide for frequent-connection-disconnection and improve performance.

6. *N-tier system (NTS)*: In a NTS (inter-galactic client-server), the middle tier of a TTS is not implemented as a monolithic program but as a collection of components that are used in a variety of client-initiated business transactions. Each such component realises a small business function.

A comparison of the above mentioned six models is given in Table 1. From Table 1 we see that the agent-based system provides for know-how, tools, and self-services (except for resources) in a more comprehensive manner than the CS model. Also, mobile agents simplify protocols by partitioning the tasks among many agents, each having a different functionality and reducing communication. Adding mobility balances message exchange and code dispatching. Management agents co-located within the network devices act like servers that communicate on request.

Mobile Agents

A mobile agent is ideally suited for performing a variety of tasks in distributed systems since it has the following properties (Knabe, 1996; Vitek & Tschudin, 1997):

1. It is a code-containing object along with data and execution context that is able to migrate autonomously and purposefully within a computer network during the execution.
2. It can react to external events.
3. It can be persistent in the sense that it can suspend execution and keep local data in stable storage. After resuming activity, an agent's execution is continued, but not necessarily at the same location.
4. A user or a program can delegate tasks to an agent and vest it with an authority (power of attorney) to act on its behalf by providing terms of reference and time deadlines.
5. Agent can make decisions, based on rules, goals, policies, and preferences set by its owner.
6. Agents can interact with host environment and owners.
7. Agents can cooperate with each other to achieve common goals.
8. Agents can support peer-peer model for distributed computing.
9. Agents can vary their roles—may act as clients or servers, observers, seekers.
10. Agents have the ability to reason and learn from interactions with other agents, owners and environment.

Suitable Model for E-Business INE

The suitability of the model depends upon the application and actual context. Therefore, provision should exist for supporting all the above system models in INE. This universal system (inter-galactic model) will enable the user to act as a client, consultant, designer, an explorer, or as a prospector in data-mining. Such a provision would make the mobile computer a very versatile tool. To develop a suitable inter-galactic model for e-business INE, the language implementation must handle architectural heterogeneity between communicating machines. Thus appropriate choice of programming paradigms and related software tools are to be made available to the mobile host so that clients can install special purpose interfaces with appropriate properties they require at the remote fixed host.

INE: REQUIREMENTS AND CHARACTERISTICS

Three major requirements for a successful INE are:

1. Facilities that can permit a mobile computer to be connected from different access points and to stay connected while on movement.
2. A good bandwidth for fast reliable communication.
3. The availability of battery power to operate a mobile computer. Since the battery life sets a limitation, we need some kind of facilities that will permit disconnection and save power without affecting the performance and reliability of the whole system.

The important characteristics in INE are:

1. Non-symmetrical nature of communications between mobile hosts and fixed servers. The hosts are subject to resource limitation (power and capacity of machine and portability). Thus generally it is cheaper for the mobile host to receive messages than sending the messages from a mobile host.
2. Long disconnection from mobile host to save power and permit the user to work at his will.
3. The mobility of a host also implies the availability of a virtual server that is available to provide an efficient service to the mobile host.

Mobile Transactions: Their Features

A transaction submitted from a mobile host in INE is called a mobile transaction (Murthy, 1998). It is a distributed transaction that can be executed partly within that mobile host (MH) as internal transactions (Intran) and partly in other fixed hosts (FH) as external transactions (Extran). Each FH has a coordinator (FHC) that receives external transaction operations from mobile hosts and monitors their execution in the database servers within the fixed network. Similarly each MH has a coordinator (MHC). In conventional transactions, the ACID properties are enforced. The ACID properties turn out to be restrictive for a mobile environment and need to be relaxed, as illustrated by the following two examples:

Example 1: Suppose we need to procure and match two or more interdependent components that have one or more matching attributes to repair a machine—say component x sold by company A, component y sold by company B and component z sold by C. To purchase such matching items we need to access three different databases in three different companies. These involve three transactions A, B, and C. In a conventional set-up the total global transaction succeeds only if all the three independent transactions A, B ,and C, succeed or none of them succeed, thus making only the correct purchases visible. But this is a very strong requirement that is inflexible. To relax the conditions we may be tempted to go through a conventional two-phase commit (2PC) protocol. But, the execution of a 2PC may not be possible when independent enterprises do not have visible precommit states; further, we may not be able to lock resources indefinitely, while communicating with each remote database site. To obviate this difficulty one needs to relax the ACID properties of the transaction, since we need to execute long global transactions consisting of activities, where the individual outcomes are to be made visible to the user or other transactions before the global transactions can be completed. If not all of them succeed we either cancel the successful ones by a compensating action or we can retry the failed ones thus allowing for temporary inconsistencies that are short-lived.

Example 2: Suppose we want to make a flight reservation using a mobile transaction. Here one needs to have the following collection of tasks: select a suitable airline that offers cheap fares, ensure there is vacancy, and make an advanced booking (that is to be confirmed later). These individual steps are not traditional transactions, but well-defined program pieces that can be carried out concurrently and may need to follow a predefined partial order to satisfy certain predicates (such as seat availability), invariant criteria (number of seats cannot exceed the size of aircraft), and synchronization (one step requires the completion of other step). Therefore, the steps need not be atomic, need not be immediately consistent, and need not satisfy isolation property, since intermediate non-commit states are to be made visible (called externalization). Further, such steps are liable to be cancelled eventually and require a suitable rollback preserving some local states.

Thus in contrast to the conventional transactions, the mobile transactions need to have the following properties:

1.   Due to latency in communication and disconnection, they need to be long-lived.
2.   They are error-prone due to the possibility of accidents to mobile hosts.
3.   They can have short-lived inconsistencies to permit access to a variety of databases where two-phase commit protocol and resource locking are not possible to carry out.
4.   They are also required to be distributed and heterogeneous because of host mobility and access to different databases.

NEW LOGICAL MODES FOR E-BUSINESS ENVIRONMENT

An e-business INE needs to be rich in its problem-solving capability, since it needs to serve as a virtual logical tool for the user. Such a tool is meant for effective decision making using different logical modes to cooperatively solve a business problem. In such a cooperative business environment, it is necessary to allow data exchange between some transactions during their execution, thereby necessitating the relaxation of the Isolation property used in conventional transactions. Most conventional programming use two types of logical constructs: Declarative and Imperative. In a e-business environment, in addition to these constructs, we need two other logical modes: subjunctive (what if I do this? or speculative) and abductive (how did this happen? diagnostic) programming features that add additional power to the user and provide for various forms of reasoning to aid planning, analysing, acquiring and arguing.

Subjunctive Mode

When a human solves a real-world problem or plans a task, he/ she uses an exploratory non-pre-programmed real-time procedure that uses a memory recall (Read), acquires new information and performs a memory revision (Write). Each step of solution is also provided with the facility for repair (recovery-Undo). Each partial plan is refined by a proper choice and partial ordering of operations to refine the plan further. Also, some independent or dependent information is acquired from various knowledge sources and its consistency is verified before completing a step of the solution to achieve each subtask; this process corresponds to committing a subtransaction in a distributed transaction processing system.

In e-business computing, we need a similar mechanism for experimenting with the imaginary effects of "what if I do this" changes to the database that are not permanently recorded, so that the user has the freedom to examine the impact of complex changes. This is like *forward chaining in AI (* beginning with the initial state to the goal through a set of successive transformations, each transformation achieving a subgoal that is consistent) and is analogous to planning for the future. The subjunctive logical mode arises in practical situations such as: planning, reservation, purchases and forecasting. Such a mode can be realised by using intention-action protocols.

Abductive Mode

Abduction is a reasoning that proceeds from effects to cause when there is incomplete knowledge. It is a powerful mechanism for hypothetical reasoning. In other words, if A implies B then given B, if it is consistent to assume, A does so. This is like *backward chaining* in AI (starting from goal to reach the initial state through a succession of subgoals and checking that each subgoal is consistent) and is analogous to a post-mortem. Here we need a mechanism to discuss and argue with others as to "how did this happen?" In many domains this reasoning is useful in e-business as a diagnostic tool, especially in a failure situation. We need to find pertinent facts and apply them to infer a new fact. But the fact inferred need not be unique. So we need to select among alternatives and weigh the evidence. Thus there are two issues here:

1. finding a fact for or against the conclusion (similar to finding the disease); and
2. how to piece together facts and evidences into a conclusion (similar to treating it).

For the subjunctive and abductive modes, the conventional transactional model is unsuitable due to ACID properties and serializability requirements. Atomicity is very restrictive, since all or no operations should take place indivisibly as one entity. Also, consistency may not be achievable in subjunctive and abductive reasoning situations. In addition, we may have to relax the Isolation property, since it prevents each transaction from looking into what other transactions are doing at intermediate stages; here we need data-exchanges to achieve consistency. Durability and recovery are to be supported under failures as well as under voluntary disconnection and reconnection of the mobile hand fixed hosts and have to take place through data exchange that is not atomic. Thus disconnection and reconnection are essential functions and protocols, and are to be designed using suitable logs and recovery mechanisms.

We can now outline the requirements for E-business transactions.

REQUIREMENTS FOR E-BUSINESS TRANSACTIONS

E-business transactions need to have the following properties: Attribute-Sensitivity, Attribute Tolerance, Time-criticality, and Time-tolerance and eventual consistency. Attribute and time tolerant and time-critical transactions arise in planning (subjunctive or "what-if" programming) where we execute hypothetical or pseudo-transactions to test the intention of actions for trial-error design.

As a simple example, such transactions arise in real-time transactions in E-tailing with E-shopping carts. The E-shopping cart holds a record of the selection the buyer intends to buy. At any point the buyer can review the items, remove items, or change their quantity, type and brand. It is useful to have the shopping cart in place even though the buyer leaves the Web site to do something else and come back later. Such a persistent E-shopping cart is very useful for grocery shopping. This of course requires a deadline on the availability as well as pricing, since some items can go up or down in pricing. Thus the items selected are not only controlled by the buyer, but their current availability and pricing are automatically changed by the shop at the time when intention commit becomes an action commit. The time-tolerant and eventual consistency property is used in E-tailing. To handle time-criticality, for example, inconsistency on deadlines, we need to ensure that the fixed host can meet the required deadline by determining a priori whether an incoming transaction or a part of a transaction from a mobile host is schedulable within that deadline. As a result we need to consider new approaches to relaxing serializability criteria (discussed in a later section) and also introduce suitable protocols. A bounded amount of inconsistency may be introduced to finish a task within a deadline or accept inconsistency only when the transaction is about to miss the deadline. This can be specified by condition-event-action or rule-based systems (or equivalently by scripts, protocols defined as a well-formed sentence in a formal grammar). Thus in a e-business INE, the traditional transaction model needs to be replaced by a more realistic model in which the isolation property is removed, and intermediate results are visible, precedence order in execution and other dependencies are taken care of, thereby removing the atomicity restrictions. This model is called a workflow between the customer and the trader and is supported by suitable protocols.

WORKFLOWS, AGENTS AND CONCURRENCY

A workflow is a collection of tasks organized to accomplish some business activity (Georgapoulos, 1993; Geppert, 2000). Here each task defines some unit of work to be carried out. A workflow ties together a group of tasks by specifying execution dependencies and the data-flow between tasks. Also, there may be a constraint that a particular task cannot begin until some other task ends. Such constraints can be specified by event action systems or a script. A script is a condition-event structure that describes a stereotyped sequence of events in a particular context. Scripts are useful because, in the real world, there are patterns in the occurrence of events. Events described in a script form a causal chain. In a workflow model, we need to ensure correctness and reliability of workflows. Correctness means that the concurrent execution of transactions and workflows are interleaved in such a way that incorrect results such as lost update or inconsistent retrieval do not occur. Recovery means both the tasks and the transactions are recoverable in the event of a failure. The workflow model is better suited than the conventional transactional model for e-business INE since it provides the following features:

1. A programming paradigm that supports a combination of transactions that satisfy ACID properties, and workflow tasks that do not have the ACID properties.
2. A method of managing control flow and transactions.
3. A suitable recovery model under failure of the workflow; this recovery is very complex compared to short transactions, since it will require re-instantiation and following the control flow of actions strictly.
4. Contextual information that preserves the consistency of database as well as the local state of the application.
5. Remembering the execution history and path and local states produced in the past.
6. Externalization of preliminary results: Workflow computations need to externalize their results before they are completely done. This implies that unilateral rollback is no longer possible; one needs to specify compensating actions as part of control flow description.
7. Concurrency and consistency control: Consistency can no longer be based on serializability only; it allows for application-oriented policies of synchronizing access to shared objects.

8. Conflict handling: When a resource conflict occurs it is not feasible to delay some activity until a long duration transaction has completed. Also, it is not acceptable to roll back the transaction. Therefore, if a resource conflict occurs, the control flow description should specify either how to resolve the conflict or specify an alternate strategy.

Workflow based- mobile agents (for structuring and implementing distributed systems) provide the following advantages:
1. Rapid development and maintenance;
2. Platform independence: Must run on different hardware/OS platforms; must be developed once and deployed in the desired platforms transparently;
3. Interoperability: Adapt itself to interact with peers;
4. Ease of use: Increased number of users of different expertise, user-friendly and personalizable interfaces;
5. Flexibility: Behaviour is compatible with environment, other components and user;
6. Efficiency: Use resources efficiently and provide for network management;
7. Support mobile computing: This brings the code to place where information is available; and
8. Support long-duration computation: Agents can control long-lived complex computations, in a manner analogous to a parallel programming environment with persistent local variables, accesses to shared objects, and synchronization facilities.

Concurrency and Serializability

In concurrent mobile-host programming, we need to consider how to speed up the system by permitting concurrent transactions between several mobile hosts (MH) and the fixed host (FH). This would require an analysis of how the respective internal and external transactions interfere with each other when they are applied. In order to execute the internal transactions concurrently, they must satisfy the following conditions (Murthy,1996; Murthy, 1998):
1. The set of objects in each FH(p) and in each MH(i) accessed by any two different Intran are pairwise-disjoint to prevent side effects. This condition is well-known for those familiar with database transaction handling;
2. The set of local states in MH(i) and FH(p) used by two different Intran are pair wise disjoint. This condition corresponds to the mutual exclusion of processes in concurrent programming. These aspects are taken care of by the coordinators MHC(i) and FHC(p).

Traditionally, we require that the following two conditions are to be satisfied for global serialization:
1. At each MH and FH, the local schedules are serializable; that is, the conflicting actions are performed in the order of their temporal precedence.
2. At each MH and FH, the serialization order of transactions dictated by every other MH and in FH is not violated. That is, for each pair of conflicting actions among transactions p and q , an action of p precedes an action of q in any local schedule, if and only if p precedes q in the total ordering of all transactions in all FH and in all MH.

The above two conditions require that two different MH(i) and MH(j)) do not interfere in FH(i) [we assume that two FHs do not interfere]. The Extrans are called conflict-free if they do not have any of the above dependencies. However, in a mobile environment with many mobile hosts, the above conflicts are hard to resolve due to disconnection; hence global consistency through serialization becomes an issue, and we must relax this criterion also.

Relaxing Serializability Criterion

Traditional databases use serializability as the basic notion of correctness. Serializability requires that conflicting operations are executed in a strictly sequential way. However, during cooperation, the transactions need to share data associated with the particular application. Since tasks executing from different mobile hosts may interfere in an undesirable way, it is necessary to enforce certain behaviour patterns among the members to prevent side effects. The members may themselves decide to enforce some protocol on the interaction between the members and objects to ensure consistency for each member in its own way. Also, each member can set up its own method of undoing and recovery in isolation from other members to avoid interferences and further failures. Since global serialization in an e-business INE is difficult, concurrent computations should be restricted to only business processes that are not immediately consistent but are only eventually consistent among the interested parties, such as reservations, purchases and other processes that involve negotiation between sellers and many customers. In a practical situation, two-party consistency may be adequate and can be achieved through certain protocols between each mobile client and fixed host.

PROTOCOLS REQUIRED

We mentioned that the traditional transactional model is not well suited in INE, since data consistency, deadlines, and scheduling are to be taken care of. In such systems it is preferable to have a negotiation protocol between the client and host to carry out tasks reliably. This can go through two phases called: Intention Phase and Action Phase. These phases enable us to carry out subjunctive or "what-if" programming in which we execute hypothetical or pseudo-transactions to test the intention of each party and then perform actions. The subjunctive programming paradigm is widely applicable in mobile computing, as it allows the mobile client and fixed host to interact and negotiate and carry out transactions, workflows as well as connection - disconnection protocols. Thus we need three basic protocols for the e-business (mobile computing) environment (for details refer to Murthy, 2001):

1. Intention-Action (IA) protocol for subjunctive mode that takes place between the client and the trader;
2. Disconnection-Reconnection (DC) protocol for disconnection to reconnection mode. This protocol takes care of connection establishment, data transfer and connection release; and
3. Propose-Revise (PR) protocol for abductive mode of tele-reasoning. This protocol takes place between several clients and is most effectively carried out by a three-tier system.

As described earlier, we have two forms of transactions: Extran (external transaction) that takes place between a client C and a trader T, and Intran (internal transaction) which takes place locally within each C or T. It is assumed that Intran have ACID properties, while Extran is split into intention and action transactions, where the intention transactions have ACID properties, while the action transactions are long-duration transactions supported by a recovery protocol. The intention transactions are again local to each C or T and based on the decision in this phase; the action transaction takes place through a protocol called Intention-Action (IA) Protocol provided with a time-out strategy and recovery to cope with disconnection. This protocol coordinates the control flow and also ensures reliability.

E-Shopping Cart Model

We now illustrate the application of Intention-Action Protocol for the e-shopping cart problem. The Shop database has a set of items and each item has a status available or unavailable on specified dates. The object Alloc stores the confirmed allocation of items to named shoppers and Int -alloc holds the intentional items in an e-shopping cart. We assume that each buyer has a unique ID and is not permitted to hold multiple e- shopping carts in the same shop.

The shop database has two integrity constraints:
1. The number of confirmed plus intentional reservation of items does not exceed the number of items on any date; and
2. The set of items that are unavailable on any date are those already allocated to the buyers in Alloc, plus those in Int-Alloc on those dates.

The following transactions act on the shop database:
1. Reservation request from buyer within a deadline (Extran);
2. Reservation availability from shop and intention commit (Intran);
3. Send negative intent or (positive intent + deadline) to buyer to confirm (Extran);
4. Reservation acceptance or cancellation by the buyer (Extran);
5. After cancellation by the buyer within shop deadline the intent reservations of items are cancelled and items are made available and the IntAlloc is suitably modified and committed (Intran); and
6. After confirmation by the buyer within shop-deadline the Int-Alloc items are transferred to Alloc and committed (Intran).

Note that transactions 2, 5 and 6 are transactions internal to each buyer (with ACID properties), while 1, 3 and 4 are Extrans between the buyer and the shop controlled by the I-A protocol.

FUTURE TRENDS

An important application area for the above paradigms and operational models is in multimedia cooperative mobile computing environment for diagnostic applications. In this environment, the users need to work remotely on common shared resources and applications and simultaneously communicate both visually and through audio. Such environments become more flexible and useful in an integrated wireless and wired environment that provides services for mobile hosts. Mobility of users becomes very important for many applications in telemedicine (Gomez, 1997), where doctors, specialists, and health-record officials can cooperate and discuss a particular medical treatment. In this application, we are concerned with a large data set such as radiological images, video images of signals, and text that are transferred to the host from a server. In this application we need cooperation among the participants through special communication tools for conversation and tele-pointing. The conversation can be of conferencing type where two or more participants are involved. The tele-pointers aid each participant to point out a particular segment of an image or a video image of a signal so that each of the other participants can visualize the movements of the remote pointer. This would provide for greater clarity and effectiveness of discussion about the particular image. The remote access to image and other related databases may appear like ATM transactions; however, they differ in several respects. Such telemedicine transactions are long-duration transactions which need the transfer of a large amount of data and require lengthy negotiations, cooperation, pointing, and decisions to reach a final diagnosis and therapy.

SOFTWARE TOOLS

There are several available languages (Knabe, 1996; Yourdon, 1996) for programming the different operational models, but Java seems to be ideally suited to our requirements. Java is a complete programming language that offers all the basic mechanisms for communication and synchronization between processes and guarantees portability of the code across multiple architectures and operating systems in a high performance secure way. Thus Java is useful to implement agent-based workflow. The distributed networking nature of Java permits the development of all six models of distributed systems. Also, the Java Database Connectivity Application Program interface (JDBC API) provides for simultaneous connection to several databases, transaction management, simple queries, manipulation of precompiled statements with bind variables, calls to stored procedures, streaming access to long column data, access to the database dictionary, and description of cursors. Mobile agents in Java can also be very useful in mobile computing. Java is very suitable for CORBA application development since Java and CORBA are similar in architecture; this similarity in architecture results in the near seamlessness between Java and CORBA (Orfali, Harkey & Edwards, 1996; Rosenfeld & Morville, 1998; Siegel, 1996). There is an almost direct correspondence between the use of interfaces in Java and CORBA. Java provides to CORBA the capability to develop a client-side application once and run it on many platforms. Also, CORBA provides the benefit of cross-language interoperability to Java. CORBA provides an object-oriented abstraction that permits Java-based systems to communicate with applications written in almost any language.

CONCLUSION

We described the key issues involved in the design of online E-business Transaction Processing systems in a Web-Integrated Network Environment and the solutions available for these problems using the techniques of AI, conventional database transaction processing methodology, and protocol engineering. e-business transaction processing differs from conventional transaction processing since we need to relax the ACID and serializability properties by introducing the workflow model and three additional protocols: Intention-Action (IA) protocol for subjunctive mode, Disconnection-Reconnection (DC) protocol for disconnection to reconnection mode, and Propose-Revise (PR) protocol for abductive mode of tele-reasoning. We also explained how the workflow can be realised using agents.

ACKNOWLEDGMENT

The author thanks Professor Charles Newton for his support and encouragement.

REFERENCES

Brancheau, J. & Shi, N. (2001). *Essential technologies for e-commerce*. Singapore: Prentice Hall.

Chen, Q. & Dayal, U. (2000). Multi agent cooperative transactions for e-commerce. *Lecture Notes in Computer Science*, Vol. 1901, 311-322. New York: Springer Verlag.

Dignum, F. & Sierra, C. (eds.). (2001). Agent mediated e-commerce, *lecture notes in artificial intelligence*, Vol. 1991 & Vol. 2003. New York: Springer Verlag.

Elmagarmid, A.K. (1995). *Database transaction models.* San Mateo, California: Morgan Kaufmann.

Georgapoulos, D. (1993). An extended transaction environment for workflows in distributed object computing. *IEEE Data Engineering Bulletin,* 1692.

Geppert, A. (2000). Modeling electronic workflow markets. *Lecture Notes in Computer Science*, Vol 1921, 52-63. New York: Springer Verlag.

Ghezzi, C. and Vigna, G. (1997). *Mobile code paradigms and technologies, A case study. Lecture Notes in Computer Science*, Vol. 1219, 39-49. New York: Springer Verlag.

Gomez, E.J. (1997). The Bonaparte telemedicine ATM multimedia applications. *Lecture Notes in Computer Science,* Vol. 1242, 693-708. New York: Springer-Verlag.

Knabe, F. (1996). An overview of mobile agent programming. *Lecture Notes in Computer Science,* Vol. 1192, 100-115. New York: Springer Verlag.

Krishnamurthy, E.V. & Murthy, V.K. (1991). *Transaction processing systems.* New York: Prentice Hall.

Menasce, D.A. & Almeida, V.A.F. (2000). *Scaling for e-business.* New York: Prentice Hall.

Murthy, V.K. (1996). Transactional programming for distributed agent systems. In *Proceedings IEEE International Conference on Parallel and Distributed Systems,* Japan, 64–71, New York: IEEE Computer Society Press.

Murthy, V.K. (1998). Transactional workflow paradigm for mobile computing. In *Proceedings 13th ACM Conference on Applied Computing,* 424-432. New York: ACM Press.

Murthy, V.K. (2001). Seamless mobile transaction processing: Models, protocols and software tools. In *Proceedings 8th IEEE International Conference on Parallel and Distributed Systems.* 147-154. California. New York: IEEE Computer Society Press.

Orfali, R., Harkey, D., & Edwards, J. (1996). *The essential distributed objects.* New York: John Wiley.

Rosenfeld, L. & Morville, P. (1998). *Information architecture for the World Wide Web.* Sebastopol, CA: O'Reilly.

Siegel, J. (1996). *CORBA.* New York: John Wiley.

Vitek, J. & Tschudin, C. (1997). Mobile object systems, *Lecture Notes in Computer Science,* Vol. 1222. New York: Springer Verlag.

Yourdon, E. (1996). Java, the Web, and software development. *IEEE Computer,* 29, 25-39.

Chapter XIV

System Development Methodologies for Web-Enabled E-Business: A Customization Framework

Linda V. Knight and Theresa A. Steinbach
DePaul University, USA

Vince Kellen
Blue Wolf, USA

ABSTRACT

The fast-paced, rapidly changing e-business environment, coupled with its emphasis on brand image and the human-computer interface, and the creative nature of Web development teams combine to require changes in traditional system development methodologies. This chapter explores the fit between typical Web-based information system characteristics and existing development methodologies, from the traditional System Development Life Cycle (SDLC) to some of the newer rapid-response models. It concludes that, contrary to common practice in most organizations, one standardized development methodology is not best suited for all, or even most, e-business projects. Fifteen variables that are key to identifying the best methodology for a given e-business project are distilled, and a framework is constructed to aid development teams in the process of formulating a customized development methodology to serve as a basis for project management and control. Projections are made concerning the future of e-business system development methodologies.

INTRODUCTION

As Isakowitz and Bieber (1998) noted, Web-based information systems (WISs) are sufficiently different from traditional development that they require "new approaches to design and development." These differences, which are detailed in the background section on the e-business environment, include a faster paced, more rapidly changing environment, a greater emphasis on brand image and the human-computer interface, and inclusion of a broad range of creative talent on development teams. As the following sections show, traditional system development methodologies, ranging from the Waterfall to the newest rapid-response models, were designed for vastly different environments and cannot be easily transplanted into this new Web setting. Yet, to date, little scholarly research has been published that centers on appropriate system development methodologies for e-business. In the practitioner press, however, Yourdon (2000) has called for a new "light" version of traditional methodologies for use in e-business development. This call is consistent with the widely held position that there must be a single best approach to system development for e-business. This belief, a natural extension of the fact that most organizations mandate standardized development methodology, is challenged by the research reported in this chapter.

Research Objective and Methodology

The objective of this work is to identify appropriate system development methodology for the e-business environment by exploring the fit between existing development methodologies and the characteristics of e-business. The specific research approach employed in this chapter is a theoretical rather than empirical study and is divided into three steps. In Step 1, the unique characteristics of the e-business environment are considered. In Step 2, recognized system development methodologies are examined independently of e-business, using both prior research and the inherent characteristics of each methodology to isolate and identify situations where each model is most appropriately applied. Finally, in Step 3, the characteristics of e-business are aligned with those of the development methodologies, yielding a framework for e-business system development methodology customization.

RESEARCH STEP 1: EXAMINING THE E-BUSINESS ENVIRONMENT

Six aspects of the e-business environment set it apart from traditional IT development:

(1) More Rapid Time-to-Market

The nature of Web technologies allows Web Information Systems to be developed and deployed much more quickly than many traditional IT systems. Timeframes of three months have replaced those of one or two years for major systems. The fact that Web-based technologies are often easier to implement than similar technologies in traditional systems, has led to a widespread perception that e-business systems can be implemented with lightning speed. This in turn has increased pressure on developers to make rapid design decisions and produce results quickly (Odlyzko, 2001).

(2) More Heterogeneous Technical Environment

The technological environment for Web Information Systems is typically more heterogeneous and less stable than it is for most traditional IT systems. With a typical traditional system, the organization controls all technology choices. With a Web-based system, many hardware, software, and networking choices are made by external users. Further, integration with legacy systems is a greater problem for WISs than for traditional systems because (a) Web-based technologies are less compatible with traditional technologies, and (b) Web-based technologies are continuing to develop at a much faster rate than older, more traditional technologies.

(3) Changes in IT Strategy

The e-business marketplace changes quickly. As Porter (2001) noted, " In previous generations of information technology, application development was often complex, arduous, time consuming, and hugely expensive. These traits made it harder to gain an IT advantage, but they also made it difficult for competitors to imitate information systems. The openness of the Internet, combined with advances in software architecture, development tools, and modularity, makes it much easier for companies to design and implement applications." Thus while Web Information Systems can more easily gain competitive advantage, that very competitive advantage is far less easily sustained. This situation leads to two possible conclusions. First, some argue that e-business systems need to be designed flexibly, so that they can easily handle future changes. Second, others like Porter (2001) maintain that organizations involved in e-business need to embed their distinctive strategy into their value chain in such a way that competitors find it more difficult to copy. In addition to the competitive environment, the user interface strength of Web Information Systems causes many organizations to modify their strategic IT emphasis, moving from internal operations toward a greater emphasis upon customer relationships. In addition, brand relationships, the image and culture that characterize a relationship between a company and its customers (Hatch & Schultz, 2001), are an integral part of many WISs. Personalizing the Web interface and creating online communities through such features as chat or listservs offer an organization opportunities to support and extend existing brand relationships. Further, it is critical that a WIS's brand image dovetails with the organization's traditional branding, so that, from the customer viewpoint, there is seamless integration of the company's overall strategy.

(4) Emphasis upon the Human-Computer Interface

Information architects working on WISs concentrate heavily on human-computer interface and usability issues because most e-business systems interact with users outside the organization. This is not true of most traditional IT systems.

(5) Less Reliable Time and Cost Estimates

Web Information Systems are more difficult to estimate and control than projects that are more traditional because they lack a long history of time and cost estimates.

(6) Changes in Development Team Composition

Unlike traditional teams, WIS development teams include a broad range of non-technical talent. Marketing staff, business analysts, graphical artists, human-computer interaction specialists, and branding specialists participate to a greater degree in WIS teams than in traditional development teams. This alteration in team composition changes the dynamics of the work group and the approach taken by the teams to their projects. Further, the stability and continuity that an organization gains from its common culture can be upset by the creative, more liberal culture characteristic of many of the "creative types" now involved in Web development.

RESEARCH STEP 2: EXAMINING SYSTEM DEVELOPMENT METHODOLOGIES

System development methodology refers here to the model that is used to structure, plan, and control the process of developing an information system. A wide variety of such models has been proposed over the years, beginning with the System Development Life Cycle or Waterfall model. It would take an entire book to thoroughly cover all of the models proposed or used over the years. This research categorizes the most popular models into one of five major categories: linear, iterative, parallel, disruptive, or rapid-response. In the sections that follow, each of these major approaches to system development methodology is considered in terms of its strengths and weaknesses. Then in Step 3, the applicability of each of these methodologies to the realm of e-business system development is considered.

Linear Models (Including System Development Life Cycle and Waterfall)

While Boehm (1986) tracks system development methodology to Bennington's 1956 Stagewise model and Royce's 1970 Waterfall model, other authors suggest that the System Development Life Cycle (SDLC) evolved primarily during the 1970s (Harrison, 1985), in response to organizations' needs to better organize, plan, schedule, and control projects (Hall, 1980). The use of the term SDLC is in itself confusing, since some authors use it as a generic term to refer to virtually all development methodologies, and others use it to refer specifically to some of the earliest linear models. Here the term is used in the latter sense.

The SDLC is based upon two principles: dividing projects into phases, and using written documentation and approvals to maintain control. While the exact phases in the cycle vary from one author or organization to the next, the steps generally follow this pattern: initial investigation; conception or feasibility study; requirements definition; system design; coding, unit testing, integration and system testing; and implementation, maintenance and support. A formal review and approval or signoff by user and Information Technology management marks the end of most phases. The SDLC typically is "document driven" (Weinberg, 1991). It emphasizes time schedules, target dates, budgets, and implementation of an entire system at one time. The Waterfall model, which allows some overlap and splashback between the phases, and the V Model, which emphasizes quality assurance (Plogert, 1996), are some of the variations of the SDLC. Such linear models work best in situations where requirements are stable, the solution is clear, the user is knowledgeable, and there is no pressure for immediate implementation. In addition, because of the controlled nature of the linear approaches, they are ideal for supporting less experienced teams and project leaders, or teams whose composition fluctuates. Organizations that need to conserve resources, or whose culture or policies typically require strict management approvals, may be drawn to linear models.

Iterative Models (Including Prototyping, Spiral, Rapid Application Development)

Prototyping is an iterative process that lets users work with a small-scale mock up of their system, experience how it might function in production, and request changes until it meets their requirements. Typically, once the user is satisfied with the Prototype, then the Prototype "becomes a working requirements statement" (Weinberg, 1991), and design of the actual system begins. While most Prototypes are done with the expectation that they will be discarded, it is possible to evolve from Prototype to working system. Prototyping alone is not a complete development methodology, but rather an approach to handling selected portions of traditional development. Much of the emphasis in IS literature has been upon Prototyping as a method for developing user requirements.

Prototyping works well in situations where project objectives are unclear, requirements are unstable, or users are not highly knowledgeable. Its major benefits are most evident on larger projects with many users, interrelationships, and functions, where project risk relating to requirement definition can be significantly lessened through Prototyping (Boar, 1986; Harrison, 1985). Since Prototyping's iterations add to project budgets and schedules, it is not ideal when implementation time or resources must be minimized. Further, stable, experienced teams with experienced leadership are required to guard against an unanticipated interdependency emerging late in the development cycle. Finally, Prototyping is most suitable when flexible designs are not required, since, as Weinberg warns, "the flexible designs needed to accommodate unforeseen system evolution are often not sufficiently developed during system Prototyping."

Another view of iterative development has come from Boehm as early as 1986. The Spiral model is an iterative approach that is focused on minimizing project risk. "The model holds that each cycle involves a progression through the same sequence of steps, for each portion of the product and for each of its levels of elaboration, from an overall concept-of-operation document down to the coding of each individual program" (Boehm, 1986). In Boehm's early work, each trip around the Spiral traverses four basic quadrants: (1) determine objectives, alternatives, and constraints of this iteration; (2) evaluate alternatives; identify and resolve risks; (3) develop and verify deliverables from this iteration; and (4) plan the next iteration (Boehm, 1986 and 1988). Boehm's more recent work reflects an expanded view of the Spiral, requiring identification of stakeholders and their "win" conditions at the very start of each cycle, and ending the cycle with review and commitment (Boehm, 2000).

According to Boehm, "the Spiral model can accommodate most previous models as special cases, and further provide guidance as to which combination of previous models best fits a given software iteration" (1988). Thus Boehm finds an advantage in the Spiral model's ability to help select development methodology based upon the type of project risk. Because the Spiral model is highly customized to each project, it is quite complex. A skilled and experienced project manager is required to determine how to apply it to any given project. Situations where the Spiral model is likely to be most beneficial include those where risk avoidance is a high priority, the organizational culture appreciates precision and controls, and the delivery date takes precedence over functionality, which can be added later. These situations differ significantly from those where other iterative models, like Prototyping, are likely to be most successful.

Maturity of the Prototype methodology led to a further type of iterative development model, Rapid Application Development (RAD). RAD methodologies aim at producing high quality systems quickly, primarily by using iterative Prototyping, active user involvement, and computerized development tools. These tools may include Prototyping tools, Computer-Aided Software Engineering (CASE) tools, and object-oriented programming languages. Typical RAD systems iteratively yield production software, as opposed to throwaway Prototypes. RAD generally includes Joint Application Development (JAD), where users are intensely involved in system design either through consensus building in structured workshops (Andrews, 1991), or through electronically facilitated interaction (Carmel, George, & Nunamaker., 1994).

All of the iterative approaches attempt to reduce inherent project risk by breaking the project into smaller segments and providing more ease-of-change during the development process. Perhaps the greatest benefit of all incremental development approaches is the potential for exploiting knowledge gained in an early increment as later increments are developed. As Graham (1989) has noted, "Change, which is discouraged in a monolithic model, can be turned to advantage in ...incremental models." Thus early project experiences with estimating, the user interface, or database design, for example, can be leveraged to improve performance later in the project.

Parallel Models (Including Alternative Path or Ad Agency Approaches)

With parallel models (Figures 1 and 2), different approaches are tried at the same time by different individuals or teams, and then as the project progresses, less productive paths are pruned. Alternative paths may be followed simultaneously just at the project start, or new alternative paths may be introduced when the project reaches critical points. Parallel models are used most commonly by consultancy firms. For example, a Web consultancy agency simultaneously created three separate versions of the key user-interface components of a major consumer goods retailer's Web site. Each of these versions included creative assets, separate information architecture models, some usability testing, and user feedback sessions. While the back-end system integration was not done in parallel, three versions of the site were fully designed, developed, and presented to management, who selected one to be deployed. In another example of the use of parallel methodology, a major Web consultancy firm employed this approach to build a Web-based customer information data warehouse system for a major movie studio. Because of a tight timeline, coupled with incomplete information about source file structures and content, the development team produced multiple versions of major routines based on its limited understanding, with the intent of later eliminating those versions that were less suitable for continued development.

Figure 1: Sample of an Ad Agency Model (Develop multiple competing systems and select the best solution)

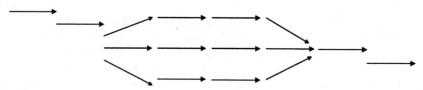

Figure 2: Sample of an Alternative Path Model (Periodically create and prune multiple paths as project progresses)

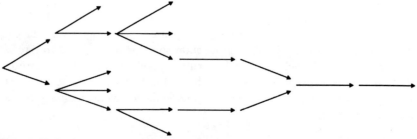

Clearly, the parallel approach is only practical when resource conservation is not a concern. It works best when the project team is solid, experienced, and stable, and both the user and the other members of the project team are flexible. The project manager must be experienced and maintain excellent communications. Team members must be strong enough to be able to see their hard work pruned in favor of competing sibling paths that either progress more quickly or offer more desirable characteristics. The parallel approach is most likely to be applied to poorly defined projects or those where time is the single most important criteria for project success.

Disruptive Models, Including Volcano Methodology

If each development phase is begun as early as possible and the phases overlap substantially, then the development methodology departs so significantly from the SDLC and Waterfall approaches that it should be given a distinct name—the Volcano methodology. When the amount of overlap between phases increases, the very concept of milestones is threatened as the lines between development phases blur and controls are weakened proportionately. Communication becomes critical. In this environment, exceptional project management and a stable, experienced, and flexible team are required. The Volcano approach is most often taken when there is a need for extremely rapid implementation, future versions are planned (and can be used to handle "clean-up"), and conservation of resources and formal approvals are not critical. Such projects are most often characterized by an atmosphere of regular upheaval. The work environment is stressful, and there is a high degree of turnover.

The Volcano methodology is not generally recognized among scholars but is found in the business environment. In one actual implementation for a major online drug Web site, a large consultancy firm used a highly overlapping methodology involving up to 120 team members in seven teams. Because of the very short timeframe, logistic considerations, and the expansive project scope, strategy, creative and technical teams worked nearly simulta-neously for the bulk of the project. Technical architecture and some programming and implementation efforts proceeded in advance of identifying a complete set of requirements. The company had an established back-end order processing system in place. Teams worked simultaneously from the user-interface towards the back-end and vice versa. As the project neared completion, the inter-team coordination required was high as both final functionality requirements and creative treatments were being set and altered close to the completion date. This is analogous to building a railroad where teams start at two coasts, but as they get closer, they have to communicate with each other more frequently to get the two tracks to line up.

Rapid-Response Models

During the late 1990s and early 2000s, a variety of new methodologies were put forth, most aimed at creating a lighter, faster, more flexible and responsive approach to development. Most of these approaches have not been subject to rigorous academic research, and it is too soon to say which of them will stand the test of time. While it would be impossible to describe all of the proposed methodologies here, a few of the most common models can be considered.

Most recent models aim for rapid-response to changing conditions. In general, they are based on breaking very large projects into many small projects, each with minimal requirements and taking just a few weeks to complete. Under Beck's Extreme Programming or XP (1999), user requirements are noted on index cards and programmers work in pairs, with two developers sharing one computer workstation, and weeding out bad code regularly through a process called refactoring. Initial studies have indicated that pair coding results in less initial productivity, but that pairs do write code with fewer defects (Radding, 2001; Williams, Kessler, Cunningham, & Jeffreies, 2000). The long-range benefits are yet to be fully assessed, although there is agreement that XP affords a unique opportunity for developers to learn from one another and for all members of a team to develop an in-depth understanding of many different aspects of their system.

Another recent model, Highsmith's Adaptive Software Development (1999), emphasizes developing a flexible team that can function in a complex, rapidly changing environment. Adaptive development grew out of Highsmith's attempt to apply Rapid Application Development techniques to larger, more complex projects. His adaptive development cycle consists of three major phases or stages: (1) speculate (project mission statement, initial requirements and cycle plan); (2) collaborate (short cycles where system components are developed concurrently and delivered); and (3) learn (review work and team's performance). At the end of the project, there is a final quality assurance and release step. Thus, Adaptive Software Development combines elements of earlier models. It has a strong iterative component with roots in RAD. Further, the order in which requirements are addressed is heavily riskbased, with the riskiest aspects tackled in early cycles. However, it also goes beyond these considerations in putting the emphasis upon the human element and development of a flexible team.

Overall, rapid-response methodologies are clearly borne out of the need for a methodology that is flexible and user-involved with a short implementation schedule, and yet well controlled. They are best employed in situations where rapid installation of the bulk of the system is not critical, users are flexible and able to make rapid, binding decisions, the team is collaborative and possesses substantial system design experience, and the project leader is experienced.

RESEARCH STEP 3: DEVELOPING A FRAMEWORK FOR E-BUSINESS DEVELOPMENT METHODOLOGY

As the prior sections have shown, each system development methodology, from the linear Waterfall to the rapid-response models, is best suited for particular situations. By examining the situations where each of these existing models is most appropriate, it is possible to distill a list of fifteen key variables that together determine the appropriateness of any development methodology. These variables, which fall into three categories—organizational, project, and team—are described in the following sections and depicted in Table 1.

Organizational Variables

The first organizational variable is culture, which varies from controlled to innovative. A controlled organization that is governed by a traditional, hierarchical structure with well-defined silos of operations relies on clear policies and procedures for most aspects of corporate functions. Documentation, approvals, and resource conservation are very important in project development. This type of organization does not function well with a methodology that requires flexibility, rapid decision making, and liberal use of resources. A linear or Spiral methodology is more suitable for its culture. At the opposite end of the spectrum, a company with a flat organizational structure that is built around cooperative innovation between business units and support departments may be inclined to favor methodologies where controls and resource conservation are secondary to flexibility and

Table 1: E-business development methodology variables

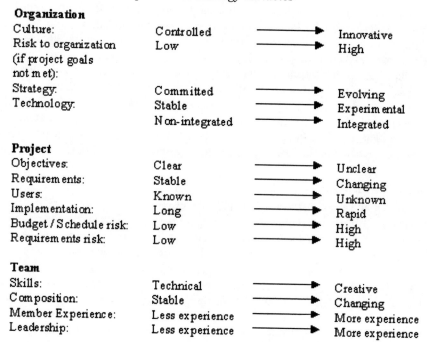

Organization

Culture:	Controlled ⟶	Innovative
Risk to organization (if project goals not met):	Low ⟶	High
Strategy:	Committed ⟶	Evolving
Technology:	Stable ⟶	Experimental
	Non-integrated ⟶	Integrated

Project

Objectives:	Clear ⟶	Unclear
Requirements:	Stable ⟶	Changing
Users:	Known ⟶	Unknown
Implementation:	Long ⟶	Rapid
Budget / Schedule risk:	Low ⟶	High
Requirements risk:	Low ⟶	High

Team

Skills:	Technical ⟶	Creative
Composition:	Stable ⟶	Changing
Member Experience:	Less experience ⟶	More experience
Leadership:	Less experience ⟶	More experience

rapid implementation. Parallel, disruptive, and rapid-response models are compatible with this culture and supportive of the core business strategy.

A second organizational variable concerns the extent to which there is a serious risk to the organization if the Web Information System's goals are not met. For example, if the very continuation of the business is dependent upon installation of the desired functionality, then either the Volcano approach, which sacrifices resources for functionality, or the Spiral method, which offers a way to control complexity and minimize risk, may be the methodology of choice. On the other hand, a linear approach would be more appropriate if there is little or no risk to the organization if the WIS goals are not met.

A third organizational variable is strategy. The importance of strategy to system development methodology was recognized by Wetherbe, Vitalri, & Mi. in 1994: "The tools and techniques that form the practice of systems development should reflect customers' immediate needs for fast business results, as well as the long-term vision of the company." Many Web Information Systems demand flexibility in adapting to continually evolving organizational strategy. This must be reflected in the development methodology. Prototyping, RAD, disruptive and rapid-response models deal well with changing functional requirements. Organizations that do not aggressively monitor the business environment and modify their strategies accordingly can successfully adopt more linear development methods.

The fourth organizational variable is technology. The organization must determine its predilection for the stability of a mature technology or the technical advantages of being on the leading edge. An added challenge is that the technology that supports Web Information Systems is continually changing, with few clear long-term dominant technologies emerging. Thus, organizations must not only consider their relative desire for stability or technical advantages, but also the relative stability level of the technologies available to them.

Organizations that plan to continue to operate in a stable technical environment with current staffing may benefit most from a linear or Spiral model, while those at the opposite end of the spectrum should consider parallel, disruptive, or rapid-response models.

Organizations must also determine the amount of integration required between their legacy systems and their WIS. The ability of these disparate systems to interact with one another, the amount of financial resources for hardware and software upgrades to be committed, and the availability and skill level of the organization's technical staff will influence this decision. Those organizations that decide their WISs and non-WISs will be kept relatively unconnected may find the linear models most compatible. On the other hand, organizations that desire full integration of their information systems components, and who want the advantages of the latest technologies may find that the Spiral model is better suited.

Project Variables

Project variables shown in Table 1 include objectives, requirements, users, implementation, and risk. When project objectives and requirements are clear and unchanging, they are more easily planned and documented. Budgets can be estimated and schedules can be forecast with a reasonable amount of certainty. Linear and Spiral models are appropriate for these conditions. If the project objectives and requirements are unclear and changing, the budget and schedule must be continually reassessed and communicated to the stakeholders and team members. Web Information Systems are characterized by an expectation, not only that the system will continue to evolve, but that fundamental changes in the system's basic functionality may be required. Parallel or rapid-response models are the most suitable for such changing functional requirements.

The third project variable is users. Many types of users with varying levels of knowledge and skill use Web Information Systems; yet, only a precise knowledge of user needs enables the development of WISs with high user value (Hahsler & Simon, 2000). Iterative models best support such situations because they provide multiple opportunities to develop, incorporate, and fine-tune understanding of the user. Linear models work best when user requirements are clear and the user is knowledgeable.

The fourth project variable is implementation timeframe. If there is no immediate need to install a Web Information System, for example in the case of an intranet whose functions are already available through other means, then the linear or Spiral models may be beneficial. Both oversee projects with more stringent controls. In addition, linear models can provide an organization with the opportunity to use the development methodology as an employee development training project, to give project leaders more experience and to acclimate users to team dynamics. Rapid implementation, on the other hand, is more likely with RAD, parallel, disruptive, and rapid-response methodologies.

The final project variables evaluate two different kinds of project risk. The more likely a project is to fail to meet its budget or schedule, the more applicable the linear and Spiral models, with their higher levels of inherent controls. On the other hand, projects whose greatest risk is of not correctly identifying and meeting functional requirements would be more likely to benefit from a Prototyping, RAD, parallel, or rapid-response methodology.

Team Variables

Team variables shown in Table 1 include skill levels, composition, experience, and leadership. Linear methodologies are particularly well suited for teams characterized by technical rather than creative skill sets, high turnover, and less experienced project leaders and team members. Other methodologies rely on a more experienced, stable team, and more easily accommodate creative talent along with technical experts.

ANALYSIS AND DISCUSSION

Table 2 is an enhancement of Table 1, showing the relationships between various development methodologies and organizational, project, and team variables. Since the fifteen variables concern specific organizations, projects, and teams, it is impossible to draw generalized e-business conclusions for all of them. Nonetheless, generalizations can be made about the relationship between e-business and eight of the fifteen variables. As described

Table 2: Framework for evaluating e-business development methodology

Organization

Culture: Controlled ⟶ Innovative / Research & Development
(Linear, Spiral) (Parallel, Disruptive, Rapid Response)

Risk to organization Low ⟶ High
if project goals not met (Linear, Prototyping, RAD) (Spiral, Volcano)

Strategy: Committed ⟶ Evolving (*)
(Linear) (Prototyping, RAD, Disruptive, Rapid Response)

Technology: Stable ⟶ Experimental (*)
(Linear, Spiral) (Parallel, Disruptive, Rapid Response)

Non-integrated ⟶ Integrated (*)
(Linear) (Spiral)

Project

Objectives: Clear ⟶ Unclear (*)
(Linear, Spiral) (Prototyping)

Requirements: Stable ⟶ Changing system fundamentals (*)
(Linear, Spiral) (Parallel, Rapid Response)

Users: Known ⟶ Unknown (*)
(Linear) (Spiral, Prototyping, RAD)

Implementation: Long ⟶ Rapid (*)
(Linear, Spiral) (RAD, Parallel, Disruptive, Rapid Response)

Budget/schedule risk: Low ⟶ High
(risk of not meeting) (Disruptive) (Linear, Spiral)

Requirements risk: Low ⟶ High
(risk of not identifying) (Linear, Spiral) (Prototyping, RAD, Parallel, Rapid Response)

Team

Skills: Technical ⟶ Creative (*)
(Linear, Spiral, Prototyping) (Parallel, Disruptive, Rapid Response)

Composition: Stable ⟶ Changing
(Prototyping, (Linear)
RAD, Parallel, Disruptive,
Rapid Response)

Member Experience: Less Experience ⟶ Highly Experienced
(Linear) (Disruptive)

Leadership: Less Experience ⟶ Highly Experienced
(Linear) (Spiral, Prototyping, RAD, Parallel, Disruptive, Rapid Response)

in the background section of this chapter, e-business tends to be characterized by evolving strategy, experimental technology with a need for integration, unclear project objectives, changing system fundamentals, unknown users, rapid implementation, and more creative teams. All of these typical characteristics of e-business are noted with an asterisk (*) in *Table 2*. A visual inspection of these eight asterisks quickly demonstrates that no one methodology is clearly most supportive of e-business development. When the other seven variables are also considered, it becomes apparent that the sheer number of variables (fifteen), coupled with the wide variance from one project to the next, dictates that no one existing development methodology will be clearly superior for all, or even most, WIS projects. Further, it is unlikely that any new methodology will ever be devised or discovered that will provide such a silver bullet. With no across-the-board solution available or on the horizon, the framework in Table 2 provides a way for an organization to determine the best practice development methodology for each of its e-business projects.

When an organization applies the framework to a particular project, considering all of its organization, project, and team variables, the framework is unlikely to align perfectly with any one methodology. At this point, the project leader may select a methodology model that is a close fit, cognizant of that model's limitations when applied to his or her project. For example, an innovative Web Information System might line up well with a rapid-response method except for the lack of experience of the project team. By using the framework, the project leader is able to identify this shortcoming and make plans in advance to compensate. Alternatively, when there is not a single methodology that is clearly the best fit, then the project leader may elect to create his or her own best practice by combining various aspects of those models that most effectively address the organization, project, and team variables.

FUTURE TRENDS AND CONSIDERATIONS

This research demonstrates that, instead of working to standardize development methodology, e-business project managers can maximize their projects' success by carefully selecting and following a customized methodology that is best suited to their organization, their project, their team, and the Web-enabled e-business environment. Such process customization is not without risk. One area for concern is whether a project manager, tailoring his or her own methodology, might not short-circuit controls in favor of autonomy. Solutions for this potential pitfall include definition of a specific methodology, including checkpoints and milestones, at the start of the project, and creation of either administrative responsibility or an oversight committee to insure that the methodology is followed throughout the life of the project.

Over time, some of the current instability inherent in e-business system development efforts is likely to subside. Technologies will stabilize, and dominant forces will emerge. Industries will absorb Internet technologies into their competitive marketplaces. Organizations will more fully integrate Web-based systems with traditional systems. IT departments will build experience in Web development. In this long-term environment, e-business development methodologies are likely to move toward greater controls, with increasing emphasis upon budgets, approvals, documentation, and milestones. Yet the very nature of e-business will continue to place a heavy emphasis upon such unique characteristics of Web Information Systems as the ability of any competitor to quickly transform the competitive environment, integration of marketing with systems analysis, rapid, iterative implementation, branding, and the importance of the user interface. Thus, e-business systems will always have unique development requirements and characteristics that require critically examining and customizing development methodologies.

Ultimately, there is no reason to believe that the system development methodology determination framework developed here applies only in the realm of Web-enabled e-business. One major area for future research involves transferring the framework to traditional system development projects. The flexible approach to project development that the Web demands at least hints at potential improvements in more traditional system development projects, where there is, after all, no reason to expect that one development methodology should be the best fit for all of an organization's projects.

CONCLUSION

The rapidly changing business and technical environment that characterizes Web-enabled e-business, coupled with the unique nature of Web development teams themselves, combine to demand a new approach to system development methodology. By examining the characteristics of existing development methodologies against the backdrop of Web Information System characteristics, this chapter has identified fifteen key variables that are central to methodology selection for e-business information systems. The combination of the large number of variables and the wide range of potential values for each establishes the fact that no existing methodology is ideally suited for all e-business development endeavors, and that it is unlikely that any one single methodology ever will be devised that will be appropriate for all, or even most, WIS development projects. Rather than continuing the search for a silver bullet, organizations seeking a best practice methodology for e-business development need to move away from the conventional wisdom of standardized procedures and toward project-based customization of development methodology. The framework presented here provides a storehouse of options from which project managers can and should select and tailor methodologies best suited to their organizations, their projects, their teams, and the unique nature of Web-enabled e-business. As this research shows, contrary to popular belief, one development methodology does not fit all systems.

REFERENCES

Andrews, D.C. (1991). JAD: A crucial dimension for rapid applications development. *Journal of Systems Management*, 42:3, 23-31.

Beck, K. (1999). *Extreme Programming Explained: Embrace Change (The XP Series)*. Upper Saddle River, NJ: Addison-Wesley.

Bennington, H.D. (1956). Productivity of large computer programs. *Proceedings ONR Symposium on Advanced Programming Methods for Digital Computers*, 15-27; also *Annals of the History of Computing*, (October 1983), 350-361.

Boar, B. (1986). Application prototyping: A Life Cycle Perspective. *Journal of Systems Management*, 37:2, 25-31.

Boehm, B. (1986). A spiral model of software development and enhancement. *ACM SigSoft Software Engineering Notes*, 11:4, 21-42.

Boehm, B. (1988, May). A spiral model of software development and enhancement. *Computer*, 61-72.

Boehm, B. (2000). Spiral development: Experience, principles, and refinements. *Spiral Development Workshop, February 9,, Special Report CMU/ SEI-2000-SR-008*.

Carmel, E., George, J.F., & Nunamaker, J.F. Jr. (1995). Examining the process of electronic-JAD. *Journal of End-User Computing*, 7:1, 13-22.

Graham, D.R. (1989). Incremental development: Review of nonmonolithic life-cycle development models. *Information and software technology*, 31:1, 7-20.

Hahsler, M. & Simon, B. (2000). User-centered navigation re-design for Web-based information systems. *Proceedings of the Americas Conference on Information Systems*, 192-198.

Hall, T.P. (1980). Systems life cycle model. *Journal of Systems Management*, 31:4, 29-31.

Harrison, R. (1985). Prototyping and the systems development life cycle. *Journal of Systems Management*, 36:8, 22-25.

Hatch, M.J. & Schultz, M. (2001). Are the strategic stars aligned for your corporate brand? *Harvard Business Review*, 79:2, 128-134.

Highsmith, J.A. III (1999). *Adaptive software development; A collaborative approach to managing complex systems*. New York: Dorset House Publishing.

Isakowitz, T. & Bieber, M.V. (1998). Web Information Systems. *Communications of the ACM*, 41:7, 78-80.

Odlyzko, A. (2001). The myth of "Internet time." *Technology Review*, 104:3, 92-93.

Plogert, K., (1996), The tailoring process in the German V-Model. *Journal of Systems Architecture*, 42:8, 601-609.

Porter, M. (2001). Strategy and the Internet. *Harvard Business Review*, 79:3, 62-78.

Radding, A. (2001). Simplicity, but with control. *Informationweek*, 831, 71-74.

Royce, W.W. (1970). Managing the development of large software systems: Concepts and techniques. *Proceedings, WESCON*.

Weinberg, R.S. (1991). Prototyping and the systems development life cycle. *Journal of Information Systems Management*, 8:2, 47-53.

Wetherbe, J.C., Vitalari, N.P., & Milner, A. (1994). Key trends in systems development in Europe and North America. *Journal of Global Information Management*, 2:2, 5-20.

Williams, L., Kessler, R.R., Cunningham, W., & Jeffries, R. (2000). Strengthening the case for pair-programmin. http://collaboration.csc.ncsu.edu/laurie/Papers/ieeeSoftware.PDF

Yourdon, E. (2000). The 'light' touch. *Computerworld*, http://www.computerworld.com/cwi/story/0,1199,NAV47_STO50363,00.html Accessed September 15, 2001

Chapter XV

Characterising Web Systems: Merging Information and Functional Architectures

David Lowe and Brian Henderson-Sellers
University of Technology, Sydney

ABSTRACT

Expenditure on Web-based initiatives has grown rapidly over the last five years, with a growing trend towards integrating these systems into the core business of many organisations. The architecture of these systems, however, tends to be quite complex – merging both a complex information architecture with a sophisticated technical architecture, with both being contextualised within new business models. An important key in achieving more effective Web system development within this rapidly changing environment will be a design approach that facilitates the creation of architectures that actively encompass both functional and informational elements, and which links both to the business model in a way that creates strong cohesion. This, in turn, requires both an appropriate architectural modelling language (particularly one that links the technology to the business model) and a process for carrying out the architectural design. In this chapter, we discuss both these aspects, looking at a model of Web systems that emphasizes the links between the various architectural elements and process-level support for design activities.

INTRODUCTION

There has been recent phenomenal growth in investment in online systems. A recent International Data Corp. report predicted that U.S. expenditure on Web-based initiatives would grow from US$12 billion in 1999 to $43.6 billion in 2002. The systems being developed are becoming increasingly important to the core business practices of many organisations and, consequently, to their business success. Essentially, they leverage the rapidly evolving infrastructure of the Internet and the increasingly complex set of Web standards, protocols and technologies to provide sophisticated business applications, including but not restricted to: business-to-business (B2B) interactions; e-commerce and electronic retailing systems; business support and workflow management; and governmental services.

These systems are much more complex than simple Web sites containing only static pages. They typically utilise Web technologies to provide a complex distributed front-end (often, though not universally, accessible through Web browsers) combined with high-performance back-end software systems that integrate the systems with critical business processes.

The architecture of these systems tends to be quite complex – merging a multifaceted information architecture with a sophisticated functional architecture. The information architecture encompasses aspects such as content and interaction modelling, informational viewpoints, user adaptation, and navigational support. The functional architecture typically has a structure composed of a diverse component-based middleware layer (Russell, 2000) with significant "glue" code, a highly customised thin front-end providing the interface and functionality to users of the system, and a highly customised back-end integrating the system with legacy and/or related systems. The component-based middleware layer usually makes extensive use of Commercial-Off-The-Shelf (COTS) subsystems with custom software created to integrate the various components.

The architecture (and in particular the technical aspects thereof) is usually highly constrained by the broader support infrastructure. For example, the requirements of having to work within the framework provided by existing Web browsers, data and document formats (such as HTML and XML), Internet limitations (such as bandwidth and security issues), etc., places tight constraints on the form that solutions may take. It also means that the solutions

Figure 1: Typical Web development process

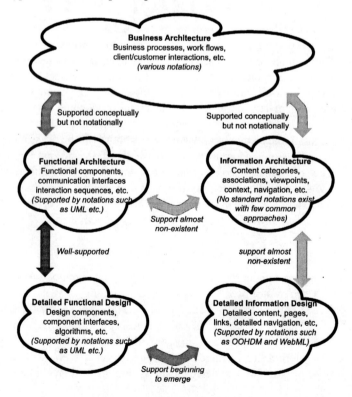

are much more directly related to the business needs being addressed and the resultant business models.

This highlights the fact that the information and functional architectures are typically tightly coupled to the business architecture. A specific business architecture (comprising aspects such as workflow support, customer management, user interaction, user management, and data management) will need to be reflected directly in both the information and functional architectures. This business architecture must, however, be a reflection of rapidly changing business needs and, indeed, of business models.

As illustrated in Figure 1, functional modelling is well supported by suitable modelling notations, and the modelling link between functional architectures and detailed functional designs is well established. Conversely, whilst modelling notations for detailed information design have begun to emerge, the equivalent notations at the architectural level are very poor and are not well linked with the detailed information design approaches.

This lack of effective modelling is particularly problematic given the particular characteristics of Web projects. These characteristics are most noticeable in the development processes that are typically adopted in commercial Web development. Industry best practice Web development tends to be highly incremental and, in particular, often removes the distinction between requirements specifications and design specifications, focussing simply on the more general concept of specification. This is partly a consequence of the domain uncertainty by both clients and developers (Sinha, 1999). With conventional IT development, developers may use both an iterative and an incremental approach to gain feedback from a client as to whether or not a particular solution addresses the clients needs (and, in doing so, improve the developers' understanding of the clients' requirements). The iterative/incremental development in Web projects, however, is intended not to evaluate solutions against a known set of needs but rather to actually help the client understand his/her own problem and formulate those needs.

As a consequence, many of the requirements are actually captured as part of an architectural specification rather than a more conventional requirements specification. This may appear to be anathema from the perspective of more conventional requirements engineering processes, but it is a reflection of the need to cope with the short development timeframes, rapid technological change, and significant client uncertainty. Merging the requirements process into the architectural design is tolerable because the architectures that are being explored are already relatively constrained by the broader infrastructure. This, nevertheless, remains a somewhat contentious issue.

This reliance on an architectural specification to form the bridge between the joint exploration of the problem and solution spaces and the incremental build cycle indicates that we need to support highly cohesive architectural models. A flaw in the specification at this point (such as the inability to adequately describe the system at a suitable level of abstraction) will result in poor specifications and inadequate solutions.

In this chapter, we explore these issues, considering approaches to developing a better cohesion between business needs and the architectural representations. Specifically, we will look at the need to couple a business architecture with both an information architecture and a functional architecture. It should be noted, before reading any further, that much of the discussion in this chapter poses questions but does not provide concrete answers to these questions. This is because, in many cases, these answers do not yet exist. This does not mean that the issues themselves can be ignored – rather that we simply need to be much more careful in acknowledging them and being aware of their consequences.

BACKGROUND: WEB ARCHITECTURAL MODELLING

Web systems typically have a number of characteristics that differentiate them from more conventional IT systems (Lowe & Henderson-Sellers, 2001; Overmyer, 2000). Possibly the most obvious difference between Web and traditional software development is seen in regard to the specific technologies that are used and the ways in which these are constrained by the inherent architectural limitations of the Internet/Web model. Partly as a consequence of this, the linkage between the business architecture and the technical design of the system is much tighter than for conventional software systems. Similarly, the information architecture (which covers aspects such as the content viewpoints, interface metaphors and navigational structures) is substantially more sophisticated than that of conventional software systems. This is partly a consequence of the fact that whereas conventional software systems focus on defining data *types*, Web systems typically have a major focus on the content itself.

Another aspect worth considering is the emphasis that is typically placed on open and modularised architectures for Web systems (Haggard, 1998; Russell, 2000; Sinha, 1999). Though not unique to Web systems, it is often more pronounced. Web systems are often constructed from multiple commercial off-the-shelf (COTS) components that are adapted and integrated together – particularly for the system back-end middleware layers. This implies that strong integration skills become much more critical in most Web projects.

The technology that underpins most Web systems is also changing very rapidly. This has several consequences. The first is that it increases the importance of creating *flexible* architectures that can be updated and migrated to new technologies with minimal effort, for example, the need for reusable data formats (such as XML) increases substantially.

Of notable significance is the importance of content. Irrespective of the sophistication of the functionality and the creativity of the interface, a site is likely to fail without appropriate, substantial, and up-to-date content. This demands an effective information design as well as suitable content management. Indeed, many Web systems, and in particular e-commerce systems, are being utilised by external users who therefore have no structured introduction to the interface. The system is typically the "public interface" for an organisation and, as such, performance and usability are key objectives, as is the need to engage users and provide much more evident satisfaction of users' needs and achievement of their objectives. The result is an increased emphasis on the information architecture and how it relates to the user interface and its associated structure and functionality.

These unique characteristics impact on the development process that is usually adopted. There are some obvious implications, such as the need to adopt a process that supports rapid development (Thomas, 2000). More subtly, however, is the impact in the relationship between requirements, architecture, and the built system. This can be seen best by looking at best practice in commercial development (Lowe & Henderson-Sellers, 2001).

Most commercial Web development follows a variant of the dual-cycle process shown in Figure 2. The first cycle iterates around a series of white sites, story-boards, and other similar exploratory design prototypes, with the aim of developing a clear specification of the system. This specification, however, typically includes not only the requirements but also the broad architectural design elements of the site (Gates, 2001; Haggard, 1998). The second cycle covers the usually fine-grained, incremental design and build process. This second cycle (and indeed elements of the first cycle) bear similarity to lightweight incremental processes like eXtreme Programming (XP) (Beck, 1999).

Figure 2: Typical Web development process

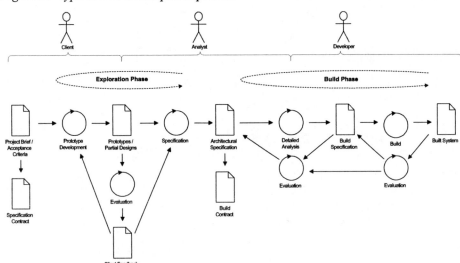

We can see the significance of this process by contrasting it with the lightweight and iterative processes that are adopted in conventional IT development. Typically, these processes support the evaluation of intermediate designs in order to obtain feedback from clients regarding the applicability of proposed solutions as a way to clarify client requirements. Even processes like XP assume that the client understands and is able to articulate his or her needs (for example, documented as *user stories* in XP) (Martin, 2000) – something that is often not true (or at least somewhat sporadic) in Web projects.

Consequently, when applied to Web development, these incremental processes have a slightly different focus (Angelique, 1999; Fournier, 1999) – supporting the development of problem domain understanding. In effect, the process (specifically the first of the two key cycles shown in Figure 2) is aimed at developing a joint understanding of the combined problem/solution domain. Developers utilise rapid prototyping and exploratory design approaches to assist clients in understanding the problem domain and how this relates to potential solutions. The result is a specification that incorporates both requirements and design elements. In particular, the specification that is used as a basis for the detailed system design and build is effectively an architectural specification that embeds many of the requirements directly into a specific architecture.

An important consequence of a process that evolves the requirements in conjunction with the emerging architecture is that the architecture needs to be highly flexible – able to evolve as the clients' understanding changes and matures. Indeed, it is our contention (one which we are continuing to explore) that this means that architecture is therefore the appropriate point to ensure consistency and integration between the business needs and the system design.

So, let us consider what should be included in the architectural specification. Figure 3 provides a generalised framework for considering the elements of an architecture and how they relate to other modelling aspects. This figure includes three different dimensions.

- *System abstraction:* This depicts the progression from viewing the system as a "black-box" that contributes to the overall business model through to the actual design and build. In particular, we can conceptualise the following abstraction levels: a business

Figure 3: Web system modelling framework

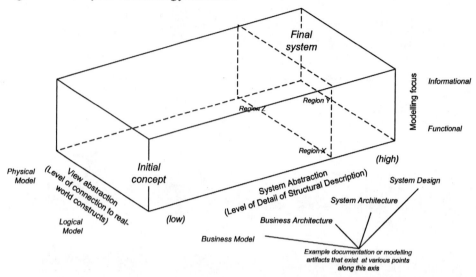

model defines the business approach and the role that the system plays in supporting the business; a business architecture defines the business processes, content, data transfers, client interactions, etc.; a system architecture defines the logical elements and physical components in the solution, the interfaces, constraints, etc.; and a system build defines the detailed structure of the solution.

- *View abstraction*: This captures the move from a logical view of the system to a physical view of the system. Note that this is independent of the system abstraction. For example, we can have a physical view of the business model that shows how the business actually operates in the context of its business environment, or we can have a logical view of the system architecture that shows the major functional components (such as user profiling, content management, session control, etc.)

- *Modelling focus*: At any given level of view of system abstraction we need to be able to focus on different modelling views. In particular, with Web systems we need to be able to model both the information being utilised, accessed or managed, as well as the functionality that supports this information.

When we construct different development models, they will typically occupy a "region" within this modelling "space". For example, we can construct a functional system architecture that shows the major logical components in the system, such as client registration, order processing and content updating (Region X in Figure 3). Alternatively, we might define a logical information architecture that shows the broad navigational structure and how this relates to the underlying information domain model (Region Y in Figure 3). One final example might be a physical model of the system functional architecture, which includes the specific Web server, how it is interconnected with a given firewall and so on. In effect, when we look at existing modelling approaches, we can consider which parts of this modelling space they effectively handle.

Finally, it is worth noting that both the business needs and the technologies that underpin these applications are complex and rapidly changing. The ability of these systems to successfully address business needs in an effective manner is highly dependent upon not only the utilization of appropriate technologies (which impacts greatly on aspects such as performance and system evolvability) but also on suitable information and functional design (both of which impact on aspects of the system such as usability) and the integration of functional architectures with information architectures.

Information Architecture

Let us consider the information architecture in a little more detail. The information architecture in Web systems is usually more complex than for conventional IT systems. This is partly a consequence of the heritage of these systems – evolving out of the early Web, which was primarily a distributed document management system that utilised hypertext concepts to support information location and retrieval.

Information architecture is an important discipline in its own right. It typically covers aspects such as: content and how it is managed; information structuring and access; user contextualisation; design of, and support for, navigation; information viewpoints; and presentation issues.

Various design approaches have been developed that focus on these aspects. For example, hypermedia design models such as RMM (Isakowitz, Stohr, & Balasubramanian, 1995) and OOHDM (Schwabe & Rossi, 1995) and, more recently, work on WebML (Ceri, Fraternali, & Bongio, 2000) emphasise the management of content and how this relates to the design of information viewpoints and the navigational structures that interconnect them. Although the details vary, these approaches typically model a Web system by commencing with a model of the underlying information, then aggregating this content into abstract views, then into specific Web pages. Similarly, work on hypermedia specifications (German & Cowan, 1999; Guell, Schwabe, & Vilain, 2000; Paulo, Augusto, Turine, Oliveira, & Masiero, 1998) tends to emphasise the specification of information structures. All these approaches largely fail to consider functional elements.

Other approaches have been emerging from the information systems literature (Rosenfeld & Morville, 1998). These tend to have less rich support for designing navigational aspects, but take a broader focus – considering not only the content and its structure but also the way in which it will be utilised, managed, controlled, accessed, updated, etc. Unfortunately these approaches are yet to become widely utilised (or even understood) within the Web development community – possibly because they are seen as too awkward and not consistent with the exploratory prototyping that currently typifies Web development.

It is worth noting, however, that these approaches tend not to differentiate between the information architecture and the detailed design – seeing it as a seamless transition. Indeed, the architecture itself is rarely considered explicitly, tending to emerge either top-down out of the broader business needs or bottom-up out of the detailed design. Furthermore, the integration of the information architecture into the technical solution is rarely considered by these methods.

Functional Architecture

The second thread of the architecture is the functional architecture. Considering solely an information architecture may be sufficient for a static Web site. However, complex dynamic Web *systems* will invariably incorporate complex functionality that also needs to be considered.

Conventional software design – and in particular Object-Oriented (OO) and Component Based Development (CBD) approaches – is often used in designing Web systems. This extends from logical architectures to detailed system designs. One of the more common modelling languages used for this purpose is Unified Modelling Language (UML) (OMG, 1999). UML, and other similar modelling languages such as Open Modelling Language (OML) (Firesmith, Henderson-Sellers, & Graham, 1997) tend to provide stronger modelling support for detailed design and largely fail to address architectural level issues – though it is possible to construct architectural diagrams that convey some of the required meaning.

Even more problematically, software modelling languages tend to focus on the functional elements and largely fail to provide suitable modelling support for the information architecture. A number of researchers have attempted to address this problem by adapting UML to Web development (Baumeister, Koch, & Mandel, 1999; Vilain, Schwabe, & Souza, 2000). In most cases the result is somewhat cumbersome. In effect, the *notation* of UML has been utilised but not the underlying modelling constructs, with the result that we have a method for diagramming navigational diagrams but not for reasoning about and manipulating the inherent models. Furthermore, these approaches have largely failed to integrate information modelling into the functional modelling.

One attempt to resolve this problem is the work by Conallen (1999). This attempts to link the informational perspective with the functional components. For example, Conallen attempts to model the connection between client-side content and behaviour, and server-side functionality. The result is a useful start but tends to focus on detailed design artifacts rather than supporting effective architectural modelling. Furthermore, the modelling of the informational aspects is rather limited. The result is an approach that is useful for visualising the functional operation and how it relates to actual Web pages, but not for supporting the design of an information architecture.

Work on functional architectures for Web systems has tended to emphasise the understanding of different business patterns and how these support linking the business domain to specific solutions, including the architecture. Patterns categorise best practice in various domains. The topic area of patterns has been maturing and expanding from the early work on object-oriented patterns (Gamma, Helm, Johnson, & Vlissides, 1995) to more recently encompassing patterns for interfaces, business models, requirements, etc. This patterns-based work has recently been extended to consider Web system business models and architectures. For example, Adams (2000) defines different patterns for the structural foundations of e-businesses: the e-channel pattern, the click-and-brick pattern, the e-portal pattern, etc. Each of these patterns requires a different supporting technical architecture. Indeed, an overriding theme in the emerging literature is the need to ensure (and the difficulty in doing so) that the business pattern matches well to the underlying technologies and the architecture into which they fit. This is captured well in IBM's Application Framework for e-Business (Lord, 2000), which encompasses a set of "patterns for e-business." This work emphasizes that there should be an understood link between the business model (as represented by a suitable pattern) and the logical and physical patterns for the design of the system. In particular, the business patterns include a set of application *topologies* that help provide these insights into the desired system architectures.

Although IBM's application framework for e-business (and similar approaches such as J2EE Blueprints) provide an effective foundation for considering e-business architectures, they do tend to focus on the functional elements of the architecture and largely overlook informational aspects.

Conversely, the work captured in the Hypermedia Pattern Repository (see http://www.designpattern.lu.unisi.ch/) collects patterns for Web systems that are largely focused on various elements of the information architecture, including navigation, interface, and interactions, but tends to overlook functional aspects, particularly at the logical and physical levels.

We can gain some insights into how we might create better cohesion between the architectural elements by looking at the development process in some detail. A number of Web and e-commerce system design approaches have been emerging over the last few years (Angelique, 1999; Burdman, 1999; De Troyer & Leune, 1997; Fournier, 1999). These tend to focus on supporting functional design and/or understanding potential usage patterns, resulting in approaches that have a very restricted focus.

In contrast to this, the authors (Haire, Henderson-Sellers, & Lowe, 2001; Henderson-Sellers, Haire, & Lowe, 2001) have been exploring the required extensions to the Object-oriented Process, Environment and Notation (OPEN) process framework (Graham, Henderson-Sellers, & Younessi, 1997) to make it more suitable for supporting Web development process. In particular, a number of tasks have been recently included that explicitly address the need to develop a cohesive architecture. These include tasks such as: "Design Web site architecture" and "Choose Architectural Pattern for Web site" (Haire et al., 2001). Whilst general software architecture design techniques can be used, specific techniques that cohesively link the design of the functional architecture with the design of the information architecture have yet to be developed.

So, where does this leave us? An important key in achieving more effective Web system development will be an architectural design approach that facilitates the creation of an architecture that actively encompasses both functional and informational elements and that links both of them to the business model in a way that creates strong cohesion. This, in turn, requires two key components: an architectural modelling language that allows representation of the link between the technology being used and the role it plays in both the business model and the underlying system architecture; and a process for carrying out the architectural design and utilizing this design suitably. Neither of these yet exists, but in the next section we will explore how we might move towards them.

IMPROVING ARCHITECTURAL MODELS

So how do we achieve improvements to the architectural models? A useful starting place is to investigate commercial Web specifications and from these data then to develop models of the evolving characteristics of Web systems. Figure 4 shows the key characteristics of Web systems as the system evolves. Consistent with the process shown in Figure 2, there are three key levels: initial acceptance criteria that form the basis of the project initiation and/or tendering; the architectural specification; and the build specification. Note that the elements of the model are referred to as characteristics rather than requirements or design elements, since the distinction is somewhat arbitrary for Web projects. The model that underlies Figure 4 also captures aspects such as the causal relationships between these characteristics – an aspect that can be important in terms of both guiding development of the emerging system and in understanding the potential implications of changes.

The model that underlies Figure 4 not only captures the key system characteristics, but also the relationships between these characteristics. For example, it allows representation of the causal link between identification of stakeholders and characterisation of users. The most significant links are those between the business architecture and the functional and information architectures. The business architecture is essentially the external view of the system, describing how the specific business needs will be met. It incorporates aspects such

Figure 4:   Characterisation diagram of Web systems

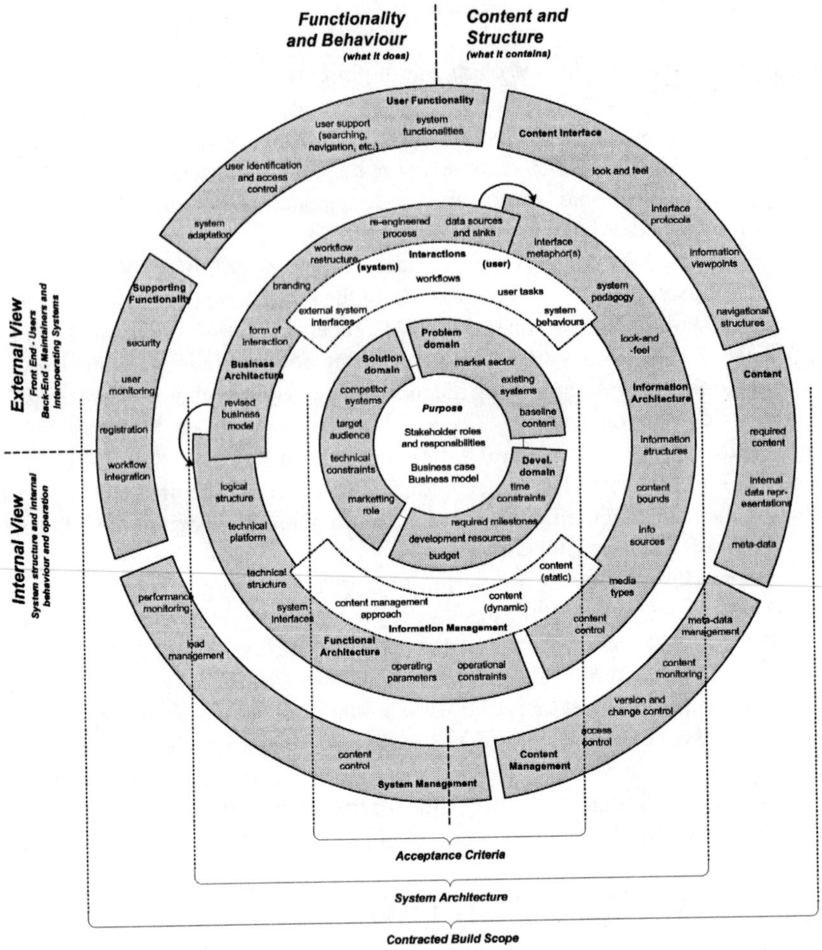

as business processes and workflows, the types of user interactions that will be supported, site branding, etc.

The business architecture, in turn, drives both the information architecture and the functional architecture. The information architecture will incorporate aspects such as interface metaphors, broad content requirements, information sources, and content access control. The functional architecture will incorporate aspects such as the logical components of the system, the system interfaces, and the core functionality as well as the key operating parameters and constraints.

This now gives us a starting point for considering the elements that need to be incorporated into an architectural specification, but we are still missing the modelling language(s) that allow us to represent these aspects. In effect, the above characterisation model provides a framework for structuring the relationships between the models, but does not provide the actual modelling language(s).

As we noted earlier, there has been some recent work in these directions, though this has tended to be limited to partial adaptation of information and hypertext modelling language [such as WebML (Ceri et al., 2000)] to incorporate some functional aspects, or adaptation of UML to incorporate information modelling [such as work by Conallen (1999)]. The elements requiring to be modelled include various kinds of Web pages: e.g., server pages, client pages. Modelling *Webpage* as a class thus leads to *serverpage* and *clientpage* as being subtypes in the model (a *serverpage* is a special kind of *Webpage*) and thus the use of the generalization relationship in the UML. Unfortunately, Conallen (1999) instead erroneously uses the UML concept of a stereotype to model a *serverpage* as a kind of *Webpage* – stereotypes in the UML refer to user-defined virtual extensions to the metamodel [the so-called M2 level (OMG, 1999)] not to subtypes in the model itself (M1 level). To use stereotypes correctly in the UML (e.g., Atkinson, Kühne, & Henderson-Sellers, 2000), we need to identify a conceptual level subtype of an existing metalevel class, such as *Class*. For example, a useful stereotype on *Class* might be <<*container*>> to denote any class that acts as a *ContainerClass* (a metalevel class not previously in existence and invented herein) – although of course container classes can be modelled in other ways directly without necessarily resorting to inventing new metatypes! Another, alternative means of depicting functional and architectural modelling elements worth future exploration would be the use of traits (Firesmith et al., 1997) which are informal groupings of model elements at the M1 (model) level.

There has also been several more recent approaches – such as the work on MESH (Lemahieu, 2001). This, along with the other approaches described above, has, however, tended to focus on linking information modelling and functional modelling at a detailed design level, rather than an architectural level. Addressing this issue remains an open research question.

IMPROVING ARCHITECTURAL PROCESSES

Figure 2 depicted some typical aspects of a Web development process in which the architecture tends to emerge from a joint client-developer exploration of prototypes and partial designs – rather than being *architected* in the conventional sense. Both functional and information architecture aspects must be strongly linked back to the business architecture (which acts to couple these together) and the architecture models built up incrementally and iteratively. In addition to the constraints of the business architecture, the more detailed architecture will rely more heavily on pre-existing architectural elements as embodied in components and collections of components, such as COTS software. These architectural elements can then be fed back to the customer in the Web prototyping mode of development described here.

One of the interesting research questions remaining is how to quantify an architecture. Derivation and application of software engineering metrics to the design would permit answers to questions such as: How detailed does the architectural specification need to become before we switch from the "exploration phase" into the "build phase"? Once we can monitor the changes in such architecture metrics, we can then understand to what extent changes might be permissible in the evolving architecture and at what stage in the incremental process. In addition, such techniques as refactoring can be evaluated for the contribution to increased quality as the architectural design evolves.

In effect, we need to be able to develop highly evolvable systems. If we consider the well-know maxim "form follows function," then, in the context of Web systems, the function continues to evolve constantly throughout the lifetime of a system, implying that the form will need to evolve. Indeed, given the initial lack of clarity (with respect to client needs) in most Web projects, the intended function of the system will evolve not only during the project lifetime but even during the initial development, again implying that the form of the system (i.e., its architecture) will need to evolve even as it is being developed.

One final issue worth considering is related to the exploration phase shown in Figure 2. During this phase, developers and clients will typically jointly explore partial designs and prototypes as a vehicle for removing client uncertainty. It is during this exploration, and the associated development of partial solutions, that the architecture begins to emerge. This means that we need to be understand what manner of prototypes will allow developers to jointly resolve requirements and develop an effective architecture.

FUTURE TRENDS AND CONCLUSIONS

In this chapter we have posed numerous questions, raised a significant number of issues, yet only provided a few answers. Unfortunately this is a reflection of the rather immature state of current understanding about handling Web system architectures, particularly in the context of the rapid evolution and client uncertainty with regard to these systems.

Nevertheless, we have at least attempted to map out the terrain associated with these issues. Specifically, a number of general conclusions become evident. Possibly the most obvious is that the field is currently very fragmented – though this is to be expected given its relatively recent emergence and its continuing rapid change. For example, although various approaches to modelling Web systems are emerging, these tend to address specific aspects of the system and little work has been done to draw them together.

Most problematically from a systems perspective is the lack of any coherence at all in addressing the broad architectural issues, despite the widespread recognition that getting the architecture correct is correct (reflected in recent attention on *infrastructure*). Certainly, aspects of the architecture are being considered (such as in the e-business frameworks work by IBM) but, when functionality is considered, information is overlooked and vice versa. Despite these problems, the current research foci certainly indicate that attention is beginning to be paid to these problems.

REFERENCES

Adams, J. (2000). *IBM Redbooks: Patterns for e-Business.*: IBM.

Angelique, E. (1999), . A lightweight development process for implementing business functions on the Web. Paper presented at the WebNet'99, (October 24-30) Honolulu, Hawaii.

Atkinson, C., Kühne, T., & Henderson-Sellers, B. (2000). To meta or not to meta—That is the question. *Journal of Object-Oriented Programming, 13*(8), 32-35.

Baumeister, H., Koch, N., & Mandel, L. (1999). Towards a UML extension for hypermedia design. Paper presented at the <<UML>> 1999: The Second International Conference on The Unified Modeling Language, Fort Collins, Colorado, USA.

Beck, K. (1999). *Extreme programming explained*: Reading, MA: Addison-Wesley.

Burdman, J. (1999). *Collaborative Web development*: New York: Addison-Wesley.

Ceri, S., Fraternali, P., & Bongio, A. (2000). *Web Modeling Language (WebML): a modeling language for designing Web sites.* Paper presented at the Proceedings of WWW9 Conference, May, Amsterdam.

Conallen, J. (1999). *Building Web Applications with UML*: Reading, MA: Addison-Wesley.

De Troyer, O., & Leune, C. (1997, 1998). *WSDM: A user-centered design method for Web sites.* Paper presented at the *7th International World Wide Web Conference,* Brisbane, Australia.

Firesmith, D. G., Henderson-Sellers, B., & Graham, I. (1997). *OPEN Modeling Language (OML) Reference Manual.* New York: SIGS Books.

Fournier, R. (1999). *Methodology for Client/Server and Web Application Development*: Englewood Cliffs, NJ: Yourdon Press.

Gamma, E., Helm, R., Johnson, R., & Vlissides, J. (1995). *Design patterns: Elements of reusable object-oriented software*: Reading, MA: Addison-Wesley.

Gates, L. (2001). Analysis and design: Critical yet complicated. *Application Development Trends, February 2001*, 40-42.

German, D. M., & Cowan, D. D. (1999). Formalizing the specification of Web applications. *Lecture Notes in Computer Science,* Springer Verlag, 1727, 281–292.

Graham, I., Henderson-Sellers, B., & Younessi, H. (1997). *The OPEN Process Specification.*: Reading, MA: Addison-Wesley.

Guell, N., Schwabe, D., & Vilain, P. (2000). Modeling interactions and navigation in Web applications. Paper presented at the *World Wild Web and Conceptual Modeling '00 Workshop* - ER'00 Conference, Salt Lake City, USA.

Haggard, M. (1998). *Survival guide to Web site development*. Microsoft Press.

Haire, B., Henderson-Sellers, B., & Lowe, D. (2001). *Supporting Web development in the OPEN process: Additional tasks*. Paper presented at the *COMPSAC'2001: International Computer Software and Applications Conference,* 8-12 Oct, Chicago, Illinois, USA.

Henderson-Sellers, B., Haire, B., & Lowe, D. (2001). Adding Web support to OPEN. *Journal of Object Oriented Programming, 14*(3), 34-38.

Isakowitz, T., Stohr, E., & Balasubramanian, P. (1995). RMM: A methodology for structured hypermedia design. *Communications of the ACM, 38*(8), 34-44.

Lemahieu, W. (2001). MESH: An object-oriented approach to hypermedia modelling and navigation. Paper presented at the *SSGRR 2001: International Conference on Advances in Infrastructure for Electronic Business, Science, and Education on the Internet,* 6-12 Aug. L'Aquila, Italy.

Lord, J. (2000). Patterns for e-business: Lessons learned from building successful e-business applications, [IBM White Paper]. IBM. Available: http://www-4.ibm.com/software/developer/library/lessons/.

Lowe, D., & Henderson-Sellers, B. (2001). *Impacts on the development process of differences between Web systems and conventional software systems*. Paper presented at the SSGRR 2001: International Conference on Advances in Infrastructure for Electronic Business, Science, and Education on the Internet, 6-12 Aug. 1L'Aquila, Italy.

Martin, R. (2000). A Case study of XP practices at work. Paper presented at the XP2000, Cagliari, June Italy.

OMG. (1999). OMG Unified Modeling Language Specification, Version 1.3 (Vol. OMG document 99-06-09).

Overmyer, S. (2000). What's different about requirements engineering for Web sites? *Requirements Engineering Journal, 5*(1), 62-65.

Paulo, F. B., Augusto, M., Turine, S., Oliveira, M. C. F. D., & Masiero, P. C. (1998). *XHMBS: A formal model to support hypermedia specification*. Paper presented at the *Ninth ACM Conference on Hypertext*.

Rosenfeld, L., & Morville, P. (1998). *Information Architecture for the World Wide Web*. Sebastopol, CA: O'Reilly.

Russell, P. (2000). *Infrastructure - Make or Break your E-Business*. Paper presented at the TOOLS-Pacific 2000: Technology of Object-Oriented Languages and Systems, November 20-23, Sydney, Australia.

Schwabe, D., & Rossi, G. (1995). The object-oriented hypermedia design model. *Communications of the ACM, 38*(8), 45-46.

Sinha, G. (1999). Build a component architecture for e-commerce. *E-Business Advisor,* March.

Thomas, D. (2000). Managing software development in Web time software. Paper presented at the XP2000, June, Cagliari, Italy.

Vilain, P., Schwabe, D., & Souza, C. S. D. (2000). *A diagrammatic tool for representing user interaction in UML.* Paper presented at the *<<UML>>2000: The Third International Conference on The Unified Modeling Language,* York, UK.

Chapter XVI

Customisation of Internet Multimedia Information Systems Design Through User Modelling

Sherry Y. Chen and Marios C. Angelides
Brunel University, UK

ABSTRACT

Internet multimedia information systems have become widespread in business and educational settings. However, much remains to be identified about how different users perceive such systems. Therefore, it is essential to build robust user models to illustrate how multimedia features are experienced by different users. Multimedia research suggests cognitive and interpersonal styles have a significant effect on the users' navigation patterns and interaction behaviour. In particular, gender difference, prior knowledge, and cognitive styles have been extensively examined in previous studies. The findings of the research review that has been done as part of this chapter are classified into three themes: (a) content information and presentation, (b) information space navigation and accessibility, and (c) user interfaces and support. A user model is then developed as a result of the analysis of the findings. Finally, implications for the design of Internet multimedia information systems are discussed.

INTRODUCTION

The freedom offered by Internet multimedia information systems often comes with a price. The most reported negative effects are "getting lost in hyperspace" and "cognitive overload" (McDonald & Spencer, 2000). Not all users appreciate the freedom of interaction and wealth of information that Internet multimedia information systems provide. Such importance has been highlighted by previous research, which indicates that users with different cognitive and interpersonal styles experience different problems and require different navigational support in Internet multimedia information systems (e.g., Ford & Chen, 2000).

It is, therefore, essential to build a robust user model by understanding the needs of users with different cognitive and interpersonal styles (Ford, 2000). Such a user model can help the designers to develop Internet multimedia information systems that can accommodate a wide range of cognitive and interpersonal styles. The paper aims to examine the application of user modelling for customising the design of Internet multimedia information systems. At first, it discusses the importance of cognitive and interpersonal styles and how differences in these influence user-interaction with Internet multimedia systems. The evidence is then analysed under three common themes: (a) content information and presentation, (b) information space navigation and accessibility and (c) user interfaces and support. Finally, a user model is developed that is comprised of three user profiles—requirements, system, and personal—that can be used in customising the design of Internet multimedia information systems.

BACKGROUND

In the past ten years, many studies have found that cognitive and interpersonal styles had significant effects on the use of information systems. Such differences include gender differences (Ford & Miller, 1996), prior knowledge (Ford & Chen, 2000), and cognitive styles (Shih & Gamon, 1999).

For gender differences, previous research showed that males have higher abilities and interest in computers than females (Busch, 1995). Koch (1994) examines the effects of gender differences on the use of technology in the classroom. She points out that many girls in school show little interest for computers. "They are socialized to view technology and technically literate people as belonging to a particular culture—the hacker culture"—which is comprised primarily of men. She also describes that women "may also see the world of technology as precise and unforgiving, often lacking in creativity and having little connection to people."

Users' prior knowledge includes previous understanding of the content area and levels of system experience appropriate to the program. A number of studies compared the differences between users with high prior knowledge and those with low prior knowledge. Table 1 classifies the familiarity with computer systems and system requirements for these two groups.

Cognitive style is an individual's preferred and habitual approach to organising and representing information (Riding & Rayner, 1998). Among the various dimensions of cognitive styles, Witkin's Field Dependence has emerged as one of the most widely studied

Table 1: Prior knowledge and system requirement (Adapted from Shneiderman, Byrd, Croft, 1997)

	Familiarity	Requirements
Low prior knowledge	Applying little specialised training to use the system. They use the interface that supports the primary functions.	Such users need an orderly structure, visible landmarks, reversibility, and safety during the processes of interacting with computer systems.
High prior knowledge	Possessing the capability to use most of the system's features. They can get the point quickly and in a straight way.	Such users demand shortcuts or macros to speed-repeated tasks and extensive services to satisfy their varied needs.

cognitive styles with the computer-based applications (Witkin, Moore, Goodenough, & Cox, 1977). This is because it reflects how well a user is able to restructure information based on the use of salient cues and field arrangement (Weller, Repman, & Rooze, 1994). Field Dependence describes the degree to which a user's perception or comprehension of information is affected by the surrounding perceptual or contextual field (Jonassen & Grabowski, 1993). Their characteristics are:

1. Field Dependence: the individuals are considered to have a more social orientation than field independent persons since they are more likely to make use of externally developed social frameworks. They tend to seek out external referents for processing and structuring their information, are more readily influenced by the opinions of others, and are affected by the approval or disapproval of authority figures (Witkin et al., 1977).

2. Field Independence: the individuals are more capable of developing their own internal referents, and they do not require an imposed external structure to process their experiences. They also tend to exhibit more individualistic behaviours since they are not in need of external referents to aid in the processing of information. In addition, they are not easily influenced by others, and they are not overly affected by the approval or disapproval of superiors (Witkin et al., 1977).

Users with different cognitive and interpersonal styles have different interaction behaviours. Such differences also influence their interactions with Internet multimedia information systems. The next section will present a comprehensive review of previous studies to illustrate how people interact with Internet multimedia information systems.

INTERNET MULTIMEDIA INFORMATION SYSTEMS

The empirical studies discussed in this section illustrate the relationships between cognitive and interpersonal styles and the use of Internet multimedia information systems and, in particular, the core themes of content information and presentation, information space navigation and accessibility, and user interface and support.

Content Information and Presentation

Multiple formats

Previous research indicated that users with different cognitive and interpersonal styles showed different preferences to presentation of information content in Internet multimedia systems. In the dimension of Field Dependence, several studies suggested that Field Independent individuals could particularly benefit from the control of media choice. A study by Chuang (1999) produced four courseware versions: animation+text, animation+voice, animation+text+voice, and free choice. The results showed that Field Independent subjects in the animation+text+voice group or in the free choice group scored significantly higher than those in the animation+text group or those in the animation+voice group. No significant presentation effect was found for the Field Dependent subjects. Similar results were obtained by Chanlin's (1998) study, which found Field Independent users did significantly better in visual control treatment, but there was no difference for Field Dependent users.

Several studies suggest that auditory cues are important to Field Dependent users. Lee (1994) investigate the effectiveness of auditory cueing of multimedia material. The result showed that Field Dependent users would perform more effectively if the auditory cues were provided. Marrison and Frick (1994) also claim similar results to that Field Dependent users indicate that sound would enhance multimedia instruction.

Furthermore, prior knowledge may be another factor that influences the preferences to the visualisation of the content in Internet multimedia information systems. Kirby and Boulter (1999) compare the learning performance of two instructional groups. A traditional group follows an approach that involves paper-and-pencil tasks and verbal instruction, and a spatial group follows an approach incorporating object manipulation and visual imagery designed to encourage spatial thinking. The interaction indicates that high prior knowledge subjects perform better in the spatial group and that low prior knowledge subjects outperform in the traditional group.

Non-linear presentation

Non-linear presentation is another feature of Internet multimedia information systems. Several studies showed that users' prior knowledge has significant effects on the attitudes and performance toward non-linear presentation. Savenye (1996) investigated the achievement and attitudinal effects of navigational behaviour patterns in using a non-linear multimedia-based instruction designed for college students. The results of this study showed that there is a positive relationship between levels of prior knowledge and learning achievement. This finding is in line with that of Ford and Chen (2000), who examined users' navigation patterns in a Web-based multimedia environment. The results also showed that users with high prior knowledge perform better than those with low prior knowledge.

In addition, Last *et al.* (1998) examined the influences of a user's prior knowledge on the difficulties and benefits associated with using multimedia. The results indicated that high levels of anxiety were common for the low prior knowledge users, especially when required to perform a specific learning task. Similar results were obtained by the study of McDonald and Stevenson (1998), who examined different multimedia topologies and compared knowledgeable and non-knowledgeable subjects on hierarchical (linear), non-linear, and mixed (a combination of hierarchical and non-linear) psychology tutorials. They discovered that non-knowledgeable subjects seem overwhelmed by the number of choices offered by non-linear text while knowledgeable users seem most comfortable with that set-up. They suggest that novices should have a more structured learning environment to guide them through the material. The findings of these two studies echo the views of Demetriadis and Pombortsis (1999) that a more structured instruction should be provided for novices and complexity should be kept at a minimum for them.

The aforementioned studies reveal that users with different cognitive and interpersonal styles may have different information needs and may require different information presentations. The choice of media is advantageous to Field Independent users, while sound is an important cue to Field Dependent users. Text-based environments are favourable to users with low prior knowledge; conversely, image-based environments are useful to users with high prior knowledge. Non-linear interaction will be beneficial to users with high prior knowledge; on the other hand, linear presentation will be suitable to users with low prior knowledge.

Information Space Navigation and Accessibility
Navigation strategies

Most of Internet multimedia information systems provide various navigation tools to allow users to structure their navigation strategies with multiple approaches. With multiple tools given in multimedia information systems, how do individuals with different cognitive and interpersonal styles make use of these tools? User preferences are likely to be an important factor in determining whether a particular tool is useful.

A number of empirical studies evaluated the effectiveness of different navigation tools for high and low prior knowledge users. Farrell and Moore (2001) investigated whether the use of different navigation tools (linear, main menu, and search engine) would influence users' achievement and attitude. The results indicate a significant difference for high prior knowledge subjects using the search engine. A significant difference in positive attitude was found for all users using the main menu.

Several studies also found that there are significant relationships between users' cognitive styles and their navigation strategies. Ford and Chen (2000) examined the effects of cognitive styles on the use of multimedia systems. They found significant differences in navigation strategies used by Field Dependent and Field Independent users. Field Independent users make greater use of the index to locate a particular item. Conversely, Field Dependent users favour using the map to get the whole picture of the context. This may be because using the map can provide users with a structured interface that can adapt to the more global approach of Field Dependent users. Kim (1997) investigated how users with different cognitive styles navigate the Web differently. The author reported that the cognitive styles affect users' search strategies. Field Independent users tend to use search engines, the *find* option and URLs more frequently to reach the desired Web sites. On the other hand, Field Dependent users tended to use the *home* or *backward/forward* keys more frequently. This implies that Field Independent users tend to engage in search tasks with more active and analytic strategies. In contrast, Field Dependent users do not feel comfortable with using tools for jumping around different nodes and navigate the Web in a linear mode.

In addition, previous research indicates that gender differences influence users' navigation strategies in Internet multimedia information systems. Schwarz (2001) found that females and males request different kinds of support when locating particular information. Male users need a larger frame of reference, while female users ask procedural directions. Furthermore, Cutmore, Hines, Maberly, Langford, and Hawgood (2000) examined the influence of gender differences on the knowledge acquisition with two types of navigational cues: landmark information and compass heading. Landmark information provides navigators with location rather than orientation, and it is used as the basis of the acquisition of route knowledge. On the other hand, compass heading provides orientation cues to facilitate the development of survey knowledge. Their results showed that men acquire route knowledge from landmarks faster than women. Women do also, but require more trials to achieve a similar level of performance.

This suggests that users' cognitive styles and prior knowledge have detrimental effects on their selection of navigational strategies. Males, Field Independent users' and users with high prior knowledge have a higher ability to engage in freedom of navigation. Index, query searching, or other tools that allow active engagement should be made available to them. Conversely, females, Field Dependent users and users with low prior knowledge tend to adopt a passive approach and to require more structural information. The system should provide them with authoritative guidance or present the context with well-structured tools such as maps and menus, etc.

Disorientation problems

One of the potential benefits of Internet multimedia information systems is that users can decide their own navigation paths. However, without the existence of fixed paths, users may get lost within the information space. Such problems seem especially serious to females, who experience more disorientation problems. Chen and Ford (1998) examined the effects of individual differences on the use of Web-based multimedia programs. The results indicated that females frequently get lost on the Web. This finding does concur with that of Ford and Miller (1996) who investigated users' perceptions of the Internet. They also found that women reported significantly more disorientation than males when searching for information on the Internet.

Furthermore, McDonald and Spencer (2000) examined gender differences in Web navigation. The results indicated that males express a greater degree of confidence non-linear navigation than females. In addition, Felix (2001) examined the potential of the Web as a medium of language instruction and finds that female users have higher demands from human tutors. According to the outcomes of these studies, males have higher confidence and interest in navigating in multimedia information systems than females. Hence, there may be a need to provide females with extra support.

The aforementioned studies suggest that users' cognitive styles and prior knowledge have detrimental effects on their selection of navigation tools, while gender difference influences the levels of disorientation problems. These findings have implications for the design of navigational tools that can support the differing navigational strategies favoured by users with different cognitive and interpersonal styles.

User Interface and Support

Matching and mismatching

A user interface serves as a major medium for users to engage with Internet multimedia information systems and is a major determinant factor of effective communication (Chen, 2000). Previous research reveals that a user interface that matches a user's cognitive style can potentially enhance his/her performance. Ford (1995) conducted an empirical study in which users' cognitive styles were identified with Riding's CSA. Users took computerised versions of Pask and Scott's teaching materials designed to suit Holist and Serialist learning strategies. He reported that users in the matched conditions perform better than those in the mismatched conditions. Field Dependent individuals obtain higher test scores in the Holist condition, and Field Independent individuals get higher test scores in the Serialist condition.

Similar results are reported by Ford and Chen (2001), who compared the effects of matching condition with those of mismatching conditions. Two versions of Internet multimedia information systems were designed with program control paths, including the Breadth-first and the Depth-first versions. In the Depth-first version, each topic is presented in detail before the next topic (i.e., Serialist condition). In contrast, the Breadth-first version gives an overview of all material prior to introducing detail (i.e., Holist condition). Their results also showed that, significantly, users whose cognitive styles match the design of Internet multimedia information systems attain higher post-test and gain scores. Field Dependent users in the Breadth-first version perform better than in the Depth-first version. Conversely, Field Independent users outperform in the Depth-first version than in the Breadth-first version.

In these two studies (Ford, 1995; Ford & Chen, 2001), the Breadth-first version provides an overview for each topic first, spanning several topics at once. This seems beneficial to Field Dependent users who tend to obtain information from a more global picture. On the other hand, the Depth-first version focuses on the detailed information. This approach is favoured by Field Independent users, who prefer to apply the operation-learning approach, which concentrates primarily on procedural details when processing information in a rich context (Pask, 1979).

Screen design

The screen design of the multimedia application is very important in conveying the content of an application (Fink & Kobsa, 2000). The colour scheme used and the integration of various media are elements of consideration in designing a professional-quality multimedia presentation. This task requires that developers have a good understanding of users' preferences. Empirical studies show that gender differences have significant effects on users' preferences in screen design. Passig and Levin (1999) examined the different preferences of boys and girls to varying interface designs. Their results indicated that boys like the whole screen changes at once whilst girls dislike this approach. They also find that boys prefer green and blue colours, whilst girls prefer red and yellow. Miller and Arnold (2000) investigate how gender differences influence the design of Web pages. They report that women favour the use of pretty images, such as flowers, contrasting with macho technical images, such as a computer favoured by men. These different preferences may be caused by their life styles. While females prefer aesthetics, males tend to be more practical.

Additional support

As described in the previous section, prior knowledge is one of the crucial factors, that affect the difficulties and benefits associated with using multimedia systems. Users with low prior knowledge have difficulties in non-linear interaction. Numerous studies examine how to provide extra support for users with low prior knowledge. Shapiro (1999) explored the effects of interactive overviews in an interactive multimedia program. The results indicate that the interactive overviews can significantly assist users with no prior knowledge in meeting learning objectives. Furthermore, Reuter, Doebner, and Moller (1998) argued that novices, who rely more on salient cues that the system provides, may get lost in the levels of the presentations. Therefore, they proposed a new information structure combining the background colours with an overall navigation system. The system points out the actual level in the content with different background colours and enables the users to jump on the different levels by identifying the colours. The results indicated that this approach could help novices go deeper into the structure of the subject content.

The empirical studies suggest that cognitive and interpersonal styles play an important role in users' interaction with Internet multimedia information systems. Individuals approach multimedia information systems with different levels of ability, experience and insight. They consequently have different user interface requirements. Therefore, understanding the relationship between multimedia features and cognitive and interpersonal styles is needed if customisation of design is to be achieved.

DEVELOPMENT OF A USER MODEL

As discussed in the previous sections, users' gender differences, prior knowledge, and cognitive styles have significant effects on their preferences toward content information and presentation, information space navigation and accessibility, user interfaces, and support of Internet multimedia information systems. This section will present user models drawn from the preceding analysis, that illustrate users' cognitive and interpersonal styles and their navigation patterns in Internet multimedia information systems. Each user model will be comprised of three user profiles: requirements, system, and personal, which may be used in customisation of Internet multimedia information systems. The *user requirements profile* models the user's requirements, both needs and preferences, as they arise from his/her own cognitive and interpersonal styles. The *user system profile* models the impact of the Internet multimedia information systems design on the user in terms of content information and presentation, information space navigation and accessibility, user interface, and support. The *user personal profile* models the outcome of matching the user requirements to the system design in order to identify how well the user requirements are served by the underlying system design.

Cognitive Styles

A major issue in identifying differences of users' cognitive styles is their global and analytical approaches. Field Dependent users process information in a global fashion and rely on cues to build the entire perceptual fields. By contrast, Field Independent users tend to be analytical and are very task-oriented (Witkin et al., 1977). Figure 1 shows a user model that describes how cognitive styles influence users' navigation patterns in Internet multimedia information systems.

As showed in this model, Field Independent and Field Dependent users employ different navigation strategies. Therefore, cognitive style is an important factor for designers in evaluating which kinds of navigation support should be provided in Internet multimedia information systems. The index and other tools that can help them to find specific information should be available to Field Independent users. On the other hand, main menu and maps that show the whole picture of context should be applied to support Field Dependent users.

In addition, Field Dependent users favour the Breadth-first structure, but Field Independent users prefer to take the Depth-first path. This finding can be applied to design links of Internet multimedia information systems with using adaptive ordering techniques that

Figure 1: User model (Cognitive styles)

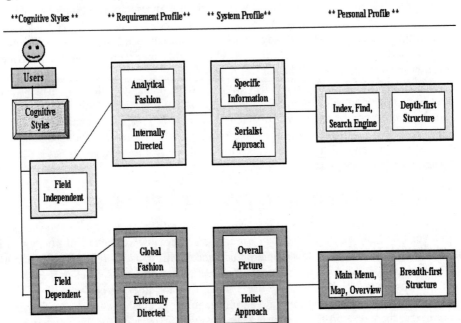

implement user models and some user criteria to adapt the order of presentation for all possible links. Such adaptive navigation support can provide users with the more relevant links according to their learning preferences and information needs (Hohl, Böcker, & Gunzenhäuser, 1996).

In terms of the presentation of multiple formats, previous works indicated that Field Independent users prefer to have visual control. By contrary, Field Dependent users prefer to have extra support from auditory cues. However, it is possible to design Internet multimedia information systems that can accommodate both Field Independent and Field Dependent users. Possible approaches include:

- Switch of Clues: In an Internet multimedia information system that provides rich content, extra-auditory cues can be provided for Field Dependent users. However, such cues can be switched off, in case they irritate Field Independent users.
- Successive Options: Internet multimedia information systems can provide a series of visual options with pop-up windows so that users can decide whether they need extra visual options by opening the windows according to their own preferences.

Multimedia information systems that are adaptive to users' cognitive styles will help them to maximise use of the systems. Such programs will be perceived as more friendly and intelligent because they tend to match with users' cognitive structure.

Prior Knowledge

In terms of non-linear interaction, it has been argued that there is a large cognitive load on users as they need to transfer textual information into their own knowledge base (Foltz, 1996). Previous research provides evidence that transfer of the users' knowledge is mainly dependent on the levels of their prior knowledge, which have significant effect on their performance. In other words, such transfer requires an understanding of subject content and navigation skills.

Figure 2 illustrates the user model for users with different levels of prior knowledge in Internet multimedia information systems. Users who have an adequate amount of prior knowledge on the subject will have higher comprehension so that they can cover most contents and appreciate non-linear interaction. However, users with low prior knowledge may not be aware of what the most important information is, so they may be easily distracted. To enhance users' interest and engage them at their level of comprehension, users' prior knowledge should be catered to within the content of Internet multimedia information systems (Kennedy, 1995).

Marshall and Irish (1989) suggested that it would make sense to provide novices with the appropriate guidance. One of the ways is to provide visual paths, which can be displayed by means of cues to indicate how far users are along a path or by giving some conceptual description for the possible sequences. The alternative way is to keep novices on the correct paths by hiding links to pages that the user is not yet prepared to understand (Eklund, Brusilovsky, & Schwarz, 1997). In this way, novices are restricted to making use of a subset of the available content before going into advanced levels.

In addition to providing an appropriate content for users, it is important to provide a clear structure of the text. Although the structure of large text may not be visualised as a whole, it may be useful to provide local information on the current page and additional information as a way of linking the page to other pages. Along with having a clear structure, providing good labels for the pages will also aid novices. Labels that clearly indicate the role of a particular page may help novices successfully decide the appropriate coherent path (Lewis & Polson, 1990).

Figure 2: User model (Prior knowledge)

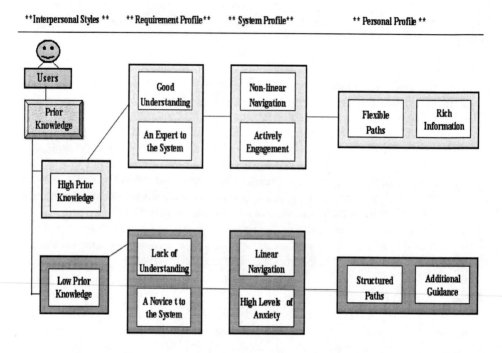

The above suggests a variety of options to support users with different levels of prior knowledge. As indicated by Linard and Zeilger (1995), every user who uses a new system needs to be supported by an initial phase of orientation and initiation in both spaces of interface and domain contents. Only catering to the needs of both novice and experts, users can then be actively involved in the navigation processes. Therefore, it is essential to adapt suitable contents for users with different levels of prior knowledge in the design of effective Internet multimedia information systems.

Gender Differences

Figure 3 shows the user model that illustrates the influence of gender differences on the use of Internet multimedia information systems. As described in this model, males are confident in freedom of navigation. However, fi nales experience more disorientation problems. Under this situation, the proper use of visual cues appears to be critical in helping them to structure the information in their minds (De La Passardiere & Dufresne, 1992). For example, highlighting of the content is a possible approach to solve disorientation problems that females meet. Proper use of font sizes and colours may also facilitate them to identify the part of the information being explored and the relative position in context. In addition, screen elements of the user interface should be an organised layout that draws attention to the important pieces. Clear and consistent icons can give them confidence that they can find what they are looking for. Moreover, Internet multimedia information systems can provide maps or hierarchical diagrams to show current location and some identical symbols. For example, a checking mark "Ö" can be allocated to the map to indicate pages visited. Furthermore, pop-up window. can be applied to present history-based annotations that outline the links to previously visited pages (Eklund, Brusilovsky, & Schwarz, 1997). These

Figure 3: User model (Gender differences)

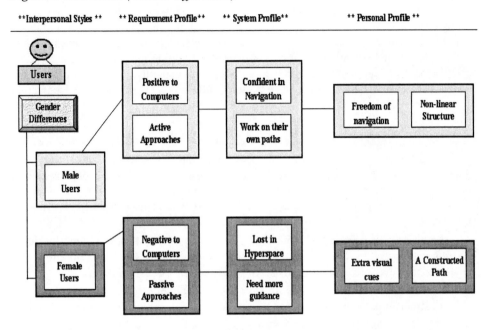

design options can help users to build a picture of what is available and what has been done. Multimedia's ease of use as a deliverable material could be achieved only if cognitive overload related to navigation is minimal (Dufresne & Turcotte, 1997).

ENGAGING THE USER MODEL IN SYSTEM DESIGN

This chapter investigates and integrates the results of the previous studies and produces a user model, which illustrates how users with different cognitive and interpersonal styles interact with Internet multimedia information systems. It has implications for the design of Internet multimedia information systems. Decisions about navigation support and user interface should consider users' cognitive and interpersonal styles.

It is the current trend that the design of Internet multimedia information systems takes a user-centred approach, instead of system-centred approach. In the user-centred design, the user is the key element in the design process. The user model produced in this chapter can help designers to implement user-centred design in two aspects: the inclusion of user requirements and the personalisation of the multimedia information system.

Inclusion of User Requirements

In order to include user requirements in Internet multimedia information systems, designers needs to know: (a) the majority profile of the users, (b) what user needs and preferences are, and (c) how the design matches user requirements. The user model can be applied to support the last two activities. With the proposed user model, the designers can recognise more easily "what" and "why" users need and, hence, identify the development constraints for including such needs and preferences.

For example, in cases where the designers need to design a system for an organisation with a majority of female users, the model will help designers cater to females frequently getting lost in navigation and preferring a constructed path. Then, the designers will know if it is important to provide users with extra navigation support. In summary, such a user model can help designers to develop a user requirement specification that can meet users' needs according to their cognitive and interpersonal styles. Consequently, the interaction between end users and system designers may be enhanced, and users' performance and satisfaction can be increased.

Personalised Multimedia Systems

Fink and Kobsa (2001) define *personalised multimedia system* as a multimedia system which adapts the content, structure, and/or presentation of the multimedia objects to each individual user's characteristics, usage behaviour and/or usage environment. The proposed user model may be applied to support the design of personalised Internet multimedia information systems, which involve the following three processes:

- *Acquisition of User Data*: to identify users' characteristics and their levels of computing skills, either by monitoring the computer usage (e.g., data mining) or by obtaining this information from external sources (e.g., questionnaires);
- *Construction of Usage Models:* to store the user model produced in this chapter to construct initial models of the user, the computer usage, and/or the usage environment;
- *Production of Personalised System*: to generate the adaptation of the content structure, navigation facilities, and user interface of multimedia information systems by matching users' data and the usage models stored in the system.

CONCLUSION AND FUTURE DIRECTIONS

This chapter attempts to incorporate cognitive and interpersonal styles into the design of Internet multimedia information systems. Based on the findings of previous studies, this chapter has presented a user model to customise the design of Internet multimedia information systems for different cognitive and interpersonal styles. The authors hope this model can help designers to decide which levels of navigation support and presentational structures work best for different types of users. This model can be applied for providing personalisation for users with different preferences. The challenge is how to effectively implement this model in the design of Internet multimedia information systems. To respond to this challenge, further research should evaluate the effectiveness of personalisation provided in Internet multimedia information systems. Therefore, it will be beneficial to examine further whether applying the model suggested by this chapter achieves personalisation and can accommodate users' individual differences or whether differences in users' interaction behaviours would remain.

REFERENCES

Busch, T., (1995). Gender differences in self-efficacy and attitudes toward computers. *Journal of Educational Computing Research, 12*(2), 147-158.

Chen, S.Y., (2000). *The role of individual differences and levels of learner control in hypermedia learning environments*. Unpublished Ph.D. Thesis, University of Sheffield, Sheffield, UK.

Chen, S. Y., & Ford, N.J., (1998). Modelling user navigation behaviours in a hypermedia-based learning system: An individual differences approach. *International Journal of Knowledge Organization, 25(3),* 67-78.

Chuang, Y-R., (1999). *Teaching in a multimedia computer environment: A study of effects of learning style, gender, and math achievement* [On-line]. Available: http://imej.wfu.edu./articles/1999/1/10/.

Cutmore, T.R.H., Hine, T.J., Maberly, K.J., Langford, N.M., & Hawgood, G., (2000). Cognitive and gender factors influencing navigation in a virtual environment. *International Journal of Human-Computer Studies, 53*(2), 223-249.

De La Passardière, B. & Dufresne, A., (1992). *Adaptive navigational tools for educational hypermedia. Computer Assisted Learning.* 555-567. Berlin, New York: Springer-Verlag. 1992. [On-line]. Available: http://mistral.ere.umontreal.ca/~dufresne/Publications/ical91.htm.

Demetriadis, S., & Pombortsis, A., (1999). Novice student learning in case-based hypermedia environment: A quantitative study. *Journal of Educational Multimedia and Hypermedia, 8*(2), 241-269.

Dufresne, A., & Turcotte, S., (1997). Cognitive style and its implications for navigation strategies. In, B. Boulay and R. Mizoguchi (eds.) *Artifical intelligence in education knowledge and media learning system,* 287-293, Kobe (Japan): Amsterdam IOS Press.

Eklund, J., Brusilovsky, P., & Schwarz, E., (1997). Adaptive Textbooks on the WWW, in: *Proceedings of AUSWEB97 - The Third Australian Conference on the World Wide Web,* pp. 186–192, Queensland, Australia.

Farrell, I.H., & Moore, D.M., (2001). The effect of navigation tools on learners' achievement and attitude in a hypermedia environment. *Journal of Educational Technology Systems, 29*(2), 169-181.

Felix, U., (2001). A multivariate analysis of students' experience of Web-based learning. *Australian Journal of Educational Technology, 17*(1):21-36.

Fink, J. & Kobsa, A., (2000). A review and analysis of commercial user modeling servers for personalization on the World Wide Web. *User Modeling and User-Adapted Interaction, 9*(34), 209-249.

Foltz, P. W., (1996). Comprehension, coherence, and strategies in hypertext and linear text." In *Hypertext and Cognition.* 109-136. Mahwah, NJ: Lawrence Erlbaum Associates.

Ford, N., (1995). Levels and types of mediation in instructional systems: An individual difference approach. *International Journal of Human-Computer Studies, 43,* 243-259.

Ford, N. & Chen, S.Y., (2000). Individual differences, hypermedia navigation and learning: an empirical study. *Journal of Educational Multimedia and Hypermedia, 9*(4), 281-312.

Ford, N. & Chen, S.Y., (2001) Matching/mismatching revisited: An empirical study of learning and teaching styles. *British Journal of Educational Technology, 32*(1), 5-22.

Ford, N., & Miller, D., (1996). Gender differences in Internet perceptions and use. *Aslib Proceedings, 48,* 183-92.

Hohl, H., Böcker, H. & Gunzenhäuser, R., (1996). Hypadapter: An adaptive hypertext system for exploratory learning and programming. *User Modeling and User Adapted Interaction, 6*(2/3), 131-156.

Jonassen, D.H., & Grabowski, B.L., (1993). *Handbook of individual differences, learning, and instruction.* Hillsdale, NJ: Lawrence Erlbaum Associates.

Kennedy, D.M,. (1995). Students' prior knowledge: Implications for instructional design of interactive multimedia. In J. M. Pearce, A. Ellis, C. McNaught, & G. Hart (Eds.), *Learning with technology*: ASCILITE '95. *Proceedings of the Australian Society for Computers in Learning in Tertiary Education Conference*. 288-296. The University of Melbourne: The Science Multimedia Teaching Unit.

Kim, K.S., (1997). *Effects of cognitive and problem-solving styles on information-seeking behavior in the WWW: A case study*. [Online]. Available: http://www.edb.utexas.edu/mmresearch/Students07/Kim.

Kirby J.R., & Boulter, D.R., (1999). Spatial ability and transformational geometry. *European Journal of Psychology Of Education, 14*(2):283-294.

Koch, M., (1994). No girls allowed! *Technos, 3,* 14-19.

Last, D.A., O'Donnell, A.M., & Kelly, A.E., (1998). Using hypermedia: Effects of prior knowledge and goal strength. In *SITE 98: Society for Information Technology & Teacher Education International Conference (9th, Washington, DC, March 10-14, 1998) Proceedings*; 6 p.

Lee, C.H., (1994). *The effects of auditory cues in interactive multimedia and cognitive style on reading skills of third graders*. Unpublished Ed.D. Dissertation. University Of Pittsburgh, UK.

Lewis, C. & Polson, P.G., (1990). Theory-based design for easily learned interfaces. *HCI, 5,* 191-220.

Linard, M. & Zeillger, G., (1995). Designing navigational support for educational software. *Proceedings of Human Computer Interactions*. 63-78.

Marrison, D.L., & Frick, M.J., (1994). The effect of agricultural students' learning styles on academic achievement and their perceptions of two methods of instruction. *Journal of Agricultural Education, 35*(1), 26-30 .

Marshall, C.C., & Irish, P.M., (1989). Guided tours and online presentations: How authors make existing hypertext intelligible for readers. In *Proceedings of Hypertext '89*, 15-26. Pittsburgh, PA. New York: ACM.

McDonald, S., & Spencer, L., (2000). Gender differences in Web navigation: Strategies, efficiency and confidence. *Proceedings of 7th International IFIP Conference on Women, Work and Computerization*, 174-181.

McDonald, S., & Stevenson, R., (1998). Effects of text structure and prior knowledge of the learner on navigation in hypertext. *Human Factors, 40*(1), 18-27.

Miller, H., & Arnold, J., (2000). Gender and Web home pages. *Computers & Education,* 34(3/4),335-339.

Nielsen, J., (1995). *Multimedia and hypertext: The Internet and beyond.* Cambridge MA: Academic Press.

Pask, G., (1979). *Final report of S.S.R.C. Research Programme HR 2708*. Richmond (Surrey): System Research Ltd.

Passig, D., & Levin, H., (1999). Gender interest differences with multimedia learning interfaces. *Computers in Human Behaviour, 15*(2), 173-83.

Reuter, M., Doebner, D., & Moller, D.P.F., (1998). First experiences with ergonomic-cognitive structures for the WWW–presentation of the University of Clausthal. 6th European Congress on Intelligent Techniques and Soft Computing. *EUFIT '98* (2) 141-1146.

Riding R., & Rayner, S.G., (1998). *Cognitive Styles and Learning Strategies.* London: David Fulton Publisher.

Savenye, W.C., (1996). Learner navigation patterns and incentive on achievement and attitudes in hypermedia-based CAI. *Proceedings of Selected Research and Development Presentations at the 1996 National Convention of the Association for Educational Communications and Technology* (18th, Indianapolis, IN).

Schwarz, J., (2001). *Lost in virtual space: Gender differences are magnified.* [Online]. Available: http://www.washington.edu/newsroom/news/2001archive/06-01archive/k061301.html.

Shapiro, A.M., (1999). The relationship between prior knowledge and interactive overviews during hypermedia-aided learning. *Journal of Educational Computing Research, 20*(2), 143-167.

Shih, C., & Gamon, J., (1999). *Student learning styles, motivation, learning strategies, and achievement in Web-based courses.* [Online]. Available: http://iccel.wfu.edu/publications/journals/jcel/jcel990305/ccshih.htm.

Shneiderman, B., Byrd, D., & Croft, W.B., (1997). Clarifying search: A user-interface framework for text searches. *D-Lib Magazine.* [Online]. Available: http://www.dlib.org/dlib/january97/retrieval/01shneiderman.html) [12/09/1998].

Weller, H.G., Repman, J., & Rooze, G.E., (1994). The relationship of learning, behavior, and cognitive styles in hypermedia-based instruction: Implications for design of HBI. *Computers in the Schools, 10* (3/4), 401-420.

Witkin, H.A., Moore, C.A., Goodenough, D.R., & Cox., P.W., (1977). Field-dependent and field-independent cognitive styles and their educational implications. *Review of Educational Research, 47*(1), 1-64.

Chapter XVII

A Software Model, Architecture and Environment to Support Web-Based Applications

David Kearney and Weiquan Zhao
University of South Australia, Australia

ABSTRACT

Designed originally for document delivery, the Web is now being widely used as a platform for electronic commerce application software. The ad hoc enhancements that have made Web application software possible (for example, CGI and Java Script) have created an application support infrastructure where application software upgrades and maintenance are very complex. Yet the Web is the preferred platform for applications that have continuous ongoing development needs. In this chapter, we describe a model, an architecture, and an associated Web Application Support Environment (WASE) that both hides the low-level complexity of the existing Web infrastructure and, at the same time, empowers enterprise Web application programmers in their objective of writing modular and easily maintainable software applications for electronic commerce. WASE is not a compiler and does not completely abstract away the unique features of Web infrastructure. It is being constructed using XML documents in its API, to allow the function and configurability of applications to be defined in a Web-like fashion.

INTRODUCTION

There is a great demand to deploy electronic commerce applications on the Web. This demand is somehow stimulated and made possible by the services the Web itself provides and, at the same time, it is driving the Web's development. However, not all innovations to assist application development on the Web have been good software engineering, partly because the Web was not originally designed for this purpose, as has been widely recognized (Gellersen & Gaedke, 1999). Despite many enhancements that have been made to the Web, difficulties and inefficiencies in development and maintenance are still prominent, especially with the deployment of large-scale and sophisticated applications. A mechanism is needed to fill the gap between the Web used as an application infrastructure for hypermedia and the needs of complex business applications. Many approaches, for example, (Barta &Schranz, 1998; Fraternali & Paolini, 1998; Schwabe & Rossi, 1998; Diaz, Isakowitz, Maiorana & Gilabert, 1995) have been proposed. These studies either do not address large-scale Web-based applications at all or have not made a detailed study of the Web infrastructure and its relationship to large-scale application requirements. In this chapter we begin with an in-depth investigation of the Web infrastructure and proposed applications and then devise a model and architecture of Web applications together with a support environment. The architecture aims to make Web applications not only easy to implement but also easy to maintain. The chapter is organized as follows. We begin by discussing the unique aspects of the Web that impact on application development are described. Then, a completely fresh model and architecture of Web-based applications is described. This is followed by a support environment is designed to fulfil the requirements of this model, and finally, we report initial progress on implementing the architecture and our experience writing applications for it.

WEB-BASED APPLICATIONS

The Web has been used for deploying applications beyond delivering information and hypermedia only, which was its original purpose when devised about a decade ago. We define *Web-based applications* as applications that rely on the Web as the application infrastructure to perform their functionality (Kristensen, 1998) and have significant complexity in logic processing, as opposed to just hypermedia or data intensive content. We distinguish *Web-based applications* from the more common *Web applications*, which use hypermedia extensively and may have no business logic at all. Web-based applications rely on Web browsers to interact with users and employ Web protocols, mainly HTTP, to enable user interaction in the form of Web pages, delivered and connected to the rest of the application. They may range in scale and complexity from a message board utility in a personal Web site to a worldwide enterprise-level business system. The fact that the Web has been chosen to perform functions for which it was not originally designed means that this "new platform" was not devised from a fundamental requirements analysis, as was the case with CORBA (Object Management Group, 2002), for example. This explains well why the Web has been patched up with a family of technologies such as CGI and JavaScript, and a series of revisions of HTTP has been developed and innovation conducted to enhance the Web for its new role. This has made the Web different from traditional application platforms, posing a new set of challenges for development and maintenance. In this section, we compare the deployment of the same application on a traditional platform and the Web in an effort to distill the unique features of Web-based applications and define the issues raised by the existing Web infrastructure.

Web Infrastructure and Web-based Applications

If we regard the Web as a new kind of application platform then Web applications could theoretically be designed almost independently of the underlying Web. They could be deployed on an abstract application platform which hides unique features of the Web from the developer, no matter at what cost. The functionality of Web-based applications might then be implemented as if the Web never existed. But the Web has significant and unique features, that are so fundamentally different from other platforms that they cannot be entirely hidden. We argue that the factors described in this section make a totally abstract application platform unworkable. In the next few paragraphs, we wish to highlight some of these key differences between the Web and traditional platforms. Our methodology is based on answering the following questions. What are the differences if we implement the same application on the current Web infrastructure as compared to traditional platforms and what causes them? What would be the consequences of hiding all the differences theoretically allowing those methodologies now used for high-level application development on traditional platforms to be applied to the Web? If we cannot hide the unique properties of the Web, then what particular aspects of the Web should be hidden by abstraction and what should be left exposed? In answering these questions we are particularly interested in enhancing our ability to maintain applications and to continuously extend their functionality to meet the expanding demands of the enterprise.

We will take as our example an online catalogue, a very common application found in many e-business systems based on the Web. End users can specify search criteria or choose a category with the inquiry page and then get the search result or browse content displayed in the answer page. Users only need a browser. The process of searching and page preparation is done at the server side. The general arrangement is shown in Figure 1. If the Web were *not* used for such online catalogue, then a likely traditional application architecture may be a two-tiered (client-server) or three-tiered distributed application. The three-tiered architecture is shown in Figure 2 where a client executable resides on users' machine communicating with its counterpart at the server side via a proprietary protocol. In Figure 3 the Web based equivalent of the three tiered architecture is shown.

Major aspects of the Web application deployment are revealed by comparing the deployment of the same application as shown in figures 2 and 3.

Figure 1: A two-tiered architecture for an online catalogue

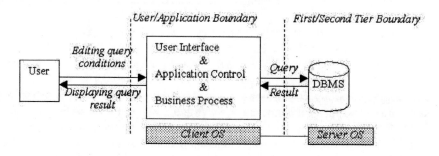

Figure 2: Non-Web-based three-tiered application architecture

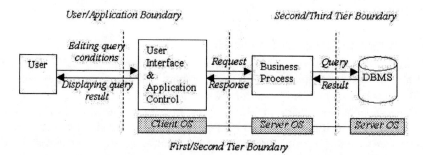

Figure 3: Web-based three-tiered application architecture

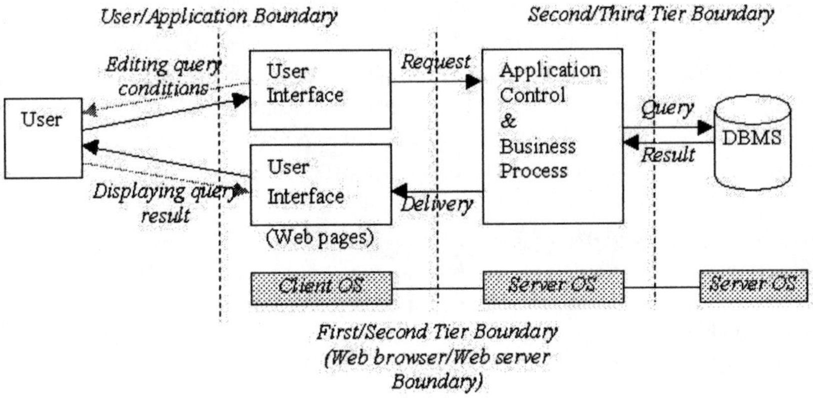

Locality distribution

Web-based applications are no doubt distributed applications and hence are at least two-tiered. In some sense, the Web is a means for deploying the client component of distributed application and connecting it to its counterpart at the back end. It must be noted that the Web does not define the architecture of components behind the Web server (HTTP server), but a clear definition is the key issue in enabling the Web to be extended into an application platform. Yet the capability of the client platform and the communication protocol, HTML (and its extensions) and HTTP respectively, determines how Web-based applications are partitioned and distributed against locality. So application developers must address the two main aspects of the partition by answering the following questions: What tasks can be performed at each tier? How are the parts at different tiers going to inter-operate?

In a typical traditional multitiered application like the one shown in Figure 2, the client component maintains the control logic of the whole application in a master-slave relationship with its server-side counterpart (which may be further tiered). However, in Web-based applications the situation is totally different due to the limitations of the browser and the HTTP protocol. The client component, normally in the form of a Web page, can perform only a small portion of the task usually related to user interaction, and most of the work including global control and state management falls on the server side. Moreover, the client component cannot intelligently process messages from its server-side counterpart. They are thus not working in a request-and-response manner at the level of abstraction of the application programmer, even though they work this way at the lower infrastructure level. In this sense, Web-based applications are not client/server applications as is usually understood by the term. If we examine the first tiers in Figure 2, we can find a large portion of the first tier in the traditional application has been "pushed" back to the server side in the Web-based version, leaving a very "thin" client.

This tiering scheme induced by making use of the Web as an application platform does not match the layering scheme that best suits traditional multitiered applications. This poses a challenge to developers who have gotten used to the traditional tiering scheme. They must take this into consideration when designing Web-based applications unless this mismatch can be completely hidden by some means.

A consequence of the Web's uneven location distribution is the inevitable complexity in implementing of server-side components, as they are now burdened with tasks that used to be in the first tier. This will cause difficulties in both development and maintenance if a single component is employed to carry out multiple roles of different types, which may be developed and maintained by different personnel with different skills at different times. Thus it is important to have a proper model and architecture for server-side components in which the concerns of tasks of a different nature can be clearly identified and separated into different components. The situation is similar to that of separating content and layout in a hypermedia only Web site, except that in the case of Web-based applications the separation is likely to be more difficult and to involve more subtle trade-offs.

Execution segmentation

The limitation of Web browsers has another consequence in Web-based applications—the segmentation of the client component against the execution process. Since the Web browser can deal with only one interaction at a time, it is normally impossible to squeeze the whole client component into one page. It must be divided into many pieces as a set of Web pages and delivered to the client side one by one. This is totally different from traditional applications whose client component is deployed in place as a monolithic one prior to execution. At the client side, the *execution* of a Web-based application is artificially sequential and interlaced by the *deployment* of the client components, which brings about a lot of unexpected overhead. This poses a challenge for the developer of Web-based applications in choosing proper granularity of client components in order to alleviate the performance drawback caused by their deployment.

The segmentation also results in another problem, which we call the *multiple access points* of Web-based applications. Users can almost activate any step of an application at any time by sending directly the server side a request that should have been issued by the client component in correct sequence. The intermediate steps cannot be hidden completely from users. This is also different from traditional applications, which have full control of their execution sequence. As a result, it is made more difficult for Web-based applications to conduct their state and session management.

Interface granularity

When end users are presented with interfaces to more than one task within a single window or screen, we refer to this as *interface composition*. A typical example is that in a desktop Windows-based application, a menu bar is always displayed in the main window in spite of the current application task. It gives users great convenience to access other functions of the application whenever desired. Apart from requirements on screen resource management and internal coordination, on most platforms it is no problem at all to provide interface composition. But for Web-based applications this must be carefully dealt with, as otherwise it will cause additional overhead, especially in deploying the same portion in a series of client components. Frame technology can assist in solving this problem to certain, extent but problems still exist in compatibility between frame-used and frame-less versions of the same application.

Network performance variability

The bandwidth of the Internet supporting applications and the liveness of nodes connected to it is not well defined or uniform. This means that an application designer must anticipate a wide range of possibilities in the user experience of the software that has little to do with its inherent design. One way to handle this is to establish a range of contexts for applications that specify some quality of service factor associated with users or user locations. This special adaptation seems to be unique to Web applications, and there seems no obvious way to abstract away all its effects.

A wide range of user capabilities and user requirements for the same application

On the Web, the user community is most likely bigger but more diverse than for traditional application platforms. Thus, as part of any Web application, it is necessary to establish who the user is before significant interaction commences. Identification of users might be achieved by a combination of automatic collection of user information, such as location and Web browser version, or manual questions, such as what language to use. A user *type* becomes an important part of the context of the application and seems to be unique to the Web environment. The establishment of the user's identity and credentials is also heavily dependent on a complex state transition system's defining steps in an type of logon procedure (either explicit or not). This reinforces the extra needs that Web applications have for managing state and persistence.

In summary, all these special features of Web-based applications are at the root of what we call the "Web dilemma." That is, how to provide an environment for applications that must be implemented on an infrastructure that was not originally designed to support them and which has unique features that ordinary application platforms do not exhibit. In next section, we will explore in more detail the "Web dilemma."

Web Infrastructure and Web Application Servers

Strictly speaking, based on the observations above, the Web is not an application platform because it has a lack of key mechanisms necessary to support application execution, and, moreover, a large part of a Web-based application must run directly on host operating systems at the server side. To some extent, the Web infrastructure is a sort of middle-ware that Web-based applications use to interconnect their components at the client side and server side. The Web, together with all enhancements made to it and associated extension technologies, is best described as an *infrastructure* that Web-based applications must rely on for their execution. The infrastructure of Web-based applications should also be considered to include operating systems at the server side, which is one of the few items they share with traditional applications. Without the support of an environment built upon the Web infrastructure, any Web-based application must itself take care of the following aspects needed to be a full-fledged application:

–   State management: To keep track of application execution;
–   Session management: To distinguish among application instances;
–   User identification: To distinguish among different users (configurations); and
–   Service access: To provide application services in a consistent way (APIs).

The situation has been much improved by the family of products now called *Web application servers*. They normally provide an environment on the top of the Web infrastructure with some of the missing facilities. We can quite safely call the Web infrastructure, "topped up" with services provided by application servers as an application platform since application run-time requirements are mostly fulfilled within this environment. However, these application servers have less to contribute in establishing a systematic application model that facilitates good software engineering than might have been hoped when they first appeared. Even with an application server adapting modern applications to the unique infrastructure of the Web (especially those that are logic centric rather than data or content centric) and performing subsequent maintenance and upgrading appears to be a very complex task compared with more traditional platforms. The reason for this may be that the application server community has taken a bottom-up approach to architecture development. In short, some application server architectures continue to provide the missing links in the Web infrastructure without considering the big picture. But even if Web application servers had taken good ideas from traditional application software architectures, they may still have had difficulties since, as we will see in the next section, the software development process for Web-based applications is significantly different than for traditional platforms.

Software Development Processes for Web-based Applications

The process of development and maintenance of Web-based applications has unique elements. They are related to two characteristics that seem to be unique to the process of Web application development. First, almost all Web development is a mixture of development with maintenance or iterative and incremental (ever-evolving) development. This means that maintainability is a key requirement, perhaps more important than performance and meeting exactly the requirements in the original specification. Maintainability can be achieved by having an easy to understand, top-down definition of the architecture of the application. Second, a team carries out development on the Web. This team has a mixture of very different skill sets in the same project. Not all team members are software developers in the normal sense of the word. A traditional system engineering solution to this type of complex task is to have the whole system, including the application and its supporting environment, modular with all components clearly defined with clearly defined interfaces. This facilitates the maintenance and evolution of the system, as well as cooperation among developers. A contribution of the work described in this chapter is the concept of a support environment that makes the Web application development process as similar to a traditional application platform process as possible, but providing a high-level model that takes into account the uniqueness of Web development process by giving more emphasis to components and interfaces. We propose an architecture for an environment comprising software and other objects, which conforms to and refines the model. We believe that this layering of abstractions fits well with the software and other artifact development processes in the domain of applications we are targeting. This domain is e-commerce and, in particular, enterprise wide applications that have a heavy reliance on logical decision making (complex business logic). Hence our environment and model are closely inter-related and tailored to the intended domain. We expect the implementation of our environment to be modular, component-oriented, with clearly defined interfaces. However, inside components we expect that well-established software development processes can be used and that the incorporation of existing software abstractions below this level will be an advantage.

Existing Models for Web Application Development

No really high-level models and very few architectures for software applications implemented on the Web, or in conjunction with Web application servers, have emerged. One popular architecture is an adaptation of the well-known "Model-View-Controller" (MVC) pattern (Buschmann, Meunier, Rohnert, Sommerlad, & Stal, 1996; Gamma, Helm, Johnson, &

Figure 4: The model view controller pattern as applied in the J2EE application server (Sun Java 2 Enterprise Edition, 2002)

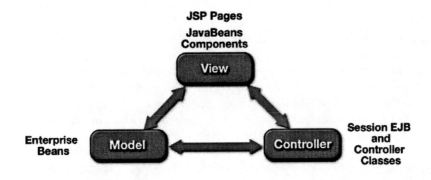

Vlissides 1995) to a higher level of abstraction. Many Web application servers use this as a suggested architecture for applications (BEA WebLogic, 2002; IBM WebSphere 2002).

Although originally created to meet the needs of user interface development, MVC has become one of the inspirations for systems that attempt the most basic separation of concerns that is demanded by hypermedia applications—that of separating presentation and content. Architectures based on the MVC pattern are also claimed to separate concerns of business logic, data, and presentation. Figure 4 shows how the MVC pattern has been applied to one particular Web application server structure. However, there is little evidence presented to support these assertions. There are also several major weaknesses associated with MVC pattern when used with the Web infrastructure. These include:

1.   Every view has to be updated when it receives an update message. Even if the view in question is not affected by the update, the view still has to process the update method. This may not be possible or very inefficient in a Web-based application.

2.   An application built according to the MVC can be very complex when a view has to depend on more than one model. This may become more common as enterprise applications become more complex.

We will return to the MVC-inspired architectures later and explain how our proposal overcomes these weaknesses of their structure.

In this section we have attempted to show that the Web's infrastructure, which has been developed in an ad hoc manner to support Web applications, is deficient in its support for Web-based applications. Web application servers and abstractions of the MVC pattern to produce basic application architectures do not provide a sound foundation for a software development process, which is in any case quite different from that of applications built on traditional platforms. The use of higher-level conceptual models of Web software is very rare. In the next section we show how this situation can be remedied by providing a top-down model that, when projected onto the Web infrastructure, gives appropriate architectures for Web-based applications.

A NEW MODEL AND ARCHITECTURE FOR WEB-BASED APPLICATIONS

We have discussed the Web being used as an application infrastructure and examined the effect of its unique attributes on the software application development process. In this section, we propose a *model* of Web-based applications and architectures which when projected from this model onto the unique characteristics of the Web provide a strong foundation for application development and more importantly maintenance. By a model we mean those aspects of the high-level design of the framework for application development that guide the choice of architectures on which applications will be deployed. The model is like a policy document for the architecture. Our model is motivated by a desire to facilitate the development and maintenance of these applications.

Any well-engineered Web-based application must be modular and have all constituent modules clearly identified, separated, and structured. But it must also adapt to the underlying Web infrastructure as well as meet the common Web driven need for ongoing evolution in requirements. Our model is aligned to a component-based software development methodology, because we believe that this will best support maintainability, rapid application development, and reuse. We note that many current lower-level Web application support environments are not component based (for example, they are often just object oriented). We contend that components are a better choice for high-level conceptualization of a complex system because of their focus on well-defined interfaces. Object-oriented technologies are, we believe, more appropriate for component internal structure below the architecture level.

Our model is constructed by first looking at the architecture of an application with no consideration of the Web. We then apply the restrictions incurred by the Web to it. In this way, we have achieved an application model that is inspired by the functionality of the application and is adapted to the unique underlying infrastructure as well.

A Generic Web Application

At a high conceptual level, we think of Web-based logic centric applications as not much different from those based on other platforms. A generic Web-based application is shown in Figure 5. On most occasions in the electronic commerce area, such a Web-based application can be regarded as an aggregation of state machine-like logic with an information system built *using* the Web. This application has user interaction, business logic, and data access.

Figure 5: Generic Web-based application as a state machine

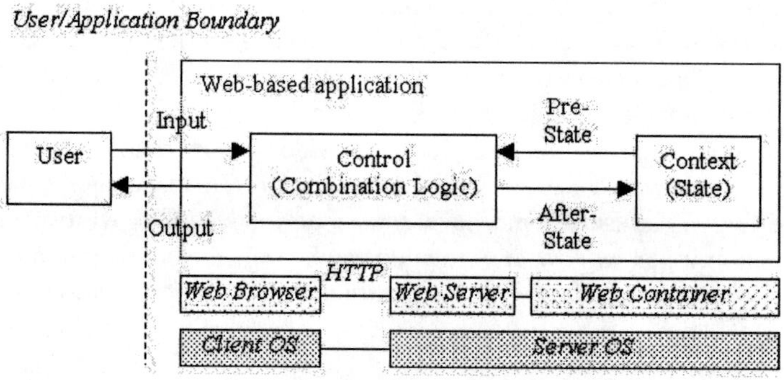

Figure 6: A conceptual model of Web applications

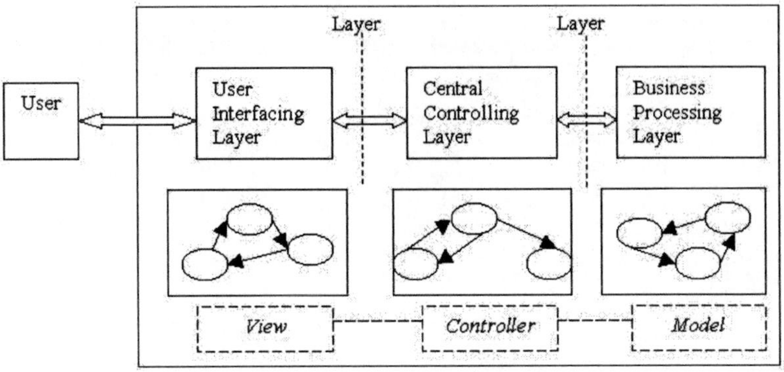

The Web-Based Application Conceptual Model

Figure 6 shows a typical three-layered application model that is widely used, especially in distributed information systems. We do not say it is built *solely on the Web* because there are very likely other application platforms involved in the whole system. On many occasions we can use *Web-based applications* interchangeably with *Web-based information systems*. If we implement an information system on both the Web and another platform, the Web-based version is not supposed to sacrifice any of the application's functionality, unless the Web by nature does not allow some feature. In this sense, we distinguish *Web-based applications* from the general *Web applications*, which could be so primitive as to have no business logic involved at all.

Figure 6 is our conceptual layering model of generic Web applications. It can have significantly different tiering schemes when implemented on various application platforms. In a stand-alone desktop application, all the three layers are put together as a monolithic one, while in a typical two-tiered distributed application, the first two layers normally fall into one single front tier with the third one behind, which is usually a data base management system (DBMS). Notice that we have used the terminology of the model view controller pattern to denote the components, but we have not followed the interconnection structure of this pattern. Rather, we have chosen to break the link between the view and the model, preferring to pass communication from view to model via the controller. Note also that both the view and the controller have state machines associated with them, indicating that we intend to allow the application programmer to decentralize detailed control of, for example, page sequence to the view component.

The Basic Web-Based Application Architecture

We *project* the conceptual model onto the unique aspects of the Web infrastructure to derive an appropriate architecture for Web-based applications. In this part we look at how the tiers of the Web infrastructure (Figure 3) influence the derivation of the architecture (Figure 7). In later parts we will examine in the same way the effect of execution segmentation and the unique needs of the Web development software process.

We can see clearly in Figure 7 the mismatch of layering of the conceptual model (Figure 6) and tiering schemes. The user-interfacing layer must be divided into two tiers due to the capability of Web browsers and HTTP, as we discussed before. The "front end" is actually

Figure 7: Basic tiered architecture of web-based applications

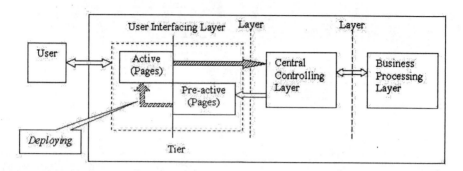

in the form of active Web pages in browsers, and a "back end" is normally the components responsible for producing deliverable pages. This front end is able to interact with users and send requests back to other tiers but not to respond to any feedback or requests, which is the responsibility of the back end. In many implementations, the back end is incorporated in a central-processing layer, which makes it difficult to properly separate concerns. We keep the back end of the user-interfacing layer in our architecture independent of the central-processing layer so as to maintain the advantages of this layering scheme. Hence, while the business processing layer has the characteristics of a model, and the application sequence is resident in the central controlling layer, and the user interface does not directly interface to the model layer.

Another important aspect where this architecture differs from many others is that we have all the active pages as part of the application. In many approaches, the application boundary is set to where the first tiering line is, thus implying that actively generated pages are the output of the application. This might be due to the fact that pages do not exist at the client side before the application to which they belong is launched and they are activated at that particular time. These approaches are still based on the primitive functionality of Web applications as page producers, and consequently client-side interaction behavior can hardly be systematically incorporated in design of the whole application. Instead, we based our architecture on a run-time image of Web-based applications by imagining those pages as being already active and interacting with users. Then a clear programming interface can be easily identified in front of central-controlling units, which are therefore freed from user interaction details and are not exposed directly to users.

The Extended Web-Based Application Architecture with Execution Segmentation

The front end of the user-interfacing layer, or the front tier, is no longer a monolithic one, as we also discussed previously. It can be in the form of a set of Web pages, each of which can perform only a small piece of a task. The execution of an application then has to be segmented into many steps. After applying this segmentation, we have the architecture as shown in Figure 8.

Unfortunately, the use of the HTTP protocol is this case causes much of the complexity of this layer because even the simplest interaction requires a page update from the server. There seem to be several ways to avoid this difficulty. The first is to use a framed page. Even though updates are performed often, most of the frames remain in place. Another way is to

Figure 8: Tiered architecture of web-based applications with execution segmented

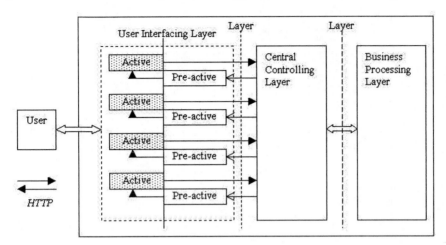

simulate frames with active pages based on templates. In this case, the user perceives the update of pages but only small parts of the page change at each update. But the complexity of the application development environment remains for both these options. A third way of managing execution segmentation is to use an alternative to the HTTP protocol for some of the more trivial interactions between the client and server. For example, a propriety protocol can be implemented between a thin client downloaded via HTTP and a server-side component. In this situation, the very detailed interaction with the user can be handled more efficiently without an HTTP update of the page every time.

The option may also allow a more familiar programming model for the user interface level based on events. Then, valid arguments exist for employing the original model view controller pattern, but only in the limited context of the implementation of the user interface layer in Figure 7.

Task Partitions: Supporting the Continual Evolution of Web-Based Applications

One of the challenges to development of Web-based applications is their ongoing evolution. It is hard to elicit their requirements completely before commencing development, due to the open user base of Web-based applications. A good architecture must be able to facilitate adding new components and modifying existing ones. In view of this we partition both central-process layer and service-providing layer into *task partitions*. Each task partition is well encapsulated and clearly interfaced, as shown in Figure 9. What is essential here is the relationship between user-interfacing units and central-processing units. Each central-processing unit manages one or more user-interfacing units, and each user-interfacing unit is responsible for only one central-processing unit. One central-processing unit together with its managed user-interfacing units performs a single task as a team, and all of these teams make up the whole application. The interaction among these teams can take place only through a central-processing unit, thus the overall application control logic is reflected in the interrelationship of central-process units. In this way, user-interfacing units are not combined with central-processing units so the scope of design, implementation, and

Figure 9: Tiered architecture of web-based applications with task partitions

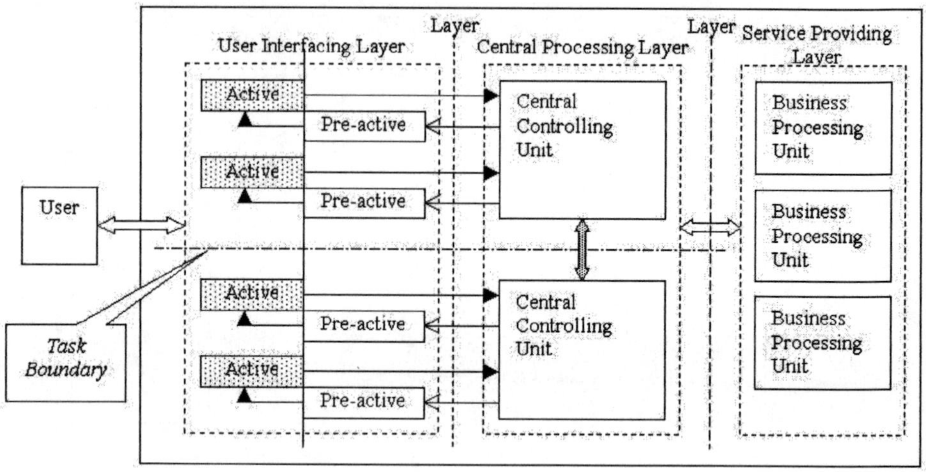

maintenance of any component is restricted. A side benefit is that presentation logic can be completely separated from application logic and business logic.

Relationship to the Model-View-Controller Pattern

MVC is a widely used pattern, and has recently been applied in distributed Web enterprise application based on Sun's EJB (Sun Enterprise Java Beans, 2002). There is no single interpretation of MVC in these settings, but our model can be regarded as using some of the components of the MVC pattern while avoiding the problems created in Web applications by its loop structure (which will induce circular dependencies between components). As shown in Figure 6, the user-interfacing layer can be regarded as the traditional MVC *view*, which holds presentation logic of an application. In this mapping, however, our view, besides having components for displaying, has also a partial "controller" that is responsible for managing behaviors very local to the view, including interacting with users and communicating with back layers. The central-processing layer is the *controller* that holds the logic relating to the steps the application must go through to interface to the user and control the execution of the whole application. Business logic falls in the service-providing layer, which can be considered as the *model* part. It holds the most essential operations for manipulating and maintaining an application's data resources. Though similar in the overall structure to MVC, our architecture is significantly different from it in the following aspects.

Firstly, our view components have no direct connections with the model components; thus, the triangle linkage of dependencies is broken. The controller takes full charge of handling requests from the view as well as providing both instruction and data information back to view components to be updated. By such decoupling, the design of interfaces for components as well as communication protocols between them can be simplified. Model components do not have to produce dual interfaces to both controller and view components. As at any time there is only one view component, active update messages are not processed by views that do not need to be changed. View components are freed from maintaining knowledge of any model components. They are fully responsible to their controllers only. The complexity that could arise when one view is dependent on more than one model is removed. View components are further released from dealing with errors or exceptions that might happen during their access to the model. It is difficult for the view component to interpret some of these errors. This is important for Web-based application in which granularity of view components is small.

The other difference is that the relationship between view components and their controllers is extended from one-to-one to many-to-one. As just stated, granularity of view components of Web-based applications is small, so it will probably cause much more overhead if we broke controller components down in similar, small-sized pieces as well. The many-to-one relationship helps group closely related view components together under a unified control. Moreover, this will also help a task-oriented incremental development using controller components as the basic unit.

A SUPPORT ENVIRONMENT FOR WEB-BASED APPLICATIONS

In the second section, we noted that the Web itself is an "incomplete" application infrastructure. The model and architecture described in the third section cannot be supported on this infrastructure alone. Thus, a new run-time support environment is required. The run-time support will be common to all applications that use the model and architecture we have described. In this section we give details of the architecture of this environment. It is proper to build the new support environment on the top of the "naked" Web, but it is not necessary to construct many parts of it from scratch because many components of existing application servers can be re-used. Thus, our support environment is an extension and elaboration of the now commonplace application servers often implemented with Java-based objects. However, we reject the application architectures that have been proposed for use with these application servers. In particular, we wish to avoid the model view controller pattern as a basis for the architecture because it tends to introduce dependence loops that will likely make maintenance difficult.

Where the application infrastructure of the Web lacks support is in areas such as state management, session management, user identification, and service access. Therefore, the support environment needs to provide these facilities for running applications. Figure 10 depicts the environment and its relationship with the upper-level applications.

The overall design is based on a conceptual model similar to Figure 5 but in which the whole application at the highest level of abstraction can be regarded as having two parts, control and context. The control part holds the whole logic of the application that determines its behavior, including its input and output with external actors and resources. The context part holds all the state data concerned with the execution of any instance of the application. We follow this style because the Web itself does not provide any facility to support context-aware applications. Context is very important to Web applications because the user base is diverse and there are security issues related to the identification of individual users. In addition, the execution of many existing Web-based applications appear to be segmented into too many small fragments. Instead of having every application component managing its own context directly on the server operating system, we provide a unified mechanism in the environment of all components. We believe this is more efficient in both application design and execution support. Application components that are free from context thus can be focused on state transitions relevant to the application logic. Other issues like persistence, we believe, could be more efficiently managed through centralized state management.

Figure 10: The architecture of a web-based application support environment (WASE)

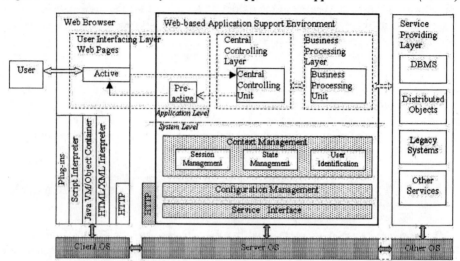

In the architecture of Figure 10, we can further divide the application level into sub-levels. Given an application, we can always break it down into levels in specialty of tasks from application specific through to application general, with many in between like domain general and domain specific ones. That is where application framework (or package or templates) comes from – we can pull out those units common in a special area in the application level and put them into a package to make a sub-level. In the system level underneath, the run-time support mechanisms are not a fixed part of the environment and the context management units are in the same form as business processing units. This idea is quite commonly applied in operating systems like Unix for system extensibility and maintainability. For instance, applications not required to distinguish users could just leave out the user identification mechanism; to avoid unnecessary run-time overhead. New support mechanism can be added and existing ones upgraded as well. In this way, the architecture can provide a wide range of applications from as simple as being stateless to sophisticated session-aware and user-aware ones.

Central-controlling units use a session-management as well a state-management mechanism to manage the context information of one application instance. The context-management utility is part of the environment responsible for initiating and coordinating application units. Communications between central-controlling units and the other two kinds of units—user-interfacing and business processing—are once and off so do not use the state-management mechanism to maintain their state.

System level applications, such as configuration management and the service interface, used for managing user level applications are built in the same way. They are at the meta-level providing system users with the facility to monitoring, configuring and maintaining upper-level applications.

IMPLEMENTATION

To evaluate our architecture we are implementing the support environment and sample applications in the context of the Java 2 Enterprise Edition (J2EE) platform (Sun Java 2

Enterprise Edition, 2002). This environment is quite self-contained and independent of any host operation systems. Moreover, it has an abundant group of technologies we can use, such as the Enterprise Java Bean framework that it is approximately component-based, that complies with the basic philosophy of our approach. All the interactions between applications and the support environment are implemented as XML messages encoding the API calls in a manner similar to the XML-RPC style, which may soon be standardized and well supported in Java as well (Sun Microsystems, 2002). This enables any part of the support environment to be distributed.

CONCLUSION

In this chapter we have explored the consequences of the Web being used as an infrastructure to support electronic business applications. We have examined the likely consequences of using the existing infrastructure and suggested architectures to support applications as they increase in terms of both scale and complexity. To facilitate adapting these applications to the infrastructure, we have proposed a new model and architecture for Web-based applications as well as a support environment that can hide some of the ad hoc complexity of the Web. The architecture and support environment are also more compliant with the development processes induced by the Web, making continuous updates and maintenance easier and less costly for application-level developers.

REFERENCES

Barta, R. & Schranz, M. (1998). JESSICA: An object-oriented hypermedia publishing processor. *Computer Networks and ISDN Systems, Special Issue on the 7th International World-Wide Web Conference 30*, 239-249. Retrieved January 26, 2002, from http://www7.scu.edu.au/programme/fullpapers/1882/com1882.htm.

BEA WebLogic (2002). Retrieved January 26, 2002, from http://www.Weblogic.com.

Buschmann, F., Meunier, R., Rohnert, H., Sommerlad, P., & Stal, M. (1996). *Pattern-oriented software architecture: A system of patterns*. New York: John Wiley & Sons.

Diaz, A., Isakowitz, T., Maiorana, V., & Gilabert, G. (1995). RMC: A tool to design WWW applications. *The 4th International World-Wide Web Conference*, Retrieved January 26, 2002, from http://www.w3.org/Conferences/WWW4/Papers/187/.

Fraternali, P. & Paolini, P. (1998). A conceptual model and a tool environment for developing more scalable, dynamic and customizable Web applications. *6th International Conference on Extending Database Technology*, 421-435. Retrieved January 26, 2002, from http://www.ing.unico.it/autoWeb/Papers/autoWeb2.zip.

Gamma, E., Helm, R., Johnson, R. & Vlissides, J. (1995). *Design patterns–Elements of reusable object-oriented software*. Reading, MA: Addison-Wesley.

Gellersen, H-W. & Gaedke, M. (1999). Object-oriented Web application development. *IEEE Internet Computing, 3*(1), 60-68. Retrieved January 26, 2002, from http://computer.org/internet/ic1999/w1toc.htm.

IBM WebSphere (2002). Retrieved January 26, 2002, from http://www.ibm.com/Websphere.

Kristensen, A. (1998). Developing HTML-based Web applications. *First International Workshop on Web Engineering, WWW7 Conference*. Retrieved January 26, 2002, from http://www-uk.hpl.hp.com/people/ak/doc/Webe98.html.

Object Management Group. (2002). *CORBA specification*. Retrieved January 26, 2002, from http://www.omg.org/gettingstarted/specintro.htm#CORBA.

Schwabe, D. & Rossi, G. (1998). An object-oriented approach to Web-based application design. *Theory and Practice of Object Systems, 4*(4). Retrieved January 26, 2002, from http://www-di.inf.puc-rio.br/~schwabe//papers/TAPOSRevised.pdf.

Sun Enterprise Java Beans (2002). Retrieved January 26, 2002, from http://java.sun.com/products/ejb/index.html.

Sun Java 2 Enterprise Edition (2002). Retrieved January 26, 2002, from http://java.sun.com/j2ee/index.html.

Sun Microsystems (2002). *Sun Java API for XML-based RPC (JAX-RPC)*. Retrieved January 26, 2002, from http://java.sun.com/xml/xml_jaxrpc.html.

Chapter XVIII

XML - Digital Glue for the Modern World

Electronic Business Standards Fuelling Intra- and Inter-Enterprise Interoperability for Global Collaboration

Frank Jung
Software AG, Germany

ABSTRACT

This chapter provides information about current XML-related standards for the electronic interchange of business documents. The reader is introduced to the principles of the major standards in this area, such as XML, DTDs, XML Schema, XSL, XSLT, XPath, XPointer, DOM, and SAX. Furthermore, it is discussed why XML is not only an ideal data interchange format, but is very likely to earn its merits as a very effective format for persistently storing XML-based documents required in the modern e-business world. Finally, the chapter provides a brief introduction to industry initiatives aimed at optimizing the standardized exchange of business documents, such as BizTalk, ebXML, and others.

INTRODUCTION

Currently, we are facing a very challenging moment in the development of electronic business processes for cross-company collaboration. The Internet itself has driven us to develop open public standards across a wide range of individuals and companies, no matter where they are located. Though the rise and fall of the new economy created and swept away an incredible amount of business and investments, the initial reason for introducing electronic business in enterprises is still evident: if companies wish to continue their business successfully in times of global trading, pervasive networking, and constant change, they need to coordinate their business processes optimally with one another.

With Internet standards such as TCP/IP, HTTP, SGML, HTML and the globally recognized information exchange standard XML (eXtensible Markup Language), the Internet community will continue to provide an ideal basis for successfully streamlining all business processes. XML is user-driven and text-based, and frees information from computing systems and applications. It is based on simple rules that are just as responsible for bringing about the success of XML as the associated substandards or proposals that were submitted to and discussed and passed by the World Wide Web Consortium (W3C). It is these substandards that enable the actual potential of XML to be put into practice in effective applications.

ELECTRONIC BUSINESS IS ALL ABOUT COLLABORATION
Electronic business is more than just e-commerce!

The Internet will continue to be the driving force behind the ever more rapid expansion of e-commerce. Consequently, only those enterprises that realize the necessity of being able to access internal and external data quickly, to integrate and manage this data effectively, and to make it available both within the company and externally over the Web will be able to maintain and extend their lead over their rivals. Therefore, companies will create ideal conditions for ensuring their own survival in the age of the Internet if they begin now to adjust their business processes towards electronic business. Only then will they be able to respond to the future demands in today's fast-moving, global market. Whoever carries this through systematically will very probably be rewarded with excellent, way-above-average growth prospects. Now, what does electronic business really mean?

Electronic business can be viewed as transactions that are handled electronically and that support the corporate business process. Such transactions can take place either within companies, such as between departments, teams, or individual members of staff, or even across company boundaries, such as between business partners. When all direct contact with the customer takes place electronically—that is, for example, electronic orders are placed over the Internet (i.e. business to consumer, B2C), and the entire purchasing and delivery processes of all the companies involved in the manufacturing and delivery process are also handled by electronic means (that is, business to business, B2B), then we speak of electronic business. It is clear that automating many separate, interlinked business processes across the entire value-added chain results in a multitude of speed-related advantages and cost savings that every company hopes for from implementing electronic business processes.

We do indeed already have powerful, economically priced computers and high-bandwidth networks today, but it is only through the rapid development of Internet technology and the introduction of XML that it has become possible to put the exchange of data and information on a uniform, standardized basis that is totally independent of the platforms and applications used. This development was absolutely essential, since the actual problem today no longer lies with the capability of the technology, but far more with the limited capability of a global army of programmers. Until now, these people have had to waste a great deal of energy, time, and resources getting different heterogeneous and, for the most part, incompatible systems to communicate with one another by means of specially developed interfaces and protocols. It comes, therefore, as no surprise that IT-Analysts tell us that nowadays companies typically spend between 35% and 40% of their annual IT budget on developing, maintaining, and improving new programs, the sole purpose of which is to ensure the smooth exchange of information between databases and IT applications. Furthermore, Debra Logan (2000) of the Gartner Group stated:

> Major savings in efficiency and improvements in data quality come from XML's ability to represent and manipulate data that can be processed by multiple applications without corrupting or modifying the source data models. This is an essential feature in achieving "straight through processing"—one pass data transformation along a continuous process chain.

In order to be able to satisfy the demands made by your customers in an ever quicker, more comprehensible and ubiquitous manner, you will nowadays scarcely be able to avoid getting involved in electronic business. And in times of stagnating economies a commonly accepted, Internet-based interoperability technology, such as XML, helps keep enterprises in the profitability zone, or, at least, allows them to turn back to profitability quickly, thanks to enormously reduced costs for interfacing of IT components in heterogeneous infrastructures. Besides the technology factor, one other thing is important: true collaboration requires enterprises to open themselves up. Only those who master this challenge of cooperation, probably by partly opening their enterprises to the competitor, will reap the benefits of global trade and increased productivity based on electronic business and XML.

Limiting Factors of Electronic Business

Those managers who have decided to introduce electronic business in their company will come up against certain obstacles and restrictions. These will essentially be data format incompatibilities, transformation of information, management of disparate business data, and inflexible Internet solutions.

Data format incompatibilities

Since there has been no flexible and universally recognized data interchange format so far, a large number of incompatible and proprietary data formats have to be converted to one another. Today, for instance, placing orders with manufacturers is performed in various ways, such as by mail, fax, phone, or even telephone messages recorded on answering machines. The information transmitted in these ways can be of differing types, be written in different languages, and have different layouts.

The method currently being used to master this data chaos after receiving new orders is to manually enter the data of each and every order in an order processing system. Hence, a uniform data format, such as XML, is necessary in order to achieve the desired degree of automation for a manufacturer-customer relationship based on electronic business. XML enables the transmission, utilization, and storage of data over the Internet and across company and state boundaries.

Transformation of information

Even if two business partners have come to a joint agreement as to how each of them can access the data of the other, implementation of this agreement often fails due to different data formats, incompatible security systems, heterogeneous IT infrastructures, and the large number of "homemade" solutions. With the help of a platform- and application-independent meta language such as XML, all the different data types and pieces of information used in the transactions can be transformed into one another.

Management of disparate business data

The majority of companies interested in going into electronic business have large volumes of data that are stored in different formats and at different locations. Access to and the ability to search for specific details are often restricted by the actual data format itself, by the type of database being used, or by the operating system environment. Without a uniform database concept, you quickly put yourself in danger of having to fragment your data and consequently, in the long term, of losing the original context in which the pieces of data once stood. With XML and a solid database concept around it, it now becomes relatively simple to access distributed, differently structured data. A modern DBMS combines two technologies to solve a single problem: "providing unified access and management of structured content from across the enterprise and a control point for recording and directing incoming data from external sources." Hence, such a system would ideally store all possible data types and formats and present itself as a single database, accessing data from multiple back-end sources as if they were internal data stores. The latter is what the analysts at International Data Corporation (IDC) call a "virtual DBMS" (Goldfarb & Prescod, 1999; Olofson, 2000).

Inflexible Internet solutions

Many companies have started to eliminate their problems with complex and expensive scripting and gateway technologies (e.g., CGI). XML greatly simplifies the task of gaining access to distributed data. The error-prone and costly programming of task-specific, maintenance-intensive gateway scripts to read data from different storage media, files and databases in order to process them together, can be avoided by employing common standards, such as XML. One thing does become evident: in anticipation of the massive increase in business transactions that will be taking place in the near future, those Internet solutions created and put to use in the past will, in the short and medium term, certainly not be seen as the first choice for guaranteeing reliability, maximum performance, and scalability for electronic business.

THE XML STANDARD – "DIGITAL GLUE" FOR INTEROPERABILITY

XML has been developed with the aim of eliminating the restrictions cited above and of making the dream of global electronic business come true. In addition to this, what is essential are applications that enable the exchange of data between different database systems, that are able to process the data received with a minimum of manual intervention, that give different users different views of data already generated, (e.g., by means of a browser), and those that are able to tailor information searches to the needs of users using intelligent methods.

XML is actually not new. XML has been derived as a lightweight subset of the rather complex Standard Generalized Markup Language (SGML) passed in 1986 and 100% SGML-compliant (30 page XML specs versus 500 SGML pages). The concept of HTML was likewise derived from SGML, the difference being that it is not a subset of SGML, but an application of the SGML rules with a specifically defined number of specific HTML tags. When it defined

XML, the W3C did indeed succeed in making available 80% of the original SGML functionality, while at the same time reducing the complexity and the amount of effort required to implement it to 20%. Since XML reached W3C recommendation status in February 1998, it has become increasingly more popular in all branches of industry.

Even though its name lets us assume so, in truth the XML language is not a markup language! XML is far more a meta language that allows the definition of markup languages for different designated uses. XML is based on simple rules that are just as responsible for the success of XML as the associated co-related standards that enable the actual potential of XML to be put into practice in effective applications.

The "digital glue" — as part of the headline of this chapter — is used symbolically for XML and its associated co-related standards that have meanwhile become recognized as being ideally suited for scalable and most effective implementation of system interoperability across heterogeneous electronic business environments. Below is a brief summary of the main XML rules:

- Individual elements (or entire document sections) are enclosed by start and end tags.
- Tags must not be left out. Note: This is a major difference from HTML!
- A distinction is always made between upper- and lower-case characters (case sensitivity!).
- All tags used must begin with "<" and end with ">".
- Associated attribute values must likewise be set between angle brackets.
- With an empty element tag, an additional end tag is not expected. It looks as follows: *<identifier />*.
- Every "non-empty" element must have both a start tag and an end tag: *<identifier>element</identifier>*.
- Nested tags must not overlap (e.g., *<a>incorrect</a>*).
- DTDs (or XML schemas) are not absolutely necessary. If DTDs are not taken in account, a correctly specified XML document is only "well-formed."

The spread of the "eXtensible Markup Language" around the world within such a short time is no accident. In the run-up to this development, Internet standards such as TCP/IP, HTTP, SGML and HTML had set up an ideal basis on which XML has been able to build and expand just as successfully, and indeed will be able to continue expanding at a even greater rate. The triumphal march of the markup languages actually began with the launch of the easy-to-understand but somewhat limited-in-use HTML standard for Web pages. HTML has been in use for over 10 years, initially for exchanging scientific text documents and then successfully for developing pure presentation platforms for corporate and product information. Due to the increased level of interactivity on the Internet, the limits of what can be achieved with HTML have already been reached. Since the well-defined HTML markup had been designed for presentation purposes in order to make data look good on a browser screen, it is not possible to have users redefine the tags for their own purposes and in a more meaningful way. Changing the content of HTML pages generally requires error-prone and time-consuming manual adaptation, since data and formatting information are intermingled rigidly. It is just as impossible to convey the meaning of certain pieces of information with HTML as it is to automatically evaluate data. Therefore, the W3C proposed a lightweight derivative of SGML that is capable of separating the presentation of data from its actual content and at the same time of giving the documents a useful and logical structure - XML.

XML Adds Meaning to the Data and is Easy to Learn

Introduced to the general public in February 1998, XML is a text-based meta-language and already represents a universal, platform-independent means of transport for information of all types. It has already been extolled by many as the ASCII of the third millennium, because it is easy to read both for humans and "machines." This turns it into a potential solution for making the exchange of electronic documents over the Internet simple. First hand, the XML standard owes the level of its success to the independence of data from its presentation. Only when the content (data) is strictly separated from instructions relating to how the data is to be presented does it become possible to reuse XML-formatted data flexibly and repeatedly. The rules of the XML standard, however, only specify the grammar that is to be used for uniform data interchange. What vocabulary is used in the respective communication, for instance for a trade, must be agreed on between the communicating parties for the particular case in question. Three things must be guaranteed in order to ensure transactions will function:

- the parties communicating with one another interpret the rules of business in the same way;
- the object being traded is clearly described;
- it must be possible for the requester (e.g., and a purchaser in a trading situation) to express his expectations briefly and clearly in order to avoid misunderstandings before the transaction is concluded.

People contemplate and talk to one another in order to comply with the above-mentioned rules and to make absolutely sure of what each other means, seen against the backdrop of the different social and cultural environments in which they live. Machines, however, are not capable of thinking ahead and merely keep to the communication rules made available to them in the form of unambiguous instructions. In order to ensure that electronic business really are a success and are able to facilitate the fully automatic, computerized handling of business transactions, these rules must be standardized depending on the purpose being pursued; i.e., the trading parties must not only coordinate and agree on these rules, they must also describe them absolutely clearly and in unambiguous terms. To be able to satisfy these variable requirements of electronic business, great value was placed during the development of the XML standard on ensuring that the standard is extensible – a point which in the end has also been reflected in the given name. This should enable unused document elements to be deleted in the simplest way possible and new elements to be added simply to the documents transmitted or stored, without, for example, machine-to-machine communication coming to a standstill.

The flexibility of being able to define a variety of open, self-descriptive tags yourself depending on the particular needs is in fact one of the biggest advantages of the XML standard. In particular, this facilitates the commercial use of XML, because XML can be adapted to meet the needs of any branch of industry. At the same time, however, this capability is also seen as being the biggest disadvantage of XML. This flexibility runs contrary to the idea of a uniform mode of data interchange and conceals a danger of leading to the splitting-up of the language into countless dialects that are demanded by industry-specific structure definitions, that is, document type definitions (DTD) or XML Schema. XML schemas will supercede those DTDs still mainly in use and can be developed for almost any purpose. There is already a countless number of these definitions, such as the XML-based Chemical Markup Language (CML) used for representing complicated chemical structures, and the Synchronized Multimedia Integration Language (SMIL) used for managing multimedia contents. And there are many more.

In principle, XML is an easy-to-learn, open standard that can be put to good use wherever the job at hand is to put information into some sort of useful order. In addition to being used for transferring business documents, scientific and commercially used databases are also predestined for XML, and finally, even the entire chaotic knowledge network that has arisen with the World Wide Web. With the aid of the tags that describe the content, it is now possible to search for information far more successfully than before; in addition to full-text searches, XML supports the querying of specific terms from within the context and in this way enables an enormous improvement in the search processes employed over the Internet.

As a rule, searching for data in specially developed "native" XML data management systems, such as Tamino XML Server from Software AG, that can store XML documents in their original hierarchical structure, leads to the search results being displayed far more quickly than with other database types. The simple reason for this is that native XML DBMSs can do this without a complex conversion process that has to be run through with relational database systems not only for indexed saving but also every time search results are returned in XML format. Far more important than the slowness of speed displaying results is the amount of work involved with relational systems before XML document data with a large number of hierarchical levels can even be saved initially or its structure changed after subsequent updates. It is easy to imagine the entire database structure having to be completely redefined before the changes can be used. It goes without saying that such a redefinition is not necessary with "pure" XML storage in database systems designed for this purpose. Thus, masses of time and money can be saved.

XML AS A DATA STORAGE FORMAT
Document-Centric and Data-Centric Documents

It is evident that XML-based business documents exchanged over the Internet tend to have a quite complex structure. XML elements can be nested and can include multiple attributes. The main characteristic of so-called *document-centric* documents is that they are organized as a hierarchical tree of elements providing for an unlimited number of hierarchy levels and recursions. In contrast, current data management systems for the interchange of business data operate with *data-centric* documents. With their relatively flat structure, data-centric and document-centric documents can be optimally mapped to the row-column-table model of relational databases (Bourret, 2001a). Besides their complexity, business documents are very likely to be monitored and analyzed during active transactions or thereafter. In order to fulfill legal requirements after having the transactions completed, these documents must be stored in their entirety for a long time, while at the same time maintaining the ability to be efficiently searched on their content. This requires a document-centric treatment for storage and retrieval; hence, other ways than storing XML in a relational database (RDBMS) are needed.

Why Traditional Databases Are
Not Ideally Suited for XML

Relational databases (RDBMS) and object databases (ODBMS) utilize external XML parsers to map XML data into the format required for storing the document elements in the respective database. The internal structure of ODBMSs is very closely related to the principles of XML—they can store and retrieve hierarchically structured XML documents quite easily. However, these systems are not very well suited for e-business applications due to some major road blocks; integration of data from external systems, such as RDBMSs or file systems is very limited. Also, RDBMSs have particular disadvantages:

- For storing incoming XML documents in a relational database, documents must be broken down into a multitude of RDBMS tables and be dissected into single elements, fitting to the table-internal row-column model. This always requires conformance to a pre-existing structure given by a document type definition (DTD) or a respective XML schema document, for which application programmers have to program the appropriate storage logic (Bourret, 2001). Such a model is inflexible with regard to frequent and unpredictable schema changes following at a later date.
- For retrieving complex XML documents along with their nested element hierarchies, RDBMSs require complex joins to be performed when querying across various tables. The more complex the document gets, the higher the performance degradation will be.
- Locking is another problem area for RDBMSs. Most RDBMSs lock at the table-row level in order to safeguard parts of a document from being accessed and manipulated by another party while being written on, read, updated, or deleted by a first accessor. Thus, because of the original XML document being stored in many tables, updating an XML document in an RDBMS would require many locks to be set. At the end of a transaction, all these locks have to be reset. This results in further performance degradation.
- Additional problems arise when changing a schema. Even if only one single additional tag is required, the database administrator (programmer) must insert new columns or entire tables into the RDBMS, or worst case, he is required to redesign the entire data model. Moreover, he has to adapt the storage logic and the mapping to the new elements - obviously an enormous development and maintenance effort.

Mismatches Between XML and RDBMS Technology

Finally, what remains is the conclusion that relational and object-oriented databases are not suited to leverage all the advantages provided by XML (Champion, Jung, & Hearn, 2001). For reaping the benefits of XML and its potential in Web-based applications, a native XML server with integrated XML data store is required to avoid unnecessary performance degradations and development efforts otherwise resulting from squeezing the square peg (XML) into a round hole (non-native XML storage solutions). Such an XML server is a preventive measure against the aforementioned pitfalls. Since XML documents are processed in their original format, no format conversion is necessary for storing or retrieving hierarchically structured XML documents. In general, native XML servers will provide enterprises with persistent storage and high-performance search capabilities for global interoperability. The advantage of native XML storage will increase further, the deeper the

Table 1: Mismatches between XML data and RDBMS

XML	RDBMS (normalized)
• Nested hierarchies of elements • Elements are ordered • A formal schema is optional • Ordinary business documents can be represented, stored and retrieved as a single object • XPath and XQuery standards provide common query languages for locating data	• Data in multiple tables • Cells have a single value • Atomic cell values • Row/column order not defined • Schema always required • Joins necessary to retrieve simple documents • Query with SQL retrofitted for XML

element hierarchies of the business documents become that need to be stored and the more changes on related schemas are expected.

*W3C status: **Feb. 10, 1998 - XML 1.0 Recommendation** - http://www.w3.org/TR/REC-xml*
*   **Oct. 6, 2000 - XML 1.0 Release 2 - Recommendation***
*   (also look at http://www.w3.org/XML/xml-19980210-errata).*
*   The error list of Release 2: http://www.w3.org/XML/xml-V10-2e-errata .*

CO-RELATED XML STANDARDS

A number of important and necessary co-standards play a decisive role for XML's success: DTDs or XML schemas serve to define document structures; XSL is for document formatting and XSLT for transformation to other document structures; XPath, DOM and SAX enable the programmer to navigate through XML element trees; XLink (XML Linking Language, not discussed in this chapter) can be seen as an extension of the hyperlink functionality familiar from HTML that enables, for example, references to be made to several different target documents; and XPointer governs navigation within a document, either directly by means of pointers to specified words or phrases or indirectly by specifying a path.

DTD and XML Schema

DTDs or schemas represent documents that can be used to check whether or not document elements used and their contents or layout satisfy a previously concluded agreement (i.e., valid). Especially in XML schemas, it is possible to determine data types for elements and attributes. DTDs (like XML) have been derived from the document-oriented SGML standard and are used solely for defining the structure and attributes. DTDs provide no data types other than characters (CDATA) or parsed characters (PCDATA), which is a major disadvantage compared with the XML schema standard that has been ratified recently. After receiving XML-formatted data, applications using DTDs must generate the data types (e.g., integer) themselves, in order to be able to use this data to carry out calculations, for example.

This situation is made worse by the fact that DTDs are not XML standard-compliant, because they do not obey the rules of XML 1.0. XML documents are called "well-formed" XML if the syntax of XML data transmitted conforms only to the rules of XML 1.0. A non-validating parser analyzes and checks the document transmitted only with respect to the correctness of its elements in relation to the rules laid down in XML 1.0. No check is run with regard to compliance with specified structural characteristics. "Valid" XML documents have been successfully checked by means of a validating parser for conformity with structural definitions specified in DTDs or XML schemas.

XML Schema provides mechanisms for declaring, defining, and modifying data types. For simplicity reasons you can consider W3C XML Schema as DTDs + data types + namespace. But due to its flexibility and comprehensiveness, its inherent complexity leaves many XML activists still in doubt, as to whether XML Schema will replace DTDs in the long term or not. For the coming years, the widespread use of DTDs until now will make this unlikely, since for an average programmer it is more difficult to understand the XML Schema specification. This is a fact that will presumably favor the continued use of DTDs.

*W3C status: **May 2, 2001 - XML Schema 1.0 Recommendation** -*
*   (Part 0:Primer; Part 1:Structures; Part 2:Datatypes) - http://www.w3.org/*
*   TdR/xmlschema-0/*

From CSS to XSL

When XML 1.0 was adopted, the XML standard specified that the contents and the presentation of XML documents must be written separately from one another. This required a further standard for the definition of the additional formatting information. In an initial attempt to find a solution to this problem, the Cascading Style Sheets standard (CSS) was used. CSS was already being applied successfully for formatting HTML pages and should be familiar to all HTML programmers. This standard allows tag-based formatting of documents that are to be displayed and has contributed to the successful introduction of XML thanks to the extent to which it is known. That said, the formatting possibilities with respect to the sequence of the tags in the source document were seen as being too inflexible to be good enough for use with XML. After making a great number of modifications to the specifications, the W3C introduced eXtensible Stylesheet Language (XSL), governing the presentation of XML documents.

When the first XSL standardization proposal was submitted back in August 1997, XSL still stood for "eXtensible *Style* Language," but today the finally proposed recommendation carries the name "eXtensible *Stylesheet* Language." In April 1999, the subset known as XSL Transformations (XSLT) was split off from the specification as a separate proposal for a further standard. Then, on July 9, 1999, XPath was separated from the XSLT draft. XPath has already been able to establish itself as a standard for locating elements and attributes within a document and is described further below. Due to the extensive changes made to the XSL specification, early implementations of the standard are to a large extent incompatible with today's versions of the XSL and XSLT standards.

XSL Stylesheets

XSL stylesheets are XML-compliant documents for organizing formatting instructions, that is, rules for producing optimum presentation of the contents of referenced elements on different output media. With such stylesheets, the contents of an individual source document (it contains the data to be formatted with the aid of stylesheets) can be displayed in different ways or be optimally adapted to various formats supported by display devices a user wants to use. Stylesheets allow for displaying a Web site with the aid of a standard browser or for printing out this Web site and writing it to a CD-ROM or even for outputing it on small displays such as those of mobile phones, Personal Digital Assistants (PDA), or Pocket PCs.

By providing different stylesheets applied to one set of data, several display variants can be generated concurrently and for various output devices. If changes have to be made to the content of the source document, normally all that needs to be changed is this document and not the associated stylesheets.

XSLT - eXtensible Stylesheet Language Transformations

XSLT is a language designed for transforming an XML document of any structure into another XML document. Although XSLT can be applied on its own, that is, independent of XSL, there is no intention to employ XSLT as a complete, multi-purpose XML transformation language. Based on a document tree that is generated from an XML source document, an application referred to as an XSLT stylesheet processor (e.g., XT from James Clark, written in Java) creates, with the aid of the rules defined in a stylesheet, a target document tree that can be saved either in XML, HTML, or as ASCII text. The target format can be defined by means of the XSLT language element "<xsl:output>". The text output method allows it to generate any other text-based output format such as "comma-separated values" files, PDF documents, EDI messages or the WML format for output on mobile devices. In general, the transformation process creates a result tree from two basic documents (XML and XSLT), with the tree itself also possibly being an XML document.

Template rules count among the most important constituent parts of the XSLT standard and XSLT documents. They specify the criteria according to which elements of a source tree are selected. They also contain the process instructions that enable the source tree elements to be restructured into those of the target tree. A "template rule" consists of two parts: a pattern and a template. The pattern is compared with source tree elements in order to find out which document nodes come into question for further processing with the associated template. Path operators (specified in XPath) are used to select document nodes. On the other hand, the template contains instructions with which the content found by means of the search pattern can be processed. Each template rule generates subtrees not only containing the markup but also the content, which is put together in accordance with the given rules. The complete result tree of an XSL transformation is then built up from the partial results in the specified order.

W3C status: Nov. 16, 1999 - XSLT 1.0 Recommendation - http://www.w3.org/TR/xslt

XSL- eXtensible Stylesheet Language

The XSL specification itself is put together from XSLT and XSL Formatting Objects (FO). An XSL stylesheet therefore contains two types of instructions. Whereas in the case of XSLT instructions, the elements to be formatted have to be found and selected first, FO uses XML-compliant instructions to describe the appearance the XML elements specified beforehand are to have when displayed in the target document. To format the output, stylesheets might contain HTML tags, printer control instructions, etc.

W3C status: Aug. 28, 2001 - XSL 1.0 Proposed Recommendation -
       http://www.w3.org/TR/xsl/

XPath - XML Path Language

XPath is the result of an attempt to bestow a common syntax and meaning to mutual functionalities of the XSL Transformation and XPath standards. XPath is basically a language for addressing parts of an XML document and also enables manipulation of strings, numbers and Boolean variables. XPath works at the level of abstract, logical XML document structures and defines a navigation path through the XML document tree, and builds on the Common Path Expression Syntax that is also used in XSLT, XPointer and XLink. XPath is used by XSLT to identify or localize document elements through specified search patterns with path expressions that are presented with a syntax that is not XML-compliant. Addressing nodes within an XML tree takes place either by specifying absolute node names, the relative position, the node type (e.g., text node), conditions that the node must fulfill (filter expressions), or by specifying axes (predecessor, successor, child). More complex XPath expressions can be formulated using logical and arithmetic operators. If standardized query expressions are used, the possibility of further using not only the document but also the application program code is increased, because XPath is used with XLink, XSLT, XML Schema and many other substandards.

W3C status: Oct. 18, 2000 - XSLT / XPath Update - New working draft,
       Nov.16, 1999 - XPath 1.0 Recommendation - http://www.w3.org/TR/xpath

XPointer

XPath uses XPointer for node addressing within a document. An equivalent familiar from the world of HTML is the fragment identifier (anchor), "#", which can be used to jump directly to specific positions within a document. Referencing already familiar from HTML looks, for example, like this:

<A href="http://www.xyz.com/abc/docsearchedfor.xml#bookmark">

Furthermore, XPointer allows the accessing of elements and attributes depending on the logical document structure, such as to branch within a book to a branching location that can be found, for example, under the 2nd section, in the 3rd paragraph at the 5th word position. *W3C status: Jun. 7, 2000 - XPointer 1.0 Candidate Recommendation - rejected due to major flaws.*
Jan. 8, 2001 - XPointer 1.0 Working Draft Last Call - *http://www.w3.org/TR/WD-xptr*

DOM – Document Object Model

DOM and SAX are standardized application programming interfaces (APIs) for platform- and programming-language-independent access to XML documents and for processing such documents. Since the elements of an XML document are hierarchically nested, a document can be displayed as a document tree. DOM is a tree-based API with which all elements of XML or HTML documents, too, first have to be created (modeled) in the form of a tree structure in the RAM of the computer. Only then is an application able to navigate beyond the tree elements and access the elements mapped in them, in order to modify their contents, for instance. Sub-elements and attributes then appear as sub-nodes to a higher-level element. The fact that a copy of the original XML document or of its structure is available quasi-statically in RAM has both advantages and disadvantages. One indisputable advantage is the ability to modify the elements directly, that is, to change, delete or insert totally new, individual elements or their contents, or even to copy entire subtrees. This advantageous capability, however, brings with it the disadvantage that it consumes massive amounts of resources. The longer the document is, the more difficult (and slower) it becomes to remodel it as an object model.
W3C status: Oct. 1, 1998 - DOM Level 1.0 Recommendation -
http://www.w3.org/TR/rec-dom-level-1/
Aug. 30, 2001 - DOM Level 3.0 (XPath specification) Working Draft -
http://www.w3.org/TR/DOM-Level-3-XPath/

SAX – Simple API For XML

SAX is supported by the majority of parsers and is used not only to access XML documents, but to process them as well. In contrast to the DOM, SAX is an event-based API that gives an application control over a document even while parsing is still in progress—doing so by communicating events. SAX makes it easy to check the status of the parser while it is analyzing XML documents. Depending on whether a document element searched for is available or not, or whether certain contents have been found or not, corresponding events can be sent back to the application. The events described are called, for example, "startDocument," "startElement," "characters," "endElement" or "endDocument," and the data sent back can contain the associated values to which the application can respond promptly. A querying application can then respond immediately.

The advantage compared with a DOM solution is quite clearly the fact that with SAX, documents can be parsed that are far larger than the RAM available. Moreover, SAX delivers results far quicker wherever individual elements (or their contents) of a document are to be read out. It is not necessary to remodel the complete document every time.

The latest variant, SAX 2.0, adds fourteen new interface modules and classes.

Status: ***May 5, 2000 - SAX 2.0 - XML-DEV Mailing List Member Specification,***
Megginson Technologies - http://www.megginson.com/SAX/index.html

XML-BASED STANDARDS FOR ELECTRONIC DATA INTERCHANGE

The idea of handling business processes quicker and cheaper and, therefore, more effectively overall with the aid of electronic data interchange is not new. But even though electronic data interchange (EDI) has been in use for precisely this purpose for more than 25 years, primarily in large enterprises, it does not necessarily enjoy the highest degree of popularity. Especially for small-and medium-sized companies, this technology is too expensive; data traffic can indeed be processed right through entire supply chains, but only via private value-added networks (VAN). It is true that data interchange over a VAN can, for all intents and purposes, be classified as "secure" with respect to protection against unauthorized access and manipulation, but EDI is not particularly robust. Furthermore, the almost cryptic coding of the messages to be exchanged makes it necessary to employ highly paid specialists and purchase expensive tools.

It comes, therefore, as no great surprise that EDI has a global share of just around 2% of all transactions taking place (Fickus & Loeken, 2001). Regarding inter-company data interchange, two definitive EDI dialects have managed to establish themselves—these being ANSI X.12 in North America and EDIFACT (today UN/CEFACT) in Europe and almost all of the rest of the world. Whereas large corporations have profited from the possibilities offered by EDI for a long time now, small-and medium-sized companies are still processing their orders mostly by means of phone calls, faxes, and correspondence for cost-related reasons. It is easy to imagine how unreliable it is to transfer the data required for an order received by fax to the order processing system by hand –and that after the data contained in the fax received has possibly even been printed out beforehand with the aid of a computer. Without a doubt, this costs money and slows down the purchasing and sales processes considerably. Such high costs are disadvantageous not only for small-and medium-sized companies, but also for developing countries who are increasingly becoming involved in trade relations with the industrialized nations. The Internet is enjoying increasing popularity all around the world and can be tapped into relatively inexpensively and from practically anywhere to feed data in or call it up. XML is playing a key role in this, because global adoption of a standardized and uniform exchange format gives small-and medium-sized companies the chance to tag onto the already established processes of the big players. This gives them the chance to profit from the savings possibilities and competitive advantages one hopes for from the application of B2B in the company. In this context, the hybrid data interchange standards, XEDI and XML/ EDI, convert the familiar EDI rules and vocabularies on the basis of XML and are becoming ever more popular. The fact that EDI is moving towards XML and the Internet is, however, not the only application being found for XML in today's e-commerce. Whereas EDI was originally designed and used more for interchanging data over point-to-point connections, XML and the Internet permit the creation of networked solutions for optimizing purchasing conditions and trade with goods of all kinds via electronic market places, auctions, or exchanges. Companies such as Ariba with its cXML protocol and Commerce One with xCBL have developed standards for Internet-based, B2B e-commerce transactions that lead the world. The specifications of these XML-based protocols contain all the information necessary to be able to conduct Internet-based transactions. To this end, the actual message to be transmitted is completely "packed" into a well-defined, electronic envelope and sent over the Internet to the recipient. Despite all the flexibility offered when implementing business

Table 2: XML-based Transaction Standards Categories (Vollmer, 2000)

Standard	Description	Status
Industry-specific XML-based standards		
RosettaNet PIPs	New standard developed by RosettaNet Consortium to support general business activity in the high-tech manufacturing sector (computers) on a global basis. PIPs define related Partner Interface Processes and provide a mechanism for creating, canceling/exchanging purchase orders between business partners.	More than 100 PIPs developed (with limited scope). Some of them used in the IT manufacturers sector.
FpML	New XML-based standard that has been developed to enable e-commerce in the financial derivatives sector.	FpML 1.0 recommendation released on May 14, 2001. FpML Architecture 1.0 rec. released on March 16, 2001.
Many more	More than 100 other standards based on XML are currently being developed for usage in 40 different industry branches.	Variable progress. For details, see also www.xml.org.
Application-specific XML-based standards		
cXML	XML-based standard used for Ariba's e-commerce applications	In use.
xCBL	XML-based standard used for Commerce One's e-commerce applications	In use.
Universally usable XML-based standards		
BizTalk Framework BizTalk.org (Library)	A Microsoft-led effort that represents a guideline for how to publish schemas in XML and how to use XML messages to integrate software programs.	BizTalk Developer's Tool Kit has been available since May 3, 2000.
ebXML	New general business standard being jointly developed by the United Nations and the Oasis Consortium. The main objective of ebXML is to lower the barrier of entry to electronic business in order to facilitate trade. See also http://www.ebxml.org/specs/index.htm	ebXML Technical Architecture Specification v1.04 approved on Feb. 16, 2001. Business Process Specification Schema v1.01; ebXML Requirements Specs v1.06; some more approved on May 11, 2001.
Hybrid Standards (EDI / XML)		
XEDI	This standard traditionally encapsulates X12 and EDIFACT transactions in XML. Has been developed by the XEDI Organization.	In use. Support for converting RosettaNet PIPs to X12 or EDIFACT standards.Announced May 11, 2000.
XML/EDI	Another standard that encapsulates X12 and converts EDIFACT transactions to XML. Developed by the XML/EDI Group.	Currently being tested.

processes with XML, a technical specification on its own can not guarantee the interoperability of business applications. A smooth interchange of business-related data between a large number of parties involved in the business process is only possible if standardized vocabularies are made available that are clearly tailored to the needs of their respective user groups and is coordinated with and agreed on with them beforehand. These vocabularies are defined using XML and associated DTDs or schemas. Business partners involved in the process must then be notified of the vocabularies and given simple access to them. In order to put the exchange of different document types across company boundaries on a common footing, many companies have already made an attempt to package the content data in a "proprietary" electronic envelope. As in real life when delivering letters, such an envelope carries information identifying where the message has come from and the address to which it is to be delivered. It is precisely with respect to these specifications where the approaches of Microsoft's BizTalk (Framework and Library), Open Buying on the Internet (OBI), RosettaNet, XML.ORG, the ebXML initiative and the EDI message envelope specifications differ.

To summarize, Table 2 gives a brief overview of the current initiatives for XML-based schema repositories, which can be split up into four classes in which they now compete among themselves. These classes are either industry-specific, application-specific, general data interchange rules, or hybrid EDI, that is, rules such as those that have already been introduced for EDIFACT and X12 standards within the framework of efforts to standardize EDI.

CONCLUSION

XML is the key technology that makes information understandable and accessible and already makes the Internet an important economic factor. XML is accepted all around the world and really does have a chance of becoming the motor of tomorrow's World Wide Web. Thanks to XML, information becomes platform-independent and can be accessed via the Internet from anywhere in the world and be put to use immediately. For the benefit of a globally interconnected IT-world, XML and its co-related standards allow a far more effective exchange of documents between machines than would be possible between intelligent, but "slower and more expensive" humans. This increase in effectiveness would be most desirable, because it would enable all of us to work and communicate with one another in an optimum way, that is, with a minimum of frictional losses. Using the scarce resources available for more important tasks than the "pointless" conversion of formats is without doubt a course of action that will not hinder us from further increasing our effectiveness in going about our business!

Along with the acceptance of XML as the universal standard for data exchange, XML also turns out to be a perfect data format for storage and retrieval of data. As such, storing exchanged XML documents in persistent repositories provides for a range of benefits: it allows for fast and efficient searches, requires far less development effort than other data storage solutions (e.g., RDBMS), and gives easy access to stored data via an unlimited range of end-user devices. Since the presentation of a document is decoupled from its content, displaying it on a specific end device just depends on a device-specific style sheet. The latter is retrieved from the XML server along with the queried content. A high degree of agreement has already been reached with respect to the XML standards presented in this chapter, but what remains to be seen is whether or not present efforts to draw up a universally utilizable vocabulary for business communication (see ebXML) will lead to an equally successful and globally accepted electronic business standard. This also applies to the current move towards the implementation of Web services and the UDDI initiative.

REFERENCES

Bourret, Ronald P. (2001a). *XML and Databases*. Available at http://www.rpbourret.com/xml/XMLAndDatabases.htm.

Bourret, R. P. (2001b). *XML Database Products*. Available at http://www.rpbourret.com/xml/XMLDatabaseProds.htm#native.

Champion, M., Jung, F., & Hearn, C. (2001). *Tamino XML Server White Paper*, Software AG: INS-WP06E0901, [Brochure]. Page 9. Available at http://www.softwareag.com/tamino/brochures.htm.

Fickus, W. & Loeken, N. (Jan. 16, 2001*)*. *XML - Die Evolution des Internet zur integrierten Computerplattform*. WestLB Panmure Report [Brochure]. Pg. 20/21.

Goldfarb, C.F. & Prescod, P. (1999). *XML Handbuch*. Pg. 396 ff. Upper Saddle Rivers, NJ: Prentice Hall.

Logan, D. (2000). *Gartner Symposium ITxpo 2000*, Cannes/France. Nov. 6-9, Pg. 6.

Olofson, Carl. (2000). *IDC Bulletin: XML and virtual DBMS Market Forecast and Analysis, 2000-2004*. Pg. 2.

Vollmer, Ken. (2000). *Giga Information Group Planning Assumption: XML's Role in the EDI world*. Pg. 3. Available at http://www.gigaweb.com.

Additional Information Sources

www.xml.com, *www.xml.com/pub/q/stdlistdate*, *www.xmlsoftware.com*, *www.w3.org*, *www.xml.org*

Section VII:

E-Marketing and Virtual Marketplace

Chapter XIX

Designing Agent-Based Negotiation for E-Marketing

V. K. Murthy
University of New South Wales at ADFA, Australia

ABSTRACT

This chapter describes how to design agent-based negotiation systems in e-marketing. Such a negotiation scheme requires the construction of a suitable set of rules, called a protocol, among the participating agents. The construction of the protocol is carried out in two stages: first expressing a program into an object-based rule system and then converting the rule applications into a set of agent-based transactions on a database of active objects represented using high-level data structures. We also describe how to detect the termination of the negotiation process based on Commission-Savings-Tally Algorithm.

A simple example illustrates how a set of agents can participate in a negotiation protocol to find the shortest travel route on a map of cities represented as a directed weighted graph.

INTRODUCTION

In Chapter 13, "E-business Transaction Management in Web Integrated Network Environment," we described the applications of agents in e-business transaction. As described there, agents consist of information objects and an associated script that knows what to do with the information and how to deal with the environment. They behave like actors and have intentions and actions. Agents are autonomous and they have a built in control to act only if they want to. In addition, agents are flexible, proactive, and have multithreaded control. In this chapter, we describe in detail how a set of agents can be used for negotiation in e-marketing. For this purpose we need to have a model of the multi-agent-based paradigm for executing the negotiation process in a manner very similar to what human beings do.

An important model of multi-agent paradigm that is suitable for our purpose is from Fisher (1995). This model is applicable to design a concurrent multi-agent negotiation paradigm based on the transactional logic model (Bonner & Kifer, 1994). Although other models of the multi-agent system have also been proposed (Figure1) (Chen & Dayal, 2000; Dignum & Sierra, 2001; Genesereth & Nilsson, 1987; Ishida, 1994), Fisher's model has the simplicity and adaptability for realization as a distributed transaction-based paradigm for negotiation.

Figure 1: Model of the multi-agent system

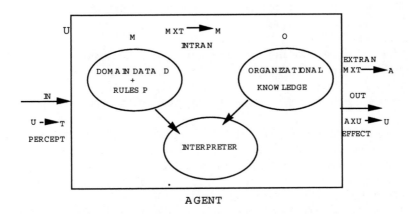

A GENT

A multi-agent system consists of the following subsystems:

(1) Worldly states or environment U: Those states that completely describe the universe containing all the agents.

(2) Percept: Depending upon the sensory capabilities (input interface to the universe or environment), an agent can partition U into a standard set of messages T, using a sensory function Perception (PERCEPT): PERCEPT :U→ T.

PERCEPT can involve various types of perception: see, read, hear, smell. The messages are assumed to be of standard types based on an interaction language that is interpreted identically by all agents.

(3) Epistemic states or Mind M: We assume that the agent has a mind M (that is essentially a problem domain knowledge consisting of an internal database for the problem domain data and a set of problem domain rules) that can be clearly understood by the agent without involving any sensory function. The database D sentences are in first order predicate calculus (also known as extensional database) and agents' mental actions are viewed as inferences arising from the associated rules that result in an intentional database that changes (revises or updates) D.

The agent's state of belief, or a representation of an agent's state of belief at a certain time, is represented by an ordered pair of elements (D, P). D is a set of beliefs about objects, their attributes, and relationships stored as an internal database, and P is a set of rules expressed as preconditions and consequences (conditions and actions). When T is input, if the conditions given on the left-hand side of P match T, the elements from D that correspond to the right-hand side are taken from D, and suitable actions are carried out locally (in M) as well as on the environment.

(4) Organizational Knowledge (O): Since each agent needs to communicate with the external world or other agents, we assume that O contains all the information about the relationships among the different agents. For example, the connectivity relationship for communication, the data dependencies between agents, interference among agents with respect to rules, and information about the location of different domain rules are in O.

(5) INTRAN: M is suitably revised or updated by the function called Internal Transaction (INTRAN). Revision means acquisition of new information about the world state, while update means change of the agent's view of the world. Revision of M corresponds to a transformation of U due to occurrence of events and transforming an agent's view due to acquisition of new information that modifies rules in P or their mode of application (deterministic, nondeterministic or probabilistic) and corresponding changes in database D. Updates to M correspond to changes in U due to the occurrence of events that changes D but not P. That is: INTRAN: M X T → M.

(6) EXTRAN: External action is defined through a function called global or external transaction (EXTRAN) that maps an epistemic state and a partition from an external state into an action performed by the agent. That is: EXTRAN: M X T → A.

This means that the current state of mind and a new input activates an external action from A.

(7) EFFECT: The agent also has an effectory capability on U by performing an action from a set of actions A (ask, tell, hear, read, write, speak, send, smell, taste, receive, silent), or more complex actions. Such actions are carried out according to a particular agent's role and governed by an etiquette called protocols. The effect of these actions is defined by a function EFFECT, that modifies the world states through the actions of an agent:

EFFECT: A X U → U; EFFECT can involve additions, deletions and modifications to U.

Thus an agent is defined by a 9-tuple:

(U,T,M(P,D),O,A,PERCEPT,INTRAN,EXTRAN,EFFECT).

The interpreter repeatedly executes selected rules in P, until no rule can be fired.

We can interpret all the abstract machine models (such as a Finite state machine or a Turing machine) and parallel computational models (such as classifier systems) as subclasses of the agents, by suitably formulating the definitions. Thus agents can exhibit the same computational power as a nondeterministic Turing machine (Murthy, 1996), which is a very powerful computational model for solving many real-life problems that arise in Artificial Intelligence applications to e-marketing.

The nature of internal production rules P, their mode of application, and the action set A determines whether an agent is deterministic, nondeterministic, probabilistic or fuzzy. Rule application policy in a production system P can be modified by:
1.   assigning probabilities/fuzziness for applying the rule;
2.   assigning strength to each rule by using a measure of its past success; and
3.   introducing a support for each rule by using a measure of its likely relevance to the current situation.

The above three factors provide for competition and cooperation among the different rules (Murthy & Krishnamurthy, 1995a). Such a model is useful for negotiation in e-marketing that involves interactions between many agents.

WHAT IS NEGOTIATION?

"Negotiation" is an interactive process among a number of agents that results in varying degrees of cooperation, competition, and ultimately commitment that leads to a total agreement, consensus or a disagreement. Accordingly, a negotiation protocol is viewed as a set of public rules that dictate the conduct of an agent with other agents to achieve a desired final outcome.

A negotiation protocol among agents involves the following actions or conversational states:
1.   Propose: One puts forward for consideration a set of intentions called a proposal.

2.   Accept: The proposal is accepted for execution into actions.
3.   Refuse: The proposal is rejected for execution into actions.
4.   Modify: This alters some of the intentions of the proposer and suggests a modified proposal, that is, at the worst it can be, a Refuse and a New proposal, or a partial acceptance and new additions.
5.   No proposal: No negotiation.
6.   Abort: Quit negotiation.
7.   Report agreement: This is the termination point for negotiation in order to begin executing actions.
8.   Report failure (agree to disagree): Negotiation breaks down.
       Note that the above actions are not simple exchange of messages but may involve some intelligent or smart computation.
       The syntax of the negotiation action can be represented in Backus-Naur form (BNF):
       Negotiation:= { Open Transaction |Closed transaction}
       Open Transaction := {Propose | Accept | Refuse | Revise |No-proposal |}
       Closed Transaction := {Abort |Report Agreement |Failure}

A directed graph can be used to represent a negotiation process with the Open transaction as the initial state and the closed transaction as the final state. Such a directed graph that expresses the connectivity relationship among the agents can be real or imaginary and can be dynamic or static depending upon the problem at hand.

Multi-agents can cooperate to achieve a common goal to complete a transaction to aid the customer. The negotiation follows rule-based strategies that are computed locally by its host server. Here competing offers are to be considered; occasionally cooperation may be required. Special rules may be needed to take care of risk factors, domain knowledge dependencies between attributes, and positive and negative end conditions. When making a transaction, several agents have to negotiate and converge to some final set of values that satisfies their common goal. Such a goal should also be cost effective so that it is in an agreed state at the minimum cost or a utility function. To choose an optimal strategy, each agent must build a plan of action and communicate with other agents. We will later illustrate this situation by converting a distributed greedy algorithm that finds a minimal cost path in a graph, into a negotiation problem. In this case, the system is deterministic and the negotiation reaches a stable state. However, it is possible that a system is nondeterministic or stochastic and has many stable states, as in e-market trading. In an e-market situation, such a negotiation can lead to a speculation bubble or a crash, or a stagnation and a phase transition among such states, as discussed in a later section.

NEGOTIATION AS A TRANSACTIONAL PARADIGM

Problem solving consists of finding a partially ordered sequence of application of desired operators that can transform a given starting or initial state of the solution to a desired final state - called goal- that provides the solution to the desired problem. Reaching a goal through a sequence of totally ordered subgoals is called a linear solution. For many problems, such a totally ordered sequential assembly (or concatenation) of subgoals may not exist. Such problems require a nondeterministic search. A solution based on a nondeterministic search strategy is called a nonlinear solution. A nonlinear solution uses an act-verify strategy.

Human problem solving also uses this act-verify strategy through preconditions and actions (Murthy & Krishnamurthy,1995b). When a human solves a problem, the solution process has a similarity to the transaction handling problem; for each transaction is an exploratory, non-pre-programmed real-time procedure that uses a memory recall (Read), acquires new information, and performs a memory revision (Write). Each transaction is also provided with the facility for repair (recovery-Undo) much like the repair process encountered in human problem solving. In human problem solving, several pieces of independent or dependent information are acquired from various knowledge sources, and their consistency is verified before completing a step of the solution to achieve each subgoal; this process corresponds to committing a subtransaction in a distributed transaction processing system, before proceeding to reach the next level of subgoal arranged in a hierarchy. Thus the transactional approach provides for a propose, act, and verify strategy by offering a nonprocedural style of programming (called "subjunctive programming") in which a hypothetical proposal or action (what-if changes) is followed by verification, commitment or abort, and restoration. So this paradigm is well-suited for agent-based computations.

OBJECT-BASED RULES AND TRANSACTIONS

The multi-agent negotiation is based on post production system model, and the related language (Weerasooriya, Rao & Ramamohanarao, 1995). It is well known that the production system paradigm occupies a prominent place in AI. This system consists of a set of rewrite rules consisting of a left-hand-side expression (LHS) and a right-hand-side expression (RHS). Given any string drawn from a database that matches the LHS, the corresponding RHS is substituted. Thus we may substitute expressions, constants, or null elements permitting update, evaluation , insertion, or deletion operations. The implementation of a production system operates in three-phase cycles: matching, selecting, and execution. The cycle halts when the database fulfils a termination condition. The task of the match phase is similar to query matching - that is, unification of the rules with the database. This phase returns a conflict set that satisfies the conditions of different rules. In the select phase, we select those compatible rules after conflict resolution. In the execution phase; all selected rules are fired and actions are implemented.

In order to use the production system as the basis for transactional multi-agent negotiation, we need to analyze how the rules (and hence the respective transactions) interfere with each other when they are applied. There are several ways in which the rules can interfere when we consider object-based production rule systems (OPRUS) (Ishida, 1994; Murthy & Krishnamurthy, 1995a, 1995b). Here we assume that the rules do not interfere during the negotiation process or their interference is suitably controlled (Woolridge, Muller & Tambe, 1996).

OPRUS can be implemented as transactions, by identifying every rule that fires as a transaction. We can find a direct correspondence between concurrent transaction processing systems and concurrently enabled rule systems. Therefore, much of the known results in concurrency control in transaction processing can be directly applied. That is, we can identify inter-rule and intra-rule consistency with inter-transaction and intra-transaction consistency. This approach is therefore useful for multi-agent production systems in distributed computing.

In the transactional implementation, the serializability of transactions guarantees correctness. The notion of serializability is essentially concerned with the conflict equivalence of an interleaved schedule to a serial schedule (namely, the conflicting actions in the non-aborted transactions are performed in the same temporal order). Hence, it ensures a priori (from what is before) consistency in a competitive environment.

PLANNING, REASONING AND NEGOTIATION

The negotiation process is usually preceded by two other cooperating interactive processes: planning and reasoning. The ability to plan ahead for solving a problem is the key aspect of intelligent behavior. To solve a problem through negotiation, we start with a set of desired properties and try to devise a plan that results in a final state with the desired properties. For this purpose, we define an initial state where we begin an operation and also define a desirable goal state or a set of goal states. Simultaneously, we use a reasoning scheme and define a set of intended actions that can convert a given initial state to a desired goal state or states. Such a set of intended actions, the plan, exists if and only if it can achieve a goal state starting from an initial state and moving through a succession of states. Therefore, to begin the negotiation process, we need to look for a precondition that is a negation of the goal state and look for actions that can achieve the goal. This strategy is used widely in AI and forms the basis to plan a negotiation (Genersereth & Nilsson, 1987). Such planning is possible for clear-cut algorithmic problems. For general AI problems, however, we can only generate a plan that may or may not work; if the plan does not work, we need to either modify the plan or devise a new plan. The same approach is used for devising a multi-agent negotiation (MAN) protocol.

To systematically derive a multi-agent negotiation (MAN) protocol we use the following rules that are widely used in the logic and algebra of specification (Bauer & Brauer, 1993):

1. Transform the specification into an invariant (an invariant for a set of successively enabled rules is a logical formula that is true initially and is true when every enabled rule fires sequentially or in parallel) and a termination condition (Bonner & Kifer, 1994; Murthy, 1996). The specification is the key feature for plan construction. Its precondition (or a priori condition) describes the initial states; its postcondition (or a posteriori condition) describes the final states. We need to introduce suitable actions in order to bring the final state (or desired plan) to satisfy the postcondition through a set of agent transitions.

2. Derive a precondition of a rule as a negation of the termination condition so that the precondition exhibits the desired local property that can be checked as a local operation.

3. Devise the actions to modify the database in such a way that the termination conditions can be locally validated, while maintaining the invariant.

4. Ensure that the rule applications and the different pathways used for reasoning ultimately unite (confluence); that is, the associated transactions commit and are serializable.

Note that the application of the above rules produce the desired effect of ensuring that the union of all preconditions is logically equivalent to the negation of the termination condition, and the union of all actions is equivalent to the termination condition, and each action maintains the invariant in every rule.

To choose granularity and levels of parallelism, we need to split the precondition, action, and postcondition into a sequence of events. This is called refinement (the refinement corresponds to decomposing goals into subgoals in order to simplify the solution process). In a refinement, a specification is improved:

1. by strengthening its postcondition so that the new postcondition implies the old, and
2. weakening the precondition so that the old precondition implies the new.

The refinement enables us to choose simpler actions.

To verify that MAN satisfies the specification, we need to prove that when MAN begins executing from an initial state, it will eventually satisfy the postcondition and once the final state is reached, the postcondition can never turn false. That is, MAN begins with a specified initial data space. On each execution step, several transactions operate, satisfying the concurrency control restrictions, and eventually MAN halts when no more transactions are executable. The fact that the transactional paradigm is commit, abort, and recovery-oriented provides the MAN with an embedded assertional reasoning system (Murthy, 1996).

The implementation of rule-based-system requires that the application of the rules eventually terminate and are confluent; that is, for each initial database state, the pathways used for application of the rules or the rule execution order is immaterial. Termination of a rule set is guaranteed if rule processing always reaches a stable state in which no rules will be enabled through "false" conditions. Therefore, rule processing does not terminate if and only if the rules provide new conditions to fire indefinitely. The complexity of MAN can be reduced by constructing minimally dependent rules or maximally independent rules.

DESIGN OF AN AGENT NEGOTIATION PROTOCOL

A protocol is a language L whose vocabulary V is the set of all possible messages. V* denotes the set of all combinations of elements of V, the set of all possible message sequences. A negotiation protocol should have the following properties:
1. The negotiation leads to a finite number of states.
2. Every kind of protocol message is used.
3. The protocol leads to a negotiation process in which no message is unused.
4. The negotiation process does not enter cyclic or infinite sequences but always reaches a terminal state.

A protocol has the following phases:
1. Identifying message types.
2. Explaining the possible sequences among the participants.
3. Identifying various conversational states.
4. Drawing the transition diagram.

A multi-agent system consists of a fixed set of agents, a fixed set of channels, and a local memory for each agent. An agent can only read or write from its local memory. Channels are assumed error-free and deliver messages in the order they were sent. For each channel there is exactly one agent that sends messages along that channel and exactly one agent that receives the messages across that channel. Associated with each channel is a buffer. For each channel the only action that can be taken by the sending agent is to send a message (data message and other messages) if the buffer is not full, and the only action that can be taken by the receiving agent is to receive the message, if the buffer is not empty.

We will now describe how to carry out distributed multi-agent negotiation by sending, receiving, handshaking, and acknowledging messages, and performing some local computations. A multi-agent negotiation has the following features (Dignum & Sierra, 2001):
1. There is a seeding agent who initiates the negotiation.
2. Each agent can be active or inactive.

3.   Initially all agents are inactive except for a specified seeding agent that initiates the computation.
4.   An active agent can do local computation, send and receive messages, and can spontaneously become inactive.
5.   An inactive agent becomes active, if and only if, it receives a message.
6.   Each agent may retain its current belief or revise its belief as a result of receiving a new message by performing a local computation. If it revises its belief, it communicates its revised state of belief to other concerned agents, or else it does not revise its solution and remains silent.

We now illustrate how a set of agents can participate in a negotiation protocol to find the shortest travel route or lowest cost path on a map of cities represented as a directed weighted graph.

Example
Consider the problem of finding a lowest cost path between any two vertices in a directed graph whose edges have a certain assigned positive costs (Figure 2). The lowest cost path problem requires the entity set of vertices, the relationship set of ordered pairs of vertices (x,y) representing edges, and the attribute of cost c for each member of the relationship set, denoted by (x,y,c). Given a graph G, the program should give for each pair of vertices (x,y) the smallest sum of costs path from x to y. The vertex from which the lowest cost paths to other vertices are required is called the root vertex r (vertex 1 in this example). Let c denote the cost between any two adjacent vertices x and y, and let s denote the sum of costs along the path from the root to y; we assume that c (and hence s) is positive. This information is described by the ordered 4-tuple (x,y,c,s): (vertex label, vertex label, cost, sum of costs from root). The fourth member of the 4-tuple, namely the sum of costs from a specified root, remains initially undefined and we set this to a large number *. We then use the production rules to modify these tuples or to remove them. To find the lowest cost path to

Figure 2: Locating a lowest cost path between vertices in a directed graph with certain assigned positive costs

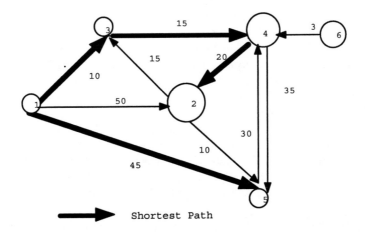

2

all vertices from a specified root r, we use the MAN for tuple processing and let the 4-tuples interact; this interaction results in either the generation of modified 4-tuples or the removal of some 4-tuples of the representation.

Specification to find the shortest path

Let $C(i,j)$ be the cost of path (i,j). A better path is one that can pass through some vertex k such that: $C(i,k)+C(k,j)<C(i,j)$.

That is, our production rule is:

If $C(i,k)+C(k,j)<C(i,j)$ then delete $C(i,j)$ and set $C(i,j)=C(i,k)+C(k,j)$.

The invariant is: if $C(i,j)$ is the initial cost then all the costs are always less than or equal to $C(i,j)$. We refine this by using the rule: If $C(i,k)<C(p,k)$, delete $C(p,k)$ and retain $C(i,k)$. Thus the following three production rules result:

Rule 1: If there are tuples of the form $(r,r,0,0)$ and $(r,y,c,*)$, replace $(r,y,c,*)$ by (r,y,c,c) and retain $(r,r,0,0)$.

Rule 1 defines the sum of costs for vertices adjacent to the root, by deleting * and defining the values.

Rule 2: If there are tuples of the form $(x,y,c1,s1)$ and $(y,z,c2,s2)$, where $s2>s1+c2$ then replace $(y,z,c2,s2)$ by $(y,z,c2,s1+c2)$; or else do nothing.

Rule 2 states that if $s2>s1+c2$ we can find a lower cost path to z through y.

Rule 3: If there are tuples of the form $(x,y,c1,s1)$ and $(z,y,c2,s2)$ and if $s1<s2$, then remove $(z,y,c2,s2)$ from the tuple set; or else do nothing.

Rule 3 states that for a given vertex y that has two paths, one from x and another from z, we can eliminate that 4-tuple that has a higher sum of costs from the root.

The above three rules provide for nondeterministic local computation by many agents, and we are left with those tuples that precisely describe the lowest cost path from the root. We assume that there are n agents with names identical to the nodes in the graph and each agent is connected to other agents in an isomorphic manner to the given graph. Such an assumption on the topology of the network simplifies the organizational knowledge O. Using O, each agent knows the identity of its neighbors, the direction and cost of connection of the outgoing edges. Thus, for the given directed graph, the outdegree of each node is the number of sending channels and the indegree is the number of receiving channels.

The revised production rules for multi-agent computation are as follows (Figure 3):

a. Agent 1 (root) sends to all its neighbors x the tuple $(1,x,c,c)$ describing the name of the root, and the distance of x from the root (c); all the neighbors of the root handshake, receive, and store it. This corresponds to the initialization of beliefs.

b. Each agent x sends its neighbor y at a distance c1 from it the tuple $(x,y,c1,c+c1)$ describing its name, its distance to y, and the distance of y from the root through x using its distance to the root c. This is the initial set of beliefs of the agents.

c. Each agent y compares an earlier tuple $(x,y,c1,s1)$ received from a neighbor x, or the root, with the new tuple $(z,y,c1',s1')$ from another neighbor z. If $s1<s1'$, then y retains $(x,y,c1,s1)$ and remains silent; or else it stores $(z,y,c1',s1')$ and sends out the tuple $(y,w,c2,s1'+c2)$ to its neighbor w at a distance c2, advising w to revise its distance from the root. That is, each agent revises its beliefs and communicates the beliefs to concerned agents.

d. An agent does not send messages if it receives a message from another agent that reports a higher value for its distance from the root and ignores the message; i.e., it does not revise its beliefs. Thus it contains only the lowest distance from the root. All the agents halt when no more messages are in circulation and the system stabilizes. An algorithm to detect the termination of negotiation is described below.

NEGOTIATION TERMINATION DETECTION

In order for the negotiation protocol to be successful we need to ensure that the negotiation process ultimately terminates. For this purpose, we now describe an algorithm called "Commission-Savings-Tally Algorithm" (COSTA) that can detect the global termination of a negotiation protocol. This is a general algorithm. We will apply this algorithm to the above example to illustrate that the negotiation based on rule applications terminated.

Let us assume that the N agents are connected through a communication network represented by a directed graph G with N nodes and M directed arcs. Let us also denote the outdegree of each node i by Oud (i) and indegree by Ind(i). Also we assume that an initiator or a seeding agent exists to initiate the transactions. The seeding agent (SA) holds an initial amount of money C.

When the SA sends a data message to other agents, it pays a commission: C/(Oud (SA) + 1) to each of its agents and retains the same amount for itself. When an agent receives a credit, it does the following:

a. Let agent j receive a credit C(M(i)) due to some data message M(i) sent from agent i. If j passes on data messages to other agents, j retains C((M(i))/(Oud(j)+1) for its credit and distributes the remaining amount to other Oud(j) agents. If there is no data message from agent j to others, then j credits C(M(i)) for that message in its own savings account, but this savings will not be passed on to any other agent, even if some other message is eventually received from another agent.

b. When no messages are received and no messages are sent out by any agent, it waits for a time-out and sends or broadcasts or writes on a transactional blackboard its savings account balance to the initiator.

c. The initiator on receiving the message broadcast adds up all the agents' savings account, and its own and verifies whether the total tallies to C.

d. In order to store savings and transmit commission, we use an ordered pair of integers to denote a rational number and assume that each agent has a provision to handle exact rational arithmetic. If we assume C=1, we only need to carry out multiplication and store the denominator of the rational number.

We prove the following theorems to describe the validity of the above algorithm:

Theorem 1: If there are negotiation cycles that correspond to indefinite arguments among the agents (including the initiator itself), then the initiator cannot tally its sum to C.

Proof: Assume that two agents i and j are engaged in a rule-dependent argument cycle. This means i and j are revising their beliefs forever, without coming to an agreement, and wasting the common resource C. Let the initial credit of i be x. If i passes a message to j, then i holds x/2 and j gets x/2. If eventually j passes a message to i ,then its credit is x/4 and i has a credit x.3/4 ; if there is continuous exchange of messages for ever then their total credit remains (x - x/ 2k) with x/ 2k being carried away by the message at k the exchange. Hence the total sum will never tally in a finite time.

Theorem 2: The above algorithm (COSTA) terminates if and only if the initiator tallies the sum of all the agents' savings to C.

Proof: If part: If the initiator tallies the sum to C this implies that all the agents have sent their savings, no message is in transit carrying some credit, and there is no chattering among agents.

Figure 3: Multi-agent negotiation

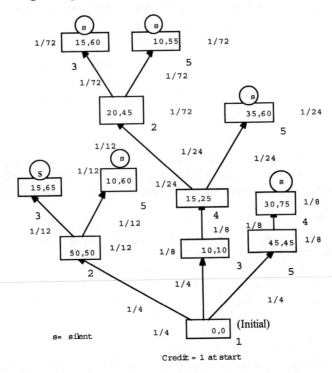

Only if part: The credit assigned can be only distributed in the following manner:

a. An agent has received a message and credit in a buffer; if it has sent a message then a part of the credit is lost; otherwise it holds the credit in savings.

b. Each message carries a credit, so if a message is lost in transit or communication fails then total credit cannot be recovered.

Thus termination can happen only if the total sum tallies to C, i.e., the common resource is not wasted, and all the agents have reached an agreement on their beliefs.

Figure 3 illustrates this algorithm for the above example; the credits are indicated on the nodes and arcs. Note that at the termination of the algorithm the nodes have the following savings adding up to 1:

Node 1: 18/72; Node 2: 7/72; Node 3: 16/72; Node 4: 12/72; Node 5: 19/72.

MODELING E-MARKET

The agent negotiation system can be used to model the e-market with many traders (agents), popularly known as buyers and sellers. These agents negotiate over the Internet to sell or buy shares or stocks in a stock market. In an e-market situation, it is possible that the negotiation ultimately leads to self-organization and criticality causing crashes. That is, individual agents that correspond to a microscopic system can emerge as a self-organizing macroscopic system corresponding to a "percolation model" (Paul & Baschnagel, 1999).

In an e-market situation (see Figure 1), initially, the domain data D, rules P and organizational knowledge O can be based on three factors:

(i)   the experience and economics knowledge of an agent deployed by a trader based totally on individualistic idiosyncratic criteria;

(ii)   the traders acquired knowledge through communication with other selected agents (such a trader is called a fundamentalist); and

(iii) the traders acquired knowledge by observing the market trends from a collective opinion of other traders (such a trader is called a trend chaser). In practice a trader is influenced by all the above factors and the modified knowledge is incorporated in D, P and O.

In e-market at any time a trader can adopt three possible states of action: Buy, Sell, or Wait, respectively represented by three states 1, -1 and 0. Each agent corresponding to a trader can communicate with one another, and this creates an imaginary bond or connectivity relationship among them modifying the organizational knowledge O. This bond is created with a certain probability determined by a single parameter that characterizes the willingness of an agent to comply with others.

Since detailed information about the mechanism of bond formation is difficult to know, we can assume that any two agents are randomly connected with a certain probability. This divides the agents into clusters of different sizes whose members are linked either directly or indirectly via a chain of intermediate agents. These groups are coalitions of market participants who share the same opinion about their activity. The decision of each group is independent of its size and the decision taken by other clusters.

Using percolation theory (Paul & Baschnagel, 1999; Sahimi, 1994), it can be shown that when every trader is on average connected to another, more and more traders join the spanning cluster, and the cluster begins to dominate the overall behavior of the system. This gives rise to a "speculation bubble" (if the members all decide to buy), a crash (if the members all decide to sell), or a stagnation (if the members all decide to wait). Crash is a highly cooperative phenomenon and depends upon trading rules, exchange of information, the speed and volume, and the connectivity relationship. Accordingly, an analogy exists between stock market crashes and critical phenomena or phase transitions in physics. Thus a distributed agent system can eventually enter into a phase transition-like situation (Bak, 1996).

FEATURES OF MULTI-AGENT NEGOTIATION PARADIGM

The multi-agent negotiation paradigm described here provides the following desirable features:

1.   The production system provides a programming methodology free from control management. The transactional implementation of rules provides for the propose-verify-revise strategy.

2.   It provides for the application of locality principle in protocol construction.

3.   It will have applications in programming as well as design of multi-agent architectures consisting of agents that serve as processes, functions, relations, or constraints, depending upon the context. Therefore, they can be used for realizing algorithms based on divide-conquer, greedy approach, and dynamic programming.

CONCLUSION

This chapter explained the use of multi-agent-based planning, reasoning, and negotiation in E-Marketing. We explained how to use the techniques of AI planning, the logic and algebra of specification, to devise the multi-agent-based negotiation protocol.

ACKNOWLEDGMENT

The author thanks Professor Charles Newton for his support and encouragement.

REFERENCES

Bak, B. (1996). *How nature works: The science of self-organized criticality*. New York: Springer.

Bauer, F.L., &Brauer, W. (1993). *Logic and algebra of specification*. New York: Springer-Verlag.

Bonner, A.J. & Kifer, M. (1994). Application of transaction logic to knowledge representation. *Lecture Notes in Computer Science*, Vol. 827, pp. 67-81. New York: Springer-Verlag.

Chen, Q. & Dayal, U. (2000). Multi agent cooperative transactions for e-commerce. *Lecture Notes in Computer Science,* Vol. 1901, pp. 311-322. New York: Springer Verlag.

Dignum, F. & Sierra, C. (eds.). (2001). Agent Mediated E-Commerce. *Lecture Notes in Artificial Intelligence*, Vol. 1991 & Vol. 2003. New York: Springer Verlag.

Fisher, M. (1995). Representing and executing agent-based systems. *Lecture Notes in Computer Science*, Vol. 890, pp. 307-323. New York: Springer-Verlag.

Genesereth ,M.R. & Nilsson, N.J. (1987). *Logical foundations of AI*. New York: Morgan Kaufmann.

Ishida, T. (1994). Parallel, distributed and multiagent production systems. *Lecture Notes in Computer Science*, Vol. 878. New York: Springer Verlag.

Murthy, V.K. & Krishnamurthy, E.V. (1995a). Probabilistic parallel programming based on multiset transformation. *Future Generation Computer Systems*, 11, 283-293.

Murthy, V.K. & Krishnamurthy, E.V. (1995b). Automating problem solving using transactional paradigm. *Proc. Intl. Conf. on AI & Expert Systems*, 721-729. New York: Gordon Breach.

Murthy, V.K. (1996). Transactional programming for distributed agent systems. In *Proc. IEEE Intl. Conf. on Parallel and Distributed Systems*, Japan, pp 64-71. New York: IEEE Computer Society Press.

Paul, W. & Baschnagel, J. (1999). *Stochastic processes*. New York: Springer-Verlag.

Sahimi, M. (1994). *Applications of percolation theory*. London: Taylor and Francis.

Weerasooriya, D., Rao, A. & Ramamohanarao, K. (1995). Design of a concurrent agent-oriented language. *Lecture Notes in Computer Science*, Vol. 890, pp. 386-401. New York: Springer-Verlag.

Woolridge, M., Muller, J.P., & Tambe, M. (eds.). (1996). Intelligent Agents II. *Lecture Notes in Computer Science*, Vol. 1037. New York: Springer-Verlag.

Chapter XX

Virtual Marketplace for Agent-Based Electronic Commerce

Chuen Hwee Ng, Sheng-Uei Guan, and Fangming Zhu
National University of Singapore

ABSTRACT

This chapter proposes the architecture for a mobile agent-based virtual marketplace. As the Internet grows, the potential for conducting electronic commerce grows as well. However, given the explosion of online shopping, searching for particular products amongst the sea of commercial content could become a fundamental obstacle for Internet electronic commerce. Hence, an agent-based virtual marketplace is seen as the solution. The agents in the marketplace are autonomous, and so there is no need for user intervention once the agents have been deployed with the assigned task. The architecture of the marketplace has been specifically designed to facilitate agent negotiations by providing a trusted and secure environment. A novel dynamic pricing mechanism has also been implemented in the context of the airline ticketing industry and found to be rather successful.

INTRODUCTION

With the ever-increasing amount of available online resources in general, information overload has become a very real problem. One possible solution is the application of software agents in e-commerce. Intelligent agents are already on the Web, freeing us from some of the drudgework of searching and automatically keeping us up to date. There are now many examples of software agents currently available on the Web. Shopping agents like BargainBot, Excite's Jango, and Andersen Consulting's BargainFinder are but a few. However, they have their shortcomings, such as lack of purchasing capability and limited range of product selection. Furthermore, the current Web front end to an online storefront is not conducive to autonomous browsing by search agents.

A more comprehensive solution would, therefore, be to build a virtual marketplace whereby producers and consumers can come together and, with the help of software agents, actively participate and conduct e-commerce.   Software agents have already been in development since the mid 1990s, but with recent advances in software agent technologies, their potential and capabilities have been greatly enhanced.

There are currently several agent-based marketplace systems that have been developed for purposes of electronic commerce, and these include Kasbah (Chavez & Maes, 1996), MAGMA (Tsvetovatyy & Gini, 1996) and MAGNET (Collins, Youngdahl, Jamison, Mobasher, & Gini, 1998). Kasbah was developed in 1996 by the Software Agents Group of the MIT Media Lab as an agent-based consumer-to-consumer marketplace where users can create autonomous agents that help buy and sell goods on their behalf. Once these agents are created and released into the marketplace, it negotiates and makes decisions on its own without the need for user intervention.   In preliminary experiments on Kasbah, users preferred simple, predictable agents with predetermined negotiation strategies over "smarter" agents that continuously adapted their behavior according to their analysis of the marketplace. A strength of the Kasbah system is the straightforwardness of its negotiation strategies, as this simplicity made it easy for users to understand the workings of their agents and subsequently they were able to trust their agents to perform the necessary transactions on their behalf. However, one weakness of the Kasbah system architecture was that it did not include any form of payment mechanisms, and this hampered users from effectively concluding transactions after a deal had been struck.

The University of Minnesota's Multi-Agent Negotiation Testbed (MAGNET) is a generalized market architecture that was designed to provide support for a variety of types of transactions, from simple buying and selling of goods and services to complex multi-agent contract negotiations. The MAGNET architecture is organized around three basic components: the Exchange, the Market, and the Session. An important fundamental concept in the MAGNET architecture is its market Session. Because the session is contained within the market, and because it maintains, independently of the initiator and any clients, a persistent record of the activities encompassed by the session, it is able to discourage value-based counter-speculation by acting as a trusted auctioneer. More importantly, however, it can record commitments made by all parties and, within the limits of its enforcement powers, ensure performance against those commitments.

The MAGMA architecture is an earlier prototype of a virtual marketplace designed by the team that developed MAGNET. This virtual marketplace architecture was designed to exhibit many of the properties attributed to physical marketplaces. It therefore includes several elements simulating a real market.   These elements include a communication infrastructure, a mechanism for the storage and transfer of goods, advertising and a banking system. The MAGMA system consists of a relay server written in Allegro Common Lisp and a set of agents written in Java that work over the World Wide Web.   The current implementation of MAGMA includes multiple trader agents, an advertising server, and a bank. The advertising server provides a classified service that includes search and retrieval ads by category. The banking system is able to provide a basic set of banking services including checking accounts and lines of credit. However, a shortcoming of the architecture is the fact that all agents within the system communicate to one another through socket connections. In order to facilitate communications between agents, a relay server maintains all socket connections and routes messages between the agents based on unique agent names. This architecture is felt to be rather expensive on network bandwidth and the system performance is heavily reliant on network latencies. Moreover, the scalability of this approach is also questionable.

The objective of our research work is to build a new virtual marketplace prototype whereby producers and consumers can meet and conduct e-commerce in cyberspace with the help of software agents. We chose airline ticket purchasing as an application area for prototype design and implementation, because airlines today already perform limited dynamic pricing and consumers are accustomed to the idea of different pricing for different flights and changing prices over time.

GENERAL MARKETPLACE ARCHITECTURE

A marketplace is a place where buying and selling agents meet to negotiate transactions. It is important, therefore, that the architecture of the virtual marketplace is designed to facilitate interactions between agents by providing a secure and reliable environment for the conduction of electronic commerce. A Business-to-Consumer model has been adopted for implementation in the virtual marketplace. The architecture of the virtual marketplace can be divided into three separate elements. These are the Control Center, Business Center, and Financial Center (Figure 1). Specialist agents reside in each module and work independently as well as collaboratively with the other agents in the virtual marketplace to achieve their goals and objectives.

Figure 1: Virtual market architecture overview

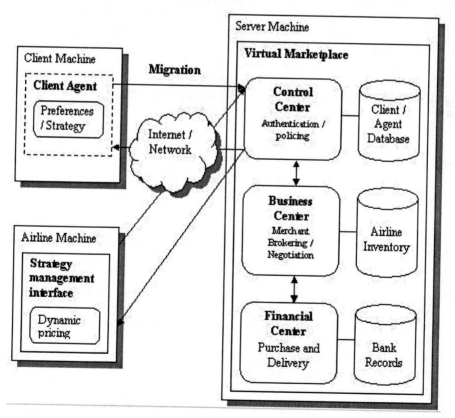

Figure 2: Architecture of Financial Center

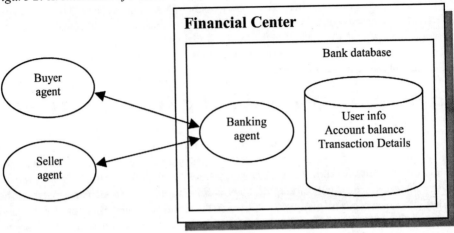

Financial Center

If a marketplace is to become anything more than a toy, it needs to provide the necessary banking and financial services that are required by the transacting agents (Tsvetovatyy & Gini, 1996). The Financial Center (Figure 2) is aimed at achieving these objectives by housing within it various authorized banks, which are able to provide these services. It is a virtual financial hub that handles all necessary payment activities within the virtual marketplace. The individual banks themselves are represented by their own agents. These agent representatives handle such tasks as verification of legal transactions and assisting in fund transfers from the parties involved in the transaction. They also manage their clients' bank accounts and help carry out the necessary paperwork involved in marketplace transactions. Communication within the Financial Center, especially between agent-to-bank or bank-to-bank, needs to be encrypted and secure.

Control Center

The Control Centers (Figure 3) role is to act as the administrative center of the virtual marketplace. This is the main gateway that is used by all agents roaming to and from the marketplace. For reasons of security, all potential users of the virtual marketplace will first have to register an account with the Control Center before its agents are allowed to participate in marketplace activities. Once registered, important user information will then be stored in the market database, and these are later retrieved for various purposes such as user authentication and user alert notifications. Besides clients, the airlines themselves can also log into the marketplace for purposes of viewing and updating their own customized negotiation strategies. The Control Center accepts airline connections on a different port to distinguish between client and airline access. To gain access to the server, the airlines will still have to be authenticated.

The Control Center also keeps a list of all active buyer agents that are currently residing within the virtual marketplace, and it also acts as the policing authority within the virtual marketplace. The agent and transaction monitoring capability is the most important function of the Control Center. From the time a buyer agent enters the marketplace till the time it returns home to the client machine, the Control Center keeps a record of all its activities. Details such

Figure 3: Control center architecture

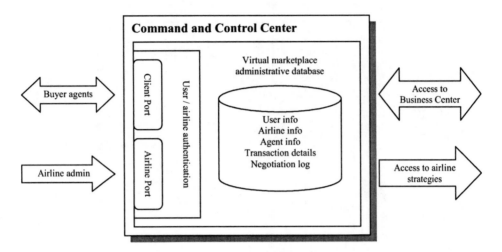

as the time the agent entered and left the marketplace, the duration of stay, and the owner of the agent are all noted and recorded into the database. If a successful transaction was completed by the buyer agent, the Control Center will also keep a record of the exact details, in this case, details such as flight times, number and cost of each ticket bought, the time the transaction was completed, etc. The Control Center goes a step further by keeping a log of the entire negotiation process that took place between the negotiating parties, regardless of whether any sale was concluded.

With such a monitoring mechanism in place, it is hoped that fraud and misrepresentation by agents (both buyers and sellers) can be more effectively controlled within the virtual marketplace. This in turn will help increase the level of trust and confidence that users will have in the system.

Business Center

This is the heart of the virtual marketplace where all buyer and seller agents meet to negotiate deals. This research work has been modeled after the Business-to-Consumer model of electronic commerce. Therefore, clients are only capable of sending buyer agents into the marketplace to negotiate for items that they would like to purchase. The Business Center (Figure 4) consists of several virtual storefronts belonging to the various airlines. These are controlled by seller agents representing the various airlines. Virtual stores are tied into their own individual inventory databases, and they maintain a permanent presence in the marketplace. The agents controlling the stores are akin to sales personnel, and may adopt different marketing strategies based on preferences set by the individual airlines themselves.

After a buyer agent has been authenticated by the Control Center, it arrives at the Business Center where it is matched to the relevant seller agents by marketplace merchant brokers. By providing this brokering service, the marketplace frees the agents from having to do this additional work. This is important as incorporating too many functions will inevitably increase the size of the buyer agent, making them more costly to transport through the network. More importantly, it reduces the security risks by not allowing the buyer agent to gain access to the virtual marketplace's database and other system resources. This step

Figure 4: Business center architecture

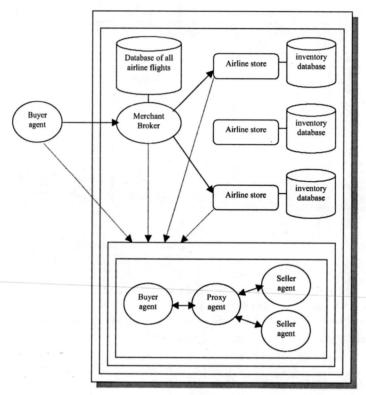

can be classified under the Merchant Brokering stage of the Consumer Buying Behaviour (CBB) model that has been proposed by the Software Agents Group at MIT Media Lab (Maes, Guttmam, & Moukas, 1999).

Once potential merchants have been identified, buyer and seller agents can then commence their negotiations. This constitutes the Negotiation stage of the CBB. All negotiations take place in their own particular negotiation *Session* container. This *Session* serves as an encapsulation for a transaction in the marketplace. Furthermore, negotiations between buyer and seller agents in the virtual marketplace take place through an intermediary that is appointed by the marketplace itself, and this is done for reasons of trust, security and transaction monitoring. This intermediary, which resides within the *Session*, is the marketplace's proxy agent.

After negotiations have been concluded, the finalized deal, together with the respective seller and buyer, are then passed over to the banking agent in the Financial Center for payment. This forms the final Purchase and Delivery stage of the CBB. Once the final stage in the buying process has been completed, the buyer agent will then be returned to the client.

SOFTWARE AGENTS

Since agents in the marketplace are designed to be autonomous, implementing them as threads is seen as the natural solution. As executing threads, individual agents will be able to operate independently and asynchronously of the other entities in the marketplace. This also allows all agents in the marketplace to operate concurrently, and, as such, it is advantageous in reducing processing time and permits more flexibility in implementing various negotiation protocols. Although this is more challenging to implement due to synchronization issues, this approach is superior to simulating agents running "in parallel" using a marketplace scheduler as in the case of Kasbah (Chavez et al., 1996).

Each agent in the marketplace is also assigned a unique agent identification. By adopting this identification scheme, it allows the virtual marketplace to uniquely identify agents belonging to registered users and sellers. What is more significant, however, is that this allows the airlines in the marketplace to identify their clients. This is very useful when the airline wants to personalize its strategy to each individual client.

When agents in the marketplace need to communicate with one another, they employ one of two available methods, depending on the nature of their relationship. For reasons of security and policing efforts, all forms of communication between buyer and seller agents go through a proxy agent and are never direct. This negotiation process between buyer and seller is encapsulated within a negotiation session.

All other forms of communication, for example between the marketplace's proxy agent and the banking agents, are direct, because agents generated by the marketplace itself are assumed to be trusted and non-malicious.

Buyer Agent

The buyer agent is designed to be an autonomous entity that is capable of migrating across networks to accomplish the task assigned by its owner. In the current implementation, only the buyer agent has the capability to migrate across networks. Agent migration in this work is done through serialization of the buyer agent, together with all its associated objects, using object serialization. All buyer agents are created and owned by users (Figure 5). The agent itself contains the necessary negotiation protocols and reasoning functions that help it communicate and decide on its course of action within the marketplace.

Each buyer agent carries with it its own shopping list and negotiation strategy (Figure 6). At present, these negotiation strategies are set by the user and consist of a time-based price increment function, similar to those employed in the Kasbah system (Chavez et al., 1996). Currently, there are three different price negotiation functions that the user may choose. These are "anxious," "normal," and "frugal," and the differences are contained in the various shapes of the price function curve.

Figure 5: Agent creation process

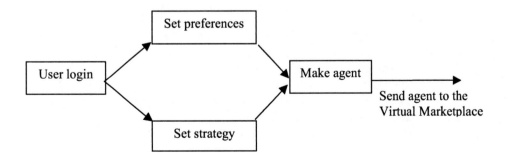

Figure 6: Anatomy of a buyer agent

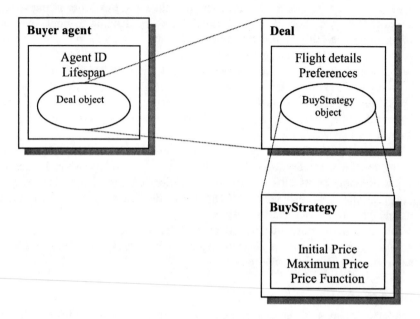

The buyer agent is the only agent in the marketplace to have a lifespan attribute. This is set by the user, in number of days, and is indicative of the deadline by which the agent should conclude all negotiations and return with a result. This is not just critical to the user, but also important to prevent buyer agents from residing in the virtual marketplace for an indefinite period of time, thus crowding out the server and slowing down the overall application by using up valuable resources. Once the expiration time of a buyer agent is reached, it is forced by the virtual marketplace to cease all negotiations, and once payment has been concluded, the agent thread is stopped and put into a waiting area pending return to the client's machine.

Seller Agent

Although there are various different airlines in the marketplace, all the airlines utilize the same generic seller to represent them, albeit with differently customized strategies. A seller agent (Figure 7) is created by the respective airline each time an available flight in the airline's database is found that matches a buyer's preferences. Once spawned by the airline, the seller agent is completely autonomous and does not require any further control during its negotiation cycles with the buyer agent. Like the buyer agent, the agent itself contains the necessary negotiation protocols and reasoning functions that help it communicate and decide on its course of action within the marketplace.

The negotiation strategy of the seller agent is of particular interest because it is derived in a just-in-time, individualized analysis manner, which allows the airline to maximize revenue over each plane flight with more precision. This dynamic pricing mechanism is one of the important features of the marketplace architecture. This is further elaborated in the following section.

Figure 7: Anatomy of a seller agent

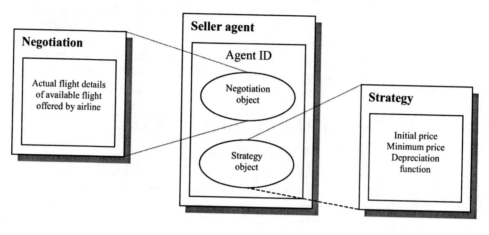

Proxy Agent

The proxy agent is the sole agent that is created and owned by the virtual marketplace itself. This agent plays a vital role in the marketplace by acting as an intermediary between the buyer and seller agents during negotiation sessions. The proxy agent is the entity that maintains a *Session* and, while doing so, closely monitors the activities of the participating agents. Once started, the proxy agent is completely autonomous and will continue to execute and assist in negotiations until the *Session* has ceased.

The proxy agent is also responsible for maintaining a constant connection to the client machine whenever the client is connected to the virtual marketplace. It is through this stream that all output, like session updates, are sent back to the user across the network. This allows the user to view the progress of his/her agent's negotiations in real time as it takes place in the virtual marketplace.

Another function of the proxy agent is to implement the two client alert mechanisms that the marketplace offers, which are e-mail notification and sms alerts. These notification mechanisms are used to alert the disconnected client to important events occurring within the virtual marketplace that require the user's attention. For example, if the buyer agent has completed negotiations and needs to obtain the user's permission before payment, but the object has detected that the client is no longer connected to the marketplace, it will then send out an e-mail notification as well as an sms alert message to the user. This is an important feature of the virtual marketplace design because it gives the user the freedom to disconnect from the server at any time and still be notified of important events that require the user's intervention. This frees the user from having to continuously monitor ongoing negotiations, which is extremely time-consuming and therefore defeats the purpose of using agents to reduce his/her workload in the first place!

Banking Agent

The role of the banking agent is to assist the buyer agent with payment for a negotiated item. When a buyer agent requests payment to be made to the seller agent, the respective bank where the buyer has an account first verifies the identity of the agent owner. Once the authentication has been completed, the bank then checks its database to see if there are sufficient funds in the user's account to make payment to the seller. If funds are deemed sufficient, the banking agent then keeps a record of the transaction details in its database and withdraws the necessary funds to pay the airline.

The payment mechanism is not the main focus of this research work and, as such, only a simple banking system has been implemented for purposes of aiding in the completion of transactions. More details on e-payment can be referred to in Hua (2000).

CLIENT APPLICATION AND AIRLINE MANAGEMENT

The design of the client application for the virtual marketplace architecture is crucial. A well-designed client application will facilitate the acceptance and adoption of the application. To facilitate use, it is designed with a user-friendly GUI (Figure 8) that allows easy configuration of the agent parameters and monitoring of agent activities in the virtual marketplace. It consists of various functions, such as agent retrieval and termination. As a Business-to-Consumer model has been adopted for this research, the user's role is solely as a buyer looking to purchase airlines tickets that match his/her preferences in the virtual marketplace. Besides flight preferences, the user is also able to configure a custom negotiation strategy.

Airlines are also able to manage their stores within the virtual marketplace via a strategy management interface (Figure 9). To be granted access to the airline's strategy settings, the airline administrator must first log in and be authenticated by the Control Center. This strategy management tool allows the individual airlines to customize and personalize their pricing strategy using real-time, individualized analysis. This dynamic pricing capability is an important feature of the virtual marketplace architecture.

Figure 8: Client application interface

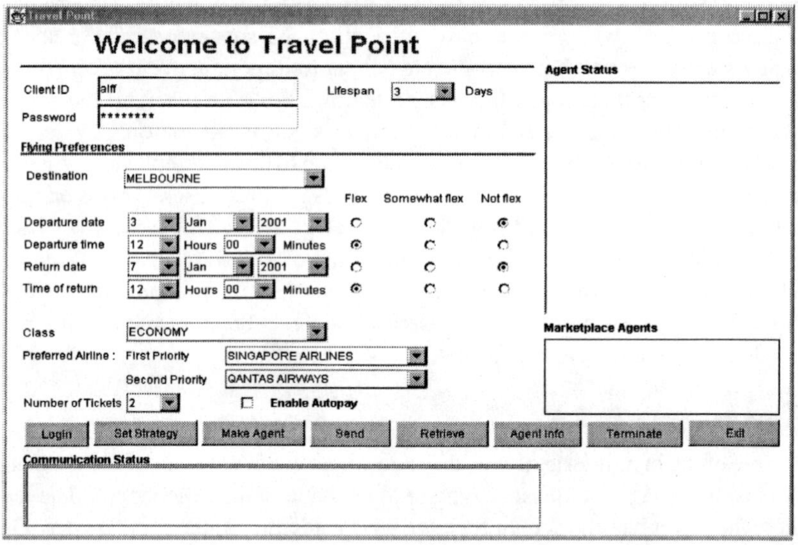

Figure 9: Screenshot of airline pricing strategy management

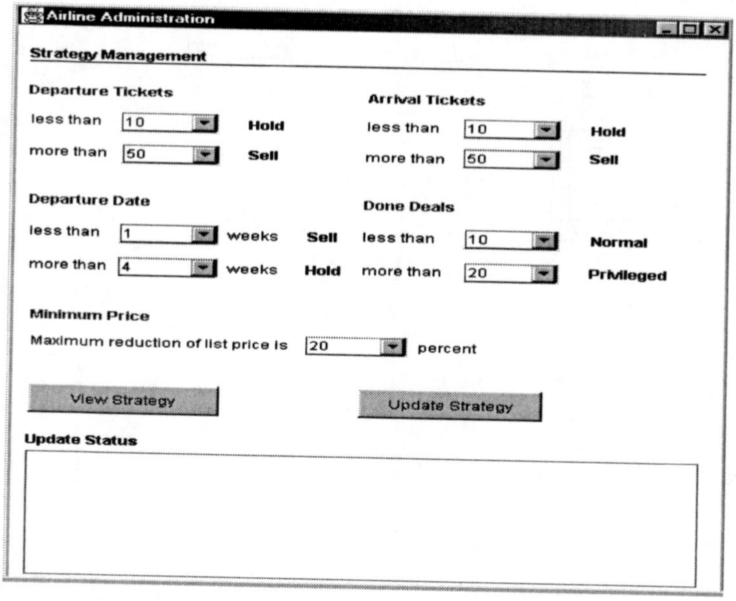

IMPORTANT ARCHITECTURAL FEATURES

There are three features of the marketplace architecture that deserve special attention. These are the negotiation session, the dynamic pricing mechanism, and issues on security, trust, and privacy.

Negotiation Session

A *Session* is created with the creation and starting of the proxy agent (Figure 10). To join the *Session*, the buyer or seller agent must first register with the proxy agent. This is done by providing the proxy with an individual unique agent identification and a reference to itself. The proxy agent thus maintains a list of all agents participating in the *Session*. Initially, the buyer agent is the only party in the *Session*, and it waits patiently for the respective airlines to send forth their representative sellers into the *Session*. Negotiations commence as soon as the first seller agent enters the *Session* and initiates with an offer to sell. It is always the seller agent that initiates the negotiation process. Thereafter, all arriving seller agents will also initiate their own negotiation process. The buyer agent thus has to simultaneously keep track of each individual negotiation with each individual seller agent. Each negotiation process between the buyer and a particular seller is independent of other concurrent negotiations within the *Session*.

The *Session* thus serves as an encapsulation for a transaction in the marketplace. This is where all the negotiations between buyer and sellers take place. The *Session* always contains only one buyer agent but may house several different sellers. Due to security issues, these negotiations take place through an intermediary designated by the virtual marketplace, which is the proxy agent. Doing so has two obvious benefits. First, the agents never have a direct reference to one another and, as such, the security risks posed by malicious agents are reduced considerably. Secondly, the marketplace itself is able to closely monitor and log

Figure 10: Session negotiation mechanism

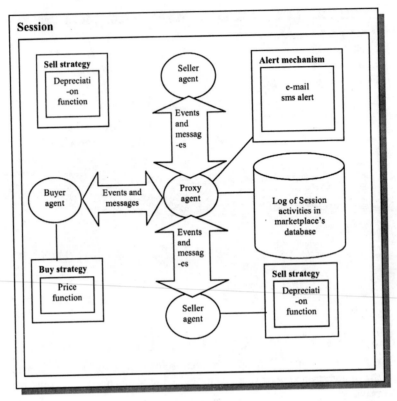

all agent negotiations, and this instills an element of trust and confidence in the system by guarding against cases of misrepresentation and repudiation.

Another unique feature of the Session is that negotiation is a non-binding agreement, thus allowing the buyer agent to negotiate concurrently on several items, and thereby increasing the chances of obtaining a successful match and a better deal (Morris & Maes, 2000). The motivation for adopting this design approach stems from a limitation in the Kasbah system.

In the Kasbah architecture, once an agent makes a deal, it ceases to negotiate with other agents and is removed from the active list (Chavez et al., 1997). A major drawback of this approach is that during experiments conducted on the Kasbah prototype, users were disappointed because the agents always accepted the first offer that met their asking price, even though there might be another offer that was even better if somehow the agent had waited to take that into consideration.

Because of the disadvantages of the Kasbah approach, the buyer agent in our virtual marketplace has been designed to wait until all concurrent negotiations have been concluded before reaching a decision on which ticket to purchase. By allowing the buyer agent the capability to wait until all negotiations have concluded before making a comparison, the agent is able to make an informed decision on which is really the best deal or offer as it is able to compare the various finalized offers instead of just picking the first acceptable offer.

The *Session* is concluded when the buyer agent finally pays for a ticket or rejects all the offers and decides not to purchase anything. Subsequently, all agents associated with the *Session* are stopped and terminated, and the buyer agent is returned to the client machine.

Dynamic Pricing Mechanism

Although at present the negotiation process tends to favour the buyer, the virtual marketplace architecture benefits the airlines by providing them with a strategy management tool which allows them to formulate a negotiation strategy based on complex criteria and real-time data, not just price alone (Figure 9). There are currently four non-price criteria by which the airlines configure their pricing strategy. These are the number of departure flight tickets remaining, the number of arrival flight tickets remaining, the time left to the departure date of the flight, and the number of previous deals that the user has completed with the airline.

Each time a seller agent is dispatched into the Session to negotiate with the buyer, the airline store will have to first set the selling strategy of that seller agent. With the dynamic pricing mechanism in place, the airline itself can customize the pricing strategy of each and every flight ticket it sells based on a set of criteria and real-time data from its inventory database. Such criteria will include real-time factors such as the number of tickets left for the particular flight in question, and the length of time left to the actual departure date. What is more, by taking into account the client's personal details such as previously completed transactions, an airline is also able to personalize and tailor its strategy to each individual buyer agent by giving valued customers a better price discount.

As an example, consider a flight that is less than a week away and has more than 50 tickets remaining. If a fixed pricing strategy was adopted for all tickets, the seller might be unable to sell this ticket at the end of the day, which would result in a revenue loss because the unsold seat cannot be sold after the flight date. However, with the aid of the dynamic pricing mechanism, the airline would have been able to indicate to its sales representative (seller agent) that it should adopt a more eager approach to selling that ticket, and as a consequence, would have been able to offer the ticket for a cheaper price and eventually made the sale. Therefore, by allowing airlines to formulate their strategies based on a just-in-time, individualized analysis of the immediate situation, the dynamic pricing mechanism gives the airlines a greater ability to maximize revenue over each flight with better precision (Morris and Maes, 2000). Dynamic pricing thus gives an airline an important advantage when negotiating within the marketplace.

Security, Trust, and Privacy

Security, trust, and privacy are important considerations given any electronic commerce application (Corradi, Montanari, & Stefanelli, 1999; Greenberg, Byington, & Harper 1998; Marques, Silva, & Sylvia, 1999). Furthermore, with the introduction of agent autonomy, these issues become even more crucial. If the trading mechanism cannot be trusted or is perceived to be insecure to protect privacy, then acceptance of the application will be severely limited. To address these, the following design issues have been adopted.

Financial Credibility

All clients that wish to trade within the virtual marketplace must first have a valid bank account with one of the virtual marketplace's authorized banks. By implementing this policy, the credibility of all buyer agents is increased. This also enhances traceability in cases of fraud and will deter insincere users from participating in transactions.

Indirect Agent Negotiations

As agents have a high degree of autonomy and capability, the potential for them to breach the integrity of fellow agents to gain an unfair advantage is a serious threat. Therefore, in an effort to reduce the likelihood of such incidents, buyer and seller agents within the marketplace should not be allowed to negotiate with each other directly. By introducing an intermediary to control and monitor negotiations, this not only reduces the risk of a security breach amongst agents, it also helps to ensure fair practices and non-repudiation of concluded transactions. This helps to increase the trust that parties will have in the marketplace, and it also reduces the possibility that each agent may access the private information of other agents. This means the private information is only available to the controller of the virtual marketplace and is carefully protected against illegal access.

Secure Transport and Agent Integrity

Due to the fact that this application is based on a mobile agent concept, the agent and its data will be susceptible to "attack" while it transverses the network, especially if this application is deployed over the Internet. Therefore, a secure transport mechanism is required (Guan & Yang, 1999), for example, encryption of the agent before transportation. Agent integrity can also be achieved using a similar mechanism as discussed by Wang, Guan, and Chan (2001).

Trusted Client Applications

Not only fellow agents, but also the virtual marketplace itself has to be protected from malignant agents. To ensure that only trusted agents are allowed into the marketplace, only agents manufactured from trusted agent factories (Guan, 2000; Guan & Zhu, 2001; Zhu, Guan, & Yang, 2000) are allowed into the server. In this particular implementation, only agents constructed and verified by the provided client applications are granted access to the marketplace. The disadvantage of doing so is that this does not allow clients to custom build their own agents that might have greater intelligence and negotiation capabilities, but this downside is seen as minimal since most users would not bother to go through the complexities to do so anyway.

IMPLEMENTATION DISCUSSIONS

Agent Identification

Each agent in the marketplace is assigned a unique agent identification. This is accomplished by appending the agent's name with a six-digit random number. The agent's name is, in the case of the buyer and seller agents, indicative of its respective owner. For example, if a user with user id alff creates an agent, its agent identification will be alff_123456. By adopting this identification scheme, the virtual marketplace can uniquely identify agents belonging to registered users and sellers. What is more significant, this allows the airlines in the marketplace to identify their clients. This is very useful when an airline wants to customize its marketing strategy to each individual user.

Event-Driven Model

All agents created in the virtual marketplace are Java EventListeners. To achieve this, all agent classes extend the parent class VMAgent. VMAgent, in turn, implements a custom EventListener interface called VMAgentEventListener.

Figure 11: Format of a VMAgentMessage object

```
VMAgentMessage

Performative : "offer"
Sender : seller ID
Receiver : buyer ID
Price : XXX
```

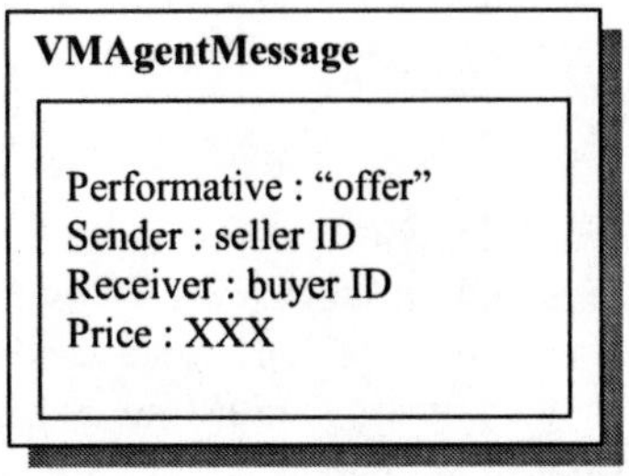

As an EventListener, an agent is able to continuously monitor for any incoming events that are being triggered by fellow agents. Agents in the marketplace use this method to signal an event that requires the attention of the target agent. This alerts the target agent which then processes the incoming event once it awakes.

Agent Communication

Together with the event object VMAgentEvent that is passed to the target agent during an event trigger is a VMAgentMessage object. The VMAgentMessage object is modeled in a similar format to a KQML message packet. As with KQML, the VMAgentMessage uses performatives to indicate the intention of the sending agent and the actions that it wants the target agent to take. The set of performatives that agents support at the moment are limited, but these can be expanded further to increase the complexity of possible actions that agents may take or respond to. Figure 11 shows the contents of a sample VMAgentMessage.

Buyer-Agent Migration

Agent migration in this research work is done through serialization of the agent, together with all its associated objects, using object serialization. The object serialization computes the transitive closure of all objects belonging to the agent and creates a system-independent representation of the agent. This serialized version of the agent is then sent to the virtual marketplace through a socket connection, and the agent is reinstantiated over on the server. As object serialization is used, all objects referenced by the buyer agent implement the Serializable interface.

Shopping List

When a buyer agent is created, the agent creates a shopping list of all the items the user wishes to purchase. Within the list are individual Deal objects (Figure 6) which specify the details of the particular item in question. For air tickets, the Deal object stores such information as specific flight times, preferred airlines, and the number of tickets to purchase.

If items of varying categories are to be specified, then the Deal object will have to explicitly state which ontology is being used. This may be applicable to a marketplace that hosts sellers dealing in many different types of products requiring different specifications.

Purchasing Strategy

For every Deal object that is created, a corresponding BuyStrategy object is also created and is contained within the Deal. This allows the user to customize a specific strategy for each item that the user wishes to purchase. The BuyStrategy object contains the initial price, the maximum permissible price, and the time-based price increment function for that particular item.

Selling Strategy

The seller agent's negotiation strategy is contained in a Strategy object. This object is used by an airline to customize the selling strategy of its representative seller agents. There is a marked difference in the way the buyer and seller agents use their strategies to determine their current offer prices. Because the buyer agent's strategy has knowledge of the initial price, maximum price, and the lifespan of the agent, it is able to calculate the exact offer price at each stage of the negotiation given the elapsed time. The Strategy object of the seller agent is unable to do this because, unlike the buyer agent, it has no foreknowledge of the lifespan of the buyer or the length of the negotiation, and therefore the Strategy object can only advise the seller on an appropriate depreciation function.

CONCLUSION AND FUTURE WORK

In this research work, an agent-based virtual marketplace architecture based on a Business-to-Consumer electronic commerce model has been designed and implemented. Its purpose is to provide a conducive environment for self-interested agents from businesses and clients to interact safely and autonomously with one another for the purposes of negotiating agreements on the behalf of their owners.

The three fundamental elements of the marketplace architecture are the Control Center, the Business Center, and the Financial Center. This implementation has been concentrated on development of the Control and Business Centers. Of particular interest are two of the design elements that warrant greater attention. These are the negotiation session mechanism and the dynamic pricing strategy management scheme that was implemented.

The importance of the negotiation session mechanism within the marketplace architecture as a means to increase the trust and security of the overall system can be seen by its ability to combat fraud and misrepresentation. The nature of the negotiation protocol also allows the buyer to arrive at a more informed decision for the product that he/she is purchasing by allowing for simultaneous, non-binding agreements. The marketplace has also provided the opportunity to catch a glimpse into the potential benefits of implementing a dynamic pricing scheme using a just-in-time, individualized analysis of real-time data to maximize profits with greater precision.

At present, the pricing strategy of the buyer agents is still limited and based on some simple time-based functions. Future work should therefore try to address this issue and work on enhancing the buyer agent's pricing strategy with greater room for customizability by the owner.

Also, other than the priority airline settings, users are only able to evaluate an item based on its price. This price-based paradigm is a disservice to both buyers and sellers because it does not allow other value-added services to be brought into the equation. Further work needs to be done in this area to address this limitation. A possible solution would be to set up a rating system similar to the "Better Business Bureau" currently in use in the Kasbah system (Chavez et al., 1996). This new system should allow buyers to rate the airlines on factors such as punctuality, flight service, food, etc. Users will then be able to evaluate air tickets based on more than just the price, and can include the above criteria listed within the rating system.

Finally, in the current implementation, all sellers (and buyers) are assumed to reside within a single marketplace. This does not fully illustrate the migration capability of buyer/seller agents. Future work should accommodate this aspect.

REFERENCES

Chavez, A., Dreilinger, D., Guttman, R., & Maes, P., (1997). A real-life experiment in creating an agent marketplace. *Proceedings of the Second International Conference on the Practical Application of Intelligent Agents and Multi-Agent Technology (PAAM'97)*, London, UK.

Chavez, A. & Maes, P., (1996). Kasbah: An agent marketplace for buying and selling goods. *Proceedings of the First International Conference on the Practical Application of Intelligent Agents and Multi-Agent Technology (PAAM'96)*, 75-90, London, UK.

Collins, J., Youngdahl, B., Jamison, S., Mobasher, B., & Gini, M., (1998). A market architecture for multi-agent contracting. *Proceedings of the Second International Conference on Autonomous Agents*, 285-292.

Corradi, A., Montanari, R., & Stefanelli, C., (1999). Mobile agents integrity in e-commerce applications. *Proceedings of 19th IEEE International Conference on Distributed Computing Systems*, 59-64.

Greenberg, M.S., Byington, J.C., & Harper, D.G., (1998). Mobile agents and security. *IEEE Communications Magazine,* 36(7), 76-85.

Guan, S.U., Ng, C.H., & Liu, F., (2002). Virtual marketplace for agent-based electronic commerce, *IMSA2002 Conference,* Hawaii.

Guan, S.U. & Yang, Y., (1999). SAFE: secure-roaming agent for e-commerce. *Proceedings of the 26th International Conference on Computers & Industrial Engineering*, Melbourne, Australia, 33-37.

Guan, S.U. & Zhu, F.M., (2001). Agent fabrication and its implementation for agent-based electronic commerce. To appear in *Journal of Applied Systems Studies.*

Guan, S.U., Zhu, F.M., & Ko, C.C., (2000). Agent fabrication and authorization in agent-based electronic commerce. *Proceedings of International ICSC Symposium on Multi-Agents and Mobile Agents in Virtual Organizations and E-Commerce*, Wollongong, Australia, 528-534.

Hua, F. & Guan, S.U., (2000). Agent and payment systems in e-commerce. In *Internet Commerce and Software Agents: Cases, Technologies and Opportunities,* S.M. Rahman, S.M. & R.J. Bignall, (eds), 317-330. Hershey, PA: Idea Group Publishing.

Maes, P., Guttman, R.H., & Moukas, A.G., (1999). Agents that buy and sell: transforming commerce as we know it. *Communications of the ACM,* (3).

Marques, P.J., Silva, L.M., & Silva, J.G., (1999). Security mechanisms for using mobile agents in electronic commerce. *Proceedings of the 18th IEEE Symposium on Reliable Distributed Systems,* 378-383.

Morris, J. & Maes, P., (2000). Sardine: An agent-facilitated airline ticket bidding system. *Proceedings of the Fourth International Conference on Autonomous Agents,* Barcelona, Spain.

Morris, J. & Maes, P., (2000). Negotiating beyond the bid price. *Proceedings of the Conference on Human Factors in Computing Systems (CHI 2000),* Hague, the Netherlands.

Tsvetovatyy, M. & Gini, M., (1996). Toward a virtual marketplace: Architectures and strategies. *Proceedings of the First International Conference on the Practical*

Application of Intelligent Agents and Multi-Agent Technology (PAAM'96), 597-613, London, UK.

Wang, T.H., Guan, S.U., & Chan, T.K., (2001). Integrity protection for code-on-demand mobile agents in e-commerce. To appear in *Special Issue of Journal of Systems and Software.*

Zhu, F.M., Guan, S.U., & Yang, Y. (2000)., SAFER e-commerce: secure agent fabrication, evolution & roaming for e-commerce. In S.M. Rahman, & R.J. Bignall, (eds.), *Internet Commerce and Software Agents: Cases, Technologies and Opportunities,* 190-206. Hershey, PA: Idea Group Publishing.

Chapter XXI

Integrated E-Marketing – A Strategy-Driven Technical Analysis Framework

Simpson Poon, Irfan Altas and Geoff Fellows
Charles Sturt University, New South Wales, Australia

ABSTRACT

E-marketing is considered to be one of the key applications in e-business but so far there has been no sure-fire formula for success. One of the problems is that although we can gather visitor information through behaviours online (e.g., cookies and Weblogs), often there is not an integrated approach to link up strategy formulation with empirical data. In this chapter, we propose a framework that addresses the issue of real-time objective-driven e-marketing. We present approaches that combine real-time data packet analysis integrated with data mining techniques to create a responsive e-marketing campaign. Finally, we discuss some of the potential problems facing e-marketers in the future.

INTRODUCTION

E-marketing in this chapter can be broadly defined as carrying out marketing activities using the Web and Internet-based technologies. Since the inception of e-commerce, e-marketing (together with e-advertising) has contributed to the majority of discussions, and was believed to hold huge potential for the new economy. After billions of dollars were spent to support and promote products online, the results were less than encouraging. Although methods and tricks such as using bright colours, posing questions, call to action, etc., (DoubleClick, 2001) had been devised to attract customers and induce decisions, the overall trend is that we were often guessing what customers were thinking and wanting.

Technologies are now available to customise e-advertising and e-marketing campaigns. For example, e-customers, Inc., offers a total solution called Enterprise Customer Response Systems that combines the online behaviours of customers, intentions of merchants, and decision rules as input to a data-warehousing application (see Figure 1). In addition, DoubleClick (www.doubleclick.net) offers products such as DART that help to manage online advertising campaigns.

Figure 1: Enterprise customer response technology. Source: www.customers.com/tech/ index.htm

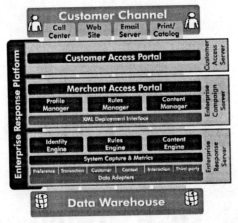

One of the difficulties of marketing online is to align marketing objectives with marketing technology and data mining techniques. This three-stage approach is critical to the success of online marketing because failure to set up key marketing objectives is often the reason for online marketing failure, such as overspending on marketing activities that contribute little to the overall result. Consequently, it is important to formulate clear and tangible marketing objectives before deploying e-marketing solutions and data mining techniques. At the same time, allow empirical data to generate meanings to verify marketing objectives performances. Figure 2 depicts a three-stage model of objective-driven e-marketing with feedback mechanisms.

Objective-driven e-marketing starts with identifying the objectives of the marketing campaign as the key to successful E-marketing, as well as with a goal (or a strategic goal) based on the organisation's mission. For example, a goal can be "to obtain at least 50% of the market among the online interactive game players." This is then factored into a number of objectives. An objective is a management directive of what is to be achieved in an e-marketing campaign.

Figure 2: A three-stage model of objective-driven e-marketing with feedback mechanisms

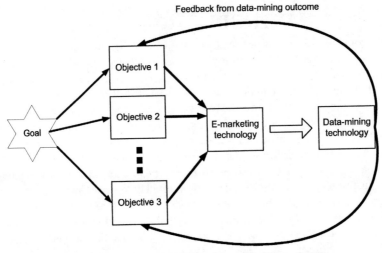

An example of such objective is to "use a cost-effective way to make an impression of Product X on teenagers who play online games over the Internet." In this context, the difference between a goal and an objective is that a goal addresses strategic issues while an objective tactical.

Often an e-marketing campaign includes multiple objectives and together constitutes the goal of the campaign. In order to achieve such a goal, it is necessary to deploy e-marketing technology and data mining techniques to provide feedback to measure the achievement of objectives. Not very often, an e-marketing technology is chosen based on close examination of e-marketing objectives. One just hopes that the objectives are somehow satisfied. However, it is increasingly important to have an e-marketing solution that helps to monitor if whether the original objectives are satisfied; if not, there should be sufficient feedback on what additional steps should be taken to ensure this is achieved.

In the following sections, we first provide a discussion on the various e-marketing solutions ranging from simple Weblog analysis to real-time packet analysis. We then discuss their strengths and weaknesses together with their suitability in the context of various e-marketing scenarios. Finally, we explain how these solutions can be interfaced with various data mining techniques to provide feedback. The feedback will be analysed to ensure designated marketing objectives are being achieved and if not, what should be done.

Technical Analysis Methods for E-Marketers

Even though Web designers can make visually appealing Web sites by following the advice of interface designers such as Nielsen (2001), reality has shown that this is insufficient to make a B2C or B2B site successful in terms of financial viability. More importantly, it is how to correctly analyse the data generated on visitors to Web sites. Monitoring and continuously interpreting visitor behaviours can help a site to uncover vital feedback that can help determine if the visitor is likely to purchase.

Essentially, there are two guiding principles to extract information out of visitor behaviours: the type (what information) and range (duration and spread) of data left behind as well as the relationship between these data clusters. Compared to the early days of benchmarking the delivery performance of Web servers, the emphasis is on understanding customer satisfaction based on hard data. Analysis of log files can yield extensive information, but by using Java and JavaScript applets, user behaviours can be sent back to the Web server and provide near real-time analysis. Another alternative is to have separate servers monitoring the raw network transactions, determining the types of interactions, and doing more complex analyses.

Log File Analysis

The very first Web servers were often implemented on hardware running Unix operating systems. These systems provided text-based log files similar to other system services such as e-mail, FTP, and telnet. Typically, there were two log files: access_log and error_log. The error_log is useful to determine if there are missing pages or graphics, misspelled links and so on.

The data in the access_log is a record of items delivered by the server. For example, two lines were taken from the server access_log on a server called *farrer.csu.edu.au*. is:

203.10.72.216--[18/Apr/2001:10:02:52+1000] "GET /ASGAP/banksia.html HTTP/1.0" 20027495

203.10.72.216--[18/Apr/2001:10:02:53+1000]"GET/ASGAP/gif/diag1c.gifHTTP/1.0"
200 6258.

They indicate the transfer of an HTML page and online image on that page. The first segment gives the host name of the client or just IP address to cut down on the workload of the local Domain Name Server (DNS). The second and third segments are optional items and often they are blank. The fourth column is a date stamp indicating when the event occurred. The fifth segment is the HyperText Transport Protocol (HTTP) command given by the client (or Web browser). The sixth segment is the return status number indicating the result of the request, and the seventh segment is the number of bytes transferred.

With log files like these, it is possible to do some simple analyses. A simple measure would be just to count the lines in the access_log file. This is a measure of the total activity of the server. A better measure would be the lines that have a GET command and an HTML file name that would indicate pages delivered. The Web server on farrer delivered on 18th April 31537 items but only 3048 HTML pages. Another more complex analysis is to sort by client fully-qualified host names (as determined from IP address) in reverse and get an indication where the clients are geographically (for country-based names) or which organisation (.com, .gov, .edu, etc.). This is an important indication for early server operators to see how global their impact was. From a business perspective, it might be important to know if there was interest from customers in a certain region, hence, adjusting the advertising strategy in a more focused manner.

One of the most popular, freely available Web server log analysis programs is called *Analog* (Turner, 2001a). It offers a wide range of reports, including the number of pages requested within a certain time period (hourly, daily, monthly, etc.), breakdown of client operating system and browser type, breakdown of client domain names, among others (University of Cambridge, 2001). Charts can be generated to provide visual information. A useful report is the one that shows the ranking of pages. This helps to decide if changes are required. Popular pages should be easy to download but still compelling. Perhaps the least popular pages should be changed or even deleted by moving their content.

Another very useful analysis in marketing is how long a visitor stayed on a page and which pages they went to from that page. A graph of page links, also known as a click-stream, correlating with client's cookie and time sequence would provide further information about the intention of the visitor. However, this only provides the "footprints" of the visitor and further psychological, cognitive, and behavioural analyses are needed.

Turner has an excellent description (2001b) of how the Web works and includes his discussion on what can and can't be gleaned from Web site log file data analysis. He gives reasons why the type of analysis that marketers would demand can be difficult to be interpreted from a log file. For example, visitor's identity can only be known if you can tie a "cookie" (Lavoie & Nielsen 1999; Netscape, 1999) to information entered on a "Free to Join" form. Once a visitor fills out that form, the server can send a cookie to the client's browser and every time that client's browser asks for a new page the request includes the cookie identification. This can be tied to a visitor database, which includes the details from the online form and past behaviours. Host name cannot be used because often this is in the proxy server cache used by client's ISP, and a different IP address may be assigned each time they connect. Turner reports American On Line may change the IP address of the proxy server used by a client's browser on each request for elements of a Web document. Turner also points out that the click-stream analysis will be muddied by the browser's and the ISP's cache.

Web Servers "add-ons"

As well as having server-side scripting for accessing database back-ends and other Common Gateway Interface (CGI) programming, it is possible for server-side scripts to gather "click-stream" data. Application Program Interfaces (APIs) have been traditionally used to enhance the functionality of a basic Web server. These days Web pages containing VBScript, PERL, Java Servlets, or PHP scripts are used as an alternative to slower CGI scripts. CGI scripts are slower because they are separate child processes and not part of the parent request handling process. The advantage of CGI scripts is that any programming language can be used to build them. Using a script embedded in the HTML which is interpreted by a module that is part of the server is faster because a separate process is not required to be created and later destroyed. Another method is to have a separate "back-end" server to which the Web server is a client.

Other server-side scripts can interact with client-side scripts embedded in Web documents. This arrangement can add an extra channel of interaction between the client and the server programs to overcome some of the limitations of the HyperText Transport Protocol (HTTP) (Fielding et al., 1999). This channel might provide data about mouse movement, which is not normally captured until a link is clicked.

Network "wire-tap" Data Gathering and Analysis

Because of the need to maximise Web server response time, the process of tracking visitor behaviours can be off-loaded to another server. The network sniffer is on the local network and captures the raw data packets that make up the interaction between the visitor and the Web server. This separate server could be the server on the other end of the extra channel mentioned in the previous section. It reconstructs and then analyses the visitor's behaviour (including that from the extra channel), combines that with previous behaviour from the visitor database, and produces a high-level suggestion to the Web server for remedial actions. Cooley (2000) describes several methods on how this can be achieved. One scenario is that the visitor may decide to make a purchase. However, if a long time lapse occurs since the purchase button was presented and if this lapse time is longer than a predefined waiting period, say, 15 seconds, it suggests that the customer is reviewing his/her decision to purchase. A pop-up window containing further information can be presented for assistance.

"On the Internet, nobody knows you're a dog." This caption of a classic Steiner cartoon describes the marketer's dilemma: you don't know anything about your Web site visitors apart from their behaviours (McClure, 2001). Unless one can convince a visitor to accurately fill out a form using some sort of incentive, one doesn't know who the visitor is beyond the person's click-stream. Once he/she fills out the form, the server can send a "cookie" to the client's browser. Anonymous click-streams provide useful data for analysing page sequences but are less effective when trying to close sales. This can be tied to a visitor database that includes the details from the online form and past behaviours.

FROM ANALYSIS TO DATA MINING TECHNIQUES

So far the discussion has been focusing on analysis techniques and what to analyse. In this section, the "how to carry out" question is addressed. Nowadays there is a

Figure 3: Stages in a data mining technique

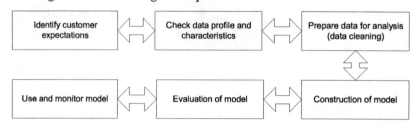

considerable amount of effort to convert a mountain of data collected from Web servers into competitive intelligence that can improve a business' performance.

"Web data mining" is about extracting previously unknown, actionable intelligence from a Web site's interactions. Similar to a typical data mining exercise, this type of information may be obtained from the analysis of behavioural and transaction data captured at the server level as it is outlined in the previous sections. The data, coupled with a collaborative filtering engine, external demographic, and household information, allow a business to profile its users and discover their preferences, their online behaviours, and purchasing patterns.

There are a number of techniques available to gain an insight into the behaviours and features of users to a Web site. There are also different stages of data mining processes within a particular data mining technique (Mena, 1999; Thuraisingham, 1999) as illustrated in Figure 3.

Identify Customer Expectations

Based on the objective-based e-marketing framework (see Figure 1), it is important to have a clear statement of the data-mining objective (i.e., what are we mining?). This will affect the model employed as well as the evaluation criteria of the data mining process. In addition, this helps to justify the costs and allocates financial and personnel resources appropriately.

Check Data Profile and Characteristics

After identifying the objectives, it is important to examine if the necessary data set is available and suitable for a certain goal of analysis. It is also important to examine data by employing a visualisation package such as SAS (www.sas.com) to capture some essential semantics.

Prepare Data for Analysis

After preliminary checks are done, it is essential to consolidate data and repair problematic data areas identified in the previous step, such as missing values, outliers, inaccuracies, and uncertain data. Select the data that is suitable for one's model (for example, choosing dependent-independent variables for a predictive model) before using visualisation packages to identify relationships in data. Sometimes data transformation is needed to bring the data set into the "right" forms.

Construction of Model

Broadly speaking data mining models deployed for e-marketing can be classified into two types:

Prediction-Type Models (Supervised Learning)

- Classification: identify key characteristics of cases for grouping purposes (for example, how do I recognize high propensity to purchase users?).
- Regression: use existing values, likely to be those belonging to the key characteristics, to forecast what other values will be.
- Time series forecasting: similar to regression but takes into account the distinctive properties of time (for example, what probability this new user on my Web site will be a loyal customer over time?).

Description-Type Models (Unsupervised Learning)

- Clustering: to divide a database into different groups, clustering aims to identify groups that are different from each other, as well as the very similar (for example, what attributes describe high return users to my Web site?). It may be useful to state the difference between clustering and classification: Classification classifies an entity based on some predefined values of attributes, whereas clustering groups similar records not based on some predefined values.
- Associations: items that occur together in a given event or record (for example, what relationship does user gender have to sales at my site?).
- Sequence discovery: is closely related to associations, except that the related items are spread over time (for example, if a user to my Web site buys Product A, will (s)he buys Product B and C and when?).

Many algorithms/technologies/tools are available that can be used to construct models such as: neural networks, decision trees, genetic algorithms, collaborative filtering, regression and its variations, generalized additive models, and visualization.

Evaluation of Model

In order to answer questions such as "What do we do with results/patterns? Are there analysts who can understand what the output data are about? Are there domain experts who can interpret the significance of the results?," the right model needs to be selected and deployed. The output from the model should be evaluated using sample data with tools such as confusion matrix and lift chart. Assessing the viability of a model is crucial to its success, since patterns may be attractive/interesting but acting upon it may cost more than the revenue generated.

Use and Monitor the Model

After acting upon the results from the model, it is important to determine the benefits and costs of implementing the model in full by re-evaluating the whole process. This helps to improve the next data mining cycle if new algorithms emerge or fine-tuning the model if the data set has changed.

DATA MINING TOOLS AND ALGORITHMS FOR E-MARKETING

There are tools and algorithms specifically related to e-marketing applications. One family of such algorithms is called "item-based collaborative filtering recommendation algorithms." Collaborative filtering is one of the most promising tools to implement real-time Web data mining (Sarwar, Karypis, Konstan, & Reidl, 2000a). The main function of a recommender system is to recommend products that are likely to meet a visitor's needs based on information about the visitor as well as the visitor's past behaviours (e.g., buying/ browsing behaviours).

Recommender systems apply data mining techniques to come up with product recommendations during a live customer interaction on a Web site. This is a challenging problem for a Web site when there are millions of customers and thousands of products such as movies, music CDs/videos, books, and news stories being considered. However, the same approach can readily be implemented as a dynamic Web page presentation tool for visitors of a Web site by assuming Web pages as products and visitors as customers.

The techniques implemented in recommendation systems can be categorised as content-based and collaborative methods (Billsus & Pazzani, 1998). Content-based approaches use textual description of the items to be recommended by implementing techniques from machine learning and information retrieval areas. A content-based method creates a profile for a user by analysing a set of documents rated by the individual user. The content of these documents is used to recommend additional products of interest to the user. On the other hand, collaborative methods recommend items based on combined user ratings of those items, independent of their textual description. A collection of commercial Web data mining software can be found at http://www.kdnuggets.com/software/Web.html including "Analog" and "WUM" that are available freely.

One of the successful recommender systems in an interactive environment is collaborative filtering that works by matching customer preferences to other customers' to make recommendations. The principle for these algorithms is that predictions for a user may be based on the similarities between the interest profile of the user and those of other users. Once we have data indicating users' interest in a product as numeric scale, they can be used to measure similarities of user preferences in items. The concept of measuring similarity (usually referred to as resemblance coefficients in information retrieval context) is investigated in the context of information retrieval to measure the resemblance of documents, and a brief survey on the topic can be found in Lindley (1996). Similarity measurements can be classified into four classes: distance, probabilistic, correlation, and association coefficient. A probabilistic similarity measurement implementation for textual documents can be found in Lindley, Atlas, & Wilson, 1998).

Pearson correlation coefficient is proposed by Shardanand and Maes (1995) to measure similarities of user profiles. All users whose similarities are greater than a certain threshold are identified and predictions for a product are computed as a weighted average of the ratings of those similar users for the product. Some major shortcomings of correlation-based approaches are identified in Billsus and Pazzani (1998). Correlation between two user profiles is calculated when both users rate a product via an online evaluation form. However, as users might choose any item to rate, given the thousands of items on the many millions of B2C sites, there will be overlaps between two sets of user ratings. Thus, correlation measure may not be a promising means to measure similarities as some can happen by chance. Furthermore, if there is no direct overlap between the set of ratings of two users due to a transitive similarity relationship, two users with reasonable similarity may not be identified. For example, Users A and B are highly correlated as are Users B and C. This relation implies a similarity between user profiles of A and C. However, if there were no direct overlap in the ratings of Users A and C, a correlation-based method would not detect this relation.

As an alternative to correlation-based approach, collaborative filtering can be treated as a classification model to classify products in a discrete scale for a user (e.g., likes and dislikes) or as a regression model in case user ratings are predicted based on a continuous scale. In this approach, the main idea is to come up with a model that classifies unseen items into two or more classes for each user. Unlike correlation-based methods, which operate on pairs of users, classification model approach usually operates on the whole data set that is organised into a matrix form. For example, rows represent users, columns correspond to items, and entries of the matrix are user ratings or some other kind of measurement of the relation between a particular user and a product. By employing this matrix, it is possible to calculate a similarity measure between a particular user and product (Billsus & Pazzani, 1998). Some techniques such as cover coefficients were already developed in the context of information retrieval to measure similarities for this type of data, (e.g., rows represent documents, columns represent some terms in a document, and matrix entries show whether a particular term is contained in a document or not). Cover coefficients technique is based on a probabilistic similarity measurement, and details can be found in Can and Ozkarahan (1990). Another similarity measurement approach is implemented in collaborative filtering as well as information retrieval contexts called cosine. In this approach, the similarity between two users (or two rows) is evaluated by treating two rows as vectors and calculating the cosine of the angle between two vectors (Sarwar et al., 2000b; Willet, 1983).

Billsus and Pazzani (1998) created a set of feature vectors for each user from the original matrix by employing a learning algorithm. After converting a data set of user ratings in matrix form for feature vectors, they claim that many supervised prediction-type algorithms from machine learning can be applied.

Scalability Issue

Recommender systems apply knowledge discovery techniques to the problems of making product recommendations during a live customer interaction. Although these systems are achieving some success in e-marketing nowadays, the exponential growth of users (customers) and products (items) makes scalability of recommender algorithms a challenge. With millions of customers and thousands of products, an interactive (Web-based) recommender algorithm can suffer serious scalability problem very quickly. The amount of data points needed to approximate a concept in **d** dimensions grows exponentially with **d**, a phenomenon commonly referred to as "curse of dimensionality" (Bellman, 1961).

In order to illustrate the problem, let us assume that an algorithm implemented using the *nearest neighbourhood algorithm* (Eldershaw & Hegland, 1997) to classify users with certain properties. Let us examine the figure on the following page, which is taken from http://cslab.anu.edu.au/ml/dm/index.html.

In the left figure of Figure 4, the nearest neighbours of a random point to 1 million normally distributed points are displayed in the case of two dimensions. The right figure of Figure 4 shows the same for 100 dimensions that have been projected to two dimensions such that the distance to the random point is maintained. Note how in high dimensions all the points have very similar distances and thus all are *nearest neighbours*. This example clearly shows that data mining algorithms must be able to cope with the high dimensionality of the data as well as scale from smaller to larger data sizes that are addressed by scalable data-mining predictive algorithms implementing regression techniques (Christen, Hegland, Nielsen, Roberts, & Altas, 2000).

Also, scalable algorithms in collaborative filtering context are presented in Billsus and Pazzani (1998) and Sarwa et al. (2000b), based on singular value decomposition (SVD)

Figure 4: Comparison of the effect of dimensionality on neighbourhood algorithms' effectiveness

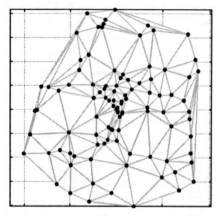 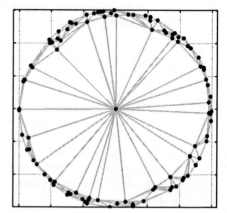

technique. The original data matrix is preprocessed to remove all features that appear less than twice in the data. Thus, the new form of the data matrix, say A, contains many zeros (no rating for items from the user) and at least two ones (rated items by the user) in its every row. By implementing SVD, the matrix A can be written as the factor of three matrices $A=USV^T$ where U and V are two orthogonal matrices and S is a diagonal matrix of size (r x r) containing all singular values of A. Here, r denotes the rank of the original matrix A and is usually much smaller than the dimensions of the original matrix A. Through this factorisation procedure, it is possible to obtain a new user and item matrix with reduced dimensions in the item column.

It has the form $R=US^{1/2}$. Note that the singular values of A are stored in decreasing order in S and dimensions of R can be reduced further by omitting singular values of A that are less than a certain threshold. Then, a similarity measurement technique such as cosine can be implemented over R to calculate similarity measures of a particular user to the rest.

CONCLUSION

Objective-driven e-marketing coupled with multiple analysis methods and sophisticated data-mining techniques can be a very effective way to target online marketing efforts. By first setting up the objectives of the e-marketing campaign, e-marketers are better prepared for the outcomes. Monitoring customer behaviours can be started at the traditional Web-logs level right up to monitoring data packets in real-time using network "wire-tap" strategy. On top of the understanding of "what" to analyse, we also discuss "how" to carry out the analysis – applying viable data-mining techniques. We have outlined a strategy to proceed with data mining and how the various approaches (e.g., collaborative filtering) are applied to extract meaning out of data. We then suggested what could be done to address the scalability issues due to increase in dimensionality. This chapter has only explored some preliminary concepts of objective-driven e-marketing, and the challenge is how to integrate the business and technology strategies to maximize the understanding of e-marketing in a dynamic way.

REFERENCES

Bellman, R., (1961). *Adaptive control processes: A guided tour,* Princeton, New Jersey: Princeton University Press.

Billsus, D., & Pazzani, J.M., (1998). Learning collaborative information filters. In *Proceedings of Recommender Systems Workshop*. Tech. Report WS-98-08. Madison, WI: AAAI press.

Can, F., & Ozkarahan, E.A., (1990). Concepts and effectiveness of the cover-coefficient based clustering methodology for text based databases. *ACM Transactions on Database Systems*, 15(4), 483-517.

Christen, P., Hegland, M., Nielsen, O., Roberts, S. & Altas, I., (2000). Scalable parallel algorithms for predictive modelling. In *Data Mining II*, N. Ebecken & C.A. Brebbia, (eds). Southampton, UK: WIT press, .

Cooley, R.W., (2000). *Web usage mining: Discovery and applications of interesting patterns from Web data*. Ph.D. Thesis. University of Minnesota.

DoubleClick (2001) Effective Tips. Available: http://www.doubleclick.net/us/resource-center/RCstreamlined.asp?asp_object_1=&pageID=311&parentID=-13.

Eldershaw, C., & Hegland, M., (1997). Cluster analysis using triangulation. In B.J. Noye, M.D. Teubner & A.W. Gill, (Eds), *Computational Techniques and Applications: CTAC97*, 201-208. Singapore, World Scientific.

Gettys, J., Mogul, J., Frystyk, H., Masinter, L., Leach, P., & Berners-Lee, T., (1999). Hypertext Transfer Protocol—HTTP/1.1 http://www.w3.org/Protocols/rfc2616/rfc2616.txt [Accessed 7th Sept 2001].

Lavoie, B., & Nielsen, H.F., eds, (1999), Web characterization terminology & definitions sheet http://www.w3.org/1999/05/WCA-terms/ [Accessed 7th Sept 2001].

Lindley, D., (1996). Interactive classification of dynamic document collections, Ph.D. Thesis. The University of New South Wales, Australia.

Lindley, D., Altas, I., & Wilson, C.S., (1998). Discovering knowledge by recognising concepts from word distribution patterns in dynamic document collections. In E. Alpaydin & C. Fyfe, (eds) *Proceedings of Independence and Artificial Networks*, 1112-1118.

McClure, M., Web traffic analysis software (online) http://www.businesswire.com/emk/mwave3.htm [Accessed 3rd Sept 2001].

Mena, J., (1999). Data mining your website, Melbourne: Digital Press.

Netscape (1999). Persistent client state: HTTP Cookies. (online) http://home.mcom.com/newsref/std/cookie_spec.html [Accessed 5th Sept 2001].

Nielsen, J., Usable information technology. (online) http://useit.com [Accessed 20th June 2001].

Web Usage Mining: Discovery and Application of Interesting Patterns from Web Data. Doctoral Thesis. University of Minnesota (online)from http://citeseer.nj.nec.com/426030.html [Accessed 7th Sept 2001].

Sarwar, B.M., Karypis, G., Konstan J., & Riedl, J., (2000a). Analysis of recommendation algorithms for e-commerce. In *Proceedings of the 2nd ACM conference on Electronic Commerce*, October 17-20, Minneapolis, USA. ACM Digital Library, 158-167, www.acm.org/pubs/contents/proceedings/ecomm/352871.

Sarwar, B.M., Karypis, G., Konstan J., & Riedl, J., (2000b). Application of dimensionality reduction in recommender systems – A case study. In *ACM WebKDD 2000 Workshop*.

Shardanand, U., & Maes, P., (1995). Social information filtering: Algorithms for automating "Word of Mouth." In *Proceedings of Human Factors in Computing Systems*, 210-217, New York: ACM Press.

Steiner, P., (1993). Cartoon with caption "On the Internet nobody, knows you're a dog." *The New Yorker*, 69 (LXIX) 20: 61, July 5. Archived at http://www.unc.edu/courses/jomc050/idog.html.

Thuraisingham, B., (1999). Data mining technologies, techniques, tools and trends, New York: CRC Press.

Turner, S., (2001a). Analog (software). http://www.analog.org/loganalysis/ [Accessed 5th Sept 2001].

Turner, S., (2001b). How the Web works. July 5th. http://www.analog.org/loganalysis/docs/Webworks.html [Accessed 5th Sept 2001].

University of Cambridge Statistical Laboratory, (2001). 2001 statistics. http://www.statslab.cam.ac.uk/~sret1/stats/stats.html [accessed 5th Sept 2001].

Willet, P., (1983). Similarity coefficients and weighting functions for automatic document classification: an empirical comparison. *International Classification,* 10(3), 138-142.

Chapter XXII

An Agent-Based Architecture for Product Selection and Evaluation Under E-Commerce

Leng Woon Sim and Sheng-Uei Guan
National University of Singapore

ABSTRACT

This chapter proposes the establishment of a trusted Trade Services entity within the electronic commerce agent framework. A Trade Services entity may be set up for each agent community. All products to be sold in the framework are to be registered with the Trade Services. The main objective of the Trade Services is to extend the current use of agents from product selection to include product evaluation in the purchase decision. To take advantage of the agent framework, the Trade Services can be a logical entity that is implemented by a community of expert agents. Each expert agent must be capable of learning about the product category it is designed to handle, as well as the ability to evaluate a specific product in the category. An approach that combines statistical analysis and fuzzy logic reasoning is proposed as one of the learning methodologies for determining the rules for product evaluation. Each feature of the registered product is statistically analyzed for any correlation with the price of the product. A regression model is then fitted to the observed data. The assumption of an intrinsically linear function for a non-linear regression model will simplify the efforts to obtain a suitable model to fit the data. The model is then used as the input membership function to indicate the desirability of the feature in the product evaluation, and the appropriate fuzzy reasoning techniques may be applied accordingly to the inputs thus obtained to arrive at a conclusion.

INTRODUCTION

The Internet and World Wide Web is becoming an increasingly important channel for retail commerce as well as business-to-business (B2B) transactions. Online marketplaces provide an opportunity for retailers and merchants to advertise and sell their products to customers anywhere, anytime. For the consumers, the Web represents an easy channel to obtain information (e.g., product price and specification) that will assist them in their purchase decisions. However, despite the rapid growth of e-commerce and the hype surrounding it, there remain a few fundamental problems that need to be solved before e-commerce can really be a true alternative to the conventional shopping experience. One of the reasons why the potential of the Internet for truly transforming commerce is largely unrealized to date is because most electronic purchases are still largely non-automated. User presence is still required in all stages of the buying process. According to the nomenclature of Maes' group in the MIT Media Labs (Maes, 1994; Guttman & Maes, 1999), the common commerce behavior can be described with the Consumer Buying Behaviour (CBB) model, which consists of six stages, namely, need identification, product brokering, merchant brokering, negotiation, purchase and delivery, and product service and evaluation.

This adds to the transaction costs. The solution to automating electronic purchases could lie in the employment of software agents and relevant AI technologies in e-commerce. Software agent technologies can be used to automate several of the most time-consuming stages of the buying process like product information gathering and comparison. Unlike "traditional" software, software agents are personalized, continuously running, and semi-autonomous. These qualities are conducive for optimizing the whole buying experience and revolutionizing commerce, as we know it today. Software agents could monitor quantity and usage patterns, collect information on vendors and products that may fit the needs of the owner, evaluate different offerings, make decisions on which merchants and products to pursue, negotiate the terms of transactions with these merchants, and finally place orders and make automated payments (Hua, 2000). The ultimate goal of agents is to reduce the minimum degree of human involvement required for online purchases.

At present, there are some software agents like BargainFinder, Jango, and Firefly providing ranked lists based on the prices of merchant products. However, these shopping agents fail to resolve the challenges presented below.

Seller Differentiation

Currently, the most common basis for comparison between products via the e-commerce channel is through price differentiation. Through our personal experience, we know that this is not the most indicative basis for product comparison. In fact, product comparisons are usually performed over a number of purchase criteria. Many merchants deny entry of such comparison agents into their site and refuse to be rated by these agents for this reason. Unless product comparisons can be performed in a multi-dimensional way, merchants will continue to show strong resistance towards admitting software agents with product comparison functions into their sites.

Buyer Differentiation

Current e-commerce architecture places too much emphasis on the price as the single most important factor in purchase decisions. This simplistic assumption fails to capture the essence of the product selection process. Although comparison between products based on price and features is currently available on the Internet, this feature is only useful to the buyer with relevant product knowledge. What is truly needed is a means of selecting products that match the user's purchase requirements and preferences. For example, a user may consider whether a product is popular or well received in addition to the price factor when making his decision. Generally, users are inclined to choose a well-known product even if it has a higher price than others. These preferential purchase values include affordability, portability, brand loyalty, and other high-level values that a user would usually consider in the normal purchase process.

Differentiation Change

In today's world of rapid technological innovation, product features that are desirable yesterday may not be desirable today. Therefore, product recommendation models must be adaptable to the dynamic, changing nature of feature desirability.

The current agents also do not have complete interpretation capability of the products because vendor information is described in unstructured HTML files in a natural language. Finally, there is also the issue that the agents may need a long time in order to locate the relevant product information, given the vast amounts of information available online. A more coordinated structure is required to ensure faster search time and more meaningful basis for product comparison. It is, therefore, the aim of this chapter to propose a methodology for agent learning that determines the desirability of a product and to propose an agent framework for meaningful product definition to enable value-based product evaluation and selection.

LITERATURE REVIEW

In this section, we consider some of the online solutions that are currently applied on the Internet for product comparison and recommendation and a number of agent architectures proposed for electronic commerce.

Internet Models

The most common Internet model for e-commerce product selection is feature-based product comparison. The constraints on product features essentially reduce the search scope for the product. Most search engines are able to collate the relevant product information for a specified number of the filtered products and present the outcome in the form of a comparison table. The drawback from this scheme is that it is usually only able to make comparisons between a specified number of products. There is also no strong basis for making product recommendations based only on the product features without consideration for the user's preferences.

Several dot.com startups like allExperts.com and epinions.com use a network of Web users who contribute their opinions about a specific product to assist a user to make product purchase decisions. The drawback from this scheme is that the process of product filtering, which is the precursor to product evaluation, is usually absent. There exists a need to have a separate process for product filtration from which the opinions regarding the filtered products are individually considered by the user. Furthermore, the opinions of the contributors could be based on different value judgements. Thus, what may be desirable to one user might not be so for another user. In essence, this model suffers from a lack of personalization.

It is felt that an approach that considers the user's consideration of the relative importance of product features is a more reasonable way to handle product purchase decisions.

Agent Frameworks

A case for the continued existence of intermediaries in the electronic marketplace and their functionalities were presented in Sarker (1995). Decker *et al.* (1996) examined the agent roles and behaviors required to achieve the intermediary functions of agent matchmaking and brokering in their work.

Little research has been done in this area, however, there are a number of operations research techniques available to consider for this purpose. The UNIK agent framework proposed by Jae Kyu Lee and Woongkyu Lee (1998) makes use of some of these techniques, like Constraint and Rules Satisfaction Problem (CRSP) with interactive reasoning capability approach. Other techniques that can be considered include Multi-Attribute Utility Theory and Analytical Hierarchy Process (AHP) (Taylor, 1999).

The main problem with the agent frameworks mentioned thus far is that the product domains are distinct and separate. However, for a complex system like a personal computer system where component level information is widely available, it would be a definite advantage to be able to mobilize the relevant product agents together to give a better evaluation of the given product. There is therefore insufficient agent integration towards product recommendation. The cause of this problem most probably lies in the form of knowledge representation for the products. It is probably for this purpose that the UNIK agent framework also proposes an agent communication mechanism on product specification level. This consideration forms one of the important factors for the proposed design of our work.

TRADE SERVICES UNDER SAFER

SAFER - *Secure Agent Fabrication, Evolution and Roaming* for electronic commerce (Guan & Yang, 1999) is an infrastructure to serve agents in e-commerce and establish the necessary mechanisms to manipulate them. SAFER has been proposed as an infrastructure for intelligent mobile-agent mediated E-commerce. The proposed Trade Services is best positioned based on such an infrastructure, which offers services such as agent administration, agent migration, agent fabrication, e-banking, etc. The goal of SAFER is to construct standard, dynamic and evolutionary agent systems for e-commerce. The SAFER architecture consists of different communities as shown in Figure 1. Agents can be grouped into many communities based on certain criteria. To distinguish agents in the SAFER architecture from those that are not, we divide them into SAFER communities and non-SAFER communities. Each SAFER community consists of the following components: Owner, Butler, Agent, Agent Factory, Community Administration Center, Agent Charger, Agent Immigration, Bank,

Figure 1: SAFER architecture

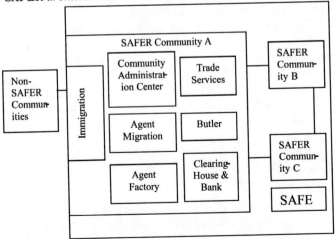

Clearing House, and Trade Services. In the following, we only elaborate those entities that are related to our Trade Services framework.

Community Administration Center

To become a SAFER community member, an applicant should apply to his local community administration center. The center will issue a certification to the applicant whenever it accepts the application. A digital certificate will be issued to prove the status of the applicant. To decide whether an individual belongs to a community, one can look up the roster in the community administration center. It is also required that each agent in the SAFER architecture has a unique identification number. A registered agent in one community may migrate into another community so that it can carry out tasks in a foreign community. When an agent roams from one SAFER community to another, it will be checked by agent migration with regard to its identification and security privileges before it can perform any action in this community.

Owner & Butler

The Owner is the real participant during transactions. He doesn't need to be online all the time, but assigns tasks and makes requests to agents via his Agent Butler. Depending on the authorization given, Agent Butler can make decisions on behalf of the Owner during his absence, and manage various agents. An agent butler assists its agent owner in coordinating agents for him. In the absence of the agent owner, an agent butler will, depending on the authorization given, make decisions on behalf of the agent owner.

Agent Factory

Agent factory is the kernel of SAFER, as it undertakes the primary task of "creating" agents. In addition, agent factory has the responsibility to fix and check agents, which is an indispensable function in agent evolution and security. Agent factory will have a database including various ontology structures and standard modules to assemble different agents.

Clearing House & Bank

Clearing House & Bank, as the financial institutions in a SAFER community, link all value-representations to real money.

Trade Services

This is the place where product selection and evaluation can be conducted. We elaborate it in the following sections.

ARCHITECTURE OF AGENT-BASED TRADE SERVICES

The central design questions raised are: How does a purchase agent locate relevant vendor agents among the sea of agents in the World Wide Web? After the products have been found, how does the agent evaluate the performance and desirability of a particular product and make good recommendations? Our solution would be an Agent-based Trade Services entity.

Trade Services

A trusted Trade Services entity is proposed for each agent community (Zhu, Guam, & Yang, 2000). All the vendors participating in the framework are to be registered with the Trade Services, and the products to be sold within the agent framework are also to be registered. In thus doing, the approach also overcomes the potential problem of an overtly long product searching process when there is no known directory for the purchase agents to locate a product and related vendor information quickly. The Trade Services, in this role, acts as an intermediary between the purchase agents and the vendor agents and provides the facilities for agent matchmaking and agent brokering. The Agent Naming Service provides the mapping of agent names and their locations, while the Agent Broker maintains the mapping of agents and their capabilities within the framework.

The Trade Services is proposed to be a neutral, logical entity that embodies a collection of autonomous expert agents, each capable of handling a specific domain. However, the Trade Services needs not play a merely passive role as a routing mechanism in a client-server framework that connects the purchase agent to the relevant expert agent. It also plays an active role in providing interconnectivity between the various expert agents in order to achieve a better evaluation of the product. This "divide-and-conquer" approach will be especially useful in evaluating complex, composite products like the PC, where reliable evaluation of individual components could be the key to a reliable overall recommendation. This could mean that the Trade Services needs to have some meta-knowledge about the relationships between products, and these relationships could be built into the knowledge base by the manner the product information was represented.

The advantages to a multi-agent Trade Services approach are:
- Lower search cost and waiting time–if each expert agent handles its own knowledge

Figure 2: Agent-based trade services

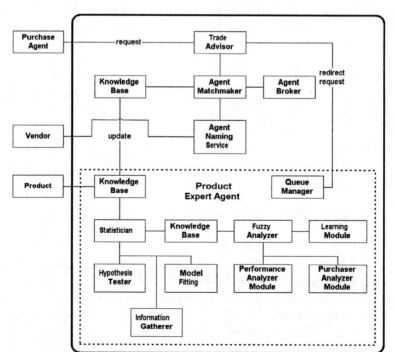

base, the extent for a search is greatly limited, leading to a faster search time. The queue for services from the Trade Services could be split into shorter queues for individual expert agents, thus reducing the mean waiting time for requests. This again will lead to superior performance from the system.

- Knowledge representation of the domain can be uniquely determined. Ambiguity that may arise from similar terminology employed for different products is avoided. Specific ontology for agent communication on product specification level can also be established along product lines.

Expert Agent

Each expert agent handles requests for its services with regards to its specialization. In the realistic situation, there could be many simultaneous requests for the services of the same expert agent. Thus, a queue needs to be managed, and this calls for the existence of a Queue Manager.

Each expert agent maintains it own knowledge base from which reasoning and inference of the facts in the database can be performed. An agent conducts its own learning based on the statistics and inferences derived from the acquired knowledge. It should be an autonomous entity. Based on these requirements, the expert agent should have a knowledge base, a statistics-gathering module, one or more learning mechanisms, and a reasoning engine that is capable of handling uncertainty in the knowledge. A knowledge base is chosen over a relational database as the means for storing product and vendor information in the expert agent because it provides the means for which inferences and reasoning can be performed on the data. AI techniques like backward chaining and forward chaining can be operated on the information. Rules and inheritance relationships can also be expressed to allow greater flexibility in working with this information. Fuzzy logic is introduced to handle the uncertainty that exists in the knowledge, and the linguistic properties it introduces allow greater flexibility in purchase decisions. Ultimately, this could culminate in a form of values-based purchase decision process where the user only needs to specify the need and the value judgments in a particular purchase.

The Statistician entity acting in the Information Gatherer role extracts salient information about the product category like the maximum, minimum, and the mean values of the product features. Statistics on the frequency of occurrence of product features may lead to conclusions about whether the feature is proprietary or standard. Higher order statistics like the variance, the covariance, the Pearson's Coefficient, the Spearman's Rank Correlation Coefficient (Devore, 2000) can also be calculated to assist in the analysis of the product category and rule formation in the Rule-Former. In acting as a Hypothesis Tester, the Statistician can test hypothese made about the product. The conclusions arrived from the Hypothesis Tester are useful for the Rule-Former in formulating the necessary rules for product evaluation. Finally, in the model-fitting role, the Statistician tries to fit a mathematical model to the observed price-attribute correlation. This involves the determination of parameter values to best fit a model curve to the observed data. The conclusions made in the Hypothesis Tester role can sometimes help to reduce the amount of work required here, since it can determine whether the underlying correlation is linear or non-linear.

The Performance Analyzer Module is one of two fuzzy logic-based modules that exist within the agent. The Performance Analyzer Module serves to determine the performance of the product based on the feature values of the product that affect its operational performance. The module returns the defuzzified value of the resultant fuzzy set after the operations of approximate reasoning has been performed. This defuzzified value (Performance Index) serves as an index to indicate the performance rating of the product. A higher Performance Index indicates a product with higher performance.

The other fuzzy logic-based component implemented within the agent is the Purchase Analyzer Module. The purpose of this module is to make recommendations of the products that meet the feature specifications dictated by the user. The recommendation takes into account the relative importance of the high-level purchase values like affordability and product performance in the user's purchase decision. Therefore, the recommendation index for the same product will be different when the relative importance of purchase values differ. This is more reflective of the reality where the evaluation of a product is highly dependent on the personal value judgement of an individual buyer. The performance index from the Performance Analyzer Module can be used as an input to the Purchase Analyzer Module when one of the purchase values is product performance. The output from the Purchase Analyzer Module (Recommendation Index) is again the defuzzified result of the resultant fuzzy set. The Recommendation Index of a product is an indication of the desirability of the product after the personal value preferences of the user has been factored into the recommendation process. The higher the recommendation index, the more desirable the product is.

Product Evaluation Methodology

In many situations, a human buyer depends on heuristics or rules of thumb to make purchase decisions. In general, decisions based on these heuristics are sufficient conditions to make a good purchase decision. For an agent equipped with relevant learning algorithms and statistical knowledge, it should not be too difficult a task to arrive at these rules of thumb.

Whilst the price of a product may not be an absolutely accurate indication of the desirability or the performance of the product, it is nevertheless a very good indicator in most cases. Therefore, in order to ascertain the desirability of a certain product feature, the relationship between the feature value and the price of the product may be used as a heuristic. After the salient features of a product are determined, statistical tests may be conducted to ascertain the correlation that exists between the feature value and the price of a product. A possible method of determining if a feature is useful in the purchase decision is to consider the frequency of occurrence of that feature in all the registered products in the specified category. An alternative approach is to use the concepts of information theory in the same way it is being applied to decision trees, that is, to determine those factors that contribute the most information about the product.

Spearman's Rank Correlation Test is then performed on the ranked list of products in the category to determine whether any form of correlation exists between the price of a product and the attribute value for each of its features. The Spearman's Rank Correlation Coefficient may be determined by the equation below.

$$p_s = 1 - \frac{6 \sum d_i^2}{n\left(n^2 - 1\right)}$$

where d_i is the difference in ranks scored by the item between the two variables, i.e., price and the feature value under test.

The Spearman's Rank Correlation Coefficient test essentially considers whether a high ranking in one of the lists leads to high ranking in the other list. It is a very general purpose test that is unaffected by the nature of the underlying correlation relationship, whether it is linear or non-linear. The Spearman's Rank Correlation Coefficient obtained needs to be compared to the critical levels at various levels of significance to determine if the hypotheses are to be accepted or rejected. A reasonable level of significance that can be employed is at 5%, indicating an important decision with consequences of a wrong decision at less than $100,000 (Devore, 2000).

This correlation forms useful heuristics to allow the Rule-Former to determine the rules that evaluate product performance and desirability. A method that the Rule-Former can adopt to formulate the rules is to assign a ranking system for the possible states that the antecedents may consists of. For example, 3 points may be assigned to the value of *High* in the antecedent, and 2 points for *Medium,* and so forth. The desirability of a set of input conditions can be taken to be the aggregate sum of the points accumulated by each of the individual input antecedents. The aggregate sum is then utilized to determine which term the conclusion part of the rule takes on.

After the general correlation is obtained, the feature-price model can be fitted with either a linear or non-linear regression model. Linear correlation can be easily obtained from Pearson correlation coefficients and linear regression model techniques. For the non-linear correlation model, it is observed that most of the price-attribute correlations exist in a monotonic manner. Therefore, we only need to consider intrinsically linear functions to model the relationship. This greatly simplifies the mathematical modeling complexity as the choice of the model can be reduced to merely three main categories – the logarithmic model, the exponential model and the power model, for which the parameters can be easily obtained.

It is further argued that the correlation model obtained is an indication of the desirability of the product feature. That is, we can assume the price-attribute correlation to be equivalent to the desirability-attribute correlation for a product feature. This correlation can then be assigned as the membership function of a fuzzy logic variable upon which fuzzy inferences and reasoning can be performed to evaluate the product.

Agent Learning

Where there are established benchmarks for evaluating product performances, these data could be used to train the agent and tune the membership functions for the fuzzy components. Tuning of fuzzy membership functions is usually done with genetic algorithms. To determine the outcome of learning, k-fold cross validation can be applied. A large proportion of the total available data is used as training set while the remaining proportion is used as a validation set to test the results from learning. This procedure is repeated a number of times for the same data set. However, a common practice would be to perform five repetitions, hence the name 5-fold cross validation. Genetic algorithms can also be considered to tune the membership functions.

System Operation

The first event that must occur is the registration of a vendor to the Trade Services. Information about the new vendor is added to the existing knowledge base maintained by the Trade Services. Upon successful registration of the vendor, the Trade Services will request the Agent Factory (13) to produce a Seller Agent for the registered vendor. The Seller agent, being the main agent for the registered vendor to conduct trade in the community, should be equipped with the relevant modules for electronic transactions. The location and the capabilities of this agent should be registered with the Agent Naming Service and with the Agent Broker. A data mining agent needs to be allowed periodic access to the vendor's Web site to update information about the products, especially the price of the product. This operation ensures that the prices of the products are kept up to date for valid product recommendations.

When a user intends to purchase a type of product, the intention is made known to his Agent Butler who would then instruct a purchase agent to proceed to the Trade Services to conduct queries about the product. The Trade Services determines the type of product for which the query is made and redirects the purchase agent to the relevant product expert agent. This requires the involvement of the Agent Broker to determine the type of product query made and then match that request to the capability of the agents listed with it. After the appropriate matching is determined, the exact location of the agent needs to be located to start a session. The Agent Matchmaker looks up the Agent Naming Service and returns the location of the relevant expert agent. The purchase agent then starts a session with the expert agent, and the Agent Broker and Matchmaker are freed to handle the requests of other purchase agents. The request of the purchase agent may be place on a locally managed queue by the expert agent, which implements a queue manager. Each expert agent could monitor its volume of requests. A suitable scheme based on the volume of requests can be derived to determine when an expert agent needs to clone itself to optimally handle the requests so that the average waiting time is not too long.

In handling the request of the purchase agent, the expert agent first checks its knowledge base for the list of products that satisfy the requirements. These products are then subjected to evaluation to obtain a recommendation index for each product. The recommendation index could be obtained in a number of ways with varying degrees of complexity and accuracy, depending on the approach used. An implementation based on fuzzy logic is employed. This approach allows uncertainty in the information and the incompleteness of the product knowledge to be elegantly handled. The product information, as well as the recommendation index is returned to the purchase agent who returns to its owner.

Position of Trade Services

Finally, the position of the Trade Services in the architecture is considered. It is possible that the Trade Services and indeed an entire community can be implemented and managed by a third party in a business-oriented manner. The third party can employ a few possible business models to ensure profitability of implementing the SAFER community. First, it can charge an initial startup fee during vendor registration for the costs of fabricating agents held by the vendor in the framework. The third party, by virtue of implementing the Bank, the Clearinghouse, and the Trade Services, is in the center of all agent transactions. Thus, it is in a good position to analyze purchasing trends for any product category. The third party could exploit this position to charge the registered vendors for product trend analysis, which is crucial information, otherwise unavailable to the vendors. The easy availability of product trend analysis could be the major push factor to participate in this architecture, because to employ consultants for such purposes would be a very expensive alternative.

However, despite the advantages of a third-party implementation, there will certainly be questions raised about the trustworthiness of the third party. With profitability as the bottom-line, would the third party be maneuvered to place certain major players in positions that are more favorable? This could lead to suspicion from other registered vendors, especially the minor vendors, who might suspect their interests would be compromised. Such suspicion could seriously undermine the trust in the Trade Services and thus affect the applicability of the Trade Services. Therefore, it is thought that any complications that may result from a third-party implementation of the Trade Services may be reduced if the implementation of the Trade Services were endorsed or undertaken by a government body overlooking trade development. Furthermore, the move would tie in with the increasing e-government trend currently employed in many developed countries.

RESULTS AND DISCUSSIONS

A prototype was developed to provide for a test of concept. The prototype handles the purchase of a CPU processor. The performance of each processor was evaluated with a fuzzy

Table 1: Performance comparison of CPUs

Processor Speed	Cache size	Bus-speed	ICMP 3.0 Performance		Performance Analyzer Performance	
			Raw Score	Percentage	Raw Score	Normalized
533	512	133	1721	52.47	75.8	88.45
600	256	133	1930	58.84	50.0	58.34
667	256	133	2320	70.73	52.4	61.14
733	256	133	2510	76.52	65.4	76.31
800	256	133	2760	84.15	83.1	96.97
866	256	133	2949	89.91	84.8	98.95
450	512	100	1500	45.73	56.4	65.81
500	512	100	1650	50.30	66.8	77.95
550	512	100	1780	54.27	76.3	89.03
600	256	100	2110	64.33	50.0	58.34
650	256	100	2270	69.21	51.8	60.44
700	256	100	2420	73.78	56.5	65.93
800	256	100	2760	84.15	80.2	93.58
850	256	100	2790	85.06	80.4	93.82
1000	256	133	3280	100.00	85.7	100.00
533	256	133	1850	56.40	50.0	58.34
600	256	133	2108	64.27	50.0	58.34
667	256	133	2214	67.50	52.4	61.14
800	256	133	2690	82.01	83.1	96.97
866	256	133	2890	88.11	84.8	98.95
933	256	133	3100	94.51	85.6	99.88
550	256	100	1900	57.93	50.0	58.34
650	256	100	1922	58.60	51.8	60.44
700	256	100	2420	73.78	56.5	65.93
750	256	100	2540	77.44	71.7	83.66
800	256	100	2690	82.01	80.2	93.58
533	128	66	1517	46.25	39.7	46.32
566	128	66	1631	49.73	46.7	54.49
600	128	66	1749	53.32	50.0	58.34
633	128	66	1863	56.80	50.0	58.34
667	128	66	1980	60.37	50.0	58.34
700	128	66	2094	63.84	50.0	58.34
766	128	66	2322	70.79	50.0	58.34
800	128	66	2459	74.97	50.0	58.34

Figure 3: Performance analyzer results

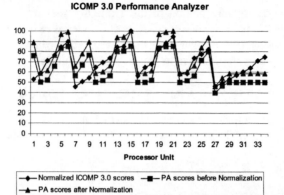

logic-reasoning engine employing Mamdani implication and Center-of-Gravity defuzzification. The results obtained are shown in Table 1.

The performance rating for the processors, as determined by the Performance Analyzer module, is compared against the official processor benchmark values as given by the manufacturers. This benchmark is based on the ICOMP 3.0 (http://cpuscorecard.com) benchmark adopted by Intel.

The ICOMP 3.0 scores were normalized against the maximum value obtained to establish a basis for comparison with the results from the Performance Analyzer. When the raw scores from the Performance Analyzer were compared against that of the normalized ICMP 3.0 scores, the results did not appear to be too encouraging as the difference in values seems to be rather wide. The maximum value provided by the Performance Analyzer is only 85.7. This is a drawback of using the product-moment defuzzification scheme for fuzzy logic systems. A possible way around this problem is to normalize the results, and after doing so, the results from the Performance Analyzer were quite similar to that of ICOMP 3.0. To ascertain if positive correlation exists between the two sets of ratings, the Spearman's Rank Correlation Coefficient was calculated. It was found to have a value of 0.703. This is much greater than the critical value of 0.432 required at 1-% significance level. Therefore, we claim that the results from the Performance Analyzer show positive correlation with the ICOMP 3.0 results.

However, it was observed that the fuzzy module showed a low level of sensitivity when the cachesize and bus speed are low. An analysis of the surface plot for the bus-cache relationship when the processor speed was set to 600 MHz revealed a relatively flat surface over a wide range of values, thus accounting for the insensitivity.

CONCLUSION

In conclusion, it was shown through the prototype implementation that intelligent agent is a feasible approach to handle the uncertainty involved in product selection and evaluation. This could be a step towards embedding more intelligence in e-commerce. The knowledge base implementation of Trade Services for product services caters to the possibility of further reasoning using AI techniques like forward chaining and backward chaining. The proposed architecture for Trade Services as a logical entity comprising of a group of intelligent agents allows greater integration of the expert agents towards product evaluation where component-wise evaluation of a complex product is possible.

Finally, the performances of the fuzzy logic modules could be improved by fine-tuning using genetic algorithms. The most important features of a product can be determined using decision trees and extracting those attributes that contribute the most information. Case-based learning algorithms can also be implemented into agents to handle situations where all the user's criteria cannot be met simultaneously.

REFERENCES

allExperts.com Web site: http://www.allexperts.com.

Besterfield, D.H., (1999). *Experimental Design,* Upper Saddle River, NJ: Prentice Hall.

CPU processor benchmark ICOMP 3.0: http://cpuscorecard.com.

Decker, K., (1996). Matchmaking and brokering, In *Proceedings of the 2nd International Conference on Multi-Agent Systems (ICMAS).*

Devore, J.L., (2000). Probability and Statistics for Engineering and Sciences, 5th Edition, Pacific Grove, CA: Brooks/Cole.

epinion.com Web site: http://www.epinion.com.

Guan, S.U., & Zhu, F.M., Agent fabrication and its implementation for agent-based electronic commerce, to appear in the *Journal of Applied Systems Studies.*

Guan, S.U., &. Yang, Y., (1999). SAFE: Secure-roaming agent for e-commerce. *Proceedings of the 26th International Conference on Computers and Industrial Engineering,* Australia.

Guttman, R.H. & Maes, P., (1999). Agent-mediated negotiation for retail electronic commerce, *Agent.* In P. Noriega & C. Sierra, (eds). 70-90. *Mediated Electronic Commerce: First International Workshop on Agent Mediated Electronic Trading,* Berlin: Springer-Verlag.

Hua, F., & Guan, S.U., (2000). Agents and payment systems in e-commerce. In S.M. Rahman & R.J. Bignall (eds). *Internet Commerce and Software Agents: Cases, Technologies and Opportunities,* 317-330. Hershey, PA: Idea Group Publishing.

Lee, J.K., & Lee, W., (1998). An intelligent agent-based competitive contract process: UNIK agent. *International Journal of Intelligent Systems in Account, Finance and Management,* (7), 91-105.

Maes, P., (1994). Agents that reduce work and information overload. *Communication of the ACM,* 37(7), 31-40.

Nwana, H.S. (1996). Software agents: An overview. *Knowledge Engineering Review* 2(3), 31-40.

Poh, T.K., & Guan, S.U., (2000). Internet-enabled smart card agent environment and applications. In S.M. Rahman & R.J. Bignall, (eds). *Internet Commerce and Software Agents: Cases, Technologies and Opportunities,* 190-206, Hershey, PA: Idea Group Publishing.

Sarkar, M.B., (1995). A continuing role for mediating players in the electronic marketplace. *Journal of Computer Mediated Communication,* 1(3).

Taylor III, W., (1999). *Introduction to Management Science* 6th Edition: Upper Sadle River, NJ: Prentice Hall.

Wang, T., Guan, S.U., & Chan, T.K. Integrity protection for code-on-demand mobile agents in e-commerce, to appear in the *Journal of Systems and Software.*

Yang, Y., & Guan, S.U., (1999). Intelligent mobile agents for e-commerce: Security issues and agent transport, In S.M. Rahman & R.J. Bignall, (eds). *Electronic Commerce: Opportunities and Challenges,* 321-336. Hershey, PA: Idea Group Publishing.

Zhu, F.M., Guan, S.U., & Yang, Y., (2000). SAFER e-commerce: A new architecture for agent-based electronic commerce. In S.M. Rahman, and R.J. Bignall, (eds). *Internet Commerce and Software Agents: Cases, Technologies and Opportunities,* 190-206. Hershey, PA: Idea Group Publishing.

Section VIII:

Security Architecture

Chapter XXIII

An Architecture for Authentication and Authorization of Mobile Agents in E-Commerce

Wee Chye Yeo, Sheng-Uei Guan, and Fangming Zhu
National University of Singapore

ABSTRACT

Agent-based e-commerce is a new technology being researched extensively by many academic and industrial organizations. The mobility and autonomy properties of agents have offered a new approach of doing business online. To fully exploit the advantages of this new technology, a secure system to authenticate and authorize mobile agents must be in place. In this chapter, an architecture to ensure a proper authentication and authorization of agents has been proposed. The Public Key Infrastructure (PKI) is used as the underlying crypto-graphic scheme. An agent is digitally signed by the Agent Factory and its signature is authenticated at hosts using the corresponding public key. Agents can also authenticate the hosts to make sure that they are not heading to a wrong place. When an agent visits a host, agent's expiry date, host trace, and the factory's trustworthiness are checked during the authentication process. According to the level of authentication that the incoming agent has passed, the agent will be categorized and associated with a relevant security policy during the authorization phase. The corresponding security policy will be enforced on the agent to restrict its operations at the host. The prototype has been implemented with Java.

INTRODUCTION

With the increasing world-wide usage of the Internet, electronic commerce (e-commerce) has been catching on fast in a lot of businesses. As e-commerce booms, there comes a demand for a better system to manage and carry out transactions. This has led to the development of agent-based e-commerce. In this new approach, agents are employed on behalf of users to carry out various e-commerce activities, such as auction, brokering, negotiation, payment, etc.

Although the tradeoff of employing mobile agents is still a contentious topic (Milojicic, 1999), using mobile agents in e-commerce attracts much research effort as it may improve the potential of their applications in e-commerce. There are many advantages for employing mobile agents. First, communication cost can be reduced, because the agents will travel to the destination and transfer only the necessary information. This saves the bandwidth and reduces the chances of clogging the network. Second, users can let their agents travel asynchronously to their destinations and collect information or execute other applications while the user can disconnect from the network (Wong, Paciorek, & Moore, 1999).

Having seen the advantages of this emerging technology, the major factor that is still holding people back from employing agents in e-commerce is the security issues involved. On the one hand, hosts cannot trust incoming agents belonging to unknown owners, because malicious agents may launch attacks on the hosts and other agents. On the other hand, agents may also have concerns on the reliability of hosts and will be reluctant to expose their secrets to distrustful hosts.

There are two broad categories of security issues to be considered in the research field of mobile agents: misuse of hosts by mobile agents and misuse of mobile agents by hosts or other mobile agents. In the first category, a host is exposed to attacks from visiting agents. The various kinds of attacks include theft of information, denial of services, damage to local resources, etc. For instance, with the attack of denial of services, a malicious agent may overload some local resource or service, blocking the host's access to other agents or applications. In the scenario of the second category, when an agent is executing in a malicious host's environment, it is exposed to possible attacks from that host and other agents residing in the host.

To build bilateral trust in an e-commerce environment, the authorization and authentication schemes for mobile agents should be well designed. Authentication checks the credentials of an agent before processing the agent's requests. If the agent is found to be suspicious, the host may decide to deny its service requests. Authorization refers to the permissions granted for the agent to access whichever resource it requested. The Public Key Infrastructure (PKI) is used as the basic cryptographic method in our design, and Java is selected as the implementation language. Digital signature is used for authentication purpose, and authorization is achieved using the security manager provided by Java. To restrict the access to resources, user-defined security policies have to be designed and used in conjunction with the security manager. Based on the authentication results, the host can decide the type of privileges to offer to various authenticated agents.

In our previous work, we have proposed a Secure Agent Fabrication, Evolution & Roaming (SAFER) architecture (Zhu, Guam, & Yang, 2000), which aims to construct an open, dynamic and evolutionary agent system for e-commerce. It provides a framework for agents in e-commerce and establishes a rich set of mechanisms to manage and secure them. We have already elaborated agent fabrication, evolution, and roaming in Guan and Zhu (2001), Guan, Zhu, and Ko (2000), Wang, Guam, and Chan (2001), Zhu and Guan (2001), and Guan and Yang (1999). This chapter elaborates the design and implementation of authentication and authorization issues on the basis of the SAFER architecture.

The remainder of the chapter is organized as follows. Section 2 presents background on agent-based e-commerce, mobile agent systems, and PKI. Section 3 elaborates the design of agent authentication and authorization. Section 4 describes the implementation of the proposed design. Section 5 discusses the advantages and limitations of the implemented approach in comparison with the related work. The final section concludes the chapter and discusses the possible future work.

BACKGROUND

Many intelligent agent-based systems have been designed to support various aspects of e-commerce applications in recent years. The Maes group in the MIT Media Lab has conducted several projects in Agent mediated E-Commerce (AmEC). These projects focus on creating e-commerce infrastructures for dynamic virtual marketplaces and higher-level aspects of agent mediation. One typical project is Kasbah (Chavez & Maes,, 1998), which is an online marketplace where buying and selling agents can interact. The Minnesota AGent Marketplace Architecture (MAGMA) (Tsvetovatyy, Mobasher, Gini, & Wieckowski, 1997) is a prototype for a virtual marketplace which includes the infrastructure required for conducting commerce on the Internet, supports communication among agents, and allows for various forms of automated and human-controlled transactions. MAgNet (Dasgupta, Narasimha, Moser, & Melliar-Smith, 1999) is a system for networked electronic trading with mobile agents. It is based on the pull model of marketing in which buyer agents approach supplier agents of products with their requirements.

Currently, mobile code technologies can be divided into two categories, the weakly mobile technologies and the strongly mobile technologies (Oppliger, 1999). Weakly mobile technologies allow the code to migrate from site to site, but the execution state cannot be migrated to the new site. An example is the Java applets. On the contrary, strongly mobile technologies allow the code and the state to migrate to a new execution environment, and to resume execution at the destination site. Mobile agent system is an example of a strongly mobile technology. Here, we introduce three mobile agent systems and focus on their methods of authenticating and authorizing mobile agents.

D'Agents (Gray, Kotz, Cybenko, & Rus, 1998) is a mobile agent system developed by Dartmouth College. It employs the PKI for authentication purposes, and uses the Rivest, Shamir, and Adleman (RSA) public key cryptography (1978) to generate the public-private key pair. After the identity of an agent is determined, the system decides what access rights to assign to the agent. Then, it sets up the appropriate execution environment for the agent. A stationary agent plays the role of a resource manager. Each resource manager defines its own security policy. The manager will check each request against an access list and accept or reject the request.

IBM Aglets (Lange & Oshima, 1998) are Java-based mobile agents. Each aglet has a globally unique name and a travel itinerary. The IBM Aglets Workbench (AWB) consists of a development kit for aglets and a platform for aglet execution. Aglets travel to various places that are defined as context in IBM Aglets. The context owner is responsible for keeping the underlying operating system secure, mainly protecting it from malicious aglets. Therefore, he defines the security policy for the context. He will authenticate the aglet and restrict the aglet under the context's security policy. The IBM AWB has a configurable Java security manager that can restrict the activities of the aglet in the same way as the default security manager is used to restrict the activities of an applet.

Ajanta is also a Java-based mobile agent system developed at University of Minnesota (Karnik & Tripathis, 1999). Ajanta employs a challenge-response based authentication protocol. Each entity in Ajanta registers its public key with Ajanta's name service. A client has to be authenticated by obtaining a ticket from the server. The Ajanta Security Manager is responsible for the agents' access to system resources. There is an access control list created based on the users' Uniform Resource Names (URNs). The Ajanta Security Manager grants permissions to resources based on this access control list.

The PKI is not only used in mobile agent systems discussed above, but also in e-commerce applications due to its powerful features for security. Under PKI, each entity may possess a public-private key pair. The public key is known to all, while the private key is only known to the key owner. Information encrypted with the public key can only be decrypted with the corresponding private key. In the same note, information signed by the private key can only be verified with the corresponding public key (Rivest et al., 1978; Simonds, 1996).

There are several algorithms that can be used to generate these key pairs. The default algorithm available in a standard Java package is the Digital Signature Algorithm (DSA). A digital signature works like a signature on a contract. The signature is unique, so that the other party can be sure that you are the only person who can produce it.

The above-mentioned mobile agent systems are all general platforms. They are mainly concerned about issues such as agent mobility, scalability, operability, etc. Security issues for mobile agents are not a focus in these systems. However, in e-commerce application systems with mobile agents, the security issues become more important. Unfortunately, most current agent-based systems such as Kasbah and MAGMA are serving only stationary agents. Although MAgNet employs mobile agents, it does not consider security issues in its architecture. This motivates us to deal with the security issues of launching mobile agents in e-commerce systems, especially on the aspects of agent authentication and authorization.

DESIGN OF AGENT AUTHENTICATION AND AUTHORIZATION

Overview of the SAFER Architecture

Our design and implementation of agent authentication and authorization are based on our previous work — the SAFER architecture. SAFER (Zhu et al., 2000) refers to a Secure Agent Fabrication, Evolution and Roaming architecture for agent-based e-commerce. It is an infrastructure to facilitate agent-based e-commerce, to create agents, to dispatch them out on missions, and to make the whole process secure so that the agents and the hosts will not be subject to malicious attacks.

The SAFER architecture comprises various communities and each community consists of the following components (shown in Figure 1): Agent Owner, Agent Factory, Agent Butler, Community Administration Center, Virtual Marketplace, etc.

Figure 1: SAFER architecture

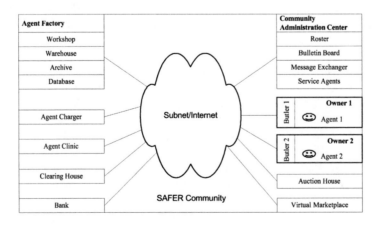

The Agent Owner is the initiator in the SAFER environment. The Owner can request the Agent Factory to fabricate the agents he requires. He is also the one who will dispatch his agents out for their missions.

The Agent Butler is a representative of the Agent Owner. He is authorized by the owner to coordinate the agents that are dispatched, and is present all the time. The purpose for this is so the Owner can go offline after dispatching his agents, and thereafter the butler can take over the coordination of his agents that have been dispatched.

The Agent Factory is the entity that fabricates all the agents. This is the birthplace of agents and is thus considered a good source to check whether an agent is malicious or not. It plays a major role in agent certification. A reputable and trusted Agent Factory is deemed to manufacture agents that can be trusted. However, trust can be subjective. For example, a host may not trust the Factory that fabricates agents for his competitors. Therefore every host will keep a list of his/her trusted factories. The Factory will normally check whether the Owner is a registered community member before it agrees to fabricate an agent for him. The FactoryID, AgentID, AgentExpiryDate will be hard-coded into the agent during fabrication. It will then be signed with the Factory's private key before it is delivered to the Owner.

The Community Administration Center (CAC) is the administrative body in the agent community. It has a roster that keeps the data of the agents that are in the community. It also collects information, such as addresses of new sites that agents can roam to.

Agent Structure and Cryptographic Schemes

In SAFER, mobile agents have a uniform structure. Here, we mainly discuss the components which are closely related to authentication and authorization. The agent credentials are the most important part of the agent body, and they are immutable. The necessary components in this immutable part include FactoryID, AgentID, Expiry Date, etc. During the fabrication process, the agent's credentials will be hard-coded into the agent (Guan & Zhu, 2001; Guan et al., 2000). This immutable part is then signed by the Agent Factory. When the agent is subsequently sent out on its mission, the hosts can only view but not modify this immutable part. When the receiving host accepts this agent, it can verify with the Agent Factory's public key whether the agent's credentials have been modified.

The mutable part of the agent includes the Host Trace, and any encrypted data that is appended to the agent body by the hosts it visited. The Host Trace stores a list of names of the hosts that the agent has visited so far. At every host that the agent visits, the host will check if the agent has visited any distrusted host sites before arriving at its site. If any distrusted host is found in the agent's Host Trace, the current host may decide not to trust this agent and impose a stricter security policy on it to restrict its operations. After an agent finishes its mission at the host, the host will add its identity to the Host Trace. This is to allow the next host to verify the integrity of the agent.

In SAFER, the main cryptographic technology used is the PKI. When the agent owner uses his private key to sign an agent, it produces a digital signature that no one else can forge without knowing his private key. An external party can now verify the digital signature by retrieving the owner's public key, and use it to verify the digital signature in the agent. If the agent or signature has been tampered with, the verification will fail, because no other party would have the private key to sign the tampered agent and pass it off as the original one.

In the SAFER design, the public keys are stored in a common database located in the CAC, where the public has read-access, but no access to modify existing records. When a receiving party needs to verify a digital signature, he can retrieve the relevant public key from the common database and use it to verify that the signature indeed originates from this particular host or factory. This method works because only the signing party has the correct private key to sign the agent. Any other public key will render the verification false. Therefore, if the verification returns true, then the agent must have been signed by the particular party.

Authentication Process

Authenticating Host

Before roaming to the next host, it is the duty of the agent to authenticate the next host to make sure that the host it is visiting is a genuine one. There could be malicious hosts out there masquerading as the host that the agent wishes to visit. If the agent were to travel to these hosts, it could be endangered by them.

To prevent that from happening, a handshaking method is devised to authenticate hosts. The agent sends its request to a host asking for permission to visit. The host will sign on the agent's request message with its private key and send it back to the agent. The agent can then verify the host's identity by extracting the host's public key from the common database and authenticating the signature. If the authentication is successful, then the agent will know that it is communicating with the genuine host and starts to ship itself over to the host.

Authenticating Agent

Authentication of an agent involves two major steps. One is to verify the agent's credentials, which is hard-coded and signed by the Agent Factory's private key during fabrication. The other step is to verify the mutable part of the agent, checking whether it has been tampered with by anyone in its roaming process.

Figure 2: Authentication and authorization procedure

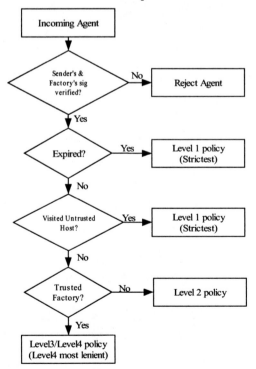

The authentication procedure is shown in Figure 2. Firstly, the agent will be checked for its expiry date. If it has not expired, its host trace will be examined to see if it has been to any distrusted host. Each site keeps a database of distrusted hosts that it uses to check with the agent's host trace. If the agent passes these two tests, the final test is to check the trustworthiness of the factory that has manufactured it.

Authorization Process

After the host accepts an agent, it has to determine what resources the agent is allowed to access based on the level of authentication that the agent has passed. Four levels of authorization has been designed, with Level 1 being the strictest and Level 4 the most lenient. Level 1 authority is given to agents that the host does not have much trust on. An agent that passes all levels of authentication and is deemed to be trusted may be awarded the Level 4 authority.

To implement the authorization module, four sets of security policies have to be defined to cater to the four authorization levels. A security manager is set on the agent's applications to enforce the security policy (according to the level of authorization awarded) for the particular agent. In this way, an agent that is not very trusted by the host will not have the permissions to perform a lot of functions, while a trusted agent will get more freedom in using the host's resources.

Table 1 shows the four policies and the restrictions imposed on each policy. The permissions can be customized to meet the requirements of different hosts. For example, the Level 4 policy, being the most lenient, has the most permissions granted. This includes the file read/write permission, AWT permission that allows it to pop up windows on the screen, socket permission to listen, accept, and connect to the ports, and runtime permission to create/set security manager and to queue print jobs. In contrast, the strictest policy (Level 1) only has file read permission.

Table 1: Definition of the various security policies

Level of leniency	Policy name	Permissions
Level 4 (Most lenient)	Polfile.policy	FilePermission (Read, write)
		AWT Permission
		Socket Permission (Accept, Listen, Connect)
		Runtime Permission(create/set SecurityManager, queue PrintJob)
Level 3	Pol1.policy	FilePermission (Read, write)
		AWT Permission
		Socket Permission (Accept, Listen, Connect)
		Runtime Permission(create SecurityManager, queue PrintJob)
Level 2	Pol2.policy	FilePermission (Read only)
		AWT Permission
		Socket Permission (Accept, Connect)
		Runtime Permission(create SecurityManager)
Level 1 (Most Strict)	Pol3.policy	FilePermission (Read only)
		No AWT Permission
		No Socket Permission
		No Runtime Permission

IMPLEMENTATION

Implementation of agent authentication and authorization was done using the Java programming language. The Java Security API and the Java Cryptography Extension were widely used in the implementation. The Graphical User Interfaces were designed using the Java Swing components.

Generation of Keys

Every new user who wishes to make use of the SAFER system has to register and has a set of public-private key pair generated. The user has to store his own private key in his own password-protected database. The public key will be stored in a public database where everyone has access to read and retrieve the public key, but they would not have the authority to modify the entries in the database.

Figure 3 shows the user interface when a new user generates a new pair of public-private keys. The new user can click on the "Generate Keypair" button. The user then enters the name of the database to store his private key, the database username and password, and of course his new user ID and password that he needs in order to retrieve his keys in future. After that, he would press "Register" and the keypair will be generated and then stored in the respective databases.

Signing of Agent

The party signing the agent will use his private key to sign the agent. He will enter his UserID and password to retrieve his private key from the key database. Figure 4 shows an example of the Agent Factory signing the agent before sending it to the Agent Owner.

After entering the necessary fields, the "Sign Agent" button can be clicked. The private key of the factory is retrieved from the key database and used to sign the agent. A signature file will be created, which will be sent together with the agent to the Agent Owner for verification purposes.

Figure 3: Generation of keys

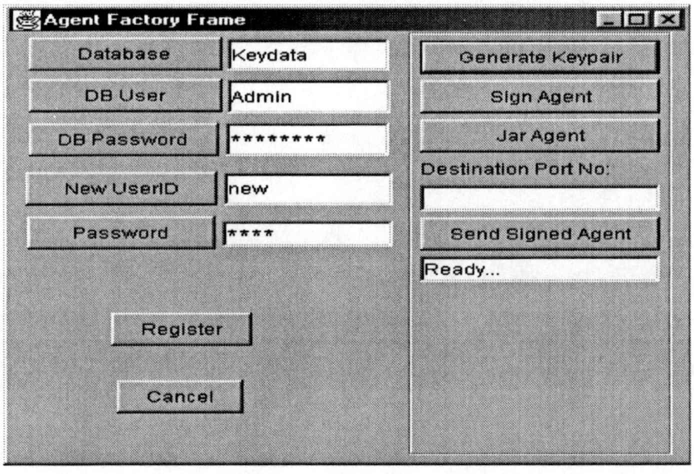

Figure 4: Signing of agent

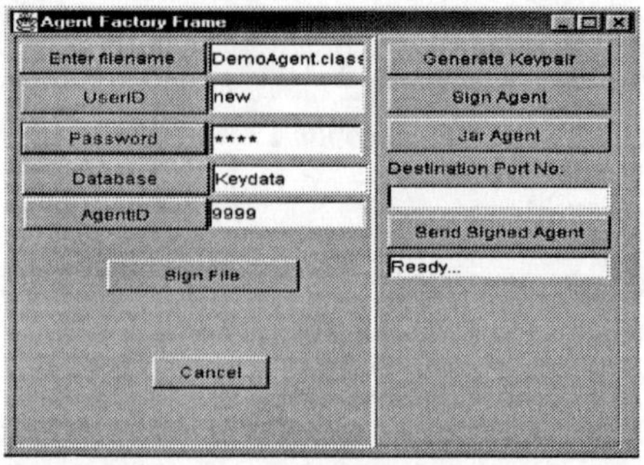

Authentication of Host by Agent

Before the agent is dispatched to the destination, it can authenticate that the host it is going to is indeed the right destination. This step is shown in Figure 5. The current address and the Sender ID fields are automatically updated. The user has to enter the destination address. A dummy file called request.txt has to be created too. When the information is sent to the host, the host will automatically sign on the request.txt and send it back together with the signature to the sending party.

When the sending party receives the signature and request.txt, these will be automatically authenticated (Figure 6). In this way, the sending party can be sure whether the destination host is a genuine or a bogus one.

Figure 5: Sending an authentication request to the host

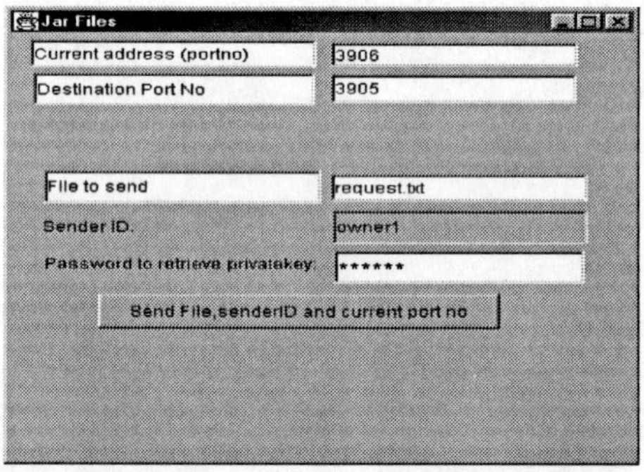

Figure 6: Sender of the request receiving the host authentication

Figure 7: Signature of the sending party verified

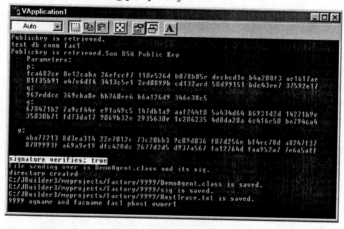

Sending Signed Agent to Destination

After the agent is signed and the destination host is tested to be credible, the agent can be dispatched to its destination. When the agent is being sent over, the receiving party will verify with the sending party's public key that the agent being sent over has not been tampered with across the channel. Refer to Figure 7 for the verification results. He will also verify with the Agent Factory's public key that the agent's credentials have not been modified since its creation. When both these conditions are satisfied, the next step - authentication of the agent's credentials - will continue.

Authentication of Agent's Credentials

This phase is normally automated. The host will check the agent's expiry date, host trace and the manufacturing factory. It will then assign a suitable policy to enforce on the agent and run the agent based on the assigned policy. Figure 8 shows a manual version of the program where the host administrator can select the authentication procedures to apply on the agent, simply by checking the boxes. The authentication results will be shown in the text box and a security policy recommended to the host administrator. The host administrator can then run the agent under the recommended policy or he may manually select another policy to run on the agent. He may click on the "Definition of Policies" to see what kinds of restrictions are imposed by each policy.

Figure 8: Authenticating and running agent

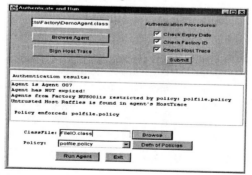

DISCUSSIONS

We have implemented the prototype for authentication and authorization of mobile agents in e-commerce, which has been integrated into our SAFER architecture. We do not intend to compare our prototype with mobile agent systems such as D'Agents and Aglets on detail benchmarks, as the focus of our approach is on the security issues in the context of e-commerce applications, which is quite different from the focus of these general mobile agent platforms. Here, we present our features in comparison to related work, and discuss the advantages and limitations of our system in the following subsections.

Our approach has some features that are similar to the related systems discussed in section 2. For example, the authentication mechanism is based on PKI. The authorization mechanism is implemented using the Java security manager and some user-defined security policies. The major features of our approach lie in the method of authorization. Some agent systems authorize agents based on a role-based access control list, and some are based on the identity of the agent. For the D'Agents system, each resource defines its own security policy and enforces the same policy on all agents. The SAFER system is different in that it allocates a different security policy based on the identity of the agent and the level of authentication it has passed. The level of authentication is decided by whether the agent has expired, whether it has visited any distrusted host, and whether it was manufactured by a distrusted factory. For these purposes, each host will keep a list of distrusted hosts and a list of trusted factories. Every agent also has its factory ID hard-coded within the agent body, and it also carries a host trace that monitors its itinerary. In this way, the hosts can authenticate the agent and assign to it appropriate security policies.

Advantages of Our Infrastructure

Storage of Keys

One of the principal advantages of the prototype implemented is that there is no sending of keys over the network. This enhances the security of the system since it is impossible for keys to get intercepted and replaced.

The database storage of the public keys also allows an efficient method of retrieval of keys. This facilitates the verification of all previous signatures in the agent by the current host. For example, the owner may want to verify the signatures of all the previous hosts that the agent has visited. Instead of having all these hosts append their public keys to the agent (which may be compromised later), the owner can simply retrieve the keys from the database according to the hosts' ID. To prevent illegal modification of records, the database is set in a read-only mode, hence no malicious party can modify the entries without the administrator's password.

Examining the Agent's Host Trace

The agent's host trace keeps a list of hosts that the agent has visited prior to the current place. Every host is required to sign on the agent's host trace before it is dispatched to the next destination. The IDs of the hosts visited are compared with the distrusted host list that each host would keep. If a distrusted host were found, the host would then take special precautions against these agents by imposing a stricter security policy on its operations.

Automation of the Authentication and Authorization Process

Automation of the authentication and authorization process would allow a higher traffic of agents to operate at the host. The beauty of this system is that it can be automated or run manually when the need arises. In the automatic configuration, when an agent is sent over, the host will do the authentication and assign an appropriate security policy to the agent. If the execution is successful, the host signs the agent and adds its identity on the host trace, before sending it out to the next host. In the manual configuration, all the authentication and authorization procedures need prompting from the host owner. The advantage is that the host has more control on what methods to authenticate and what authorization level and policy to enforce on the agent.

Limitations of Our Infrastructure

Predetermined Security Policies

In the current design, the agent is assigned to the security policy based on the authentication process. Having predetermined security policies may be stifling to the operations of an agent. One scenario could be that the agent may just require a "read" File Permission to gather the price information from the host. It would be useless if the agent is denied the read access but instead is granted other permissions that it does not need.

The limitation here is that the mechanism to customize the permission for each agent has not been developed. Having pre-determined security policies are simpler to implement for large-scale systems. Each agent needs not be tested for all the permissions that it is requesting. However, the compromise is lack of flexibility in that the agent has no freedom to request the permissions it requires.

Difficulty in Identifying a Malicious Host

The current implementation does not have a way of identifying the host that is causing the attacks on the agent. The agent owner can only detect that certain information has been tampered, but he does not know exactly which host caused the disparity. Without this information, the malicious host will never be identified in the network, and the agent owner would not be able to warn the other agents in the community of the malicious host.

CONCLUSIONS AND FUTURE WORK

With the development of the Internet and software agent technologies, agent-based e-commerce systems are being developed by many academic and industrial organizations. However, the advantages of employing mobile agents can be manifested only if there is a secure and robust system in place.

In this chapter, the design and implementation of agent authentication and authorization are elaborated. By combining the features of the Java security environment and the Java Cryptographic Extensions, a secure and robust infrastructure is built. PKI is the main technology used in the authentication module. In developing this module, care was taken to protect the public and private keys generated. To verify the integrity of the agent, digital signature is used. The receiving party would use the public keys of the relevant parties to verify that all the information on the agent is intact. In the authorization module, the agent is checked regarding its trustworthiness and a suitable user-defined security policy will be recommended based on the level of authentication the agent has passed. This policy controls the amount of resources to be granted to the agent. The agent will be run under the security manager and the prescribed security policy. If it ever tried to access beyond what the security policy allows, a security exception will be thrown and the execution will fail.

Overall, the implementation of the prototype has provided a basic infrastructure to authenticate and authorize agents. We are improving our approaches and implementation in two aspects. First, to make the system more flexible in enforcing restrictions on agents, a possible improvement is to let the agent specify the security policy that it requires for its operation at the particular host. It is desirable to have a personalized system with the agent stating what it needs and the host deciding on whether to grant the permission or not. Second, the protection of agents against other agents can be another important issue. The authentication and authorization aspects between communicating agents are similar to that of host-to-agent and agent-to-host processes. We are designing certain mechanisms for this type of protection.

REFERENCES

Chavez, A. & Maes, P., (1998). Kasbah: An agent marketplace for buying and selling goods. *Proceedings of First International Conference on Practical Application of Intelligent Agents and Multi-Agent Technology*, London, 75-90.

Corradi, A., Montanari, R., & Stefanelli, C., (1999). Mobile agents integrity in e-commerce applications. *Proceedings of 19th IEEE International Conference on Distributed Computing Systems*, 59-64.

Dasgupta, P., Narasimhan, N., Moser, L.E., & Melliar-Smith, P.M., (1999). MAgNET: Mobile agents for networked electronic trading. *IEEE Transactions on Knowledge and Data Engineering*, 11(4), 509-525.

Gray, R.S., Kotz, D., Cybenko, G., & Rus, D., (1998). D'Agents: Security in a multiple-language, mobile-agent system. , In G. Vigna, (Eds.), *Mobile Agents and Security* Lecture Notes in Computer Science, Springer-Verlag.

Greenberg, M.S., Byington, J.C., & Harper, D.G., (1998). Mobile agents and security. *IEEE Communications Magazine*, 36(7), 76-85.

Guan, S.U. & Yang, Y., (1999). SAFE: Secure-roaming agent for e-commerce. *Proceedings of the 26th International Conference on Computers and Industrial Engineering*, Melbourne, Australia, 33-37.

Guan, S.U., Zhu, F.M., & Ko, C.C., (2000). Agent fabrication and authorization in agent-based electronic commerce. *Proceedings of International ICSC Symposium on Multi-Agents and Mobile Agents in Virtual Organizations and E-Commerce*, Wollongong, Australia, 528-534.

Guan, S.U. & Zhu, F.M., (2001). Agent fabrication and is Implementation for agent-based electronic commerce. To appear in *Journal of Applied Systems Studies*.

Hua, F. & Guan, S.U., (2000). Agent and payment systems in e-commerce, In S.M. Rahman, & R.J. Bignall, (Eds.) *Internet Commerce and Software Agents: Cases, Technologies and Opportunities*, Hershey, PA: Idea Group Publishing, 317-330.

Jardin, C.A., (1997). *Java electronic commerce sourcebook*, New York: Wiley Computer Publishing.

Karnik, N., & Tripathi, A., (1999). *Security in the ajanta mobile agent system*, Technical Report, Department of Computer Science, University of Minnesota.

Lange, D.B., & Oshima, M., (1998). *Programming and deploying JAVA mobile agents with aglets*, Reading, MA: Addison-Wesley.

Marques, P.J., Silva, L.M., & Silva, J.G., (1999). Security mechanisms for using mobile agents in electronic commerce. *Proceedings of the 18th IEEE Symposium on Reliable Distributed Systems*, 378-383.

Milojicic, D., (1999). Mobile agent applications. *IEEE Concurrency, 7*(3), 80-90.

Oppliger, R., (1999). Security issues related to mobile code and agent-based systems. *Computer Communications*, 22(12), 1165-1170.

Pistoia, M., Reller, D.F., Gupta, D., Nagnur, M., & Ramani, A.K., (1999). *Java 2 Network Security*, Upper Saddle River, NJ: Prentice Hall.

Poh, T.K., & Guan, S.U., (2000). Internet-enabled smart card agent environment and applications. *Electronic Commerce: Opportunities and Challenges,* S.M. Rahman, & M. Raisinghani, (Eds.), 246-260. Hershey, PA: Idea Group Publishing.

Rivest, R.L., Shamir, A., & Adleman, L.M., (1978). A method for obtaining digital signatures and public-key cryptosystems. *Communications of the ACM.*

Simonds, F., (1996). *Network Security: Data and Voice Communications*, New York: McGraw-Hill.

Tsvetovatyy, M., Mobasher, B., Gini, M., & Wieckowski, Z., (1997). MAGMA: An agent based virtual market for electronic commerce. *Applied Artificial Intelligence*, 11(6), 501-524.

Wang, T., Guan, S.U., & Chan, T.K., (2001). Integrity protection for code-on-demand mobile agents in e-commerce. To appear in *Journal of Systems and Software.*

Wayner, P., (1995). *Agent unleashed: A public domain look at agent technology,* London: Academic Press.

Wong, D., Paciorek, N., & Moore, D., (1999). Java-based mobile agents. *Communications of the ACM,* 42(3), 92-102.

Zhu, F.M., & Guan, S.U., (2001). Towards evolution of software agents in electronic commerce. *Proceedings of the IEEE Congress on Evolutionary Computation 2001,* Seoul, Korea, 1303-1308.

Zhu, F.M., Guan, S.U., & Yang, Y., (2000). SAFER e-commerce: Secure agent fabrication, evolution & roaming for e-commerce. In S.M Rahman, & R.J. Bignall, (Eds.), *Internet Commerce and Software Agents: Cases, Technologies and Opportunities.* Hershey, PA: Idea Group Publishing, 190-206.

Chapter XXIV

Security and Trust of Online Auction Systems in E-Commerce

P.W. Lei, C.R. Chatwin, and R.C.D. Young
University of Sussex, UK

L.K. Lo
University of Nottingham, UK

M.I. Heywood and N. Zincir-Heywood
Dalhousie University, Canada

ABSTRACT

Internet trading is an irresistible business activity, which nevertheless is constrained by unresolved security issues. With e-tailers like amazon.com having a storefront for auction and the two largest traditional auction houses in the world, Christie's and Sotheby's, operating online auctions too; online auction systems are now playing an increasingly important role in e-commerce. However, online auction fraud has been reported in several high profile cases; this chapter offers some solutions for problems identified in online auction trading; which is largely unregulated and in which small auction sites have very little security. A secure architecture for online auction systems will greatly reduce the problems. The discussion herein is restricted to those factors that are deemed critical for ensuring that consumers gain the confidence required to participate in online auctions, and hence a broader spectrum of businesses are able to invest in integrating online auction systems into their commercial operations.

INTRODUCTION

What are Auctions?

An auction is a market with an explicit set of rules determining resource allocation and prices on the basis of bids from market participants (McAfee & McMillan, 1987). Generally speaking, an auction is the standard means for performing an aggregation of supply and demand in the marketplace to effectively establish a price for a product or service. It establishes prices according to participants' bids for buying and selling commodities, and the commodities are sold to the highest bidder. Simply stated, an auction is a method for allocating scarce goods—a method that is based upon competition among the participants. It is the purest of markets: a seller wishes to obtain as much money as possible for the commodity offered, and a buyer wants to pay as little as necessary for the same commodity. Traditionally, there are three role players in the auction: sellers, buyers, and auctioneers. An auction offers the advantage of simplicity in determining market-based prices. It is efficient in the sense that an auction usually ensures that resources accrue to those who value them most highly and ensures also that sellers receive the collective assessment of the value.

Current Electronic Auctions Hosted on the World Wide Web

As indicated above, traditional auctions are held at physical auction sites at which the majority of participants need to actually attend in order to contribute. Information technology however is changing this. In particular, the Internet is changing the way business-to-consumer and business-to-business interactions are expedited. The Internet has the potential to provide a Virtual Marketplace in which the entire global business may participate. It has dramatically changed how people sell and buy goods. The very nature of the Internet as an auction medium expands the scope of potential participants beyond those typically able to physically attend. Electronic auctions have existed for several years. Examples include the auctioning of pigs in Taiwan and Singapore and the auctioning of flowers in Holland, which was computerized in 1995 (Turban, 1997), but these were only for local area networks (i.e., subject to the same physical constraints as a classical auction market).

Auctions on the Internet have been available since 1995, one of the most successful online auctions is eBay's Auction Web (www.ebay.com), which purports to have about 29.7 million registered users. It enables trade on a local, national, and international basis, there are six million items listed for sale daily on eBay across thousands of categories. Bidnask.com (www.bidnask.com) is an online retail service that operates an interactive, real time, electronic "Trading Floor" for the purchase and sale of financial instruments with an initial focus on equities. Yahoo! Auction (auctions.yahoo.com) is a further site rapidly gaining popularity.

In all these cases, the Internet auction acts as the collection of rules governing the exchange of goods. These include those legislated, the pricing model used, the bidding rules, and security requirements. Businesses communicate with customers and partners through many channels, but the Internet is one of the newest and, for many purposes the best business communication channel. It is fast, reasonably reliable, inexpensive, and universally accessible. The Internet provides an infrastructure for executing auctions much cheaper and faster. Consumer interest in online auctions is growing.

Existing Problems

Online auctions have become very popular. In the U.S., there are 35.6 million people participating in online auctions. Most auctions are open to the public. Whatever you want, you can find. Given the rapid success of the virtual market, no de facto standards exist as to the bidding rules and policies governing the online auction business. Although online auctions have been developing for many years, there are still two major problems: trustworthy transactions, and security and safety, summarized as follows:

Trustworthy transactions. Many auction sites describe themselves merely as meeting places for buyers and sellers. They simply allow sellers to list merchandise offered for trade and do not verify that the merchandise actually exists or is accurately described. They only use an email address to identify the traders—buyers and sellers. After the auction is over, it is the seller's responsibility to deal directly with the buyer concerning payment and delivery. The auction companies do not hold any responsibility in the transaction. Auction fraud is therefore an increasingly difficult problem in the Virtual Market. The common types of auction fraud are as follows (National Consumer League, 2001):

1)   Failure to deliver: Buyers pay for an item, that is never received.
2)   Misrepresentation: Items received do not match up to the original description.
3)   Shill bidding: A seller, or an associate, places a fake bid intended to drive up prices.
4)   Selling black-market goods: The goods are typically delivered without authentic merchandize, warranty, or instructions.

Among the complaints that the Federal Trade Commission (FTC) receives about auction fraud, the two most frequent are "Failure to deliver" and "Misrepresentation." However, in the last few years there is a new trend of increased "shill bidding." These problems effectively prevent some Internet users from participating in Internet auctions. According to FTC's May Auction Fraud Report, Internet auction fraud entails 64% of all Internet fraud that is reported (FBI Internet Fraud Complaint Center, 2001). Internet auction fraud has become a significant problem.

Security and Safety. Security is naturally a big concern for any business on the Internet. Since data is being transported over public networks, this makes it possible for third parties to snoop and derive critical information. Security and safety is an important topic in conducting business on the Internet. Online auctions are no exception. During the auction, buyers and sellers have to submit their personal information to the system as well as providing electronic payment for their goods. Hundreds and perhaps thousands of credit card numbers, home addresses, and phone numbers were exposed for months through a security hole on many Internet auction sites. Few auction sites provide security features such as SSL and Verisign security. In the survey of protections on smaller auction sites, there is less than 20% implementing security technology (Selis, Ramasastry, & Wright, 2001).

On the other hand, most online auctions do not enforce strong authentication, relying instead on a user ID and password or maybe an e-mail account to establish the validity of a client. Once this minimal information is supplied, people are free to enter into the online auction system and participate in bidding. Moreover, no minimally acceptable standard exists for ensuring that auctioneers protect users against the loss of personal information by the auctioneer. There are no established minimum-security standards or licensing bodies to protect the privacy rights of customers. People are risking their personal information. Ensuring security and trust in electronic communication is a principal requirement for achieving the trust necessary to gain widespread acceptance of Internet auction systems as a medium for commerce.

ONLINE AUCTION SYSTEM (OAS)

OAS versus Physical Auction System

Physical Auction System. Auctions are conducted in accordance with formal rules for governing market access, trade interaction, price determination and trade generation. The consolidated market institutions (Friedman, 1993) represented by such a collection of rules are traditionally applied to facilitate: the exchange of numerous kinds of commodities, and the determination of prices for individual objects including pieces of fine art, buildings or large vessels. In the case of a traditional physical auction, a seller will choose an auction house based on the service: the form of licensing, the availability of suitable insurance, suitable descriptions and access to the commodities, payment terms, and security of goods before and during the auction process. Physical auction is still popular in the auction marketplace. It provides a traditional face-to-face business environment, eye contact, a handshake, and discussion between multiple parties provides the knowledge necessary to facilitate deal making. However, traditional auctions suffer from all the drawbacks and inefficiencies associated with commuting to work rather than working from home and the time the actual auction takes, which can be considerable. It is fragmented and regional in nature, which makes it expensive for buyers and sellers to meet, exchange information and complete transactions. In short, rather than the market coming to the customer, the customer needs to come to the market. Hence, sellers, bidders, and auction houses lose out.

Online Auction System (OAS). Online auction systems provide immediate access advantages with respect to their physical auction systems counterpart. Participants may join an online auction system effectively placing bids using a computer on an anywhere-anytime basis. The access is not only limited to computers but is also available to mobile phones. However, in 2000, less than 0.1 percent of mobile phone users bought goods using wireless data services in the US, which is the largest base of mobile phone users according to Jupiter Media Metrix (Mahony, 2001). In reality, m-commerce is still in its infancy. In this chapter, we will discuss the security features in e-commerce.

In online auctions, transactions take place based on information (product descriptions), and the products move from seller directly to buyers only after on-line transactions are completed. It facilitates buyers and sellers in: meeting, the listing of items for sale independent of physical location, exchanging information, interacting with each other and ultimately completing transactions. It offers significant convenience, allowing trading at all hours and providing continually updated information. They allow buyers and sellers to trade directly, by bypassing traditional intermediaries and lowering costs for both parties. Online auctions are global in reach, offering buyers a significantly broader selection of goods to purchase, and providing sellers the opportunity to sell their goods efficiently to a broader base of buyers. More and more businesses are being drawn to the online auction arena such as Yahoo! (originally a search engine) and Amazon (originally an online bookstore). There are two major reasons. First, the cost to participate is minimal compared to that of a physical environment. It is possible to become a seller at most major auctions sites for next to nothing, and then pay only based on your actual sales. The other reason for the e-business growth in online auctions is the equally low cost of promoting your products.

Factors that make online auctions attractive may also present disadvantages. Many online auctions simply list the items for sale. No attempt is made to verify and check that the merchandise actually exists or that the description is accurate. The issue of transaction trustworthiness is a significant problem, the issues have already been described in the section on Trustworthy Transactions and the security issues in the section of Security and Safety. Surveys of consumer groups indicate that most people still do not trust online security systems. In the specific case of auction frauds, it is the seller who is typically responsible for perpetrating the fraud. Requiring registration and password access enables the logging of visitors, but if exchange of information is not secured, data can be intercepted online. Moreover, the verification of information supplied is often impossible.

Categories of Electronic Commerce and Various Forms of Auctions

Categories of Electronic Commerce. Over the years, auctions have matured into several different protocols. This heritage has carried over into online auctions. Here, a classification is developed depending on application context, in accordance with entities involved in the transaction (buyer–seller) (Barbosa & Silva, 2001). Classification:

1. Customer-to-Customer (C2C) - implies applications that support direct commercial transactions between consumers. In this category, product or services are offered directly between individuals. The concept of an enterprise or legal entity are therefore minimal. Virtual auctions, like ebay, are examples of this category.

2. Business-to-Business (B2B) - are online auctions involving a transaction from one business to another via the Internet. No customer is involved in the transaction. A strict and legal entity is required between businesses. All sellers are registered and cleared as a certified business or commercial identity. Isteelasia.com is a market for many sellers and buyers, which is suited for a special community of business such as the steel industry, whereas Gmsupplypower.com is a market for one buyer and many sellers (suppliers), which suits the requirements of a large corporation such as General Motors.

3. Business-to-Customer (B2C) - supports commercial transactions among final customers and enterprises. Through these Web sites, the final consumer can place electronic orders and pay for them. Web sites such as Amazon and Dell are examples of this category.

4. Customer-to-Business (C2B) - is a commercial activity in which the consumer takes the initiative to contact the business establishment. The auction site is initiated by a consumer the business is between a consumer and a business. The consumer initiates commerce with consumers using businesses as an intermediary. Priceline.com is the example of this category. In B2C category, the process is opposite: the enterprise gives the exact price of their products.

Each one of these categories has particular characteristics that should be analyzed and treated differently. These differences are reflected in the different entities and therefore the different types of relationships, perceptions, and requirements these entities bring to the auction. Most of the categories can be operated through an auction system, except B2C where the price is fixed by the enterprise.

Various Forms of Online Auctions. The above was a categorization of electronic commerce from the perspective of the participants. In this section, the case of auction types applicable to C2C and B2B contexts is investigated further. Most auctions differ in the protocol and information provided a priori. The following are the most common auction forms on the Internet:

1. English Auction - is by far the most popular auction method. Bidding takes the form of an ascending price auction where a bid must be higher in price than an existing bid in order to win the auction.

2. Reserve Auction - in this case the seller sets a reserve price, or the lowest price on which the seller is willing to transact.

3. Dutch Auction - Dutch auction is a popular kind of auction at many sites. It is commonly used when a seller has a number of the same item to sell e.g., selling ten posters. The auctioneer starts with a high asking price. The seller then gradually decreases the offer price, and the first person to bid is the winner.

4. Continuous Double Auction - In the above mentioned formats, there is only one seller but many buyers. In continuous double auction, there are many sellers and buyers, which is well suited to B2B conditions. Under double auction rules, both the bid and sale offers are publicly announced to the market. Buyers are free at any time to accept offers and raise or lower their bids. Sellers can accept any bid and raise or lower their offer. Naturally sales are made when a buyer accepts an offer or seller accepts a bid.

5. Proxy Bidding - this is an attempt to reduce the barrier of actually having to physically monitor the online auction. To do so a confidential maximum bid value is submitted to the auction service which will automatically increase the bid to make the winning bid. The proxy bidding will stop when the bid has won the auction or reached the declared bid limit.

OAS sites often support multiple modes of auction as a method of marketing and differentiating the site from competitors. For instance, eBay trademarked its automated bidding system as Proxy Bidding.

Mechanisms of Online Auctions

An online auction system is considered to be formed from four components: auctioneer, bidder, seller, and auction items. The role of the auctioneer in online auctions, however, requires some explanation. In a physical market, auctioneers attempt to provide sufficient information about auction items to attract both buyers and sellers and provide the institutional setting of the auction for the different transaction phases of the trading process, which includes information exchange, price determination, the trade execution, and settlement. In electronic auctions, the role of the auctioneer is replaced by OAS. OAS acts as the intermediary. The OAS mechanism is illustrated by Figure 1. The rules for online auctions are as follows (Feldman, 2000):

Figure 1: Mechanism of an online auction

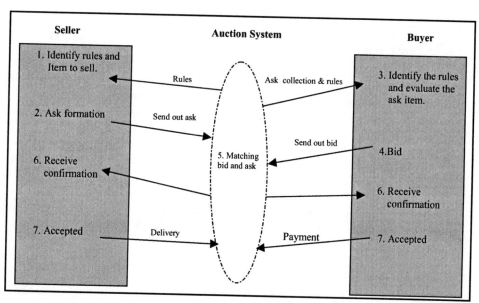

1.   Bidding rules - Bidding rules determine what actions participants can take, particularly the conditions under which they introduce, modify, or withdraw bids.
2.   Clearing rules - Clearing rules deal with what happens at the time an auction closes, that is, what are the trades and at what price.
3.   Information revelation rules - These rules determine the information participants receive during the auction process.

SECURITY AND CONFIDENTIALITY

Security Consideration

As mentioned before, security is central to both increasing the degree of trust between participants and reducing the likelihood of fraudulent activities on OAS. Bad software, poor configuration, and the lack of a clearly defined security strategy are the basic causes of the majority of security-related problems that arise. With the development of advanced technology on the Internet, Web servers have become a large, complex application that can, and often do, contain security holes. Moreover, TCP/IP protocol was not designed with security in mind. Online auction systems are therefore vulnerable to network eavesdropping. Unlike other online auction categories, in C2C or B2B auction data exchange is not only between buyers and OAS, but also the buyers and sellers. It is necessary to provide a secure channel for sellers to post their goods to the OAS, and the OAS also needs to guarantee that the message transmitted between seller and buyer is secret, especially with regards to payment and contact information. In addition to ensuring that only the winning bid and sell participants can read the message; the auctioneer should not be aware of the message contents. A safe information exchange transaction is a fundamental key to establishing user satisfaction. Without this, business transactions are effectively taking place in an open and insecure environment.

Fundamental Security Needs for Online Auction Systems

The challenge in building an online auction system is to provide safe communication and collaboration for legitimate users. The following summarises the fundamental security needs for OAS:
1.   The need to identify and authenticate legitimate users, thus identifying and granting access to bid information, content, and supporting services.
2.   Provision of a security system with fine-grained access control that will allow, on the one hand, legitimate users access to resources, whilst on the other, protecting sensitive information from hackers and unauthorized users (i.e., all other users).
3.   OAS should ensure that private, tamperproof communication channels for auction participants exist. Hence processing of their transaction is secure.
4.   OAS should provide auditing and logging facilities to track site security and misuse.
5.   OAS should provide secure data transaction from sellers to OAS and from OAS to buyers.
6.   Database system security is another consideration in OAS. In order to make sure that no unauthorized or authorized user can access any data in the database system, OAS should clearly identify data held, conditions for release of information, and the duration for which information is held.

Technologies in OAS

Authentication is often considered the single most important technology for OAS. It should be computationally intractable for a person to pretend to be someone else when logging in to OAS. It should be impossible for a third party to alter email addresses, digital signatures (see below), or the content of any document without detection. In addition, it should be equally difficult for someone to mimic the Internet address of a computer when connecting to the OAS. Various authentication technologies are available for determining and validating the authenticity of users, network nodes, files, and messages; several levels of authentication must be considered. Here, we explicitly identify validation, co-ordination payments and network integrity. Validating the identity of users during the login process to the system is supported by encryption technologies to support authentication. Technologies facilitating OAS coordination are grouped under the heading of workflow systems, cooperative work systems, tracking e-mail system, or coordination systems. These systems cooperate to facilitate the transparent operation of transaction processes. Based on the implementation of authentication and coordination, secure payment transactions could be possible for the auction participants. Finally, the technologies for securing network integrity of the Internet itself, the medium for all transactions, will include methods for detecting criminal acts, resisting viruses, and recovering from computer and connection failures.

Cryptography Technology

Encryption is the fundamental technology that protects information as it travels over the Internet. Four properties are used to describe the majority of encryption functions of interest to OAS. These are: confidentiality, authentication, integrity , non-repudiation. A cryptosystem comes with two procedures, one for encryption and one for decryption (Garfinkel, 1995). Different cryptographic systems are summarised as follows:

1. Secure Sockets Layer (SSL) - Because the Web is a public network, there is a danger of eavesdropping and losing information. SSL is one way of overcoming this problem. SSL protocol provides secure links over the Internet between a Web browser and a server. SSL was developed by Netscape Communications in 1995 and is embedded in Web browsers. Its adoption has been widespread as it is relatively inexpensive.

2. Public Key Infrastructure (PKI) - is an Internet trust model based on public key cryptography (encryption is conducted with a dual key system: a public key known to everyone, and a private key known only to the recipient of the message). PKI offers the advantages of authentication and non-repudiation, which SSL lacks. Digital certificates are used to authenticate both parties. Certificate authorities (CAs) must issue these certificates. These are trusted third parties that have carried out identity checks on their certificate holders and are prepared to accept a degree of liability for any losses due to fraud. The CA also issues the public and private keys.

3. Secure Electronic Transaction (SET) - Despite SSL's popularity, MasterCard, Visa, and several other companies developed SET. Released in 1997, SET v1.0 established a standard specifically for handling electronic payments, describing field formats, message types, protocol handshaking, and encryption mechanisms. The key difference between SET and SSL is that SET has digital certificates for all involved parties as an integral part of its design. In SSL, client/customer/authentication is an optional feature. Furthermore, the encryption and decryption in SET is more complicated than that in SSL.

In B2B, most transactions are paid offline as the buyers still prefer to have credit terms and receive payment by a letter of credit issued by a bank. Problems with B2B mainly arise if the transaction involves multiple countries. "Cross border" transactions involve taxes, duties, customs procedures, and legalities. Most countries lack the legal framework for such electronic transactions. The Philippines is only currently considering the enactment of the "Rules on the Electronic Evidence" (REE) (Disini, 2001). The REE says that electronic documentary evidence shall be the functional equivalent of a written document under existing laws. In effect, it will become difficult to conduct commerce with companies in other countries if the country has no such legislation. Supplier-buyer enablement (B2B) is easy to support in Singapore and Hong Kong, but it is still in its infancy in the Philippines, Indonesia, India, and China (Choy, 2000). The legal framework will need a much longer time to become established in these countries.

Certification of Participants

A C2C online auction system is designed for sellers and buyers; the online auction site acts as an intermediary. Sellers and buyers will interact with each other for their payment transaction. In order to prevent transaction problems, OAS should provide a mechanism for trustworthiness such that the identity of the parties is established/verified. An anonymous user is not allowed to take part in the auction process. The most common way to identify sellers and buyers is through the registration process. Sellers and buyers are required to be registered as a member of the OAS before they bid on the auction items. In fact, almost every online business makes use of registration to identify and classify their customers. However, the difficulty lies in identifying information, which can be readily verified, which is also unique, difficult to fabricate, and not reducing the potential customer base. Most systems, therefore, are relatively weak at ensuring the validity of information offered to identify registrants. At best, systems are capable of identifying when data has been entered in the wrong field.

Trustworthy Online Registration

The limits for ensuring trustworthy online registration are principally set by the availability of online verification services. The OAS may be able to do data field-type checking (validate post codes or names). The one verifiable piece of information under current systems might be the customer email address. If the ISP for the customer email system is the same as the OAS, then cross referencing of other information may be possible. In practice, the only sure way of ensuring customer trustworthiness might be to limit the customer base to a set of certified users.

1) Becoming an Buyer

To help ensure a safer environment for auction users, it is required that all users provide verification of their credit card (ability to pay). Through credit card verification, OAS can ensure that the buyers will act in accordance with the Terms of Service defined at the online auction site, and that sellers are of a legal age to sell and conduct business online. It will also be possible to take legal action against anyone posting illegal items or conducting in illegal activity on the auction site. Moreover, this may provide a first line of defence against fraudulent or irresponsible participants from participating in the site in the future.

2) Becoming a Seller

Selling at an auction is a different matter – verification of items for sale becomes steadily more difficult as the product becomes more unique. Particular examples of this include descriptions of houses or cars, in which there can be a wide disparity between description and "goods delivered." Here significant effort is necessary to ensure enforcement of minimum customer (buyer) rights. Furthermore, doing so across the boundary of multiple countries is presently rather difficult.

Establishing Payment Systems

Banking plays a critical role in commerce and therefore auction systems, as it typically represents the authority responsible for policing the final settlement of payment (c.f. SET). In e-commerce as a whole, however, banks often lag behind the rate of technological change in other sectors of commerce. First, banks only began to deploy Internet-friendly applications in the Internet boom of 1999, and therefore are still playing catch up. In the beginning, banks provided personal e-banking services to their own customers using dial-up Intranet services limited to a comparatively local area. In such a system, customers can check account balances and transfer funds from one account to another account. This has advanced to the point where secure access is possible at anywhere and anytime. In effect, the aim here is to move services currently offered by banking tellers to e-personal services, hence reducing the cost of processing a transaction. E-banking services to business accounts, however, are under development, as business accounts involve trade activities such as a letter of credit. Second, the banks have a legal obligation to protect their customers' account. For instance, the duties of a bank to customers when dealing with cheque payment take two principal forms:

1. To advise a customer immediately if it suspects his/her cheques are being forged; and
2. To exercise proper care and diligence, especially with cheques.

Third, business users prefer cheques for payments, and this is reflected in the large amount of paper still in use in the payment systems (Lipscombe & Pond, 1999). The underlying perception is that cheques provide evidence of receipt and evidence of non-payment should they be returned unpaid, this provides significant support for trust in the transaction system.

Credit Card

Buyers may have several payment options, including credit card, debit card, personal check, cashier's check, money order, cash on delivery and escrow services. Credit cards offer buyers the most protection, including the right to seek credit from the credit card issuer if the product is not delivered or if the product received is not the product ordered. Many sellers in C2C auctions do not accept it. There are several reasons for this. From the seller's perspective, there will be a charge on them and the average values of most purchases was US $100 or less (National Consumer League, 2001). The use of a credit card for payment will add cost to the sellers. From the buyer's perspective, it is very dangerous to disclose the credit card information to a person that he or she has never met before. They may use your credit card information for mischief. Payment by check, cashier's check or money order directly to the seller accounts for 69% of payment methods. However, those methods have no protection for the buyers.

Money can be electronicaly transferred between buyers and sellers in a fast and low cost-way. The E-payment methods are shown in Figure 2 and are classified as:

1. Proprietary payment: A proprietary payment system is a system in which the buyer pays a payment company rather than the seller and the payments company pays the sellers. Examples are ebay's Billpoint and Yahoo's PayDirect. Proprietary payment systems offer an attractive alternative to credit cards as they charge a buyer's credit card. This

Figure 2: E-Payment systems

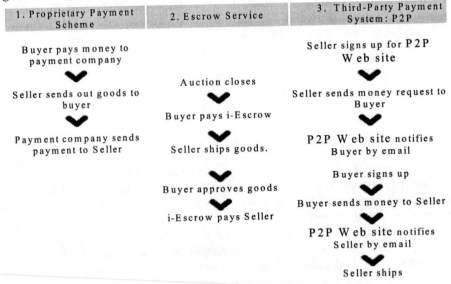

approach leaves the payment company to collect any disputed charges from the seller. The services are free to buyers but sites charge sellers for using the services. It is up to the seller to accept this kind of payment or not.

2. Escrow services: Allows buyers to deposit money in trust with a company, who will not release the funds to a seller until certain conditions are met or verified. It is estimated that only 1% of auction buyers use escrow services. Buyers use it when the amount is high. The low rate of usage is due to the charge or a fee — generally 5% of the cost of the item—paid by the buyer, and the delay to the deal. As with any business transactions, it is necessary to investigate the reputation of escrow service before signing on to the service. Examples are tradenable (www.tradenable.com) and escrow (www.escrow.com).

3. Third party payment: Person to Person (P2P) payment has been available on the Web as a service for almost a year, but its popularity seems to have taken off in just the last few months. In order to use a P2P payment system, it is first necessary for the payer to registers with a P2P Web site, giving the payment provider authorization to debit a personal bank or credit card account; Second, the payer enters the amount of the payment, gives the name of the recipient and the recipient's email address to the P2P provider; Thirdly, the bank representing the payer's account or credit card is debited; the recipient is notified by email that he or she has a payment and from whom; Finally, the recipient goes to the P2P Web site and defines the manner in which the payment needs to be made, either by providing an account number to receive an Automated Clearing House (ACH) credit or by offering a mailing address to receive a check. Example is Paypal (www.paypal.com).

E-payment enables the transfer of money from buyers to sellers in a fast and cost-effective way. However, it doesn't have the same protections that consumers have learned to expect from credit cards. In the U.S., credit card users aren't liable for more than US$50 in unauthorized charges. By contrast, online payment services tend to restrict the dollar amounts they must pay out, rather than limiting a consumer's liability to US$50 (Livingston, 2001).

CONCLUSION

Except for some notable large auction systems, most small online auction systems do not implement any security technology, which is the foundation for trusted transactions. Should international legislation be drafted for law enforcement of Internet auctions? It may be likened to legislation for road safety, e.g., it is illegal for drivers and passengers to ride a car without wearing a seat belts. In other words, the online auction systems should only be operated with essential security features such as SSL and a privacy policy. Nowadays, the C2C online auction systems are attracting a significant base of customers. The major difference between online auction systems and a physical auction house is the management approach. The traditional auction houses not only provide a meeting place for buyers and sellers but also act as middlemen to safeguard the transactions between buyer and seller. In addition, an auctioneer will monitor the bidding process, running it in a fair and open environment. However, the online auction markets merely provide virtual meeting places for their global customers, and the settlement of the transaction is put in the hands of the buyer and seller.

Credit cards give the best protection to the customers, however, the risk is high as the buyer's information about the seller is limited to an email address. P2P provides a free and adequate protection for transactions under US$200. Over this amount, it is safer for an individual buyer to pay through an escrow service, which charges a fee. For high-value transactions, bringing in the rules of the traditional auction house may be a trend to maintain the confidence of both buyers and sellers. In July 2000, eBay invoked new rules for baseball card auctioning in reaction to Sotheby's new online auction site (Wolverton, 2000). To bid on it, the bidder must agree to some rules including pre-registering with the sellers, making a US$100,000 deposit and agreeing to pay a 15% buyer's premium. At present, consumers have various ways to protect themselves from auction fraud. It is important to educate them about the choices of payment methods related to the degree of protection available. There is always a tradeoff between cost and risk.

B2B transactions are growing very fast. Gartner has estimated that B2B sales in the Asia Pacific region will rise from US$9 million in 1999 to $992 million by 2004. In the world B2B e-commerce will reach $919 billion in 2001 and $1.9 trillion in 2002 (Enos, 2001). The trading within B2B is usually limited to a group of traders within an industry or registered users. In other words, the identity of traders is known. This is unlike C2C, where the identity of traders is based on an email address or credit card number. However, the payment is still largely based on paper, a letter of credit issued by a bank. It is perhaps because of the large amounts of cash exchanged. The processing of a letter of credit is very costly. Business communities need to find an effective e-payment method to minimize the cost. The availability of e-payment is limited in B2B when comparing it to C2C. Tradecard seems to be the only choice (Morphy, 2001). It is a B2B financial product that claims to replace the traditional letter of credit and collection process. The degree of security and trust will be evaluated by business users. Cooperation among banking, financial institutions, and business communities will result in a cost-effective and secure e-payment method to cater for the inevitable exponential growth in the near future.

Another major problem facing both C2C and B2B online auction systems is the legal framework under which they operate, since it is not limited to one nation but is "cross border."

In C2C, a perpetrator of fraudulent transactions may be from another country. It may thus be difficult to take legal action against him/her. While in B2B, besides the issues of taxation and currency exchange, there are difficult issues relating to legal authority. Who will arbitrate or convene legal hearings in B2B? Online auction systems account for 55% of e-marketplace activity; it is therefore an important channel for trading. In order to make it a secure and a trusted marketplace, there is an urgent requirement for international management and control.

ACKNOWLEDGMENT

The authors would like to thank the reviewers for their helpful comments and valuable suggestions that contributed to improve the quality of this paper.

REFERENCES

Barbosa, G. P. & Silva, F.Q.B., (2001). An electronic marketplace architecture based on the technology of intelligent agents & knowledge. In J. Liu & Y.Ye, (Eds). *E-commerce Agents: Marketplaces solutions, Security Issues and Supply and Demand.* 39-60. LNAI 2033, Berlin Heidelberg: Springer-Verlag.

Choy, J., (2000). Asian E-marketplaces Faces Challenges. *Asia Computer Weekly.* (December 11-17).

Disini, J.J., (2001). Philippines: New rules on electronic evidence. In e-lawasi@, *Asia's Global IT & E-commerce News Forum,* 2(6), .5-6.

Enos, L., (2001). The biggest myths about B2B. *E-commerce Times,* (www.ecommercetimes.com).

FBI Internet Fraud Complaint Centers (2001). Auction fraud report (www.ftc.gov).

Feldman, S., (2000).Electronic Marketplaces, *IEEE Internet Computing,* July-August, 93–95.

Friedman, D., (1993). The double auction market institution: A survey. In D. Friedman and J. Rust (Eds.), The double auction market institutions, theories and evidence (3-26). Santa Fe Institute Studies in the Science of Complexity, Reading, MA: Addison-Wesley Publishing Company.

Garfinkel, S., (1995). *PGP: Pretty good privacy.* Sebastopoli, CA: O'Reilly & Associates.

Lipscombe, G. & Pond, K., (1999). *The business of banking : An introduction to the modern financial services industry.* 3rd edition. Chartered Institute of Bankers.

Livingston, B., (2001). Sticking it to auction winners. February 16. CNET news.com (news.cnet.com).

Mahony, M., (2001). Whatever Happened to M-Commerce?. E-commerce Times. November 30. (www.ecommercetimes.com).

McAfee, R. P. & McMillan, J., (1987). Auctions and bidding. *Journal of Economic Literature,* 699–738. June.

Morphy, E., (2001). Easy payments crucial for B2B success. CRMDaily.com, part of the News Factor Network (www.CRMDaily.com), September 24.

National Consumer League (2001). Online auction survey summary. January 31. (www.nclnet.org/onlineauctins/auctionsurvey2001.htm).

Selis, P., Ramasastry, A., & Wright, C.S., (2001). Bidder beware: Toward a fraud free marketplace – Best practices for the online auction industry. Center for Law, Commerce & Technology, School of Law, University of Washington (www.law.washington.edu/lct/publications.html), April 17.

Turban, E., (1997). Auction and bidding on the Internet: An assessment. *Electronic Markets*, 7(4) (www.electronicmarkets.org).

Wolverton, T., (2000). E-bay invokes new rules for baseball card auction. CNET news.com (news.cent.com). July 5.

Section IX:

E-Business Applications

Chapter XXV

E-Commerce and Digital Libraries

Suliman Al-Hawamdeh and Schubert Foo
Nanyang Technological University, Singapore

ABSTRACT

Until recently, digital libraries have provided free access to either limited resources owned by an organization or information available in the public domain. For digital libraries to provide access to copyrighted material, an access control and charging mechanism needs to be put in place. Electronic commerce provides digital libraries with the mechanism to provide access to copyrighted material in a way that will protect the interest of both the copyright owner and the digital library. In fact, many organizations, such as the Association for Computing Machinery (ACM) and the Institute of Electrical and Electronics Engineers (IEEE), have already started to make their collections available online. The subscription model seems to be the favourable option at this point of time. However, for many ad hoc users, the subscription model can be expensive and not an option. In order to cater to a wider range of users, digital libraries need to go beyond the subscription models and explore other possibilities, such as the use of micro payments, that appear to be an alternative logical solution. But, even before that can happen, digital libraries will need to foremost address a number of outstanding issues, among which including access control, content management, information organization, and so on. This chapter discusses these issues and challenges confronting digital libraries in their adoption of e-commerce, including e-commerce charging models.

INTRODUCTION

Digital Library Research Initiatives in the United States and the increased interested in digital libraries by computer science researchers has provided the impetus for the growing proliferation of digital libraries around the world. Most existing digital libraries have mainly focused on digitizing individual collections and making them available on the Web for users to search, access ,and use. They are providing a new means of fast and effective access to information in different forms and formats. Nonetheless, the development of digital libraries also translates into significant financial requirements, which, in the past, has been borne largely by government funding agencies, academic institutions, and other non-profit organizations.

By virtue of the basic principles of economics and business, digital libraries are looking for alternative forms of revenue generation in order to meet the ever-increasing needs of users through the provision of new value-added services and products. In this respect, e-commerce can provide digital libraries with the means to support their operation and provide them with a sustainable source of funding. This is a natural evolution in the use of digital libraries, as content management and electronic publishing are gaining momentum and popularity.

However, before digital libraries can engage in e-commerce activities, many issues need to be addressed. Some of these issues include intellectual property, access control, backup and archiving, and micro payments. In this chapter, we will look at these issues and highlight problems and opportunities related to digital libraries as a viable e-commerce business model.

CHARACTERISTICS OF DIGITAL LIBRARIES

The "digital library" is a term that implies the use of digital technologies by libraries and information resource centers to acquire, store, conserve, and provide access to information. But with the increased interest in other areas such as electronic commerce and knowledge management, the concept of digital library has gone beyond the digitization of library collections. It has been expanded to encompass the whole impact of digital and networking technologies on libraries and the wider information field. Researchers from many fields including computer science, engineering, library and information science are investigating not only the digitization of catalogues and collections or the effective use of networked resources but also the meaning of these developments for both information providers and users alike. Beside the technical issues that engineers are dealing with, there are a number of issues such as acquisition, content management, charging, and intellectual property that require the help of business and legal experts.

As digital libraries are being embraced by many communities, the definitions and characteristics of digital libraries vary rom one community to another. To the engineering and computer science community, digital library is a metaphor for the new kinds of distributed database services that manage unstructured multimedia. It is a digital working environment that integrates various resources and makes them available to the users. From the business community perspective, digital library presents a new opportunity and a new marketplace for the world's information resources and services. From the library and information science perspective, it has been seen as "the logical extensions and augmentations of physical libraries in the electronic information society. Extensions amplify existing resources and services and augmentations enable new kinds of human solving and expression" (Marchionini, 1999).

According to the Digital Library Federation (DLF), digital libraries are "organizations that provide the resources, including the specialized staff, to select, structure, offer intellectual access to, interpret, distribute, preserve the integrity of, and ensure the persistence over time of collections of digital works so that they are readily and economically available for use by a defined community or set of communities" (Digital Library Federation, 2001). From the above, it is clear that the stakeholders of digital libraries are many and wide-ranging. They include publishers, individual authors and creators, librarians, commercial information providers, federal, state and local governments, schools, colleges, universities and research centers, corporate technology providers, and major information user organizations in both the public and private sectors. With this, it is not surprising to find a myriad of different definitions and interpretations of a digital library. It could be a service, an architecture, information resources, databases, text, numbers, graphics, sound, video or a set of tools and capabilities to locate, retrieve, and utilize the available information resources. It is a coordinated collection of services, which is based on collections of materials, some of which may not be directly under the control of the organization providing a service in which they play a role. However, this should not be confused with virtual libraries or resource gateways that merely provide a link to external resources without any extra effort to manage those resources. As those resources are normally not under the control of the organization, maintaining content and keeping the links up to date is extremely difficult.

But while the definition of the digital library is still evolving, it might be easier to look at the characteristic and functionality provided by the digital library. Garrett (1993) outlined some of these characteristics that are worth noting :

- Ubiquity. At lease some set of services must be accessible at any time from any physical location.
- Transparency. The internal functioning of infrastructure components and interactions must be invisible to users. Users must be able to access services using their user interface of choice.
- Robustness and scalability. The infrastructure must be powerful enough to withstand a wide range of potential risks and continue to function without disruption to users and service providers.
- Security and confidentiality. The infrastructure must include mechanisms which ensure that parties to any transaction can reliably be identified to each other, that confidentiality of the parties and the transaction can be assured where appropriate, and that the system cannot be easily compromised.
- Billing, payment, and contracting. The infrastructure must support both financial transactions in payment for goods and services and the delivery and utilization of electronically generated and managed tokens (e.g., digital cash).
- Searching and discovery. The infrastructure must provide for a wide range of resource identification strategies, from highly specific searches to generic browsing.

Clearly, the above characteristics involve access to information, content management, search and retrieval of information, payments, security and confidentiality, technology and infrastructure. While some of these issues sound manageable, other issues such as payments and intellectual property still pose significant challenges and are still candidates for further research and development. The following sections address some of these issues confronting digital library development, and, in particular, those affecting the electronic commerce aspect of the digital library.

ISSUES CONFRONTING DIGITAL LIBRARIES
Content Management

Content management is an important and critical activity in digital libraries. It involves the creation, storage, and subsequent retrieval and dissemination of information or metadata. In this respect, content management can be closely linked to online search services. While most of the collections in digital libraries are still text-based, this is expected to change in future as more and more material will be made available in multimedia format. As the content is expected to come from various sources, it will also come in different formats, such as word processor files, spreadsheet files, PDF files, CAD/CAM files, and so on. However, Rowley (1998) pointed out that despite the growing importance of multimedia approaches, most of the collections are still text based. The volume of text-based information is increasing at an alarming rate, and its diversity of form—from the relatively unstructured memos, letters or journal articles, to the more formally structured reports, directories or books—is continually broadening. The management of content will also involve capturing and validating information. Nonetheless, issues related to ownership and intellectual property will continue to hamper the development of digital libraries. Most of the digital libraries that exist today either own the content or just provide a link to the information resource. Access control and intellectual property are therefore fundamental issues in the operation of large digital libraries.

Issues Facing the Content Organization in Digital Format

Information organization is an area that is still evolving and will continue to do so for some time. Statistical-based information storage retrieval models have failed to provide an effective approach to the organization of large amounts of digital information. On the other hand, more effective tools, which have been used manually by the librarians to organize information in the traditional libraries, are considered slow, tedious, and very expensive. Given the vast amount of information available today, it is important to organize it in a way that allows for modification in the retrieval system. This is highlighted by Arms, Banchi, and Overly (1997) where flexible organization of information is one of the key design challenges in any digital library. The purpose of the information architecture is to represent the richness and variety of library information, using them as building blocks of the digital library system. With the different types of material in a digital library, information can be organized using a hybrid approach that combines the statistical-based techniques with manual organization tools. Many companies are developing tools that will enable libraries to create taxonomies and organize information in a more meaningful and useful way.

The growth in size and heterogeneity represents one set of challenges for designers of search and retrieval tools. The ability of these tools to cope with the exponential increase of information will impact directly on the content management of the digital systems. Another challenge pertains to searcher behaviour. Recent studies have shown that users have difficulty in finding the resources they are seeking. Using log file analysis, Catledge and Pitkow (1995) found that users typically did not know the location of the documents they sought and used various heuristic techniques to navigate the Internet, with the use of hyperlinks being the most popular method. They also found that users rarely cross more than two layers in a hypertext structure before returning to their entry point. This shows the importance of information organization and content management in digital libraries.

The organization of information is still an issue in content management that needs to be addressed. Some outstanding issues include the following:

- The nature of digital materials and the relationship between different components. A digitized document may consist of pages, folders, index, graphics, or illustration in the form of multimedia information. A computer program, for example, is assembled from many files, both source and binary, with complex rules of inclusion. Materials belonging to collections can be a collections in the traditional, custodial sense or may be a compound document with components maintained and physically located in different places, although it appears to the user as one entity, in reality it can be put together as a collection of links or an executable component.

- Digital collections can be stored in several formats that require different tools to interpret and display. Sometimes, these formats are standard and it is possible to convert from one format to another. At other times, the different formats contain proprietary information that requires special tools for display and conversion, thereby creating content management and maintenance problems.

- Since digital information is easy to manipulate, different versions can be created at any time. Versions can differ by one single bit resulting in duplicate information. Also digital information can exist in different levels of resolution. For example, a scanned photograph may have a high-resolution archival version, a medium-quality version, and a thumbnail. In many cases, this is required if we want to address the retrieval and display issues on one hand, and printing quality issues on the other hand.

- Each element of digital information may have different access rights associated with it. This is essential if digital libraries are used in an environment were information needs to be filtered according to confidentiality or is sold at different prices.

- The manner in which the user wishes to access material may depend upon the characteristics of the computer systems and networks, and the size of the material. For example, a user connected to the digital library over a high-speed network may have a different pattern of work than the same user when using a dial-up line. Thus, taking into account the response time and the speed by which information can be delivered to the users becomes another factor of consideration.

It is clear from the above that the organization of information should take into consideration many issues. Borgman (1997) noted that the issues of interoperability, portability, and data exchange related to multi-lingual character sets have received little attention except in Europe. Supporting searching and display in multiple languages is an increasingly important issue for all digital libraries accessible on the Internet. Even if a digital library contains materials in only one language, the content needs to be searchable and displayable on computers in countries speaking other languages. Data needs to be exchanged between digital libraries, whether in a single language or in multiple languages. Data exchanges may be large batch updates or interactive hyperlinks. In any of these cases, character sets must be represented in a consistent manner if exchanges are to succeed.

Information retrieval in a multimedia environment is normally more complex. Most of the information systems available today (including digital libraries) still rely on keywords and database attributes for the retrieval of images and sound. No matter how good the image descriptions used for indexing is a lot of information in the image will still not be accessible. Croft (1995) noted that general solutions to multimedia indexing are very difficult, and those that do exist tend to be of limited utility. The most progress is being made in well-defined applications in a single medium, such as searching for music or for photographs of faces.

Copyright and Intellectual Property

Digital libraries as any other Web applications are still not protected from copying, downloading, and reuse. Digital technology makes reproduction of electronic documents easy and inexpensive. A copy of an original electronic document is also original, making it difficult to preserve the original document or treat it different from the other copies. In a central depository system where the original document is normally stored, the digital library system will have to make copies of this document for viewing or editing purposes whenever users access the document. In the Web environment, a copy is normally downloaded to the users machines and sometimes cached into the temporary directory for subsequent access.

The ease in which copies can be made and distributed prompted many to predict that electronic publishing will not prevail, as there might not be many people willing to put their works on the Web due to lack of protection. As legislators grapple with the issues of copyright, electronic document delivery is already taking place both within and outside the restrictions of copyright. The sentiments expressed by Oppenheim (1992) reflect those of many with regard to copyright in that

> "the information world is essentially a global one ... and the legal framework in which the industry operates is in places very confused, and in some cases, such as data protection, it is unwittingly swept up by legislation not aimed at it all. In other areas such as liability and confidentiality of searches, it will face increasing pressures from its consumers in the coming years."

Although the copyright issues in many areas have not been fully addressed, attempts have been made recently to introduce greater restrictions upon copyright and intellectual property. One such notable effort is by the Clinton Administration's Intellectual Property Working Group, which issued its Copyright Amendment recommendation code named "Green Paper." The Green Paper recommends amending the copyright law to guard against unauthorized digital transmission of copyrighted materials (Mohideen, 1996). The four main principal implications of the law include:

- Copyright should proscribe the authorized copying of these works
- Copyright should in no way inhibit the rightful use of these works
- Copyright should not block the development of dissemination of these works
- Copyright should not grant anyone more economic power than is necessary to achieve the incentives to create

Based on these principles, the U.S. Copyright Commission concluded that making some changes to the Copyright Act of 1976 could develop protection of computer programs. Congress has accepted the recommendations.

The question of *Intellectual Property* versus the *Freedom of Information* has been widely debated. There are two opposing views to this issue. One is that creators of information should be amply rewarded for their works. On the other hand, there is the notion that nobody really owns information, and society would be better off if knowledge is available for all. In the old system, copyrights always protected the physical entities by prohibiting the reproduction of the work without permission from the author. This also includes photocopying with the exception of fair use for educational purpose. In the Internet environment, downloading and printing is not much different from photocopying, although controlling this activity is extremely difficult.

In the past, copyright and patent laws were developed to compensate the *Inventors* for their creations. The systems of both law and practice were based on physical expression. In the absence of successful new models for non-physical transaction, how can we create reliable payment for mental works? In cyberspace, with no clear national and local boundaries to contain the scene of a crime and determine the method of prosecution, there are no clear cultural agreements on what a crime might be (Barlow, 1995).

Intellectual Property Management

For digital libraries to succeed, an intellectual property system needs to be developed to manage copyrighted material and ensure that the rights of authors and creators are protected. Garett (1993) proposed having an Intellectual Property Management System to manage intellectual property in a distributed networked environment. This system should assure copyright owners that users would not be allowed to create derivative works without permission or to disseminate the information beyond what is permitted. Besides controlling the copying of information, owners and users also would like to ensure that information has not been intercepted or altered in anyway. To be able to achieve this, Garett suggested that the Intellectual Property Management System must be capable of the following:

- Provide for confidential, automated rights and royalty exchange;
- Ensure owners and users that information is protected from unauthorized, accidental or intentional misattribution, alteration, or misuse;
- Ensure rapid, seamless, efficient linking of requests to authorizations; and
- Include efficient and secure billing and accounting mechanisms.

Another method of protecting intellectual property and copyright as proposed by Marchionini (1999) is through using technical solutions. The solutions are in the form of encryption algorithms and digital watermarking. So far, techniques have been developed whereby visible or hidden watermarks on digital objects have been incorporated into commercial products. According to Marchionini, these techniques insure the veracity of an object and may discourage the copying and distribution in the open market place. Examples of such systems currently being tested include Cybercash, Digicash, and Netbill. Cybercash use a third party intermediary to effect transfer of property and payment while Digicash issues money in the form of bit stream tokens that are exchanged for Intellectual Property. Netbill uses prefunded accounts to enable intellectual property transfer.

Cataloguing and Indexing

The exponential growth of the Web has made available vast amount of information on a huge range of topics. But the technology and the methods of accessing this information have not advanced sufficiently to deal with the influx of information. There is a growing awareness and consensus that the information on the Web is very poorly organized and of variable quality and stability, so that it is difficult to conceptualize, browse, search, filter, or reference (Levy, 1995). Traditionally, librarians have made use of established information organization tools such as the Anglo-American Cataloging Rules (AACR2) to organize, index, and catalog library resources. This works fine with the printed material by providing access to the bibliographic information only. When it comes to content indexing on the Web, these tools are inadequate and expensive to use due to the large amount of information available on the Web. The other major problem with the traditional approach is the fact that it is a largely intellectual manual process and that the costs can be prohibitive in the Web environment. This is further exacerbated that information on the Web is prone to sudden and instant updates and changes. An automated indexing process is therefore more useful and suitable. The success of automatic indexing should therefore lead to fast access and lower costs. The other major difference between traditional libraries and digital libraries is the content and format of the information stored. Digital libraries contain multimedia information, images, graphics, and other objects where traditional cataloging rules do not deal with.

Currently, indexing and retrieval of images is carried out using textual description or database attributes assigned to the image at the time of indexing. Indexing and retrieval based on image content is still very much in the research stage. In the Web environment, metadata is used to provide a description of an object for indexing purposes. Metadata is data about data, which is highly structured like its MARC (MAchine Readable Catalogue) counterpart in order for retrieval software to understand exactly how to treat each descriptive element in order to limit a search to a particular field.

Some of the digital libraries, such as the State Library of Victoria Multimedia Catalogue, attempted to use the MARC format to catalog digital objects only to find that it did not work adequately. In some cases, it becomes very complex requiring highly trained staff and specialized input systems. Digital librarians have identified three categories of metadata information about digital resources: descriptive (or intellectual), structural, and administrative. Of these categories, MARC only works well with intellectual metadata. Descriptive metadata includes the creator of the resource, its title, and appropriate subject headings. Structural metadata describes how the item is structured. In a book, pages follow one another, but as a digital object, if each page is scanned as an image, metadata must "bind" hundreds of separate image files together into a logical whole and provide ways to navigate the digital document. Administrative metadata could include information on how the digital file was produced and its ownership. Unlike MARC, which is a standard specified by AACR2, metadata standards are still evolving and there is still no consensus on a particular standard to follow (Tennant, 1997).

The other main concern with cataloging and indexing is the hefty cost involved. Basically, the cost to assign values to index attributes depends on the amount of work that is needed to determine what information to post. If the index is prepared before scanning, such as filling out a form, then adding index records to the database is strictly a data entry effort. However, if the information is derived from a reading or the document or an analysis of photographs, it will be very costly indeed. According to a report prepared for the Washington State Library Council (1999), a 15-element index record with 500 characters of entry may take between 30 seconds and a few minutes to complete. For thousands or hundred of thousands of items, this translates into very high costs.

Access Control

Access to most digital libraries was initially free to promote the site and attract users. Materials available on these sites are limited due to the lack of an appropriate and good access control system. When digital libraries deal with copyrighted material or private information, they are faced with the necessary task of developing access control facilities. A good example is the course reserve system developed by many universities to manage courseware. Most course reserve systems provide different levels of access control depending on the type of material and the enrollment of the students. Another reason for having a flexible and good access control system is the need for cross-organizational access management for Web-based resources. This is another area of great interest to information consuming institutions and information-resource providers. These organizations would like to enable access to a particular networked resource or to a particular member of an institutional consumer community. While access to users should be easy and flexible, it should also protect the privacy of the user and should not depend entirely on the user's location or network address but rather on the user's membership in appropriate communities. It should also provide the necessary management and demographic information to institutional consumer administrators and to resource providers.

A flexible and good access management system should do more than provide the technical infrastructure. It should also address a number of other difficult issues such as access policies and deployment of technology. Two important technical infrastructure components are required for an institutional access management system. First is the ability of a user to obtain an identity on the network, known as authentication, and the second is the ability to correlate a user's identity with rights and permissions to use various services, called authorization.

Given the problem surrounding the development of a good access control in digital libraries, there are a number of issues that need to be taken into consideration when developing and deploying an access control infrastructure:

- The system must address real-world situations. It should take into consideration the technology being used to verify users' as well as the level of user expertise. In the Internet and e-commerce environment, verification of users is rather difficult and a Public Key Infrastructure (PKI) might be needed to address the security and trust problems.

- The system should protect users' privacy and protect users' information from illegal or inappropriate use.

- It should provide different level of access to information depending on the type and nature of that information. Some services might be made accessible to the public while others can be restricted to paid users, managers, or heads of divisions.

- Access to information should not be hampered by technology and made difficult as a result of security or access right measures. It should remain efficient and simple.

- It should be easy to control and manage. Web-based user registration and verification reduces the time and cost involved in administering the system. It should be as painless to manage and to scale as current technology permits.

For libraries to engage in e-commerce activities, they need to deploy an access control system, not only to protect information resources but to also enable them to charge and collect money. Thus, access control in digital libraries will need to be integrated with payment and intellectual property management.

E-COMMERCE IN LIBRARIES

Libraries have so far been very slow to embrace electronic commerce. This is largely due to that fact that most libraries are originally institutionalized as non-profit organizations. Furthermore, the cost of setting up an e-commerce infrastructure is a barrier as libraries are generally not cash-rich organizations. However, electronic commerce and Internet have played a significant role in the way libraries operate and the way library services have developed. Many libraries have made their presence felt on the Web by making their collections searchable and their services accessible. The web sites of the New York Public Library (NYPL), the British Library, and Singapore National Library Board (NLB) are good examples of libraries using current technology to enhance and extend their services to current and future clientele.

Whether in a digital or traditional environment, libraries were set to provide various mechanisms for knowledge archiving, preservation, and maintenance of culture, knowledge sharing, information retrieval, education and social interaction. Barker (1994) states that as an educational knowledge transfer system, a library fulfils a number of important requirements, these being:

- The library is a meeting place – a place where people can interact and exchange ideas.
- The library provides a range of resources to which access is otherwise difficult.
- The library provides an effective mechanism for information acquisition and dissemination.
- The library provides access to experts in different fields and helps users to locate relevant information.
- The library is an educational institution and plays an important educational role in the fulfillment of lifelong learning.

In keeping up with the changes and advances in technology and the need to create self-sustaining entities, some libraries are changing their practices and adapting to the new environment by starting to charge their users for certain classes of value-added services, such as document delivery, reference services, and information research. The Canadian Institute for Scientific and Technical Information (CISTI) is an example of such a library or resource center that charges the public for value-added services (Song, 1999). In Singapore, the Library 2000 Report recommended that basic library services remain free, however value-added services such as translating, analyzing, and repackaging information will be chargeable (Fong, 1997). Currently, the National Library Board (NLB) of Singapore has adopted and implemented cashless payments through the use of the cash-cards. The use of cash-cards at NLB branches for all transactions was introduced in 1998 in an effort to automate payment processing. Although the introduction of cash-card systems at NLB branches initially drew some negative responses, the majority of library users soon grew accustomed to this mode of payment.

The cash-card system developed by Network for Electronic Transfers (S) Pte Ltd (NETS) and Kent Ridge Digital Laboratories (KRDL) of Singapore enabled the cash-card to be conveniently used at NLB branches. C-ONE, Singapore's first attempt at developing an electronic commerce system to enable cash card payments over the Internet, was introduced at some NLB libraries in 1999. The cash-card, which is basically a stored-value card, is useful for micro-payments. The value of the card can be topped at machines through the use of bankcards. However, the main drawback of the cash card and NETS is that they are only usable in Singapore.

As another example, the Library of Virginia introduced electronic commerce by enabling its patrons to adopt a book or shop online from its gift shop via its Web site that is credit card enabled (Harris, 2000). In more noticeable emerging trends, some libraries have begun to develop partnerships with vendors such as booksellers. The Tacoma Public Library is one such library where it allows its patrons to order books from the online bookseller, Amazon.com, via its online public access catalogue (OPAC) system. For each transaction, it earns 15% commission on the sale (Fialkoff, 1998).

Digital libraries are being developed for the preservation and access of heritage material through digitization efforts. At the same time, the digitized documents are potential revenue generators for these digital libraries. In addition, the digital library is an avenue through which electronic publications and value-added services can be accessed. With the presence of NetLibrary, many options are available to libraries (physical and digital) to offer electronic books for access to their members. NetLibrary goes through the process of acquiring the distribution rights to books from publishers and has made approximately 14,000 books available for access. Some of these books can be accessed for free while others require payment (Breeding, 2000). Electronic commerce and digital libraries are complementary in that "a digital library may require the transactional aspects of EC to manage the purchasing and distribution of its content, while a digital library can be used as a resource in electronic commerce to manage products, services and consumers" (Adam & Yesha, 1996).

The platform for libraries to innovate within their designated roles is reaching new heights with the aid of technology and electronic commerce. Traditional methods of doing things can be performed more effectively through an electronic exposure. The World Wide Web has created new avenues of delivering traditional services and created an environment of creative business development within the realms of the library world.

CHARGING MODELS FOR DIGITAL LIBRARIES

Since the definition of a digital library is till evolving, there is no prevailing e-commerce model for digital libraries. However, most of the goods sold on digital libraries are content such as electronic journals and databases. But there is no reason that digital libraries cannot sell physical goods such as postcards, books, T-shirts, mugs and other forms of goods. Given that, digital libraries might have to adopt different charging models. These charging models need to be integrated into a seamless and convenient interface. Some of the charging models that can be used for digital libraries include the prepaid subscription model, pay later subscription model, and pay now or as you use model.

Prepaid Subscription Model

In this model, the buyer maintains a virtual account with the seller that has been debited with a certain amount that is normally the annual or monthly subscription value. Depending on the terms and conditions of the subscription arrangement, the account can then be used for subsequent payments during payment transaction. This provides a very convenient form of payment where a user need not submit payment details each time to effect a transaction.

Pay Later Subscription Model

This is similar to the prepaid subscription model with the exception of "use first and pay later." This model also requires users (buyers) to register with the service provided. A virtual account is created and maintained. At the end of the subscription period, a bill is sent to the user for payment. Payment methods using credit cards fall in this category. In the case of e-commerce, credit card is a very common and convenient payment type and will be expected to be available in the digital library by many users. Most of the e-commerce Web sites operating under this model require the user credit card number upon registration. The credit card will be charged at the end of the subscription period.

Pay Now or As You Use Model

This model requires the user to pay immediately after completing the transaction. For example, if the payment method selected by the buyer is the cash card, then the amount of the transaction will be immediately deducted from the cash card and deposited into the electronic wallet of the seller. In the context of digital libraries, this type of payment mode is appropriate where payment must be collected before a user can access a service, such as downloading of documents, articles, software, etc. The problem with this model is that some of the payment techniques used, such as cash cards and NETS, are not standard and users cannot use them from abroad. Since credit card payments are not suitable for micro-payments and small amounts, there is a need for a standardized charging mechanism, such as cybercash or digital cash. Currently none of these charging techniques are accepted as a standard.

In fact, the issue of micro-payment is not restricted to libraries but to many sprouting new businesses on the Web.

According to the micro-payment model of Amazon.com, a micro-payment constitutes an amount of US$2 or less. It was cited that these payments are difficult for many sites to collect because the cost of processing such small transactions is higher than the fee itself (Regan, 2001). This issue greatly impacts the libraries, as they are generally non-profit, so that they are effectively incurring more costs to provide such a service to allow users to make micro-payments online.

Given that, how can consumers pay for such micro-payments at their convenience that does not incur a high overhead for the online merchant? In respect to this, many various commercial suppliers (such as CyberCoin of CyberCash.com, MicroPayment by IBM and Millicent by Compaq) have developed products in response to addressing the need for micro-payment transaction and processing.

These suppliers attempt to connect buyers and sellers on the Internet to a worldwide microcommerce environment. For the example of MilliCent (Compaq Computer Corporation, 2001), buyers will first need to open an account with them or through authorised brokers, and fund it in one of three ways, namely, through an online credit card or debit card transaction, by direct billing their monthly Internet Service Provider (ISP) statement or telephone bill, or through pre-paid cards purchased anonymously through convenience stores. Funds are held in the account in any currency until needed and then spent at vendor Web sites with the simple click of a mouse. The system takes care of the actual payment, handles currency conversion if required, resolves content delivery problems, and automatically processes refund requests. On the part of the seller, they open vendor accounts by first selecting a licensed payment hosting provider from the MilliCent Web site. This might be their ISP, a preferred Commerce Hosting Provider (CSP), or MilliCent itself. Once the account is opened, the vendor is "live" as part of the network. Using their browser, vendors assign prices to individual objects to be sold or to groups of objects. As a final step, vendors generally update their Web site HTML pages to visually reflect pricing to Web site visitors. Alternatively, vendors are allowed to integrate the software directly into their Web sites. By directly controlling their own payment processing, advanced vendors can increase their Web site responsiveness for end-users, better integrate MilliCent into their day-to-day operations, and eliminate any fees charged by MilliCent payment hosting providers.

Micro-payment is also an issue facing digital libraries as a direct result of intellectual property management. Digital libraries will not be able to provide services for copyrighted material unless a charging mechanism that takes intellectual property into account is put in place. Monash University implemented a course reserve system as well as a formula to calculate charges for copyright materials in an electronic course reserve system (Hawamdeh, 1999). The formula takes into account the number of pages scanned, viewed or printed, the retail price of the printed material or monographs, and the number of users enrolled in the course. This could form a basis for licensing and use of copyrighted material in universities and large corporations. Implementing such a formula can help the library to provide copyright clearance and manage charges when necessary.

XML MIGHT HOLD THE KEY

Digital libraries have started recently to take advantage of XML to better organize and manage digital resources. XML or Extensible Markup Language came about as a result of combining Standard Generalized Markup Language (SGML) and the Web. Due to the limitations inherited in HyperText Markup Language (HTML), there is a need to extend HTML capabilities to better display and manipulate Web pages. SGML, on the other hand, is powerful but too complicated. XML achieves much of the power of SGML but without the complexity associated with the use and implementation of SGML.

XML promises to solve many of the problems associated with diverse data types by allowing for user-defined markup rather than browser-defined markup. It provides markup that describes the content similar to that of SGML and goes beyond merely describing the format. This description of content has implications for extracting and reusing the content in ways that allows micro-payments and charge-per-use mechanisms. For example, a book marked in XML can then be displayed and manipulated in various ways. It can be displayed chapter-by-chapter, in sections or even paragraphs. XML-encoded material can be viewed both on the Web and personal devices such as e-book readers and personal digital assistants. The Open eBook Forum is working on a standard method of encoding e-books in XML specifically to provide an easy method for interchanging books across reading devices (www.openebook.org).

The efforts to provide an open XML-based infrastructure enabling the global use of electronic business information in an interoperable and secure environment are underway. ebXML, sponsored by UN/CEFACT and OASIS, is a modular suite of specifications that enables enterprises of any size and in any geographical location to conduct business over the Internet (http://www.ebxml.org/geninfo.htm). By taking advantage of these efforts, digital libraries will be in a better position to implement electronic commerce and micro-payment systems.

CONCLUSION

In this chapter we addressed some of the issues and challenges facing digital libraries in their adoption of e-commerce. Some of these issues can be resolved using technology such as access control, cataloging, and indexing. Others, such as content management, quality of information, copyright and intellectual property, go beyond technical issues and extend to policies and regulation. To make e-commerce a viable option for digital libraries, the issue of to micro-payments and charging must first be resolved. Such an issue is not restricted to digital libraries but also to many businesses on the Web that deal with content such as music and gaming. It is obviously infeasible to collect small amounts when the cost of processing such small transactions is higher than the fee to be collected itself. As technology advances, digital libraries will continue to look for new ways in which content and other services can be delivered and a fee correspondingly collected. This could be achieved through new charging mechanisms, such as CyberCash and across-country NETS mechanism.

REFERENCES

Adam, N. & Yesha, Y., (1996). Electronic commerce and digital libraries: Towards a digital agora. *ACM Computing Surveys.*

Al-Hawamdeh, S., (1999). Integrating electronic course reserve into the digital library framework. *Singapore Journal of Library and Information Management.* 28, 64-72.

Arms, W.Y., Banchi, C., & Overly, E.A., (1997). An architecture for information in digital libraries. *D-Lib Magazine,* February, [Online] http://www.dlib.org/dlib/february97/cnri/02arms1.html.

Barker, P., (1994). Electronic libraries – Visions of the future. *The Electronic Library,* 12(4), 221-230.

Barlow, J.P., (1995). Selling wine without bottles. *Proceedings of Digital Libraries Conference : Moving forward into the information era,* Singapore.

Breeding, M., (2000). NetLibrary, Innovative interfaces to add to e-books to library collections. *Information Today,* 17(3), 1-3.

Borgman, C.L., (1997). Multi media, multi cultural and multi lingual digital libraries. *D-Lib Magazine,* June [Online] http://www.dlib.org/dlib/june97/06borgman.html.

Catledge, L.D. & Pitkow, J.E., (1995). Characterizing browsing strategies in the World-Wide Web. *Proceedings of the 3rd International World Wide Web Conference, Volume 28 of Computer Networks and ISDN Systems,* April 10-14, Darmstadt, Germany. [Online] http://www.igd.fhg.de/archive/1995_www95/proceedings/papers/80/userpatterns/UserPatterns.Paper4.formatted.html.

Compaq Computer Corporation, (2001). The MilliCent microcommerce network [Online] http://www.millicent.com/home.html.

Croft, W.B. (1995). What do people want from information retrieval? (The top 10 research issues for companies that use and sell IR systems). *D-Lib Magazine,* November. [Online] http://www.dlib.org/dlib/november95/11croft.html.

Digital Library Federation (2001). [Online] http://www.clir.org/diglib/dlfhomepage.htm.

Fialkoff, F., (1998). Linking to online booksellers. *Library Journal,* 123(11), 68.

Fong, W.W., (1997). Library information and technology in Southeast Asia. *Information Technology and Libraries,* 16(1), 20-27.

Garrett, J., (1993). Digital libraries: The grand challenges. [Online] http://www.ifla.org/documents/libraries/net/garrett.txt.

Harris, L.E., (2000). Libraries and e-commerce: Improving information services and beyond. *Information Outlook,* 4(3), 24-30.

Levy, D.M., (1995). Cataloging in the digital order. [Online] http: //csdl.tamu.edu/DL95/papers/levy/levy.html.

Marchionini, G., (1999). Research development in digital libraries [Online]. http://www.glue.umd.edu/~march/digital_library_R_and_D.html.

Mohideen, H., (1996). Dealing with copyright issues in digital libraries. Libraries in national development, *Proceedings of Tenth Congress of Southeast Asian Librarians.* Kuala Lumpur.

Oppenheim, C., (1992). *The legal and regulatory environment for electronic information.* Calne, Wilts., Calne, UK: Infonortics Ltd.

Regan, K., (2001) Amazon testing micropayments via music downloads. [Online] http://www.ecommercetimes.com/perl/story/7822.html.

Rowley, J., (1998). *The electronic library.* London: *Library* Association Publishing. 263.

Song, S., (1999). Electronic commerce and its impacts to library and information profession. [Online] http://www.slis.ualberta.ca/538-99/ssong/termproj.htm.

Tennant, R., (1997). Digital potential and pitfalls. *Library Journal,* 122(19), 21-22. Also available in Library Journal Digital, InfoTech News: Digital Libraries, November 15. [Online] http://www.libraryjournal.com/articles/infotech/digitallibraries/19971115_2014.asp.

Washington State Library Council (1999). *Issues in Digitization: A report prepared for the Washington State Library Council,* Jan 5.

Chapter XXVI

Electronic Business Over Wireless Device: A Case Study

Richi Nayak
Queensland University of Technology, Australia

Anurag Nayak·
IT Consultant, Australia

ABSTRACT

Research and practices in electronic businesses over wireless devices have recently seen an exponential growth. This chapter presents the basic concepts necessary to understand m-business applications and a case study of the voice driven airline-ticketing system that can be accessed at any time, anywhere by mobile phones. This application offers maximum functionality while still maintaining a high level of user convenience in terms of input and navigation.

INTRODUCTION

Research and practices in electronic business (e-business) have witnessed an exponential growth in the last couple of years (Huff, 2000; Liautand & Hammond, 2001; McKie, 2001; Wimmer, Traunmüller, & Lenk, 2001). At its broadest, e-business is any type of business transaction or interaction in which the participants operate or transact business or conduct their trade electronically.

Over the last decade, deployment of wireless communications in Asia, Europe, and North America has also been phenomenal (Boyd & Park, 1998; Garg & Wilkes, 1996; Shafi, 2001; Schneiderman, 1997). Wireless technology has evolved a logical path, from simple first generation analog products designed for business use, to second generation digital wireless telecommunications systems for residential and business environments, to emerging radio-active signal-based third generation of wireless communications.

The explosive growth of mobile computing and e-business has created a new concept of mobile electronic business or electronic business over wireless devices (m-business).

Mobile e-business is a new way of advertising, buying, selling and, in some cases, delivering goods and services. It includes a range of online business activities, business-to-business and business-to-consumer, for products and services through wireless devices such as mobile phones with display screens, personal digital assistant (PDA), two-way pagers, and low-end or reduced size laptops.

Significant benefits of m-business to consumers are convenience, portability, safety, integrating existing mobile phones with mobile computing technology, verifiable receipts and transaction records that can be made available instantly and permanently on the smartcard (Inglis & Mosely, 2000; Keller, Zavagli, Hartmann, & Williams, 1998). Significant advantages of m-business to service providers and/or content providers include driving additional revenue and decreasing consumer attrition by offering new m-business services.

This chapter presents a case study of an airline ticketing system, which can be accessed by users via a mobile phone voice browser. The specific goals for this system are to allow users to search for flight information and then purchase an airline ticket to a destination while still being mobile. The objective of this chapter is to present this m-business case study in detail. Before presenting this case study, the desirability of development of m-business applications is discussed.

BASIC CONCEPTS OF M-BUSINESS

The applications and services that were envisioned for the m-business marketplace are becoming a reality today. Example applications are mobile ticketing and receipting, banking, mobile gaming, mobile weather forecast, sport scores access, movie database access, television guide access, stock exchange information, ordering of books and other daily needs such as food and groceries. Widespread adoption of m-business proves to be a more efficient mode of doing business. Figure 1 illustrates a typical platform that enables m-business services.

Technologies to Enable M-Business

The Internet standards require large amounts of (mainly) text-based data to be sent over the network. These standards are inefficient over mobile networks due to constraints such as low bandwidth, low computing processing, instable connection, etc. (Tsalgatidou, Veijalainen, & Pitoura, 2000). Techniques and protocols are required to conduct e-business for the unique constraints of the wireless computing environment.

Wireless Application Protocol - A commonly used approach to bridge the gap between e-business and mobile computing environments is Wireless Application Protocol (WAP).

Figure 1: A typical platform enabling m-business services

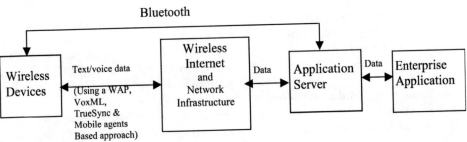

WAP makes it possible to link wireless devices to the Internet by optimising Internet information so it can be displayed on the small screen of a portable device.[1]

There are many components to WAP - the client, the gateway, and the server. The client is a person using a WAP-enabled mobile portal, a device containing a WAP browser much like Internet Explorer for a PC. A WAP gateway is an intermediary between the Internet and the mobile network. It converts WAP requests into Web (HTML) requests when information is requested from a mobile device and vice versa. A standard WAP server can be a HTTP Server capable of delivering wireless markup language (WML) files. Web pages accessed by WAP-enabled mobile portals during m-business transactions must be written in WML.[2] Characteristics of WML, based on XML principles, such as simplifying download times and presentation of web sites on mobile portals, make it most appropriate for developing applications.

It is not sure how well WAP will be able to proliferate (Tsalgatidou et al., 2000). Developments such as third-generation mobile communications and XYPOINT WebWirelessNow applications (Wen, 2001) already allow mobile phone users to experience the web services without WAP.

VoxML - Wireless Internet connecting technologies that offer textual interface, e.g., WAP, significantly suffer from the constraints of wireless communication such as having small display screen, less computation power, etc. An alternative solution is to provide voice access to users for the contents available on web via wireless Internet and network infrastructure. Advances in speech recognition and text-to-speech technologies have made voice-based communication possible between computers and users over the phone.

The voice access to web contents can be achieved by using an Interactive Voice Response system. Historically these systems have been very proprietary and therefore unsuitable for allowing access to web-based content. A better solution is to write web scripts in voice markup languages and follow the same development model as traditional web-based development. Existing markup languages (even with style sheets) are not well suited for developing voice dialogues. Even with sophisticated speech synthesis (using text-to-speech technology), it is not practical to read web pages developed for typical graphical browsing on the web. The free-form input elements of HTML forms do not align well with rigid telephone-grade speech recognition. For these reasons VoxML,[3] based on the W3C XML standard, is designed to support interactive dialogues. VoxML masks the technology behind the voice-to-voice communications by using XML data-tagging structures to link the text-to-speech that generates audio with the speech-recognition software that interprets a user's command (2001).

VoxML technology enables the application interface to be in the form of dialogues; navigation and input is produced via automatic speech recognition of end-user's voice; and output is delivered via text-to-speech software and recorded voice. For example, a user calls a VoxML server from a phone over an ordinary voice call. The user's own voice is actually data in this system. On the server, gateway translates the user's voice input, retrieves requested information from voice-enabled web sites via HTTP, performs actions based on the interpreted VoxML page, and can also read the relevant data (from the VoxML page) to the end user (2001).

There are some obvious drawbacks of this technology. There is extra overhead for content providers to offer the same web service through different channels, e.g., providing voice-enabled browser for their wireless customers along with the HTML/XML/WML browser. A manageable architecture using XML can solve this problem (2001). Another overhead is the processing power that speech recognition requires. The increasing CPU speed is the solution of this problem. Also this type of data transfer mode is not appropriate for applications with confidential data where one could be overheard. Overall the success of this technology depends on public acceptance of mobile phones as data delivering tools and type of applications best suited to its use.

Bluetooth - The Bluetooth technology[4] further enhances the sphere of mobility by conducting m-business without a heavy network infrastructure unlike WAP and VoxML technologies. The Bluetooth technology is designed to allow low-cost, short-range data (asynchronous) and voice (synchronous) radio link (2.4 GHz, 1 Mb/sec) to facilitate protected connections for stationary (homes, buildings, shopping centres, restaurants, cars, etc.) and mobile (phones, PDAs) computing environments. A simple example of a Bluetooth application is to automatically update mobile phone contents such as phone list, emails and memos without any user involvement when the phone comes within the range of the home/office PC.

The Bluetooth technology allows for the replacement of the many proprietary cables that connect one device to another with one universal short-range radio link.[5] The Bluetooth networks providing m-business services are limited to 30 feet only. A promising future of Bluetooth technology is its integration with WAP or VoxML. Some work in this direction is currently under way.[6]

TrueSync - The TrueSync technology is an approach providing a complete customised SyncML-enabled synchronization and integration of infrastructure and software solutions for wireless and wired devices. The TrueSync technology platform is designed to: (1) provide multi-point synchronization - one-step synchronization of wireless and wired devices, desktop applications and server-based applications and servers; (2) allow users to enter information once anywhere, and synchronize it everywhere; (3) enable the rapid development of ultra-thin, wearable products without sacrificing performance or quality; (4) optimise battery life and memory requirements of wired and wireless devices; (5) integrate with the new digital wireless infrastructure; and (6) operate seamlessly with standard enterprise software applications.[7]

Mobile Agent Paradigm - Mobile agent technology offers a new computing paradigm in which a program, in the form of software agents, initiated at the host, can suspend its execution on a host computer, launch itself to another agent-enabled host on the network, resume execution on the new host, and return back to its host with the result (Cockayne, 1998; Hayzelden & Bigham, 1999; Rothermel & Hohl, 1998).

This type of paradigm advocates the client/server model where the client is a mobile portal and server is a fixed network. The server hides the vendor-specific aspects of its host platform and offers standardized services to a mobile agent that is migrated to such a server from its mobile portal host. The mobile agent performs various optimisations on the server in lieu of its mobile portal to reduce the problems such as C-autonomy, limited bandwidth, and limited computational power. The fixed network offers its services to the agent, such as access to local resources and applications, the local exchange of information between agents via message passing, basic security services, creation of new agents, etc.

Many research papers emphasis that one of the most promising approaches for developing e-business applications is mobile agent technology (Dikaiakos & Samaras, 2001; Tsalgatidou et al., 2000). Influenced with this success, m-business applications supported by personalized agents (such as search agents to locate appropriate service around a geographical location) do not seem to be far away from realization. Such agents in m-business environments are initiated at the mobile host, migrated at the fixed network to perform a specified task, and return to the mobile host with the result.

Technical, Business and Legal Issues in M-Business and Their Ramifications

Analysing demands and opportunities in increasing revenue, network operators and companies have started offering m-business services to mobile subscribers. Innovative applications such as news, travel, mobile banking, etc., have been developed to attract subscribers. However, it is not easy to develop m-business applications due to some technical and legal issues involved.

Limited environment of mobile device - From the technical point of view, the mobile devices are a limited environment for user convenient purposes. These devices usually have limited display size, limited input capabilities, limited data transfer rate, limited computation power, limited power usage, etc.

Application partitioning can be effectively used over a wireless link to deal with these limitations. Much like a client/server application design, the application and its functionality are divided into two separate interacting parts. How much of the application is run on the client side versus the server side can be decided dynamically based upon the available bandwidth. Another solution to reduce the need and amount of transferring unnecessary data to consumer is locating the position of the consumer and then, sending only the most relevant information to that current geographical location (Pfeifer, Magedanz, & Hubener, 1998; Ratsimor, Korolev, Joshi, & Finin, 2001; Terziyan, 2001). This eliminates the need of burdening mobile users with extraneous information for services in remote locations.

Security - Consumers should feel the same sense of security when they shop using a mobile phone, as when they shop in the physical world. Two approaches, Secure Sockets Layer (SSL) and Secure HTTP (SHTTP), that provide secure electronic cash transactions for e-business by encrypting all web network traffic, do not apply in m-business applications (Freier, Karrton, & Kocher, 1996). There are some problems using these protocols, such as: (1) these protocols cannot generate signed messages or signed receipts, which naturally makes them unsuitable for electronic online payment and contract signing tasks; (2) these protocols do not allow WWW browsers to tell users in a simple way with whom exactly they are communicating over an establishes secure channel; (3) mobile portals may not have efficient encryption algorithms installed due to limited computing processing and input storage; and (4) the mobile portal and the content provider may not be using the same security protocol. In this case, gateway server requires the message to decrypt and encrypt again, and the message resides on the server in its original form for sometimes. (Chari, Kermani, Smith, & Tassiulas, 2001; Lacoste, Pfitzmann, Steiner, & Waidner, 2000)

There are various encryption and integrity mechanisms available to protect digitally encoded speech and control information in m-business services. Once a shared secret key is established between two entities across an interface (such as a mobile portal and a fixed network server), protocols dealing with transactional requirements for the business model deployed in m-business applications are responsible for authenticating the entities involved.[8]

Identification is another issue that is related with m-businesses, as mobile devices are prone to be stolen. Usually a person using m-business services is identified with an SIM card or device identity. Although the device is protected with security PIN, what if the device is stolen while on or along with its PIN, which is usually the case. Identification can be based on personal identity such as finger or eye prints or voice recognition (easy and preferred method if VoxML is used.

Transactional issues - Usually transactional models with Atomicity, Consistency, Isolation and Durability problems (ACID) assist an application developer in providing powerful abstraction and semantics to concurrent executions and recovery in transaction management. M-business transactions require these properties to be redefined due to additional requirements such as (1) the need for transferring money and goods along with data transfer, and (2) increased risk of incomplete transactions as mobile terminals can easily lose network connections (C-autonomous).[9] Approaches such as the asymmetric cryptographic algorithms (also called Public Key algorithms) with certification authorities are used to fulfil ACID properties of m-business transactions (Tsalgatidou & Veijalainen, 2000; Veijalainen, 1999).

Legal issues - From the legal point of view, consumers' mobility poses new challenges. Every country has its own legislation about conducting e-businesses. A consumer may be in USA while doing a business transaction in Europe with his/her mobile portal. The question arises that the business should be conducted according to which legislation - legislation of the residence country of the content provider, or the service provider, or the consumer. This problem calls for restructuring the m-business conducting regulatory framework worldwide. The geographical location of mobile users can be identified and used in charging for m-business services according to an appropriate legislation. (Tsalgatidou & Veijalainen, 2000; Veijalainen, 1999)

A CASE STUDY

This section describes a case study that allows users to search for flight tickets and to purchase online using voice-driven mobile portals. Instead of using HTML (or WML) pages to browse flight information, users will be interacting with the web site through a voice browser.

Figure 2: The voice-driven airline-ticketing system (a simple presentation)

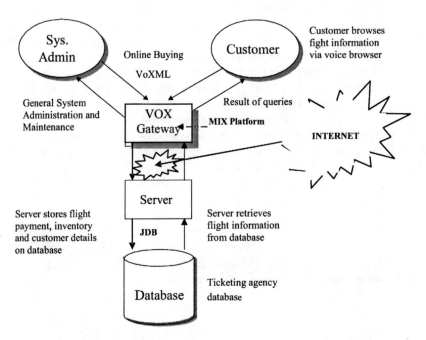

Main Components

The Voice-Driven Mobile Airline-Ticketing System illustrated in Figure 2 consists of four main components: User, Gateway, Application Server, and Application Database. This m-business application is developed using Mobile Application Development Kit (MADK 2.0).[10] Following is the description of components of this application.

VOX (Voice) Gateway - MIX Platform - The Mobile Internet Exchange Platform[11] (MIX communications platform) offers capabilities ranging from voice dialling of phone numbers to allowing a user to read or listen to Internet content or email while mobile. The MIX platform has two gateways to channel the type of information coming into the gateway server. When the server detects incoming data-based information, the Wireless Application Protocol

```
<?xml version="1.0"?>
<!-- Prototype Source Code -->
<DIALOG>
<CLASS NAME="help_generic">
<HELP> Your choices are <OPTIONS/>. </HELP>
<ERROR TYPE="ALL"> Your choices are <OPTIONS/>. </ERROR>
</CLASS>
        <!-- MOVING TO "init" step    -->
<STEP NAME="init">
<PROMPT>
This is an example of what a voice driven ticketing application
might sound like.
</PROMPT>
<INPUT TYPE="NONE" NEXT="\#intro"/>
</STEP>
        <!-- MOVING TO "intro" step    -->
<STEP NAME="intro" PARENT="help_generic">
<PROMPT>
Hello, and welcome to <BREAK MSECS="250"/> The voice driven airline
ticketing system. <BREAK MSECS="250"/> Please say your name or say Main
Menu to return to the main menu.
</PROMPT>
<INPUT TYPE="OPTIONLIST" NAME="userName">
<OPTION NEXT="\#userGreeting" VALUE="Richi Nayak"> Richi Nayak </
OPTION>
<OPTION NEXT="\#top.vml\#top"> main menu </OPTION>
</INPUT>
</STEP>
        <!-- MOVING TO "userGreeting" step    -->
<STEP NAME="userGreeting">
<PROMPT>
Welcome <VALUE NAME="userName"/>
</PROMPT>
<INPUT TYPE="NONE" NEXT="\#pid"/>
</STEP>
</DIALOG>
```

(WAP) gateway activates. Likewise, when voice-based information is detected, the VOX (voice) gateway is activated.

We utilize the VOX gateway to transfer the message (voice) between the mobile phone and the fixed network server. The scalability, reliability, security, and performance of this application depend on the protocols implemented in MIX platform. An example VoxML script that allows interactions with users is:

Application Server - The application server is a communications module between the ticketing agency database and the user. The server performs the following tasks: (1) receives the VoxML request, retrieves search information and returns it to the user, and (2) receives purchase information, such as user details, relevant flight and payment details, while monitoring seat inventory.

This case study uses JRUN of j2ee application server for implementation. With its modular design, JRUN is especially suitable for the development of e-business applications using Java Server Pages and Java Servlets, among others. The alternative solution can be ORACLE 9ais, BEA WebLogic, IBM WebSphere application server, etc. The developed application mainly depends on server-side processing in developing dynamic pages as client-side processing is considered to be slow and not advantageous looking at the limited environmental characteristics of mobile portals.

Database - The foundation of the developed application relies on the database (currently implemented as a dummy database) underneath in which it uses server side processing and an interface between the server and the database in generating dynamic pages for the voice browser of the client.

System Operation

In this system, a user requests a flight status for a specific flight by making a phone call to an online service provider and logging into the system. Upon connection, the user is presented with a dialog sequence stating a range of voice-driven services provided. The user selects the type of service, in this case, "flights information," which allows the user to either search for flight information and/or book a flight and/or purchase an airline ticket. The voice browser recognizes the voice request and translates it into a URL for a travel service provider's Web application server. The Web application server processes the request to determine the status for the specified flight, as it would process a request from a Web browser, and responds with a VoxML page. The voice browser interprets the VoxML page to relay flight information to the user via audio voice.

Depending on the results of the search, the user can either repeat a search query or move on to another search sequence. If search information matches the user's preferred flying schedule, the system will then prompt the user to confirm acceptance and finalize ticket purchase by making a permanent reservation. When the user selects to make and pay for a booking, the system prompts the user to complete the transaction by providing credit card details. The system then interacts with the financial institute to validate cardholder details and verifies funds. Once successful, the system credits the cardholder with the airfare and then executes a credit entry into the system's bank account. The system then allocates a new booking number and inserts the booking into the database. On completion, the system allocates a passenger number. Together with the booking number, the system inserts passenger details into the database. The interaction is transparent to the user, much like surfing the Web is via the computer on a desk today.

Figure 3: The Voice-driven airline-ticketing system (A detailed presentation)

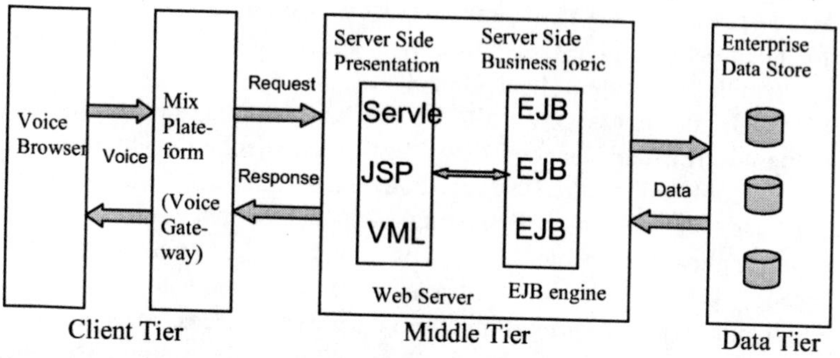

The user interface of the project is implemented through the User Interface Simulator (UIS) of the Motorola Mobile Applications Development Kit, a speech agent, that speaks dialogs written within VoxML tags, and a transcript window that displays the interchange between the user and the system. Figure 3 illustrates each component of this case study in detail.

System Benefits

The system enables users to search for flight information and reserve/buy airline tickets anytime, anywhere. The application offers maximum functionality while still maintaining a high level of user convenience in terms of input and navigation. Most of the computing processing is on server side. Also, the use of VoxML technique enables the user to interact with mobile portals through voice browser. Otherwise, the user convenience (implementing user interface menu using HREF anchor tags and back buttons of WML) is compromised because of the small display screen of a mobile device environment.

RELATED WORK

A number of public and private initiatives are underway to offer efficient m-business services to customers worldwide. The Global Mobile Commerce Forum (GMCF)[12] was established in 1997 by a diverse group of companies from around the world to promote the development of mobile commerce services around the world, for the benefit of consumers and the companies involved. The Wireless Data Forum (WDF)[13] was established in 1999 to help the wireless industry develop new e-business products and services and to use the Internet to sell products and services.

As there are not many m-business applications using VoxML, attempts have been made to search voice-activated business applications on the Internet or high quality WAP applications related to the air-line system explained in this chapter.

Voice Activated M-Business or E-Business

A handful of businesses are using VoxML or equivalent (VoiceML or IBM's SpeechML) techniques to provide voice-enabled services.

One such business is Tellme Network[14] that combines the power and flexibility of open Internet standards with world-class voice recognition technology. The Tellme Voice Application Network combines carrier-grade Network Infrastructure, the premier VoiceXML Application Platform, and the Voice Advantage suite of unique voice technologies. The company claims that (1) the voice applications can be deployed up to 90% faster than with traditional voice-enabled IVR systems, and (2) voice applications are at scale, easy, and cost-effective for businesses to give their customers self-service access to powerful voice-activated applications any time from any telephone.

Another such business is BeVocal[15] creating voice portal applications that can be personalized based on a caller's location, delivered to any device, and customized. BeVocal's applications and tools utilize the BeVocal Foundation Platform that supports both the VoiceXML 1.0 and Java standards for delivering voice-enabled enhanced services. BeVocal's voice-activated applications enable callers to use simple spoken commands and keywords to access location and travel services, information services, and entertainment services.

America Online's new AOLbyPhone[16] service provides access to its members to their AOL account from any phone, anytime, anywhere, simply by speaking. This system also provides facilities like getting movie listings, bar/restaurant guides, news, stock quotes, sports scores and international weather updates. The AOL/Quack voice platform utilizes voice recognition technology provided by SpeechWorks International and its Speechify's Text-to-Speech engine.

Related WAP Applications

There are a number of Internet sites with WML browser. Following are some of the high quality WML Internet sites in terms of user convenience.

Qantas Airways[17] offers information such as providing real-time flight timetables to users with mobile devices. This site mainly implements drop-down menu and back button for the site navigation. This site attempts to offer the user text input to search for flight numbers.

Weather Online[18] offers comprehensive current weather and forecast information worldwide. Navigation on the site is provided using HREF anchors and the options and previous buttons. No user text inputs seem to be available, and thus site navigation is straightforward, choosing the anchors provided.

Go2Online[19] offers a wide range of services such as the directory/location service (in terms of distances, street names, etc.) for restaurants, cinemas, shops, etc. inside the United States to mobile users. Navigation is mainly done using the options button and anchor tags on a single card.

Microguides[20] offers guidance (in terms of basic contact information of address and phone numbers) to specific important places such as consultants, hospitals, hotlines, etc worldwide. Navigation on this site is pretty straightforward, using many HREF anchor tags, and pages on this site load faster.

Most of these sites use databases and server-side processing to dynamically generate WML pages. Overall, these sites are capable of satisfying users needing relevant information considering the limitations of wireless applications.

SUMMARY AND CONCLUSION

This chapter attempts to present the basic concepts and issues associated with m-business. This chapter also discusses a working prototype of a voice-driven airline-ticketing system. This system allows consumer to use the service with voice browsing. This improves the value of the service for the providers and gives an easy and natural interfacing and interacting to the users with mobile portals. Considering it is difficult to provide full convenience due to the limited nature of the wireless devices, the application seems to be able to offer ease of navigation in providing real-time flight timetable information to users of mobile devices, anytime and anywhere. We are currently working on improving this system. We are expanding our knowledge base of airline tickets. We are also looking into making this system more distributed and fault tolerant.

Many optimists see m-business as a technology that is just one step away from becoming everyday use. Analyst and consulting company, Ovum Limited, predicts that the market potential for m-business in Asia-Pacific is expected to hit US$67 billion in 2005 (Businessworld, 2001), where it is highly adopted as compared to Europe or North America. Many pessimists see many unsolved problems and predict that m-business will not break through in the next few years (Martin, 2001). As usual, the truth lies somewhere in the middle.

Basic techniques are already available. Millions of people are already using mobile portals. Businesses are making profits—by moving on to e-business solutions. The potential of m-business is enormous. So why not integrate them all? Major mobile service providers are taking initiatives (such as MeT^{2,1} GMCF, WDF) to make this technology flourish. The remaining tasks are rigorous testing and refining of protocols especially suited for m-business applications, and resolving the related technical, business, and legal issues, thus winning the trust of consumers to use m-business services.

ACKNOWLEDGMENT

First, we would like to thank Ameesh Baxi and Giri Selvaduri for their valuable time to implement this case study with us. We also wish to thank Nevill Inglis, Madhav Shivdas, and Andrew Boey from the e-commerce and smart card group at Motorola Application Software Centre, Adelaide, Australia, for their technical assistance. Finally, we would like to thank Jill Slay and the School of Computing and Information Science, University of South Australia, Adelaide, for providing us resources.

REFERENCES

Boyd, C. & Mathuria, A., (1998). Key establishment protocols for secure mobile communications: A selective survey. In *Information security and privacy*, Vol. 1438 of *Lecture Notes in Computer Science,* 344-355. New York: Springer-Verlag.

Boyd, C. & Park, D., (1998). Public key protocols for wireless communications. In *Proceedings of the 1st International Conference on Information Security and Cryptology* (ICISC 98), 47-57.

Businessworld (2001)., Visa Int'l launches secure mobile. In *Financial Times Information Limited,* Manila. October 1.

Chari, S., Kermani, P., Smith, S., & Tassiulas, L., (2001). Security issues in m-commerce: A usage-based taxonomy. In Liu, J. & Te, Ye. (Eds). *E-Commerce agents,* vol. 2033 of *Lecture Notes in Artificial Intelligence.* 264-282. New York: Springer-Verlag.

Cockayne, W. R., (1998). *Mobile agents.*

Dikaiakos, M. D. & Samaras, G., (2001). Performance evaluation of mobile agents: Issues and approaches. In R. Dumke et al., (Eds). *Performance Engineering,* volume 2047 of *Lecture Notes in Computer Science* 148-166. New York: Springer-Verlag.

Freier, A. O., Kartton, P., & Kocher, P. C., (1996). The SSL protocol version 3.0. Technical report, *IFTF Transport Layer Security Working Group.*

Garg, V. & Wilkes, J. E., (1996). *Wireless and Personal Communications Systems.* Upper Saddle River, NJ: Prentice Hall.

Hayzelden, A., & Bigham, J., (1999). *Software agents for future communication systems.* Berlin; New York: Springer-Verlag.

Huff, S. L. (2000). *Cases in electronic commerce*. New York: McGraw-Hill.

Inglis, N. & Moseley, P., (2000). Towards secure e-commerce over wireless devices. Technical report, *Motorola Application Software Centre,* Adelaide, Australia.

Keller, R., Zavagli, G., Hartmann, J., & Williams, F., (1998). Mobile electronic commerce: GeldKarte loading functionality in wireless wallets. In *International IFIP/GI Working Conference: Trends in Electronic Commerce*, Hamburg.

Lacoste, G., Pfitzmann, B., Steiner, M. & Waidner, M., (Eds.) (2000). *SEMPER - Secure electronic marketplace for Europe*, vol 1854 of *Lecture Notes in Computer Science*. New York: Springer Verlag.

Liautaud, B. & Hammond, M., (2001). *E-business intelligence: Turning information into knowledge into profit*. New York; London: McGraw-Hill.

Martin, Z., (2001). Mobile commerce is coming, but experts can't say when. *Card Marketing, 5*(8). October 3. New York: Thomson Financial.

McKie, S., (2001). *E-business best practices: Leveraging technology for business advantage*. New York; Chichester: Wiley.

Pfeifer, T., Magedanz, T., & Hubener, S., (1998). Mobile guide - Location-aware applications from the Lab to the Market. In *Lecture Notes in Computer Science*, vol. 1483, 15-28. New York: Springer-Verlag.

Ratsimor, O., Korolev, V., Joshi, A., & Finin, T., (2001). Agents2Go: An infrastructure for location-dependent service discovery in the mobile electronic commerce environment. In *ACM Mobile Commerce Workshop*. Retrieved October 5, 2001, from citeseer.nj.nec.com/455113.html.

Rothermel, K. & Hohl, F. (Eds.)., (1998). *Mobile agents: Second international workshop*. Berlin; New York: Springer. Stuttgart, Germany, September 9-11.

Schneiderman, R., (1997). *Future talk: The changing Wireless game*. New York: IEEE Press.

Shafi, M., (2001). *Wireless communication in the 21st century*. New York: John Wiley-IEEE Press.

Terziyan, V., (2001). Architecture for mobile p-commerce: Multilevel profiling framework. In IJCAI 01 *Workshop on E-business and the Intelligent Web*.

Tsalgatidou, A. & Veijalainen, J., (2000). Mobile electronic commerce: Emerging issues. In *Proceedings of 1st International Conference on E-commerce and Web Technologies* (EC-Web), London-Greenwich, U.K.

Tsalgatidou, A., Veijalainen, J,. & Pitoura, E., (2000). Challenges in mobile electronic commerce. In *Proceedings of 3rd International Conference on Innovation through E-commerce* (IeC). Manchester, UK.

Veijalainen, J., (1999). Transactions in mobile electronic commerce. In *Transactions and Database Dynamics*, volume 1773 of *Lecture Notes in Computer Science*. G. Saake, K. Schwarz, & C. Trker, (Eds.). New York: Springer Verlag.

Wen, H., (2001). Doing the Web without WAP: A Discussion with XYPoint's Patrick Carey. In *The Wireless Communication Channel*. Retrieved October 1, 2001, from http://www.wirelessdevnet.com/channels/lbs/features/xypoint.html.

Wimmer, M., Traunmüller, R., & Lenk, K. (2001). Electronic business invading the public sector: Considerations on change, and design. In *Proceedings of the 34th Annual Hawaii International Conference on System Sciences*.

The wireless communication channel (2001). . Retrieved October 1, 2001, from http://www.wirelessdevnet.com/channels/voice/training/voicexmloverview.html.

ENDNOTES

[1] Edited and retrieved, September 28, 2001 from http://www.wapforum.org/

[2] Edited and retrieved, September 25, 2001 from http://www.oasis-open.org/over/wap-wml.html

[3] http://voxml.mot.com/

[4] http://www.bluetooth.com

[5] Edited from "Technology Overview", retrieved October 1, 2001 from http://www.bluetooth.com/v2/document

[6] http://www.wapforum.org/

[7] Edited from "Technology Overview", retrieved October 1, 2001 from http://www.starfish.com/products/truetech/truetech.html

[8] Several security protocol improvements exist but this discussion goes beyond the scope of this chapter. Secure Electronic Transactions (SET) [http://www.setco.org/] is probably the best-known commercially developed standard. Interesting readers can refer (Boyd & Mathuria, 1998; Chari et al., 2001) for detailed study of security issues in m-business.

[9] Interesting readers can refer (Veijalainen, 1999) for a detailed study of transaction issues in m-business.

[10] http://www.motorola.com/MIMS/ISG/cgi-bin/dev_madk_wp.cgi

[11] http://mix.motorola.com/

[12] http://www.gmcforum.com/

[13] http://www.wirelessdata.org

[14] http://www.tellme.com

[15] http://www.bevocal.com/index.html

[16] http://www.quake.com

[17] http://www.qantas.com.au/wap/dyn/Main

[18] http://wap.weatheronline.co.uk

[19] http://wap.go2online.com

[20] http://www.waptown.net/main.wml

[21] MeT, http://www.mobiletransaction.org/, targets to establish a framework for secure mobile transactions, ensuring a consistent user experience independent of device, service and network.

About the Authors

Nan Si Shi, has a Ph.D. in Information Systems Management (University of South Australia), Master in Computer Networks (Nanyang Technological University), and more than 20 years of experience in the Information Systems field, including industry practice and academic research, including teaching an MBA course *Competitiveness Through Information Management.* He is the coauthor of the book *Essential Technologies for E-Commerce* (Prentice Hall), and he has published a number of research papers, contributed several chapters in various books and international journals and conferences. He is a member of the International Board of Editors for the *Journal of Information Technology Education.* He is currently responsible for the area of Corporate IT Strategy Planning, E-Business, Mobile Commerce, IT Security Policy, Information Management, etc. He also is Adjunct Research Associate, Division of Business and Enterprise, University of South Australia.

V.K. Murthy is Senior Lecturer at the School of Computer Science, University of New South Wales at ADFA. Earlier, he was Associate Professor in Hong Kong and a Visiting Fellow at the Australian National University. He has extensive experience in the areas of distributed systems/Internet technologies, database and E-commerce systems. Also, he has software engineering and project management experience with Fujitsu R&D. Dr. Murthy has an extensive publication record in high-profile international journals and conferences, and he is the coauthor of the book *Transaction Processing Systems,* (Prentice-Hall). He is Program Chair and Program committee member in several major international conferences. He is one of the principal foundation editors of the ACM IT Journal on Education.

* * *

Hussein Abdel-Wahab received a Ph.D. in 1976 and an M.S. in 1973 both from the University of Waterloo in Computer Communications and a B.S. in Electrical Engineering from Cairo University in 1969. Currently, he is a full-time Professor of Computer Science at Old Dominion University. In addition, he is an Adjunct Professor of Computer Science at the University of North Carolina at Chapel Hill and a faculty member at the Information Technology Lab of the

National Institute of Standards and Technology. Prior to that, he held faculty positions at North Carolina State University, the University of Maryland, and Rochester Institute of Technology. He served as a consultant to many organizations including IBM, MCNC and MITRE Corp. He is the principal investigator in designing and implementation of XTV, a pioneer X-window-based Teleconferencing system. His main research interests are collaborative desktop multimedia conferencing systems, and real-time distributed information sharing. His research has been supported by NSF, ONR, IBM, MCNC, MITRE, ARPA ,among others. He is a senior member of IEEE Computer Society and a member of the Association for Computing Machinery.

Suliman Al-Hawamdeh is an Associate Professor and Programme Director of the Master of Science in Knowledge Management programme, School of Communication and Information at Nanyang Technological University, Singapore. He has more than 20 years of teaching and industrial experience in areas such as knowledge management, electronic commerce, document imaging, information retrieval, Internet, and digital library. He holds a master's degree from University of Michigan, Ann Arbor and a Ph.D. from University of Sheffield in UK. He is the founder and president of Information and Knowledge Management Society *(iKMS)*. He is also the author of a book, *Information and Knowledge Society* published by McGraw-Hill.

Irfan Altas is Associate Professor at Charles Sturt University, Australia. He received his Ph.D. from University of Saskatchewan, Canada. His research interests include: Data Mining, Parallel Processing, Using Technology in Education, Image Processing and Numerical Solution of Partial Differential Equations. He has published many articles in scholarly and professional journals and conference proceedings in these areas. He has been a consultant in data mining and information technology projects.

Marios C. Angelides is Professor of Computing in the Department of Information Systems and Computing at Brunel University. He holds a B.Sc. in Computing and a Ph.D. in Information Systems both from The London School of Economics and Political Science where he began his academic career as a Lecturer in Information Systems in 1990. His research interests are multimedia information systems and superhighways. He is the author of *Multimedia Information Systems* published by Kluwer and is an editorial board member of *Multimedia Tools and Applications* by Kluwer. He is a member of the ACM, IEEE Computer Society, and British Computer Society.

Daniel Brandon, Jr. is a Professor and Department Chairperson in the Information Technology Management (ITM) Department at Christian Brothers University (CBU) in Memphis, TN. His education includes a B.S. in Engineering from Case Western University, M.S. in Engineering from the University of Connecticut, and a Ph.D. from the University of Connecticut, specializing in computer control and simulation. He also has the Project Management Professional (PMP) certification. His research interest is focused on software development, both on the technical side (analysis, design, and programming) and on the management side. In addition to his seven years at CBU, Dr. Brandon has over twenty years experience in the information systems industry including experience in management, operations, research, and development. He was the Director of Information Systems for the Prime Technical Contractor at the NASA Stennis Space Center for six years, MIS manager for Film Transit Corporation in Memphis for ten years, and affiliated with Control Data Corporation in Minneapolis for six years in several positions including Manager of Applications Development. He has also been an independent consultant and software developer in several industries including: Medicine, Transportation/Logistics, Finance, Law, and Entertainment.

K. Selçuk Candan is a tenure-track Assistant Professor at the Department of Computer Science and Engineering at the Arizona State University. He joined the department in August 1997, after receiving his Ph.D. from the Computer Science Department at the University of Maryland at College Park. His dissertation research concentrated on multimedia document authoring, presentation, and retrieval in distributed collaborative environments. He received the 1997 ACM DC Chapter award of Samuel N. Alexander Fellowship for his Ph.D. work. His research interests include development of formal models, indexing schemes, and retrieval algorithms for multimedia and Web information, and development of novel query optimization and processing algorithms. He has published various articles in respected journals and conferences in related areas. He received his B.S. degree, ranked first in the department, in Computer Science from Bilkent University in Turkey in 1993.

C. R. Chatwin holds the Chair of Industrial Informatics and Manufacturing Systems at the University of Sussex, UK, where, inter alia, he is Director of the South East Advanced Technology Hub (SEATH), the Research Centre, and the Laser and Photonic Systems Research Group. Before moving to Sussex, Professor Chatwin spent 15 years at the University of Glasgow, Engineering Faculty, Scotland, where as a Reader he was head of the Laser and Optical Systems Engineering Centre and Industrial Informatics Research Group. He has published two research level books: one on numerical methods, the other on hybrid optical/digital computing - and more than one hundred and fifty international papers which focus on: optics, optical computing, signal processing, optical filtering, holography, laser materials processing, laser systems and power supply design, laser physics beam/target interactions, heat transfer, knowledge-based control systems, expert systems, computer integrated manufacture, CIM scheduling, manufacturing communication systems, computational numerical methods, genetic algorithms, maximum entropy algorithms, chaos, robotics, instrumentation, digital image processing, intelligent digital control systems and digital electronics.

Sherry Y. Chen is a Lecturer of Computing in the Department of Information Systems and Computing at Brunel University, UK. She holds a master's degree from the University of Maryland and a Ph.D. from the University of Sheffield, UK. Her major research interests focus on hypermedia-based learning environments and human-computer interaction. She has published widely in these areas. Her current research project, funded by the Engineering and Physical Science Research Council (EPSRC), UK, investigates human factors in the design of adaptive hypermedia systems. She is a member of the ACM and the British HCI group.

Zhixiang Chen is an Associate Professor in the Department of Computer Science at the University of Texas-Pan American in Edinburg, Texas. He received his Ph.D. in Computer Science from Boston University in January 1996. He was an Assistant Professor at Southwest State University from August 1995 to September 1997. He also studied and worked at University of Illinois and Huazhong University of Science and Technology. His research interests include intelligent Web search, machine learning, information retrieval, data mining, Web mining, AI, and applied algorithms and complexity. He has published over 60 papers in refereed journals and conference proceedings.

Nikhilesh Dholakia is a Professor in the Marketing, E-Commerce, and Management Information Systems Areas in the College of Business Administration at the University of Rhode Island, USA. He is also the Associate Director of the Research Institute for Telecommunications and Information Marketing (RITIM) at the University of Rhode Island. His current research is on the strategic and cultural aspects of m-commerce, e-commerce, and the Internet.

Geoff Fellows is Lecturer at Charles Sturt University, Australia. He has a Master of Information Technology from Charles Sturt University. His research interests include: E-commerce, World Wide Web and human-computer interaction. He has published some articles in these areas. He is the Executive Director of the Internet Special Projects Group.

Schubert Foo is the Head of the Division of Information Studies and Programme Director of the Master of Science in Information Studies programme, School of Communication and Information at Nanyang Technological University (NTU), Singapore. He received his B.Sc. (Hons) in Mechanical Engineering, a Ph.D. in Materials Engineering, and an M.B.A. from the University of Strathclyde in 1982, 1985 and 1989, respectively. He joined NTU in 1990 and over the years, lectured in the Divisions of Computer Technology, Software Systems and Information Studies. His research interests include Internet and multimedia technologies, information retrieval, and digital libraries. He has published over 100 international journals and conference papers to date in these areas.

Sheng-Uei Guan received his M.Sc. and Ph.D. from the University of North Carolina at Chapel Hill. He is currently an Associate Professor of the Electrical Engineering Department at National University of Singapore. Professor Guan has also worked in a prestigious R&D organization for several years, serving as a design engineer, project leader, and manager. He has also served as a member on the R.O.C. Information & Communication National Standard Draft Committee. After leaving the industry, he joined Yuan-Ze University in Taiwan for three and half years. He served as Deputy Director for the Computing Center, and also as the Chairman for the Department of Information & Communication Technology. Later he joined La Trobe University with the Department of Computer Science & Computer Engineering where he helped to create a new Multimedia Systems stream.

Professor Brian Henderson-Sellers is Director of the Centre for Object Technology Applications and Research and Professor of Information Systems at the University of Technology, Sydney (UTS). He is author of ten books on object technology and is well-known for his work in OO methodologies (MOSES, COMMA and OPEN) and in OO metrics. Brian has been Regional Editor of *Object-Oriented Systems*, a member of the editorial board of *Object Magazine/Component Strategies and Object Expert*. He was the Founder of the Object-Oriented Special Interest Group of the Australian Computer Society (NSW Branch) and Chairman of the Computerworld Object Developers' Awards Committee for ObjectWorld 94 and 95 (Sydney). He is a frequent, invited speaker at international OT conferences. In 1999, he was voted Number 3 in the *Who's Who of Object Technology* (Handbook of Object Technology, CRC Press, Appendix N). He is currently a member of the Review Panel for the OMG's Software Process Engineering Model (SPEM) standards initiative. In July 2001, Professor Henderson-Sellers was awarded a Doctor of Science (D.Sc.) from the University of London for his research contributions in object-oriented methodologies.

Malcolm Heywood received the Ph.D. from University of Essex, United Kingdom. He is currently an Associate Professor of Computer Science in Dalhousie University. His research interests include genetic programming, neural networks, soft-computing with applications in spatial and/or temporal reasoning, reconfigurable computing.

Wen-Chen Hu received a B.E. degree in Computer Science from Tamkang University, Taiwan, in 1984, an M.E. degree in Electronic and Information Engineering from the National Central University, Taiwan, in 1986, an M.S. degree in Computer Science from the University of Iowa, Iowa City, in 1993, and a Ph.D. in Computer and Information Science and Engineering from the University of Florida, Gainesville, in 1998. He is currently in the Department of Computer Science at the University of North Dakota. His current research interests are in the World Wide Web research and applications including information retrieval, especially search engines, data mining, and databases.

Roland Hübscher is an Assistant Professor of Computer Science at Auburn University. His research interests are human-computer interaction with focus on learner-centered design, cognitive science, and artificial intelligence. His projects include adaptive hypermedia and e-commerce where he is focusing on navigational issues. He is frequently collaborating with researchers from psychology and education departments. He received a Ph.D. in Computer Science from University of Colorado and an M.S. in Computer Science from the Swiss Federal Institute of Technology.

Frank Jung is Product Marketing Manager for Tamino XML Server products at Software AG Headquarters in Darmstadt, Germany. His multi-faceted career encompasses assignments including research and advanced development engineering in the area of professional HDTV and digital SDTV television studio equipment, product management and database management. Frank joined Software AG in 1999 and is responsible for the company's Tamino XML Server product marketing. His main tasks include strategic planning issues for the Tamino XML Server product line, as well as international public presentations about XML and Software AG's XML Server technology. Since 1999, numerous related articles have been published by him in renowned national and international IT magazines around the world.

David Kearney received his Bachelor's degree with first class honours from the University of New South Wales and his doctorate from the Queensland University of Technology. He has published 47 refereed papers in conferences, books and journals in areas relating to Computer Science and Engineering. He is currently the leader of the Systems Architecture and Security Research Group within the School of Computer and Information Science at the University of South Australia, where he is also the Director of the Reconfigurable Computing Laboratory. His research interests include languages and software architectures for advanced computing systems with particular emphasis on Internet-based computing.

Vince Kellen is President of Blue Wolf, a firm specializing in customer relationship management solutions. Prior to that, he served as vice president of customer knowledge management and analytics with Scient, Inc. and as a data warehouse practice leader for USWeb, an Internet consultancy. Mr. Kellen is an international speaker on CRM, the Internet and technology issues and the author of four books on database technology. He is also an adjunct faculty member for DePaul University's M.S. in e-Commerce degree program, one of the first graduate programs in the U.S. in e-Commerce.

Linda V. Knight is Associate Dean of DePaul University's School of Computer Science, Telecommunications, and Information Systems. She teaches and conducts research in the area of e-commerce business strategy, development, and implementation. In addition to acting as Associate Editor of the *Journal of IT Education*, she also serves on the Editorial Review Board of the *Information Resources Management Journal*. An entrepreneur and IT consultant, she has held industry positions in IT management and Quality Assurance management. She holds a Ph.D. in Computer Science from DePaul University, as well as a B.A. in Mathematics and an M.B.A., both from Dominican University.

Shonali Krishnaswamy is a Ph.D. candidate in the School of Computer Science and Software Engineering at Monash University. Her research interests are in the areas of e-services, e-marketplaces, distributed data mining, XML data management, and software agents. She received her B.Sc. in Computer Science from Madras University (India) in 1996 and her master's degree in Computing from Monash University (Australia) in 1998.

Nir Kshetri is an Assistant Professor at the School of Management, Kathmandu University, Nepal, and a doctoral candidate in Marketing and E-Commerce areas at the College of Business Administration, University of Rhode Island. He is the winner of the 2001 Association for Consumer Research/Sheth Foundation Dissertation Award, the first prize of the 2001 Pacific Telecommunications Essay (PTC) Competition, and second prize of the PTC 2000 essay competition. His papers on the Internet and e-commerce have appeared in such journals as *Electronic Markets* and *Pacific Telecommunications Review*.

Patricia Lanford is currently a second-year Ph.D. student in the Department of Computer Science and Software Engineering at Auburn University. Her research area is in human-computer interaction, specifically, e-commerce. She plans on focusing her research on developing methods and tools for collecting trust-related data pertaining to the checkout process of online stores. She received her B.S. in Computer Science from Auburn University in 2000 and was a cooperative education student from 1996 to 1998.

P.W. Lei or **Pouwan Lei** is a Lecturer in the Department of Business Information Systems in the Faculty of Business Administration in the University of Macao, Macao, since 1995. Before she was employed as system administrator in Adsale Group, Hong Kong. Her responsibilities involved formulating IT strategy, database security, user control, and system testing and implementation. Currently, she is pursuing a Ph.D. in the School of Engineering and Information Technology at the University of Sussex, United Kingdom. Her research interests include multi-agent systems, auction market model, supply chain management, and the management of IT.

Wen-Syan Li is a Senior Research Staff Member at Computers & Communications Research Laboratories (CCRL), NEC USA Inc. He received his Ph.D. in Computer Science from Northwestern University in December 1995. He also holds an M.B.A. degree. His main research interests include content delivery network, multimedia/hypermedia/document databases, WWW, E-Commerce, and information retrieval. He is leading the CachePortal project at NEC USA Venture Development Center, and Content Awareness Network project at NEC CCRL in San Jose. Wen-Syan is the recipient of the first NEC USA Achievement Award for his contributions in technology innovation.

Xue Li is a Senior Lecturer in Information Technology and Electrical Engineering at the University of Queensland in Brisbane Australia. He has a master's degree in Computer Science and a Ph.D. in Information Systems. His research interests include programming, object-oriented databases and Web Information Systems, and he has published many articles in these areas. Xue has had more than 18 years' experience in Information Technology. He has programmed numerous commercial database applications and network applications. Among other interesting projects, Xue was involved in programming the first Fortran compiler for Chinese machines. He has also consulted for a number of firms. Currently Xue is a principal supervisor for a few Ph.D. research projects and also involved in teaching Advanced Data Networks and Advanced Database Systems.

Laikin Lo received a B.A. degree in Business Information Systems from University of Macao, Macao, and an M.Sc. degree in Information Technology from Nottingham Univeristy, United Kingdom in 1998 and 2001, respectively. Between 1998 and 1999, he was employed as Support Engineer in Trade Development Council in Hong Kong. Then he worked as System Developer in NetComm Technology Co., Hong Kong. He was responsible for the development of client/server applications, systems implementation and supervising project on Web database systems (Extranet/Internet/Intranet).

Seng Wai Loke is currently a Lecturer in the School of Computer Science and Information Technology at RMIT University, Australia. He was formerly Senior Research Scientist at the Australian Cooperative Research Center on Enterprise Distributed Systems Technology. His current endeavours are in the areas of intelligent agents, innovative e-commerce technologies, and pervasive computing. His previous research yielded LogicWeb, integrating logic programming with the World Wide Web.

David Lowe is the Associate Dean (Teaching and Learning) in the Faculty of Engineering at the University of Technology, Sydney. He has active research interests in the areas of Web development and technologies, hypermedia, and software engineering. In particular, he focuses on Web development processes and Web project specification and scoping, and information contextualisation. He has published widely in the area, including several texts (Lowe and Hall, *Hypermedia and the Web: An Engineering Approach,* Wiley, 1999, and Wilde and Lowe, *Transcluding the Web: Linking and XML,* Addison-Wesley, currently in preparation). He has published over 65 refereed papers and attracted over $1,300,000 in funding, including a recent grant for research into Web project specification processes. He is on numerous Web conference committees and is the information management theme editor for the *Journal of Digital Information.* He has undertaken numerous consultancies related to software evaluation, Web development (especially project planning and evaluation) and Web technologies.

Xiannong Meng is an Associate Professor in the Department of Computer Science at Bucknell University in Lewisburg, Pennsylvania. His research interests include distributed computing, data mining, intelligent Web search, operating systems and computer networks. He received his Ph.D. in Computer Science from Worcester Polytechnic Institute in Worcester, Massachusetts. He was an Assistant and then Associate Professor in the Computer Science Department of the University of Texas – Pan American in Edinburg, Texas. He is a member of ACM and IEEE Computer Society.

Mohammed A. Moharrum received His B.Sc. Computer Science from Alexanderia University, Egypt, 1997. Received His M.Sc. Computer Science from Alexanderia University, Egypt, 2000. He is currently a Ph.D. student at Computer Science Department, Old Dominion University. Research Interests: 1-Multimedia Datbase Systems, 2-Network Security.

Anurag Nayak has a postgraduate degree in Computing and Information Science (2001) from the University of South Australia, Adelaide, Australia. He also has a Ph.D. (2000) from the University of Queensland, Australia, a master's degree (1994) from the University of Roorkee, India, and a bachelor's degree (1990) in Engineering. Currently he is working as an IT consultant specializing in j2ee applications. His research interests are e-business, distributed computing and 3G mobile technologies.

Richi Nayak has a Ph.D. (2000) in Information Technology from the Queensland University of Technology, Brisbane, Australia, a Master's degree (1999) in Power System Engineering from the University of Roorkee, India, and a Bachelor's degree (1992) in Electrical Engineering from the Govt.Eng.College, Bilaspur, India. Currently she is working as a Lecturer in the School of Information Systems, Queensland University of Technology, Brisbane, Australia. Her research interests are knowledge discovery and data mining and artificial intelligence and artificial neural networks technologies.

Chuen Hwee Ng received his B. Eng. (Electrical) from the National University of Singapore. During his industrial attachment, he worked in the Advanced Distributed Systems Group at the British Telecommunications Laboratories in Ipswich, UK, on an Application Level Active Networking (ALAN) project. During that time, he designed and developed a WAP-based ALAN demonstrator for the Programmable Networks Lab. After his graduation from the University, he now works in an IT start-up firm as a Software Analyst.

Stephan Olariu received the M.Sc. and Ph.D. degrees in Computer Science from McGill University, Montreal, in 1983 and 1986, respectively. In 1986 he joined the Computer Science Department at Old Dominion University where he is now a professor. Dr. Olariu has published extensively in various archival journals, book chapters, and conference proceedings. His research interests include wireless networks and mobile computing, parallel and distributed systems, peer-to-peer networks, and performance evaluation. Dr. Olariu serves on the editorial board of several journals including *IEEE Transactions on Parallel and Distributed Systems, Journal of Parallel and Distributed Computing, International Journal of Foundations of Computer Science, International Journal of Computer Mathematics, VLSI Design,* and *Parallel Algorithms and Applications.*

Michael J. Oudshoorn completed his Ph.D. at the University of Adelaide in 1992. He is now an Associate Professor in the Department of Computer Science at the University of Adelaide, as well as the Associate Dean (International) for the Faculty of Engineering, Computer and Mathematical Sciences. His research interests include concurrent and distributed systems, software engineering, and compiler construction. He is an active member of the Australian Computer Society, ISCA, ACM, and the IEEE. He serves on numerous conference program committees and journal editorial boards.

Tony Pittarese is a Computer Science and Marketing Instructor at Pensacola Christian College. His research interest is in bridging the gap between marketing and brick-and-mortar retailing concepts and computer implementation in electronic commerce. His dissertation work which is in progress is tentatively entitled "Effective Merchandising in an Online Retail Environment Based on the Customer Decision-Making Process." He received both an M.B.A. in Marketing and an M.S. in Computer Science and Software Engineering from the University of West Florida.

Simpson Poon is Professor, Chair of Information Systems at Charles Sturt University, Australia. He received his Ph.D. from Monash University, Australia. His research interests include: E-Business strategy, E-marketing, small business E-Commerce adoption and networked organisations. He is an E-Business strategist and researcher and was the Founding Director of the Centre for E-Commerce and Internet Studies at Murdoch University, Australia. He has published many articles in scholarly and professional journals in both E-Business and E-marketing. He has been a consultant with public and private organisations engaging in E-Business consulting projects over the last decade.

Anthony Scimé is currently an Assistant Professor of Computer Science at the State University of New York College at Brockport. His interests include the World Wide Web as an information system for the creation, discovery, storage, and dissemination of knowledge. He has over 20 years of academic, industry, and government experience in applying information systems to solve large-scale problems. He has supervised multiple large and small software development projects as well as complex hardware/telecommunications designs and installations.

Leng Woon Sim received his B. Eng. (Electrical) from the National University of Singapore. During his industrial attachment, he worked in the Network Software Development Division Group at the Fujitsu Singapore Limited on an SNMP (Simple Network Management) project. He is currently working in an IT consultancy firm as an analyst.

Theresa A. Steinbach is an Instructor at DePaul University's School of Computer Science, Telecommunications and Information Systems. She teaches Web-based scripting as well as teaching and conducting research in traditional and e-commerce systems analysis and design. As owner of an IT consulting firm, she provided turnkey solutions for small and medium size enterprises. Ms. Steinbach is currently completing her Ph.D. in Computer Science from DePaul University. She holds a B.A. in Mathematics, an M.B.A in Quantitative Economics and an M.S. in Information Systems from DePaul University.

Jyh-Haw Yeh was born in Taiwan on May 20, 1966. He received his Bachelor of Science degree from National Chung-Hsin University, Taichung, Taiwan, in 1988. He received his Master of Science degree from Cleveland State University, Cleveland, Ohio, in 1993. He received his Doctor of Philosophy degree in Computer and Information Science and Engineering at the University of Florida, Gainesville, Florida, in December 1999. Currently, he is an Assistant Professor in the Department of Computer Science of Boise State University, Boise, Idaho. His research area is computer systems with specialties in network security, network access control, and Internet technologies.

Wee Chye Yeo received his B. Eng. (Electrical) from the National University of Singapore. During his industrial attachment, he worked in the Information Technology Group at the Development Bank of Singapore on a Data Warehousing project. In his Final Year Project, he was involved in the development of an architecture for the Authentication and Authorization of Mobile Agents in E-commerce. Since his graduation from the University, Wee Chye works in the Development Bank of Singapore as a Credit Analyst.

Rupert Young obtained both his undergraduate and Ph.D. degrees from Glasgow University Engineering Faculty. Until 1993 he was employed within the Laser and Optical Systems Engineering Research Centre at Glasgow, during which time he gained wide experience in optical systems engineering and image/signal processing techniques. He participated in two European funded electro-optical projects involving pan-European collaboration between leading European Universities and Industry. The second of the projects was proposed and led by Glasgow University. In April 1995, he was appointed a Lecturer in the School of Engineering at the University of Sussex, a Senior Lecturer in October 1998, and a Reader in October 1999. There, he is continuing research into various aspects of optical pattern recognition, digital image processing and electro-optics system design, and applying this to a wide range of problems of industrial relevance. He has over 70 publications in peer-reviewed academic Journals and international conferences, many of them invited as papers to special issues, and has been invited as a keynote speaker to several conference sessions. He chairs sessions in the conference on Optical Pattern Recognition held each year by SPIE in Orlando, Florida. He is a member of the Society of Photo-Optical Instrumentation Engineers (SPIE), the Optical Society of America, and the IEEE.

Arkady Zaslavsky received an M.Sc. in Applied Mathematics majoring in Computer Science from the Tbilisi State University (Georgia, USSR) in 1976 and Ph.D. in Computer Science from the USSR Academy of Sciences in 1987. He holds a position of Associate Professor with the School of Computer Science and Software Engineering of Monash University. His research interests include mobile computing, distributed and mobile agents and objects, distributed computing and database systems, distributed object technology and mobile commerce. He is a member of ACS, ACM and IEEE Computer and Communications Societies.

Weiquan Zhao received his bachelor's and master's degrees in Computer Science from the Xi'an Jiaotong University in the People's Republic of China. He is currently with The School of Computer and Information Science at the University of South Australia where he is a doctoral candidate. Mr. Zhao has previously published in the area of web engineering and advanced architectures for web-based applications. Mr. Zhao has extensive teaching experience in universities in both China and Australia in the area of formal methods and web based information systems and has acted as a consultant in web engineering for organizations in China.

Binhai Zhu obtained a PhD in computer science from McGill University in 1994. He is now an Associate Professor with the Computer Science Department, Montana State University at Bozeman, MT. From 1994 to 1996, he was a post-doctoral research associate with Los Alamos National Laboratory, NM. From 1996 to 2000, he was an Assistant Professor at City University of Hong Kong. His research interests are algorithms, geometric computing, and Web-based computing.

Fangming Zhu received his B.S. and M.S. degrees from Shanghai Jiaotong University, China, in 1994 and 1997 respectively. After graduation, he joined Shanghai Ricoh Facsimile Co. Ltd. as a research engineer. He is now a PhD candidate in the Department of Electrical and

Computer Engineering at National University of Singapore. His current research interests include electronic commerce, software agents, and evolutionary computation. He is a student member of the IEEE.

Nur Zincir-Heywood received a Ph.D. from Ege University, Turkey, in 1998. She is an Assistant Professor of Computer Science in Dalhousie University. Her research interests include network information retrieval, network management, network applications, and e-commerce, managing Internet information services, multilingual Internet applications and Web engineering, globalization and socio-economic factors.

Index

X

XML 11, 165, 230, 271, 274, 388
XML schema 278
XSL stylesheets 282

Y

Yarrow 140

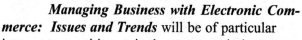